THE WRIT
Theobald Wolfe Tone
1763–98

THE WRITINGS OF THEOBALD WOLFE TONE, 1763–98

13th

Talleyrand Perigord sent for Lewines this morning to tell him that the Directory were positively determined on our business, that the arrangements were all concluded upon, and every thing would be ready for April next, viz about four months from this; all this is very good.

17th

Called with Lewines on Genl Desaix and gave him a letter from Genl Daendels; Desaix repeated the assurances which Talleyrand had given on the 13th, and told us further that Buonaparte and the Directory were now occupied in the organization of the marine and the funds and that when that was arranged, the military part of the business would be easily settled; finally he desired us to set our hearts at ease, for that every thing was going on as well as we could possibly desire it; ——

21st

Genl Desaix brought Lewines and me this morning and introduced us to Buonaparte, at his house in the Rue Chantereine; he lives in the greatest simplicity, his house is small, but neat, and all the furniture and ornaments in the most classical taste; he is about five feet six inches high, slender and well made but stoops considerably; he looks at least ten years older than he is, owing to the great fatigue he underwent in his immortal campaign of Italy; his face is that of a profound thinker, but with no marks of that great enthusiasm and that incessant activity by which he is so much distinguished; it is rather to my mind the countenance

Page of Theobald Wolfe Tone's diary for December 1797
(T.C.D., Tone papers, MS 2049, f. 285^r)
Reproduced by courtesy of the Board of Trinity College, Dublin

THE WRITINGS OF
Theobald Wolfe Tone
1763–98

VOLUME III

France, the Rhine, Lough Swilly and death of Tone,
January 1797 to November 1798

Edited by

T. W. MOODY, R. B. McDOWELL

and

C. J. WOODS

CLARENDON PRESS · OXFORD

OXFORD
UNIVERSITY PRESS

Great Clarendon Street, Oxford OX2 6DP

Oxford University Press is a department of the University of Oxford.
It furthers the University's objective of excellence in research, scholarship,
and education by publishing worldwide in

Oxford New York

Auckland Cape Town Dar es Salaam Hong Kong Karachi
Kuala Lumpur Madrid Melbourne Mexico City Nairobi
New Delhi Shanghai Taipei Toronto

With offices in

Argentina Austria Brazil Chile Czech Republic France Greece
Guatemala Hungary Italy Japan Poland Portugal Singapore
South Korea Switzerland Thailand Turkey Ukraine Vietnam

Oxford is a registered trade mark of Oxford University Press
in the UK and in certain other countries

Published in the United States
by Oxford University Press Inc., New York

© Oxford University Press, 2007

The moral rights of the authors have been asserted
Database right Oxford University Press (maker)

First published 2007

First published in paperback 2009

British Library Cataloguing in Publication Data

Data available

Library of Congress Cataloging in Publication Data

Data available

Typeset by Newgen Imaging Systems (P) Ltd., Chennai, India

Printed and bound in Great Britain by
CPI Antony Rowe, Chippenham, Wiltshire

1 3 5 7 9 10 8 6 4 2

ISBN 978-0-19956408-8 (Pbk)
ISBN 978-0-19-820880-8 (Hbk)

EDITORS' PREFACE

THIS edition of the writings of Theobald Wolfe Tone (1763–98), barrister, United Irishman, agent of the Catholic Committee and later an officer in the French revolutionary army, the first volume of which appeared in October 1998 and the second in November 2001, is intended to be complete and largely to supersede the two-volume *Life of Theobald Wolfe Tone . . . written by himself and edited by his son, William* (Washington, 1826). This, the third and final volume ('France, the Rhine, Lough Swilly and death of Tone, January 1797 to November 1798'), consists mainly of Tone's correspondence and diaries together with documents relating to his arrest, trial and death; like the earlier volumes, it is based on the original MSS if extant or on the most reliable printed version. The diaries are held by Trinity College, Dublin, together with a letter-book. The most important part of the correspondence (51 letters addressed by Tone to his wife, Matilda), for many years in the possession of his great-great granddaughter, Katherine Dickason (1903–95) of Short Hills, New Jersey, is now held by Mrs Dickason's granddaughter, Mrs Katherine Prendergast; most of the other letters, mainly of military interest, are in archives in Paris. This volume contains also additional documents for the period to December 1796, some physical descriptions of Tone and his wife, an iconography, a genealogy, a chronology, addenda and corrigenda to volumes I and II, a comprehensive bibliography, and an index to all three volumes. Facsimiles of MSS printed by us have been deposited in the manuscript department of the library of Trinity College, as have English translations of some of the French documents.

Editorial practice

The editors' intention has been to publish all of Tone's writings together with letters to him and some contemporary documents relating to his career. All matter in each document (e.g. date, address, etc. of letters) has been printed with a few exceptions (as indicated). The arrangement is strictly chronological. Letters and other documents whose dates fall within those of a diary sequence have been inserted in their appropriate places within the sequence. The original spelling has been retained. Punctuation and use of capitals have been silently standardised. Dates have been supplied in some cases, as explained in headnotes. The eighteenth-century practice of underlining or italicising names of persons and places, direct speech and literary quotations has been followed only for literary quotations, which are italicised, as are French and Latin words in documents largely in English. In the case of French official documents the republican calendar (in which the year begins on 22 September and is divided into ten months, each with a name taken from the season) has been silently converted to the Gregorian in the headings and notes. The dating of Tone's diaries (but not of other documents) has been standardised in the form '22 Feb. 1797'. Numerous footnotes are supplied to elucidate the text of the documents. We have followed the conventions in T. W. Moody, 'Rules for contributors to *Irish Historical Studies*' in *I.H.S.*, suppl. I (Jan. 1968), except that references to the first and second volumes are in the form 'see above, vol. II, pp 367–9'.

Acknowledgements

We are grateful to the board of Trinity College, Dublin, for permission to publish documents in the Tone, Madden, Sirr and Courts-martial papers; to Mrs Katherine Prendergast of Minneapolis, Minnesota, for permission to publish documents in the Tone family papers; to the director of the National Archives (Ireland) for permission to publish documents in the Rebellion papers; to the trustees of the National Archives, Kew, for permission to publish documents in the Home Office papers; to the director of the National Library of Ireland for permission to publish documents acquired from the McPeake collection; to the director of the National Museum of Ireland for permission to publish the inscription on a pocket-book of Tone; to the trustees of the British Library for permission to publish part of the diary of Sir John Moore; to the director of the Archives Nationales, Rue des Francs-Bourgeois, Paris, for permission to publish or quote from documents in the records of the Police Générale; to the director of the Archives des Affaires Étrangères, Quai d'Orsay, Paris, for permission to publish letters in the series Correspondance Politique, Angleterre; and to the director of the Service Historique de la Défense, Château de Vincennes, Val-de-Marne, for permission to publish various letters and to cite information in the *dossiers personnels* series.

The number of people who over the years have helped in one way or another is so large that we cannot attempt to thank them all by name without inadvertently omitting some. We can only acknowledge that our debt of gratitude to them is immense and hope that the final result of their assistance gives satisfaction. We must however mention Dr Sylvie Kleinman, whose expertise and enthusiasm during the final stages of our work, as well as her contribution of source-materials not previously known to us, are greatly appreciated.

The project of editing Tone's writings was begun in 1963. One of the editors, T. W. Moody, died on 11 February 1984.

R. B. McDowell
C. J. Woods

20 September 2007

CONTENTS

Contents

[1797 continued]

Contents

[1798 continued]

[1798 continued]

ADDITIONAL DOCUMENTS

ABBREVIATIONS

Archives de la Guerre	Service Historique de la Défense, Château de Vincennes, Val-de-Marne
Archives des Affaires Étrangères	Archives du Département des Affaires Étrangères, quai d'Orsay, Paris
Archives Nationales	Archives Nationales, rue des Francs-Bourgeois, Paris
B.L.	British Library
Castlereagh corr.	*Memoirs and correspondence of Viscount Castlereagh, second marquess of Londonderry*, ed. Charles Vane, marquess of Londonderry (12 vols, London, 1848–53)
Commons' jn. Ire.	*Journals of the house of commons of the kingdom of Ireland* (19 vols, Dublin, 1796–1800)
D.A.B.	*Dictionary of American biography* (20 vols, New York and London, 1928–37)
D.N.B.	*Dictionary of national biography* (66 vols, London, 1908–09)
Dict. biog. franç.	*Dictionnaire de biographie française* (Paris, 1933–)
Dict. parl. franç.	Adolphe Robert and Gaston Cougny, *Dictionnaire de parlementaires français* (5 vols, Paris, 1889–91)
Drennan–McTier letters	*The Drennan–McTier letters*, ed. Jean Agnew (3 vols, Dublin, 1998–9)
Enciclopedia universal	*Enciclopedia universal ilustrada europeo-americana* (70 vols, Madrid, 1908–30)
Gent. Mag.	*Gentleman's Magazine*
Life	*Life of Theobald Wolfe Tone . . . written by himself and . . . edited by his son, William* (2 vols, Washington, 1826)
McPeake papers	Miscellaneous papers collected by the late Brendan McPeake
Madden, *United Irishmen*	R. R. Madden, *The United Irishmen: their lives and times* (1st ed., 3 ser. in 7 vols, Dublin, 1842–6; 2nd ed. in 4 vols, London, 1857–60)
Nat. Arch. (Ire.)	National Archives (Ireland), Dublin
N.L.I.	National Library of Ireland
Nieuw Nederlandsch biografisch woordenboek	*Nieuw Nederlandsch biografisch woordenboek* (10 vols, Leiden, 1911–37)

Nouv. biog. gén.	*Nouvelle biographie générale* (46 vols, Paris, 1855–66)
P.R.O.	National Archives, Kew, Surrey (formerly Public Record Office, London)
P.R.O.N.I.	Public Record Office of Northern Ireland
R.I.A.	Royal Irish Academy
Six, *Dict. des généraux & amiraux*	Georges Six, *Dictionnaire biographique des généraux et amiraux français de la Révolution et de l'Empire, 1792–1814* (2 vols, Paris, 1934)
T.C.D.	Trinity College, Dublin
Tone (Dickason) papers	Tone family papers in the possession of the late Mrs Katherine Dickason
Wolfe Tone letters	*The letters of Wolfe Tone*, ed. Bulmer Hobson (Dublin, [1920]).

FRANCE, THE RHINE, LOUGH SWILLY
AND DEATH OF TONE,
JANUARY 1797 TO
NOVEMBER 1798

Between Theobald Wolfe Tone's return to Brest from Bantry Bay at the beginning of January 1797 and his departure from France in General Jean Hardy's expedition to Ireland in the middle of September 1798, there stretched a period of twenty-one months. For Tone it was a time of intense, varied and ultimately futile activity. He continued pressing the French to send help to Ireland. He travelled in the course of duty fairly widely, visiting the Rhine and the Netherlands. He served as a staff officer attached to the *armée de Sambre-et-Meuse* and the *armée d'Angleterre*. And, to his intense satisfaction, he managed to get his wife, Matilda, and their three children settled in France.

About 20 December 1796, Matilda Tone, with her children and sister-in-law, Mary Tone, arrived in Hamburg from America 'after a tedious and rough passage of two months'.[1] Hamburg, being a free city and neutral, provided a gateway through which British and Irish radicals could pass to France. On the crossing from America the small party had met a young Swiss merchant, Jean Frédéric Giauque, whom Mary Tone, after a very short engagement, married in Hamburg. Matilda Tone shared her husband's political ideals and literary enthusiasms, responding easily to the play of his mind. And it is clear from his letters what inestimable difference to his happiness her arrival in France made. Politics apart, his existence centred on the small household he and his wife established, first at Nanterre, a village near the Seine about 12 kilometres north-west of Paris, and then at Chaillot, a suburb.

But Tone could spend only short periods at home. Fortunately, though home-loving he was not over-domesticated, and had a lively enjoyment of social life, and so he quickly found army life congenial and inspiring. The French army, an amalgam of the old royal army and of revolutionary levies, hardened by a series of campaigns in which victory had often been snatched by desperate efforts from defeat, had developed immense *élan* and *esprit de corps*. Of its officers, some at the beginning of the revolution had been civilians, many had been serving in the ranks, some had been officers in the pre-revolutionary army—and the fact they had accepted the revolution suggests men of independent mind. Among such a body of men, drawn from such varied backgrounds but held together by common loyalties, ideas must

---

[1] *Life*, ii, 337.

still have circulated fairly freely while the tendency towards intellectual rigidity and the respect for conformity, which often characterise an officer corps, had scarcely set in. Tone was fascinated by this bold, self-confident, cheerful world. He threw himself into the life of the mess; he took soldiering seriously and he certainly thought of making a military career if fate prevented him returning to Ireland.

During 1797 and 1798 Tone's main objective continued to be a French invasion of Ireland. The French government had not been discouraged by the failure of Lazare Hoche's expedition. After all, the expedition had come remarkably near to success and the ships were scarcely back before another attempt was being talked of. But there were good reasons why a French expedition to Ireland had to be postponed. At the beginning of the campaigning season of 1797 it was clear that Austria, reeling from the blows inflicted by Napoleon Bonaparte, was preparing to advance in northern Italy. Hoche, who had been transferred to the command of the army of the Sambre-et-Meuse, hurried to take up his new command on the Rhine. Hoche remained intensely interested in Ireland. But stepping up the pressure on Austria would probably produce decisive strategic results in the near future, and from the personal point of view Hoche could not permit Bonaparte to make a monopoly of available laurels. Moreover, there was a sound negative reason for concentrating the French military effort against Austria. The navy was not ready to undertake a new Irish expedition. Hoche's expedition had revealed serious deficiencies in material and personnel, and though in January 1797 thirty ships of the line were gathered at Brest, a year later it was estimated that only about ten were ready for sea. There was a lack of all sorts of equipment, trained seamen could not be found in sufficient numbers and delay and despondency pervaded the dockyards.[1]

But if there was no hope of staging, in the immediate future, an invasion of Ireland from France, there was another possibility. It was thought that a Dutch fleet and Dutch troops might be employed in a thrust against the British Isles. Early in 1795 the United Provinces had been overrun by the French. After prolonged negotiations, the 'Batavian Republic' (as the Dutch Netherlands were henceforth to be known) became an ally of France, ceding some territory, paying a large indemnity and promising to maintain a French army of 25,000 men stationed in the country. In March 1796 a constituent assembly met to draft a constitution for the new republic. Constitutional conflict had been inherent in Dutch life for centuries and the debates in the assembly waxed warm between the federalists (supporters of provincial rights), and the unitarians (who supported centralisation).

In April 1797, Tone, passing through the Hague on his way to Groninguen to meet his wife, visited the assembly, but he took only a passing interest in

---

[1] Édouard Desbrière, *Projets et tentatives de débarquement aux îles Britanniques, 1793–1805* (Paris, 1900–2), ii, 296–7.

Dutch politics. He was far more interested in the possibility of a Dutch expedition to Ireland. At the end of June he was back at the Hague accompanying Hoche, who had come to discuss with the Dutch government an Irish expedition—a Dutch fleet from the Texel to convey a force composed of 15,000 Dutch and 5,000 French troops—the latter detached from Hoche's army. Hoche soon realised that the Dutch, concerned with the recovery of national prestige, wanted the expedition from the Texel to be purely Dutch. So he withdrew the proposal that French troops should be employed, and— a generous gesture—implicitly renounced command of the expedition. In fact, he had in mind a scheme which would have put him in control of the invading force. He planned to move a detachment from his army to Brest and embark it for Ireland. He calculated that this force under his command would reach Ireland shortly after the Dutch force from the Texel and then there would be little doubt who would have supreme command of the invading army. But Hoche's scheme became entangled in the complexities of French politics. His troops moving during July from the east to Brest came unconstitutionally near to Paris. Right-wing politicians were alarmed, Hoche was severely rebuked by Carnot, and returned to his Rhine headquarters, a sick and harassed man.[1]

On 4 July, Tone arriving at the Hague, after an interview with Hoche at Coblence, found the Dutch general Wilhelm Daendels, who was to command the Dutch expeditionary force, at the point of leaving for the Texel. But already a superb opportunity had been lost. During May and early June the British navy in home waters was immobilised by mutiny and, for a time, Admiral Duncan's squadron blockading the Texel was reduced to two ships. Duncan would have fought to the end but the odds against him would have been overwhelming. By the time, however, that the Dutch expedition was ready to sail, most of his ships had rejoined him. In addition, with 'a foul wind', Tone again discovered to what an exasperating extent wind and weather could interfere with strategy. Early in September, Tone was sent by Daendels to Wetzlar to place before Hoche a new plan of invasion. A Dutch force having landed in Scotland at Leith was to strike across to the Clyde from where it could effect a landing in the north of Ireland. But on 19 September, Hoche, the victim of galloping consumption, died. And three weeks later, the Dutch admiral Dewinter, putting out to sea from the Texel, was completely defeated by Duncan at Camperdown.

Hoche, who had campaigned both in the Low Countries and in the west of France, had his eyes firmly fixed on England, and Tone seems to have inspired him with a genuine desire to be the liberator of Ireland. His death left Bonaparte unrivalled among French generals and Bonaparte, a Corsican, had fought only in the south of France and Italy. For the moment, however, it looked as if he was going to direct his energies against the British Isles.

---

[1] M. R. Reinhard, *Le grand Carnot* (Paris, 1952), iii, 232–4.

In October 1797, the Directory announced the formation of the *armée d'Angleterre*, under the command of General Bonaparte, and units were steadily moved towards the west of France. Plans were made to collect a fleet which would protect the crossing of an expeditionary force, the collection and construction of small ships in which troops could be ferried across was hurried forward and the Dutch were asked to co-operate. But Bonaparte himself was, until the end of 1798, preoccupied with Franco-Austrian relations and the settlement of Italy. It was not until the beginning of February 1798 that he paid a visit to the Channel coast, and shortly afterwards in a masterly memorandum, dated 23 February 1798, he emphasised that 'carrying out a landing in England without being master of the sea would be the most daring and difficult operation made'. He then listed in depressing detail the preparations which would have to be completed before the crossing could be attempted. Finally, he drew attention to two other operations that he thought feasible: an attack on Hamburg and Hanover; or an expedition to the Levant, which would threaten British trade with India.[1]

The decision was soon made and preparations were begun for an eastern expedition. The Toulon fleet, conveying Bonaparte's army, started on its voyage to Egypt on 19 May, a few days before insurrection broke out in Ireland. The French government was naturally anxious to assist an insurrection, which might become very dangerous to Great Britain. But it was not in a position to intervene decisively. The ships were not available, and with central European problems becoming a matter of growing concern, the Directory could not spare much thought for Ireland. In the end, as will be seen, its efforts to assist the insurgents amounted to little more than a few comparatively small expeditions intended to keep up the spirits of the insurgents. The secret of Bonaparte's intentions was well kept and, until the middle of April, Tone seems to have believed that a great attack was being mounted against the British Isles. Then he began to realise the great emphasis that was being placed on the Mediterranean theatre of operations and could only wait with growing impatience and despair as news of events in Ireland reached France.

By the beginning of 1798 the French had definitely decided in favour of the indirect approach, planning by an eastward thrust to deprive Great Britain of much of its commercial strength. But the Irish insurrection, which began on 23 May and continued for several weeks, offered an opportunity to strike a damaging blow at British power. During the summer efforts were hastily made to mount an Irish expedition. An optimistic assessment of the situation would suggest that such an expedition might attain a considerable degree of success. The *armée d'Angleterre* could spare the men and, from reports

---

[1] *Correspondance de Napoléon 1ᵉʳ* (Paris, 1858–69), iii, 644–8. The words quoted are the editors' translation; the original reads: 'opérer une descente en Angleterre sans être maître de la mer est l'opération la plus hardie et la plus difficile qui ait été faite'.

reaching France, it seemed that the insurgents would be greatly invigorated by the arrival of French assistance. There was, however, a problem. How, with the French navy weak and ill prepared, was that assistance to reach Ireland?

In July, General Jean Hardy was appointed provisional commander of the *armée d'Irlande* and Admiral Jean-Baptiste Bompard, commanding a squadron at Brest, was instructed to transport his force to Ireland, Killybegs being suggested as a landing place. Another squadron, consisting of three frigates commanded by Admiral Daniel Savary and transporting 1,019 men under the command of General Jean Joseph Humbert, left La Rochelle on 6 August. Bompard's squadron consisted of a ship of the line, the *Hoche* (80 guns), six frigates and a brig. The force directly under Hardy's command, 2,800 men, was distributed among the ships of the squadron, 640 men, including the headquarters staff to which Theobald Wolfe Tone was attached, being on the *Hoche*.[1]

On 1 August, Tone, having been placed on Hardy's staff, joined him at Brest, and for the third time found himself condemned to weeks of frustration and exasperating delay. The wind was adverse, the blockading ships alert. It was not until 16 September that, with a change of wind, Bompard put out to sea on a course that took him due west about 650 kilometres into the Atlantic before he turned north and made for the Irish coast. At daybreak on 17 September, his ships were sighted sailing west by Captain Richard Keats of the *Boadicea*, who concluded from the number of men on board that they had troops embarked. Keats, a very able officer and a future admiral, immediately took steps to inform Admiral Gardiner, cruising off the French coast, and so the Admiralty, that the French were at sea. He also detached the *Ethalion* (38 guns) and *Sylph*, a brig, to observe the French. They were soon joined by the *Amelia* (44) and the *Anson* (44) and kept a close watch on the French ships, the *Ethalion* noting that 'some of them sail indifferently, particularly the line of battle ship'. On 20 September, Bridport, who commanded the Channel fleet, having intercepted Keats's message to the Admiralty, sent four ships of the line to cruise off Ushant, instructing the captain of one of them, the *Caesar* (80), that if the enemy were not soon found to cruise off Cape Clear for ten days. On the 23rd Gardiner received orders from the Admiralty to detach three ships of the line and a frigate to cruise off Cape Clear, the squadron being under the command of Sir John Borlase Warren, flying his flag in the *Canada* (74).[2]

On 10 October the *Amelia* joined Warren with news of the enemy, and on the 11th, discerning the French ships to the north-west, he gave the

---

[1] For accounts of Hardy's expedition, see General Hardy to Directory, 19 Nov. 1798 (below, pp 425–8), and Desbrière, *Projets & tentatives*, ii, 134–71.

[2] Dispatches and Admiralty instructions (P.R.O., Adm. 1/111). Warren's dispatch describing the action off the Rosses was published in *London Gazette*, 21 Oct. 1798.

signal for a general chase. But the French were to windward and a 'hollow sea' made it hard to come up with them. At 7.30 a.m. on 12 October, in 'bad boisterous weather', Warren came up with the French squadron and engaged it with the Rosses bearing 5 leagues south-south-west. The *Hoche*, after what Warren generously described as 'a gallant defence', struck at 11 a.m. with many guns dismantled and 5 feet of water in the hold. Three of the French frigates were taken during the action and three others subsequently in single-ship actions.

Owing to the prevalent bad weather, it was some time before the disabled *Hoche* could be brought into Lough Swilly and Tone, who had commanded a group of guns during the engagement, was not landed until 3 November. On coming ashore at Buncrana, he was immediately arrested and lodged in Londonderry jail for two days before being sent up to Dublin under escort. Arriving there on 8 November, he was confined in the provost's marshalsea,[1] and on the 10th he was brought before a court martial, charged with being in arms against the king. Tone, who admitted with pride that he held a commission in the French army, having delivered a short and eloquent apologia for his political career, asked that he should be granted a soldier's death. The court martial, having heard his statement, found him guilty and sentenced him to be hanged.[2]

Almost immediately the competency of the court martial to hear his case was challenged. For well over a century, even during the rebellions of '15 and '45, military courts had never in Great Britain and Ireland been permitted to exercise jurisdiction over civilians. The jurisdiction of courts martial was strictly limited to persons subject to the mutiny act (serving officers and soldiers charged with military offences). But it was generally agreed that, in a grave emergency, insurrection or invasion, the crown exercising its prerogative powers could take whatever action was deemed necessary for the safety of the realm, and obviously during such an emergency commanding officers might try and regulate the use of the force at their disposal by setting up military tribunals which could investigate the cases of persons charged with being rebels in arms. What should be the relationship of these tribunals to the ordinary courts of law was undetermined. In Ireland after the outbreak of insurrection in May 1798 military tribunals, termed courts martial, acting under a viceregal proclamation, began to sit and determine cases brought before them. But the ordinary courts remained open. During the rising, term began at the Four Courts and the autumn assizes were held (except in Wexford and Wicklow), though they had to be postponed for some weeks in the west. It could therefore be argued in November that the state of emergency which would justify military tribunals inquiring into the conduct of civilians no longer existed. On the other hand, it could be contended that

---

[1] *Faulkner's Dublin Journal*, 10 Nov. 1798.
[2] For accounts of the court martial, see below (pp 374–98)

many areas were seriously disturbed, and that the ordinary courts could function only if protected by military force and supplemented by special tribunals—an argument which was to receive legislative sanction by the passing of the suppression of rebellion act early in 1799.[1]

On 9 November it was rumoured in Dublin that Tone's friends intended to ask the king's bench to grant a prohibition against his being brought before a court martial. The court martial, however, sat too early in the day 'to render such a motion if granted useful'.[2] But on Monday 12 November, J. P. Curran moved in the king's bench for a writ of habeas corpus on Tone's behalf, arguing that with the courts open 'a court sitting under the authority of martial law had no jurisdiction over civilians'.[3] It was said that Curran intended that if Tone were brought before the king's bench to argue that, since he had already been brought by the crown before the wrong tribunal, tried and sentenced, he must now be discharged, otherwise he would be placed in double jeopardy.[4] Lord Kilwarden, the chief justice of the king's bench, agreed to grant the writ, but when it was served on William Sandys, the brigade major of Dublin, he refused to obey it, stating that 'he acted under the orders of the general of the garrison'. Kilwarden, on being informed of Sandys's attitude, took decisive steps to uphold the authority of his court, ordering the sheriff to go to the barracks and take Tone and his detainers into custody. When the sheriff appeared at the barracks he was met by Lieutenant-General Peter Craig and a return was made that Tone had attempted suicide, had severely injured himself and could not, with safety, be moved. On the evening of 11 November, Tone had been informed that the court martial's sentence had been confirmed by the lord lieutenant. With a strong sense of honour and dignity, he was bound to prefer suicide to an ignominious death—a course sanctioned by classical antiquity. About 4 a.m. on the 12th, Major Sandys was informed that Tone had cut his throat.[5] Tone's attempt at suicide infuriated strong conservatives, who wanted the competency of the military tribunals to deal with suspected rebels to be upheld by bold action.[6] But the law officers at some stage (probably on 12 November) advised the administration that a writ of habeas corpus must be obeyed.[7] Cornwallis certainly did not want to provoke a clash of jurisdictions

---

[1] For the principles governing the use of military force in an emergency, see William Blackstone, *Commentaries on the laws of England* (6th ed., London, 1774), i, 251; *Charge of the lord chief justice of England to the grand jury . . . in the case of the queen against Nelson and Brand* (2nd ed., London, 1867); *Halsbury's laws of England* (1st ed., London, 1909), vi, 402–03; F. W. Maitland, *The constitutional history of England* (Cambridge, 1931), pp 266–8, 324–5, 490–92.

[2] *Morning Post*, 14 Nov. 1798.   [3] Ibid., 17 Nov. 1798.

[4] *Morning Chronicle*, 19 Nov. 1798.

[5] *Morning Post*, 17 Nov. 1798; *Faulkner's Dublin Journal*, 13 Nov. 1798.

[6] Marquis of Buckingham to Lord Grenville, 13 Nov. 1798 (below, pp 417–18); Sir George Hill to Edward Cooke, 15 Nov. 1798 (below, pp 418–20); R. Brownrigg to duke of York, 16 Nov. 1798 (P.R.O., WO 133/2).

[7] *Cornwallis corr.*, iii, 11; Cornwallis to Portland, 10 Dec. 1798 (P.R.O., HO 100/79).

and from the middle of November 1798 until the suppression of rebellion act became law in March 1799 civilians were rarely brought before a military tribunal.

Tone, after lingering some days, died on 19 November 1798 and was buried in the Tone family grave at Bodenstown in County Kildare.

To Matilda Tone, 13 January 1797

Tone (Dickason) papers; *Life*, ii, 381–4.

Paris, 13 January, 1797

My dearest Love,

I have this instant received your letter, which I have read with a mixture of pleasure and pain which I cannot describe. Thank God, you are safe thus far with our darling babies! I will not hear, I will not believe, that your health is not in the best possible state; at the same time, I entreat you, as you value *my* life, that you may take all possible care of yourself, for you know very well, if anything were to happen you, I could not survive you, and then what would become of the little things? But let me tell you first about myself. I am only this morning arrived at Paris from Brest, whence I was dispatched by the general commanding the army intended for Ireland, in the absence of Gen[era]l Hoche, in order to communicate with the Executive Directory.[1] I am at present Adjutant General and I can live on my appointments; and when the peace comes, we will rent a cabin and a garden and be as happy as emperors on my half-pay; at the same time I am not without hopes that the government here may do something better for me; but, for all this, it is indispensable that you be in rude health. Who will milk the cows, or make the butter, if you are not stout? Indeed, my dearest love, I cannot write with the least connexion when there is question of your safety.

Let me begin again. The 16th of last month we sailed from Brest with 17 sail of the line besides frigates &c., to the number in all of 43 sail, having on board 15,000 troops and 45,000 stand of arms with artillery &c. We were intended for Ireland, but no unfortunate fleet was ever so tossed by storm and tempest; at length the division on which I embarked was forced to return to Brest, the 2d of this month, after lying eight days in Bantry Bay, near Cork, without being able to put a man ashore. We brought back about 5,000 men and, as the General has not yet returned, we are in great hopes that he has effected a landing with the other 10,000, in which case we shall retrieve everything. In the meantime I am here waiting the orders of the Gov[ernmen]t. If the expedition be renewed, I shall of course return to Brest; if not, I will wait your arrival at Paris. This is a hasty sketch of my affairs, but I have a *journal* for you in eleven little volumes.[2] I have only to add that I am in the

---

[1] The allusion is to General Emmanuel Grouchy, who took over the military command of the Bantry Bay expedition when General Lazare Hoche was separated from the main force, his ship being blown far to the west.

[2] It was written during the period 2 Feb. 1796 to 1 Jan. 1797 and is printed above (vol. II).

highest health and should be in as good spirits if it were not for these two cruel lines where you speak of yourself.[1]

Let me come now to your affairs, or rather Mary's.[2] I will give my opinion in one word by saying that I leave everything to her own decision; I have no right and, if I had, I have no wish to put the smallest constraint upon her inclination; I certainly feel a satisfaction at the prospect of her being settled and I entreat her to receive my most earnest and anxious wishes for her future happiness. As far therefore as my consent may be necessary, I give it in the fullest and freest manner, and I write to Mons[ieu]r Giauque[3] accordingly by the same post which brings you this. When an affair of that kind is once determined upon I do not see the use of delay and therefore I think they had better be married in Hambourg; but I hope Mons[ieu]r Giauque will have the goodness to see you safe into France when the season is sufficiently advanced to admit of your travelling, for I will not hear of your exposing yourself and our children in this dreadful season. Indeed, at any rate until my business here is decided, you had better remain at Hamburgh [*sic*], or some village in the neighbourhood, according as you find most agreeable to your health and circumstances; the expense will be much the same as in France and you will not hazard your safety. I shall soon know now whether our affair will be prosecuted or not; if it is, I am of course compelled to take my share and must return to my post; if it is not, I will go for you myself to Hamburgh; but in all events I positively desire and enjoin you not to stir until the season will admit of your travelling without injury to your health, and I hope the marriage of Mons[ieu]r Giauque and Mary may render your stay for a short period both convenient and agreeable.

I return to my own affairs. You desire me to write something comfortable and in consequence I tell you, in the first place, that I doat upon you and the Babs and, in the next place, that my pay and appointments amount to near 8,000 livres a year, of which one fourth is paid in cash and the remainder in paper, so that I receive now about £84 ster[lin]g a year, and

---

[1] It appears that Matilda Tone suffered a miscarriage (cf. above, vol. II, pp 340, 403).

[2] Mary Tone, his sister. She had accompanied him and his family to America and later accompanied Matilda Tone back to Europe. She made the acquaintance of Jean Frédéric Giauque (see below, n. 3) on the voyage from America in 1796; they married in Hamburg on 29 Jan. 1797 and lived there for about two years, first at Rödingsmarkt, then at Speenshörn. In April 1798 they were in Paris. Later, according to William Tone, 'Mary followed her husband to St Domingo and died of the yellow fever, during the siege of Cap Français, attending a sick friend' (*Neues Hamburger und Altonaer Adress-Buch*, 1797 and 1798 (Hamburg, 1797–8); *Life*, ii, 546; Paul Weber, *On the road to rebellion: the United Irishmen and Hamburg, 1796–1803* (Dublin, 1997), p. 57; Hamburger Staatsarchiv, Kämmerei I, no. 225, Fremdenschoßbücher, Bd 2, 1793–1811, Seite 150; Wedd I, no. 29, Bd 78, Hochzeitenprotokoll de anno 1797; Tone to Mathew Tone, 18, 23 Apr. 1798 (below, pp 236–7, 242–3).

[3] Jean Frédéric Giauque, merchant, said to be from Neuchâtel, Switzerland. Very little is known about him. In Sept. 1799, when he was living at No. 906, rue Rousselet, Paris, his name appeared with those of six United Irishmen (Thomas Corbet, James Joseph MacDonnell, William Henry Hamilton, Anthony MacCann, John Donovan and Thomas Howard) in a notarial document supporting their request for a widow's pension for Matilda Tone (Archives de la Guerre, 17 yd 14, Généraux prétendus, Dossier personnel of T. W. Tone; see also above, n. 2).

when we come to be paid all in cash, as we shall be some time or other, my pay will be about £350 a year; but supposing it be no more than £84 a year, I will rent a cottage and a few acres of land within a few miles of Paris in order to be on the spot, and with our £84 a year, a couple of cows, a hog and some poultry, you will see whether we will not be happy. That is the worst that can happen us; but if our expedition succeeds, of which as yet I know nothing but which a very few days must now decide, only think what a change that will make in our affairs, and even if anything should happen me, in that event you and the Babies will be the care of the nation; so let me entreat of you not to give way to any gloomy ideas. I look upon Mary's marriage, supposing the young man to have a good character and an amiable temper, which I trust he has from your report, to be a very fortunate circumstance; for as to riches you and I well know by our experience how independant happiness is of wealth.

When I tell you that, after tossing three weeks on a stormy sea, I have passed the last seven days in a carriage almost without sleep, you will not wonder at the want of connexion in this letter, but I am obliged to write in order to catch the post. Your letter is dated, *generally*, Hamburgh, but I put mine in a train that I hope it will reach you. Henceforward I will direct to you at the Post Office, where you must send Mons[ieu]r Giauque to look for my letters. I will write to you again by the next post but one, by which time I hope to have some news, one way or other, for you. Direct your answer to *Le Citoyen Smith, Petite Rue St Roch, Poissonnière, No. 7, à Paris*. Once more, keep up your spirits; be sure that if I am not ordered on the affair you wot of, I will go myself and fetch you from Hamburgh and, as the weather will not admit of your stirring for a short period, there is no time lost. My sincere love to Mary and the little ones. God Almighty forever bless you, because I doat on you.

Yours ever,
J. Smith

Let Mons[ieu]r Giauque give his address & yours to the gentleman who will hand you this in case I should find it necessary to write by the same channel.

À Madame Smith
À Hambourg

To Matilda Tone, 17 January 1797

Tone (Dickason) papers; *Life*, ii, 384–8.

Petite Rue St Roch, Poissonnière, No. 7
Paris, Jany 17, 1797

Dearest Love,

I wrote to you the 13th ins[tan]t,[1] being the day after my arrival at Paris from Brest, whence I was dispatched by the General with letters to the Directoire. My mind was so affected then (and still is) by the apprehension of your illness that I scarcely know what I wrote to you and I do not believe my present letter will be more connected. To begin with what interests me most, your health, I positively enjoin you not to attempt coming to France until I give you further orders. I suppose I need not say that my impatience to embrace you and our dear little ones is fully equal to that which I know you feel to see me once more, but I cannot permit you to undertake a journey of that nature in this dreadful season, when there are so few conveniences for travelling, when your health is so delicate, and you have three children whose constitution cannot possibly support the fatigue and the cold. I desire you may immediately, and on the most economical system, take a lodging for yourself and the Babies and make it out as well as you can until the beginning of April. In this, Mons[ieu]r Giauque, to whom I wrote in vile French by the last post, will of course assist you. I presume you will be accom[m]odated equally well and much cheaper in some of the villages within a few leagues of Hamburgh than in the city; but you will decide for yourself. My wish is, however, that you should rather be in a village, if it were only for the purity of the air and the convenience of having new milk, of which I beg you make the principal part of your diet; the children too will be better. By the beginning of April the stormy season will be over, and then I think your best method will be to come in a Danish vessell or any other neutral bottom to Havre de Grâce. It will be much cheaper, especially if you have any baggage, much shorter and, what I think more of, will fatigue you and the children infinitely less than a journey of a thousand miles by land. I speak in this manner on the supposition that I should be at that time *on service*, of which as yet I know nothing; if I am not, the moment I am satisfied that I can quit the army with honor, I will the same instant set off for Hamburgh and bring you with me to France. In my last I wrote you three words on the fate of the expedition. What the further decision of the Government here may be, I know not; but at any rate I am almost sure I shall receive within three or four days orders to return to Brest to Headquarters, and probably some time will elapse after, before we know whether anything further will be done or attempted in the business; so that you see by remaining, as I desire, at Hamburgh, you lose nothing, for if you were even in France we could not for some time be together and the expense will be just the same. If I find the expedition will not take place, I will apply immediately for leave of absence and join you; so once more I positively desire you may not attempt to expose yourself and the children to the perils and fatigues of such a journey at this time of year. Only think if you were taken ill by the road!

---

[1] Above, pp 1–2.

On your allegiance do not stir until further orders, and count upon my impatience in the meantime being equal to yours, which is saying enough.

With regard to your finances, all I have to say is that

> *When both house & land is spent*
> *Then learning is most excellent.*[1]

I desired Reynolds in my letter[2] to get you specie for your stock and not to meddle with bills of exchange, and I see he did not pay the least attention to my request, *'for which his own gods damn him!'*.[3] I do not well understand that part of your letter where you speak of your *having* a bill on London for 500 dollars *which is not received*. However, as Mons[ieu]r Giauque is, or is about to be, one of our family, and as he is a man used to commercial affairs, of which I know nothing, I presume he will do his best to recover the money for you; but if it should be lost, let it go! We shall be rich enough to make ourselves peasants, and I will buy you a handsome pair of *sabots* (in English, *wooden shoes*) and another for myself, and you will see, with my half-pay, which is the worst that can happen us, we shall be as happy as the day is long. I will, the moment I am clear of the business in which I am engaged, devote the remainder of my life to making you happy and educating our little ones; and I know you well enough to be convinced that when we are once together all stations in life are indifferent to you. If you are lucky enough to recover your 500 dollars, do not take another bill of exchange, but keep your money by you until you hear again from me.

I am surprised you did not receive my last letter addressed to you at Princeton,[4] because I *enclosed it* in one to Reynolds and Rowan jointly which it seems they received, which is a little extraordinary; however as it happens it is no great matter, for it was little more than a duplicate of the one you got by way of Havre.[5]

I am heartily glad that Matt[6] is safe and well. If I had him here now I could make him a captain and my aid-du-camp for a word's speaking to the General; so that, if he has any wish for a military life it is unlucky that he did not come with you as I desired in my letter to you which miscarried; but perhaps it is all for the better, and at any rate it is now too late to write

---

[1] Samuel Foote, *Taste* (1752), i, 1.

[2] Either the letter to Reynolds mentioned in his diary for 26 May 1796, or that to Rowan mentioned in his diary for 30 July 1796 (see above, vol. II, pp 190, 258).

[3] Tone may have been recalling these words from John Hawkesworth, *Orounoko* (1759), act V, final scene.

[4] Apparently the letter to his wife which he began on 17 July 'desiring her to sell off everything and embark in the first vessel for Havre de Grâce'; he gave it to the American consul-general, Fulwar Skipwith, on 29 July 1796 together with one for Rowan (see above, vol. II, pp 239, 258, 403). Matilda Tone wrote in her letter to Thomas Russell of 11 Sept. 1796 (above, vol. II, p. 312): 'I had a letter from Tone about a fortnight since. We are all to join him . . . this fall.'

[5] Perhaps the letter to Matilda Tone dated 30 Nov. and 2 Dec. 1796 which Tone sent under cover to Nicholas Madgett (above, vol. II, pp 403–8). In *Life*, ii, 386, at this point there is a footnote: 'these letters contained directions to my mother to carry the papers and everything from America. Can it be that Reynolds already meditated to keep them?'   [6] Mathew Tone.

for him on that topic. If we succeed, by and bye, I shall be able to provide for him and all my friends who need my assistance and who luckily are not many. Our expedition is at present but suspended; it may be resumed and if we once reach our destination I have no doubt of success, and in that case I will reserve for Matt the very first company of grenadiers in the army; so Mary will have two brothers in that case of the *état militaire* instead of one; and perhaps she may have three, for Arthur (of whom I have not heard one word since he left Philadelphia) is now old enough to carry a pair of colors.

The uncertainty in which I am with regard to the expedition embarrasses me a good deal in writing to you. If it goes on, I proceed of course with the army; and in that case I have the warmest expectations of success, which will set us at once at our ease; if it is laid aside, that instant I will set out to join you; and console yourself for the delay by the reflection that, for the reasons I have already given you, we lose no time, for at present it is absolutely impossible that you should travel.

In my last, as well as in my letter to Mons[ieu]r Giauque, I gave my consent fully to his marriage with Mary. I presume, in consequence, they will make no delay. If they should be married when you receive this, give them my warmest and sincerest wishes for their happiness. Mary knows how well I love her, and I hope and trust she has made a proper choice. I rely upon the friendship of Mons[ieu]r Giauque to shew you all possible assistance and attention during your stay at Hambourg.

Adieu, dearest Love. I send this under cover to a gentleman at Hambourg who will I hope find you out. Write to me instantly and tell me that you are well and as happy as you can be while we are separated. Kiss the babies for me ten thousand times. If I am ordered off, as I expect, I will write again before I leave Paris. God Almighty for ever bless you, my dearest Life & Soul.

Yours ever,
J. Smith, Adj[utan]t Gen[era]l!!!!

I send you the names of several villages in the neighbourhood of Hambourg,[1] viz. Altona;[2] Grindel, *hors de la porte de* Damthore;[3] Eimsbüttel,[4] *hors de la porte d'*Altona; Ham, *hors de la porte de* Steinthor;[5] Eppendorf,[6] *hors de la porte de* Damthor. The address of the person who will (I hope) deliver you this is Mons[ieu]r Holterman,[7] *demeurant* Neuen-Wall,[8] No. 123. If you remove, as I beg you may, to a village in the neighbourhood, it will be to him I shall direct my letters, so you will take care to give him your

---

[1] The information that follows seems to have been taken from a gazetteer.

[2] In fact Altona was a town with a population of 20,000 in 1790; it lay only 2 km west of Hamburg (Paul Weber, *On the road to rebellion: the United Irishmen and Hamburg* (Dublin, 1997), pp 24–5).

[3] *Recte* Damthor. Grindel is about 2 km north of the Neustadt.

[4] Eimsbüttel is about 3 km north-west of the Neustadt.

[5] The Steinthor was the gate to the east of the Neustadt; Ham lay just beyond.

[6] Eppendorf is about 4.5 km north-north-west of the Altstadt.

[7] Not further identified. [8] *Recte* Neuer Wall, which is in the Neustadt.

address. In all this, Mons[ieu]r Giauque will, of course, assist you. Adieu, once more, my dearest love. *Do not attempt to quit Hambourg until I desire you, as you value my affection.* I will not attempt to express the admiration I feel for your courage; but remember, courage and rashness are two different things. For my sake, and for the sake of our dear babies, take care of your health. I am in a state of anxiety on your account which no words can express. I doat upon you; my life lies in you; I could not survive you four and twenty hours. If you do not wish to deprive our children of both their parents, do not attempt to stir until I permit you. Count upon my love for you, and our dear, dear babies. The tears gush into my eyes, so that I can scarcely see what I write and I am not very subject to that weakness. I trust in God it is only the fatigue of the journey from Cuxhaven that has affected you.[1] Dear, dear Love, take care of yourself, and do not let your impatience to see me induce you to expose your health. If all that will not do, I order you, *as a general*, not to quit your post without my permission.

J. S.

À Madame Smith
À Hambourg

To Colonel William Tate, 19 January 1797

Tone (Dickason) papers; *Castlereagh corr.*, i, 434–5.

Mrs Katherine Dickason believed that this letter was purchased by Miss Katherine Anne Maxwell.

Petite Rue Roch, Poissonnière, no. 7
30 Nivôse, an 5

Dear Colonel,

I was in hopes to have had a line from you before this. I have been now at Paris seven days, and I have not one syllable of news but what I have learned from the gazettes. You know my old and laudable custom, to ask no questions, so I can of course give you nothing but my own conjectures, and I am sorry to say they are not favourable to the probability of a second trial.[2] The Government *may* take up our business again, but I much fear it; it is so easy to find fault *after* the event, and so easy to demonstrate that an expedition which has actually failed could by no possibility have succeeded! Well, I will if possible think no more about it; I have acted all along to the best of my judgement, I have made great sacrifices (great, in proportion to my means) in the cause of my country and the Republic, and if we have not succeeded, I have the consolation at least to think that it is not my fault.

---

[1] William Tone states that 'after a tedious and rough passage of two months', Matilda Tone and her children 'landed at the mouth of the frozen Elbe and proceeded to Hamburgh in an open post wagon' (*Life*, ii, 337).   [2] i.e. expedition.

My mind is in a situation which I cannot describe, and to aggravate my distress I have just received a letter from my wife, dated at Hamburgh, where she arrived before Christmass, which gives me the most dreadful alarms as to her health; the remnant of my fortune is by unforeseen circumstances diminished *one half* since I saw you, but that is the least of my concerns. In short I am at present in a situation which I would recommend to my enemies, if I have any, to come and indulge themselves with the prospect.

I am here waiting the orders of the Minister at War. Perhaps I may be sent back to Brest, but I doubt it. In the meantime I think, all desperate as I am of your business, if it be taken up, and if I can get my wife and children once safe in France, I think more and more of taking a part in it. In that case I may perhaps (but God knows) be of some use to you; at least you may trust to my discretion that if I cannot be of use I will at least be of no prejudice to you; if therefore you think proper, send me such papers and memorandums as may enable me to speak, with information, on the subject, for I believe if I do not deceive myself, I have a channel open by which I can come at the fountain head. Perhaps my ill star may not always be in the mood to persecute me.

Send me by return of the post an exact list of all the vessels of all sorts which have returned from our unfortunate expedition. I learn this moment that General Hoche is arrived in safety at Rochelle; that is a great point gained![1]

Once more, if you think I can be of use in your affair (to which latterly I turn my thoughts more and more) and if you have confidence in me, send me without a moment's delay such documents as may be useful and I will stretch that string as far as it will go without cracking. Adieu, dear Colonel,

Yours truly,
J. Smith

Direct to me, simply, *Au Citoyen Smith*; my address is at the top of my letter. Do not tell anyone I write to you.

Au Colonel Taite
Rue J. J. Rousseau
À Brest

[*Pencilled on back*]: General Wolfe Tone intercepted letter.
[*In ink*]: From Tate's Papers.

William Henry Tone to Peter Tone, 25 January 1797

T.C.D., Madden papers, MS 873/36; printed in R. R. Madden, *The United Irishmen*, 3rd ser. (London, 1846), i, 179–82.

[1] Hoche landed on the French coast on 13 January (Arthur Chuquet (ed.), *Quatre généraux de la Révolution: Hoche et Desaix, Kléber et Marceau* (4 vols, Paris, 1911–20), ii, 63–6).

The original was lent to Madden by a Mrs Moore, a relation of the Tone family, and a copy was made. Some obvious small errors of transcription have been silently corrected here.

There are difficulties with the dating of this document and some indications that the year should be 1798.

Bombay, January 25th, '79[1]

Dear Father,

I wrote to you by the overland dispatch which left this settlement the 1st inst[an]t, which I hope will reach you long before this can.[2] By the same conveyance I sent a bill of exchange for one hundred pounds on the house of Law & Bruce, Laurence Lane, London, and transmits [*sic*] by the ships of this season the duplicate and triplicate in case the first should miscarry. Should this be the case, you will immediately write to Messrs Bruce & Law, where you will hear of the money, which I am sure must be convenient to you; and I only hope it may do you all the good that I wish. It is with very great regret that I have to complain of the total neglect which I have been treated with by the whole family—an inattention which I cannot forbear calling unkind. I will not, however, commence this letter (which is, I believe, the twentieth which I have written to you) with any reproaches; but I trust that this will produce an answer; & I can only assure you, if you will communicate with me and apprize me of your real situation, that my purse, person and credit shall be strained for your convenience.

My present situation I shall describe as concisely as possible. I have for some time commanded a small corps in the service of Paishwa, the head of the Mahratta Empire. My pay has been tolerably liberal; but my expenses have nearly kept pace with it. I have it therefore in contemplation to go into the service of the Lomba of the Dekan, where I have an offer of a brigade. I have not as yet determined, but shall inform you more fully in my next.[3] In other respects I am very well in health, not very rich, but far above want, and have the peculiar happiness of enjoying the countenance and attention of the first characters in this country; a circumstance the more flattering, as I may say without vanity, that [it] is the consequence of my own behaviour. One circumstance has contributed very much to make me known here. I have now in the press a little book, a treatise on Mahratta institutions, which will be

---

[1] The MS reads ''79', the printed version '1779', but this is obviously incorrect.

[2] It is almost certainly the letter dated 'Bombay, 1st January' and printed in R. R. Madden, *United Irishmen*, 3rd ser. (London, 1846), i, 182. Nearly all the internal evidence suggests it is the same letter. There is, however, an apparent contradiction in remarks William Henry Tone makes about his employment in the service of the Lomba of the Dekan (see below, n. 3).

[3] He states, however, in the letter dated 1 January and printed by Madden: 'I at this time command a brigade in the service of Nizam Ali, the Lomba of the Dekan, and in high favour at court, and very much patronized by the British residents and, in one word, have a universal acquaintance and am much respected. I have had offers of commissions in the King and Company's service but prefer my present situation.'

published in the course of a month.[1] It is tolerably well written & contains a good deal of local information. I sold the copy[right] a few days ago for a thousand rupees, which is the sum I sent for your use, which you will consider the first-fruits of my literary labours. This incident has procured me great reputation and a general correspondence with our Asiatic literati, many of whom I know only by letter. The work itself I shall send you when I hear from you, and also another to Theobald in America, where I understand he is.[2] I have a very dear friend of mine returning to Boston, who has promised to find him out if he be on the continent.[3] As I am not certain whether this will reach you or not, I shall say but very little more. I have only to entreat you to write to me at large; let me candidly know your situation, which I am certain is not a splendid one. Professions are, I trust, not necessary between you & me; but be assured the last rupee I possess or can raise shall be chearfully contributed to your wants and that of the family.

Write to me whenever this reaches you and I will see what can be done; but I will positively give myself no further concern unless I receive an answer to this letter. I write constantly to our old friend Harry Douglas[4] and I am happy to be able to inform you that I have had it in my power lately to do him a small service in return for the very great one he conferred on me. He met lately with a young man, a natural son of his father's, in the ranks in Bengal and, not knowing exactly how to provide for him, I desired him to send him round to me. I very fortunately happened to be in Bombay when he arrived, and shall take him up the country with me, where I am pretty certain of being able to procure him an appointment that will be worth from two or three hundred pounds a year. This circumstance may possibly put you upon thinking of something for Arthur. I wish to God I had him here: I could, without any difficulty, get him a commission in His Majesty's service, or perhaps something better; but of this more when I hear from you.

Tell my mother, my dear Mary, & in short all the family, that I love them entirely; nor is it possible for any length of time or separation to alter me. I wish, however, to give other proofs than profession; but that totally depends

---

[1] *A letter to an officer of the Madras establishment, being an attempt to illustrate some particular institutions of the Mahratta people, principally relative to their system of war and finance; also an account of the political changes of the empire in the year 1796* (Bombay: *Courier*, 1798, 110 pp).

[2] In the letter dated 1 January he writes, 'in God's name where is ——? I have heard from the public papers of his having gone to America.'

[3] Probably John Parker Boyd (1764–1830), a native of Massachusetts, who arrived in India in 1789 and served various Indian rulers including the Nizam, Holkar and the Peishwa; he left India in 1798; he was in Paris in 1806 and returned finally to America in 1808. He was probably the General Boyd who delivered 'a packet containing probably the history, notes &c.' of William Henry Tone in India to Dr James Reynolds in Philadelphia. (*Life*, ii, 561, fn; *American national biography* (New York, 1999), iii, 311–12).

[4] Probably Henry Douglas (d. 1803), cadet, 1778; lieut., 1784; capt., 1795; major of artillery, 1798; served in second and third Mysore wars (V. C. P. Hobson, *List of the officers of the Bengal army, 1758–1834*, pt II (London, 1928), p. 75).

on the answer to this. Give my love to my poor mother and every one whom I care for. And believe me, dear Sir,

Your ever affectionate son,
W. H. Tone

Direct to me exactly 'Henry Fawcitt, Esqr, Bombay, recommended to the care of Messrs Law and Bruce, Larkins Lane, London'.

Peter Tone, Esqr, 10 Monk Place

To General Lazare Hoche, 29 January 1797

Tone (Dickason) papers.

After relating how he was of service to France by communicating with a French agent in Ireland in 1794 and (after fleeing to America) with the French ambassador in Philadelphia, as well as by coming to France in 1796 to be commissioned in the army and be with Hoche, Tone reluctantly confesses his need for money: 'if my services can still be useful to my country and to the Republic, I am ready to begin again'; if not, can he be retired on pay or be reimbursed for his expenses?

Paris, ce 10 Pluviôse an 5
reçu le 10

Mon Général

J'ai l'honneur de vous exposer que l'ancien Comité du salut public ayant envoyé une personne affidée en Irlande (en 1794)[1] pour ouvrir une communication avec les patriotes de ce pays, je lui ai donné par écrit tous les renseignemens nécessaires pour effectuer cet objet. Malheureusement il étoit trahi par un de ses amis,[2] arrêté par le gouvernement anglois, mis en jugement et condamné à la mort, en conséquence de quoi j'étois forcé de quitter ma patrie et d'aller avec toute ma famille en exil dans la Nouvelle Angleterre,[3] ayant avec la plus grande difficulté évité une mort ignominieuse.

Dès mon arrivée à Philadelphie je me suis présenté chez le Citoyen Adet, ambassadeur de la République, et après lui avoir communiqué tout ce que je croyois de plus important sur l'état actuel d'Irlande, il m'a conseillé de venir en France pour m'expliquer de vive voix avec son gouvernement, ce que je fis en conséquence, le Ministre ayant la bonté de me donner une lettre d'introduction au Directoire Exécutif, et de m'offrir d'argent pour mes dépenses, lequel j'ai refusé d'accepter.

En conséquence je suis venu en France au commencement de 1796. Je me suis présenté au Citoyen Carnot, et après, par ses ordres, au Général Clarke.

---

[1] William Jackson.   [2] John Cockayne.

[3] In fact Tone and his family landed in Delaware, spent some weeks in Pennsylvania and then settled in New Jersey; none of these states is in New England.

Ces deux citoyens sont instruits de toute ma conduite et ont entre leurs mains tous les mémoires, &c., que j'ai préparés et arrangés, d'après leurs ordres.

Enfin, l'argent que j'avois apporté avec moi étant épuisé, le Directoire eut la bonté de me nommer au grade du chef de brigade au mois de Messidor, et bientôt après je reçus des ordres de me rendre à Rennes. Depuis ca tems là, Général, ayant eu le bonheur d'être auprès de vous, je me soumets avec respect et confiance à votre decision sur ma conduite.

Si l'objet qui m'a attiré en France avoit réussi, assurément ce seroit à ma patrie que je me serois adressé pour la récompense de tous mes périls, mes souffrances et mes sacrifices. J'aurois même fidèlement rendu à la Trésorerie Nationale tous les appointements que j'aurois touché, pendant que j'avois l'honneur d'être au service de la République; mais actuellement que je me vois forcé de désespérer enfin de l'affranchissement de ma patrie, je me jette sur l'honneur, sur la justice même, du Gouvernement François pour m'accorder telle recompense qu'il pourra juger convenable, je ne dirai pas à mes services mais au moins aux sacrifices que j'ai fait dans une poursuite également interéssante à l'Irlande et à la République.

Quand j'ose faire cette demande, Général, je vous donne ma parole, la plus sacrée, que si j'avois les moyens d'exister autrement, je ne mettrai pas [*sic*] la République à la dépense d'un sous sur mon compte; mais, exilé de mon pays, avec un bien très modique, que les dépenses indispensables de ma famille (que j'ai laissée dans la Nouvelle Angleterre) et les miennes pendant mon séjour en France ont réduit presque à rien, ayant une femme et trois enfans qui dépendent de moi seul pour leur existence, je suis forcé malgré moi de m'adresser à vous, et de vous prier, Général, de me recommander à la notice du Gouvernement.

Je sais trop bien, les difficultés actuelles de la République à l'égard de ses finances et cela augmente infiniment la répugnance que je sens de vous donner cette peine, mais enfin je n'ai pas d'autre resource. C'est pour ma femme et pour mes enfans; voilà mon excuse. J'éspère que je trouverai mon meilleur avocat dans votre coeur.

Je n'ai qu'une chose de plus à vous dire—si mes services peuvent jamais être utiles à ma patrie et à la République, je suis toujours prêt à recommencer, sans être du tout rebuté, ni des difficultés, ni des dangers que j'ai essuyés jusqu'ici; mais si le Gouvernement a décidé de ne plus tenter l'entreprise à laquelle je me suis si longtems dévoué, je sens mon incapacité trop pour désirer de rester dans ma situation actuelle, quand il y a tant de braves officiers qui ont bien mérité de la République sans être arrivés au grade duquel il a plu au Directoire de m'honorer. Dans ce cas là, peut-être on m'accordera *ma retraite avec permission de garder mes appointemens*, à moins que le Gouvernement ne préfère pas de me rembourser la totalité de la somme que j'ai été forcé de dépenser ou de sacrifier dans le progrès de cette malheureuse affaire.

Encore une fois, Général, si le Gouvernement envoye jamais *dix* hommes en Irlande, je suis toujours prêt à être du nombre, *et avec peu de forces nous pourrions, au moins, y faire une belle chouannerie*; mais si il a déjà décidé autrement, il ne me reste que de me recommander à votre justice, à votre honneur, oserai-je dire à votre amitié, pour m'obtenir telle compensation que vous jugerez convenable à mes services et à la dignité de la République.

Salut et Respect,
James Smith
Adj[udan]t Gén[éra]l dans l'armée expéditionnaire

Au Général en Chef Hoche,
&c., &c., &c.[1]

Diary, 31 January 1797

T.C.D., Tone papers, MS 2049, ff 188ʳ–197ᵛ; *Life*, ii, 337–42.

No. 12
From Jan[uar]y 1st 1797 to March 25th[2]
Nil desperandum!
Paris
1797[3]

31 Jan. 1797[4]

It is exactly a month today since I wrote a line by way of memorandum.[5] It will be well supposed I had no great inclination, nor in fact have I had much to say. On our arrival at Brest, after a day or two there was a little intrigue set on foot against Gen[era]l Grouchy with a view to lessen the merit of his services, in consequence of which he determined to send me to Paris with his dispatches for the Directory and the Minister at War.[6] Simon was joined with me in commission, and Fairin was also dispatched by Chérin, who is at the head of this dirty[7] cabal. Grouchy desired me to state fairly what I thought of his conduct during our stay in Bantry Bay to the Government, and I was not a little pleased with this proof of his good opinion. We set off on the 5th of January at night and arrived without accident at Paris on the

---

[1] A note in Hoche's hand in the top right-hand corner of this letter reads: 'faire une copie pour être adressée au Directoire avec la demande de sa conservation motivée sur l'utilité dont il peut être, lui faire une réponse flatteuse, lui témoigner ma satisfaction de sa conduite'.

[2] The Diary entries for 8 Feb., 18 Feb.–5 Mar., 10–20 Mar., 24 Mar. and 25 Mar. are given as separate documents (below).

[3] The preceding headings, which Tone obviously added later than 31 Jan., are omitted from *Life*.

[4] In the MS the year is centred and the date is given as 'January 1st–31st'. The diary was evidently written up on 31 Jan. 1797.   [5] Above, vol. II, pp 434–5.

[6] Pétiet.   [7] In *Life* this word is omitted.

12th. We went immediately to the Minister at War and delivered our letters; we saw him but for an instant; thence we went to the Directory, where we were introduced and had an audience for above half an hour at which all the Directors assisted.[1] They were of opinion on that day, from the latest accounts, that Hoche had effectuated a landing with that part of the army which had been separated off Bantry Bay, and in consequence we expected orders immediately to return to Brest. From the Directory I went to Doulcet,[2] a member of the Conseil de[s] Cinq Cens, brother-in-law to Grouchy, for whom, as well as for Madame Grouchy,[3] I had letters from the General. Doulcet invited [me] to dinner and I dined accordingly very agreeably. Madame Doulcet is a charming woman;[4] her name was Le Jay, she was the wife of a bookseller, and, as the scandalous Chronicle has it, mistress to the famous Mirabeau; she is ugly, but her conversation is delightful. The next day Doulcet introduced me to Lacuée, of the Conseil des Anciens, and the chosen friend of Carnot. I took that occasion to do justice to the zeal and spirit of General Grouchy, and I hope I succeeded. At four I went to dinner with the Minister at War and at eight, by appointment, to the Luxembourg, where I had an interview with Carnot and Lacuée, for about a quarter of an hour, on the subject of MacSheehy's mission into Ireland, the general result of which I endeavoured to impress upon Carnot. I also stated in the strongest manner what I felt in favor of Grouchy, so that so far I have done my duty by him. Several days elapsed in this manner, waiting continually for news of the General,[5] until at length on the 15th he arrived, with the *Révolution* of 74, at La Rochelle so that put at once an end to my expectations of anything further being attempted, at least for the present. About the 21st the General arrived at Paris, and I had the consolation to learn from his aid-du-camp, Poitou, that my friend Mr Sheé[6] was safe and in tolerable health; he had suffered dreadfully from the gout, never having quit his bed during the whole voyage of a month but once for a quarter of an hour.[7] The morning after his arrival I saw the General, for five minutes; he received me very favorably and asked me particularly about MacSheehy's expedition, which I detailed to him, and by his orders gave him an abstract of it in writing the next morning.[8] He asked me what I was doing at Paris? I told him I was sent by General Grouchy with his dispatches, and

[1] i.e. were present. The five Directors in Jan. 1797 were Barras, Carnot, La Revellière, Letourneur and Reubell.

[2] Louis Gustave Doulcet, comte de Pontécoulant (1764–1853), member of the Convention; voted for the banishment of Louis XVI; member of the Council of Five Hundred; count of the empire, 1808; peer of France (*Dict. biog. franç.*).

[3] Cécile Félicité Célestine Le Doulcet de Pontécoulant until she married Grouchy in 1785.

[4] The words that follow as far as and including 'she is ugly' are omitted from *Life*, and 'but' is changed to 'and'.   [5] i.e. Hoche.

[6] Henry (or Henri) Shee invariably signed his name 'Sheé', i.e. with an acute accent over the second 'e'. As Tone eventually came to spell it thus, contrary to the conventional Irish spelling as well as to modern French orthography, the editorial norm in this volume is 'Sheé'.

[7] Sheé's gout caused him difficulty when disembarking, in which Hoche came to his aid (see below, p. 19, n. 2).   [8] For MacSheehy's secret mission to Ireland, see above, vol. II, pp 367–9.

that I was waiting further orders. Four or five days after the General was named to the command of the Army of Sambre and Meuse, which was decisive with regard to our expedition, I began now to think of my own situation and that of my family, of whom it is at length, surely, time to speak.

On my arrival at Paris I found a letter at Madgett's from my wife dated at Hamburgh and informing me of her safe arrival there about the 20th of December with my sister[1] and the children, my brother[2] having decided to settle at Boston in America.[3] The transports of joy I felt at the news of her arrival were most dreadfully corrected by the account she gave me of her health, which threw me into the most terrible alarms. I wrote to her instantly to remain at Hamburgh until further orders and by no means to think of exposing herself, in her present weak state, and our dear little babies to a journey from Hamburg in this dreadful season, great part of the road being thro' a wild country where there is no better accom[m]odation for travelling than open waggons. In my wife's letter there was an account of an affair relative to my sister,[4] which is perfectly in the style of the romantic adventures of our family. A person who came over in the same ship,[5] a Swiss from Neuchâtel named Giauque, a young merchant just beginning the world, with little or no property, thought proper to fall in love with my sister.[6] In consequence I received, by the same conveyance which brought my wife's letter, one from Giauque,[7] informing me of his situation and circumstances, of his love for my sister and hers for him, and praying my consent. I must say[8] there was an air of candour and honesty in his letter, which gave me a good opinion of him, and I did not consider myself as at liberty to stand in the way of her happiness, which my wife mentioned to me was deeply interested[9] in the affair. I wrote therefore to Mons[ieu]r Giauque[10] giving my full consent to their marriage, and I trust in God they may be as happy as I wish them. It is certainly a step of great hazard in favour of a man whom I do not know, but as she is passionately fond of him, and he of her, as he perfectly knows her situation and has by no means endeavoured to disguise or exaggerate his own,[11] and especially, to repeat it, from the style of his letter which interested me very much, I am in hopes they may do well. At all events I have acted with the best intentions and to the best of my judgement under the circumstances,[12] and I trust, once more, in God they will be happy, for I love my sister dearly, and she is a most valuable girl. They will, I believe, settle in Hamburgh, so there is one more of our family dispersed. I am sure if there were *five* quarters in the Globe, there would be one of us

---

[1] Mary Tone.   [2] Mathew Tone.   [3] *Life* omits 'at Boston'.

[4] i.e. Mary Tone. In *Life* what follows up to and including 'our family' is omitted.

[5] In *Life*, ii, 339, what follows has been altered to 'a young Swiss merchant just beginning the world', neither Neuchâtel nor Giauque being named.

[6] In *Life*, 'her' is substituted for 'my sister'.   [7] In *Life*, 'him' is substituted for 'Giauque'.

[8] In *Life*, 'I must say' is omitted.   [9] The following three words are omitted from *Life*.

[10] The words 'to Monsr Giauque' are omitted from *Life*.

[11] What follows up to and including 'interested me very much' is omitted from *Life*.

[12] What follows up to and including 'valuable girl' is omitted from *Life*.

perched upon the fifth. Towards the end of the month I received a second letter from my wife, dated Dec[embe]r 27th, with a postscript from my little Maria, being the first line I have seen of her writing; it brought the tears fast into my eyes. Thank God my dearest love's health is a little better, for I have been most miserable ever since I received her first letter. I hope, however, mine may arrive in time, as well as a second, which I dispatched three days after the first to prevent her leaving Hamburgh.[1]

But to return to my affairs. On the 30th I wrote to Gen[era]l Hoche on the subject of my present situation, praying him to apply to the Government to permit me to retire from the service, preserving my pay and appointments, and at the same time offering at any future period wherein I might be useful, to resume my situation. The same evening I had a note from the General desiring to see me the next morning early, and accordingly this day (the 31st) I went to the Hotel of the Minister at War,[2] where he is lodged, at eight o'clock. On my calling on his aid-du-camp, Poitou, who makes his correspondence, Poitou shewed me my letter,[3] with a note in the margin written by the General: *'Faire une copie, pour être adressée au Directoire, avec la demande de sa conservation, motivée sur l'utilité dont il peut être; lui faire une réponse flatteuse et lui témoigner ma satisfaction de sa conduite.'*[4] Nothing certainly can be more agreeable to me. Poitou also shewed me, in confidence, the copy of the General's letter to the Directory in my favor, which is worded in the most flattering and strongest manner, so I am in hopes I shall succeed in my application. From Poitou I went to the General's appartment, who received me *like a friend*, which I remarked the more because his manner in general to his officers is cold and dry; he told me he had written to the Directory, and that I should carry the letter myself to General Dupont,[5] who transacts General Clarke's business in his absence; that Dupont would present me to the Directory in consequence, and he hoped the affair would be settled to my satisfaction. I returned him my acknowledgements, and in the course of what I said I mentioned the arrival of my wife and family at Hamburgh and my intention of going thither to bring them to France. The General seemed struck when I mentioned Hamburgh and asked me again was I going thither. I replied it was my intention as soon as I had settled the affair which he was so good as to undertake for me. 'Well then', said he, 'perhaps we may find something for you to do there; there is a person there whom perhaps you may see'. I told him that there, or anywhere that I could be useful to my country and the Republic, I was ready to go at an hour's warning; I added that when I asked my retreat for the present I begged him

---

[1] In MS, ff 192, 193 and 194 each have two or three lines overscored and illegible.
[2] In the Rue de Varennes (*Almanach national de France*)   [3] Above, pp 11–13.
[4] 'Make a copy to be addressed to the Directory with a request that it be preserved on account of the use he can be; make him a warm reply and indicate to him my satisfaction at his conduct.'
[5] Pierre Dupont de l'Étang (1765–1840), officer in the Dutch army, 1784–90; lieut. in French army, 1791; general of brigade, 1793; général de division, 1797; head of the 'Cabinet topographique et historique militaire' in succession to Clarke; director, dépôt de guerre, May–Sept. 1797; count of the empire, 1808; disgraced after his surrender at Baylen, 1808 (*Six, Dict. des généraux & amiraux*).

to remember that if ever our business were resumed under any form, I was as ready and desirous as ever to take my share in it and that I did not at all despair of having the honor of serving once more under his orders. 'The affair', replied he, 'is but suspended; you know our difficulties for money: the repair of our fleet and the necessary preparations require some considerable time, and in the mean time there are 15,000 men lying idle below, and, in fact, we cannot even feed them there; the Directory has resolved in the mean time to employ them usefully elsewhere and has accepted my services; but be assured the moment the enterprise is resumed that I will return with the first *patrouille* that embarks'. I expressed the satisfaction which this assurance gave me and, after a conversation of about half an hour in which I found him as warm and steady as ever in our business, I took my leave and tomorrow I am to have my letter for the Directory. This conversation with Hoche has given me spirits to recommence my memorandums, for in fact my mind has been in a state of stupor ever since I landed at Brest from our unfortunate expedition. Perhaps Providence has not yet given us up. For my part my courage, such as it is, is not abated a single jot, tho' I see by an article in the English papers that they were in hopes to catch the vessel on board of which I was embarked, in which case they were kind enough to promise that I should be properly taken care of.[1] They may go be hanged, and I do not '*value their chariot of a rush*'.[2] Buonaparte has beaten the Austrians for the five and fortyeth time this campaign, killed 7,000 and taken 23,000.[3] I mention this because it may bring about a peace with the Emperor, in which case we shall have nothing to do but lay along side of England, and perhaps we have not done with her yet. As soon as my affair here is settled, I will set off for Hamburgh and bring my dear, dear love and our little ones, and I think I will plant myself at Nanterre,[4] beside my friend Mr Sheé, in order to keep the communication open with General Clarke when he returns, and may be I may be able to do a little mischief yet. I feel this moment like a man who is just awakened from a long, terrible dream. Who is my lover that I am to see at Hamburgh, in God's name? '*I feel once more my ancient propensities begin to revive.*'[5] We shall see.

To General Lazare Hoche, 7 or 8 February 1797

N.L.I., French invasion papers, MS 705, ff 25-26. This is a copy in a nineteenth-century official hand.

[1] On 12 Jan. 1797 the *True Briton* reported that Hamilton Rowan was certainly on board the French fleet, adding 'we ardently hope he will be taken and made an example to those traitors who favour the hostile designs of the enemy'.   [2] Henry Fielding, *Joseph Andrews* (1742), ii, chap. 12.

[3] At Rivoli in northern Italy. According to Bonaparte himself, writing to the Directory on 28 Nivôse V (17 Jan. 1797), 6,000 Austrians had been killed or wounded and 23,000 (including three generals) taken prisoner since 23 Nivôse for the loss of 700 French dead and 1,200 wounded (*Correspondance de Napoléon 1ᵉʳ* (32 vols, Paris, 1858–70), ii, 248–9).

[4] Nanterre lies about 11 km west of Notre-Dame.

[5] Source of this quotation has not been traced.

In his diary for 8 Feb. 1797 (below, p. 21), Tone seems to imply that this letter was written that day.

Tone tells Hoche of reading in an English newspaper, the *Courier*, a report of a speech by Lord Clare; he refers also to an abortive royalist plot.

19 Pluviôs[e] an 5

Mon Général,

Je viens de lire dans une gazette anglaise (*The Courrier*, Jan[vie]r 26 ou 27) un discours du lord chancellier d'Irlande qui est l'organe de Pitt dans ce pays.[1] Il me fait l'honneur de parler de moi en me nommant deux fois dans son discours, et il m'accuse d'être le fondateur des *Club des Irlandais Unis* qui sont les ennemis, selon lui, les plus acharnés de la domination anglaise, ce qui, en effet, est bien vrai. Cette *grande colère* du Lord Chancelier à la vérité ne me fait pas beaucoup de peine, surtout quand je vois dans la même feuille qu'il s'est permis de faire une sortie furieuse contre *vous aussi*, Général. C'est un honneur trop flatteur pour moi, que de m'y trouver compris, avec vous, dans le nombre des ennemis d'Angleterre; je l'acheterais volontiers au prix de mon sang. Il y a encore une chose dans le même discours qui me paraît digne de notre observation. Tout en louant le zèle et la loyauté générale des Irlandais, il fait une exception en parlant des habitants du parti du Nord, et il dit nettement *qu'il craint beaucoup qu'il ne devient nécessaire de les ramener à leurs devoirs en faisant couler leur sang.* Ces paroles sont trop remarquables pour être dites par hazard, et je crains beaucoup que le ministre anglais ne soit décidé de mettre le plus grand parti de ce pays sous exécution militaire comme il a déjà fait dans plusieurs districts, et dans ce cas là, Dieu sait quel en sera la conséquence. Oh! mon Général, plût aux cieux que vous étiez à Londonderrie aujourd'hui même, avec une seule demi-brigade, et l'artillerie légère nous mettrions bientôt à la raison le Lord Chancelier et tous ses adhérens.

Je présume que le Directoire est présentement trop occupé de la conspiration royaliste,[2] qui vient heureusement d'avorter, pour qu'il soit décidé de mon application. Souvenez-vous de moi, je vous en prie, Général. Je vous assure que je suis bien gêné à cette heure même, et j'espère que je ne serai pas laissé dans la misère par le Gouvernement français en même temps que je suis chassé de ma patrie et calomnié même dans la chambre des Pairs par les agents de Pitt pour avoir été dévoué au service de la République.

Je ne sais pas, Général, si vous saurez lire mon français; je l'écris si exécrablement, mais si vous pouvez le déchiffrer, vous me ferez un grand service en m'apprenant le résultat de votre application au Directoire en ma faveur. Je vous assure que je suis actuellement dans un état d'incertitude si pénible que je ne sais si un refus absolu le serait plus.

---

[1] In the debate on the address on 17 January 1797, Lord Clare referred to Tone as one of the founders of the United Irishmen clubs and as the writer of the well-known letter of 9 July 1791 (*Faulkner's Dublin Journal*, 19 Jan. 1797). [2] See above, introduction.

Salut et respect
J. Smith

N'ayant pas sous mes yeux le journal anglais, je ne cite que la substance, et par les expressions du Lord Chancelier. Je ne suis pas sûr même du *date* mais c'est quelque jour entre le 29 et le 29[1] Janvier et vous pouvez facilement trouver les *Couriers* de ce date chez le Directoire.

Diary, 8 February 1797

T.C.D., Tone papers, MS 2049, ff 198ʳ–201ʳ; *Life*, ii, 342–4.

8 Feb. 1797

Yesterday morning I heard of the arrival of my friend Mr Sheé from Rochelle. I ran off immediately and found him at Gen[era]l Clarke's apartments; he was delighted to see me. It seems they had a dreadful voyage of it in the *Fraternité*; they sailed at one time four and twenty hours unnoticed in the very middle of the English fleet.[2] We soon came to our business in which he seems as hearty as ever; he tells me he is in hopes the Government will renew it by and bye on a grand scale, and that we shall have the co-operation, so long wished for, of the Spanish marine. If that be so all may be yet recovered. He told me also that he had seen Gen[era]l Hoche and spoken to him about me in the strongest manner; that the General had the best opinion of me and had applied personally to the Directory and to Gen[era]l Dupont, in whose department such business lies during the absence of Gen[era]l Clarke, to have me continued on the *Tableau* of the Army; that the General also told him of my desire to go to Hamburgh to bring my wife and family to France, to which he (Mr Sheé) observed that I might be more usefully employed elsewhere, and that he knew me so well that he would take upon him to answer for me, that no personal considerations would prevent me going where I could be of most service to the cause. I told Mr Sheé that I waived going to Hamburgh notwithstanding the situation of my wife's health, and was ready in an hour to go wherever the General might think proper to order me. I then mentioned to him Gen[era]l Grouchy's motives for send-ing me to Paris, and I begged of him, if he found an opportunity, to express to Gen[era]l Hoche the favourable opinion I held of Grouchy's conduct. Mr Sheé told me he was very glad I had mentioned that circumstance, as it gave him the key to one or two things which appeared unaccountable to him; that Grouchy was at present rather down in the General's opinion, which he saw now must

---

[1] Second digit in these dates appears to be '9' in both cases, which would obviously be an error.

[2] The return to the French coast was also dreadful. On approaching land, on a dark night in a raging sea, howling wind and rain, the launch of the *Fraternité* struck rocks, forcing the sailors and passengers to jump into the sea and wade ashore one league from La Rochelle; Sheé being struck down by an attack of gout, Hoche carried him on his shoulders (Alexandre Rousselin, *Vie de Lazare Hoche* (4th ed., Paris, 1800), pp 220–22).

be in consequence of the cabal I spoke of, but that he would endeavour, discreetly, to set him right, so I am in hopes I have been of use to my lover[1] Grouchy in this business. I do not know very much of him, but he behaves like a gentleman, and his conduct in Bantry Bay was as spirited as I could desire, and besides I hate the dirty spirit of cabal which is working against him. I then left Mr Sheé, having fixed to call on him again this morning, which I did accordingly, but we had not much conversation, being interrupted by a young general who lost a leg at Rastadt[2] in the last campaign on the Rhine; however I gave him MacSheehy's report,[3] Grouchy's proclamation to the Irish,[4] and my own opinion at the council of war held in Bantry Bay.[5] I also gave him a memorandum of the names of the *Northern Star, Dublin Evening Post* and *Cork Gazette*, which I strongly pressed him to have procured for the Directory, and he went immediately to speak to Gen[era]l Dupont on the subject. I am to see him tomorrow at 12. On my return I was hailed by Gen[era]l Hoche, who was driving thro' the Rue Montmartre, and informed me that my affair was settled, so now I am fixed in the French service, if nothing better offers in my own country; I returned the General my acknowledgements and so we parted.

Altogether things do not look so gloomy just now as they did a fortnight ago. If the Spaniards and the Directory act with spirit and decision, all may yet do well, and Ireland be independant. As to myself, I can at least exist on my appointments and if I had my family here, I could be as happy as the richest man in Europe; but the state of my dearest Love's health keeps me in the most mortal inquietude; two nights successively I have started out of my sleep in a cold sweat with horrible dreams regarding her. I have read her two letters a thousand times and there is not a phrase regarding her health that I have not turned a thousand different ways to torment myself; in short, I am truly miserable on her account. Tomorrow I will demand of Mr Sheé whether I am to be employed here or not; if not, the moment I receive my appointments I will set out to meet her; if I am employed, I think I will order her to stay at Hamburgh until the 1st of May, which is about three months, and then to come in a neutral vessel to Havre de Grâce, or Dunkirk, and so to Paris. I hope in God I shall have a letter from her now in two or three days in answer to mine of the [ ][6] January; it is today 26 days since I wrote, and I think I must soon have an answer now. Apropos[7] of letters! I had one yesterday from Reynolds,[8]

---

[1] Meaning here 'friend'.

[2] Jacques Nicolas Bellavène (1770–1826), general, 1796; baron of the empire, 1813 (*Moniteur*, 15 July 1796; *Dict. biog. franç.*).   [3] See above, vol. II, p. 369, n. 4.

[4] Above, vol. II, pp 426–7.

[5] Possibly Tone's proposal 'to sally out with all our forces, to mount to the Shannon and disembark the troops, to make a forced march to Limerick' which he put in writing for Chérin and others in Bantry Bay on 25 Dec. 1796 (see above, vol. II, p. 430). At a council of war at which Tone was present two days later 'it was unanimously agreed to quit Bantry Bay directly and to proceed for the mouth of the Shannon without delay . . . [and] there we will determine according to the means in our hands what part we shall take' (see above, vol. II, p. 433).

[6] Blotted out. The date should be 13 January, as supplied in *Life*, ii, 344. The letter referred to is above (pp 1–3).   [7] *Life* omits from 'Apropos' to 'honest!', several lines below.

[8] James Reynolds, who was in America.

dated *nowhere* and not even the month or year prefixed, but I conjecture it was written about the 1st November last. That carelessness is so like him! It contains little or no news but what I was already acquainted with, yet I was *very glad* to receive it. It is so long since I have had a line from one of my friends! And Reynolds, with all his enthusiasm, is so sincerely honest! I see also in the English papers that in a late debate in the Irish parliament the Lord Chancellor (my old friend Fitzgibbon, who is now Earl of Clare) did me the favor to abuse me twice, by name, as the father of the United Irishmen.[1] I thought he had forgot me; but if we had got safe into Ireland, with the blessing of God, I would have refreshed his memory. In the same debate he called Gen[era]l Hoche a *monster*,[2] so at least I had the pleasure to be abused in good company. I wrote a witty note[3] (in an unknown language which I please myself to call *French*) to the General thereupon, consoling him for the disgrace &c., &c. I think I am growing sprightly once more, but *'God knows the heart'*.[4]

To Matilda Tone, 11 February 1797

Tone (Dickason) papers; *Life*, ii, 388–91, 392.

[Paris], 11th Feb^y, 1797

My dearest Life and Soul,

Your letter of the 26 of last month has taken a mountain off my breast. I hope and trust you are daily getting better and that the terrible apprehensions which I have been under since the receipt of your first will be belied by the event. You do not know, you ugly thing, how much I love you. I hope you are by this settled somewhere near Hamburgh, where you may live at less expense than you can in the city and with more comfort. Live with the greatest economy, unless where your health is concerned, and in that case spare nothing. Drink new milk, and if it disagrees, as perhaps it may, with your stomach, you are in the very country to get Seltzer water; and I beg you may lay in a little stock and mix it with your milk. I remember you used to like it formerly. If you have a cough, put on a flannel waistcoat under your chemise and, if necessary, a slight blister between your shoulders; above all things, avoid wetting your feet or anything in short that can give you cold. Make veal broth so strong as to be in jelly when it cools, and take a small bason of it two or three times a day. In one word, take the greatest possible

---

[1] See above, p. 18, n. 1.

[2] It was reported that Lord Clare in his speech in the house of lords of 17 January 1797, after quoting from Hoche's address to his army, went on to say 'this is the language of Hoche, this the professed friendship and commiseration for this country, of a man, a monster I should say, whose sanguinary massacres and wide wasting devastations are yet felt and mourned in the reeking plains and ruined habitations of La Vendée' (*Northern Star*, 24 Jan. 1797).   [3] Above, pp 18–19.

[4] Cf. 'God knows my heart' (Isaac Bickerstaffe, *The life and strange adventures of Ambrose Gwinett* (1770?), p. 15).

care of yourself for ten thousand reasons, one of which is that if anything were to happen you, I could not, I think, live without you. When I have lately been forced, once or twice, to contemplate that most terrible of all events, you cannot imagine to yourself what a dreary wilderness the world appeared to me, and how helpless and desolate I seemed to myself. But let us quit this dispiriting subject and turn to another more encouraging.

I gave you in my last a short sketch of our unlucky expedition, for the failure of which we are, ultimately, to accuse the winds alone, for as to an enemy we saw none. In the event, the British took but one frigate and two or three transports; so you see the rhodomontades which you read in the English papers were utterly false. I mentioned to you that I had been sent by Gen[era]l Grouchy with his dispatches to the Directoire Exécutif, which you are not to wonder at, for I am highly esteemed by the said general; inasmuch as *'the first day I marched before him thinking of you I missed the step and threw the whole line into confusion, upon which I determined to retrieve my credit and exerted myself so much that at the end of the review the General thanked me for my behaviour'*. I hope you remember that quotation, which is a choice one.[1] I thought at the time I wrote that I should be ordered back to Brest, but Gen[era]l Hoche, who commanded our expedition in chief, has, it seems, taken a liking to me, for this very blessed day he caused to be signified to me that he thought of taking me in his family to the army of Sambre and Meuse, which he is appointed to command; to which I replied, as in duty bound, that I was at all times ready to obey his orders. So I fancy, go I shall. I did not calculate for a campaign on the Rhine, tho' I was prepared for one on the Shannon; however, my honour is now engaged and therefore (sings)

> Were the whole army lost in smoke,
> Were these the last words that I spoke,
> I swear (and damn me if I joke)
> I had rather be with you.[2]

If I go, as I believe I shall, you may be very sure that I shall take all care of myself that may be consistent with my duty; and, besides, as I shall be in the General's family and immediately attached to his person, I shall be the less exposed, and finally *'dost think that Hawser Trunnion, who has stood the fire of so many floating batteries, runs any risque from the lousy pops of a landsman?'*[3] I rely upon your courage on this, as on every former occasion in our lives; our situation is today a thousand times more desirable than when I left you in Princeton. Between ourselves, I think I have not done badly since my arrival in France; and so you will say when you read my memorandums. I came here knowing not a single soul and scarcely a word of the language. I have had the good fortune, thus far, to obtain the confidence of the Government, so far as was necessary for our affair and to secure the

---

[1] Its source has not been traced. [2] Charles Dibdin, *Poor Vulcan* (1778), II, iii.
[3] Tobias Smollett, *Peregrine Pickle* (1751), bk I, ch. 32.

good opinion of my superior officers, as appears by the station I hold. It is not every stranger that comes into France and is made Adjutant General, 'with *two* points on his shoulder',[1] as you say right enough; but that is nothing to what is, I hope, to come. (Sings) *'Zounds, I will soon be a brigadier!'*.[2] If I join the army of Sambre and Meuse, I shall be nearer to you than I am here, and we can correspond, so that in that respect we lose nothing; and, as my lot is cast in the army, I must learn a little of the business, because I am *not at all without very well founded expectation* that we may have occasion to display our military talents *elsewhere.* In the meantime I am in the best school and under one of the best masters in Europe. I cannot explain myself further to you by letter; remember the motto of our arms, 'Never despair!', and I see as little, and *infinitely less reason*, to despair this day than I did six months after my first arrival in France, so (sings) *'Madam, you know my trade is war!'*.[3] I think this is a very musical letter.

I have written by this post to Mons[ieu]r Giauque with a postscript to Mary on the supposition that they are married.[4] I most sincerely wish them happy; yet I cannot help thinking how oddly we are dispersed at this moment; no two of us together! I am sure if there were *five* quarters in the globe, one of us would be perched upon the fifth. M[onsieur] Giauque wrote to me about a claim he has on the French Government. If I had staid at Paris, I would have exerted myself to the utmost, tho[ugh] I cannot say I should have succeeded, for we have here infinitely more glory than cash; however, I hope I should at least have got an answer; but now as I go to the army (probably) there is nobody here whom I can trust with the application; so I have written to him to keep the papers &c. till my return, when I will do everything possible to recover the money, or at least a part of it. If I should not, after all, be ordered to the banks of the Rhine, I will immediately write him word, and in that case I will lose no time to make the proper application.

As to Arthur, I am sorry for the account you give me of him. Without going into a history of my reasons, I would advise you *not* to send for him until further advice. A few months hence will do as well and in the meantime my advice is to let him remain as he is. If I had him *here*, actually with me, on the spot, I might be able, by and bye, to place him; but we have not the time to wait, and so once again let him for the present remain.

As to Russel, I have known of his situation near three months.[5] Judge of the distress I have felt and feel on his account and that of his fellow sufferers. One of the greatest pleasures I had proposed to myself, if our expedition had succeeded, was to break their chains and to make an example of their oppressors. I would give anything to see the letter which you found in the

---

[1] *2 Henry IV*, II, iv.   [2] John O'Keeffe, *Love in a camp* (1785), I, ii.
[3] Charles Dibdin, *Poor Vulcan* (1778), II, iii.
[4] They were married on 29 Jan. 1797 (see above, p. 2, n. 2).
[5] Thomas Russell was arrested on 16 Sept. 1796. See Diary for 29 Oct. 1796 (above, vol. II, p. 360).

papers.[1] If you can lay hands on it, or a copy of it, enclose it to me in your next; make Giauque or Mr Wilson[2] search for it. (Apropos! I have been at Madgett's about Mr Wilson's letters, but they are not yet arrived.) I am hammering at the possibility of writing a line to one or two friends of mine by way of Hamburgh. Do you know whether Giauque has *a safe correspond-ent* in London? Consult with him as to this, but with the most profound secrecy. If he can be serviceable, it may have a beneficial effect with regard to his claim here, for obvious reasons. I hope and rely he is a man in whom I may confide, especially in an affair which may materially serve him and can put him to no possible inconvenience. Let me see how well you will arrange all this.

As I shall remain, at all events, for a few days at Paris, I will write to you once or twice more before my departure. I must take up the remainder of this with a line to a young lady of my acquaintance who has done me the honor to begin a correspondance with me.

Your ever affectionate husband,
J. S., Adj[utan]t Gen[era]l!! Huzza, huzza!

[P.S.]. Get thin paper like this to write upon, and fold your letters square, like mine; or, rather, let M[onsieu]r Giauque do it for you. Let him also pay Mr Holterman the postage of my letters to you.

À Madame Smith
À Hambourg

To Maria Tone, 11 February 1797

Tone (Dickason) papers; *Life*, ii, 391–2; added to the preceding letter.

This is the earliest known letter from Tone to his daughter Maria, then aged ten.

Dearest Baby,

You are a darling little thing for writing to me, and I doat upon you, and when I read your pretty letter, it brought the tears into my eyes; I was so glad. I am delighted with the account you give me of your brothers. I think

---

[1] Russell wrote a public letter, dated from Newgate Prison, 19 Dec. 1796, published in the *Dublin Evening Post*, 22 Dec. 1796, and *Northern Star* (Belfast), 26 Dec. 1796.

[2] Thomas Wilson (1758?–1824) of Edinburgh and later of Dullatur, Lanarkshire, Scotland, admitted to the Faculty of Advocates, 1781 (Sir Francis Grant (ed.), *The Faculty of Advocates in Scotland, 1532–1943, with genealogical notes* (Scottish Record Society CXLV, Edinburgh, 1944)). After Tone's death he looked after Matilda Tone's financial affairs and eventually, on 19 Aug. 1816, married her, emigrating to America with her some months later; he seems to have met her either in America or on her voyage from New York to Hamburg; he moved to Paris, probably in Dec. 1797 or Jan. 1798, and there went by the name of 'Theodore Wilkins' (Cf. *Life*, ii, 563, 576, 593, 671, 673, and mentions below of 'Wilson' and 'Wilkins').

it is high time that William should begin to cultivate his understanding, and therefore I beg you may teach him his letters, if he does not know them already, that he may be able to write to me by and bye. I am not surprised that Frank is a bully, and I suppose he and I will have fifty battles when we meet. Has he got into a jacket and trowsers yet? Tell your Mama, from me, *'we do defer it most shamefully, Mr Shandy'*.[1] I hope you take great care of your poor Mama, who, I am afraid, is not well; but I need not say that, for I am sure you do, because you are a darling good child, and I love you more than all the world. Kiss your Mama and your two little brothers for me ten thousand times, and love me, as you promise, *as long as you live*.

Your affec[tiona]te Fadoff
J. Smith

Extract by Claude Pétiet, 16 February 1797, from the register of the Executive Directory (16 July 1796)

Tone (Dickason) papers.

Pétiet notes an extract from the register of the Executive Directory dated 28 Messidor an 5 (16 July 1796) containing a decree commissioning Tone as *chef de brigade d'infanterie* from the previous 1 Messidor (19 June). See Pétiet to Tone, 17 July 1796 (above, vol. II, p. 240).

4e Division.	LIBERTÉ ÉGALITÉ
2e Subdivision	DÉPARTEMENT DE LA GUERRE
Bureau	
d_____	

Paris, le 28 Pluviôse an 5 de la République française

Ampliation

Extrait des Registres du Directoire Exécutif
du 28 Messidor de l'an 4e [*sic*] de la République Française
une et indivisible

Le Directoire Exécutif arrête ce qui suit:

Le citoyen Theobald Wolfe Tone est promu au grade de chef de brigade d'infanterie, à prendre date du premier Messidor dernier.

Il jouira à Paris du traitement et des rations affectés à ce grade.

---

[1] Cf. ' "We should begin", said my father . . . , "to think, Mrs Shandy, of putting this boy into breeches". "We should so", said my mother. "We defer it, my dear", quoth my father, shamefully. "I think we do, Mr Shandy", said my mother.' (Laurence Sterne, *Tristram Shandy* (1759), ii, ch. 18).

Pour expédition conforme, signé Carnot président, par le Directoire Exécutif, le secrétaire général, signé Lagarde.

Pour copie conforme
Le Ministre de la Guerre
Pétiet

Diary, 18 February–5 March 1797

T.C.D., Tone papers, MS 2049, ff 202ʳ–211ʳ; *Life*, ii, 344–9.

18 Feb. 1797

This day I removed to the Hotel des États Unis, Rue Tournon, near the Luxembourg, as I have been very inconveniently off at Mlle Boivert's, my ancient landlady.[1] The 10th inst. I had the unspeakable satisfaction to receive a letter from my dearest love acquainting me that her health was much better. She had received my two letters;[2] she tells me my sister's marriage was fixed for the second day after, and M. Giauque writes me to the same effect, so I am in hopes she is settled and I trust in God she will be happy; it is a great uneasiness off my mind.[3] Wrote a long letter to my wife and to Giauque, with a P.S. for Mary, on the 11th. Gen[era]l Hoche set off for the Army on the 13th. Before his departure he asked Mr Sheé whether he thought I would like to come to the Army of Sambre and Meuse, to which he answered, as before, that he was sure I would be ready to go wherever the General thought I could be useful, on which the General desired him to propose it to me. This was in consequence of a conversation I had with Mr Sheé wherein I mentioned to him that I thought we might be able, in consequence of my sister's marriage, to open a communication with Ireland thro' Hamburgh (as I hope we may), at which Gen[era]l Hoche caught directly. It was fixed in consequence that I should make this campaign with the Army of Sambre and Meuse in order to be near his person, and he made application accordingly to the Directory and the Minister at War for my brevet as *adjudant général* and an order to join forthwith. I learned in one of the Minister's bureaux that I am described as the officer 'charged with the General's foreign correspondance'. That has a lofty sound! Bruicks,[4] who is *Major Général de l'armée navale* and who in fact conducted the naval part of our expedition, is arrived at Paris in order to confer with the Directory and the Minister of Marine. He tells Mr Sheé that if the Government will grant 8,000,000#[5] for the Navy, he will engage in six

---

[1] He means 'my former landlady'. She was presumably his landlady at No. 7, Petite Rue St Roch, Poissonnière, his address on 13 and 17 Jan. 1797 (see above, p. 3).

[2] Dated 13 and 17 Jan. 1797 (above, pp 1–7).

[3] Around here four short lines, all relating in some way to Giauque, are omitted from *Life*.

[4] Corrected to 'Bruix' in *Life*, ii, 344.   [5] Spelt out '8,000,000 livres' in ibid.

months to have 35 sail of the line ready to put to sea—8,000,000[1] is about £350,000. I trust and rely the money will be found, and indeed Truguet, the Minister, told Mr Sheé that he had made out some part already and had hopes to secure the remainder. The Spaniards, I believe, will give us 25 sail of the line and if we can make out even 25 more, that will be 50 sail. Come, all is not desperate yet! In the meantime I see in the English papers that Government is arresting all the world in Ireland: Arthur O'Connor, who it seems is canvassing the Co. Antrim, is taken up, but I believe only for a libel.[2] It seems he was walking with Lord Edw[ar]d Fitzgerald when he was arrested. It is not for nothing that these two young gentlemen were walking together! I would give a great deal for an hour's conversation with O'Connor, I see he has thrown himself, body and soul, into the revolution of his country. Well, if we succeed, he will obtain, and he deserves, one of the first stations in the Government; he is a noble fellow, that is the truth of it. I am now waiting for my brevet and my order to join, and eke for my *gratification d'entrée de campagne*, w[hi]ch amounts to 800#,[3] together with two months' pay which will make (*en numéraire*) 330# more; and my trunk is not yet arrived from Brest and will not be here this month, and before that time I may be at Cologne, where our Headquarters are fixed, and in my trunk are two gold watches and chains and my flute, and my papers, and all that makes life dear to me, and so I am in '*perplexity and doubtful dilemma*'.[4] I must see and spin out the time, if possible, until my trunk arrives, or I shall be in a state of anxiety thereupon, which will be truly alarming. I called on my friend Monroe ere yesterday. He is recalled, and the Directory has refused (very properly)[5] to acknowledge Pinckney,[6] who was named to succeed him; he leaves Paris in ten days for America, and I am to write by him to Reynolds and my brother. If Matt were here now, I could name him my adjoint directly. I think I will leave his coming to his own option; he can at any rate at all times return to America, so I believe I will write to him, rather, to come at once.

22 Feb. 1797

I see by the *Courier* of the 14th inst. that Rob[er]t and W[illia]m Simms are arrested for publishing Arthur O'Connor's letter,[7] as it should seem, for

---

[1] Spelt out '8,000,000 livres' in ibid.

[2] O'Connor was arrested in Dublin on 2 Feb. 1797 for publishing an address to the electors of County Antrim asserting that it was absurd to summon Irishmen to resist invasion when they were already oppressed by an invader (Frank MacDermot, 'Arthur O'Connor' in *Irish Historical Studies*, xv, no. 57 (Mar. 1966), pp 54–5).

[3] Spelt out 'which amounts to 800 livres' in *Life*.   [4] *Merry wives of Windsor*, IV, v, 85–6.

[5] The words 'very properly' are omitted from *Life*.

[6] Charles Cotesworth Pinckney (1746–1825), soldier, statesman and diplomat. He arrived in Paris in Dec. 1796 but the Directory refused to recognise his diplomatic status. Upon being notified by the police in Feb. 1797 that unless he secured a residence permit he was liable to arrest, he left Paris but later returned on a special mission. (*D.A.B.*).

[7] On 5 Feb. Robert and William Simms were committed to Newgate for, it was reported, publishing O'Connor's address in the *Northern Star* (*Dublin Evening Post*, 7 Feb. 1797).

the account is rather confused. I collect from another paragraph in the same paper that they were released on the 9th, but O'Connor remains in custody. He has proposed himself as candidate for the County Antrim and I have no doubt will be returned, and it is for a letter to the electors of that county that he has been arrested. Government will move Heaven and Earth to keep him out. There is now scarcely one of my friends in Ireland but is in prison and most of them in peril of their lives, for the system of Terror is carried as far there as ever it was in France in the time of Robespierre. I think I will call on Carnot today, and propose to him to write to Reynolds to have some person on whom we can depend sent over from Ireland in order to confer with the government here. It may be easily done, and my letter will go in perfect safety by Monroe. *Allons!*

23 Feb. 1797

Called on Gen[era]l Dupont yesterday in order to go with him to Carnot. I have already observed he transacts Gen[era]l Clarke's business during his absence. Instead of bringing me to Carnot, he took upon himself to give me instructions as to what I should write, and I found his instructions very frivolous. I will write now upon my own plan.

24 Feb. 1797

This day[1] I called on Monroe and gave him a letter of eight pages for Reynolds,[2] in which I give a detailed account of our expedition and assure him of the determination of the French government to persevere in our business; I likewise offer him a rapid sketch of the present posture of the great powers in Europe, in order to satisfy him of the permanency of the Republic, together with a brief view of our comparative resources as to England; finally I desire him, observing the most profound secresy and rigid caution, to write to Ireland, and by preference, if it be possible, to Rob[er]t Simms, to send a proper person to Hamburgh, addressed to the French resident there, in order to come on to Paris and confer with the Directory; I calculate, if nothing extraordinary happens to delay him, that that person may be here by the middle of July next; finally I desire him to assure our friends that we have stronger hopes than ever of success, and to entreat them, in the meantime, to remain quiet and not by a premature explosion to give the English government a pretext to let loose the dragoons upon them. Such is the substance of my letter, which I have every reason to hope will go safe.

---

[1] In the margin a hand is drawn pointing to 'this day'.

[2] This seems to have been the letter Emmet, O'Connor and MacNeven refer to in their 'Memoir or detailed statement' of 4 Aug. 1798 as having reached Ireland about May 1797 and 'assured us the French would come again and requesting that a person should be sent over to make previous arrangements . . . The person departed in the latter end of June 1797.' (W. J. MacNeven, *Pieces of Irish history* (256 pp ed., New York, 1807), pp 189–90.)

25 Feb. 1797

Walked out to Nanterre to see my friend Col[one]l Sheé, with whom I will spend two days.

26 Feb. 1797

At work with Mr Sheé writing a memorial relating to our business which is to be given to Lacuée[1] of the *Conseil des Anciens*, with whom I am already a little acquainted. He is particularly connected with Carnot, which is the reason we address ourselves to him; it is in the form of a letter from Mr Sheé to Gen[era]l Clarke.

27 Feb. 1797

Returned this morning to Paris.

28 Feb. 1797

Called on Lacuée with the memorial; found him busy engaged with his secretary; left him the paper, and fixed to call on him in two or three days.

3 Mar. 1797

I lead the life of a dog here in Paris, where I am as much alone as in the deserts of Arabia. This night is downright wretchedness. I am come to a tavern where I write this memorandum in a little box by myself. It is miserable! I wonder shall I ever be so happy as to see my dearest Love and our little ones once more. My mind is overgrown with docks and thistles for want of cultivation, and I cannot help it, for I have not a soul to speak to that I care a farthing about. There are about half a dozen Irishmen here in Paris that I have seen, but they are sad vulgar wretches, and I have been used to rather better company in all respects. Well let me change the subject. I have been lately introduced to the famous Thomas Paine[2] and I like him very well. He is vain beyond all belief, but he has reason to be vain and for my part I forgive him. He has done wonders for the cause of liberty, both in America and Europe, and I believe him to be conscientiously an honest man. He converses extremely well, and I find him wittier in discourse than in his writings, where his humour is clumsy enough. He read me some passages from a reply to the Bishop of Landaff,[3] which he is preparing for the press, in which he belabours

---

[1] Jean-Gérard Lacuée (1752–1841), army officer; writer on military subjects; général de brigade, 1793; member of Council of Ancients (*Dict. parl. franç.*).

[2] Paine was probably staying with Monroe (*The writings of James Monroe* (New York, 1899–1903), ii, 440, iii, 20).

[3] Richard Watson (1737–1816), bishop of Llandaff, published a reply to *The age of reason* in 1796. Paine started writing a rejoinder in 1796 which was not published until 1810. (*D.N.B.; The writings of Thomas Paine*, ed. M. D. Conway (4 vols, London, 1894–6), iv, 258–60).

the prelate without mercy. He seems to plume himself more on his theology than his politics, in which I am not prepared to agree with him, whatever my private opinion of the Christian religion may be. I mentioned to him that I had known Burke in England and I spoke of the shattered state of Burke's mind in consequence of the death of his only son, Richard.[1] Paine immediately said that it was the *Rights of man* that had broke his heart, and that the death of his son gave him occasion to develope the chagrin which had preyed upon him ever since the appearance of that work. I am sure the *Rights of man* have tormented Burke exceedingly, but I have seen myself the workings of a father's grief on his spirit, and I could not be deceived. *'Paine has no children!'*[2] Oh my little babies; if I were to lose my Will or my little Fantom![3] Poor little souls! I doat upon them, and on their darling mother, whom I love ten thousand times more than my existence. Darling little things![4] they are never out of my thoughts. But to return to Paine. He drinks like a fish, a misfortune which I have known to befal other justly[5] celebrated Patriots. I am told that the true time to see him to advantage is about ten at night with a bottle of brandy and water before him, which I can very well conceive, but I have not as yet had that advantage; however I must contrive, if I can, to sup with him at least one night before I set off for the army. Three days ago I saw 60 stand of the Emperor's colours presented by General Augereau[6] of the Army of Italy. They were taken in Mantua, and the President of the Directory, Reubell, presented Augereau in return with the colours of the 62d demi-brigade which he had planted on the bridge of Arcola[7] under the fire of the enemy, and which had been voted to him in consequence by the *Conseil des Cinq Cens*. It was a glorious spectacle, and, what rendered it more interesting, the father and mother of Augereau[8] (his father is an old soldier, his mother *a bonne bourgeoise*) were close beside him at the moment, and his brother[9] attended him as his aid-du-camp. What a crowd of ideas did the groupe produce instantaneously in my mind! Well, if we had succeeded in our expedition—but no matter. *'Tout ce qui est différé, n'est pas perdu.'* We shall see yet what turn things may take. The colours were carried by sixty old soldiers, and I was delighted with the *fierté* with which the veterans presented themselves. I find the spirit of enthusiasm abate daily in my mind. *'Le tems et le malheur ont flétri mon âme.'*[10]

---

[1] Tone met Burke when visiting England with delegates of the Dublin catholics in Mar. 1795. Richard Burke had died of tuberculosis on 2 Aug. 1794. (*The correspondence of Edmund Burke*, vii, ed. P. J. Marshall and John A. Woods (Cambridge, 1968), pp 561–9, 580–98; ibid., ix, ed. R. B. McDowell and John A. Woods (Cambridge, 1970), p. 115).
[2] Cf. 'Macbeth has no children!' (*Macbeth*, IV, iii).   [3] i.e. his sons William and Frank.
[4] The words 'darling little things!' are omitted from *Life*.
[5] The word 'justly' is omitted from *Life*.
[6] Pierre François Charles Augereau (1757–1816) enlisted as a private, *c.*1774; *général de division*, 1793; marshal, 1804 (*Dict. biog. franç.*).
[7] In *Life*, ii, 348, William Tone corrects 'Lodi' to 'Arcola'.
[8] Augereau's father had been a domestic servant and his mother a *fruitière*; his mother died when the future general was only a youth (*Dict. biog. franç.*).   [9] Not identified.
[10] 'Time and hardship have withered my soul.'

Yet I could not be insensible to this spectacle which brought the tears into my eyes more than once. I thought of my own father; he would be proud enough of me[1] if we were to succeed in Ireland. Well, all in good time.

5 Mar. 1797

Gave Mr Monroe a letter for my brother,[2] under cover to Reynolds, in which I recommend to him to come to France, but without pressing him very strongly. I wish to God he were here tonight. Monroe will set off now in four or five days.[3]

From Claude Pétiet, 9 March 1797

Tone (Dickason) papers.

Pétiet informs Tone that he has sent his papers to Hoche and that he should proceed as soon as possible to his posting.

4ᵉ Division
 Bureau
  des
Officiers
Généraux

LIBERTÉ [crest] ÉGALITÉ

Paris, le 19 Ventôse *an* 5ᵉᵐᵉ *de*
la République Française, une et indivisible

Le Ministre de la Guerre
Au Citoyen James Smith, chef de brigade.

LE DIRECTOIRE EXÉCUTIF ayant jugé à propos, Citoyen, de vous employer dans le grade d'Adjudant-Général près les troupes qui composent l'armée de Sambre et Meuse et spécialement près le G[ener]al en chef Hoche, j'adresse en conséquence les lettres de service qui vous ont été expédiées, au dit général commandant en chef qui vous les remettra avec ses instructions sur les fonctions que vous aurez à remplir sous ses ordres. Le bien du service exige que vous vous rendiez le plus promptement possible au poste qui vous est assigné.

Vous voudrez bien m'accuser la réception de cette lettre, et m'informer de l'époque de votre arrivée à votre destination.

Salut et Fraternité
Pétiet

---

[1] Amended in *Life*, ii, 349, to 'how proud he would be of me'.   [2] Mathew Tone.
[3] Monroe had been recalled to Philadelphia in Nov. 1796.

To Matilda Tone, 10–11 March 1797

Tone (Dickason) papers; *Life*, ii, 392–5.

Paris, March 10th, 1797

My dearest Life and Soul,

I have *this instant* received your letter, and you see with what eagerness I fly to answer it. You are, however, to consider this but as the prologue to another, which will follow it in four or five days. I must again begin with what interests me more than all other things on earth, your health. Let me intreat you, light of my eyes and pulse of my heart, to have all possible care of yourself. You know well that I only exist in your well being, and, tho' I desire you to live and take care of our babies, whatever becomes of me, I feel at the same moment that I am giving counsel which I have not firmness myself to follow. You know the effect the imagination has on the constitution; only believe yourself better; count upon my ever increasing admiration of your virtues and love for your person; think how dear you are to me—but that is too little; think that you are indispensable to my existence; look at our little children, whom you have the unspeakable happiness to see around you; remember that my very soul is wrapt up in you and them, and—but I need add no more; I know your love for me and I know your courage. We will both do what becomes us.

In reading the history of your complaints, I have at least the melancholy consolation to see that that horrible disorder which of all others I most dreaded makes no part of them.[1] Thank God, you have no cough! If I were with you, I am sure, what with my attentions about you, and what with my prescriptions (for I think, in your case, I would become no mean physician), I should soon have the unspeakable happiness to see you as well as ever. Rely upon it that I will force the impossible to join you; but, if I cannot succeed (without a forfeiture of character, which you would not desire nor I submit to) we must endeavour to accom[m]odate ourselves to a few months' additional separation, which, after all, considering what we have so long and so often experienced, we may well submit to. This very day the Executive Directory has ratified the nomination of Gen[era]l Hoche, and I am to all intents and purposes Adjutant General destined for the army of Sambre and Meuse. It is barely possible that I may be able to change, or at least to postpone, my joining the army for some time, in which case, need I say, you may rely upon my going to seek you; if, however, I should not be able to effectuate this point, I count once more upon your courage to sustain a separation which is nothing in comparison of what we have suffered hitherto.

---

[1] Tuberculosis?

I purpose dedicating the next week to a negociation in order to see if I can *honorably* avoid joining the army, which after all I may *by possibility* be able to do, and in that case I will *'fly upon the wings of love in the Exeter waggon'*[1] to join you and the little things whom I doat upon. If I fail, I fail, and in one case or the other I will write to you instantly to let you know the result. But remember, dearest love and life, that, circumstanced as I am here, my duty supersedes and *must* supersede every other consideration.

I look over your letter (*malgré* certain passages thereof) with delight. *'Jack, thou'rt a* ——, *thou'rt a* ——, *thou'rt a toper, let's have t'other quart.'*[2] (I beg you may sing that passage, or the beauty of the quotation is lost.) What do you think I would give to *crack a bottle* with you and Mary tonight? By-the-bye, you are two envious pusses, for in my last letter to her there were divers quotations well worth their weight in gold of which neither of you have the honesty to take notice, tho[ugh] I laughed myself excessively at writing, as I have no doubt you did at reading them; but I see green envy gnawed your souls. Between ourselves, I grudge you the *'three pounds five shillings and two pence'*[3] which I confess would fairly purchase all the wit in my last letter. Well, God knows the heart. (Sings) *'When as I sat in Pabilon—and a thousand vragrant posies! Passion of my heart, I have a greater mind to cry.'*[4]

March 11th

This letter, which I began last night, is in the style of all well-written novels, including, if I mistake not, *Belmont Castle*,[5] where you always find two or three different dates in the same epistle. If you like it yourself, I can have not the least objection to your visiting at the Minister's,[6] for I am sure in your present circumstances you ought not to refuse yourself any relaxation that was proper, and that is both proper and respectable. I need not, at the same time, observe to you the necessity of your being extremely guarded in your conduct in all respects for a thousand reasons; but this is unnecessary.

The more I think of it, the more I fear I shall not be able to join you before this campaign is finished. *'Madam, you know my trade is war.'*[7] At the same time it is not my intention to keep you in press at Hamburgh if you do not yourself desire it. The beginning of May, if you find yourself stout,[8] you may come by sea in a neutral bottom to Havre de Grâce, as M[onsieu]r Giauque will fix for you, and so on to Paris, or fix yourself for the summer in some of the villages near the seaside, as you see best; but this we will settle hereafter. What have you done with your bill on London? I suppose you know by this that the Bank of England has stopped payment,[9] and God knows what confusion that may produce in the commercial world; perhaps

---

[1] Richard Cumberland, *The brothers* (1770), II, xii. [2] George Powell, *Bonduca* (1696), II, i.
[3] Goldsmith, *The vicar of Wakefield* (1766), ch. 12. [4] *Merry wives of Windsor*, III, i.
[5] Tone's novel. [6] Perhaps the French minister in Hamburg.
[7] Charles Dibdin, *Poor Vulcan* (1778), II, iii. [8] i.e. strong.
[9] The Bank of England stopped cash payments in Feb. 1797.

we may lose all, which will be truly agreeable; let me know about this in your next. I have written by a safe hand to America, to Reynolds and Matt,[1] and I have left it to them to decide whether the latter gentleman shall come on or not. The dog, if he were here now, I could make him my aid-de-camp for a word's speaking. Mr Wilson's letters never came to hand. Dear love, I cannot express to you how weary I am of this eternal separation, and how I long once more to see you and the Babies. I would give a great deal of honor now for a little domestic comfort, but what can I do? You know my duty, and I need say no more. You know I am now in the pay of the Republic. (Sings) *'Here is a guinea and a crown, beside the Lord knows what renown'*,[2] and besides——, but what need I multiply reasons. I rely always upon your courage, and you may be sure on my part. I shall expose myself to no unnecessary dangers; the campaign too will probably be pacific enough on our side, for it should seem the great push will be made in Italy. I must finish this with a line to the Bab. God bless you. I will write again in a week, but do you in the meantime answer this.

J. Smith

To Maria Tone, 10 March 1797

Tone (Dickason) papers; *Life*, ii, 395; added to preceding letter.

Dearest Baby,

I cannot express to you the pleasure I feel at receiving a letter from Mama with a postscript of your writing. I am delighted that your boys are well and good. I desire you may not let William forget his Fadoff; as for Sir Fantom, I can hardly promise myself he will remember me. Take all the care in the world of your darling Mama, because you know there is nobody in the world that either you or I love half so much; above all things, do not let her catch cold. Have you any books to divert yourself with? How do you like Hamburgh? Which would you rather be, there or in Princeton? Write to me as soon as you get this. God bless you, my dearest baby.

J. S.

À Madame Smith
À Hambourg

---

[1] i.e. to James Reynolds and Mathew Tone.

[2] 'A golden guinea and a crown / Besides the Lord knows what renown' (Charles Dibdin, *Poor Vulcan* (1778), I, ii.

Diary, 10–20 March 1797

T.C.D., Tone papers, MS 2049, ff 211ʳ–214ʳ; *Life*, ii, 349–50.

10 Mar. 1797

Received a letter from Giauque informing me of his marriage with Mary and with a P.S. from her, written evidently with a contented heart.[1] I trust in God she will be happy. Inclosed was a letter from my poor dear Love, about whose health I am in most dreadful anxiety; she has removed to the suburbs of Hamburgh, where I hope she will be better. Maria wrote me a little P.S.; she writes like a little angel. Answered the two letters immediately,[2] but the Post will not leave till the 13th. Received my *gratification à l'entrée de campagne*,[3] as *chef de brigade*, çy 800ℳ = £32 ster[lin]g.

12 Mar. 1797

Applied today and got an order for my arrears since the 1st Nivôse. In the margin of the order I observed the following note *'Nota: L'activité et la grande utilité de cet officier ont été attestées par le Bureau d'Officiers Généraux.'* That is very handsome.[4]

20 Mar. 1797

Dined today with Chérin, who sets off tonight for the Army of Sambre and Meuse. I hope to follow him in a week at farthest, as I am promised my *frais de route* by that time. Came home after dinner and sat some time all alone, and devoured with the spleen. Opened my desk and read over all my dearest Love's letters; they are my constant refuge but latterly I am most terribly alarmed for her health. If I were so miserable as to lose her I do not think I could survive it, and then what would become of our dearest little babies! Darling little things, I doat on them! My poor Maria! there are two postscripts of her writing! It is impossible to express how dearly I love them all. Shall I ever have the happiness to see them again? Well, I must not think of that now. Sent out for a lemon and sugar and determined to play the part of Lord B——. *'I must have my punch.'*[5] Oh that my dearest Love were at the other side of the

---

[1] In *Life*, ii, 349, this sentence reads: 'Received a letter from Mary informing me of her marriage and written evidently with a contented heart'.   [2] Above, pp 32–4.

[3] Corrected to 'gratification d'entrée en campagne' in *Life*, ii, 349, which omits 'as *chef de brigade*' and amends what follows to '800 L = £32 sterling'.

[4] In the MS at this point (f. 211ᵛ) appear the words: 'Rue de Clery, No. 285, depuis le 15 Ventôse (*5th March*)'.

[5] The literary source of this quotation and of the allusions in the preceding sentence has not been traced.

little table at which I write this! *'Quanquam oh!'*[1] There is one thing which I have had occasion to remark tonight, and a thousand times before since my arrival in France, viz. *'that it is not good for man to be alone'.*[2] If I had my dear and unfortunate friend Russell beside me, to consult on every occasion, I should have, no doubt, conducted myself infinitely better and, at all events, I should have had infinitely more enjoyment.[3] I have read a good deal latterly, but with very little profit; in reading, an observation has struck me! Very well! But I have nobody to communicate it to; I cannot discuss it, nor follow it up to its consequences. In an hour it is lost, and I remember it no more, whereas, if I had a friend to whom I could open myself it would have become a principle. All this is not my fault. Of all the privations I have ever suffered, *that* which I most sensibly feel is the want of a friend since my arrival in France to whom I could open my heart. If William,[4] if Matt,[5] if Russell were here, what a difference would it make in my situation tonight! Well, I will go to my dreary bed! I declare I am weary of my existence.

From Colonel Henri Sheé, 22 March 1797

Tone (Dickason) papers.

Cologne, ye 2nd Germinal 5[th] Year

Not hearing from you, My Dear friend, since you left my house I imagined some sudden order had compelled you to set off immediately for the army & was much surprised not to find you here on my arrival. I asked Gen[er]al Hoche whether he had any account from you; he answered not & wondered you were not come.

I therefore intreat you to arrive the soonest possible for the operations of the campaign will begin very early & you know that first come first served.

I remain yours most affectionately
Sheé[6]

P.S. The road by Valenciennes, Bruxelles, Liège & Aix la Chapelle is the best & shortest & presents the most conveniences.

I must tell you that I am named président perpétuel de la Commission Intermédiaire pour l'Administration Civile des Pays Conquis.[7]

---

[1] For an explanation of this expression, see above vol. II, p. 397, n. 2. At this point in the MS (f. 212ᵛ), Tone draws a hand followed by '(In continuation): The writing on the other side exhibits the strongest internal evidence that it was executed *after dinner*. April 30, 1797. J.S.'
[2] Genesis, 2: 18.   [3] Tone's friend Thomas Russell was held in prison in Dublin.
[4] His brother, William Henry Tone.   [5] Mathew Tone.
[6] For the spelling of Sheé's name, see above, p. 14, n. 6.
[7] i.e. 'permanent president of the intermediary commission for the civil administration of the conquered lands'.

Au Citoyen Smith
Adjutant Général de l'armée
de Sambre et Meuse
Petite Rue St Roch Poissonière, No. 7
À Paris

Diary, 24 March 1797

T.C.D., Tone papers, MS 2049, f. 214ʳ; *Life*, ii, 350.

The diary entry for this date is indecipherably crossed out in the MS. The text given here is taken from *Life*, ii, 350.

24 Mar. 1797

Received this day a letter from my sister which has thrown me into the greatest distress. I much fear that I shall lose my best beloved wife. I cannot write.

This text seems to be a translation of the Latin quotation written by Tone on the facing page (f. 213ᵛ):

'Epistolam hodie recepi a sorore mea quae me in mairorum profundissimum jacit. Maxime timeo quod nunquam revidebo uxorem meam dilectissimam; nequeo scribere——.' Cicero, *De officiis.*

To Matilda Tone, 25 March 1797

Tone (Dickason) papers; *Life*, ii, 395–6, 397.

Paris, March 25th, 1797

Dearest Love,

I wrote to you, I think it was the 12th ins[tan]t,[1] so today, according to all probability, you should have my letter. I promised you to write again before I left Paris, and you see I keep my word. I received yesterday my order to join and the money for my expenses, and I was in hopes to have set off today, but unluckily all the places in the diligence were taken, which, together with some trifling preparations which I have still to make, prevented me; however, I have secured my seat for the 29th, which makes only four days' difference, and I hope to be in Cologne by the 3d of next month. From Cologne to Hamburgh is not as far as from New York to Paris, and I give you my word most solemnly that the instant I see Gen[era]l Hoche I will demand permission[2] to go and

---

[1] In fact it was the 10th.   [2] i.e. leave.

see you, and I hardly think he will refuse me, for reasons which I will explain to you when we meet, which I hope and trust we may now expect about the latter end of April at farthest, viz. in a month from this. Dearest Love, you cannot conceive the impatience I feel to join you and the little babies once more, an impatience which is multiplied a thousandfold by the anxiety which I feel unceasingly on account of your health; I am more unhappy on that score than I am able to express. I hope you take great care of yourself and that you have advice, if it be necessary, tho', after all, I am sure I would be your best physician. If I succeed in the arrangement I meditate with the General, I shall stay for perhaps two, or it may be three, months in Hamburgh, and then I will bring you and the little things with me into France, and we shall have a most delicious journey thro' Holland and the Low Countries in the fine season; but in order to execute the aforesaid journey it is absolutely necessary that you preserve your health and keep up *especially* your spirits. I have five hundred little things to occupy me before I set off; you must be contented with a very short letter, which you need not answer, for the reasons herein before set forth. *'Oh, I have business would employ an age and have not half an hour to do it in.'*[1] Adieu, Dearest Life and Soul, and light of my eyes, I shall have a budget of news for you when we meet. Oh how I long for that meeting! God almighty, forever bless you and preserve you for me and our darling babies!

Your ever affectionate,
J. S.

[P.S.] *Do not say a word to mortal that you expect me in Hamburgh*, nor do not be unhappy if I am not there to the hour I mention; it may be a few days later; but your own good sense will suggest all that. Once more, adieu!

À Madame Smith
À Hambourg

To Maria Tone, 25 March 1797

Tone (Dickason) papers; *Life*, ii, 396; added to preceding letter.

Dear Baby,

I wrote you a few lines in my last,[2] and I hope you got them safe. Kiss your Mama for me ten thousand times, and the little Daffs,[3] the ugly little things! I know you hate them and your Fadoff.[4] But what will you say one of these fine mornings when I walk in and catch you all together? Do you

---

[1] *Recte* 'Oh, speak and leave me, for I have business would employ an age and have but a minute's time to get it done in' (Nicholas Rowe, *Jane Shore* (1714), IV, i). [2] Above, p. 34.
[3] Maria Tone's young brothers, William and Frank. [4] Tone himself.

know that I intend going to Hamburgh very soon and that I will bring you all with me to Paris and fix you delightfully? Will you love me then, you ugly thing? I hope you nurse your poor dear Mama, for my sake, for I love her even more than I love you, Miss Baby. I doat upon you all, you little things. God Almighty bless you, my darling child.

Your affectionate father,
J. S.

Diary, 25 March 1797

T.C.D., Tone papers, MS 2049, f. 214ʳ; *Life*, ii, 350.

25 Mar. 1797

Wrote to my wife and sister, promising to join them in a month if possible. Took my place in the diligence for Liège for the 29th having received my *frais de route* yesterday.

Paris—1797
J. Smith *fecit*.

To Matilda Tone, 29 March 1797

Tone (Dickason) papers; *Life*, ii, 397–8.

Paris, 29th March 1797

Dearest Love,

I wrote to you on the 25th instant[1] informing you of my speedy departure from Paris. I have settled all my affairs here and today at three o'clock I set off for Liège, whence I proceed directly to Cologne. I suppose I shall reach Cologne in eight days, and from the moment of my arrival I shall take my measures for joining you as speedily as possible. I hardly think I shall be refused, and you may be sure that nothing short of a peremptory order to remain shall keep me from you; at the same time that I do not disguise from you that I make a very great sacrifice in acting thus, and such as nothing but the intolerable anxiety I feel for your health could induce me to submit to; but when that is at stake I would sacrifice all the world to you.

I received your letter, with poor Tom's address,[2] two days ago; it was a long time coming, for it was dated the third ins[tan]t. I beg you will return

---

[1] Above, pp 37–8.

[2] On 12 Jan. 1797 the *Morning Chronicle* published a letter from Thomas Russell, dated Newgate, 19 Dec. 1796, outlining his political principles and denying that he had any connexion with France.

my thanks to Mr Wilson for the trouble he was so kind as to take in transcribing Russell's letter. The pacquet addressed to him never came to hand.

Monsieur Benard,[1] the gentleman who delivered me your last and who is Giauque's correspondent in Paris, spoke to me of his (Giauque's) claim on the French government, and told me that he was in some negotiation with some person who had, or pretended to have, influence here, and who was to assist him in recovering the money. I did not conceal my opinion from Mon[sieu]r Benard, for I know that Paris swarms with adventurers and especially of that class who, like Mr Lofty,[2] pretend to influence with persons whom they never saw; so that the Directory and Ministers have more than once advertised the public in the papers to be on their guard against all such. I wish therefore Giauque, unless he has very good reason to be satisfied that he is at present in a safe and good track, would suspend all further pursuit until my return to Paris, especially as I expect to see him in person in a month or six weeks; perhaps I may be able to be of use to him, but at all events he will be sure his affairs will be in the hands of a person on whom he can rely. I write to him by this opportunity to that effect.

Having written to you so very lately I have nothing to add. Dearest Love, keep up your spirits, and be in good health, and let me find you getting daily stronger and better. I love you and the little things more than all the world, ten thousand times; kiss them all for me and love me ever as I love you.

J. S.

Do not say a word to mortal of my visit to Hamburgh, for I shall keep a close incognito, and caution Giauque and Mary to that effect. 'Sarvice to Saul and the kitten.'[3]
You ugly thing, I doat on you.

To Maria Tone, 29 March 1797

Tone (Dickason) papers; *Life*, ii, 398; added to preceding letter.

Baby!

Kiss your little boys for me a thousand times and take care of poor Mama, because we both love her so much. I expect to see you in a month. God bless you.

J. Smith

---

[1] John Joseph Bernard (d. *a.*1839) seems to have set up a business house in Paris in 1796 which failed in Nov. 1797, creditors receiving about a third (*Dict. biog. franç.*).
[2] A character in Goldsmith's *The good-natur'd man* (1768).
[3] Smollett, *Humphry Clinker* (1771), ii.

Diary, 29 March–13 April 1797

T.C.D., Tone papers, MS 2049, ff 215ʳ–222ᵛ; *Life*, ii, 350–59.
The first few entries show signs of having been written up in arrears.

No. 13
From March 29 to May 14 inclusive[1]
Nil desperandum!
Amsterdam
1797[2]

29 Mar. 1797

Set off from Paris at 3 o'clock in the afternoon in the diligence for Liège; travelled all night.

30 Mar. 1797

Breakfasted at Soissons. Supped at Rheims, which from the little I saw of it seems to me a delightful spot. Visited the Cathedral where the Kings of France used to be consecrated; it is a noble Gothic structure but I fancy it will be some time before that ceremony will be again performed there.[3] Drank some excellent red champaign, which is called *vin rosé*, and set off. Travelled all night again.

31 Mar. 1797

Dined at Launoy, a village, and arrived in the evening at Mézières as tired as a horse; got to bed early and slept like a top.

1 Apr. 1797

Slept at Rocroy, famous for the battle gained in 16[43][4] by the great Condé,[5] in which he annihilated the Spanish infantry and thereby changed the destiny of Europe. I should have observed that we crossed the Meuse at Mézières, where it is not very considerable. I have now traversed Champagne and have

---

[1] No. 13 does not in fact end with 14 May but continues to 11 June. The Diary entries for 16–17 Apr., 18 Apr., 20–24 Apr., 25 Apr.–26 May, 4 June and 11 June are given as separate documents (below).

[2] The preceding headings, which Tone seems to have added when in Amsterdam on 14 May (see below, p. 74), are omitted from *Life*.

[3] It was to be just over 28 years. Charles X was crowned at Rheims in May 1825.

[4] In the MS a gap is left for the last two digits of the year, which is given in full in *Life*, ii, 351.

[5] Louis de Bourbon, prince de Condé (1621–86).

seen nothing remarkable; it is a flat country only interesting from the high state of its cultivation; Rheims is the best thing in it.

2 Apr. 1797

Slept at Givet, immediately over which is Charlemont, a place, I should judge impregnable from its situation on a rock, great part of which is inaccessible. There are three noble barracks at Givet, one for cavalry and two for infantry. In the beginning of the war the Austrians penetrated as far as the hills opposite Givet, but upon observing Charlemont with their perspectives, it held out so little temptation to them that they soon retired.[1] Crossed the Meuse again which is beginning to grow interesting. The banks on each side rise boldly and in many places are covered with wood. Passed a chateau belonging to the ci-devant Duc de Beaufort,[2] who has had the good sense not to emigrate; it is a most delicious spot, on the edge of the river, highly fertile and cultivated which is well contrasted by the lofty rocks which rise bare and perpendicular on the opposite bank to an immense[3] height. Entered the Forest of Ardennes, which brought Touchstone immediately into my mind. *'Well, now I am in Arden, the more fool I; when I was at home, I was in a better place.'*[4] A most infernal road, but a most romantic country. Dined at Fumay,[5] which is completely Llangollen.[6] I never saw a completer Welsh landscape for mountains, wood and water.

3 Apr. 1797

Breakfasted at Dinant, on the road to which, close to the edge of the Meuse, is a remarkable sugar loaf rock which rises to an immense height; the road passes between this sugar loaf and an immense pile of rocks on the other side, and there is not, I am sure, a foot more than the breadth of the carriage; the passage was opened by Louis 14 . Opposite to Dinant is Bouvines, famous for the victory gained by Bayard in [ ].[7] This country is a sort of

---

[1] Tone might also have stated that Givet had until recently been the last town in France before her frontier with the Austrian Netherlands. In July 1794 France invaded the Austrian Netherlands and prince-bishopric of Liège, and on 1 Oct. 1795 incorporated them in the French republic.

[2] Frédéric Auguste Alexandre, duc de Beaufort-Spontin (1751–1817), being out of sympathy with Joseph II's policy, withdrew to Spain, 1790–92, but moved to Vienna in 1796 (*Biographie nationale . . . de Belgique* (27 vols, Brussels, 1866–1938)).

[3] *Life*, ii, 351, reads 'uncommon' instead of 'immense'.

[4] *As you like it*, II, iv. *Life*, ii, 351, reads 'Ardennes' instead of 'Arden'.

[5] As Tone points out in his diary for 6 April (below, pp 44–5), he passed through Fumay *before* Givet. *Life*, ii, 351, reads 'Feray'.

[6] A picturesque town in Wales, surrounded by hills, on the road from Holyhead to Shrewsbury.

[7] Tone may be confusing the battle of Bouvines and the siege of Mézières. At Bouvines on 27 July 1214 Philip Augustus of France defeated an imperial army led by Otto IV; Mézières in 1521 was successfully defended by Pierre Terrail, seigneur de Bayard (1473–1524), against a large imperial army. Another possibility is that Tone is thinking of a legendary horse named Bayard belonging to the four children of Aymon which threw itself into the Meuse at Dinant rather than surrender to Charlemagne.

classic ground for a French officer. Since I have last crossed the Meuse, things are beginning to take a Flemish appearance. Passed thro' Ciney where there was a fair not very much unlike an English or Irish one. Slept at Fréneux.[1]

4 Apr. 1797

Crossed the Meuse again and arrived at Liège about ten o'clock. On the road near Liège is a most magnificient Abbey of Benedictins,[2] which is in fact a palace. At present however the French have laid their ungodly hands on the revenues, so I do not know how the reverend fathers make it out. The approach to Liège put me in mind of that to Birmingham, not that the face of the country is the same but that in both cases there is a great number of neat country boxes extremely well kept, that the fields are well dressed and the gardens highly cultivated, a proof that the inhabitants are at their ease as is generally the case in great manufacturing towns.[3] Liège its self is a melancholy, dirty spot; the palace of the Prince Bishop has the air of a convent; it is a square building, the inside of which forms a court round which runs an arcade where there are little shops of divers sorts. By the bye, even in the Palais Royal at Paris, the ground floor of the Duke of Orleans's appartments is laid out in shops, which has often surprised me. An English nobleman would not suffer the interior of his palace to be so shabbily occupied. Walked about the town, which offers nothing remarkable, except the number of little boys who exercise the trade of pimping and handle the caduceus with great dexterity; a stranger is beset with them at every corner; the instant he arrives, three or four of them surround him. '*Monsieur, monsieur, voulez-vous que je vous conduise? Quinze ans, quinze ans, la plus jolie femme de la ville!*'[4] Yet Liège has always been under an ecclesisastical government! The Cathedral was, I believe, magnificent, but the French have demolished it, and now it is heap of ruins.[5] The courts of justice &c. are held in the Episcopal Palace. Supped in company with a Pole, named Mokosky,[6] who was the secretary to Kotsciusko;[7] found him extremely interesting, which might in some degree perhaps result from the similarity of our situations, each of us banished from our country and seeking refuge in France from the same motives. Sat late with him; the only pleasant evening I have had on my journey. I like him very much; he idolizes Kotsciusko, and speaks of him as of a being of a superior order; his conversation

---

[1] Now spelt 'Fraineux'.

[2] In fact the Cistercian abbey of Val-Saint-Lambert, situated just before Liège, founded in 1202 and suppressed in 1796.   [3] Both were centres of metallurgy.

[4] 'Sir, Sir, would you like me to take you? Fifteen years, fifteen, the prettiest woman in the city!'

[5] The demolition of the cathedral of Saint-Lambert began a few days after the French conquest of Liège on 27 July 1794; the initiative was taken by Léonard Defrance, a Liégeois.

[6] Possibly Casimir Malachowski (1765–1845) who after the failure of the 1795 rising in Poland took refuge in France and served in the French army (*Nouv. biog. gén.*).

[7] Tadeusz Andrzej Bonawentura Kościuszko (1746–1817), Polish soldier and patriot.

brought a thousand ideas fresh into my mind. Well, let me have done with that subject for the present; there is a time for all things, and mine may come yet. The country about Liège, especially the gardens belonging to the bourgeois, is in the highest possible state of cultivation; thus far I have remarked no trace of the ravages of war, except a part of one of the faubourgs which has been destroyed by the fire of the Austrians.[1]

5 Apr. 1797

Traversed the Duché de Limbourg, a rich pasture country,[2] the verdure of which is not exceeded by that of Ireland and which is kept with an exactness and propriety of cultivation which I have not remarked even in the finest parts of England. The peasants are sturdy and tall, well fed and well clothed; most of them wear blue smock frocks; the farm-houses are capital mansions, and everything wears the appearance of ease and plenty; the horses are remarkably well kept; in short I thought myself in the very finest part of Yorkshire, but Limbourg has the advantage in point of cultivation. Arrived in the evening at Aix-la-Chapelle, but too late to see anything. Everything now is German.

6 Apr. 1797

Set off this morning in an open carriage, with the wind in my face and a snow storm. Traversed the Duché de Juliers, a corn country, well cultivated but very inferior to Limburg in the appearance of everything especially the farmhouses, which in Juliers are very mean and grow worse as they approach Cologne, where we arrived at six in the evening. *Hic finis longae chartaeque, viaeque.*[3] In the course of this journey I am surprised at the fairness and insignificance of the observations which presented themselves to me; in fact my journal is the counterpart of Kit Codling's remarks, *'Memorandum, feathers will swim in the salt sea'*,[4] but many reasons concur to render my tour barren. In the first place my mind is totally occupied by the state of my dearest love's health to the exclusion of all other objects; I can safely say that since I left Paris she has never been one instant out of my thoughts; I am more unhappy about her than I can express. She is the delight of my eyes, the joy of my heart, the only object for which I wish to live; I doat upon her to distraction. We are now twelve years nearly married, and I love her ten thousand times more than the first hour of our union. Oh my life, my love! What should I do, if I were so miserable as to lose you? Let me, if possible, banish that horrible idea. In the next place, I apprehend I have not the talent for observation, nor perhaps the

---

[1] After the French captured Liège the commander of the retreating Austrian army, Coburg, bombed the *faubourg* of Amercoeur.

[2] This duchy of Limburg, which had been part of the Austrian Netherlands, lay to the east of Liège; it is not to be confused with the present-day Dutch province of Limburg, which lies to the north. [3] 'Here ends a long letter and journey' (Horace, *Satires*, 1, v, 104).

[4] Samuel Foote, *A trip to Calais: a comedy* (1778), act 1.

knowledge requisite or rather, the *reading*; for I perceive that tours, to borrow Sterne's comparison, as well as books, are made like apothecaries' mixtures, by pouring out of one vessel into another.[1] There are five hundred *Vademecums*, by the aid of which I see anybody may write a tour, but for my part I am *'heinously unprovided'*[2] being that I have not even the *Livre de postes*, for the want of which I have in my journal of the 2d inst. placed Fumay after Givet,[3] whereas any well-informed tourist who will only take the trouble, without quitting his fireside, to open his eyes and look on the map will see that Fumey precedes Givet, whereby I am convicted of an unpardonable error in geography, and such as may raise in disinterested minds a doubt whether in fact I ever visited those remote countries of which I pretend to speak. In the next place I am quite alone, without a soul to speak to that I care one farthing about or that cares one farthing about me. If I were to make the tour of Europe to my mind, I would chuse for my *compagnons de voyage* my wife, Russell and George Knox. It would be a most delicious party. I love George Knox dearly; for my wife and Russell, they make, I may say, a part of my existence. Well, when the peace comes we shall see more. In the last place I have been shut up all along in an execrable *diligence* from which it is almost impossible to see anything; and when we arrived in the evening at our station, I was generally so fatigued that my first object was to get to bed as soon as possible. I therefore refer my dearest Love and my little babies (for whom, and for Russell, alone I write these memorandums) to the innumerable tours which have been and may be written, thro' France and the Pays Bas, for that information in which I am so scandalously deficient, notwithstanding that I have spent eight or nine whole days in the stage coach between Paris and Cologne, and have traversed at least 400 miles of the territory of the Republic.

7 Apr. 1797, Cologne!

That I take to be in the true style of a modern tourist! In Cologne I see as yet nothing remarkable. Went with the Adj[utan]t Gen[era]l Gastines, with whom I travelled, to the *Quartier Général*. The General[4] busy and could not see us, but sent to invite us to dinner. Dinner very pleasant. I should be as happy as an emperor, if it were not for the unceasing[5] anxiety which I feel for my dearest life and soul, which at every instant shoots across my mind. If ever I feel myself for a moment disposed to enjoy anything that cruel idea recurs to me and sinks me at once. My situation is most cruel at this moment. Just at the opening of the campaign I am obliged, if I can without disgrace, to quit the army, or, if I stay I risque the death of my wife, to me the most terrible of all events, and I leave my three little children at Hamburgh without the protection of father or mother, depending solely on the friendship of my sister, who is herself depending on her husband, to whom I am an utter

---

[1] *Tristram Shandy* (1759), V, ch. 1.   [2] *1 Henry IV*, III, iii.   [3] See above, p. 42.
[4] Lazare Hoche.   [5] William Tone substitutes 'increasing' for 'unceasing' (*Life*, ii, 355).

stranger. It is terrible! I have already written twice to my dearest love that I will, if possible, proceed from Cologne to join her.[1] I must see now how that can be done with honor; if it cannot be done with honor, it is not my fault, and in that case, if we must all perish, we must, and there is no remedy. My mind is distracted tonight with a thousand opposite thoughts and I know not where to fix. I am truly miserable. Went to the spectacle, for want of other idleness. Saw *Oedipe à Colonne* butchered. A wicked punster behind me said it was truly *Oedipe à Cologne*.

8 Apr. 1797

Mr Sheé is at Bonn, five leagues from this. He is appointed by the General president of the commission of administration of the *Pays Conquis*. Took leave of the General and set off for Bonn at two o'clock in the diligence. Found Mr Sheé in the gout, in his bed, and his brother commissioners at work about him. Fixed to see him early tomorrow, when I will, if I can, settle with him what I am to do under the present painful circumstances.

9 Apr. 1797

Called on Mr Sheé early and mentioned to him my present situation. After turning it in all possible lights we agreed that I should write a letter to the General suggesting to him the necessity of opening a communication with [ ][2] and offering, in case he had not otherwise disposed of me, to go in person to Hamburgh for that purpose. Wrote the letter accordingly, which Mr Sheé translated and I signed. Left Mr Sheé with his commissioners and walked about Bonn, which is a charming little town. It was the residence of the Elector of Cologne, who has a most superb palace; indeed except the Château de Versailles, it is by much the finest I ever saw; the King of England has nothing like it. It is now converted into an hospital for the French soldiers and I am sorry to see it already a good deal damaged. The garden is likewise metamorphosed into a park of artillery, in which however there are at present but a few caissons. About a quarter of a mile from the town, there is a second palace, not so magnificent as the first but which I should certainly prefer for a residence, called Poppelsdorff;[3] it was the Elector's country seat and it has, I am told, a handsome *jardin anglois*; it is also converted into an hospital. Before the war the road from Cologne to Bonn, being fifteen miles, was planted on both sides, like an avenue, but all the trees are now cut down and the beauty of the road is lost. But this is one of the least inconveniences of war. Opposite to Bonn, on the other side of the Rhine, are the Seven Mountains,[4] which

---

[1] Tone to Matilda Tone, 25 and 29 Mar. 1797 (above, pp 37–8, 39–40).
[2] Blank in MS, 'Ireland' being inserted in *Life*, ii, 355. Probably Tone had in mind the names of certain leaders of the United Irishmen.
[3] The Schloss at Poppelsdorf was erected early in the eighteenth century.
[4] The Siebengebirge.

form a very striking and picturesque object; three of them are surmounted by castles and furnished in former days a retreat to the famous Robert, *chef de brigands*.[1] The Rhine itself here presents nothing very remarkable; it seems to me something, but not much, larger than the Shannon at Athlone. The water just now is muddy, but I do not know that it is always so. On the opposite bank is also the abbey of Siegburg,[2] situated on the summit of a hill, and forms a very striking object. Entered one or two of the churches, in which there is abundance of very middling pictures and execrably bad statuary. Dined with Messieurs the commissioners very agreeably. From the windows of the dining room I saw the advanced post of the enemy on the other side of the Rhine. It is only a small detachment of O'Donnell's free corps;[3] they are dressed in green jackets and red pantaloons, with caps and white belts. Came home early and went to bed. I am not at all well. The continual chagrin and uneasiness of my mind in a certain degree affects my health. What a difference would it make in the day I have spent at Bonn if I had my poor Love with me! What shall I do if the General does not send me to Hamburgh?

10 Apr. 1797

Called on Mr Sheé early and found him engaged. All the places in the *diligence* for Cologne are taken for today, so now I must wait till tomorrow, confound it! I am in the utmost impatience to know what decision the General will take with regard to my application. Walked round the town and in the environs for two hours; it is fortified after a manner, but they are I believe the most peaceable fortifications in Europe; the fossé is converted into a number of little gardens, which are admirably well kept; the interior of the bastions form also so many gardens, in each of which is a handsome summer-house. One of them contains the *hortus botanicus*, with a delightful house in the middle. I have not seen anything so pretty of a long time. I thought immediately if I had that house and garden, with a decent competence and my dearest Love and our little babies about me, I should be the happiest man in Europe. Spent half an hour contemplating the Sept Montagnes,[4] which appear more and more picturesque and striking. Higher up the river is a hill, not very high but which rises abruptly, the top of which is crowned with a castle of considerable extent. I do not know its name,[5] but it is a noble object in the landscape. On my return discovered a delightful little farm-house with a patch of woodland behind and a few acres of excellent land about it, which would suit me to a miracle. I think I am grown covetous

[1] The play *Robert, chef de brigands*, seems in fact to have been set in Franconia.
[2] At Siegburg, 5 km east of Bonn, there was a Benedictine abbey.
[3] Charles O'Donnell (1754–1805) of Oughty, Co. Mayo; entered Austrian service, 1778; colonel of free corps, 1790 (R. S. O Cochláin, 'The O'Donnells in Austria' in *Irish Sword*, v (1961–2), p. 200). [4] The Siebengebirge.
[5] Possibly the castle was Godesburg, Drachenfels or Rolandseck (Karl Baedeker, *The Rhine from Rotterdam to Constance* (14th ed., Leipzig, 1900), pp 67 et seq.).

today. I want everything I see. Altogether the town and environs of Bonn are charming and, if my mind were at ease, I should enjoy this little trip exceedingly. What would I give to have my poor love with me today! Well, come what will, I will not speak of her again, if possible, until we meet. I am weary of complaints, which profit me nothing. Let me see now what General Hoche will determine. I hear the campaign will open the 15th. It is a good time for me to propose going to Hamburgh! I cannot conceive a situation much more painful than mine is at this moment.

11 Apr. 1797

Returned today to Cologne and dined at the *Quartier général*. Gave my letter to Poitou, so tomorrow I suppose I shall have an answer. One way or other I shall know my destination soon.

12 Apr. 1797

Saw the General today before dinner[1] for an instant. He told me he had read my letter and approved of the plan and that he had in consequence desired Poitou to make out a *permission*[2] for me to go to Hamburgh. I did not like the word *permission*, and therefore I took an opportunity to speak to him again after dinner, when I told him that I did not desire to go to Hamburgh unless he himself thought it adviseable, and in that case I requested he would give me *an order* specifically for that purpose, as otherwise it might appear that I had applied for a *congé*[3] at the very opening of the campaign, which was not the case. He entered into my view of the business directly and promised me to have the order made out accordingly, so I am in hopes that affair will be settled to my mind. I took this occasion to ask him if he had any particular directions to give me, or any particular person to whom he wished I should address myself. He told me not; that all I had to do was to assure my friends that both the French government and himself individually were as much bent as ever on the emancipation of Ireland; that preparations were making for a second attempt, which would be made as speedily as the urgency of affairs would admit; that it was a business which the Republic never would give up, and that if three more expeditions failed they would try a fourth, and ever, until they succeeded; he desired me also to recommend that this determination should be made known thro' the medium of the patriotic prints in Ireland in order to satisfy the people that we had not lost sight of them. I then took my leave, and we wished each other mutually a good voyage. I am very well satisfied with the turn that this business is like to take, and especially I am infinitely indebted to General Hoche for his kindness to me personally. On leaving the General,

---

[1] *Life* omits 'before dinner'.   [2] i.e. leave in a military sense.
[3] i.e. leave in a more general sense.

I called on Poitou and mentioned to him what I had said about the order. I likewise wrote a line to the General, requesting my *frais de route*, but I doubt my success in this application, as our military chest here is heinously unfurnished. At all events I have money enough to carry me to Hamburgh.[1] Come! all is not lost that is in danger. I have now the General's word that our business will be undertaken again.

13 Apr. 1797

Today the General set off for Coblentz. Walked all the forenoon about Cologne and entered into divers churches; saw a procession of priests carrying the Host. To a devout catholic it must appear very striking, but to me, who am not a devout catholic,[2] it was no great things; however I am glad I have seen it, for one must see everything. Saw sundry live friars and monks, *'black, white, and grey, with all their trumpery'*.[3] Visited the port and went on board a Dutch galliot,[4] where there was an appartment of four little rooms, the neatest and prettiest things I ever saw. I should delight to make a voyage down the Rhine with my dearest love aboard such another. Yesterday and today above 6,000 men with a train of artillery have entered Cologne, including the Légion de[s] Francs and the 24th demi-brigade of light infantry, both of which were embarked in our expedition; they are to be incorporated and to serve, with a company of light artillery, on the advanced guard, and as they have been trained to the *petite guerre* in La Vendée, I think they will be a match for an equal number of the light troops of the enemy. Met several of my *connaissances expéditionnaires*, among the rest Vaudré,[5] of the *artillerie légère*, who was with me on board the *Indomptable* and whom I liked very much. He asked me was I of the army de Sambre et Meuse, and when I told him I was, 'Eh bien', said he, 'c'est un brave homme de plus'. It was handsomely said of him. It seems in the distribution of offices I am charged (being attached to the État-major) with the *armement, équippement et habillement des troupes*. I know no more than my boot what I shall have to do, but I know that I have, at least, 80,000 men to arm, clothe and equip. *'By'r lakin, a parlous fear!'*[6] I have occasion for two intelligent adjoints, and instead thereof Gen[era]l Chérin has saddled me with MacSheehy, who is a sad blockhead and who latterly is turning out the most insufferable coxcomb I ever saw—he pesters my life out; he is the neat pattern of a vulgar, impudent, ignorant, Irish dunce, with great pretentions. I will move heaven and earth to get rid of him, confound him! I wish he was up to his neck in the

---

[1] On 2 Apr. 1797, Hoche requested the Directory to order a number of officers, including Adjutant General Smitt, who had been assigned to his army to join it. On 11 Apr. the Directory took steps to have the required orders issued. (Archives Nationales, AF III, dossier 2584, ff 33–4).

[2] *Life* omits 'devout'. [3] Milton, *Paradise lost* (1674), bk III, line 474.

[4] The meaning here seems to be 'barge'. [5] Corrected in *Life*, ii, 359, to 'Waudré'.

[6] *A midsummer-night's dream*, III, i. The lines which follow up to and including 'with all my heart' are omitted from *Life*.

Rhine; with all my heart. I have not got my order, nor my *frais de route* yet, but Poitou has promised me to send me, at least, the order from Bonn, and I have written a line to Mr Sheé regarding the money, but I have no violent hopes of success. It costs me a very hard struggle to quit the army just now, and nothing under heaven but the state of my poor Love's health could induce me to make such a sacrifice; but when that is at stake, every other consideration must give way. I would sacrifice my soul for her.

To General Louis Nicolas Hyacinthe Chérin, 14 April 1797

T.C.D., Tone papers, MS 2050, f. 3^r.

Tone states that MacSheehy is unsuitable as his adjoint and asks for Citizen Jonvolle instead.

À Cologne, ce 25 Germinal an 5

Général,

Je viens d'apprendre que vous avez nommé pour mon adjoint le C[itoy]en MacSheehy, et je suis très sensible à la bonté qui vous a dicté cet choix [*sic*]; cependant il faut vous dire que ce citoyen ne me convient pas du tout. Ayant moi-même très peu d'expérience, ignorant pour ainsi dire les détails de mon emploi, j'ai besoin d'un adjoint qui, ayant l'habitude du travail et connoissant la routine des bureaux, pourra, par ses lumières et son expérience, supplier à mes défauts—ainsi je vous prie, Général, de bien vouloir me choisir un autre, tel que j'ai désigné, car assurément le C[itoy]en MacSheehy me sera fort peu d'utilité; je ne parle pas du tout de ses talens, mais il manque absolument les connoissances qu'il m'est indispensable de trouver dans mon adjoint.

Si vous n'avez pas déja destiné le Cit[oye]n Jonvolle à quelque autre emploi, et s'il n'y a rien d'irrégulier dans la demande, vous me ferez en même tems un grand service et un grand plaisir en le nommant pour mon adjoint.

Je vous prie, Gén[éra]l, de me pardonner la liberté que je viens de prendre; vous voyez ma difficulté actuelle, et je me soumets à votre décision.

Salut et respects,
J. Smith
adj[udan]t gén[éra]l

Au Gén[éra]l Chérin, Chef de l'État-Major de l'armée de Sambre et Meuse, &c.

From General Lazare Hoche, 15 April 1797

Tone (Dickason) papers

Hoche grants Tone leave to go to Hamburg and converts it, as desired, into an order. He adds that he has a plan to send to England a man he has with him but awaits orders from the Directory.

Au quartier général à Coblentz,
le 26 Germinal, 5ᵉ année répu[blicain]e

Le Général en chef de l'armée de Sambre et Meuse
à l'adjudant général Smith

Je vous accorde très volontiers, mon cher Smith, la permission que vous me demandez d'aller à Hambourg. Je la convertis en un ordre comme vous le désirez. Je le joins ici.[1] Vous me trouverez toujours disposé à seconder vos vues pour le grand objet dont vous me parlez dans une de vos lettres.[2] Je m'en occupe souvent. J'ai même le projet d'envoyer en Angleterre un homme[3] de confiance que j'ai avec moi, mais j'attends pour l'exécuter les ordres du Directoire, à qui je l'ai communiqué.

L. Hoche

Order from General Lazare Hoche, 15 April 1797

Tone (Dickason) papers.
Covered by Hoche to Tone, 15 Apr. 1797 (above).

Au quartier général à Coblentz,
le 26 Germinal 5ᵉ année répu[blicain]e

ARMÉE DE
SAMBRE ET MEUSE

Il est ordonné au Citoyen Smith, adjudant général attaché à l'État-major de l'armée de Sambre et Meuse, de se rendre à Hambourg pour y remplir une mission dont je l'ai chargé et où il restera jusqu'à ce qu'elle soit terminée.

Le Général en chef de l'armée
de Sambre et Meuse
L. Hoche

Diary, 16–17 April 1797

T.C.D., Tone papers, MS 2049, ff 222ᵛ–223ᵛ; *Life*, ii, 359.

---

[1] This order is given as the following document (below).
[2] Not identified. Probably Tone had written to Hoche with another Irish expedition in mind.
[3] Not identified.

16 Apr. 1797

I have been lounging these three days about Cologne. Stupid enough. Yesterday I entered a church, alone, for I visit all the churches. There happened to be nobody in the place but myself, and as I was gazing about I perceived the corner of a green silk curtain, behind a thick iron lattice, lifted up and some one behind it. I drew near in order to discover who it might be, and it proved to be a nun, young I am sure and I believe handsome, for I saw only her mouth and chin, but a more beautiful mouth I never saw. We continued gazing on one another in this manner for five minutes, when a villainous overgrown friar entering to say his mass put her to the rout. Poor soul! I pitied her from the very bottom of my heart and, laying aside all grosser considerations, I should have rejoiced to have battered down the gates of the convent and rescued her from her prison. They are most infernal institutions, these convents; but at the peace I trust the Republic will settle that business here, where by the bye the people are dreadfully superstitious. All this last week we have had nothing but religious processions, particularly on the 14th, being Good Friday. Went today, being Easter Sunday, and heard high mass in the Cathedral, but the ceremony was very modest. I fancy they have concealed their plate and ornaments for fear of us, and they are much in the right of it. After mass went to another church and saw a Capucin friar preach. Crossed the Rhine today on the *pont volant*[1] and took possession of the *rive droite* in the name of the Republic. '*Thus far we have advanced into the bowels of the land.*'[2] There is great talk of an armistice with the Emperor, but I doubt it; it is too good news to be true. Oh, if we had once peace with him, we could bend all our attention and all our resources on England. I wonder I have heard nothing yet about my order.

17 Apr. 1797

This day Fairin, aid-du-camp of Gen[era]l Chérin, brought me the order for my departure enclosed in a very friendly letter from the general in chief.[3] I do not see anything concerning my *frais de route*, so I presume that part of the business is refused. It is well it is no worse. Walked out in the evening to a *guinguette*,[4] which is delightfully situated on the banks of the Rhine and drank a bottle of Hock. *Pas mal!*

To Matilda Tone, 18 April 1797

Dickason (Tone papers); *Life*, ii, 398–9.

Cologne, April 18, 1797

[1] i.e. a pontoon.
[2] 'Thus far into the bowels of the land have we march'd on without impediment' (*Richard III*, v, ii).
[3] Above, pp 50–51.
[4] A suburban place of refreshment with music and dancing.

Dearest Life,

I have this moment obtained my leave of absence and the day after tomorrow I set out to join you. I shall proceed thro' Holland as far as the frontiers of Germany, but as George the third, by the grace of God, happens to be also Elector of Hanover, I will not trust my person in his dominions. You will therefore, on receipt of this, prepare to set off to meet me at the place which I shall point out to you in my next letter, but which I do not as yet myself know. I rely on the friendship of Giauque to escort you, and if Mary can be of the party I need not say it will infinitely increase the pleasure I shall feel at our meeting. It is absolutely necessary I should see Giauque, for reasons which I will explain to him, when I have the pleasure to see him. I write to him by this post.

You will of course bring all your baggage, and your money, if any you have. I am not very rich you may well conceive, but I learn that from the first Floréal (viz. the day after tomorrow) the army will be paid entirely in specie,[1] and if so I shall be able to carry on the war tolerably.

'*The cloak which I left behind me at Tarsus, when thou comest bring with thee, and likewise the books, but especially the parchments.*'[2] In plain English, take care to bring my papers.

Dear Love, I cannot express the joy I feel at the prospect of seeing you once again! I have an immensity of news for you, and all *good news*, both public and private. I say nothing of your health, because I will not suppose that you are not well. I hope you have before this two letters[3] I wrote you before my departure from Paris. I will write to you again most probably from Amsterdam. I have voyaged so much of late that I think now I could go round the world in a hop, step and a jump; and my voyages are not finished yet. (Sings), '*In Italy, Germany, France I have been*'.[4] I do not know so great a voyager, except Master Fantom,[5] who had crossed the Atlantic twice before he was three years old. Robinson Crusoe was a fool to me. I am writing sad nonsense, but I am so happy at the thought of seeing you that I cannot help it. I have every reason in the world to be pleased with my situation and so you will say when we meet, which I hope now will be in about three weeks.

Adieu, Dearest Life and Soul, I must go now about my lawful occasions, and to prepare for my journey. I embrace you with all my heart and soul. Kiss the babies for me ten thousand times. You shall have my next with full directions four or five days after this. My love to Mary.

---

[1] Gold or silver coin.
[2] *Recte* 'The cloak that I left at Troas with Carpus, when thou comest, bring with thee, and the books, but especially the parchments' (2 Timothy, 4: 13).　　　[3] Above, pp 32–4, 37–8.
[4] Isaac Bickerstaffe, *Lionel and Clarissa* (1748), II, ix. It is said that Tone was taken by his mother to see this play at the age of three or four (R. R. Madden, *United Irishmen*, 3rd ser. (Dublin, 1846), i, 123). In fact its first performance in Dublin was on 2 Apr. 1770, when Tone was aged six (T. J. Walsh, *Opera in Dublin, 1705–1797* (Dublin, 1973), p. 152).　　　[5] i.e. his son Frank.

Your ever affectionate
J. Smith
Adj[utan]t Gen[era]l &c.

À Madame Smith
À Hambourg

To Maria Tone, 18 April 1797

Tone (Dickason) papers; *Life*, ii, 399; added to preceding letter.

Dearest Baby,

I am just setting off to join you and Mama, and I hope to have you both in my arms in a fortnight or three weeks. Love your boys for me, and let me see that you bring them and Mama safe and well to your affectionate Fadoff

J. S.

Remember it is you that have the charge of the family on you.

Daffy Bab! Daffy Bab! I suppose all my words are out of date and that you have got new ones—but no matter! I will soon learn them. Kiss your boys for me, my dearest Baby. I doat on you.

Diary, 18 April 1797

T.C.D., Tone papers, MS 2049, f. 223ᵛ; *Life*, ii, 360.

18 Apr. 1797

Wrote this morning to my dearest Love,[1] to Giauque[2] and to Mr Sheé, to notify my intended departure. I think I will go no farther than the frontiers of Hanover, where I have desired Giauque and[3] my family to meet me. Called on Gen[era]l Coulanges,[4] *sous chef de l'état-major*, to apprise him of my departure. Took my place in the diligence for Nimeguen, from whence I proceed by Utrecht to Amsterdam. By the time all my voyaging is finished I shall have made a pretty handsome tour of it.

---

[1] Tone to Matilda Tone, 18 Apr. 1797 (above, pp 52–4).   [2] *Life* omits 'to Giauque'.
[3] *Life* omits 'Giauque and'.
[4] Joseph Philippe Coulange (1749–1803) enlisted in 19th regiment, 1765; sergeant, 1767; ensign, 1778; quartier-maître, 1783; captain, 1791; adjutant-general and chef de bataillon, 1794; inspector of revenues, Nivôse an X (Archives de la Guerre, dossier).

From Colonel Henri Sheé, 18 April 1797

Tone (Dickason) papers.

ADMINISTRATION
GÉNÉRALE
DES PAYS-CONQUIS
À BONN, CE 29 Germinal l'an 5 DE LA
RÉPUBLIQUE FRANÇAISE
[crest]

Le Présid[en]t de LA COMMISSION INTERMÉDIAIRE

*A*u Citoyen Smith, Adjudant Général

I am glad, my dear friend, to find you have got your order[1] for setting out on your proposed journey. What delayed you was the want of understanding your meaning in the French letter you wrote to the Gen[er]al, by which he understood you desired to conduct a person to Paris from where you were going. This letter was shewn to me by honest [*word not deciphered*] his and the Gen[era]l's comments. I explained the mistake & set things right again.

I wish you a safe journey & speedy return with your spouse & children. It will be time enough for me to write to my wife when you'll [hear] of their being on their way to Nanterre in order to procure them proper lodgings, & at the worst they would find beds in my house & a friendly welcome until they can be better provided for.

I am not as incredulous as you about an armistice & a peace even with the Emperor,[2] for he is in a sad position & the devil mend him I say as well as his warm friends the English, who I hope will soon have their turn for an Irish jigg, to which I shall play up with all my heart untill my fingers are benummed.

God bless you,
Sheé

Certificate from Adjutant-General Joseph Philippe Coulange, 19 April 1797

Tone (Dickason) papers.

Coulange certifies Tone's appointment as adjutant-general.

ARMÉE
DE
SAMBRE ET MEUSE
ÉTAT-MAJOR GÉNÉRAL

---

[1] Above, p. 51.
[2] An armistice between the Emperor and France was signed at Leoben on 18 Apr. 1797.

Au Quartier-Général à Cologne
le 30 germinal *l'an* 5 *de la*
République Française, une et indivisible

LIBERTÉ, ÉGALITÉ, FRATERNITÉ

L'adjudant général sous-chef de l'état-major certifie que l'adjudant général Smith a été porté en cette qualité sur la revue du mois de germinal.

Coulange

Diary, 20–24 April 1797

T.C.D., Tone papers, MS 2049, ff 224ʳ–229ʳ; *Life*, ii, 360–67.

20 Apr. 1797

Set out from Cologne at 5 in the morning, '*by most of the clocks*',[1] on my way to join my dearest love. Dined at Neuss, an inconsiderable town at [7] leagues from Cologne. At three reached Crevelt, the most beautiful village I ever saw. The country all around it is flat, but highly cultivated. As to the town itself it is a most delicious spot; there is a considerable manufactory of silk goods carried on there, which considerably enlivens the place; the inhabitants, it is easy to see, are rich and comfortable, 4 leagues; travelled all night.

21 Apr. 1797

Passed Geuldres, the capital of the Duché of that name, in a broken slumber. I can assure all those whom it may concern that a German post-waggon is not the most eligible contrivance for sleeping in. I am at this moment *éreinté*, as the French say.[2] Breakfasted at Cleves and made my toilette to refresh me. Shaved by a surgeon, for three pence, for in Germany the ancient fraternity between the barbers and surgeons still subsists. Thought of Partridge's lamentation on their separation.[3] Set off again in my waggon at one. At four, entered the territory of the Batavian republic. At six reached Nimeguen, which is my first halt. Secured my place in the Utrecht diligence for tomorrow morning. Walked about the town for an hour. I am enchanted with it! I never saw anything so neat and well kept, and a young German who is my fellow traveller assures me that, as we proceed, I shall find the cleanliness and exactitude increase. Passed by two or three corps de garde. The Dutch troops very handsome fine fellows and extremely well kept. It is to be remembered

---

[1] 'The Kilruddery hunt', printed in T. C. Croker, *The popular songs of Ireland* (London, 1839), p. 39. The presumed author was Thomas Mozeen (d. 1768) (*D.N.B.*). [2] i.e. 'worn out'. [3] Fielding, *Tom Jones* (1749), bk VIII, ch. 6.

tho' that our ragamuffins made them fly like chaff before the wind. The Dutch officers wear gold-laced hats, like the British and our generals; the French plan is better in all respects. Saw several young Dutch women at their windows and doors, who seem to me to be charming creatures, well dressed and with taste. I find already that I had a very erroneous idea of Holland. Well, after all, there is nothing like travelling to dispel prejudice, with which observation, as it is perfectly original, and I [am] sure never occurred to anybody before, I will finish this day's journal.

22 Apr. 1797

Set out from Nimeguen in the Utrecht diligence between seven and eight. A Dutch officer of dragoons who travels with me tells me in a barbarous jargon, worse than my own, that a letter is just arrived at the Municipality with the news that an armistice with the Emperor for four months is agreed upon. I hope in God the news is true. It would make a marvellous change for the better in our affairs. I am exceedingly pleased with my tour. There is something after all in the view of Holland, notwithstanding its monotony, which, to me at least, is not disagreeable. The features of a Dutch landscaper [*sic*], an immense tract of meadows, till the view is lost in the distance, intersected either by deep and wide ditches, or by fences of wicker, made as neat as basket work; large plantations of willows; small brick farmhouses, covered with red tiles, and in excellent order; here and there a château of a seigneur, surrounded by a garden, in the true Dutch taste. I am not clear that, for a *small* garden, that taste is a bad one; its neatness, exactitude and regularity agree admirably with what one expects to find there. It is true it has not the picturesque beauties of an English garden, but it has notwithstanding its own peculiar merits, and in short I like it well enough *in miniature*. In a Dutch garden, all is straight lines and right angles, in an English one all is sinuosity. The Dutch garden is that of a mathematician, the English is that of a poet. No question the English taste is far superior, but all I contend for is that the Dutch is not without its beauties, and by no means merits the undiscriminating ridicule which is attempted to be thrown upon it; but I am writing an essay on gardening, of which I know nothing. To return, I never saw such neat farming as in Holland; the English brag very much of their farming and, to hear themselves talk, they are the first agriculturists in the world, as well as the bravest, the wittiest, the wisest and the greatest people which has ever existed. I am no practical farmer, but to my eye everything in a Dutch farm is beyond all comparison neater than in an English one, and especially that striking and important article, the fences, to form which it is that they make such immense plantations of willows; the pasturage seems most luxuriant, and everything in short in a Dutch farm wears the appearance of ease and plenty. There is however a striking contrast between the neatness and beauty of the farm-houses and the mean and rustic appearance of the owners. I saw several very ordinary looking boors lodged in mansions which with us would suit a gentleman of from £300 up to £1,000 a year. A great number of these cottages have apiaries of 20, 30, 40, and one or two I remarked of above 100, hives. I cannot see, or rather I see plain enough, why our poor peasantry have not beas, which require so little expence and of which their children, of which they never fail to have plenty, might take care. I made the same remark with regard to the orchards in Normandy when I first arrived in France;[1] but he who can barely find potatoes for his family is little sollicitous about apples; he whose constant beverage is water dreams of neither cyder nor mead. Well, if we succeed, may be we may put my poor countrymen on somewhat a better establishment. We shall see; but to return. The storks here, who are never disturbed, build on the barns and churches; I saw several at work on their nests; it is a superstition of the country.

Breakfasted at Wyck. On the back of our post-waggon was painted a representation of Noah's Ark. I thought it no bad allusion to the interior of the machine, and if the painter intended it, I give him credit. The guard at Wyck in blue, faced sky blue, and, as at Nimeguen, very handsome fine fellows. After passing Wyck, remarked that there was considerably more corn grown than I had hitherto observed, but the neatness of cultivation continues invariably. At seven in the evening arrived at Utrecht, of which I saw almost nothing, as I alit at one gate and traversed, without stopping, a part of the town to the canal from whence proceeded the barge for Amsterdam. I remarked however that, as at Bonn, the bastions were converted into little gardens and summer houses, but at Utrecht they [are] infinitely more in number, neater kept, and higher ornamented. The quarter thro' which I passed put me strongly in mind of Philadelphia, which, to my eye, it resembles exceedingly in the exterior of the houses, the footways paved with brick, the trees planted in the streets, the fountains, and even the appearance of the inhabitants, which is very like that of the American quakers. I am very apt to see analogies and likenesses between places and individuals, which I fancy exist often in my imagination only. Be that as it may, Utrecht put me strongly in mind of Philadelphia. At eight set off in the trackschuyte, a villainous barge which is to the Grand Canal packet boat what a German post-waggon is to a neat, well-hung, English chariot.[2] The grand cabin (which is very small) being hired, I was stowed away '*among the common lumber*'.[3] We were about thirty passengers, one half Jews, every man with his pipe in his mouth. I was suffocated! I thought my entry in the boat would have been solemnised by a battle. Having nothing but French money, when I came to pay for my passage, the skipper refused my coin, which threw me into unspeakable confusion. A young Jew, seeing my difficulty, offered to

---

[1] See his diary for 10 Feb. 1796 (above, vol. II, p. 45).

[2] A treckschuyt, or track-boat, was 'a covered barge divided into two apartments, the after one, called the roof, which is superior in point of accommodations, contains from eight to a dozen persons, and the other from forty to fifty' (R. Fell, *A tour through the Batavian Republic during the latter part of the year 1800* (London, 1801), p. 143).   [3] Thomas Otway, *Venice preserv'd* (1682), I, i.

change me a piece of five livres into Dutch money. I thanked him and accepted his offer. It is to be observed that at par the Dutch *sol* is exactly double the French one;[1] consequently *one hundred* French sous should procure *fifty* Dutch. But my Jew knew the course of exchange too well for that traffic, and taking my *pièce de 100 sous*, he gravely handed me *38 sous d'Hollande*, by which I should have lost exactly 24 sous.[2] I was at first rather surprised at his impudence, but recollecting myself immediately I looked him mildly in the face and with great gravity required him instantly to refund. All Jew as he was, this threw him out of his play and he immediately offered me *4 sous d'Hollande* more. I told him that I perceived he was a Hebrew and that if he would give me one hundred, he should not have the piece, on which he submitted. All this is '*matter of inducement*'. (How the duce came I to remember so much law?) Immediately after, a man would enter the boat perforce, and sat himself down in the lap of another, who repelled him with great violence and threw him upon me, as I was endeavouring to compose myself to sleep, of which I had great need. I rose immediately and seizing him by the collar was proceeding to inflict an unheard of chastisement upon him, to which my adventure of the Biscayner at Trenton[3] would have been nothing, when my Jew, who had not digested his affront and his loss, thought proper to interfere, on which I instantly quit my antagonist and attacked the Hebrew with great violence. All the world knows that a Dutch *trackschuyte* is a most inconvenient scene for a battle, for, to go no farther, it is in the first place impossible to stand upright therein, and we were besides stowed away in bulk, like so many herrings. I could therefore do little more than swear and call names, which I did in broken French, to the great astonishment of the Dutchmen and terror of the Israelite, whom I threatened with I know not what degree of punishment. That should make him an example for ever to all the posterity of Abraham. He demanded pardon with great marks of contrition, which I at length accorded him, and, the intruder, who was the first cause of the dispute, being turned out by common consent, the tranquillity of the packet boat was restored. My sleep was however fled, and the smoking continued with great perseverance, so that I was devoured with *ennui*. Opposite me was placed a fat Dutchman with his mistress (I believe), so to divert myself and to support the honor of the Republic I determined to act the Celadon[4] with Mademoiselle, who did not know one word of French. That did not however prevent [me] making great way in her good graces, and Hans, who perceived he was losing ground fast, very wisely determined to renounce the contest, to which he found himself unequal, pulled his cap down over his eyes and composed himself to sleep. I laid my head down without ceremony in the lap of Mademoiselle and in five minutes was as fast as a church.

---

[1] i.e. the French *sol* or *sou*, of which there were 20 to the *livre*.

[2] He would have lost 24 French *sous* or 12 Dutch *sous*.

[3] Nothing more has been ascertained of this incident. By 'Biscayner' he means a 'Biscayan' or person from Biscay. Trenton, New Jersey, is about 15 km from Princeton.

[4] Character in *L'Astrée* by Honoré d'Urfé (1568–1625).

The lady followed the example of her two lovers, and in this manner at five in the morning we reached Amsterdam. I had no right in the world to teize poor Hans, but *'des chevaliers français, tel est le caractère'*; besides that he seemed *'not to be made of penetrable stuff'*.[1] I will not venture to say as much of Mademoiselle, who, by the bye, was very pretty.

23 Apr. 1797

At six reached the auberge, *'L'Étoile'*, in the Neuss, or Neiss, for I am not sure of the orthography, and got immediately into bed, of which I had great occasion, for I have not had a good night's sleep since I left Cologne. Of three nights, I have passed two in the waggon and the trackschuyte and the intervening one, at Nimeguen, I passed very badly, from the reflexion that I had to get up very early the next morning, a circumstance which always spoils my rest, and indeed was the case the night before I left Cologne, so I may say I have passed *four nights* without a good sleep, and that is too much, and I am as tired as a dog. My journey from Cologne to Amsterdam, including expenses of all kinds, has cost me about thirty-six livres of France, or £1 10[s]. o[d]. sterl[in]g. It is extremely cheap and inconvenient.

Rose at ten. *'Mem; hands but not face.'* It is today Sunday. Dined at the *table d'hôte* very agreeably at one. Drank a bottle of *'delicate wine of Lucona'* or rather indeed most excellent claret, and set out alone to see the lions.[2] The state house a most magnificent building which perfectly satisfied the conception I had formed of it. Beside it is the New Church, so called I presume because it was new when it was built by the Spaniards before the foundation of the Dutch republic. Assisted at[3] divine service, with which I was much pleased. The people here seem devout, but I remarked the congregation consisted entirely of persons advanced in life or of children; I believe I was the youngest man in the church. The organ is the largest and most magnificent I ever saw; it is truly a noble instrument. When the minister prayed, everyone took off his hat, and when he read the Scriptures, put it on again. I do not understand the *etiquette* of that. Is it that they think it would not be respectful to God almighty to address him with the hat on? But surely, if the Scriptures be the word of God, it is not respectful to listen, no more than to speak to your superiors, with your hat on. Saw the tombs of de Ruyter[4] and Van Gaalen.[5] That of De Ruyter is in the place where, in a Catholic church, would be the high altar. The tomb of that brave man occupies it much more honorably. He is represented lying, as well as Van Gaalen. I wished, at first, he had been in an erect posture, but on second thoughts I believe it is better as it is. I was exceedingly affected by the figure of Van Gaalen, who is represented as dead, with his truncheon

---

[1] 'If it be made of penetrable stuff' (*Hamlet*, III, iv).   [2] i.e. the sights.   [3] i.e. attended.
[4] Michiel Adriaanszoon de Ruyter (1607–76), Dutch admiral (*Nieuw Nederlandsch biographisch woordenboek* (10 vols, Leiden, 1911–37), v, 628–32).
[5] Jan van Galen (1604–53), Dutch hero in the Anglo-Dutch war (ibid.).

grasped in his right hand and his left on his breast; it is a glorious reward, a monument erected to the memory of a brave man by his country. I am rather afraid that we have but few Van Tromps[1] and de Ruyters in the Dutch navy of the present day. Walked round by the quays, which are kept, as everything in Holland is kept, with an astonishing neatness. Looked into the cellars where the sailors eat. The cleanliness of everything in them might tempt the appetite of a prince. I thought of George's Quay,[2] and '*Ship's kettles cooked here*', with some little humiliation. In point of cleanliness, to speak the truth, we are most terribly behind the Dutch. Coffee house; read the papers. It is fated that my national pride is to be humbled today. In the *Leyden Gazette* I had the mortification to read the following observation relative to the peaceable disarming of the province of Ulster. '*Quelques menacantes que soient souvent les dispositions des Irlandois, rarement on les a vu produire des bien terribles effets.*' The devil of it is that the observation is founded. Fitzgibbon had reason when he said we were a people easily roused and easily appeased.[3]

24 Apr. 1797

I am more and more pleased with Amsterdam. It is the first city in the world to walk in, and in that respect I prefer it infinitely to either London or Paris. Visited the *Stadt Huys* again. It is a most magnificent structure and one of the few public buildings that I have seen which completely answered my idea of it; it is exactly what it ought to be, vast, simple and grand. I know nothing in the world of architecture, but I have scarcely ever been so pleased with anything as with the State House of Amsterdam. There is a set of bells in the dome that ornaments the front of the building which execute airs and short pieces of music with an inconceivable precision. In general I detest the sound of a bell, so that when I was at the Temple, in London, surrounded by five or six churches, I often wished myself in Turkey, or some peaceable Mahometan country, where bells are forbidden; but the chimes of the State House are quite another affair. I stood today twice for near half an hour and listened to them with the greatest pleasure. The hackney coaches are here fixed upon sledges and drawn by one horse; they are convenient and ugly, but the horses are superb. Traversed the Warmoes Straat, which is the Rue St Honoré of Paris, the Strand of London, and the Dame Street of Dublin. The Kalver Straat may be called the Cheapside of Amsterdam. I had a very high notion of the dignity of commerce from seeing the City of London, but I have a much higher one now since my visit to Holland. What must the trade of this city have been before the war! Bought a set of duets at

---

[1] Maarten Harpertszoon Tromp (1598–1653), Dutch admiral (ibid., v, 969–71).
[2] In Dublin.
[3] In the Irish house of commons on 15 Aug. 1785, Fitzgibbon had remarked: 'in this perhaps lies the difference between the two nations—Ireland is easily rouzed, but she is easily appeased; England is not easily rouzed, nor easily appeased' (*The parliamentary register; or, Debates of the house of commons of Ireland* (17 vols, Dublin, 1782–1801), v, 468).

Hummel's,[1] on the Zok-kin, to have it to say that I had been in the first musical magazine in the world. Subscribed for a proof impression of a mezzotinte of Buonaparte, eight livres. I do not know whether it is like, but it is a very good print. Called on the artist, who is an Englishman, one Hodges,[2] and sat half an hour chatting with him; he has promised to chuse me out a choice impression. I have the *cacoethes emendi*[3] strongly on me today, but luck-ily I have so little money that the disease will expire for lack of nourishment.

To Matilda Tone, 25 April 1797

Tone (Dickason) papers; *Life*, ii, 400.

Amsterdam, April 25, 1797

Dear Love.

I trust you have received my letter[4] from Cologne of the 18th inst., and that you have made your preparations to set out without delay to join me. All things considered, I find I cannot prudently advance beyond the Dutch territory and therefore I have written to Giauque, by this post, to conduct you by the shortest route to Groninguen, which is the town the nearest to you that I could fix upon. You will have this letter, I trust, the 29th, and if so, and nothing unfore-seen happens to prevent you, you may be, I learn here, at Groninguen in three days; but I allow one or two days for accidents, so I hope, deducting all rea-sonable deduction, to see you about the 3d or 4th of next month, at which time I shall be in waiting at Groninguen. I rather suspect I need not press you to lose no time, as I judge of your impatience for our meeting by my own.

I hope to see you so soon that I will not write you a long letter. All I have to tell you is that everything is going on to my mind. Kiss my babies for me ten thousand times and make great haste, but not more than good speed, to join me. I insist upon your not over fatiguing yourself; a day, more or less, makes little or no difference, and may materially affect your health.

Adieu, Dearest Love. God bless you.

J. S.

I send this under cover to Mons[ieu]r Holterman;[5] that to Giauque I enclose to Victor Pretre.[6] *Remember to take leave of the French Minister.*[7]

---

[1] Johann Julius Hummel (d. 1798), music publisher, was established at Amsterdam from about 1766. Later he also had an establishment in Berlin. The business was dissolved in 1821. (Charles Burney, *A general history of music* . . . (4 vols, London, 1776–89), iv, 606; *Grove's dictionary of music and musicians*, 5th ed. by Eric Blom (9 vols, London, 1954).)

[2] Charles Howard Hodges (1764–1837), portrait painter and mezzotint engraver, settled in Amsterdam by 1794 (*D.N.B.*).   [3] Meaning 'an itch for improvement'.

[4] Above, pp 52–4.   [5] Not identified.   [6] Not identified.

[7] Charles Frédéric Reinhard (1761–1837), French minister to the Hanseatic towns; he was born in Württemberg and was later 'chef de la troisième division au Département des Affaires Étrangères' (*Biographie universelle* (21 vols, Brussels, 1843–7), viii).

À Madame Smith
À Hambourg
très pressé.

To Maria Tone, 25 April 1797

Tone (Dickason) papers; *Life*, ii, 400; added to preceding letter.

Dear Baby,

I have nothing to add.

Your affec[tiona]t[e] Fadoff
J. Smith

To M[ademoise]lle Maria Smith, &c., &c.
À Hambourg

[P.S.] My best respects to the young gentlemen your brothers.

Diary, 25 April–15 May 1797

T.C.D., Tone papers, MS 2049, ff 229ᵛ–240ʳ; *Life*, ii, 367–80.

25 Apr. 1797

Rose at nine. '*Chid Ralph for mislaying my tobacco stopper.*'[1] Wrote to my dearest Love,[2] and to Giauque,[3] appointing to meet them at Groninguen the 3d or 4th of next month.[4] Changed fifteen louis d'or for Dutch money; lost thereby nine livres, which is just six pence p[er] louis; it is not much. At the coffee-house. Found the English papers down to the 14th inst.; nothing very material, but it was a great enjoyment to me. Several United Irishmen, whose names are however not mentioned, have been acquitted.[5] There is a schism in the yeomanry corps, many of them being disgusted by the tyranny which is exercised over the people in the North, and especially by some proclamation lately published by Gen[era]l Lake,[6] which I should be glad to see and which

---

[1] *Spectator*, no. 317 (4 Mar. 1712).   [2] Tone to Matilda Tone, 25 Apr. 1797 (above).

[3] *Life* omits 'and to Giauque'.

[4] 'M[onsieur] Giauque, the brother-in-law of the Irishman Smith who was with General Hoche', later told the French minister at Hamburg that he had seen his brother-in-law at Groninguen, 'where he had conducted Mrs Smith', and that 'Smith' had told him to welcome the United Irish emissary Edward Lewines (Reinhard to minister of foreign affairs, 19 May 1797, Archives de la Guerre, Bᴵᴵ 1; see below, pp 86–7).

[5] Acquittals of persons charged with sedition in the north of Ireland were reported in the *Morning Chronicle*, 7, 14 Apr. 1797.

[6] Gerard Lake (1744–1808), appointed to command in Ulster, Dec. 1796. His proclamation of 13 Jan. 1797 requiring the surrender of privately held arms was denounced by the whigs in the Irish and British houses of commons. Between Apr. and June 1798 he was commander-in-chief in Ireland. (*D.N.B.*).

appears to be very violent. There have been in consequence resolutions and counter-resolutions and protests,[1] and in short there is a feud in the enemy's camp, and the English government can count no more upon the yeomanry corps. Mr Pitt has dispatched Mr Hammond[2] to Vienna either to negociate, or, which I rather think, to hinder the Emperor from negociating with the French government. The outcry for peace is universal and petitions pouring in to that effect from all parts. There is one from the city of Dublin, moved by Grattan and seconded by Ponsonby, at an aggregate meeting of the citizens and carried without a dissenting voice.[3] I see those illustrious patriots are at last forced to bolt out of the House of Commons and to come among the people,[4] as John Keogh advised Grattan to do long since. An attempt was made to declare the Co. Armagh in a state of disturbance but the scheme was defeated, and altogether there seems to be a faint appearance of a better spirit rising in that unfortunate country. I do not however build an inch high on it. The King and Pitt seem determined to die hard. He has refused to receive the address of the City of London sitting on the throne, and the Livery to the number of 5,000 have voted unanimously that it is the inherent right of the City to present their petitions in that manner, and so they are at issue. If they carry their point (which they will not do) the King will be obliged to give an answer, which is the ground of the dispute.[5] The stocks were as low as $49\frac{7}{8}$, but Hammond's mission have screwed them up to 52. For my part I look on it as a mere tub, while the loan is negociating, which is for £15,000,000; but nothing is too improbable for John Bull to believe, especially when he desires it. '*Mem. Mr Nisby's opinion thereupon.*'[6]

26 Apr. 1797

Having three or four days to dispose of, I resolved to see the *Convention Batave*, and in consequence I set off this morning, at five, in the trackschuyte for the Hague. At Haarlem saw a regiment of Dutch troops preparing for the parade; uniform blue faced red, and the men in general of a very good appearance; their arms, clothes and accoutrements in excellent order. Travelled as far as Leyden with a Dutch admiral who had the politeness to invite me

---

[1] Several yeomanry corps in Belfast resolved that the sole motive for their enrolment was to repel invasion (*Dublin Evening Post*, 16 Mar. 1797).

[2] Hammond, the under-secretary for foreign affairs, was sent to Vienna to persuade the Austrian government to act with Great Britain in the peace negotiations.

[3] On 8 Apr. a Dublin aggregate meeting with Henry Grattan in the chair on the motion of Benjamin Wills, seconded by Francis Burroughs, adopted a petition requesting the king to dismiss his ministers. George Ponsonby supported the petition. (*Dublin Evening Post*, 11 Apr. 1797).

[4] On 15 May, Grattan declared that if the house of commons rejected William Ponsonby's scheme of parliamentary reform, the Irish whigs would no longer attend the house. The scheme was rejected.

[5] The sheriffs were informed that the king would not receive 'upon the throne' a petition from the city of London unless presented by the corporation. A petition from the livery would be received in 'the ordinary manner' at a levee. (*Annual Register*, 1797, Chronicle, pp 14–15).

[6] *Spectator*, no. 317 (4 Mar. 1712).

into the state room which he had hired for himself; I do not know his name, but he spoke very good French, '*much better French than you or I, gentlemen of the jury*'.[1] I found his conversation very agreeable; his uniform was blue, with a red cape and cuffs embroidered in gold, and a white ostrich feather all round his hat. He is just returned from the Texel, where there are fifteen sail of the line ready and full manned for sea. That would be very good, but unfortunately the Dutch seamen have manifested such a terrible spirit of meeting, insubordination and ill will that there is no reckoning upon them; witness their running way with the *Jason* frigate and their infamous behaviour under Admiral Lucas at the Cape of Good Hope.[2] By the bye, I have never been thoroughly satisfied with regard to the conduct of the said admiral in that expedition. God knows, but may be it is a present of fifteen sail of the line that we are making the English. I asked the admiral what he thought of Cordova's[3] battle with Jervis the other day when with 27 sail of the line he contrived to be beaten by 15 and to lose four ships, and whether he thought it was thro' cowardice or ignorance. The Dutchman bluntly answered me, 'Both', and I believe he had reason. He also told me that the celebrated navigator, Bougainville,[4] is named to the command of the fleet at Brest. I am heartily glad of it. To return to my voyage. All along the banks of the canal I observed a prodigious number of wild fowl, who indeed could hardly be called *wild*, for they let us pass within twenty yards of them without seeming to take notice of us. Having been in the days of my youth something of a sportsman, I felt '*my ancient propensities begin to revive*'.[5] There were green and grey plover, red shanks, snipes, stairs &c., &c. without number. They are little disturbed, for the law here is that every man is to sport on his own ground only, and I conclude the Dutch are either too busy or too lazy to follow much that amusement. I wonder shall I ever have a day's partridge shooting in Ireland again? The last day I was out was with my dear friend Russell—poor fellow! God knows what may be his situation this day, or whether he has not been sacrificed by that infernal government of Ireland. Well, let me think no more of that. The banks of the canal, as we approached the Hague, are covered with villas as thick as they can stand and kept with an astonishing neatness; under the local difficulties of situation, it is astonishing how much they have contrived to make of their country. They have '*turned diseases to commodity*';[6] but to judge all this, it is necessary to be on the spot and to see what they have done; nothing short of Dutch patience, perseverance and resolution could have commenced, continued and concluded

---

[1] Source of this quotation not traced.

[2] Rear Admiral Engelbertus Lucas was in command of a Dutch squadron sent out to recover Cape Colony in 1796. On being discovered by a superior British squadron in Saldanha Bay, he immediately capitulated. (*London Gazette*, 4 Nov. 1796).

[3] José de Córdoba y Ramos (d. 1809) in Feb. 1797 engaged Jervis's squadron but, being defeated, was deprived of his command for incompetence (*Enciclopedia Universal*).

[4] Louis Antoine de Bougainville (1729–1811), French naval officer and circumnavigator; imprisoned during Terror (*Dict. biog. franç.*).   [5] Source of this quotation not traced.

[6] *2 Henry IV*, 1, ii.

the astonishing works which are executed everywhere in Holland. A Dutchman cultivates his garden with a precision inconceivable and brings it to a state of absolute perfection, and within fifty yards he has a windmill built for pumping off the water which is constantly at work, and if it were to cease he and his garden would be inundated in four and twenty hours. I have remarked twenty villas built, literally, in the water, to which the master entered by a bridge, and they were the neatest boxes I ever saw.

Arrived at the Hague at five o'clock. My journey of 13 leagues has lasted twelve hours and cost me [   ].[1] To Monastereven from Dublin, which is pretty nearly the same distance, it occupies nearly, as I remember, the same time and costs five shillings.[2] In the Dutch canal there are no locks; the boat, which is much inferior to our packet boats in size, beauty and all other respects, is drawn by one horse, who makes regularly about 3 miles an hour, so that here they say indifferently 'such a place is so many leagues or so many hours off'. Set up at the Seven Churches, which however the intelligent reader who knows his geography will be careful not to confound with a place of the same denomination in the County Wicklow, which is called by the natives Glandealough. Dined at the *table d'hôte* with nine members of the Dutch Convention, very plain and respectable looking men, and put me exceedingly in mind of my old and much and ever respected masters of the General Committee.[3] I feel the tears gush in my eyes and my pulse beat fast at writing that sentence! After dinner walked out alone to see the town. Visited sundry places of which I know not yet the names; found myself at last in a wood intersected by a noble avenue on the right side of which was a Dutch regiment (the 1st, blue faced white) at exercise, and on the left a battalion of French. The Dutch exercise beyond all comparison with more precision than our troops; they are taller and stouter men; better dressed and kept, their armes and accoutrements in better order. At fifty yards' distance, to see them together, there is no man that at the first blush would not give the preference to the Dutch; but I looked closer at them, when the exercise was over, and saw at once in the French something of a fire and animation that spoke that ardent and impetuous courage that is their peculiar characteristic and which the others totally wanted. I would not, after that glance, hesitate an instant with our little battalion to attack the Dutch regiment, which was at least twice as strong, and we would beat them. It was very amusing to me to observe the *fierté* of our soldiers, as they marched by the

---

[1] *Life* omits 'and cost me [   ]'. Thirteen leagues is about 60 km.

[2] Tone went by the Grand Canal from Dublin to Monastereven, a journey of about 65 km, on 26 Sept. 1792 (see above, vol. I, p. 295). In the early or mid 1790s the fare for travel in the first cabin was 1s. 1d., or 9d. back cabin, per stage of about 8 Irish miles (about 16 km). A Frenchman who visited Ireland in 1796 stated, 'the canal boats are very comfortable, being indeed very like those of Holland, but the cost here is nearly double'. In 1798 the fares were revised, the new fare from Dublin to Monastereven being 7s. 7d. (Jacques Louis de Bougrenet, chevalier de La Tocnaye, *A Frenchman's walk through Ireland, 1796–7*, trans. John Stevenson (Belfast, 1917), p. 15; Ruth Delany, *The Grand Canal of Ireland* (Newton Abbot, 1973), p. 105).

[3] i.e. the Catholic Committee.

others; there was a saucy air of civil superiority which made me laugh excessively both then and since. The physiognomy of the French is sharp, quick and penetrating; that of the Dutch is round, honest and unmeaning; their step, their air, their manner is free and assured; they are the true stuff whereof to make soldiers. There are however some important points to be considered. You must leave the French grenadier free permission to wear a very large cravat, if it be the fashion, tied just as he likes; his hat is likewise his absolute property in the disposition of which he is by no means to be interrupted or constrained; he must try it on in all possible shapes and forms, and wear it absolutely in that position which he conceives best becomes the cut of his figure. When satisfied in these important, indeed indispensable points, he is ready for everything, and Caesar himself was not so brave as these *petits maîtres*, for every soldier in France is a *petit maître*. I have seen them, God knows, ragged enough, but I never saw them but with their cravat well and fashionably arranged, and their hat cocked and put on with an air. To return. Once again, it was curious to see them march by the Dutch and the manner with which they regarded the others, most of whom were the head and shoulders taller than they; there was a certain assurance which pleased me exceedingly; the Dutchmen looked, to me, like so many taylors beside them. Saw a *corps de garde* of Dutch cavalry; uniform white, faced black and lined red; buff vest and breeches, buff cross and waistbelt, black cockades. So many colours had not a good effect. I should like however to see the regiment mounted.

27 Apr. 1797

Visited this morning the *Convention Batave*. It is held in the palace of the çi-devant *Stadthouder*, in the room which was formerly the ball room, the *orchestres* whereof are converted into the *tribunes*, as they are called here and in France, or galleries, with us. The *tribunes* are open and no introduction by a member is necessary. The room is handsome, but has nothing particularly striking; it is an oblong of, I judge, about 120 feet by fifty illuminated by six large and as many smaller windows over the others of plate glass. The President is placed on a *banquet*, raised four steps, open to the front and railed in on the other three sides. On his right and left hand are two tables and seats for four secretaries; opposite to him is the bar; his table is covered with a crimson velvet cloth laced with gold, and his chair is covered and trimmed in like manner; he wears a silk scarf of red and white, passed over his right shoulder and round his waist, and he is furnished with a middling-sized ivory mallet, with which he announces the decision of the Assembly by a stroke on the table. The mallet I do not like; it gives the President terribly the air of an auctioneer, but nobody here minds it. On his right hand, but on the floor, is a small kind of pulpit from which all reports of committees are read by the respective chairmen. The members, who are 126 in number, are placed round the three sides of the room; there are five rows of benches raised one above the other covered with green cloth; each member has before him paper, pen and ink; the places are all numbered, and every fifteen days, at the election of the President, whose office lasts no longer, the members draw for their seats, by which means they avoid the denomination of *right and left side, government and opposition side, &c.* They receive 10 florins a day, which is the same as in France, nearly, being about 16s. 8d. English. It is moderate enough, if it be not too moderate, for my principle is that public functionaries should be liberally paid, but with no fees of office. When you pay liberally you can insist that he whom you employ shall do his duty, and fewer hands infinitely are necessary. I have seen sufficiently in France the mischief of a different system, where for want of being able to pay the public functionaries, everyone was careless and it was necessary to have 10 persons to do that, and do it ill, which might be well done by one and for the fourth of the expence in the upshot. Liberality is in many instances the true economy. The members were extremely decorous in their manner and appearance, and order is sufficiently kept; infinitely better, for example, than in the *Conseil des Cinq-cens*, but not quite as well as in an English house of commons. I observed very few members that were not at least five and thirty years of age, and most of them seemed to me to be forty and upwards; they wear no distinctive mark of any kind. Altogether I was extremely pleased with the decorum and appearance both of the Assembly and the auditors. The *tribunes* were full, but not crowded; there were some women of a decent appearance, and in the *tribune* opposite the President, which is reserved for the friends of the members, there were some very handsome and well dressed. When I entered, the House was, as we would say, in committee, on some ordinary business, and the President, *pro tempore*, wore a black velvet scarf over his right shoulder with the words '*République Batave*' embroidered in gold on the front. At twelve the House resumed and the President took the chair, as I have described. The question for discussion was whether the Dutch people should or should not be obliged by the Constitution to pay the clergy. I know not what may be, but I know very well what ought to be, their decision. In France, where there is no religion, there is no salary settled by law for the priests. In America, where there is a great deal of religion, there is no salary settled by law for the clergy. The Catholic priests and the Dissenting ministers of Ireland are paid by the voluntary subscriptions of their hearers; and after all those examples I have no doubt as to the inconvenience of a church establishment. By the bye there are several of the clergy members of the Convention Batave; I saw today a Catholic priest and three Protestant ministers sitting in their places, and the priest spoke in the debate. I know not what he said, but he made the assembly laugh heartily. There are likewise some of the noblesse in the Convention, and I find they do not vote as a *caste*; some of these are patriots, and others aristocrats. All this information was given me by an honest Dutch patriot who, seeing me in a French uniform, was so good as to do me the honors of the assembly and to point out to me the most distinguished members, particularly Van Kasteele,[1] who is the leader of the Democratic interest. It seems the principle which divides the assembly is unity or federalism? The Democrats are for the first, the Aristocrats for the latter, and they have succeeded in carrying their point in the plan of the intended constitution; but my Dutch friend tells me he hopes that, for that very reason, the constitution will be rejected by the people in their primary assemblies. He likewise informed me that under the intended constitution the clergy are to be excluded from seats in the legislature, and that he wished to God they would exclude the lawyers also, who were intriguers and caballers, and, from being more in the habit of public speaking and of confounding right and wrong, were often able to confute and silence abler and honester men than themselves. I could not help laughing internally at this sketch of my *ci-devant* brethren of the Dutch bar. I find a lawyer is a lawyer all over the world. The most scandalously corrupt and unprincipled body, politically speaking, that I ever knew, is the Irish bar. I was a black sheep in their body, and I bless God that I am well rid of them. Rot them! I hate the very memory of the Four Courts, even at this distance. Well with God's blessing no man will ever see me again in a black gown and a nonsensical big wig, so let the profession of the law go and be hanged! I am happily done with it. To return. I have now seen the Parliament of Ireland, the Parliament of England, the Congress of the United States of America, the *Corps Législatif* of France, and the *Convention Batave*. I have likewise seen our shabby Volunteer convention in 1783, and the General Committee of the Catholics in 1793,[2] so that I have seen, in the way of deliberative bodies, as many, I believe, as most men, and of all those I have mentioned, beyond all comparison the most shamelessly profligate and abandoned by all sense of virtue, principle or even common decency is the legislature of my own unfortunate country; the scoundrels! I lose my temper every time I think of them.

Dined at my auberge. At the desert there entered a sort of a band of music, consisting of four women, two of whom were pretty, and two men; one of the women had a *tambour de Basque*, the rest had violins. They played and sung alternately and not ill. I observed they sung in parts, first, second and bass; they finished with the Marseillois hymn in their *patois*, and the prettiest of the women then went round with a plate to make her collection, I am not sure that I should have been as much pleased by better music; I thought, at the time, of the ballad singers of Ormond Quay[3] and blushed. Went to the coffee house and read the Paris papers, viz. the Royalist ones, which were the only ones I could find; excessively disgusted with their dullness and impudence. The liberty of the press is not yet understood in France; it is

---

[1] Pieter Leonard van de Kasteele (1748–1810), president of the Dutch national assembly, Mar.–Apr. 1796 and Aug.–Sept. 1797 (*Nieuw Nederlandsch biografisch woordenboek*, viii, 948–51).
[2] i.e. the Catholic Convention, which met in Dec. 1792 and again in Apr. 1793 (see above, vol. I, esp. pp 346–71, 431–43, 464–84).
[3] In Dublin.

scandalous and abominable, the indecent attacks that are made with impunity on the Government. In England, there is not one of those scoundrelly journalists but would be sent to Newgate for two years for the fiftieth part of the libels which are published day after day in Paris with the most perfect impunity; yet the rascals cry out that they are enslaved and call the Directory tyrants and oppressers, whereas the proof that the most unbounded liberty or, to speak more properly, the most outrageous licenciousness[1] exists in France, is that such audacious libels are published and that the authors are not instantly sent to the gallies. All over Europe there is not a tyrant whose subjects dare outrage him with impunity, and it is hard that in the only government emanating from the choice of the people, liberty should be made the instrument of her own destruction. But would I destroy the liberty of the press? No! but I would most certainly restrain it within just and reasonable limits. All fair and cool discussion I would not only permit but encourage; but the infamous personalities, the gross and vulgar abuse that disgraces the Paris journals, I would most severely punish. Liberty of the press, somebody has very well said, is like the liberty to carry a stick, which no man should be hindered to do; but if he chuses to employ it in breaking his neighbours' heads, or their windows, it is no breach of his liberty to make him answer for the mischief he has committed.[2] In short I am of opinion—and if ever I have the opportunity I will endeavour to reduce that opinion to practice—that the government of a republic, properly organized and freely and frequently chosen by the people, should be *a strong government*. It is the interest and the security of the people themselves, and the truest and best support of their liberty, that the government which they have chosen should not be insulted with impunity; it is the people themselves who are degraded and insulted in the persons of their government. I would therefore have strong and severe laws against libels and calomny; and I do not apprehend the least danger to the just and reasonable liberty of the press from the execution of those laws, where the magistrates, the judges and the jury are freely named by the people. The very same laws which under the English constitution I regard as tyrannous and unjust, I would in a free republic preserve and even strengthen. It is because the King names the judges and the sheriffs, because the sheriffs pack the jury and a thousand other obvious reasons, that I regard the English trials, in many instances, as a mockery of justice; it is not that in theory the law is bad, but that in practical execution it is tyrannical, and, as I have already said, I do not see why tyrants alone should be protected by the laws, and liberty left unprotected and defenceless. I hope I am deceived, but I much fear the French government will have reason sorely to repent their extravagant caution with

---

[1] *Life*, ii, 375, has 'license' instead of 'licenciousness'.

[2] Benjamin Franklin wrote in the *Federal Gazette*, 12 Sept. 1789: 'my proposal then is to leave the liberty of the press untouched, to be exercised in its full extent, force and vigour; but to permit *the liberty* of the *cudgel* to go with it *pari passu* (*The works of Benjamin Franklin* (10 vols, London and New York, 1887–8), x, 144).

regard to infringing the liberty of the press; it is less dangerous for a government to be feared, or even hated, than despised, and I do not see how a government which suffers itself day after day without remission to be insulted in the most outrageous manner with the most perfect impunity can avoid in the long run falling into disrepute and contempt. In America such gross indecency would not be permitted to pass unpunished, and surely, if rational liberty exists upon the earth, it is in the United States. Here endeth the first lesson on the liberty of the press. I have now disburthened my soul of the indignation which was kindled within me by those execrable libels.

To return. Walked forth into the wood in quest of the palace of the *ci-devant* Stadthouder, but could not find it, so that must be for tomorrow. Returned to my auberge, somewhat afflicted with the blue devils. Remembered one of Voltaire's precept[s] in such case, '*Ou bien buvez; c'est un parti fort sage*'.[1] Determined to put it in practice. Got off my boots and coat, into my wrapper and slippers, and determined to enjoy myself. I do not see why I should come to the Hague without tasting some Holland gin. '*The liquor, when alive, whose very smell, I did detest and loath.*'[2] Called for gin, water and sugar, '*on which the waiter disappeared and returned instantly with the noggin*'.[3] Performed the part of Lord B———[4] with infinite address. Drank to the health of my dearest love; '*Our friends in Ireland*'; '*the French Republic*', with three times three; '*a speedy republic to Ireland*', with loud and universal acclamations; '*General Hoche and the army of Sambre and Meuse*', with divers other loyal and constitutional toasts. The evening concluded with the utmost festivity.

28 Apr. 1797

Worked up my journal of yesterday. As I am about to leave the Hague tomorrow, bought *The traveller's guide* in order to amuse myself in the boat by reading what I *ought* to have seen while I was there. I do not much see the good sense of my purchase; but I perceive I am of that class, respectable at least for its numbers, who are celebrated for their facility in parting with their money, of which, by the bye, it may be supposed I am just now afflicted with a prodigious quantity. Dinner as usual but the company more mixed. At the lower end of the table sat a member of the Convention, who is worth a plumb,[5] and a sta[u]nch patriot; next him, in order, were three plain men, '*said they were farmers, indeed looked like farmers, in boots, and spattered*'.[6] They and the representative of the people had a long discussion. I observed he listened to them with great attention and took notes of their remarks. That is as it ought to be. After dinner, a concert as yesterday, but the band differently composed.

---

[1] 'Imbibe, the wisest thing!'   [2] Henry Fielding, *Tom Thumb* (1731), III, ii.
[3] Cf. above, vol. II, p. 246, n. 1.
[4] Perhaps Lord Burleigh, a character in Sheridan's *The critic* (1779).
[5] 'A plum in the cant of the city' was worth £100,000 (Samuel Johnson, *Dictionary* (1755)).
[6] The source of this quotation has not been traced.

'*On n'y voyait, ni tettons, ni beaux yeux.*'[1] In plain English, the performers were men, excepting one woman, who sung agreeably two or three duos, the other part being performed by a little *bossu*,[2] about three feet high but who was penetrated to the very soul by his music. I was exceeding amused by his style of singing and acting (for he acted also) and at the end of the concert I gave him a trifle for himself. I could not help thinking what a choice morceau Sterne[3] would have made out of one of those concerts and this poor little *bossu*, who seemed a sort of enthusiast in his act. These ambulant musicians, if you think of the opera, are nothing; but if you think of the ballad singers of other countries, they are highly respectable; and in fact I remarked two or three among them whom I would have been very glad to equal on their instruments. After dinner strolled out about the Hague. '*People may say this and that of being in Newgate, but for my part I find Holland as pleasant a place as ever I was in, in my life.*'[4] It is delicious. I am tempted, as I walk about the Hague, to cry out, '*Thou almost persuadest me to be a Dutchman*'.[5] Whoever may be ambassador from the Republic of Ireland in Holland will not be the worst off of the future *corps diplomatique*. Returned to my auberge. Demanded of the waiter '*if he could help me to a glass of genever, or so?*' (I defy man, woman, or child, to track me in that quotation.)[6] The waiter produced the needful. Lord B—— &c., &c.[7]

29 Apr. 1797

Set off this morning in the trackschuyte for Amsterdam. Saw two storks, male and female, at work at building their nest; it was a delightful emblem of a *bon ménage*, and I cannot express the pleasure I felt in observing how intent they were on their work and the assistance they mutually gave each other. How my dearest love would have enjoyed it! Travelled with *le citoyen* Van Amstel,[8] a deputy to the Convention, whom I had already met at dinner and who had been pointed out to me, when I went to the Assembly, by my Dutch acquaintance, '*whose name I know not, but whose person I reverence*',[9] as a most excellent patriot and republican. We soon found one another out; he tells me that the Committee for Foreign Affairs have received an express from Gen[era]l Daendels,[10] commander-in-chief, that the preliminaries of the peace,

---

[1] *Recte* 'tétons'; *anglice* 'Neither breasts nor beautiful eyes were to be seen'.

[2] Meaning 'hunchback'.   [3] Laurence Sterne (1713–68), humorist (*D.N.B.*).

[4] The heroine in Defoe's *Moll Flanders* (1722) was in both Newgate and Holland, but the words Tone quotes have not been found in that work.

[5] Cf. 'Almost thou persuadest me to be a Christian' (Acts of the Apostles, 26: 28).

[6] It has not been traced by the editors.   [7] See above, p. 71, n. 4.

[8] Adrianus Ploos van Amstel (1749–1816), president of the Dutch national assembly, Sept.–Oct. 1797; he represented Amsterdam (*True Briton*, 1 Apr. 1796).

[9] 'Whose profession I honour, but whose person I know not' (Dryden, *The Spanish fryar* (1681)).

[10] Herman Willem (or Hermann Wilhelm) Daendels (1762–1813), born at Hattem, Gelderland; fled to France after failure of rebellion against stadtholder, 1787; lieut.-col., 4th battalion of Légion franche étrangère, 1792, part of *armée du Nord* which invaded Holland, 1793; *général de brigade*, Apr. 1794; *général de division*, Dec. 1794; commanded Dutch division on the Rhine, 1796; later governor of Dutch East Indies (*Nieuw Nederlandsch biografisch woordenboek; Dict. biog. franç.*).

between the French republic and the Emperor, are certainly signed,[1] and that they have no doubt but the fact is so. If so, it is most excellent news, indeed the best we could desire; but I have a mighty good rule, from which I will not now depart, which is to believe most excellent news always four and twenty hours after all mankind is convinced of its certainty. He gives me another piece of intelligence, which, *if it be true*, I regard as scarcely of less importance than the peace with the Emperor, viz. that there has been a mutiny aboard the English fleet;[2] that the seamen had nearly thrown their admiral overboard; and that they had tried, condemned and hanged one of their comrades for opposing their measures. This is too good news to be true, and I long most anxiously to see it explained. It has been communicated to the *Comité des Relations Extérieures* from Hamburgh, so I shall probably learn the truth when I meet my brother-in-law[3] at Groninguen. At our parting Van Amstel requested to see me on my return by the Hague and offered his services, if he could be of any convenience to me then, on which I '*flourished my hands three times over my head in the most graceful manner*'[4] and took my leave. I think I will ask him to introduce my dearest love into the grand gallery of the Convention. Returned to my '*old hutch*' in the Neuss, where by the bye I am very well and reasonably lodged.[5] I like the Dutch inns mightily.

30 Apr. 1797

Set off on my journey for Groninguen, where I have given my wife and babies a rendezvous. Crossed the Zuyder See in the night. It took us just 12 hours.

1 May 1797

Arrive at Lemmer at 8 in the morning and set off instantly in the trackschuyte for Strobosch; a delightful day and beautiful breeze all the way; immense quantities of game all along the canals. Planned a voyage, to be executed God knows when, by my wife, Russell and myself. To hire a trackschuyte for a month certain, to go where we liked and stop where we liked; to live aboard our boat; to bring guns, fishing tackle &c. and in this manner to make a tour thro' a great part of Holland. It would be delicious— '*a very pretty journey indeed—besides where's the money?*'.[6] Oh Lord, oh Lord!

2 May 1797

Slept last night at Strobosch in a six-bedded room, the other five beds being occupied by five snoring Dutchmen. Genteel and agreeable. Arrived

---

[1] Peace preliminaries had been signed by France and Austria at Leoben on 18 Apr. 1797.
[2] Mutinies at Spithead and the Nore lasted from 16 Apr. to 15 June 1797.
[3] Jean Frédéric Giauque. In *Life*, ii, 378, William Tone substitutes 'family' for 'brother-in-law'.
[4] Source of this quotation has not been traced.
[5] Cf. 'A satisfaction it was to me to come into my old hutch and lie down' (Daniel Defoe, *Robinson Crusoe* (1719)).   [6] Source of this quotation has not been traced.

at Groninguen at 12 o'clock. The town extremely neat, like all the Dutch towns, but not as handsome as most of those I have seen. Put up at the Nieuwe Mûnster.

3, 4, 5, 6 May 1797

Tormented with the most terrible apprehensions on account of the absence of my dearest Love, about whom I heard nothing.[1] Walked out every day to the canal two or three times a day to meet the boats coming from Nieuschans,[2] where she will arrive. No Love, No Love! I never was so unhappy in all my life. One evening went to the Dutch comedy. I am enraged to see every instant how unjustly the Dutch are treated by other nations. This was but a strolling company, and the theatre was patched of boards, being a temporary building raised for the fair only, which lasts here three weeks. They played however a translation of Voltaire's *Mérope* very decently, and the after piece, which was the *tableau parlant*, exceedingly well; better for example than I have seen it played in French at Rennes and at Brest. Saw a battalion of Chasseurs in dark green coat, waistcoat and breeches, with crimson cape and cuffs; two or three companies were armed with rifles, with which I saw them fire at the target very badly, tho' they had a machine to rest their [firelocks] upon, which is a vile custom; at 150 yards not one in ten of them struck a target of three or four feet over, and not one of them, by any chance, the bull's eye. The 4th Dutch demi-brigade is here in garrison, blue faced pale yellow, and makes a very good appearance; there is likewise a regiment of hussars in dark blue, like our 6th reg[imen]t, and looks very well.

7 May 1797

At last this day in the evening, as I was taking my usual walk along the canal, I had the unspeakable satisfaction to see my dearest love and our little babies, my sister and her husband, arrive all safe and well. It is impossible to describe the pleasure I felt.

Here is an end of my journals now, for some time at least. Since I came to France, which is now above fourteen months, I have continued them pretty regularly for the amusement of my dearest love. As we are now together once more it is unnecessary. We must wait for another separation.[3]

15 May 1797, Amsterdam[4]

---

[1] In the letter he wrote to his wife from Amsterdam on 25 April he gave her a rendezvous at Groninguen on 3 or 4 May (see above, p. 62).   [2] *Recte* Nieuweschans.
[3] In a note William Tone states (*Life*, ii, 405): 'my father's meeting with his family was short and delightful. He travelled with us about a fortnight through Holland and Belgium, left us at Brussels, and on the 26th May was already returned to headquarters at Cologne, whilst we proceeded on to Paris.'
[4] It appears that Tone was at Amsterdam again when travelling with his family from Groninguen to Brussels. In the MS the date and place ('Amsterdam, May 15, 1797') appear at the foot of the entry.

Diary, 26 May 1797

T.C.D., Tone papers, MS 2049, f. 241ʳ; *Life*, ii, 405.

Cologne, 26 May 1797

I see today, in the *Journal Général*, an article copied from an English paper dated about a fortnight ago, which mentions that a discovery had been made in Ireland of a communication between the discontented party there and the French; that one[1] of the party had turned traitor and impeached the rest, and that on his indication near fifty persons in and near Belfast had been arrested, one of them a dissenting clergyman; that their papers had been all seized and that, on the motion of Mr Pelham,[2] the English Secretary, they were to be submitted to the inspection of a secret committee of fifteen members of the House of Commons. All this looks very serious.[3] There has been a formal message from the government on this business. For my part, all I can say is that if communications have been had, it is without my knowledge, but even so, I am heartily glad of it. The dissenting clergyman is Sinclaire Kelburne, as I saw in a newspaper at Amsterdam, but I wonder who is the traitor? Methinks I should be curious to see him!

To Matilda Tone, 2 June 1797

Tone (Dickason) papers; *Life*, ii, 401–02.

William Tone observes in a footnote that this letter, as well as that of 13 June 1797 (below, pp 81–2), was 'written on my father's return to the army of Sambre et Meuse'.

ÉTAT-MAJOR GÉNÉRAL

ARMÉE	*Au Quartier-Général à* Friedberg[4]
DE	*le* 14 *Prairial l'an* 5 *de la République*
SAMBRE ET MEUSE	*Française, une et indivisible*

---

[1] Edward John Newell (1771–98), a native of Downpatrick and portrait painter (*The apostacy of Newell . . . by himself* ([Belfast], 1798); Madden, *United Irishmen*, 2nd ed., i (1857), pp 531–80; *D.N.B.*).

[2] Thomas Pelham (1756–1826), chief secretary for Ireland, 1795–8; succeeded as 2nd earl of Chichester, 1805 (*D.N.B.*).

[3] Twenty-one United Irishmen were arrested at the house of John Alexander in Belfast on 7 Apr. 1797 (Mary Ann McCracken to Henry Joy McCracken, 13 Apr. 1797, in Mary McNeill, *The life and times of Mary Ann McCracken* (Dublin, 1960), pp 117–18). Altogether 'numerous men of character and credit' were arrested in the north of Ireland during the next few days (*Dublin Evening Post*, 20, 25, 27 Apr. 1797).

[4] Friedberg, situated in Hesse midway between Wetzlar and Frankfurt, was a *Reichsstadt*, or imperial free city, under French occupation.

LIBERTÉ ÉGALITÉ FRATERNITÉ

Dearest Love,

You see what a flourishing sheet of paper I write to you on, but the fact is I have got no other.[1] I arrived here yesterday evening safe and sound, which is in one word all the news I have to communicate to you. The General is out on a tour which may detain him five or six days, so I have not seen him yet.[2] In the meantime I have got very good quarters, and as we all live in one family at the État-major, I am as well and as happy as I can reasonably expect to be in your absence.[3] It is much more to the credit of the French than it is to mine that I have the good fortune to stand perfectly well with all my comrades. You may judge how a Frenchman in England would find himself in similar circumstances — but this observation I believe I made to you already.

Dear Love, I look back on our last tour with the greatest delight. I never was, I think, so happy, and more happy I never can expect to be in future, whatever change for the better may take place (if any does take place) in our circumstances. It was delightful. I recal, with pleasure, every spot where we past together. I never will forget it.

But that is not what I sat down to write about. How is your health at present? How are your spirits? Are you at Nanterre? Have you seen Madame Sheé?[4] How do you like Mademoiselle?[5] Are you fixed in lodgings to your mind? Have you heard from Mary? Has Giauque got you your money? Have you bought your musical glasses? How are the Babies? Does Maria pick at her guitar? Is Will as good as ever? Is Frank as great a tyrant?

> *Are the groves and the vallies as fair?*
> *Are the shepherds as gentle as ours?*[6]

I desire you may answer all these questions, especially the two last, which I look upon as of the most importance, and have therefore put into verse,

---

[1] On it, below 'Liberté, Égalité, Fraternité', are printed also the words 'Le Général [ ], chef de l'État-Major Général de l'Armée de Sambre & Meuse', which, however, are scored through.

[2] Hoche and Tone were badly out of touch. Hoche had written to the Directory from Friedberg on 30 May: 'Le citoyen Reinhard, votre ministre près les villes hanséatiques, vient de m'envoyer Monsieur James Thompson . . . à l'effet de recevoir de lui des renseignements positifs sur l'état de l'Irlande . . . Depuis fort longtemps l'adjudant général Smith est à Hambourg, et peut-être est-il passé en Angleterre. J'attends de ses nouvelles. Quoi qu'il en soit, il ne contribuera pas peu à occuper Monsieur Pitt et compagnie.' (Arthur Chuquet (ed.), *Quatre généraux de la Révolution* (Paris, 1911–20), iii, 177). 'James Thompson' was a nom de guerre of Edward Lewines (Lewines memorial, Archives des Affaires Étrangères, AE IV 1671, ff 100–05).

[3] General Hoche and his staff were quartered in great comfort at the imperial castle; Hoche wrote at the end of May 1797 that their plates were heaped up and 'as much wine spilt as drunk', all of which was at the expense of the locality (Klaus-Dieter Rack, *Friedberg in Hessen: die Geschichte der Stadt, Band ii: vom Dreißigjährigen Krieg bis zum Ende des Alten Reiches* (Friedberg, 1999), p. 154).

[4] Probably Marie Madelaine née Hardouin (d. 1823), wife of Henri Sheé (*Burke's landed gentry of Great Britain and Ireland* (London, 1858), p. 896; 'Shea of Munster', B.L., Add. MS 45576).

[5] Apparently Françoise or Fanny Sheé, only daughter of Henri Sheé; she married Count Jean Wulfram d'Alton and by him had a son, Edward (b. 1810), who became Count d'Alton Shee (ibid.).

[6] William Shenstone, *A pastoral ballad* (1755).

it being acknowledged that poetry is easier and longer retained in the memory than prose. I desire, I say, that you may answer them categorically, as also the following:

Have you seen Madgett? Have you seen Sullivan,[1] his nephew? Have you seen anybody else whom I do, or do not, know? How did you stand the journey in that plaguy diligence? Were the poor little babies tired to death? Were your *compagnons de voyage* civil? Finally, how do you like France in general and Paris in particular?

I have now given you a reasonable litany of questions, which I beg you may answer the day you receive this. Madame Sheé will tell you how she forwards her letters, and do you adopt the same plan.

For news, we have none here; we presume the peace will go on; but if it should not, you need not be in the least uneasy on the score of my personal safety, for we, of the État-Major, being the gentlemen of the quill, remain always in our bureaux quietly, two or three days' march in the rear of the army, not only out of reach, but out of hearing of the cannon. I beg, therefore, whether we have war or peace, that you may not make yourself unhappy by needless apprehensions.

I have done for the present. It will be a long fortnight before I receive your answer. Give the babies, as usual, 100,000,000 kisses for me. I send this under cover to Madgett, who will forward it.

Adieu, dearest love. God bless.

Your slave and dog.

J. S.

À la Citoyenne Smith

To Maria Tone, 2 June 1797

Tone (Dickason) papers; *Life*, ii, 402; added to preceding letter.

Baby!

'*Sincerely don't you pity us poor creatures in affairs?*'[2] I am sure I have cut you there, Baby. '*Fie, what the ignorance is!*'[3]

Your humble servant,

J. S.

---

[1] John Sullivan, whose acquaintance Tone made in Paris in 1796 (see above, vol. II, p. 143 et passim). He arrived in France in 1783 and was employed as a teacher of English and mathematics at La Flèche until 1793, when he joined republican forces in the Vendée. (Certificats de civisme, La Flèche, 21 Fructidor 2, 2 Nivôse, Lectre testimoniale du Collége de la Flèche, 21 Fructidor 3, Archives de la Guerre, sous série 2 e).

[2] Goldsmith, *The good-natur'd man* (1768), act II.   [3] *Merry wives of Windsor*, I, i.

Diary, 4 June 1797

T.C.D., Tone papers, MS 2049, ff 241ʳ–242ʳ; *Life*, ii, 406.

Friedberg, 4 June 1797

In the *Moniteur* of the 27th is a long article copied from the English papers of the 18th of May and containing the substance of the report made by the secret committee above mentioned.[1] Most of the facts contained in it I was already acquainted with; the organisation is however much completer than when I left Ireland; the most material fact is that about 100,000 United Irishmen exist in the North of Ireland, and that they have a large quantity of arms and at least 8 pieces of cannon and a mortar concealed. I presume that martial law is proclaimed long before this, as I see in the *Frankfort Gazette* an article from England of the 23d May (viz. five days after that in the *Moniteur*) which mentions two or three skirmishes between the Army and some detached parties of the people (who are denominated the *Rebels*) in which the Army had of course the advantage. I do not at all believe that the people are prepared for a serious and general insurrection and in short (why should I conceal the fact?) I do not believe they have the courage. It is not fear of the Army, but fear of the law and long habits of slavery that keep them down; it is not fear of the General but fear of the Judge that breaks their spirit. In the meantime it seems [that] Marquis Cornwallis[2] is named to the command in Ireland and that Lord O'Neill, Mr Conolly and the Duke [of] Leinster have resigned their regiments.[3] The example of the last has been followed by all the officers of the Kildare Militia.[4] This last circumstance is in some degree consolatory.

From Colonel Henri Sheé, 7 June 1797

Tone (Dickason) papers.

[1] A summary of the report of the secret committee presented to the Irish house of commons by Pelham is given in the *Moniteur*, 27 May 1797. For Tone's earlier comments, see his diary for 26 May (above, p. 75).

[2] Charles Cornwallis, 1st Marquis Cornwallis (1738–1805), served in America, 1776–81; governor-general of India, 1786–93; he was in May 1797 prematurely reported as going to Ireland as commander-in-chief; lord lieutenant of Ireland, 1798–1801 (*D.N.B.*).

[3] O'Neill, Conolly and Ormonde were reported in May 1797 to have resigned their commissions but in each case there was a denial (Sir Henry McAnally, *The Irish militia, 1793–1816* (Dublin, 1949), p. 114).

[4] After the duke of Leinster gave up his command of the Kildare militia (by 20 May), a number of officers resigned, among them Major Dominick William O'Reilly, Capt. Richard Rice, Lieut. William Aylmer and Ensign William Donnellan (Liam Chambers, *Rebellion in Kildare, 1790–1803* (Dublin, 1998), pp 49–50).

Au Citoyen Smith   Bonn, yᵉ 19th Prairial 5th year
adjudant général au
Quartier Général
à Friedberg

I am glad, My Dear Friend, that you arrived safe at Friedberg. You will have the pleasure of hearing from your wife herself that she allso got safe & sound with her dear little ones to Nanterre, as I learnt from my daughter,[1] who sent me a letter for you.

God send your fears with regard to Ireland may be ill grounded. I have hopes that as matters stand in England they will not be in a condition to overpower our countrymen, having enough to do at home, for it seems the insurrection in the English navy is becoming more serious every day. I could wish there were some hundreds of your excellent pamphlet[2] distributed among our Irish sailors who might at this juncture instead of blocking up the port of Brest steer a couple of dozen of English men-of-war into the said port to joyn the French & together sail to the relieve of the honest Irish. I believe that our cruel enemy Gill would now wish to have all his lifetime been as obscure as myself.

I was sorely vexed at finding in one of our late papers that a letter from one M. Theobald Wolf Tone was intercepted by the English Government of late, which letter contained particulars relating to the measures taken by different committees in Ireland for the success of the intended revolution & the restoration of liberty in that unhappy country.[3] I would give any thing you was in Brest at this moment where you might be of use. I told the General[4] so; I hope he will send you thither.

God bless you & the cause you have so constantly & so gallantly undergone every imaginable hardship.

I remain your affectionate friend & countryman for life.

Sheé

P.S. Young Dalton[5] sends you his kind services. His brother Alexander bearer hereof will remit you the letter from your wife & another from I know not whom.

---

[1] Françoise Sheé.

[2] Probably the leaflet or pamphlet 'To the Irishmen now serving aboard the British navy', which Tone wrote *a*. 22 Nov. 1796 (above, vol. II, pp 394–6). Sheé's knowledge of it is evident in a letter he (Sheé) wrote on 30 Nov. 1796 (see vol. II, p. 402, n. 2).

[3] Probably a confused reference to Tone's letter to Russell of 9 July 1791 (see above, vol. I, pp 106–08). A version of it was printed in 'Report of the secret committee' (*Commons' jn. Ire.*, xvii, pp cclxxviii–cclxxix). This letter was however intercepted shortly after it was written and its contents were not as indicated by Sheé.   [4] Hoche.

[5] Perhaps James William Dalton, brother of Alexandre Dalton; he was, however, the elder of the two brothers (see above, vol. II, p. 359, n. 2).

Diary, 11 June 1797

T.C.D., Tone papers, MS 2049, ff 241ᵛ–242ʳ; *Life*, ii, 406–7.

11 June 1797

The seditions continue aboard the English fleet and have reached the army. For the present however they seem to be appeased, but at the expence of dismissing a number of officers of the navy who were obnoxious to the seamen, and increasing the pay of both seamen and soldiers. When a government is forced to such concessions, it seems to me an inevitable symptom of decaying empire. Martial law is proclaimed in Dublin,[1] and I see that the presses &c., of the *Northern Star* have been broken and burned in Belfast by the Donegal militia.[2] In return it is said that Buonaparte has seized on 32 sail of the line and 26 frigates at Venice, but if the half of that, only, be true, it is a great prize. It is also, I believe, certain that Massaredo[3] has sailed from Cadiz with the Spanish fleet on the 21st of May. I wish he were safe and well in Brest water.

Today I rode out, with the rest of the *État-major*, to pay our respects to the Landgrave of Hesse-Cassel,[4] who passed by Friedberg on his way to Hanau, where he reviews his troops tomorrow. I wish I were there. There is great talk at headquarters of an immediate rupture between the Emperor and the King of Prussia, which last is supported by the Landgrave. '*Time will shew!*'[5]

Order from General Lazare Hoche, 12 June 1797

Tone (Dickason) papers.

Hoche orders Tone to Trèves via Neuwied.

Au quartier général à Friedberg
le 24 Prairial an 5

---

[1] Referring to an order of the commander-in-chief issued by the adjutant-general's office on 20 May 1797 stating that the military should disperse unlawful assemblies without waiting for directions from a magistrate, the *Dublin Evening Post* declared that the country is now completely under martial law (*D.E.P.*, 23, 25 May 1797).

[2] On 19 May 1797 the *Monaghan* militia attacked the *Northern Star* office and destroyed the types, etc. (Brian Inglis, *The freedom of the press in Ireland, 1784–1841* (London, 1954), p. 97; *Drennan-McTier letters*, ii, 314).

[3] Joseph Massaredo (d. *c.*1814), Spanish admiral, commanded the fleet blockaded in Cadiz by Jervis, 1797–8 (*Biographie nouvelle des contemporains* (Paris, 1820–25)).

[4] William IX (1743–1821), landgrave of Hesse-Cassel, 1785–1821; he made peace with France in 1795 (*Allgemeine Deutsche Biographie* (Leipzig, 1875–1912)).   [5] In MS nine blank folios follow.

Le général commandant en chef l'armée de Sambre et Meuse ordonne à l'adjudant général Schmitt de se rendre à Trêves, passant par Neuvied pour objets de service:

L. Hoche

Les commandants militaires des lieux où il passera voudront bien lui faire fournir les chevaux de correspondance dont il aura besoin, pour lui et la personne qui l'accompagne jusqu'à Coblentz.

L. Hoche

To Matilda Tone, 13 June 1797

Tone (Dickason) papers; *Life*, ii, 402–03.

Head Quarters at Friedberg
25 Prairial an 5

Dearest Love,

I have this instant received your letter of *no* date from Nanterre and I am above measure rejoiced that you and our dear little babies are arrived safe, and I hope, by this, well, for I cannot allow you to be sick. I have now finished my letter, which has at least the merit of brevity to recommend it. What, in God's name, is T—[1] doing at Paris? And especially why does he go by a name so notorious? I will whisper you that 'tis out of pure vanity; but let it go no farther. (Sings) '*Oh, 'tis thus we'll all stand by, the great Napper Tandy*'.

Allons! I am setting off this moment for Coblentz; from Coblentz I go to Trêves, and from Trêves, it may be, to Paris; but that is not yet decided, so do not say a word of it to *mortal soul living*. All I can tell you is that '*I shaved a great man's butler today*'.[2] The General made me a present yesterday of the handsomest horse in the whole *État-Major*, which has broke me, for I was, as in duty bound, obliged to buy a handsome saddle & furniture &c. So (sings) '*says this frog, I will go ride*', &c.[3]

Adieu, Dearest Love; write to me instantly, and direct to me À l'Adj[udan]t Gén[éra]l Smith, à Trêves, poste restante. The ordonnance is bawling for me, so I must break off here; but I will finish this letter (which I enclose, as before, to Madgett) at Trêves. In the meantime, I am yours and the Baby's [*sic*] most humble servant.

If the tail had been stronger
My story had been longer.[4]

[1] James Napper Tandy.
[2] Arthur Murphy, *The upholsterer* (1758), I.
[3] William Sampson, *Report of the trial of the King versus Hurdy Gurdy, alias Barrel Organ, alias Grinder* (Dublin, 1794), pp 20, 43. For the continuation of this verse, see above, vol. II, p. 230.
[4] Source of this quotation not traced.

Adieu, light of my eyes, and *not a word, upon your life, of my trip to Paris*, which may not take place.

My compliments a thousand times to Madame and Mlle Sheé.

J. Smith

À Madame Smith
chez le Citoyen Sheé
À Nanterre

From Matilda Tone, *c*.14 June 1797

Tone (Dickason) papers.
This is the only surviving letter to Tone from his wife.

My Dearest Life,

I wrote you a long letter yesterday in perplexity and doubtful dillemma about Mary's *friend*.[1] I received a note from Sullivan this morning which tells me that in all probability you understand it all by this, & desires me to expect a visit from Adjutant General Simon who has a letter from you &c. I shall trouble him with this note to let you know that we are all well & happy, as far as the most perfect content, tranquility & decency can make us. I am ashamed at hearing that the general wanted you very much while you were with me. My life, all the pleasure of our journey wou[l]d be destroyed if I thought it was disadvantageous to you in any respect. Satisfy me on this head *immediately*.

I hope you will get the letter I sent yesterday. I am afraid it has a very ridiculous direction, but it was Mrs S.[2] who dictated it. She insists it is right & I hope she knows French as well [as] I. Only *it is not so in the book*. She advised me to direct to Mr Sheé. Send me your own in a Christian form the next time you write. I have the most ardent hopes you are going *to do something*. The sufferings of poor Ireland are inconceivable. It is entirely under military government. No person is allowed to wear a green ribbon in the streets of Dublin. A party of soldiers met two ladies with green han[d]kerchiefs & tore them off.[3] How wou[l]d their husbands like that?

The sailors at Cork have turn'd their officers ashore.[4]

---

[1] Presumably her husband, Jean Frédéric Giauque.
[2] Presumably Col. Sheé's wife, Marie Madelaine.
[3] According to the *Dublin Evening Post*, a liberal newspaper, 'several ladies were rudely assaulted on Monday evening last [29 May] in Castle Street by the soldiery, who proceeded to the most unwarrantable acts of violence. No female passenger was suffered to walk that way if any part of her apparel was green. Ribbands, bonnets and handkerchiefs were wantonly torn from their persons with every aggravating circumstance of rudeness and foul language.' (*D.E.P.*, 1 June 1797). Two days later a conservative newspaper stated that the military were being maliciously misrepresented as disturbers of the public peace by an evening newspaper (*Faulkner's Dublin Journal*, 3 June 1797).
[4] The *Moniteur* of 12 June 1797 stated that the mutiny had spread to the squadron at Cork.

> Adieu, my dear love
> Salut et fraternité
> M. Smith

Miss S.[1] is in town

How do you like my Babies' letter?[2] I assure you I never saw it till it was finished. June 12 or 14. Direct to me Chez le Citoyen Du Bois à la porte St Germain, Nanterre.

À l'Adjutant Général Smith
Au Quartier-Général à Friedberg
Armée de Sambre et Meuse

From Maria Tone, *c.*14 June 1797

Tone (Dickason) papers; added to preceding letter.

This is the only surviving letter to Tone from his daughter.

My dearest Father,

I have now room to write you a long letter and tell you all that has happened since your departure from us. We were three days and one night on the road and arrived at Paris late in the evening. The next day I got a fever and kept my bed for three days, but I am now quite well. I am learning French and can write it a little. Mama is very well. I never knew her in better health and spirits. She and I read your journals and were delighted with them. I have not yet begun to write my travels. The children [are] as well as they can be, William as good, and Frank as great a tyrant as ever. I often think how happy we would be if you were with us. The other day Mama and I took a most delightful walk on the banks of the Seine. We are in a most beautiful situation. My dear Fadoff I wish it was possible for you to know how much I love you, or how much I regret your absence. The next time you write to Mama write me a long letter.

> M. Smith

To Matilda Tone, 22 June 1797

Tone (Dickason) papers.

> À Cologne, ce 4 Messidor an 5

Dear Love,

Since my last,[3] which I wrote in a great hurry from Friedberg, I have been continually in motion. You see by the date of this where I am tonight, and I

---

[1] Presumably Col. Shée's daughter or a sister.   [2] i.e. Maria's (below).   [3] Above, pp 81–2.

set off tomorrow morning at five for parts unknown, where I expect to arrive in three or four days and I will then write to you again. In consequence of my perpetual change of place I have received but your first letter, which mortifies me, for the greatest pleasure I can feel in your absence is in receiving your letters. I hope your money may hold out a very few days, and I will find a way by that time to send you some. I have it tonight in my pocket for you, but I have no mode of conveyance. If we were *tête à tête* I have a budget full of news for you which I think would give you pleasure, but I dare not write. Be assured, however, generally, that all goes to my mind and moreover, as I have already observed to you, '*I shaved a great man's butler today*'.[1]

Adieu, dearest love, I am as tired as a horse and must go to bed. You shall have a long letter within a week after this; in the meantime '*live unbruised, and love my babies*'.[2]

God almighty bless you and them.
J. Smith

À Madame Smith
À Nanterre

To Maria Tone, 22 June 1797

Tone (Dickason) papers; added to preceding letter.

Baby,

I am ashamed of writing so short a letter to Mama, but '*I can't help it now, fath and sole*'.[3] Take care of our dear Matty and your two boys. I doat upon you all because you are four little things. Tell Will I enjoyed his book hugely, and give Frank '*half a dozen*' for me. I suppose you speak French with Mlle Shee like your dragon. It is all in vain, Baby, for I cannot keep my eyes open any longer.

Your affec[tiona]te Fadoff
J. S.

To Matilda Tone, 1 July 1797

Tone (Dickason) papers.

À Cologne, ce 13 Messidor an 5
July 1st, 1797 V.S.

---

[1] Arthur Murphy, *The upholsterer* (1758), I. [2] *Much ado about nothing*, V, v.
[3] 'I could not help it now, Fath and Sole, but if you'll forgive me this time I'll never do so no more' (Samuel Foote, *The knights* (1754), act II).

Dearest Love,

Since the 13th of last month I have scarcely been two days in one place, and I am fatigued to death; but when it is for the public good *'bless those that care for their skin!'*.[1] I wrote to you from this place eight days ago, since which time I have spent four nights on the road so *'if I'm not a drudge, let all the world judge'*.[2] Tomorrow at five I set off again on *'a long gurney to the north'*,[3] [at] the end whereof I will write to you and send you some money, whereof I fear you have great need. I think you may count upon having it in ten days, by a safe hand, and I will at the same time send you a long letter of news which I do not care to trust to the post. All I can tell you at present is that I have seen Nu Frog,[4] and we are as pleased as punch with one another. He put his finger in his cheek and made it say *'Buck'* to me, the consequences whereof may be truly alarming. *'There be land rats and water rats!'*[5] Generally everything is going on as well as I could wish, and a thousand times better than I had any rational ground to expect three weeks ago.

It is far from impossible that before a month is over I may be in the dominions of King Estmere, if you know whereabouts that is;[6] if you do not, apply to your Baby. I suppose she has not quite forgot her Percy No. 1. *'Hey girl! fecks we are all upon the wing!'*[7]

You have doubtless read a great part, at least, of my journals. Well, the last fortnight has been more curious and more in the extravagant line of our history than all you have read taken together, and so you will say when you are informed of what is passed in that time.

My continual change of place has prevented my hearing from you. I have had but one letter and I dare say you have written oftener. I assure you it is a terrible privation to me, for I doat upon you more than I can express. The instant you receive this write to me, and address it, *in a legible hand, À l'adj[udan]t gén[éra]l Schmit, poste restante à la Haye*, where (viz. at the Hague) I shall be on business for some days, and whence I purpose to write my next. *Not a word of this to mortal.*

Adieu, light of my eyes, and pulse of my heart; I love you every hour more and more. God almighty for ever bless and watch over you. Adieu, dearest love.

Yours ever,
J. Smith

---

[1] Source of this quotation not traced.   [2] Swift, *My lady's lamentation* (1728).

[3] 'Mistress says, we are going on a long gurney to the north' (Smollett, *Humphry Clinker* (1771), i, 157).

[4] Perhaps an allusion to Tone's interview on 12 June with the Dutch committee for foreign affairs (see below, pp 95–6).   [5] *Merchant of Venice*, I, iii.

[6] See Thomas Percy, *Reliques of ancient English poetry* (1765), 1st ser., vi, for the ballad of King Estmere. King Estimere was king of England, but Tone seems to have believed he was king of Ireland (see Tone to Matilda Tone, 21 July 1797, below, p. 107).

[7] Smollett, *Humphry Clinker* (1771), i.

To Maria Tone, 1 July 1797

Tone (Dickason) papers; added to preceding letter.

Baby!

I have not said one word to Mama about the Boys, because I look upon them as in your department; neither, you see, do I desire Mama to take care of you, because I am sure you are able to take care of yourself and her also. I beseech you love each other for my sake, because you are two darling things. I think this is a letter of *becauses*. *En fin*, kiss your mama and your Boys for me ten thousand times, because I love you all more than my life, and with that *because* I remain

Your dutiful Fadoff
J. S.

My next shall be a letter of '*as hows*'. Have you heard from Giauque, and has he sent your poor Mama any money? Write to me! (Sings) '*Daffy Bab! Daffy Bab!*' Do you know the tune of that, my Baby?

My best respects to the young gentlemen.

Matty,[1]

There are one or two choice quotations in this letter, if you smoke them.

[*On back*]

À Madame Smith
À Nanterre

To Matilda Tone, 7 July 1797

Tone (Dickason) papers.

The Hague,
July 7, 1797

Dear Love,

This letter will be delivered to you by a person[2] whom you will be glad to see. I have also delivered him what money I could spare for you, and I

---

[1] The remainder of this letter is obviously intended for Matilda Tone.

[2] Edward Joseph Lewines (see above, vol. I, p. 438, n. 1), who on 4 July had left the Hague bound for Paris (see below, p. 99). An apprentice to a Dublin attorney, Martin Kirwan, he was in February or March 1797 instructed by a United Irish committee headed by Lord Edward Fitzgerald to go to the Continent as its ambassador to France, Holland and Spain. He arrived in Hamburg on 29 or 30 March, met the French ambassador, Reinhard, then went to Friedberg in Hesse where on 29 May he met Hoche. Lewines joined Tone on 14 June at Neuwied on the Rhine and the pair travelled together to the Hague. (Marianne Elliott, *Partners in revolution: the United Irishmen and France* (New Haven, 1982), pp 130–32; Thomas Bartlett (ed.), *Revolutionary Dublin, 1795–1801: the letters of Francis Higgins to Dublin Castle* (Dublin, 2004), p. 130; see above, p. 76, n. 2, below, p. 91).

hope it will enable you to subsist until I can send you a fresh remittance. I will write you no news, as the bearer hereof will give you an account of everything in detail and I think you will agree that I had reason when I said in one of my last letters[1] (which I hope you received) that the last month of my life has been even more singular than any former period. I am now Adjudant General in the service of the French and Batavian republics, which you will allow is droll. I expect to set off for the Texel in three days, and probably before ten I shall be ploughing the raging main. Our affairs never wore so favorable an appearance as now. You know I am not too sanguine, everything human is uncertain, but I do think we have every rational ground to expect success, and then you shall see what you shall see.

Dear Love, we know one another now. I do not make a parade of commonplace topics to support you in my absence. I am going on a just and an honorable cause; my conscience and my honor justify me in every step I have taken; if I survive, you will have no reason to blush for me, and if the worst should happen, I know my countrymen will take care of you and that my children will find a father in every honest Irishman. Impressed with these sentiments, which I know you participate, I shall embark with an alacrity beyond what I have ever felt. I offer you no consolation, for you require none; we will both do our duty.

I have now said almost all I have to say, at least on the subject of my departure. There is one circumstance which may make you less anxious for my safety. The General in chief, Daendels, to whom I am attached, embarks aboard a frigate and I go with him, so that we shall have no fighting at sea, whether we meet the English or not, for which I confess I am not sorry— at land, *à la bonheur*, but I have no stomach at all for a battle at sea.

I have not had one line from you yet, which is no fault of yours, as I am sure you have written; but it is above a month that I have been running about all Germany and Holland, without resting scarcely two days in one place, so god knows whether I shall ever get your letters. I have written to you pretty often.

Our affairs are now so situated that I think a very little time must settle them definitively, I hope and I trust favorably. In that event, need I promise you that the whole of my future life shall be dedicated to you and our babies. I am truly weary of the eternal separation in which we live, and tho' it is no fault of ours, but on the contrary a strict adherence to our respective duties which causes that separation, still I feel it most sensibly, and indeed nothing could sustain me in your absence but the conviction of the justice of that cause to which we have sacrificed and do daily sacrifice the greatest pleasure we are capable to enjoy, the happiness which we feel in each other's society.

I think this letter is growing rather grave and God knows whether I am not in high spirits and great expectation. Hang sorrow! Well once more, if we succeed, you shall see what you shall see.

---

[1] Probably the one he wrote on 1 July (above, pp 84–5).

I will finish here. I need tell you no news, for the bearer will do all that. I have written to my adjoint Macsheehy who will probably pass soon by Paris to bring you my trunk, &c., and I send you the key; you and the bearer will rummage my papers and any that he finds for his purpose, he will take. You may cut up all the clothes for the Babies and '*make waistcoats for Dick and Bill*'.[1] I have likewise written to Macsheehy to try and receive some pay due to me at the army of Sambre and Meuse, which, if he gets it, he will also bring you. He is a blockhead, but be civil to him.

Adieu, dearest life, I doat upon you; take care of the Babies, because they are little things. I will write again from the Texel. God bless you always.

> J. Smith
> Adj[udan]t Gen[era]l
> aux armées française et batave

Madame Smith
À Nanterre

To Maria Tone, 7 July 1797

Tone (Dickason) papers; added to preceding letter.

Dear Baby,

I have written you three or four letters and I have not been so happy as to receive one line in return; I long more than I can express to hear from you and especially to know how your boys are going on. I hope you like Nanterre. Have you a garden? How do you like Miss Sheé? I beg you may speak and read nothing but French, and I am sure Miss Sheé will have the goodness to lend you some books and to assist you. Return my thanks a thousand times to her and Madame Sheé for their kindness to Mama and your boys. Write me a long letter, for it is near six weeks since I heard from you.

Adieu, Baby; love me always.

> Your affec[iona]te Fadoff
> J. Smith

To Matilda Tone, 9 July 1797

Dickason (Tone) papers.

> The Hague,
> July 9th, 1797

[1] Goldsmith, *The vicar of Wakefield* (1766), i, chap. 4.

Dear Love,

As Lewines does not set off till today, I have the opportunity to write to you once more. As I know you are a good Irishwoman I am sure it will give you pleasure to hear that he and I have co-operated with the most uninterrupted harmony since we have met, and with a degree of success beyond what we could have expected. Destined as we were to be fellow labourers in the same great cause, it is an unspeakable satisfaction to me that on every point which has arisen, even to the most minute, our opinions have invariably coincided; had it been otherwise, I hope we have both of us virtue enough to sacrifice our private opinions to the public good, but fortunately we have had no occasion to display it. He will give you a detailed account of all that has passed and I am sure you will acknowledge that our adventures have been most extraordinary. I have recommended you and the Babies to his protection and we have taken a covenant on that head. Today[1] at two o'clock I set off for the Texel, where I expect to arrive tomorrow night, and I shall immediately go on board. I presume we shall sail the first fair wind after, in which case I will write to you once more.

I have made up a fine greatcoat which, like Mrs Tabitha's blankets, '*with God's assistance may be yoosed on some occasion*'.[2] It would do your heart good to see it.

Adieu, dearest Life and soul! I have my hands full for this morning. '*Oh, I have business would employ an age, and have not half an hour to do it in!*'[3] I am going off completely equipped in good health and high spirits. Take care of yourself, my dearest Love, for my sake, and of the little Babies, kiss them all round for me ten thousand times. If we arrive at our destination you will see what I will do for you and them. Once more, adieu; I doat upon you.

Theobald Wolfe Tone

It is so long since I wrote my own name that I hardly recognize it. Lewines will pay you £45. I hope MacSheehy may bring you something, and one way or other you must carry on the war till you hear from me in parts beyond the seas.

[*Addressed on reverse*]:

À Madame Smith
À Nanterre
près de Paris

To Maria Tone, 9 July 1797

Tone (Dickason) papers; added to preceding letter.

---

[1] But Tone seems to have arrived at the Texel on 8 July 1797 (see below, p. 99).

[2] 'With the blissing of Heaven they may be yoosed . . .' (Tobias Smollett, *Humphry Clinker* (1771), ii.

[3] See above, p. 38, n. 1.

Dear Baby,

I have nothing in the world to say to you, only that I love you with all my heart and soul. Learn French like a little thing; you must speak nothing else, and I think Mama may do the same. My compliments to the citizens, your brothers.

God bless you my darling child
T.W.T.

Diary, 12 June–14 July 1797

T.C.D., Tone papers, MS 2049, ff 243ʳ–255ᵛ; *Life*, ii, 407–20.
It is evident that much of this diary was written up in arrears on 10 July.

No. 14
From June 12th to August the 8th
Nil desperandum ——?
Aboard the ship *Vryheid* at the Texel
1797

Aboard the *Vryheid*, of 74 guns, commanded by Admiral de Winter,[1] at the Texel, July 10, 1797.

It is a long time since I have made a memorandum[2] notwithstanding I have been fully occupied; but the fact is I have had too much business. All I can now do is to make an imperfect abstract of what has passed that is most material within the last month.

Quartier général at Friedberg, 12 June 1797

This evening at eight the general[3] called me into the garden and told me he had some good news for me; he then asked me did I know one Lewines? I answered I did perfectly well and that I had the very highest opinion of his talents and patriotism.[4] Well, said he, he is at

---

[1] Jan Willem de Winter, known also as Jean Guillaume Dewinter (1761–1812), born at Campen, Over-Yssel; took part in an unsuccessful revolt against the house of Orange, subsequently fleeing to France; entered French service, 1788, becoming lieut-col. in the Légion Franche, 1792; returned to the Netherlands, 1795; vice-admiral of the Texel fleet; 1796–8; Dutch minister at Paris, 1798–1802; count of the empire, 1811; buried in Panthéon (*Dict. biog. franç.*).
[2] On 11 June 1797 (above, p. 80).   [3] Hoche.
[4] Charles Frédéric Reinhard, the French minister to Hamburg, writing to the minister of foreign affairs in Paris on 19 May 1797 informed him that 'M. Luines', the representative of the Irish patriots, had arrived. There had at first been doubts about Lewines's identity but these had been resolved by, amongst others, 'M. Giaut, the brother-in-law of the Irishman Smith who was with General Hoche'. Giauque told Reinhard that he had seen his brother-in-law at Groninguen, where he had escorted 'Mrs Smith', and that Smith had told him to welcome the traveller from Dublin and to bring him to General Hoche. Lewines, in conversation with Reinhard, stressed the need for French intervention if an Irish rising was to be successful. (Archives de la Guerre, B¹¹ 1).

Neuvied[1] waiting to see you; you must set off tomorrow morning; when you join him, you must go together to Trêves and wait for further orders. The next morning I set off and on the 14th, in the evening, I reached

Neuvied

where I found Lewines waiting for me. I cannot express the unspeakable satisfaction I felt at seeing him. I gave him a full account of all my labours and of everything that had happened me since I have been in France, and he informed me in return of everything of consequence relating to Ireland and especially to my friends now in jeopardy there. I cannot pretend to detail this conversation, which occupied us fully during our stay at Neuvied and our journey to

Trêves[2]

where we arrived on the 17th. What is most material is that he is sent here by the Executive Committee of the United People of Ireland to sollicit on their part the assistance in troops, arms and money necessary to enable them to take the field and assert their liberty; the organisation of the people is complete, and nothing is wanting but the *point d'appui*. His instructions are to apply to France, Holland and Spain. At Hamburgh, where he passed almost two months, he met a Señor Nava,[3] an officer of rank in the Spanish navy, sent thither by the *Prince de Paix*[4] on some mission of consequence; he opened himself to Nava, who wrote off in consequence to his court and received an answer, general it is true, but in the highest degree favorable. A circumstance which augurs well is that in forty days from the date of Nava's letter he received the answer, which is less time than he ever knew a courier to arrive in, and shews the earnestness of the Spanish minister. Lewines's instructions are to demand of Spain £500,000 and 30,000 stand of arms. At Trêves, on the 19th, Dalton,[5] the general's aid-du-camp, came express with orders for us to return to

Coblentz

where we arrived the 21st and met General Hoche. He told us then that he had, in consequence of the arrival of Lewines, sent off Simon, one of his adj[utan]t-generals and who was of our late expedition, as I have set forth in my former journals,[6] in order to press the Executive Directory and the Minister of the Marine; that he had also sent copies of all the necessary papers, including especially those lately prepared by Lewines, with his own observations, enforcing them in the strongest manner; that he had just received the answer of all parties, which were as favorable as we could wish, but that the minister of the marine was absolutely for making the expedition on a

---

[1] Neuvied is on the right bank of the Rhine, 12 km below Coblentz.

[2] Trêves, known in German as Trier, lies about 100 km to the south-west of Neuvied as the crow flies.   [3] Domingo de Nava (1738–1812), *jefe de escuadra* in 1797 (*Enciclopedia universal*).

[4] Manuel Godoy Alvarez de Faria Ríos Sánchez Zarzosa (1767–1851), Spanish prime minister; he was created prince of the peace on the conclusion of the treaty of Basle in 1795 (ibid.).

[5] Alexander Dalton.   [6] Above, vol. II, p. 416 et seq.

grand scale, for which at the very least two months would still be necessary; to which I, knowing Brest of old, and that two months in the language of the marine meant four months, if not five or six, remarked to him the necessity of an immediate exertion in order to profit of the state of mutiny and absolute disorganisation in which the English navy is at this moment, in which Lewines most heartily concurred, and we both observed that it was not a strong military force that we wanted, but arms and ammunition, with troops sufficient to serve as a *noyau d'armée* and to protect the people in their first assembling, adding that 5,000 men sent now, while the thing was feasible, was far better than 25,000 in three months, when perhaps we might find ourselves again blocked up in Brest water; and I besought the general to remember that the mutiny aboard the English fleet would most certainly be soon quelled, so that there was not a minute to lose; that if we were lucky enough to arrive in Ireland before that took place, I looked upon it as morally certain that by proper means we might gain over the seamen, who have already spoken of steering the fleet into the Irish harbours, and so settle the business without perhaps striking a blow. We both pressed these and such other arguments as occurred in the best manner we were able, to which Gen[era]l Hoche replied he saw everything precisely in the same light as we did, and that he would act accordingly and press the Directory and the minister of the marine in the strongest manner. He shewed Lewines Simon's letter, which contained the assurance of the Directory 'that they would make no peace with England wherein the interests of Ireland should not be fully discussed agreeably to the wishes of the people of that country'. This is a very strong declaration and has most probably been produced by a demand made by Lewines in his memorial 'that the French government should make it an indispensable condition of the peace that all the British troops should be withdrawn from Ireland and the people left at full liberty to declare whether they wished to continue the connexion with England or not'.[1] General Hoche then told us not to be discouraged by the arrival of a British negotiator, for that the Directory even determined to make no peace but on conditions which would put it out of the power of England longer to arrogate to herself the commerce of the world and to dictate the law to all the maritime powers. He added that preparations were making also in Holland for an expedition the particulars of which he would communicate to us in two or three days, and in the meantime he desired us to attend him at

Cologne

for which place we set and arrived the 24th.

---

[1] A letter from the Directory to Hoche dated 21 Prairial 5 (9 June) made clear its attitude to the Irish: 'notre intérêt est de les voir proclamer l'indépendance de leur île . . . mais sans garantie de notre part . . . Nous n'avons contracté aucun engagement de maintenir leur nouvel état politique, dans la crainte de nuire au rétablissement de la paix.' (Archives de la Guerre, Marine BB[4] 103).

25 June 1797

At nine o'clock at night the General sent us a letter from General Daendels, commander-in-chief of the army of the Batavian Republic, acquainting him that everything was in the greatest forwardness and would be ready in a very few days; that the army and navy were in the best possible spirit; that the committee for foreign affairs (the Directory, *per interim*, of the Batavian Republic) desired most earnestly to see him without loss of time in order to make the definitive arrangements; and especially they prayed him to bring with him the deputy of the people of Ireland, which Daendels repeated in two or three parts of his letter. In consequence of this I waited on the General, whom I found in his bed at the Cour Impériale, and received his orders to set off with Lewines without loss of time and to attend him at

The Hague

where we arrived accordingly on the 27th, having travelled day and night. In the evening we went to the *Comedie*, where we met the general in a sort of public incognito, that is to say, he had combed the powder out of his hair and was in a plain regimental frock. After the play we followed him to his lodgings, at the Lion d'Or, where he gave us a full detail of what was preparing in Holland. He began by telling us that the Dutch government, the General Daendels, and the Admiral De Winter, were sincerely actuated by a desire to effectuate something striking, which should rescue their country from the state of oblivion and *decadence* into which it had fallen; that, by the most indefatigable exertions on their part, they had got together at the Texel, sixteen sail of the line and eight or ten frigates, all ready for sea and in the highest condition; that they intended to embark 15,000 men (*the whole of their national troops*) 30,000[1] stand of arms, 80 pieces of artillery and money for their pay and subsistance for three months; that he had the best opinion of the sincerity of all parties, and of the courage and conduct of the admiral and general, but that here was the difficulty—the French government had demanded that at least 5,000 French troops, the *élite* of the army, should be embarked instead of a like member of Dutch, in which case, if the demand were acceded to, he would himself take the command of the united army and set off for the Texel directly, but that the Dutch government made very great difficulties, alledging a variety of reasons, of which some were good ones; that they said the French troops would never submit to the discipline of the Dutch navy, and that in that case they could not pretend to enforce it on the national troops without making unjust distinctions and giving a reasonable ground for jealousy and discontent to their own army &c., &c.; 'but the fact is', said Hoche, 'the Committee, Daendels, and de Winter are anxious that the Batavian Republic should have the whole glory of the expedition if it succeeds; they feel that their country has been

---

[1] *Life*, ii, 410, reads '3,000', obviously an error.

forgotten in Europe, and they are risquing everything even to their last stake (for if this fails, they are ruined) in order to restore the national character; the demand of the French government is now before the committee; if it is acceded to, I will go myself, and at all events tomorrow I will present you both to the committee, and we will probably then settle the matter definitively.' Both Lewines and I found ourselves now in a considerable difficulty. On the one side, it was an object of the greatest importance to have Hoche and the 5,000 grenadiers, and on the other it was most unreasonable to propose anything which might hurt the feelings of the Dutch people at the moment when they were making unexampled exertions in our favour and risquing, as Hoche himself said, their last ship and last shilling to emancipate us. I cursed and swore like a dragoon; it went to my very heart's blood and midriff to give up the General and our brave lads, five thousand of whom I would prefer to any ten thousand in Europe; on the other hand I could not but see that the Dutch were perfectly reasonable in the desire to have the entire reputation of an affair prepared and arranged entirely at their expence, and at such an expence! I did not know what to say. L——, however, extricated himself and me with considerable address. After stating very well our difficulty, he asked Hoche whether he thought that Daendels would serve under his orders, and if he refused what effect that might have on the Batavian troops? I will never forget the magnanimity of Hoche on this occasion. He said he believed Daendels would not, and therefore that the next morning he would withdraw the demand with regard to the French troops and leave the Dutch Government at perfect liberty to act as they thought proper. When it is considered that Hoche has a devouring passion for fame; that his great object, on which he has endeavoured to establish his reputation, is the destruction of the power of England; that he has for two years in a great degree devoted himself to our business and made the greatest exertions (including our memorable expedition) to emancipate us; that he sees at last the business likely to be accomplished by another, and of course all the glory he had promised to himself ravished from him; when, in addition to all this, it is considered that he could, by a word's speaking, prevent the possibility of that rival's moving one step, and find at the same time plausible reasons sufficient to justify his own conduct. I confess his renouncing the situation which he might command is an effort of very great virtue. It is true he is doing exactly what an honest man and a good citizen ought to do, he is preferring the interests of his country to his own private views; that does not however prevent my regarding his conduct in this instance with great admiration, and I shall never forget it. This important difficulty being removed, after a good deal of general discourse on our business we parted late, perfectly satisfied with each other, and having fixed to wait on the committee tomorrow in the forenoon. All reflexion made, the present arrangement, if it has its dark, has its bright sides also; of which hereafter.

28 June 1797

This morning at ten, Lewines and I went with General Hoche to the Committee for Foreign Affairs, which we found sitting. There were eight or nine members, of whom I do not know all the names, together with General Daendels. Those which I learned were Citizens Hahn[1] (who seems to have great influence among them), Bekker,[2] van Leyden,[3] and Grasveldt.[4] General Hoche began by stating, extremely well, the history of our affairs since he had interested himself in them; he pressed in the strongest manner that we could wish the advantages to be reaped from the emancipation of Ireland, the almost certainty of success if the attempt were once made, and the necessity of attempting it, if at all, immediately. It was Citizen Hahn who replied to him. He said he was heartily glad to find the measure sanctioned by so high an opinion as that of General Hoche; that originally the object of the Dutch government was to have invaded England in order to have operated a diversion in favor of the French army which it was hoped would have been in Ireland; that circumstances being totally changed in that regard, they had yielded to the wishes of the French government and resolved to go into Ireland; that for this purpose they had made the greatest exertions and had now at the Texel an armament of 16 sail of the line, 10 frigates, 15,000 troops in the best condition, 80 pieces of artillery and pay for the whole for three months, but that a difficulty had been raised within a few days in consequence of a requisition of the Minister of the Marine, Truguet, who wished to have 5,000 French troops instead of so many Dutch, to be disembarked in consequence; that this was a measure of extreme risque, inasmuch as the discipline of the Dutch navy was very severe, and such as the French troops would probably not submit to; that in that case, they could not pretend to enforce it with regard to their own troops, the consequence of which would be a relaxation of all discipline. This was precisely what Gen[era]l Hoche had told us last night. He immediately replied to Citizen Hahn that, that being so, he would take on himself to withdraw the demand of the Minister of the Marine and satisfy the Directory as to the justice of their observations, and that he hoped all difficulty on that head being removed they would press the embarkation without a moment's delay. It was easy to see the most lively satisfaction painted on all their faces at this declaration of Gen[era]l Hoche, which certainly does him the greatest honor. Gen[era]l Daendels especially was beyond measure delighted. They told us then that they hoped that all would be ready in a fortnight, and Hahn observed at the same time that as there was an English squadron which appeared almost every day at the mouth of the Texel it was very much to be desired that the Brest fleet should, if possible, put to sea, in order to draw off at least a part of the British fleet, because from the position

[1] Jacob George Hieronymus Hahn (1761–1822), president of states general, May–June 1795.

[2] Jan Bernd Bicker (1746–1812), president of the national convention, Apr.–May 1796; he was a member of the committee for foreign relations (*Le Moniteur*, 31 Jan. 1798).

[3] Frederic Auguste Leyden van West-Barendrecht (1768–1821).   [4] Not identified.

of the Texel, the Dutch fleet was liable to be attacked in detail in sailing out of the port, and even if they beat the enemy, it would not be possible to proceed, as they must return to refit. To this Gen[era]l Hoche replied that the French fleet could not, he understood, be ready before two months, which put it out of the question, and as to the necessity of returning to refit, he observed that during the last war, the British and French fleets had often fought, both in the East and West Indies, and kept the seas after; all that was necessary being to have on board the necessary articles of *rechange;* besides, it was certainly the business of the Dutch fleet to avoid an action by all possible means. Gen[era]l Daendels observed that Admiral de Winter desired nothing better than to measure himself with the enemy, but we all, that is to say Gen[era]l Hoche, Lewines and myself, cried out against it, his only business being to bring his convoy safe to its destination. A member of the committee then (I believe it was van Leyden) asked us, supposing everything succeeded to our wish, what was the definitive object of the Irish people? To which we replied categorically that it was to throw off the yoke of England, to break for ever the connexion now existing with that country and to constitute ourselves a free and independant people. They all expressed their satisfaction at this reply, and van Leyden observed that he had travelled thro' Ireland, and, to judge from the luxury of the rich and the extreme misery of the poor, no country in Europe had so crying a necessity for a revolution; to which Lewines and I replied (as is most religiously the truth) that one great motive of our conduct in this business was the conviction of the wretched state of our peasantry and the determination, if possible, to amend it. The political object of our visit being now nearly ascertained, Hahn, in the name of the committee, observed that he hoped either Lewines or I would be of the expedition, as our presence with the general would be indispensable; to which Hoche replied that I was ready to go, and he made the offer on my part in a manner peculiarly agreeable to my feelings. It was then fixed that I should set off for the army of Sambre and Meuse for my trunk, and especially for my papers, and that Lewines should remain at the Hague at the orders of the committee until my return, which might be seven or eight days. The meeting then broke up.[1]

We could not possibly desire to find greater attention to us personally, or, which is far more important, greater zeal and anxiety to forward their expedition,

---

[1] There is a record in the Dutch royal archives of what was said on 28 June 1797 by Tone and Lewines, though they are not named: 'Door de Ieren is te kennen gegeven dat zij reeds lang in Ierland waren werkzaam geweest on zich van Groot Britannie volkomentlijk af te zonderen, dat daattoe alle preparatien waren gemaakt en de insurrectie door het aanstelen der nodige committy en correspondentie volmaaktelijk georganiseerd, zodat dezelve dadelijk zou uitbarsten zo dra een zeker aantal reguliere troepen, al ware het ook naar 5000 man, waren gedebarkeerd, welke dan tevens een aantal geweren en de nodige ammunitie zou meebrengen voor de insurgenten; dat zij, gedeputeerden, gechargeerd waren om bij het Frans gouvernement op het geven van secoursen aan te dringen, en tevens ook om uit hoofde van het belang, dat de Bataafse Republiek er natuurlijk in moest stellen dezelve te verzoeken daarin te coöpereren' (Algemeen Rijksarchief 2/01/08, Buitenlandse zaken in de franse tijd, 174).

An English translation reads: 'The Irishmen intimated that they had been active for a long time in Ireland to separate Ireland completely from Great Britain, that all preparations had been made in this

in which the Dutch government has thrown itself, *à corps perdu*. They venture no less than the *whole* of their navy and army. As Hoche expressed it, 'they are like a man stripped to his breeches who has one shilling left, which he throws into the lottery in the hopes of being enabled to buy a coat'. The Committee are very plain men in their appearances, not unlike my old masters of the sub-committee. On our return to the auberge with Hoche, we took occasion to express our admiration of the singularly disinterested conduct which he had manifested on this occasion. He then told us his plan; that the minister of the marine had not thus far been lucky, counting from his expedition against Sardinia in the beginning of the war; that he had the greatest [desire] to do something which might give éclat to his administration; that he (Gen[era]l Hoche) had ceded to the wish of the Dutch government, principally because he would press no measure, however grateful to himself, which might cool their zeal in this great business; and in the next place because he knew that the instant the Dutch fleet was at sea, that Truguet's vanity would be piqued, that he would move heaven and earth to follow them, and instead of waiting to complete the expedition on a great scale, according to his present system, would dispatch instantly whatever was ready for sea, so that in all probability, if we reached Ireland, the French army might be there in a fortnight after us. He told us likewise that the Dutch army was not now what it had been in the commencement of the war; that they had numbers of French among them, particularly in the *artillerie légère;* that they had also a great quantity of Austrians, particularly of the garrison of Luxembourg, and especially that Daendels was an excellent officer, and as brave as Caesar, on whom we might rely; that he would send all such plans and papers as might be of service to him in this business and finally that he hoped we would all speedily meet in Ireland. The main business being finished, we talked of other matters, particularly of the present state of Paris, where the audacity of the Royalists seems to have no bounds. Hoche made use of these remarkable expressions: 'If these rascals were to succeed and to put down the government, I march my army that instant against Paris, and when I have restored the constitution, I break my sword, and I never touch it after'. Our meeting then broke up. The General set off for Headquarters at 4 o'clock, and I followed him at 6 in the evening.

1 July 1797

Arrived at Cologne, where I found the General. He told me that, as he had expected, the minister of marine[1] was piqued, and had given orders in

respect and that the insurrection had been fully organised by the appointment of the necessary committee and by correspondence so that the same would rise up as soon as a certain number of regular troops, even if that were only 5,000 men, had disembarked, bringing with them a number of weapons and the necessary ammunition for the insurgents; that they, the representatives, were charged with pressing the French government for assistance and at the same time, because of the importance of the matter, the Batavian Republic would of course be obliged to request the latter to co-operate therein.'

[1] Truguet.

consequence to prepare everything at Brest with the greatest possible expedition; that he had, if necessary, 300,000 livres at the disposal of the minister; that he had just received orders from the Directory to proceed instantly to Paris by way of Dunkirk; that from Paris he would set off for Brest, where everything would be ready in a fortnight and in a month, he hoped to be in Ireland. He then ordered me £50, with orders to return instantly to the Hague with a letter for Gen[era]l Daendels. I told him then that, if he expected to ready himself so soon, it was my wish not to quit him. He replied he had considered it, and that it was best I should serve under Daendels, on which I acquiesced. I then took an occasion to speak of a subject which has weighed very much upon my mind, I mean the degree of influence which the French might be disposed to arrogate to themselves in Ireland, and which I had great reason to fear would be greater than we might chuse to allow them. In the gazette of that day, there was a proclamation of Buonaparte's addressed to the government of Genoa,[1] which I thought most grossly improper and indecent, as trenching on the indispensable rights of the people. I read the most obnoxious passages to Hoche, and I observed that if Buonaparte commanded in Ireland and were to publish so indiscreet a proclamation as that, it would have the most ruinous effects; that in Italy such dictation might pass, but never in Ireland, where we understood our rights too well to submit to it. Hoche answered me, 'I understand you, but you may be at ease in that respect; Buonaparte has been my scholar, but he shall never be my master'. He then launched out into a very severe critique on Buonaparte's conduct, which certainly has latterly been terribly indiscreet, to say no worse of it, and observed that as to his victories, it was easy to gain victories with such troops as he commanded, especially when a general made no difficulty to sacrifice the lives of his soldiers & that his victories had cost the republic 200,000 men. A great deal of what Hoche said was very true, but I could see at the bottom a very great jealousy of Buonaparte, whom I am sorry to see losing so fast that spirit of moderation which did him as much honor as his victories. Hoche and I then talked of our own business; he said we must calculate on being opposed at the landing by 8 or 10,000 men; that if they were not there, so much the better, but we must expect them; that the British would probably act as they did in America [in the] last war, viz. to retreat and burn the towns behind them; that he did not desire more than 12 or, at most, 15,000 troops and that he had made his arrangements so that the maintenance of that force should not cost the Irish people above 12,000,000#,[2] equal to about £500,000 ster[lin]g. He then promised to send me his instructions for carrying on the war in La Vendée, which would exactly apply to our affair in Ireland, and giving me a letter for Gen[era]l Daendels, in which among other things he demanded for me the rank of adjudant-general in the service of the Batavian republic, we

---

[1] On 27 June the *Moniteur* published a letter from Bonaparte imperiously directing the Genoese to install a provisional government in office.   [2] Spelt out '12,000,000 livres' in *Life*, ii, 416.

embraced each other and parted.[1] He set off that evening for Bonn, and I the next morning at 5 for the Hague, where I arrived on the 4th in the evening.

4 July 1797

Instantly on my arrival I waited on General Daendels, whom I found on the point of setting out for the Texel.[2] He read the letter and told me everything should be settled with regard to any rank, and that I should have two months' pay in advance to equip me for the campaign. His reception of me was extremely friendly. I staid with Lewines at the Hague three or four days, while my regimentals &c. were making up, and at length, all being ready, we parted, he setting off for Paris to join Gen[era]l Hoche, and I for the Texel to join Gen[era]l Daendels.

8 July 1797

Arrived early in the morning at the Texel,[3] and went immediately on board the Admiral's ship, the *Vryheid* of 74 guns, a superb vessel. Found Gen[era]l Daendels aboard, who presented me to Admiral Winter, who commands our expedition. I am exceedingly pleased with both one and the other; there is a frankness and candor in their manner, which is highly interesting.

10 July 1797

I have been boating about the fleet and aboard several of the vessels; they are in very fine condition, incomparably better than the fleet at Brest, and I learn from all hands that the best possible spirit reigns in both soldiers and sailors. Admiral Duncan,[4] who commands the English fleet off the Texel, sent in yesterday an officer with a flag of truce, apparently with a letter, but in fact to reconnoitre our force.[5] De Winter was even with him, for he detained his messenger, and sent back the answer by an officer of his own with instructions to bring back an exact account of the force of the enemy.

---

[1] Hoche's letter to Daendels is mentioned in the minutes of the Dutch committee for foreign affairs for 5 July: 'De adjudant generaal Smith (dat is de schuilnaam van Wolfe Tone) komt met een brief van Hoche aan Daendels. "Je vous invite à l'employer dans son grade; il vous sera de la plus grande utilité, puisque c'est de lui que je tiens en partie les renseignements qui m'ont servi jusqu'à ce jour dans la conduite de l'expédition."' (Algemeen Rijksarchief 2/01/08, Buitenlandse zaken in de franse tijd, 174).

[2] Texel is an island 60 km north of Amsterdam. The strait between Texel and the mainland forms a passage to the North Sea from the Zuyderzee, where there is safe anchorage.

[3] But Tone in a letter from the Hague to his wife, 9 July 1797 (above, p. 89), states he is 'today at two o'clock' to 'set off for the Texel, where I expect to arrive tomorrow night'.

[4] Adam Duncan (1731–1804), British admiral; defeated the Dutch fleet commanded by Dewinter at Camperdown, 11 Oct. 1797; raised to the peerage as Viscount Duncan of Camperdown (*D.N.B.*).

[5] Terence O'Neill, master of the cutter *Nancy*, having been sent into the Texel on 10 July 1797 under a flag of truce, on his return to the fleet returned to Duncan the number of Dutch ships there 'as clearly as I could make out' (Earl of Camperdown, *Admiral Duncan* (London, 1898), pp 176–9).

11 July 1797

This day our flag of truce is returned, and the English officer released. Duncan's fleet is of eleven sail of the line, of which three are three-deckers. I do not yet exactly know our force, either by sea or land, but I must endeavour to learn it.

13 July 1797

I have had a good deal of discourse today with the Gen[era]l Daendels, and I am more and more pleased with him. His plan is to place such of our people as may present themselves at first in the *cadres* of the regiments which we bring out until our battalions are 1,000 strong each; that then we may form our corps, and he will give us proper officers to discipline and organise them; that he will keep the main army of 18 or 20,000 men in activity and leave the security of our communications, the guarding the passes, rivers &c., to the National troops, until they are in a certain degree disciplined. A great deal of this is good, but we must be brought more forward in the picture than that, for every reason in the world. I replied that the outline of his plan was just, but that cases might occur where it would be necessary to depart from it occasionally, for instance, if the militia were to join us, they ought not, nor would they consent, to be incorporated in the Dutch battalions. Daendels said, certainly not; that he knew what the *esprit du corps* was too well to think of it; that the militia battalions would in that case become themselves *cadres* of regiments, so that affair will be arranged to the satisfaction of all parties. We then spoke of the administration, and I gave him an idea how we had been circumstanced in that regard, on the Brest expedition, where we had a little army of commissaries, ready to eat up the country, who would sacrifice the liberty of Ireland, the interests of the Republic and the honor of the General for half a crown, and I did not restrain myself in speaking of those gentry as they deserve. Daendels replied to me that his intention was to leave all the details of supplying the army to the Irish people; that he brought out with him but five commissaries, who were to superintend the forage, the bread, the meat, &c., and that all their proceedings should be subject to his own immediate inspection, and nothing should stand good that was not authorised by his signature; that he prided himself more on his character for administration than for military talents, and that I might rely on it we should have no difficulties on that head. I was very glad to hear all this, the more because I have confidence in him. If the Brest expedition had succeeded, we should have had damned work with those scoundrelly administrations, but I had made up my mind on that head as to what we should do. With the Dutch I have by no means the same uneasiness, and this is one of the circumstances where we gain by the present expedition. But enough of this for the present. All is for the best in this best of all possible worlds.

14 July 1797

Gen[era]l Daendels shewed me today his instructions from the Dutch government. They are fair and honest, and I have no doubt he will act up to them. The spirit of them is always to maintain the character of a faithful ally; not to interfere in the domestic concerns of the people; to aid them by every means in his power to establish their liberty and independance; and to expect no condition in return but that we should throw off the English yoke, and that when all was settled on that score, we should arrange our future commerce with the Dutch republic on the basis of reciprocal advantage and accom[m]odation. Nothing can be more fair and honorable, and I am convinced from what I see of Daendels, and the frankness of his character, that he will act up to his instructions. The report today is that we shall get under way tomorrow, and I see a bustle in the ship which seems to confirm it, but I follow my good old rule to ask no questions. Several boatfulls of troops have passed us today, going on board the different vessels; the men are in the highest spirits, singing national songs and cheering the General as they pass; it is a noble sight, and I found it inexpressibly affecting. Daendels assures me that in the best days of the French revolution, he never witnessed greater enthusiasm than reigns at present in the army. It is, to be sure, glorious, the prospect of this day.

The following is our line of battle.

Avantgarde[1]

Jupiter, 74 guns,	——	Vice-admiral Reyntjis
Cerberus, 68	——	Captain Jacobson
Haarlem, 68	—— ——	Wiggerts
Alkmaar, 56	—— ——	Krafft
Delft, 56	—— ——	Verdoorn

Frigates

Mennikendam, 44	—— ——	Lancaster
Minerva, 24	—— ——	Elbracht
Daphné, 16	——	Lieut. Friederecks[2]

Corps de Bataille

Vryheid, 74	——	Adm¹ de Winter, Capⁿ van Rossum
Staaten Generaal, 74	——	Rear Admiral Story
Batavia 56	——	Capⁿ Soutre

[1] No attempt has been made by the editors to identify the Dutch naval officers listed below.

[2] William Tone inserts at this point a new line that reads: 'Five sail of the line and three frigates and sloops' (*Life*, ii, 419).

Wassenaar, 68	—— [Captain] Holland
Leyden, 68	—— —— Musquettier

Frigates

Mars, 44	—— —— Kolff
Furie,	—— —— Buschman
Galatea,	—— Lieut. Rivery
Atalanta,[1]	

Arrière Guarde

Brutus, 74	—— Rear Admiral van Treslong
Hercules, 68	—— Cap^n Reyscort
Gelijkheid, 68	—— —— Ruijsch
Admiral de Vries, 68	—— —— Zugers
Beschermer, 56	—— —— Heinst

Frigates

Embuscade, 44	—— —— Huijs
Waakzamheid, 24	—— —— Nierop
Ajax	——

with 27 sail[2] of transports, from 150 to 450 tons burden. Our land force I do not yet accurately know.

I should have remarked that two or three days ago, Noël,[3] minister of the French republic, dined aboard us with his wife. All was in grand costume, the shrouds manned &c. and 21 guns fired at his departure. He was dressed, like the *représentans du peuple aux armeés*, in blue with a tricolor sash and his hat, *à l'Henri 4*, with a band and panache, also *aux trois couleurs*. Yesterday the Swedish ambassador[4] dined with us with his *crachat*[5] &c. He is a damned dog and a dunce, and an English partizan, as I soon found out, and I understand a spy. The rascal! Today (indeed at this present writing) I can see from the cabin windows 10 sail of English ships of war, little and big, who have

---

[1] William Tone inserts at this point a new line that reads: 'Five sail of the line and 4 frigates and sloops' (ibid.).

[2] William Tone begins this line: 'Five sail of the line, and three frigates and sloops, with 27 sail . . .' (ibid.).

[3] François Joseph Michel Noël (1756–1841), a man of wide literary interests; minister to the Hague, 1795–7; married at Amsterdam, May 1797, Mlle Bogaërt, daughter of a rich banker; placed in 1798 at the head of a department of the ministry of the interior (*Dict. parl. franç.*).

[4] Friedrich Adolf, Graf von Löwenhielm (d. 1810), Swedish ambassador at the Hague, 1789–1804 (*Nouv. biog. gén.; Repertorium der diplomatischen Verträger aller Länder*, iii (Graz and Cologne, 1965)).

[5] A jocular expression meaning 'insignia'.

presented themselves off the mouth of the Texel. It put me in mind of the Goulet at Brest, where I have often been regaled in the same manner. Nobody here seems to mind them, and so *je m'en fiche. Allons!*

Order from General Louis Nicolas Hyacinthe Chérin, 14 July 1797

Tone (Dickason) papers.

Chérin instructs Citizen Fourru to give MacSheehy the allowances due to Tone for Prairial, Messidor and the last eight days of Ventôse. At the foot MacSheehy acknowledges receipt of 1,210 deniers.

ARMEÉ   ÉTAT-MAJOR GÉNÉRAL
DE
SAMBRE ET MEUSE   *Au Quartier-Général à* Wetzlar,
         le 26 Messidor *l'an* cinq *de la République Française, une et indivisible*

LIBERTÉ, ÉGALITÉ, FRATERNITÉ

LE GÉNÉRAL CHEF DE L'ÉTAT-MAJOR GÉNÉRAL DE L'ARMÉE
         au Citoyen Fourru,[1] majeur dre. à Wetzlar
   Je vous prie, citoyen, de vouloir bien donner au citoyen MacSheehy les appointemens de Prairiral et de Messidor ainsi que ceux des huit derniers jours de Ventôse, lesquels sont dûs à l'adjudant général Smith. Son adjoint vous en donnera quittance. Vous voudrez bien donner une cessation de payement à cet officier.

                       Salut
                       Chérin

Reçu en vertu du présent ordre la somme de douze cent dix [*2 or 3 words not deciphered?*] quatre deniers.

               L'adj[oin]t à l'adj[udant] g[énér]al Smith
                     MacSheehy

Wetzlar, le 26 Messidor an cinq

Diary, 15–20 July 1797

T.C.D., Tone papers, MS 2049, ff 255ᵛ–258ᵛ; *Life*, ii, 420–23.

---

[1] Citizen Fourru has not been identified.

15 July 1797

The human mind, or at least my mind, is a singular machine. I am here[1] in a situation extremely interesting, and on the result of which everything most dear to me as a man and a citizen depends, and yet I find myself in a state of indifference, or rather apathy, which I cannot myself comprehend. My sole amusement is reading an odd volume of Voltaire, which I have found by chance, and as for our expedition I declare I think no more of it than if it were destined for Japan, which indifference on my part, as I have said already, I cannot comprehend, but so it is. Yesterday I wrote to my wife, enclosing a bill, which Admiral de Winter accepted, for 250 florins, *moyennant* the like sum paid into his hands; also to Gen[era]l Hoche, to Mr Sheé, to Giauque and my sister,[2] and finally to Lewines. I have now finished all my business, and tomorrow I understand we put to sea, if the wind permits. It is strange, but I feel as if it were to set out in the trackschuyte from the Hague to go to Amsterdam. Hove up one of our anchors; it was beautiful to see the men at work, in which our chasseurs assisted heartily; all was executed in cadence to the music. Gen[era]l Daendels shewed me a letter from Gen[era]l Dupont announcing the immediate departure of Gen[era]l Hoche for Brest; he also told me that he and I would go on board a sloop of war and not mount the Admiral's ship until the issue of the affair (if any there may be) between the two fleets is determined. I am not sorry for that arrangement.

16 July 1797

The General tells me just now that a spy, sent out by the Admiral, is returned last night with the news that the English fleet is strong 24 sail of the line. A few days ago he said 19, but he explains that by saying that 5 sail had been detached to assist at the execution of Parker,[3] the mutineer. The Admiral's opinion is that the fellow is a double spy, and that this story of the 24 sail is a lie, in which I join him. In the *Morning Chronicle* of the 6th ins[tan]t there is an article which mentions that Admiral Duncan had demanded a reinforcement and that in consequence 3 sail had set off to join him, which with 10 or 11 that he had before, and perhaps 2 which he may draw from the Dogger Bank, where they are stationed to protect the fishery, may bring him up to 15 or 16 sail, and this calculation agrees with the reports made to the government and those of neutral vessels which have lately entered. Be that as it may, the Admiral summoned this morning all the admirals and captains of the fleet and gave them their last instructions,

---

[1] At the Texel. [2] *Life* omits 'Giauque and'.
[3] Richard Parker (1767–97), a leader of the mutiny at the Nore; sentenced to death, he was hanged from the yardarm on board the *Sandwich* on 30 June 1797 (*Oxford D.N.B.*).

which were that the frigates of 44 guns should fall into the line; that they should fight to the very last extremity, even to the sinking of their vessels, in which case they were to take to their boats; that if any captain were to attempt to break the line and hang back, the others should immediately fire on him. This is resolute of de Winter, and I have every reason to think his fleet will second him. He has in the meantime sent off a courier to the government to announce all this, and, if the wind springs up in our favour we will set off instantly, without waiting for the answer.

17 July 1797

Yesterday evening the Admiral told me his plan, as it is above set forth. He is a fine fellow, that is the God's truth. Received yesterday a letter from my dearest love dated the 9th. Thank God, she and the babies are well and in spirits. Today I have received two letters, one from Madgett, and the other from N[apper] Tandy dated the 13 June;[1] to which I have written two answers w[hi]ch I will not dispatch till we are just setting off. The wind is as foul as the devil! At Brest we had, against all probability, a fair wind for five weeks successively, during all which time we were not ready, and at last when we did arrive at our destination, the wind changed, and we missed our blow. Here, all is ready, and nothing is wanting but a fair wind. We are riding at single anchor. I hope the wind may not play us a trick. It is terribly foul this evening. Hang it, and damn it, for me! I am in a rage, which is truly astonishing, and I can do nothing to help myself. Well, well!

18 July 1797

The wind is as foul as possible this morning; it cannot be worse! Hell, hell, hell! Allah! allah! allah! I am in a most devouring rage! Well, what can't be cured, must be endured, as our ancestors have wisely remarked. An officer sent out in disguise to reconnoitre is just returned; his report is favorable. He saw the English fleet, strong 12 sail of the line and 7 or eight frigates. One of the frigates bore down on the Admiral and spoke him, on which he instantly made signal and the whole squadron stood to the S.W. I do not conceive what can be the reason of that manoeuvre, for it leaves us clear, if the wind would let us stir out. Perhaps they are going to reinforce the fleet before Brest; perhaps something has happened again at the Nore. I should have mentioned yesterday in its place that when the Admiral had determined to fight the enemy in the manner I have recited, he supposed them to be at least 19 sail of the line strong, which does the more honor to his courage. It is most terrible to be locked up by the wind as we are just now.

---

[1] *Life*, ii, 421, reads: 'one from Madgett and the other, dated the 13th June, from Napper Tandy'. Tandy had arrived in Paris from America via Hamburg at the end of May.

19 July 1797

Wind foul still! Horrible, horrible! Admiral de Winter and I endeavour to pass away the time playing the flute (which he does very well); we have some good duets, and that same is some relief. It is however impossible to conceive anything more irksome than waiting, as we now are, on the wind; what is still worse, the same wind which locks us up here is exactly favorable for the arrival of reinforcements to Duncan, if Lord Spencer[1] means to send him any. Naval expeditions are terrible for their uncertainty. I see in the Dutch papers (for I am beginning, with the help of a dictionary to decypher a little) that the Toulon fleet is at sea since the 20th of June, strong 6 sail of the line, viz. two of 80 and four of 74 guns, besides 6 frigates. I wish them safe and well into Brest water. There never was, and there never will be, such an expedition as ours if it succeeds; it is not merely to determine which of two despots shall sit upon a throne, or whether an island shall belong to this or that state; it is to change the destiny of Europe, to emancipate one, perhaps three nations, to open the sea to the commerce of the world, to found a new empire, to demolish an ancient one; to subvert a tyranny of six hundred years—and all this hangs today upon the wind! I cannot express the anxiety I feel. Well, no matter! I can do nothing to help myself, and that aggravates my rage. Our ships exercise at great guns and small arms, one or other of them, every day; they fire in general incomparably well, and it is a noble spectacle.

20 July 1797

This evening I had the pleasure to count 19 sail of British vessels which passed the mouth of the Texel under an easy sail. The general assures me however that there are not above 12 sail of the line[2] according to the comparison of the best accounts which have been received. Wind foul, as usual!

The following is a state of our army.[3]

Infantry 18 Battalions, a 452 each		8,136
Chasseurs 4 D°—, a 540—		2,160
Cavalry—8 Squadrons		1,650
Artillery—9 companies		1,049
Artillerie légère,[4] 2 D°—		389
État Major, &c., &c.—		160
	Total	13,544

---

[1] George John Spencer, 2nd Earl Spencer (1758–1834), first lord of the admiralty, 1794–1801 (*D.N.B.*).   [2] *Life*, ii, 423, adds 'among them'.

[3] In *Life*, ii, 423, the following seven lines are embodied in the text instead of being set out in tabular form.   [4] Translated in *Life* as 'Light Artillery'.

It is more than sufficient. Would to God we were all arrived safe and well at our destination!

To Matilda Tone, 21 July 1797

Tone (Dickason) papers.

Aboard the *Vryheid*, at the Texel, July 21, 1797
3 Thermidor, an 5

Dear Love,

At last I have got a letter from you, dated the 21 Messidor; it appears to be the fourth which you have written, but it is the only one which has come to my hands; the *second*, which you wish I may receive, is probably lost, so you will let me know in your next what was the substance of it, as it seems of some consequence.

I wrote to you and Lewines the 14th instant, and sent the letters under cover to General Dupont. In your letter was inclosed a bill for 250 florins, made by Admiral Winter, which I hope you have received by this.

Here we are, you see still, windbound. The Texel is terrible in that respect; of the thirty-two points of the compass there are not above six with which we can sail out; the other twenty-six lock us up; however it is some comfort that everything is absolutely ready and the instant the wind comes about in our favour, we will put to sea. In the meantime we divert ourselves as well as we can, but you will judge that I pass my time very badly; you can imagine nothing more disagreeable than to be, as we are here, waiting on the wind.

I presume that the arrival of Lewines has cleared up all the obscurity which you may have found in my letters. As to King Estmere's dominions, in Percy, No. 1, you will find it written: *'In Ireland far over the sea, there lived a bonny king'*, &c.[1]

I received yesterday a letter from Madgett inclosing one from Tandy, written above a month ago, which has followed me thro' Germany and Holland. I have answered them, but I will not send my answer until we are under way, because I do not chuse to let them know where I am. You do very right to pretend ignorance; continue to do so.

I am heartily glad Mary continues stout. I wrote to her the same day that I wrote last to you. I do not see why Bond[2] should not pay your bill directly, but as it happens I hope you have enough to carry on the war until he hears from America. The fact is money is very valuable in Dublin just now, and it may be convenient to him to have the use of even £120 for some weeks

---

[1] 'In Ireland, ferr over the sea/There dwelleth a bonnye kinge' (Percy, *Reliques*, 1st ser. (1765), iv).
[2] Possibly Oliver Bond, the wholesale linen draper.

and, as we can afford to lie out of it, if it serves him, so much the better. Pray try Mr Levinsworth.[1] I should be sorry that money should be lost to all parties. As to the news which you suppose I know by this and which Mary sent you, I must tell you I know absolutely nothing; since I have been aboard I have seen not a single newspaper, nor had a line but your letter; so you see I am utterly in the dark.

You gall me with keen iambics for supposing you have read a part of my journals; I am heartily glad they have amused you; there is only our own family and poor Tom[2] who will enter into the spirit of them; to anybody else they are sad stuff. I have begun again and when we meet I shall have sundry volumes more in MS to communicate to you. I wish you would divert yourself, during the many leisure hours which you must have at present on your hands, in writing your adventures since we left Belfast Lough. I do not desire you to shew them to me, unless you wish it yourself, but at all events I wish you would do it. I am delighted with the account you give me of your boys and their studies. I cannot express to you how my soul longs for the moment when we shall be once more all together and when I will share with you in your duties and your happiness; indeed, dear love, you can hardly imagine how intensely I love you and them—the babies, the babies!

I hope Baby[3] is picking up a little French. You do not speak of Mr Sheé's family in your last.[4] I hope no coolness has taken place between you. If you be still (as I hope you are) good friends, Mlle Sheé can be of great use to the Baby. Let me know about this.

I hope I may not be here to receive your answer to this, but at all events write. Lewines will forward your letter with his own. Let me know whether you have received your 250 florins. Adieu, dearest love, I will write to you once more before we leave this. God bless you and our dear Babies.

your ever affectionate
T. W. Tone

To Maria Tone, 21 July 1797

Tone (Dickason) papers; added to the preceding letter.

Dear Baby,

Mama wrote to me the other day, but there was not one word in the letter from a cruel baby. I am very sure of the fact, for I searched the letter over and over.

---

[1] Probably Mark Leavenworth (1750–1812) who graduated at Yale, 1771; he associated with Joel Barlow in business projects in France (F. B. Dexter, *Biographical sketches of the graduates of Yale College* (6 vols, New York and New Haven, 1885–1912), iii, 421–2).   [2] Thomas Russell.
[3] Maria Tone.   [4] For Sheé's family, see above, p. 76, nn 4, 5.

I am, cruel Bab, your affectionate

Fadoff
T. W. T.

My compliments to your brothers.

[*Addressed on verso*]:

À Madame Smith
À Nanterre

Diary, 23–8 July 1797

T.C.D., Tone papers, MS 2049, ff 258ᵛ–260ᵛ; *Life*, ii, 423–5.

23 July 1797

I pass my time here in an absolute torper. When I was at Brest, I was bad enough, but at least we had some conversation. But here! Well! The Admiral[1] tells me today that he has had a letter from London dated the 16th which mentions that L[or]d Bridport[2] is put in for fresh provisions and that three of his ships are still in revolt; that his destination is far before Brest; that S[i]r Edw[ar]d Pellew[3] is arrived at Falmouth, and his report is that the French fleet appears in a state not likely soon to put to sea (which by the bye de Winter believes to be the case and attributes to want of money); that Duncan has applied for a reinforcement but that the Ministers reply that they must first finish the trial of the mutineers in order to reduce the rest to a sense of their duty, from which I infer that they are afraid as yet to send the ships at the Nore to sea. However the *Warrior* of 74 guns is arrived, which brings Duncan up to 13 sail of the line. His report in England is that we have 20 sail of the line (I wish we had!) besides frigates with 15,000 troops embarked and 30,000 stand of arms but that our destination is a secret. The wind is today at N.W., which is not quite so execrable as yesterday and the day before; with a N.N.E. wind, the Admiral says we might get out; ergo, we want yet six points of the compass. Damn it, to all eternity for me! Was there ever anything so terrible? Wrote to my wife the 21st ins[tan]t.[4]

---

[1] Dewinter.
[2] Alexander Hood (1727–1814), 1st Baron Bridport, admiral; commanded Channel fleet, 1795–1800; created viscount, 1800; younger brother of Viscount Hood (*D.N.B.*).
[3] Edward Pellew (1757–1833), later 1st Viscount Exmouth, was at this time an outstanding frigate captain (*D.N.B.*).   [4] Above, pp 107–08.

26 July 1797

Today I saw in the Dutch papers that great changes have taken place in the French ministry. Tallyrand Périgord,[1] ci-devant Bishop of Autun, whom I saw in Philadelphia, is appointed to the Foreign Affairs in place of Cha[rle]s De la croix; Pléville Palet[2] to the Marine in place of Truguet; Le noir la roche[3] to the police in place of Cochon;[4] François de Neufchâteau[5] to the Interior in place of Bénézach;[6] and Hoche to the War department in place of Pétiet. Of all these new men I only know Hoche. Sat down immediately and wrote him a letter of congratulation, in which I took occasion to mention the negotiation now going on at Lisle with the English plenipotentiary Lord Malmesbury,[7] and prayed him, in case that peace was inevitable, to exert his interest to get an article inserted to restore to their country or to their liberty all the Irish patriots who are in exile, or in prison, naming especially his friend [   ],[8] and assuring him at the same time that I should never profit of such an article, as I never would return to Ireland, while she remained in slavery &c. The wind has been detestable these three days. At this moment the Admiral tells me the wind is hauling to the northward and that he will weigh one anchor tonight and heave short on the other, to be ready to profit of the first favorable breeze. God send! But I am sworn never to believe that our expedition will succeed till I am once more upon the sod. I am today eighteen days aboard, and we have not had eighteen minutes of a fair wind. Well, *'tis but in vain'.*[9]

28 July 1797

Yesterday we had a sort of a fair wind, but which came so late and was so feeble that we could not weigh anchor; at eight in the evening it came round to the westward, as bad as ever, and today it is not much better. I

---

[1] Charles Maurice de Talleyrand-Périgord (1754–1838), bishop of Autun, 1788–92; he was in exile in America from early in 1793 to the close of 1795 (*Encyclopaedia Britannica* (11th ed., London, 1912); *Life*, ii, 542).

[2] Georges René Pléville-le-Pelley (1726–1805), naval officer before the revolution; minister of marine, July 1797–Apr. 1798 (*Dict. parl. franç.*).

[3] Jean Jacques Lenoir-Laroche (1749–1825), minister of police, 16–26 July 1797 (*Dict. parl. franç.*).

[4] Charles Cochon de Lapparent (1750–1825), minister of police, Apr. 1796–July 1797 (*Dict. parl. franç.*).

[5] Nicolas Louis François de Neufchâteau (1750–1828), minister of the interior, 1797 and 1798–9 (*Dict. parl. franç.*).

[6] Pierre Bénézech (1749–1802), minister of the interior, 1795–7 (*Dict. parl. franç.*).

[7] From July to Sept. 1797, Lord Malmesbury was conducting at Lille peace negotiations which in the event proved abortive.

[8] Blank in MS. In *Life* the words 'naming especially his friend' are omitted. The 'friend' may have been Arthur O'Connor, whom Hoche had met at Angers in Aug. 1796.

[9] ''Tis but in vain for soldiers to complain' (*The buck's bottle companion* (1775)).

am weary of my life. The French are fitting out a squadron at Brest, which it now appears is to be only of 12 sail of the line. Lord Bridport's fleet is of 22 sail; ergo, he may detach with perfect security 7 sail to reinforce Duncan who will then have *at least* 19 sail against our 15; ergo, he will beat us &c., &c. Damn it to all eternity, for me. I am in a transport of rage which I cannot describe. Everything now depends on the wind, and we are totally helpless. Man is a poor being in that respect. Fifty millions of money cannot purchase us an hour's fair wind; talents and courage avail no more than money. But I am moralizing like an ass. '*Damn morality, and, let the constable be married &c.*'[1] Well (sings) "*'Tis but in vain, for soldiers to complain*' (*575th time*).[2]

Six o'clock. I am now alone in the great cabin and I see from the window two and twenty sail of English vessels, *anchored* within a league of our fleet. It is impossible to express the variety of innumerable ideas which shoot across my mind at this moment. I think I should suffer less in the middle of a sea-fight—and the wind is still foul! Suspense is more terrible than danger. Little as I am of a Quixote, loving as I do to distraction my wife and my dearest babies, I wish to heaven we were this moment under way to meet the enemy, with whom we should be up in an hour. It is terrible to see the two fleets so near, and to find ourselves so helpless! The sea is just now as smooth as a millpond. Ten times since I began this note, I have lifted my eyes to look at the enemy. Well, it cannot be that this inaction can continue long. I am now aboard twenty days and we have not had twenty minutes of a fair wind to carry us out! Hell, hell![3]

To Matilda Tone, 28, 30 July 1797

Tone (Dickason) papers.

Aboard the *Vryheid*,[4] at the Texel, July 28,
1797
10 Thermidor an 5

Dear Love

The wind is just now (at 9 o'clock at night) fair, and if it continues so, tomorrow morning at 4, we shall even be under way. I have written to you almost constantly since we parted, but especially I have written to you the

---

[1] John Vanbrugh, *The provok'd wife* (1697), III.
[2] *The buck's bottle companion* (1775). In *Life*, ii, 425, the bracketed words read 'for the 595th time'.
[3] *Life*, ii, 425, substitutes 'Well! Well!'
[4] Evidence of this is that Tone's handwriting, normally neat, is rough.

2d, the 14th, and the 21st of this month, my letter of the 14th inclosed you a bill drawn by Adm[ira]l de Winter, which I hope you received.[1]

To what I have already said to you, I have nothing to add. You know the very bottom of my soul; you know I doat upon you with a degree of fervor and animation which at our earliest union I did not feel, because I was not then so well acquainted with your virtues. Dear Love, I know not what may be the issue of this great enterprise in which we are embarked; if we fail, we fail in a great cause; we are not embarked to conquer a sugar island or a cotton-factory, but to emancipate a nation, and to change the destiny of Europe; to rescue an unhappy country from a slavery of six centuries, and to constitute her a free and independent nation. I do not think we shall fail because I believe there is a ruling, wise and beneficient providence. But if after all we should be unfortunate, I trust we have the courage to support it.

When I think of you at this crisis, and of our darling babies, I feel sensations which I cannot describe. I doat upon you all, God knows with what sincerity; but the love I feel for you and them, which never has been and never will be exceeded, will only prove a stimulant to the sense of the greater duty I owe my country. If we succeed, we shall meet with pleasure, because we shall meet with confidence, and I promise you, for the hundredth time, that in that case we will part no more.

I give you no formal rules for your conduct; act as becomes my wife and the mother of our children; whatever becomes of me, you will never act unworthily.

Adieu, Life of my life, and soul of my soul. There are no expressions in romance which come up to the love, esteem and admiration I feel for your person and your virtues. God Almighty bless you and my little babies—kiss them for me ten thousand times.

yours ever and most affectionatly,
T.W.T.

I have broke this open to tell you that this morning (the 30th) the wind is fair and we are just getting under way. God Almighty for ever bless you and our little ones. I doat on you all. The General and I go in a sloop, so whatever be the issue of the battle which we shall have in all probability today or tomorrow at farthest, you need be under no uneasiness for my safety. Once more, adieu, my dearest life. Love me always. T.W.T.

[*Addressed on verso*]:

À Madame Smith
À Nanterre

---

[1] Tone's letter to Matilda Tone of 21 July 1797 is printed above (pp 107–08). Those of 2 and 14 July have not been found.

To Maria Tone, 28 July 1797

Tone (Dickason) papers; added to preceding letter.

Dear Baby,

Love your Fadoff always, because he doats upon you. Take care of your boys and of your Matty until we meet, which I trust will be soon. In the meantime I am, with my compliments to your brothers, your dutiful

Fadoff
T. W. T.

Diary, 29 July 1797

T.C.D., Tone papers, MS 2049, ff 260ᵛ–261ᵛ; *Life*, ii, 425–6.

29 July 1797

This morning the wind is fair, but so little of it that we cannot stir. About midday it sprung up fresh, but then the tide was spent, and it was too late; for to sail out of the Texel, there must be a concurrence of wind and tide. The Admiral[1] went ashore today and mounted the Downs with his perspective glass like Robinson Crusoe; he counted 25 sail of three-masted vessels, being six luggers or cutters, of the English at anchor; he concludes they are about 15 or 16 of the line, the rest frigates. He tells me also that his idea is that if there is anything like a parity of success, in case of an action, Admiral Duncan will not push the fight to extremity, as he is on an enemy's coast, and if any of his ships are disma[s]ted, he must leave them; that in that case the action will be a cannonade until night, when both parties will draw off, sing *Te deum* and claim the victory, in which case he will immediately push off with his convoy and such of his ships as are in a state to keep the sea. I like de Winter's behaviour very much; there is nothing like *fanfaronade* in it, and I fancy Duncan will have warm work of it tomorrow morning. The wind tonight is excellent and blows fresh; if it holds, as I trust in God it may, tomorrow at eight o'clock we shall be under way, being the hour of the tide. God knows how earnestly I long for that moment. I hear nothing of our mounting a cutter, as the general mentioned to me, so I may happen to be taken in for a sea fight, against my expectation. Well, if it must be, it must be, but I had rather not. I do not love your sea fights at all; however, happy go lucky! We shall see what is to be done in that case. (Sings) *'Madam, you know my trade is war!'*[2]

---

[1] Dewinter.　　[2] Charles Dibdin, *Poor Vulcan* (1778), II, iii.

To General Lazare Hoche, 31 July 1797

Tone (Dickason) papers.

Tone informs Hoche that 'a sudden change of wind' has prevented the fleet from setting sail and developed into a storm. He considers the greater number and size of the enemy's vessels while urging him to advance the expedition from Brest.

À bord le *Vryheid*, ce 13 Thermidor, an 5

Hier j'ai eu l'honneur de vous écrire, général, pour vous annoncer que nous allions mettre à la voile. En effet tous les préparatifs étoient faits; tout le monde à leurs postes, et l'ennemi dehors du Texel à distance de deux lieues environ. Nous comptions avec toute certitude de les joindre dans trois heures, quand voilà toutes nos espérances dechouées par un changement subite du vent, à l'instant même où nous allions lever le dernier ancre! Il me seroit impossible de vous peindre la rage et la douleur qui nous a saisi tous, et surtout le général et l'amiral de Winter. Ce dernier, ne se fiant pas entièrement aux rapports de pilotes de son bord, a fait signal à tous les chefs de son armée pour savoir leur opinion s'il étoit possible de sortir avec le vent qui souffloit alors, mais leur réponse unanime étoit qu'il étoit absolument impossible; et en effet dans une heure après le vent non seulement devenoit plus défavorable, mais s'augmentoit à une telle point, avec de la tonnerre et des éclairs, que je crois que nous avons échappé un danger considérable, en ne nous laissant pas engager dans les écueils qui garnissent tous les sorties de cette malheureuse rade. Il faut bien lui donner cette appellation, car des trente-deux quarts de vent, il n'y en a que six avec lesquels il est possible de sortir. Enfin, nous voici encore à l'ancre, avec un vent de S.O., c'est-à-dire le plus détestable que nous pouvons en avoir, et Dieu sçoit quand il changera. Au moins, il n'y a pas maintenant la moindre apparence d'un changement prochain. L'amiral Duncan, qui nous attend toujours dehors, est, il est certain, aussi fort que nous par le nombre, et plus fort par la grandeur, de ses vaisseaux. On a compté, avant hier, vingt-six voiles sans y comprendre les lougres et cutters. Il faut croire donc qu'il a, au moins, seize vaisseaux de ligne et dix frégates. Nous n'avons que quinze vaisseaux et huit frégates; aussi, vous voyez, général, que le résultat de notre entreprise ne peut être que fort douteux; nous avons, il est vrai, une bien belle flotte, bien équippée, et les équipages sont dans le meilleur esprit; je compte aussi extrêmement sur le courage et les talens de nos chefs, et surtout de l'amiral de Winter; mais tout cela ne m'empêche pas d'être fort inquiet sur l'événement. Pourquoi vous dis-je tout cela, mon cher général? C'est pour vous prier instamment de ne pas perdre un instant, de votre côté, à l'égard de ce qui dépend de votre gouvernement. Soyez sur que nous, ici, ferons bien notre devoir, mais il ne faut jamais laisser rien à l'hasard. Je ne sais si les changemens récens dans votre ministère nous seront favorables ou non, et j'apprends (toujours dans les gazettes hollandoises) que la république sera encore quelque tems privée des services que vous lui aurez rendu, comme ministre de la guerre, vu que vous n'avez pas encore l'âge requis par la constitution pour remplir cette fonction. Si cela soit vrai, la république française perdra beaucoup, mais j'espère que ma patrie infortunée y gagnera. Je vous connois, général, et je sais bien le zèle que vous avez toujours manifesté dans notre cause; personne n'est plus pénétré que vous de la vaste utilité que seroit notre indépendance à la France, ni de la gloire qui en résultera pour celui qui aura le bonheur de l'effectuer, ni de la ruine absolue qu'un tel événement portera dans toutes les ressources, et surtout dans les plus importantes, de l'ennemi. Il ne faut pas vous presser sur tous ces sujets là, que vous connoissez tout aussi bien que moi. Cependant je ne puis pas m'empêcher de vous supplier, au nom de ma patrie, de la vôtre et de l'humanité même, de pousser l'expédition de Brest le plus possible. Nous avons ici perdu déjà à peu près un mois par les vents contraires, ce qui a donné à l'ennemi le tems de se renforcer; notre sortie est aujourd'hui aussi incertaine que jamais. Souvenez vous, général, que ce n'est pas un grande nombre d'hommes qu'il nous faut mais bien d'armes, et de munitions, et surtout votre présence. Cinq mille hommes que nous pouvons y transporter valent bien vingt-cinq mille que nous ne pouvons y transporter pas; d'ailleurs, il se peut qu'il n'y aura de tems à perdre. Vous savez bien que l'esprit public ne reste pas toujours monté et qu'il retrograde toujours, quand il n'avance pas. Qui pourra répondre que le désespoir de secours ne portera pas les malheureux Irlandais à une soumission absolue? J'espère bien et je crois même, que cela n'arrivera pas; cependant il faut le regarder comme un évènement au moins possible, et dont chaque jour de délai augmentera la possibilité.

Je ne vous pousserai plus, général. Je suis convaincu que, en tout ce qui dépend de vous, cela n'est pas nécessaire. J'espère en même tems que vous pardonnerez mon empressement, quand vous considerez l'inquiétude mortelle qui me dévore, et dont je ne puis vous donner la moindre idée. Je vous ai écrit assez souvent, sans avoir été aussi heureux que de recevoir de vos nouvelles; je vous prie de bien vouloir me donner une réponse à celle-ci sous l'enveloppe du général Daendels, car selon toute apparence nous resterons ici encore assez de tems pour me permettre de recevoir la lettre que j'espère vous me ferez le plaisir de m'écrire.

Salut et respect.

J. Smith

P.S.

15 Thermidor. Un officier envoyé en parlementaire chez l'Amiral Duncan vient de revenir à l'instant même; il a compté 17 vaisseaux de ligne dont deux ou trois à trois ponts. Le vent continue aussi détestable que jamais.

Au Général en chef Hoche
&c., &c.

Diary, 2–5 August 1797

T.C.D., Tone papers, MS 2049, ff 261ᵛ–264ᵛ; *Life*, ii, 426–9.

2 Aug. 1797

Everything goes on here from bad to worse, and I am tormented and unhappy more than I can express, so that I hate even to make these memorandums. Well, it cannot be helped. On the 30th, in the morning early, the wind was fair, the signal given to prepare to get under way, and everything ready, when, at the very instant when we were about to weigh the anchor and put to sea, the wind chopped about and left us. Nothing can be imagined more tormenting. The Admiral,[1] having some distrust of his pilots (for it seems the pilots here are all Orangists),[2] made signal to all the chiefs of the fleet to know if they thought it possible to get out with the wind which then blew (E.S.E.), but their answer was unanimous in the negative so there was an end of the business. In an hour after the wind hauled round more to the southward and blew a gale, with thunder and lightning, so it was well we were not caught in the shoals which environ the entry of this abominable road. At last it fixed in the S.W., almost the very worst quarter possible, where it has remained steadily ever since. Not to lose time, the Admiral sent out an officer with a letter addressed to Admiral Duncan, but in fact to reconnoitre the enemy's force.[3] He returned yesterday with a report that Duncan's fleet is of 17 sail of the line, including two or three three-deckers, which is pleasant. It is decided that we all remain aboard the *Vryheid* and take our chance, which is very brave and foolish, for there is no manner of proportion between the good to be obtained and the hazard to be run, a rule by which I am fond to examine questions. If General Daendels is killed, our expedition will be at least greatly embarrassed, and perhaps totally fail thereby; and as to my personal concerns, if I get knocked on the head, and the expedition should not take place after, both which circumstances are probable, at least, what will become of my dearest Love, and our little babies, left without protection or support? I cannot bear to think of it! If we were in Ireland, once fairly landed, and that I were killed, at least they would be taken care of by my country, but here I have no such consolation. It is terrible, but I cannot help it. *'Slave, I have set my life upon the cast, and I will stand the hazard of the die!'* [4] With all submission, it is a very idle point of honor of

---

[1] Dewinter.   [2] i.e. supporters of the exiled William V of Orange.

[3] On 7 Aug. 1797, Duncan, writing to Spencer, remarked, 'we have a little more intercourse with Admiral de Winter by a flag of truce ... My own idea is it was a frivolous excuse to see our force.' (*Private papers of George, second Earl Spencer* (4 vols [London], 1913–24), ii, 187).

[4] *Richard III*, v, iv.

General Daendels, but it is determined, so there is an end of it. One thing more! If we should happen to be taken the rest will be prisoners of war, but how will it be with me in that case? *C'est une chose à voir;* we shall see. Wrote to Gen[era]l Hoche, Lewines and my wife. Wind still South-west. Damn it, damn it, damn it! I am today twenty-five days aboard, and at a time when twenty-five hours are of importance. There seems to be a fate in this business. Five weeks, I believe six weeks, the English navy was paralyesed by the mutinies at Portsmouth, Plymouth and the Nore; the sea was open and nothing to prevent both the Dutch and French fleets to put to sea. Well, nothing was ready: that precious opportunity, which we can never expect to return, was lost and now that, at last, we are ready here, the wind is against us, the mutiny is quelled, and we are sure to be attacked by a superior force. At Brest it is, I fancy still worse. Had we been in Ireland at the moment of the insurrection at the Nore, we should, beyond a doubt, have had at least that fleet, and God only knows the influence that event might have had on the whole British navy. The destiny of all Europe might have been changed for ever; but, as I have already said, that great occasion is lost, and we must now do as well as we can. *'Le vin est tiré: il faut le boire.'*[1]

4 Aug. 1797

Wind foul. Proposed today to the Admiral to try an experiment in firing shells from the lower deck guns. He said he thought it would not answer, but that he would try notwithstanding. Nine at night. Tried the shell with a thirty-six pounder and found it answer famously. The Admiral I fancy will profit of this circumstance in case of an action with the English, and I am in hopes it will produce a considerable effect.

5 Aug. 1797

This morning arrived aboard the *Vryheid* Lowry[2] of the County Down, member of the Executive Comm[itt]ee, and John Tenent[3] of Belfast. I am in no degree delighted with the intelligence they bring. The persecution in Ireland is at its height, and the people there, seeing no prospect of succour, which has been so long promised to them, are beginning to lose confidence in themselves and their chiefs, whom they almost suspect of deceiving them. They ground their suspicions on the great crisis of the mutiny being suffered to pass by without the French government making the smallest attempt to profit of it, and I can hardly blame them. They held out till the 24th of June, the last day allowed by the English government in the proclamation offering

[1] 'The wine is drawn, it has to be drunk'.   [2] Alexander Lowry (see above, vol. I, p. 222).
[3] John Tennent (1777?–1813), wine and spirit merchant in Belfast; he left Ireland, May 1797; commissioned in French army, 1798 or 1799, and later served in Napoleon's Irish legion; killed in action at Löwenberg; he was a brother of William Tennent (*Northern Star*, 16 Jan. 1794; Madden, *United Irishmen*, 3rd ser. (1846), ii, 51–8; Eileen Black, 'John Tennent, 1777–1813, United Irishman and chevalier de la Légion d'Honneur' in *Irish Sword*, xiii, no. 56 (1978), pp 157–9).

a general pardon,[1] and that day being arrived they have almost intirely submitted and taken the oath of allegiance; most of them have likewise given up their arms, but it appears that the number of firelocks is much less than was imagined. In consequence of all this, the executive comm[itt]ee has doubled its exertions. McNeven was dispatched from Dublin to France, and sailed from Yarmouth the 7th July; of course he is, I reckon, long before this at Paris. Lowry, Tenent and Bar[tholome]w Teeling[2] came together to Hambourg, where they arrived about a fortnight ago, and finding the letter I wrote to my sister, acquainting her with my being here, Teeling immediately sailed for England, and I am in hopes he will get back safe, in which case his arrival will give courage to the people; the other two came on here. All this is very disagreeable; but, in fact, the matter depends upon one circumstance. If either the Dutch or the French can effectuate a landing, I do not believe the present submission of the people will prevent their doing what is right, and if no landing can be effectuated, no party remains for the people to adopt but submission or flight. By what Lowry and Tenent tell me, there seems to me to have been a great want of spirit in the leaders in Dublin.[3] I suspected it very much from Lewines's account, tho' I saw he put the best side out, but now I am sure of it; however I did not say so to them, for the thing is passed now, and criticising it will do no good, but the reverse. The people have been urgent more than once to begin, and at one time eight hundred of the garrison offered to give up the Barracks of Dublin, if the leaders would only give the signal and begin; the militia were almost to a man gained over, and numbers of those poor fellows have fallen victims in consequence. It is hard to judge at this distance, but it seems to me to have been an unpardonable weakness, if not downright cowardice to let such a great occasion slip. With eight hundred of the garrison and the barracks to begin with, in an hour they would have had the whole capital, and by seizing the persons of half a dozen individuals they would have paralysed the whole government, and, in my opinion, accomplished the whole revolution by a single proclamation; but as I said already, it is hard to judge at this distance. Keogh I know is not fit for a coup de main; he has got, as Lewines tells me, McCormick latterly into his hands, and besides, Dick is now past the age of adventure. I am surprised that Emmett did not shew more energy, because I know he is as brave as Cæsar of his person. It seems to me to have been such an occasion missed as we can hardly expect to see return. Lowry & Tenent say there are now at

[1] A vice-regal proclamation dated 17 May 1797 promised pardon to United Irishmen who surrendered to a magistrate and took the oath of allegiance by 24 June 1797, a date later extended to 24 July (*Dublin Gazette*, 18 May 1797, 24 June 1797).

[2] Bartholomew Teeling (1774–98), United Irishmen; went to France, 1797; took part in Humbert's expedition as his aide-de-camp and was captured and executed; he was the eldest son of Luke Teeling (*D.N.B.*).

[3] There is confirmation of this by John Hughes, referring to the position as it was towards the middle of June 1797, in the evidence he gave on 3 Aug. 1798 to the secret committee of the Irish house of lords (*Report from the secret committee of the House of Lords with an appendix* (Dublin, 1798), pp 27–8).

least 80,000 men in Ireland of British troops, including the militia and yeomanry corps, who together may make 35,000; but in this account I am sure there is great exaggeration, for I found they spoke pretty much by guess, and a number that is guessed, as Johnson remarks, is always exaggerated.[1] I suppose however there may be 50, or perhaps 55,000, of all kinds, and it is not that force, composed as it is, that would make me despair of success, if we could once get out of this damned hole, of which I see no sign; and, to comfort me still more, I hear that in general the westerly winds (which lock us up) prevail during the whole of this month, before the end of which time we shall have eat up our provisions, and probably be encumbered with sick; for it can hardly be supposed the troops will keep their health so long, cooped up as they are in transports, where they are packed like herrings. Add to this the chance of a peace being concluded with England, and I think I am not too gloomy in saying that nothing can well appear more unpromising than the appearance of things today. I have made out a list of Duncan's fleet from Steel's list of the Navy[2] and I see he has two of 98, two of 80, two of 74, eight of 64 and three of 50 guns besides frigates. Wind still foul, viz. W.S.W.

To Matilda Tone, 6 August 1797

Tone (Dickason) papers.

Aboard the *Vryheid*, at the Texel,
windbound, August 6, 1797

Dearest Love,

I am here you see still, which is truly agreeable. The elements have conspired our downfall, I believe. I am today twenty-nine days a shipboard, and I need say no more, for I presume under the circumstances you can sufficiently conceive the rage and fury which devour me. What considerably augments my vexation and anxiety is that I have not had one line from you, or any other person whatsoever, since my arrival here, notwithstanding I have written constantly, which surprises me very much. I suspect the post office, because I know by myself that you could not be so unkind as to leave me so long without hearing from you. I have written to you, under the following dates, July 1st, 14th, 21st and 30th; in my letter of the 14th I inclosed you a bill for 250 florins, which I hope you received.[3] Pray let me hear from you, and give your letter to Giauque,[4] who will forward it with his own.

---

[1] Johnson's remark has not been traced.
[2] David Steel, *Original and correct list of the Royal Navy* (179–?).
[3] Tone's letters to his wife dated 1, 21 and 30 July are given above (pp 84–5, 107–08, 111–12); none dated 14 July has been found, but Tone also wrote letters to his wife on 7 and 9 July (above, pp 86–9).
[4] In fact to Edward Joseph Lewines, who, as Tone explained to Talleyrand in a letter written on 15 Oct. 1797, had 'taken the name Giauque' (see below, p. 161). Lewines was already in Paris, while Giauque (Tone's brother-in-law) was still in Hamburg.

Hitherto I have sent all my letters under cover [to] General Dupont at Paris; perhaps they have miscarried. If this reaches you with the enclosed, write a line immediately to Giauque to come to you, and to bring with him the key of the cypher we agreed upon at parting. Do not trust the enclosed to the post office of Paris, but let him come for it.

I cannot bear to write, even to you, my mind is in such a state of uneasiness. The wind is today as bad as ever and God knows when it will change, or when we shall get out of this vile hole. Adieu, dearest Life and soul. May God for ever bless you and our dearest babies; I doat upon you all. I would give my soul for you, you ugly things. I have no pleasure but in your company and instead of that here I am at the Texel! Well, if ever I catch you all again, if I let you go, that is all! My poor little babies, I think of them ten thousand times a day—but that is *'only but just foolishness'*.[1] Well (sings), *"Tis but in vain for soldiers to complain!"* [2]

Adieu, life of my life, and soul of my soul; love me always as I love you.

Your dutiful spouse
J. S.

Baby![3] you are an ugly thing and I don't care for you. Tell Will that I found *'a fair piece of wood by the mast'*.[4]

Your dutiful Fadoff
J. S.

À Madame Smith
À Nanterre
À Paris

Diary, 8 August 1797

T.C.D., Tone papers, MS 2049, ff 265ʳ–266ʳ; *Life*, ii, 429–31 .

8 Aug. 1797

Wind foul. We have now been detained here so long that our hopes of undertaking the expedition to Ireland are beginning exceedingly to relax, and I more than suspect the General[5] is speculating on one elsewhere, for I have remarked him within these three days frequently examining a map of England, particularly the east coast about Yarmouth, and he has asked me several questions which lead that way. As Lowry and Tenent travelled that road very

---

[1] Source of this quotation not traced.   [2] *The buck's bottle companion* (1775).
[3] What follows is obviously intended for Maria Tone.   [4] Source not traced.
[5] Daendels.

lately I learn from them that there are few or no troops on that coast, except a small camp at Ipswich about half way (viz. 69 miles) to London. In consequence last night when the General and I were walking alone on the quarterdeck and cursing the wind, he began to mention his apprehensions on the score of our provisions running short, as well as the danger of attempting the passage North about so late in the season, and he began again to *moot* the point about Yarmouth. I said that if unfortunately we were driven so far into the season that the Irish expedition was utterly impracticable, it was undoubtedly desirable to try something in England, as well for the glory of the Dutch arms as that all the expense hitherto incurred in the affair might not be lost; that in that case my idea was to run over to the English coast and to debark the army, not at Yarmouth but at Harwich or nearer London, if possible; to carry nothing with us but bread for six days and ammunition; to make a desperate plunge, by forced marches, for the capital, where I did not consider it impossible but we might arrive before the enemy could be in sufficient force to oppose us, supposing the eastern coast to be as unfurnished of troops, as Lowry and Tenent had represented; that if we were once there we might defy all the force of England, for if they even assembled 100,000 men in Hyde Park, we could at all times make conditions, by threatening, in case they drove us to extremity, to set fire to the city at the four corners and defend ourselves afterwards to the last man; that I had no doubt but with such a pledge in our hands we could make our own terms, and I dwelt a good deal, I cannot however say with any great success, on the glory of such a desperate enterprise, if we had the good fortune to succeed, which seemed to me, tho' very far from certain, yet at least so possible as to deserve serious consideration. I mentioned likewise as a subordinate circumstance that, if we once reached London, we should to a certainty find a reinforcement inasmuch as a large portion of the mob, and those very desperate fellows, consisted of Irishmen to the amount of a great many thousands, who I was sure would desire nothing more than to have their will of the English. All these arguments however seemed to make no great impression on Daendels, who still recurred to his Yarmouth scheme. He seems to me to expect some co-operation there, on what grounds I know not but I fancy he will find himself egregiously deceived. If anything can be done in England, it must be, in my mind, by a *coup de main*, whereas he talks of maintaining himself for some time in the country, which with 14,000 men is flat nonsense. He asked me, if he were to land on the east coast, would it be possible for any of the Irish to effectuate a landing on the other side, cross the country and join him, when he would give them arms? To this most extravagant of all questions, I contented myself with declaring gravely that I looked upon it as impracticable. To be sure it is most egregious nonsense to suppose for an instant that such a measure could by any possibility be executed by a body of unarmed men without a single ship prepared to carry them over. Far from invading England I wish to heaven they were able to take the field in their own country.

I cannot conceive how such a wild idea could for a moment enter Daendels's head, yet he seemed to be in earnest. To return to my scheme, I think Charles 12th,[1] with 14,000 men, would execute it, supposing he could effectuate the landing, but I readily admit that it requires much such a head and heart as his to attempt such an enterprise. Certain it is that we will not try it. Daendels's answer at length was that he was of opinion the Dutch government would not consent to it, and if they even did, it would require too much time as he must in that case new model the army, which I do not understand. I think Hoche, with 15,000 French grenadiers, would effectuate it, but for the Dutch, I cannot pretend to say. It seems to me however at least possible. From Harwich to London is but 72 miles,[2] which could be made by forced marches in three days, supposing we had horses to draw the artillery, which in that case we must bring with us. But this is raving; the thing will not be done, so there is an end of it.

1797

Diary, 9–17 August 1797

T.C.D., Tone papers, MS 2049, ff 267ʳ–274ʳ; *Life*, ii, 431–9.

No. 15
From August the 8th, 1797, to January 22, 1798[3]
Nil desperandum!
The Texel, Wetzlar and Paris
1797 and 1798

Aboard the *Vryheid*, at the Texel, 1797[4]
9 Aug. 1797

This morning the General,[5] Lowry and Tenent and myself took a walk ashore for a couple of hours. He examined them particularly as to what they knew of the state of the public mind in Scotland, and the possibility of meeting support from the patriots in that country, in case that the expedition to Ireland were so long delayed as to become impracticable and that he should decide in consequence to try an attack on Scotland? They answered him very rationally. It seems emissaries have been sent from the north of

---

[1] Charles XII (1682–1718), king of Sweden, 1697–1718.   [2] About 115 km.
[3] There is no Diary entry for 8 Aug. 1797. The entries for 18–21 Aug., 23–6 Aug., 27–30 Aug., 1–3 Sept., 4–13 Sept., 14 Sept., 17 Sept., 19–22. Sept., 30 Sept.–29 Nov., 10–12 Dec., 13–17 Dec., 21–3 Dec., 1–13 Jan. 1798 and 22 Jan. 1798, are given as separate documents (below).
[4] The preceding headings, which Tone obviously added later than 9 Aug., are omitted from *Life*.
[5] Daendels.

Ireland into that country to propagate the system of the United Irishmen,[1] and that they have to a certain degree succeeded in some of the principal manufacturing towns, such as Paisley and Glasgow, where societies are already organised, and by the last accounts they had even advanced so far as to have formed a provincial committee.[2] Nevertheless they observed that these facts rested on the veracity of the agents sent from the North, the Scotch having sent none of their body in return; that they could not pretend to say whether the Scotch patriots were up to such a decided part as to take arms in case of an invasion but their opinion rather was that they were not so far advanced; as to the possibility of assistance from Ireland (on which head Daendels examined them pretty closely), they were decidedly of opinion that it was utterly impossible and not to be thought of. Certainly it is a most extravagant expectation. After discussing this question fully we parted, the General returning aboard the *Vryheid*, and Lowry, Tenent and I setting off for the Texel, where they are tolerably lodged in a little village. We walked over a great part of the island which is, by nature, one of the most barren, uncomfortable spots that can be imagined, but such are the inconceivable effects of liberty and a good government that their ungrateful soil is in a great degree reclaimed, enclosed and drained, covered with flocks and herds, filled with neat and snug dwellings, and supporting five little towns, which are beautiful in their kind. The population is inconceivable for the extent, and the peasants all well fed and clothed. I thought of Ireland a thousand times, with her admirable soil and climate, and the vast advantages w[hi]ch nature has showered down upon her, and which are all blasted by the malignant influence of her execrable government, till my blood boiled within me with rage and vexation. Well, I cannot help it, so let me think, if possible, no more of that melancholy subject. Passed two days very agreeably with Lowry and Tenent, and then returned on board. They are a couple of fine lads, especially Lowry, whom I like extremely. I think he will make a figure if ever we have the good fortune to reach our own country.

12 Aug. 1797

The General has been making an excursion ashore and is not yet returned. The wind is as foul as ever, and I begin fairly to despair of our enterprise. Tonight, Admiral de Winter took me into secresy & told me he had prepared a memorial to his government, stating that the design originally was to be

---

[1] In the spring of 1797 the Society of United Scotsmen, modelled on the United Irishmen, was being organised and was particularly strong in the Glasgow region. It was believed that it was started by delegates from the United Irishmen ('Report of the committee of secrecy [ordered to be printed 1 March 1797]', H.C. 1799 (4919), pp 35, 38–9, *House of Commons sessional papers of the eighteenth century*, ed. Sheila Lambert (Wilmington, Del., 1975–6), cxxi, 313–430).

[2] It does not appear that a 'provincial committee' was ever formed. For the situation in Scotland in 1797 and Irish influence there, see Elaine W. McFarland, *Ireland and Scotland in the age of revolution* (Edinburgh, 1994), chs 5 and 6.

ready for the beginning of July, and that everything was in consequence embarked by the 9th; that the English fleet at that time consisted of, at the very most, but 13 sail of the line, which could not make any effectual opposition; that contrary winds having prevailed ever since without an hour's intermission, the enemy had time to reinforce himself to the number of 17 sail of the line, so that he had now a superiority in force over the Dutch fleet, which of course rendered the issue of our engagement to a certain degree doubtful; that by this unforeseen delay, which might, and probably would, continue still longer, a great additional consumption of provisions had taken place so that in a very few days there would be barely sufficient for the voyage north about; that the season was rapidly passing away, and that, if the foul wind continued a fortnight longer, the voyage would become highly dangerous, if not utterly impracticable, with a fleet incumbered with so many transports and amounting to near 70 sail of all kinds, and that in consequence even a succes[s]ful action with the English would not ensure the success of the enterprise, which the very season would render impracticable; that for all these reasons his opinion was that the present plan was no longer advisable, and in consequence he proposed that it should be industriously published that the expedition was renounced; that the troops should be disembarked, except from 2,500 to 3,000 men of the *élite* of the army which, with 20 or 30 pieces of artillery and all the arms and ammunition, should remain on board the frigates and one or two of the fastest sailing transports; that, as the vigilance of the enemy would probably be relaxed in consequence, this *flotille* should profit of the first favorable moment to put to sea and push for their original destination, where they should land the men, arms and artillery, and he charged himself with the execution of this plan; that by this means, even if it failed, the republic would be at no very great loss and, if [it] succeeded, must gain exceedingly; that she would preserve her grand fleet, which was now her last stake, and during the winter would be able to augment it, so as to open the next campaign (in case peace was not made during the winter) with 20 sail of the line in the North Sea, whereas on the present system to the execution of which were opposed the superiority of the enemy, the extra-consumption of provisions, and especially the lateness of the season, a succes[s]ful engagement at sea would not ensure the success of the measure, and an unsucces[s]ful one, by ruining the fleet, would render it impossible for the republic, for a long time at least, to recover the blow. These are most certainly very strong reasons, and unfortunately the wind gives them every hour fresh weight. I answered the Admiral that I did not see at present any solid objection to propose to his system, and that all I had to say was that if the Batavian republic sent but a corporal's guard into Ireland, I was ready to make one. So here is our expedition in a hopeful way! It is most terrible! Twice within nine months has England been saved by the wind. It seems as if the very elements had conspired to perpetuate our slavery and protect the insolence and oppression of our tyrants. What can I do, at this moment? Nothing! The people of Ireland will now lose all spirit and confidence in themselves and their chiefs, and God only knows whether, if we were even able to effectuate a landing with 3,000 men, they might act with courage and decision? I hope they would, and I believe it; yet after all it is uncertain; their hopes have been so often deceived, and they have suffered such a dreadful persecution in consequence of what they have already done in this business; yet their sufferings must have only still more exasperated their minds, and I can not suppose that, if they saw the arms, they would not instantly seize and turn them on their oppressors. I cannot doubt it. At all events we should at least know the worst, and if they had not the courage to assert their liberty they deserve to suffer their present slavery and degradation, but, once again, I do not believe it. I shall in consequence, as far as in me lies, support the Admiral's plan, the more as it is, I see now, our only resource, and feeble as it is, it is still better than nothing. We must now begin, if at all, like the French in La Vendée.[1] Well, we have a good cause, and they had a bad one; we are the people and they were but a fraction of two provinces; we have powerful means and on the present plan we must use them.[2] All things considered, I do not know but there is something in the expedition proposed more analogous to my disposition and habits of thinking, which is a confession on my part more honest than wise, for I feel very sensibly there is no common sense in it, but after all, it is my disposition and I cannot help it. I am growing utterly desperate, and there are times that I would almost wish for death, if it were not for the consideration of my wife, and my darling little babies, who depend for their existence upon mine. God almighty for ever bless them! But this is a subject on which I must not think. Let me quit it here.

13 Aug. 1797

The General returned last night from his excursion, and this morning he mentioned to me the Admiral's plan in which he said he did not well see his way, and was proceeding to give me his reasons, when we were interrupted by Gen[era]l Dumonceau,[3] our second in command, and a heap of officers, who broke up our conversation. When he renews it, I will support de Winter's plan as far as I am able. The wind is as foul as ever, viz. S.W. in or near which point it has continued now 36 days that I am aboard, viz. since the 8th of July last.

At night. The General and I have been poring over the map of England, and he has been mooting a plan which in my mind is flat nonsense, viz. to land at or near Lynn in Lincolnshire[4] with his 14,000, where he thinks he

---

[1] i.e. the Vendéens, royalists, mostly peasants, in the western *départements* of Loire-Inférieure and Maine-et-Loire who waged guerrilla warfare against the republic from March 1793 until finally suppressed by Hoche in 1796.   [2] *Life*, ii, 435, reads 'use them, *all*'.
[3] Joannes Baptista Dumonceau (1760–1821), Dutch general; he had been in the French service until 1795 (*Nieuw Nederlandsche biografisch woordenboek*, i, 761–5).   [4] *Recte* Norfolk.

could maintain himself until the fleet could return and bring him a reinforcement of as many more and then he would march upon London and stand a battle. It is hardly worth combating a scheme which will certainly never be adopted; it is sufficient to observe that his plan necessarily includes that he must be absolute master of the sea during the whole time necessary for its execution, which, without going farther, is saying enough. Besides I presume it is hardly to be expected that with even 28,000 men supposing he had horses to mount his cavalry and draw his artillery (which he would not have) that he would be able to force his way thro' an enemy's country for above 100 miles, who would have time more than sufficient to collect his forces and to make the necessary dispositions to give him a warm reception. But it is unnecessary to combat this idea because, as I have said already, it will never be attempted, so let it lie there.

14 Aug. 1797

The General is gone off again on a party of pleasure in the North Holland. He invited me to accompany him but I have no stomach for pleasure or enjoyment of any kind, so I refused and set off for the Texel to see Lowry and Tenent, and to talk over the Admiral's new plan, in order to have their opinion thereupon. After dinner we walked out to a pretty little farm about half a mile from the town where they are lodged, and sat down together on a hillock whence we had a view of the fleet riding at anchor below. I then told them that I looked upon our expedition, on the present scale, as given up, and I stated the reasons assigned by De Winter and which are not to be answered. I then communicated his plan, and desired their advise and opinion on the whole and especially as to the material fact, viz. whether they thought the people would join us, if they saw no greater force than 3,000 men. After a long consultation, their opinion finally was that the scheme was practicable but difficult, and that by great exertions and hazards on the part of their chiefs, that the people might be brought forward, but that, for that it was indispensable that the landing should be effected in the counties of Down or Antrim, but especially the former, where there were, in June last, ready organised 24 regiments of 1,000 men each, with all their officers and sub-officers ready named. They mentioned at the same time that if the expedition had taken place three months ago with 500 men, it could not have failed of success, but that public spirit was exceedingly gone back in that time, and a great number of the most active and useful chiefs were either in prison or exile, which would considerably increase the difficulty of carrying into execution the present system. I saw they were a good deal dejected by the change of the plan and the consequent diminution in our means, and I did my best to encourage them. At last we all got into better spirits, consoling ourselves with the reflection that if we succeeded with such a trifling[1] force, the glory of our success would be

---

[1] In *Life*, ii, 436, William Tone substitutes 'so slender a' for 'such a trifling'.

the greater, and if we failed there would be the less reason to reproach us. We agreed that we should be, at our landing, in the case of men who had burned their ships, that we had no retreat, but must conquer or die, and we counted a good deal, and I think with reason, on the spirit of enthusiasm which we would be able to raise in the people. We likewise agreed that we would stop at no means necessary to ensure our success, but[1] would proceed, if we were driven to that necessity, even to the repartition of the entire property of the nation, rather than turn back one inch from our project. After this discussion we returned to the inn, where we supped, and after drinking divers loyal and constitutional toasts, we retired to bed at a very late hour.

15 Aug. 1797

As it will require from three weeks to a month to arrange matters for the expedition on the present plan, Lowry and Tenent have determined to go to the Hague, and, if they have the time, to Paris, in order to see McNeven and Lewines, and to join with them in endeavouring to procure assistance from France, and especially, if possible to obtain a small armament to co-operate with that from the Texel and which by spreading the alarm and distracting the attention of the enemy must produce the most beneficial effects. It is likewise their wish that I should accompany them, and if I had the time and money to spare, I should like it well enough, and I think it might do good. In consequence it was determined this morning that I should return immediately aboard the *Vryheid* and propose the measure to Admiral de Winter. I returned accordingly, but the Admiral was not on board. At my arrival I found 3 frigates and 4 armed brigs just getting under way, which surprised me a little. Late in the evening the Admiral returned and I told him of our project, which he approved highly and will give Lowry and Tenent letters of introduction to the Dutch government. I said nothing of my going until I see the General, who is not yet returned from his party. De Winter told me that the English frigates having approached very near the road and stopped two or three neutral vessels laden with timber, he had ordered out a *flotille* to the entry of the road partly to protect the commerce, and partly to give the change to the enemy on the subject of our present plan by habituating them to see the frigates going out and in, his orders being that they should never hazard an action. He has not yet received the answer of the Dutch government to his plan. Grasveldt, who came aboard the *Vryheid*, asked me what I thought of it. I answered that undoubtedly there was not an equal certainty of success, with our means so mutilated, as on the original plan, but that nevertheless there was such a probability as, comparing the object with the risque, ought to decide the government to try the enterprise, and that such was also the opinion of my two friends. Grasveldt upon this wrote a letter, which I presume was to the comm[itt]ee

---

[1] *Life* omits from 'but' to 'nation'.

for foreign affairs and in favor of De Winter's plan. I should have observed in its place that the General, when he was setting off yesterday morning, told me that he was ready on his part to undertake the command with 2,500 men, provided he saw such a probability as would acquit him in the eyes of the world of downright insanity in throwing away himself and his army, and that in consequence he would support the Admiral's plan. We must wait now to see the answer of the Dutch government, and for that reason I wish we were all three at the Hague. Perhaps our opinion might decide them.

16 Aug. 1797

Went to the Texel to see Lowry and Tenent and spent the day.

17 Aug. 1797

We all three came aboard the *Vryheid* in order to settle about our journey to the Hague and on our arrival found things as unpleasantly situated as possible. I see clearly there is a coolness pretty far advanced between the Admiral and General, whose manner towards each other is marked with a manifest dryness that bodes us no good. The General was the first that spoke to me. He said that with 4,000 men, viz. 4 battalions of Jägers,[1] 2,000, 2 D⁰ grenadiers, 1,300, 2 squadrons of hussars, 400, a company of the *artillerie légère*,[2] 150, artillerists, 100, and officers of the *état-major*, 50, he[3] would undertake the enterprise, but not with less; that if his government ordered him, he would go with one battalion, but that he would give his opinion decidedly against trying the measure with less than 4,000 men. I replied that undoubtedly the Dutch government would be decided, with regard to a military operation, by his opinion, which must necessarily influence theirs. I then addressed myself to the Admiral, to whom I communicated what the General had said with regard to the number of troops which [he] thought indispensable. The Admiral answered me at once that it was impossible and that 2,500 was the very utmost he would undertake to transport, and that even that force would require 18 sail to carry them, viz. 6 frigates which might carry 600 men, 6 sail of large transports, 1,800 men, and the remaining 100 on the 6 luggers and cutters. I think this calculation not reasonable, as at Brest we had 250 men on board each of our frigates, whereas De winter allows but 100; certainly the frigates might carry 200 each. The Admiral also objected to the hussars as being unnecessary, and their baggage requiring too much room, in which I by no means agree with him. In short our expedition seems now, independant of all other reasons, to be aground on the same shoal where so many others have been shipwrecked, I mean the disagreement between the land and sea service, about which I can no longer doubt. It is pleasant.

[1] In *Life*, ii, 438, William Tone spells this word 'yagers'. It derives from the German 'Jäger', meaning here 'riflemen'. In the MS the umlaut is omitted.
[2] *Life*, ii, 438, reads 'light artillery'.   [3] In the MS 'he' is preceded by a redundant 'that'.

To Matilda Tone, 18 August 1797

Tone (Dickason) papers.

Aboard the *Vryheid*, at the Texel,
18 August 1797

Dear Love,

I have written to you since my arrival here at least six times, and I have not had the happiness to receive one line in return, for which however I do not accuse you for I am sure you have written repeatedly. I suspect, or more than suspect, the post office. In short since I arrived at the Texel I have not received a single letter of any kind from mortal soul, which has made me very uneasy. I am here today forty-two days, without having had a fair wind; at last it seems to relent; we have at this moment a tolerable fair breeze and the signal is out to weigh anchor and put to sea. Of course long before you receive this, the fate of [the] expedition will be decided for good or evil. I confess to you, my expectations of success are considerably diminished; for the long delay, caused by the foul winds only, has given time to the enemy, whom I can see at this moment from the cabin windows, to reinforce himself to the number of 17 ships of the line, whereas we have but 15, so that the issue of the combat is very doubtful. If we are beaten, there is an end of the affair, and, if we even beat the English, it does not ensure our success, for our fleet will be to a certainty so mauled in the action that they must return to refit, as they will never be able to undertake the passage North about at this season with crippled ships. Of course even victory, tho' very glorious to the Dutch arms, will not, I fear, materially save us, and that is to me most truly mortifying. All that I have to console me is that nobody is to blame for this but the wind, for we have been ready now six weeks without being able to stir.

Dear Love, I wish I had brighter prospects for you, but you see how the facts are. Nevertheless I have seen them far worse; we are a thousand times better off today than the night we were blown out to sea from Bantry Bay, for example, and perhaps after all things may turn out better than I expect.

To all I have said to you in my former letters I have nothing to add. It is unnecessary now to assure you of the most sincere and ardent affection I bear you, and ever will; you know well I doat upon you and our little babies. God Almighty for ever bless you all. Kiss the little things for me a thousand and a thousand times.

Adieu, dearest Life and soul. A very short time must now decide our fate, and I know nothing so terrible as the suspense and anxiety I have suffered since I have been here. I hope and trust the event of our expedition may still be favorable and in that case, at our next meeting, we part no more, for this eternal separation is a price too dear to pay for almost any object, or any duty.

Once more adieu, Life of my Life; I doat upon you.

J. S.

I enclose a letter for Giauque[1] which you will take care to make reach him; the surest way will be to write to him to come to you for it. In my last I also enclosed you one for him, which I hope he got safe. I add the dates of all my letters since I have been here, viz, July 2, 14, 21, 30, Aug[us]t 6,[2] which was my last addressed to you under cover to Mme Sheé.

At this moment I have received your letter in date of the 15 Thermidor. Of course it has been 17 days on the road, instead of 6 or 7 at the outside; it is the only one I have got, and that from Giauque which you mention and refer me to is suppressed, so you see I had reason to elevate my voice and cry aloud against the post office. Dearest Love, I cannot express the satisfaction the receipt of your letter and the Baby's little postscript have given. You may tell her from me there is no love lost between us. You have whetted my curiosity a little with regard to Giauque's letter; I have written to him as often as to you, tho' in fact I had nothing to say to him, and I have not heard yet from him. Sad, sad! I write famous journals for you as usual. For your insulting remarks on my quotations, I overlook and pity them *'Your Noveds and omuns and bluetucks and stuff &c.'*[3] What do you tell a man of my time of life and rank in the armies of the two republics of your Percy No. 1.[4] (Sings, with great courage) *'Madam you know my trade is war!'*[5] That is what I call a good quotation. I am happier than I can express at the receipt of your letter because I see you keep up your spirits as I could wish. I would give sundry ducats to be beside you at the opera, if it were only to hear the baby's remarks thereupon. Take care of yourself, Dearest Life, and of the Babies and love me always as I love you, because you are the only happiness of my life. Adieu my soul and Love, God bless you.

To Maria Tone, 18 August 1797

Tone (Dickason) papers; added to the preceding.

---

[1] Here and below in this letter where he writes 'Giauque' he means Lewines, who took the pseudonym Giauque on going to Paris (see below, p. 161).

[2] In fact, 22 June from Cologne (above, pp 83–4), *1* July from Cologne (above, pp 84–5), 7 July from the Hague (above, pp 86–8), 21 July from the Texel (above, pp 107–8), *28* July from the Texel (above, pp 111–12), 6 Aug. from the Texel (above, pp 119–20). He overlooks the letter of 9 July (above, pp 88–9); those of 1 and 28 he misdates; 'here' is true only of letters from 21 July.

[3] 'Noveds and Blutrakes, and Omurs and stuff' (Swift, *The grand question debated* (1729), line 156).　　　　[4] Thomas Percy, *Reliques of ancient English poetry* (3 vols, London, 1765).

[5] Charles Dibdin, *Poor Vulcan* (1778), II, iii.

Dear Baby,

I have written you five hundred letters and have not got one answer from you, and if I knew who it was that had intercepted them and could catch hold of him, I know what I would do to him. Take care of your dearest Mama and of your boys until I see you all again, which I hope now will be soon.

Adieu, dear Baby. Love your Fadoff always.

J. S.

Diary, 18–21 August 1797

T.C.D., Tone papers, MS 2049, ff 274ʳ–275ᵛ; *Life*, ii, 439–40.

18 Aug. 1797

This morning we have had the same scene repeated which has happened to us once or twice already. At four or five in the morning the wind came round to the east; the signal was given to prepare to get under way; the cap-stern was manned; one anchor weighed and the other hove short to be ready for the tide; the Admiral and General[1] prepared their dispatches, and I wrote to Giauque and my wife.[2] At length, at nine, the wind slackened, and at ten came round to the old point, the S.W., where it stuck, so there was an end of the business. I have been so often disappointed, and so long, that I am now used to it. I therefore bore this very quietly. To console me I received a letter from my wife, which gave me unspeakable pleasure. Thank God she is well, and my poor little babies. May God almighty for ever bless them all!

20 Aug. 1797

Yesterday morning the General and Grasfeldt set off for the Hague in one carriage and Lowry, Tenent and I in another. We arrived safe this evening *'per varios casus, per tot discrimina rerum'*.[3]

21 Aug. 1797

Breakfasted with the General. He told me in the first place that the government had rejected the plan proposed by the Admiral, viz. to transport 2,500 men and the arms, stores and ammunition &c, and had determined to persist in their original design; that however in consideration of the lateness

---

[1] i.e. Dewinter and Daendels.
[2] Tone's letter to Matilda Tone of 18 Aug. 1797 is printed above (pp 129–30). The words 'Giauque and' are omitted from *Life*.
[3] 'Through all sorts of adventures and so many narrow escapes' (Virgil, *Aeneid*, bk 1, line 205).

of the season, he had prepared a memorial,[1] which he shewed me, for a new arrangement, which is shortly this; to sail out and fight Admiral Duncan; if the issue of the battle be favorable, to immediately pass over 15,000 men, or as many more as we can send in everything that will swim into Scotland; to seize in the first instance on Edinburgh, and to march right on Glasgow, taking every possible means to alarm the enemy with the idea that we mean to penetrate by the north of England, which is to be done by detaching flying parties, making requisitions &c. on that side; to maintain ourselves in the mean time behind the canal which joins the Firth of Forth to the Clyde, having our right at Dunbarton and our left at Falkirk, as I remember, for I have not at present either the map or the memorial before me; to collect all the vessels in the Clyde &c., and to pass over the army to the North of Ireland; to send round, while these military operations were going on by land, the frigates and such transports (as few as possible) as might be necessary to carry the artillery, stores &c.; finally that the English would probably be alarmed by all this for their own country, and perhaps recall a part of their troops from Ireland, which would very much facilitate the success of the enterprise. He added in addition that he waited only for Gen[era]l Dejean,[2] who commands the army of the north, in order to settle with him the military arrangements, and that in a day or two probably the government would be decided. In the meantime he desired us to wait upon Van Kasteele, president of the Convention, which we did accordingly. Van Kasteele received us of course very civilly, and said that in case the Government had any questions to propose to us, he would send to request our attendance, on which we took our leave.

From General Lazare Hoche,
19 August 1797

Tone (Dickason) papers.
Hoche expresses annoyance that contrary winds still keep Tone in the road.

Au Quartier général à Wetzlar
le 2 fructidor an 5ᵉ

Le général commandant en chef l'armée de Sambre et Meuse
à l'adjudant général Schmitt

Je suis bien fâché, mon cher Schmitt, que les vents vous soient constamment contraires et vous retiennent toujours en rade. Je voudrois bien

---

[1] A copy in Tone's hand, made apparently on Daendels's instruction for Hoche's benefit (see Diary for 3 Sept. 1797, below, p. 142), is in National Library of Ireland, MS 706, ff 32–6. It has been edited by C. J. Woods as 'A plan for a Dutch invasion of Scotland, 1797' in *Scottish Historical Review*, liii (1974), pp 108–14.

[2] Jean François Aimé Dejean (1749–1824) served as an officer before the revolution; général de division, 1795; in command 'des troupes franco-bataves', Sept. 1796–Sept. 1797; count of the empire, 1808 (Six, *Dict. des généraux & amiraux*).

vous savoir à la voile. Nos troupes sont en marche pour Brest. Je les y joindrai dès que la marine sera prête. J'attends ce moment avec bien de l'impatience.[1]

Diary, 23–6 August 1797

T.C.D., Tone papers, MS 2049, ff 275ᵛ–276ʳ; *Life*, ii, 440–41.

23 Aug. 1797

Breakfasted (viz. all three of us)[2] with Van Leyden, secretary to the committee for foreign affairs, whom I had seen, with Lewines, at my first visit to the Hague.[3] We had a good deal of conversation on the state of Ireland, but nothing new, as it consisted entirely of questions on his part and answers on ours. He was so good as to give us English papers, from the 1st July to the 10th instant,[4] with which we retired to our lodgings and set ourselves to devour them.

24 Aug. 1797

Hard at work at the newspapers. All we have found remarkable is that Roger O'Connor[5] surrendered himself and was discharged about the middle of July, Arthur O'Connor the 31st of July,[6] his sureties being Fitzgerald and Emmet, and it should seem, tho' it is not very clearly expressed, that nearly if not the whole of the other state prisoners have been also enlarged. God almighty send! If we arrive, they will be of use; if we do not, at least they are not languishing in prison.

26 Aug. 1797

The General[7] has submitted his plan to Gen[era]l Dejean, who approves of it entirely in a military point of view provided the frigates can get round to meet us; but of this, barring some very unforeseen accident, I think there can be little doubt inasmuch as the Admiral himself, who seems at present cool enough in all which concerns the expedition, has already, in his project of the 10th in[stan]t,[8] not only given his opinion in favor of the possibility of

---

[1] No signature at foot.

[2] i.e. Lowry, Tennent and Tone himself (cf. Diary entries for 16 and 17 Aug. 1797, above, p. 128).

[3] On 28 June 1797 (see Diary for that date, above, pp 95–6). In *Life* the words 'at my first visit to the Hague' are omitted. Tone's first visit was in fact towards the end of April (see above, pp 66–72).

[4] *Life*, ii, 440, reads '10th August'.

[5] Roger O'Connor (1762–1834), eldest brother of Arthur O'Connor; he was arrested in 1797 and again in 1798 (*D.N.B.*).

[6] *Life*, ii, 440, reads '3d of July'. In fact Arthur O'Connor was liberated on bail on 31 July (*Dublin Evening Post*, 1 Aug. 1797; *Faulkner's Dublin Journal*, 3 Aug. 1797).

[7] Daendels. For his plan, see Tone's diary for 21 Aug. (above, pp 131–2).

[8] Note by Tone: 'Vide Journal of the 12th instant'. This is printed above (pp 123–5).

effectuating the passage north about with frigates but even offered to command the expedition. The General's plan is now before the government with General Dejean's approbation, and he tells me he has strong hopes it will be adopted.

To Matilda Tone, 27 August 1797

Tone (Dickason) papers.

At the Hague, August the 27th, 1797

Dear Love,

Yesterday evening I received yours, of the 12th instant, another, of no date, which *'saving your favour made me suet to discyfer it'*,[1] and one from Giauque[2] of the 30th of July. It appears therefore that the last was only eight and twenty days on the road between Paris and the Hague, which considering the distance and the difficulty of communication is no way surprising; it seems likewise that you received mine of the 6th instant[3] the day before that of the 30th of July.[4] All this cannot happen by mere chance. I have no doubt but the English government has found in the post office of the republic some scoundrels base enough to betray their country and violate the sacred right of private correspondance. I hope they may open this likewise—the rascals! But to come to our affairs, I am beyond measure delighted with your present situation and with the attentions you continue to receive from my two friends.[5] Tell them both, for this letter is as much for them as for you, that I do myself a great violence in not writing to them, but you all see how it is, and I have certainly no wish to edify Lord Malmesbury with our private correspondance. For the same reason, unless some occasion occurs safer than the ordinary post, let neither of them write me a syllable that they would not wish to see in the *Messager du Soir*, or any other journal of equal reputation.

I have been here just a week and today I set off again for the Texel. What we may do there I do not know, and if I did I could not tell you, but I hope we shall do good; at least if we do not, as far as I can see we shall have nobody to accuse *'but the planets'*.[6] We have had now eight weeks of a south-westerly wind, which is truly amusing. I wrote to you three or four days ago and in my letter I gave you some grave advice, which half an hour after I thought was very foolish, but in the meantime the letter was gone and there was an end to it.[7] You are consequently to look upon the said grave advice as withdrawn, but you will I am sure approve of the principle

[1] Tobias Smollett, *Humphry Clinker* (1771), i.   [2] Lewines.
[3] Above, pp 119–20.   [4] Above, pp 111–12.
[5] Probably Henri Shee's wife, Marie Madelaine, and daughter, Françoise.
[6] Cf. 'But when the planets in evil mixture to disorder wander, what plagues, and what portents, what mutiny? What raging of the sea, shaking of earth?' (*Troilus and Cressida* (1623), I, iii).
[7] This letter has not been found.

which dictated it, as arising at the worst from perhaps a too anxious sensibility on your account. I believe it is now rather late to assure you of the unbounded (I wish I had a stronger expression) confidence that I have in your honor and discretion. I do not think I ever pretended before to give you advice, and I don't think I ever shall again, for my heart smites me at times as if I had done something unkind which God knows was the farthest of all things from my thoughts—but enough on this subject.

I am glad the Baby[1] is getting on with her French; let her speak it as often as she can, especially with Miss Sheé, whom I hope you continue to cultivate. If Mr Sheé were at home, you would find him a great accession to your stock of conversation, for he is one of the most agreeable and interesting men I have met with, and I am sure a man of the most excellent principles. I am likewise exceedingly glad that you have found an occasion to bathe the Boys which you must never neglect. Are they, or at least is Will, picking up any French?

'*Parly voo francey?—vee, madmansell!*'[2]

I pity Giauque,[3] who must be heartily embar[r]assed in his communications with Tandy and the rest; they are great *fits*. With regard to the real *men of business* whom he and his colleague Henry[4] must see occasionally, I have but one piece of advice to give him, which by the bye I all along made the rule of my own conduct, and that is to keep religiously the Highgate oath,[5] and never on any occasion to address the subaltern while he can possibly find access to the principal. My first step was in the Rue de Bacq,[6] but my *second* was plump into the Luxembourg.[7] Let him think of this. For his friend and mine, the aforesaid Citizen Henry, I am exceedingly happy upon every account, public and private, foreign and domestic, that they are together, and especially that you have acquired, as you merit, their confidence. There are no two men I more esteem and I have not forgot the honorable testimony which one of them bore in my favor in *the worst of times*.[8] What he says in his letter is I believe true. I think if everything went to our minds that I might be of use in promoting and continuing a perfect good understanding between all parties, the more so as I myself properly speaking am either of none, or of all, so equally are my friendships and connexions distributed. I am sure at least there is no one object which I should have more sincerely at heart.

Tell Citizen Giauque that there is a part of his letter which I cannot yet make out, inasmuch as my conjuring book[9] is aboard the *Vryheid*. When I am there, I shall see what it is about; in the meantime, at least so long as I do not

---

[1] Maria Tone, then aged eleven.

[2] Cf. 'Parley vow francey, vee Madmanseil' (Smollett, *Humphry Clinker* (1771), i, 157).

[3] Lewines.

[4] Probably William James MacNeven, who had arrived in France by 21 Aug. 1797 (Archives de la Guerre, Marine, GG¹, ff 261–80; see also Lewines to Barras, 25 Sept. 1797, below, pp 153–4).

[5] A jocular oath taken on entering inns in Highgate (James Thorne, *Handbook to the environs of London* (London, 1876), pp 346–7).   [6] i.e. at the ministry of foreign affairs.

[7] i.e. to the Directory.

[8] An allusion to 1794–5 when Tone was in considerable difficulties owing to the discovery of his relations with William Jackson.   [9] Key to an agreed code.

understand it, I shall observe the caution he gives me and communicate the contents to no living soul. You all know that I have here two persons in tow;[1] they are brave lads and I hope we may one day or other put them to a good use.

As for you, Madame Smith, with your apprehensions of never perhaps, seeing me any more I can only say that *'if I had not the valour of St George and the Dragon to boot, you would make me afraid'*.[2] Do you think we have escaped so many shipwrecks to founder at last in sight of port? Never be afraid; *'hang those that talk of fear!'*.[3] When I thought I was about to leave you alone in France, I was myself a little uneasy, but since the arrival of Giauque and Henry, on whose friendship I rely as on my own soul, I can safely say my anxiety is diminished nine tenths; but enough of this. I hope neither you and I need vapour of our courage, or at least our fortitude at this time of day.

I do not write to those active citizens, because this letter is in fact as much addressed to them as you. You will of course let them know as soon as you receive it, and I desire you may dine together then on the said joyful occasion; I leave you to judge whether I should be happy to be of the party. Apropos! I see in an English paper that a great number of persons have been discharged from the different state prisons in —— without trial, and especially one person[4] who was kept up alone in a round tower. His bail were a barrister well known to you all three, and a gentleman who was formerly Major of the 54th regiment[5] but dismissed the service for his politics, which were, it seems, not purely orthodox. This happened the 31st of last month. My paper is out, and considering that I had nothing to say, or more correctly, nothing that I dared say, because of my worthy friends of the *Poste*, I think you may be satisfied with the length of my letter.

Adieu then, dearest Life; love your Babies and kiss them for me ten thousand times, and duck and splash them in cold water. I have not time nor room to write to a Daff.[6] My love sincerely to Giauque and Henry[7] and believe ever your most affectionate husband

J. Smith

'Husband! I tremble at the name!'[8]

[*No address*]

To Matilda Tone, 31 August 1797

Tone (Dickason) papers.

[1] Lowry and Tennent.   [2] Sheridan, *The rivals* (1775), IV, i.   [3] *Macbeth*, V, iii.
[4] Arthur O'Connor, who was arrested in Dublin on 2 Feb. 1797 and held in solitary confinement in the Bermingham Tower at Dublin Castle until 31 July.
[5] Thomas Addis Emmet and Lord Edward Fitzgerald (see above, p. 133).
[6] i.e. to one of his children.   [7] i.e. Lewines and MacNeven.
[8] Cf. 'When I think of my husband, I tremble and am in a cold sweat' (William Wycherley, *The country wife* (1675), IV, i).

Aboard the *Vryheid*, at the Texel,
15 Fructidor, an 5.
31 August 1797[1]

Dearest Love,

I wrote to you from the Hague on the 4th and 11th instants,[2] On the 12th I set off for the Texel, where I arrived last night and found everything, the wind always included, in *statu quo*. It is today the last of August, and just fifty-four days since I came on board, during the whole of which time we have had invariably a foul wind, and every day that the season advances lessens the probability of our having a fair one In short this unfortunate delay, and other circumstances which I cannot trust to the Post Office, make me think very seriously of our situation and that of our friends.

Supposing a peace made, leaving our unfortunate country in slavery (and all that is at least possible), what are we to do? I wish you, Giauque and Henry[3] would hold a council of war on that subject.

You need not, all of you, be told that in that case, it is no country for us; not to speak of the persecutions and insults to which we should be personally exposed. I believe no generous mind could bear to exist under such a government as will be to a certainty established there. England will take care that she shall never be again exposed to danger and uneasiness from that quarter; and if the situation of Ireland before the war was such as to decide us to hazard everything to throw off the yoke, it cannot be supposed we will return and again bend our necks under it, when it will be rendered a thousand times more grievous and oppressive than ever; neither, as to many of us, would the passage be open for us to return, if we had so little true spirit as to entertain so humiliating an idea. It remains then to see what party is at once the most practicable and most becoming to us to take, and that is a question much easier proposed than answered.

If you and I had not been in America already, it would be solved at once, but after the experience we have had of that country I confess I feel not the least propensity to go thither. I leave it to you to detail to your colle[a]gues the circumstances which render it, of all the places I have yet seen, by far the most disagreeable to live in; nevertheless if no more eligible place could be found, I could make up my mind, even for that, but I confess it would be *multa gemens*, 'with many a groan'.

If the patriots of Ireland have acted really upon principle, I cannot suppose that a vast number of them will not emigrate *en masse* in the supposition of all hopes of freedom at home being lost; if they are not capable of that exertion, they have deceived themselves exceedingly in the idea that they had the energy

---

[1] In fact 15 Fructidor year 5 was 1 September 1797. Tone states in the body of this letter that 'it is today the last of August' and so it must be presumed that '15 Fructidor' was an error for '14 Fructidor', i.e 31 August as here stated.

[2] Tone's letter of 4 Fructidor has not been found; the letter of 11 Fructidor is given above, pp 134–6.

[3] i.e. Lewines and MacNeven.

which makes revolutions. When Louis 14th was at the gates of Amsterdam[1] the Dutch prepared every vessel that could swim and were determined in the last extremity to pierce their dykes, to deluge their country and set sail instantly to seek for liberty in India, if they could not enjoy it at home. Have we less courage than the Dutch, or will the situation of Ireland be less terrible than that of Holland would have been had she been conquered? Will England govern her rebels with lenity or will she ever esteem us but as rebels?

I love my country. I would hazard my life with pleasure for her independance so long as I saw a shadow of a possibility of success. It is only in the case of utter desperation, such as for example a peace between France and England, leaving us at the mercy of the latter, that I would think of a voluntary exile. I would stick by the vessel, and it would not be until the last plank sunk under me that I would think of swimming for my life; in that case I think I should desert no principle by consulting my own preservation. You and I know what exile is; it is therefore not lightly that we would propose such a measure to those we love and esteem, but surely there are things more to be dreaded than even exile. If we cannot obtain the permission to breathe in our own country but by an indecent prostration at the feet of our oppressor, surely it is time for us to think of quitting a soil no longer fit for us, nor we for it. But more, exile is terrible, I feel it well; it is however to be borne by men who have acted and suffered together, who know and respect each other's principles. I can conceive no spectacle more interesting than the emigration of such men, who have hazarded so much for their country, and who yield at last only to an inevitable necessity; and I still think there is among us enough of virtue and of resolution to embrace even banishment rather than slavery; we have at least the energy of despair.

Perhaps all this is romance, but I do not believe it is. I feel myself abundantly capable to adopt the conduct I propose and I am very far from thinking I have either more spirit or more principle than the great majority of those with whom I acted and suffered; what I can do, they may well do.

Supposing that a peace were made tomorrow, and that the measure of emigration were to be adopted by those who could neither with dignity nor safety remain in Ireland, once again where should we go?

I object to America, that is British America, if any other place can be found; at the same time I know not what better to propose, but as I am at present on a system of castle building, I will communicate my *reveries* to you and our friends, and I give you free leave to find them as extravagant as you please. Remember only that it is not from whim or fancy, but from hard necessity, that I have fallen into these speculations.

In the first place I hear a rumour that Spain has ceded Louisiana, or that part of America which lies beyond the Mississip[p]i, to France.[2] If that be so, which Giauque can soon find out, there is one of the finest countries in the

---

[1] In 1672.   [2] Spain ceded Louisiana to France in 1800.

world by all accounts, and I should have little doubt but that we should meet
with every encouragement from the French government in case we desired to
go thither. I have no books here to refer to, but let your friends rummage in
Paris, and they will certainly find a detailed account of the soil, productions,
&c., and then they will be better enabled to judge of this, my first idea.

In the next place, if the Republic retains the islands in the archipelago,
viz. Corfou, Zante, Cephalonia, &c., which formerly belonged to Venice,[1] if
I do not much mistake there are some of them where the soil, climate, &c.,
are delicious, but for this again I have no books to refer to. I am morally
certain that the French government would give us countenance and support,
and most probably allot us a proportion of territory and in that case we
should be nearer civilization than on my first plan; such of us as had money
(in which number we are not) and inclination might follow commerce &c.
In short I think this plan is reasonable enough.

In the third place there is the Isle of France,[2] also belonging to the republic,
which I merely throw out for examination, for I know nothing myself
about it.

In the fourth place, there is the Cape of Good Hope, supposing it to be
restored, as I presume it will, to the Batavian republic. It is undoubtedly in
many respects a very fine country, and I have spoken already both to the
Admiral and the General[3] about it. I am almost sure the Dutch government
would do everything that we could reasonably desire, as it would be mani-
festly their interest to procure for that colony a reinforcement of men who
certainly bear no devotion to England and who might on a future occasion
be ready to defend it. Let your colle[a]gues read Peter Kolben,[4] Vaillant,[5]
and any other voyages they can find, for I am in a most pitiable state of
ignorance and can get no books for love nor money.

In the fifth place, Gen[era]l Daendels tells me that between the provinces
of Guelders and Overyssel there is a great tract of country at the disposition of government which at present produces almost nothing but which is
easily reclaimable and at a small expence, and by opening two or three short
canals, would have a *débouché* for their productions into the interior of the
republic; he tells me also that he is sure the government would be glad to
grant a sufficient portion of this territory to a colony, such as I described
to him, and he gives it the preference over the Cape, which we also mooted
together. This plan depends for its eligibility absolutely on the nature of the
soil, of which I know nothing but by the report of Gen[era]l Daendels.

---

[1] In October 1793, by the treaty of Campo-Formio, Austria agreed to a number of Venetian islands
including Corfu becoming French possessions.   [2] Mauritius.

[3] Dewinter and Daendels.

[4] Peter Kolb (1675–1726), secretary to the Dutch East India Company; his account of the Cape
was translated into English as *The present state of the Cape of Good Hope* (London, 1731).

[5] François Le Vaillant (1753–1824), naturalist; explored Cape, 1781–4; author of *Voyage dans
l'intérieur de l'Afrique par le Cap de Bonne Espérance* (Paris, 1790; trans. London, 1790).

In the sixth place, which I keep for the last, because it is the wildest of all, there is some one or other of the islands discovered by Cook in the South Sea, and of which he has given such enchanting descriptions. Every man has a corner to go mad in, and you know my folly in regard to the Sandwich Islands.[1] Certainly however I think that, if one could get there, without umbrage to Spain, and with the consent of England guaranteed to us by France, we might lay the foundation of a republic which, tho' it would neither be great, rich nor powerful, might be very happy. There are numbers of islands where the situation, soil and climate are excellent and I confess this last plan is my favorite; but for its execution many previous steps are necessary, from the distance and other circumstances, which will naturally present themselves to you. I will only observe that it ought not to be thought of if the proposed emigration did not consist of at least one thousand persons, but this I submit.

Lastly, for the *pis aller*, there are the United States of North America, on which I need say nothing.

I beg you and your colle[a]gues may take all this, wild as I know a great part of it is, into your serious consideration. Remember I am not proposing emigration to you as a matter of choice, but merely examining where we can best go in case emigration be inevitable, and I certainly regard it as such in case a peace be made wherein we are not included.

After all, maybe I am enthusiastic in my ideas; maybe the people, maybe even their leaders will, even in that case, submit and remain in their country, degraded and oppressed as it will be, then more than ever. I confess I can hardly bring myself to suppose it. Surely there is yet such a thing as principle to which a man will sacrifice everything; when I consider that Cromwell[2] and Hamden[3] were embarked for America,[4] flying persecution and in pursuit of liberty, when I recall the times, the men, the state of the country they were about to leave, and that to which they were going, I cannot think that it is a wild supposition, that in our country men are to be found capable of a like exertion. What America was to them, some other spot may be to us; there are few more savage than New England was in 1630; we have as good a cause, we have far greater necessity, let us see if we have as much energy and courage.

My dear friends, and you, the dearest of my friends, and that I love a thousand times more than my existence, where is the country that with the society of those we love and esteem we could not be happy in? Exile I know is terrible, but so is slavery, and we have only left the melancholy option; for my part, I am decided and I most solemnly declare that no situation that could be offered me would buy me to return to Ireland while she remains

---

[1] For Tone's proposals for the colonisation of the Sandwich Islands, made in communications with the British government in 1788 and 1790, see above, vol. I, pp 10–16, 68–89, and vol. II, pp 278–9, 289–90.   [2] Oliver Cromwell (1599–1658), lord protector of England, 1653–8 (*D.N.B.*).
[3] John Hampden (1594–1643), a parliamentary opponent of Charles I (*D.N.B.*).
[4] 'If we may believe . . . two famous Royalists', Cromwell and Hampden were in 1638 on the point of emigrating to America (Daniel Neal, *The history of the Puritans* (4 vols, London, 1732–8), ii, 332).

at the mercy of her tyrant. I do not think so ill of my countrymen as to suppose that I am singular in the determination.

Let me beg of you, all three, to answer this letter as speedily as possible, and if you think me a wrongheaded enthusiast, do not scruple to tell me so, for I in some degree suspect it myself. Only write to me with the same frankness and sincerity that I address you, for you will see by this letter that I have stripped my heart naked before you. In the meantime, do not suppose that my ideas on emigration will in the smallest degree influence my conduct. I am here at my post and I will do my duty, but I think it right that we should regard our situation in all possible lights and be prepared for the very worst. Our conduct in the last extremity, when hope itself is lost (if that should arrive) will be the touchstone of our real principles, and I have no doubt but we will come out with honor from the trial.

Dear Love, this letter is grown a little volume, but it is the greatest, I might almost say the only, pleasure of my life to write to you. This you see is addressed to you and your colle[a]gues equally. Let them especially answer me at length and let me know what they think would probably be the sentiments of the friends and fellow slaves they left behind on the subject of emigration, *supposing all were desperate*, which, by the bye, you are not to infer from anything in this letter, as I write upon a pure hypothesis. Adieu, dearest Love; take care of yourself and the Babies, and kiss them for me a thousand times.

J. Smith

Tell Giauque I have made out his riddles, and that I have only to answer him in the words of Macheath: '*That Jemmy Twitcher should peach me, I own surprises me!*'.[1] I shall of course keep the secret. My best regards to Madame Sheé and family.

Diary, 27 August–3 September 1797

T.C.D., Tone papers, MS 2049, ff 276^r–277^v; *Life*, ii, 441–3.

27 Aug. 1797[2]

The General[3] set off on his return for the Texel, whither we followed him next day and arrived the 30th.

1 Sept. 1797

A new system, rendered indispensable by the course of events, has been mentioned to me today by the General, which will probably oblige me to

---

[1] John Gay, *The beggar's opera* (1728), scene 14.
[2] The entry for this date was evidently written up later, probably on 1 Sept. 1797.
[3] Daendels.

make a course to the headquarters of the army of Sambre and Meuse, and from that on to Paris. Admiral Duncan's fleet has been reinforced to 21 sail of the line, so that even if the wind came round in our favor, it would be madness in us to venture an action with such a terrible inferiority of force, in addition to which we have now, in consequence of the delay caused by the wind, not above ten days' provisions remaining for the troops on board. The plan proposed is, in fact, but an improvement on the last one, viz. to land the troops and canton them in the neighbourhood so as to be able to collect them in 48 hours; to appear to have renounced the idea of the expedition, but in the meantime to revictual the fleet with all diligence and secresy, which may occupy probably a month; to endeavour even to reinforce it by one or two vessels which might in that time be got ready for sea. All this will bring us to the time of the equinox when it will be impossible for the enemy (who will besides, it is probable, have relaxed in his vigilance, in consequence of these manoeuvres) to keep the sea. When all is ready the troops are to be reimbarked with the greatest expedition and a push to be made instantly for Scotland, as already detailed. '*Capot me, but it wears a face!*'[1] Such is the present idea, which we will probably lick still more into shape. The General talks of sending me to the Hague to confer with the Dutch government and General Dejean; from that to Wetzlar to communicate with Hoche, and thence to Paris to open the affair to the Minister of the Marine. '*A very pretty journey indeed! Besides, where's the money?*'[2] Well, I do not see how I can be so well employed for this vacant month, so in God's name I am ready.

3 Sept. 1797

This day the General gave me my instructions to set off to join General Hoche at Wetzlar and to bring him a copy of the memorial containing the plan already mentioned.[3] In addition he gave me verbal instructions to the following purport. That, in addition to the written plan, it might be expedient to follow up the first debarquation by a second of 15,000 of the French troops now in the pay of Holland, with which reinforcement the army being brought up to 30,000 men, could maintain itself in Scotland in spite of any force that could be brought against them; that they might even penetrate into England, and by that means force the enemy to a peace; that 25,000 might be employed on this service and the remaining 5,000 detached into Ireland, from which it was morally certain a great portion of the troops now there would be withdrawn to defend England herself; that if General Hoche would, in that case, take the command of the united armies, he (Daendels) desired nothing better than to serve under him; if not, he was ready to serve under any other French general, being a senior officer, in which case each army was, as to all matters of discipline, administration, &c., to remain under their respective

---

[1] The source of this quotation has not been traced.   [2] Source not traced.
[3] See Diary for 21 Aug. (above, pp 131–2).

chiefs. He mentioned Chaumont[1] as a proper person, in case Hoche declined, to command the expedition, MacDonal[2] to command the French troops, and himself, of course, the Dutch. He desired me likewise (but this was matter of great confidence) to tell Hoche that in case he approved of the plan he should write to the Directory, recommending to them to press the Dutch government strongly to the adoption of it; that to this effect the Directory should write a letter to the committee for foreign affairs at the Hague flattering and praising them extremely for what they had hitherto done and the great exertions they had made, and exhorting them to continue the same laudable zeal; reminding them that France was now negociating with England and if it were not for the interests of her allies could have an honorable peace in an hour; that the success of the enterprise in question would exceedingly strengthen her hands and infallibly secure the restitution of all the Dutch possessions in both Indies; finally to make them feel that it was incumbent on them to make every effort on their part to second the Republic at a time when she was exposing herself to a war for their interests, when she could, by renouncing them, secure a peace in all respects so necessary to herself at this moment. In addition to all this Daendels desired me to explain to Hoche the necessity of a greater degree of communication on the part of the French government, that of the Batavian Republic being in utter ignorance of the state of preparations at Brest and elsewhere, and whether any, and what degree of, support or co-operation might be expected, which naturally threw a certain degree of damp and had a sinister effect on their operations. With these instructions I set off the same day with Lowry and Tenent, who determined to take this opportunity to go to Paris. The General accompanied [us] as far as Alkmaar, where we lay that night, and pursued our journey at six the next morning.

To Matilda Tone, 8 September 1797

Tone (Dickason) papers.

À Brusselles, ce 22 Fructidor, an 5

Dear Love,

Inclosed you have a letter which I wrote to you several days since at the Hague and which I entrusted to the landlord of the hotel to put in the post office. Five days ago on my return to the Hague I found my letter lying *in statu quo*, at which I have been exceedingly vexed. Since the date thereof, I wrote to you from on board the *Vryheid* at the Texel, which letter I hope you received in course.

---

[1] Pierre Antoine Dupont-Chaumont (1759–1838), *sous–lieutenant*, 1776; lieut, 1783; aide-de-camp to La Fayette, 1789; *général de brigade*, 1793; *général de division*, 1795; condemned to death for ordering a retreat, 1795, but reprieved; inspector of infantry of the *armée du Nord*, 1796–7; served under Napoleon as inspector-general of infantry (Six, *Dict. des généraux & amiraux*).

[2] Alexandre Macdonald. William Tone adds (*Life*, ii, 442): 'Now Duke of Tarente'.

This will be delivered to you by my friends Black and Howard,[1] to whom I refer you for all manner of news, public and private.

The mail which should have been here yesterday from Paris is not yet arrived, which gives rise to sundry conjectures[2] of which I know nothing having not even seen a French newspaper of later date than the 11th instant; however I am not very uneasy on your account, as I am sure whatever may happen in France, at least the women and children will be protected, and for the men, they can shift for themselves.

Adieu, dearest Life and soul, and take care of yourself and the Babies.

Your ever affectionate
J. Smith
Adj[utan]t G[enera]l

À la Citoyenne Smith
À Nanterre

From General Hermann Wilhelm Daendels, 8 September 1797

Tone (Dickason) papers.

Daendels informs Tone that his government has agreed to disembark its troops temporarily; he welcomes the republican coup and news of 'a violent insurrection in Scotland'.

La Haye, ce 8ᵉ Septembre 1797
à onze heures du soir

Le Lieutenant-Général Daendels
à l'Adjudant-Général Smith

Notre gouvernement, mon cher Smith, s'est enfin déterminé à acquiéscer à la proposition que je lui ai faite, de débarquer provisoirement nos troupes pour les cantonner sur les côtes à proximité de la Rade de manière qu'au premier ordre dans 24 heures elles pourront être réembarquées.

Les heureuses nouvelles que nous recevons aujourd'hui de Paris, le triomphe que la République vient d'obtenir sur le royalisme,[3] persuadent notre gouvernement que celui de France va pouvoir enfin travailler avec énergie à suivre ses projets contre l'ennemi commun, et sûrement alors il s'empressera

---

[1] *Noms de guerre* of Alexander Lowry and John Tennent (see below, p. 161).

[2] An allusion to the events of 18 Fructidor (see below, n. 3).

[3] By a coup d'état carried out on 18 Fructidor (4 September 1797), with support from troops commanded by General Augereau, a triumvirate of Barras, Reubell and La Révellière expelled Carnot and Barthélemy from the Directory; subsequently fifty-three deputies were ordered to be deported, thirty-two journalists were arrested and forty-two Parisian and provincial newspapers were banned; laws against émigrés and refractory priests were reinstated; there were over a hundred executions (D. M. G. Sutherland, *France, 1789–1815: revolution and counter-revolution* (London, 1985), pp 305–6).

de le seconder de tous ses moyens, ainsi, mon cher Smith, assurez bien le Général Hoche qu'il peut compter sur nous, mais n'oubliez cependant pas de lui démontrer, ainsi que je vous en ai parlé dans notre entretien, la nécessité de la démarche que je l'ai prié de faire, et surtout, qu'il daigne nous instruire franchement de ce qu'il espère maintenant des tentatives que fera la France. Le triomphe du gouvernement sur les factions lève, je crois, tous les obstacles que la mauvaise volonté pouvoit succiter.[1] Tout concoure à rendre l'occasion maintenant plus favorable que jamais. Vos gazettes nous assurent unanimement qu'il vient de se manifester une insurrection violente dans l'Écosse,[2] ainsi la facilité du succès de l'entreprise, que vous devez communiquer de ma part au Général Hoche, devient plus que probable.

J'espère fermement que nous ne laisserons pas échapper un si heureux concours de circonstances. Je brûle d'impatience de voir cette espérance bientôt se réaliser, et je vous prie, mon cher Smith, de me donner par le retour du courrier des nouvelles positives sur tout ce dont je vous ai chargé de vous informer.

De mon côté, je vais travailler sans relâche à faire réapprovisionner la flotte et à préparer tous nos moyens.

Daendels

Diary, 4–13 September 1797

T.C.D., Tone papers, MS 2049, ff 277ᵛ–278ᵛ; *Life*, ii, 443–4.

This diary shows signs of having been written up in arrears, on 13 or 14 Sept.

4–12 Sept. 1797

These eight days I spent on the road between Alkmaar and Wetzlar. I came by Brussells, tho' it was out of my way, in order to accommodate my comrades,[3] whom I put into the diligence for Paris the 8th. At Brussells we heard the first rumour of the famous conspiracy of Carnot, Pichegru &c., and the downfal of the Royalists on the 18 fructidor.[4] Having sent them off, I proceeded by Liège &c. to Juliers, where luckily finding the *courier des armées*, I got with him into the mail and, travelling night and day, I arrived at length at Headquarters exceedingly fatigued, my journey from Brussells having cost me, one way or other, about 150 *livres*.

---

[1] *Recte* 'susciter', meaning 'give rise to'.

[2] Disturbances against the implementation of the Scottish militia act occurred in different parts of Scotland during the summer of 1797.   [3] Alexander Lowry and John Tennent.

[4] Pichegru, secretly in correspondence with émigré royalists since the autumn of 1795, was deprived of his command by the Directory in March 1796 for incompetence; he was elected a year later president of the Council of Five Hundred in which, after the elections of March 1797, royalists were numerous; but in July and August his treason to the French republic became manifest. Carnot was more a compromiser than a conspirator. (Sutherland, *France, 1789–1815*, pp 300, 303–4). For the coup d'état that followed on 18 Fructidor (4 September), see above, p. 144, n. 3.

13 Sept. 1797

This day I saw General Hoche, who was just returned from Frankfort. He has been very ill with a violent cold and has still a cough, which makes me seriously uneasy about him; he does not seem to apprehend anything himself, but I should not be surprised, for my part, if in three months he were in a rapid consumption; he is dreadfully altered and has a dry hollow cough that it is distressing to the last degree to hear him. I should be sincerely and truly sorry if anything were to happen him, but I very much fear he will scarcely throw off his present illness. I immediately explained to him the cause of my arrival, gave him Daendels's plan and the map of Scotland,[1] and such further elucidation as I was able in conversation. He shook his head at the idea of a second embarkation at the mouth of the Clyde and observed that, if we got safe into Scotland, the British would immediately detach a squadron of frigates into the Irish channel, which would arrive to a moral certainty before the Dutch frigates, which were, according to the plan proposed, to go north about and so cut off the communication with Ireland. As to the officers I named to him,[2] he observed that 'Chaumont was as much a general as he himself was that bottle', pointing to one that stood on the table before him; that as to Macdonal,[3] he was a good officer, but he knew he would not go. I replied that as to the second embarkation, I was entirely of his opinion and that I looked upon it as inexecutable; that nevertheless I thought well of the project as a measure against England; that it would, if it succeeded, embarrass her most extremely, and if it failed, the French republic would not lose a man nor a shilling, and that consequently it was, I thought, a measure that should be adopted, or at least very maturely weighed, as it might be, for example, in his hands, susceptible of great improvements. He then told me he would take it into his most serious consideration and let me know the result in three or four days; in the meantime I was to attend his orders. Our conversation ended by his desiring me to give him a note in writing of the principal events which took place on board the Dutch fleet while I lay at the Texel, and so we parted.

To General Lazare Hoche,
p. 13 September 1797

Tone (Dickason) papers.

This is a fragment of a letter, evidently the 'note in writing of the principal events which took place on board the Dutch fleet while I lay at the Texel' which Tone refers to in his diary for 13 Sept. 1797 (above).

---

[1] See Diary for 21 Aug. 1797 (above, p. 132),
[2] *Life*, ii, 444, reads 'as to the officers whom Daendels named'.   [3] Alexandre Macdonald.

pour un moment. Le signal fut encore donné pour le départ et au moment
où nous levions le second ancre le vent changea encore une fois et après
avoir varié pendant quelque tems, il se fixa enfin dans son ancien point,
S[ud]-ou[est], qui nous était précisément le plus contraire.[1]

Le 2 fructidor, je me rendis à La Haye en vertu des ordres du général;[2]
je l'y trouvai le 3.[3] Il me dit que son gouvernement avoit totalement rejetté le
plan de l'amiral.[4] Cependant, il me dit qu'en considération de la saison avancée
qui rendait le passage du Nord absolument impraticable et de la consom[m]ation
extraordinaire des provisions occasionnée par le retard, il avoit imaginé, lui-
même, un nouveau plan qui devoit s'exécuter, dans le cas d'un combat
avantageux ou même à succès égal entre les flottes anglaise et Hollandaise. Il
est inutile que j'entre dans le détail de ce plan puisque j'ai eu l'honneur de
vous l'exposer dans le courant de la conversation que j'ai eue avec vous ce
matin et de vous mettre sous les yeux une copie du Mémoire du général.

Le 10, nous retournâmes au Texel après que le général eût fourni son plan à
son gouvernement.[5] Nous trouvâmes à notre arrivée que l'escadre anglaise étoit
renforcé[e] de quatre v[aisse]aux de ligne, ce qui faisoit un total de 21 v[aisse]aux
de ligne; ainsi toute idée de forcer le passage devenoit impraticable. Cependant
comme l'équinox approchoit déjà & que l'ennemi n'oseroit pas tenir la mer, le
plan susmentionné restoit encore praticable en profitant du moment où le passage
seroit libre pour faire un effort à l'effet de gagner notre destination.

Le 17, le général me donna des instructions pour vous rejoindre.[6] Je suis
parti le même jour après avoir passé 57 jours au Texel. Pendant tout ce tems
nous eûmes des vents toujours contraires et qui soufflaient du S[ud]-ou[est] à
l'exception des deux occasions dont je vous ai déjà parlé où ils étaient favorables pour un instant.

En quittant la flotte hollandoise et afin de rendre justice aux troupes de
terre et de mer ainsi qu'à leurs commandans respectifs, je crois qu'il est de
mon devoir de vous déclarer que je les ai vus tous animés du meilleur esprit
possible & je n'ai nul doute que, si les vents l'eûssent permis, ils se seroient
distingués d'une manière à vous plaire. J'ai eu aussi la satisfaction de remarquer, à mon départ, que la froideur qui existoit entre le général et l'amiral
sembloit être, en grande partie, évanouie. J'ignore absolument, comme j'ai
déjà eu l'honneur de vous l'observer, quelle en a été la cause prémière.

Tel est, général, le résultat de mon expédition. Je n'ai pas besoin de vous
observer aue cette esquisse rapide est pour vous seul.

Salut et respect
L'adj[t] Général
J. Smith

---

[1] These events are related in Tone's diary for 18 Aug. 1797 (above, p. 131).　　[2] Daendels.
[3] Tone states in his diary for 20 Aug. that on the previous day (2 fructidor) he, Lowry and Tennent
travelled to the Hague in one carriage, Daendels and Grasfeldt in another (see above, p. 131).
[4] Dewinter.　　[5] Cf. Tone's diary for 26 Aug. (above, pp 133–4).
[6] Cf. Tone's diary for 3 Sept. (above, p. 142).

Diary, 14 September 1797

T.C.D., Tone papers, MS 2049, ff 278ᵛ–279ʳ; *Life*, ii, 444–5.

14 Sept. 1797

I have read this day a great number of the pieces relative to the last royal conspiracy. There can be no possible doubt of the guilt of Pichegru and several others. It seems so far back as three years ago, when he commanded the army of the Rhine, he was in treaty with Prince Condé[1] to proclaim Louis 18 and march upon Paris, and if it had not been for the stupid obstinacy of Condé, who refused to let the Austrians have any share in the business (which Pichegru made an indispensable condition), the treason w[oul]d have taken effect, that is, so far as Pichegru could ensure it, for I have no doubt but he would speedily have found himself deserted by his army, as that scoundrel Dumouriez was before him. Such treachery in a man of the situation, character and high reputation of Pichegru is enough to put a man out of humour with human nature. If I had any doubt of his guilt the proclamation of Moreau to his army would decide me, wherein he mentions that papers had fallen into his hands which proved the fact of correspondance, which papers he had transmitted to the Directory the 17th fructidor (viz. the day before Pichegru and the other conspirators were arrested). This testimony is the stronger inasmuch as Moreau has been the pupil and friend of Pichegru, and is at this moment on bad terms with the Directory. With regard to Carnot (who has made his escape), I see nothing in the pieces as yet published. There are two directors, Carnot and Barthélemi, about seventy deputies of both councils and as many journalists transported by order of the *Corps Législatif*. The report is they will be sent to Madagascar, for this time the Republic is triumphant. I hope in God they may know how to make a proper use of their victory.

To Matilda Tone, 15 September 1797

Tone (Dickason) papers.

Headquarters at Wetzlar, ce 29 fructidor an 5

Dear Love,

I write you just one word to apprise you of my safe arrival here two days ago. I presume you have before this seen two of my friends[2] whom I consigned

---

[1] Louis Joseph de Bourbon, prince de Condé (1736–1818), commanded the émigré army, 1792–6 (*Dict. biog. franç.*).   [2] Lowry and Tennent (see above, p. 143).

to you from Brusselles per the diligence; you are of consequence fully instructed in everything that has passed for the last three months. I have not a syllable of news of any kind to add, except that I observe the spirit of the army considerably mounted since the late events in Paris. What the general may decide with regard to me I shall not know for three or four days; the instant I am informed I will write to you. This letter is short and dry but that is no fault of mine, for I literally have not one syllable to communicate to you, as I believe it is no news to assure you that I doat upon you every day more than the last.

> You are my true and honorable wife,
> As dear to me as are the ruddy drops
> That visit my sad heart.[1]

Adieu, dearest Life and soul; remember me affectionately to all my friends, take care of yourself and our dearest babies and believe me,

Ever your most affectionate
J. Smith

You need not write until you hear from me again. Give my compliments to the active citizens your sons. '*Service to Saul and the kitten.*'[2] My love to a Bab.[3] Does she take to her French hugely?

À la citoyenne Smith
chez le citoyen Sheé
à Nanterre près de Paris.

Diary, 17 September 1797

T.C.D., Tone papers, MS 2049, ff 279ʳ–280ʳ; *Life*, ii, 445–6.

17 Sept. 1797

The General's[4] health is in a most alarming state, and nobody here seems to me to suspect it, at least to the extent that I do. I look upon it as a moral impossibility that he can hold out long if he persists to remain at the army, as he seems determined to do. As for his physician, I have no great faith in his skill, and in short I have the most serious alarms for his life. I should be very sincerely sorry, for every reason, public and private, that we were to lose him. Urgent as the affair is on which I am here, I have found it impossible to speak to him about it, and God knows when, or whether I may ever find an opportunity, which, in addition to my personal regard[5] for him, is a circumstance which very much aggravates my uneasiness. Today he has been removed by four grenadiers from one chamber to another, for he is unable to walk. It is terrible

---

[1] *Julius Caesar*, II, i.   [2] Smollett, *Humphry Clinker* (1771), ii.   [3] Maria Tone.
[4] Hoche's.   [5] *Life*, ii, 445, adds 'and love'.

to see a fine, handsome fellow in the very flower of his youth and strength so reduced. My heart bleeds for him. I am told that the late attacks made on him by the Royalists in the convention, and the journalists in their pay, prayed exceedingly on his spirits and are the probable cause of his present illness. Is it not strange that a man who has faced death a thousand times with intrepidity in the field should sink under the calumny of a rabble of miscreants? Wrote yesterday to Gen[era]l Daendels to apologize for my silence, letting him know that I found it as yet impossible to speak to Gen[era]l Hoche about our affair, partly on account of the state of his health, and partly on account of his being so extremely occupied, as well by the command of the two armies of the Rhine, and Sambre & Meuse, as by the late events in Paris, promising at the same time to write again in three or four days, and in the meantime entreating him to continue his preparations on the system we had settled at my departure from the Texel. I did not, in this letter, let him know the very dangerous state in which I consider the General to be. There is a rumour that Massaredo and Jervis have had a fight off Cadiz, and that the latter has had the worst of it. It is too good news to be true and consequently I do not believe it.[1] I remember the last drubbing the Spaniards got from Jervis was in like manner preceded for seven or eight days by the report of a grand victory. Le Tourneur and Maret[2] are recalled from Lisle, and two others (Treilhard,[3] I think, and some one else) named in their place. That does not look, in my mind, like a speedy termination of the negotiation with England. Merlin of Douai,[4] late Minister of Justice, and François de Neufchâteau, late Minister of the Interior, are named to replace, in the Directory, Barthélemi and Carnot. There is no one man in France so obnoxious to the Royalists as Merlin. Of course his nomination is a proof that they are at this moment completely down. All is quiet at Paris.

To Matilda Tone, 19 September 1797

Tone (Dickason) papers.

ÉTAT-MAJOR GÉNÉRAL

ARMÉE DE	*Au Quartier-Général à* Vetzlar
SAMBRE ET MEUSE	*le* 3me *jour complémentaire an* 5 *de la*
	République française, une et indivisible

---

[1] It was not true. The Spaniards at this time did not attempt to leave Cadiz.

[2] Bernard Hugues Maret (1763–1839), a journalist, was one of the delegation appointed before 18 fructidor to negotiate with Malmesbury at Lille; duke of the empire, 1809; peer of France, 1831 (*Nouvelle biographie générale; Dict. parl. franç.*).

[3] Jean Baptiste Treilhard (1742–1810), member of the Convention and of the Council of Five Hundred; he attended the congress of Rastadt as minister plenipotentiary (*Dict. parl. franç.*).

[4] Philippe Antoine Merlin (1754–1838), known as Merlin of Douai; member of the Convention; though a moderate, he presented the law of suspects to the assembly; member of the Council of Ancients; member of the Directory, 1797–9; count of the empire, 1810 (*Dict. parl. franç.*).

LIBERTÉ   ÉGALITÉ   FRATERNITÉ[1]

Dearest Love,

It is with the most inexpressible concern that I have to acquaint you that we have lost our brave general, Hoche. He died this morning at four o'clock, I think of what we call a galloping decay.[2] Judge of the distress and confusion we are all in, especially at this important period. No later than yesterday I had a message from him relating to our affair. Send this letter to Giauque[3] instantly and let him take his measures accordingly. I know not what I may do, myself, on this occasion, nor shall I for a few days.

Adieu, dearest Life. I am in very sincere affliction.[4]

Yours ever
J. Smith

I will write again in three or four days.

Diary, 19–22 September 1797

T.C.D., Tone papers, MS 2049, ff 280ʳ–282ʳ; *Life*, ii, 446–7.

19 Sept. 1797

My fears with regard to General Hoche were but too well founded. He died this morning at 4 o'clock. His lungs seemed to me to be quite gone. This most unfortunate event has so confounded and distressed me that I know not what to think or expect will be the consequence. Wrote to my wife[5] and General Daendels instantly. Yesterday Simon by the general's order, after communicating with me, wrote to the Minister for Foreign Affairs, and of the Marine, but I know not to what effect.

20 Sept. 1797[6]

The death of General Hoche having broken my connexion with the Army of Sambre and Meuse, where I have no longer any business, I applied this

---

[1] In the original the words in capitals are printed, as are the words in italics; under 'Fraternité' there is also printed a line reading 'Le Général chef de l'État-major général de l'armée', which however is scored through.

[2] Tone probably means galloping consumption, i.e. tuberculosis. However, Fouché, minister of police under the Directory, held that Hoche was poisoned (*Mémoires de Joseph Fouché* (Paris, 1824), p. 34).

[3] i.e. Lewines.

[4] Over a year later it was reported in an English newspaper that General Hoche was said to have expired in the arms of Mr Tone 'who wears a ring ornamented with the general's hair' (*Morning Chronicle*, 13 Nov. 1798).   [5] Above.

[6] The entries for this and the following dates were written up on 22 Sept.

day for an order to set off for Paris, which I obtained instantly from Gen[era]l Lefebvre,[1] who commands in chief per interim. Set off at four o'clock and travelled all night; arrived at 12 next day at Coblentz.

21 Sept. 1797

On the road; arrived at night at Bonn.

22 Sept. 1797

This is the 1st Vendémiaire, the anniversary of the establishment of the French republic. Called early on my friend Mr Sheé, whom I found occupied in preparing for the *fête* which is to be celebrated this day. At twelve assisted at the *fête*, where Mr Sheé pronounced a discourse as president of the *Commission Intermédiaire*. At one, accompanied the procession to the *grande place*, where the Municipality &c. planted the Trees of Liberty under the auspices of France, and proclaimed the République Cis-Rhénane. The same ceremony has taken place at Cologne, Coblentz and other cities, and the idea is to erect the country between the Meuse and Rhine into an independant republic in order to terminate the difference between the Empire and France as to that territory. After the ceremony, dined in state with the Municipality of Bonn, the *Com[m]issaire Intermédiaire*,[2] the constituted authorities &c. and drank sundry loyal and constitutional toasts &c., but not too many, as appears by this journal, which I write at my inn peaceably. After dinner Mr Sheé told me he had just received intelligence from a quarter on which he very much relied that the negotiation with England[3] was knocked on the head, which, if it be true, as it is highly probable, is excellent news. Settled to call on Mr Sheé tomorrow early and shew him sundry papers &c. Came home soberly and wrote to Gen[era]l Daendels. I had promised a very pretty woman at dinner ('whose name I know not, but whose person I reverence')[4] to meet her tonight at a grand ball given by the Municipality, but I will deceive her, like a false traitor, and go to my innocent bed; yet she is very pretty, for all that, and speaks very pretty German French, and I am sure she has not a grain of cruelty in her composition, and besides, *à la guerre, comme à la guerre*, but then I must set off tomorrow, and so, '*Oh cruel fate, that gave thee to the Moor!*',[5] &c., &c. Besides I have just received a delightful letter from my dearest love, written three months ago, which has put me out of conceit with all women but herself, so, as before, I will go to my virtuous bed.

---

[1] François Joseph Lefebvre (1755–1820), officer before the Revolution; aided Bonaparte's coup d'état; maréchal de France, 1804; besieged Danzig, 1807; created duc de Dantzig by Louis XVIII, June 1814, but supported Napoleon during Hundred Days (*Nouv. biog. gén.*).   [2] Henri Sheé.
[3] The negotiations at Lille between France and Great Britain (see above, p. 110).
[4] Cf. 'whose profession I honour, but whose person I know not' (Dryden, *The Spanish fryar* (1681)).
[5] *Recte* 'Cursed fate . . .' (*Othello*, III, iii).

Edward Joseph Lewines to Paul François Jean Nicolas Barras, 25 September 1797

McPeake papers; photocopy in P.R.O.N.I., T/3048/G/3.

Writing evidently from Paris, Lewines alludes to the death of Hoche, then reports that MacNeven ('Citizen Williams'), ambassador extraordinary of the Irish 'whose memorandum I have given to you', has returned to Ireland via Wetzlar. Lewines explains that he had given MacNeven a letter for Hoche and since has received two from MacNeven confirming Hoche's assurances concerning Ireland. MacNeven informs Lewines that Hoche had told him to inform him and, on his return, the Executive Committee of the Irish, 'that he would do the impossible to be ready to leave Brest on 20 October with 10,000 and all necessary guns, cannon, ammunition etc. and that he would not await the departure of the Dutch fleet'. Lewines seeks a meeting so that he can authoritatively inform the committee whether Hoche's death will change these plans. In a postscript Lewines reports having received a letter from Daendels, dated 30 Fructidor (16 September), telling him that Hoche intended sending Tone to Paris.

[No headings]

Je n'ai pas besoin, Citoyen Directeur, de vous dire que la mort du Héros de la Vendée sera un coup de foudre pour l'Irlande. Quelque profonde que soit la douleur de la France pour la perte de cet illustre guerrier elle ne pourra pas surpasser celle que nous éprouverons. Nous savons comme il s'intéressoit à notre sort, nous savons les périls qu'il a courus pour nous, nous savons qu'il étoit prêt à les effronter pour nous de nouveau, et nous avons tout lieu de croire qu'un des premiers voeux de son coeur étoit de donner l'indépendance à notre isle. Il voyoit dans l'accomplissement de ce seul objet, l'assujetissement de l'Angleterre, l'établissement de la liberté des mers, la consolidation de la République Françoise et des libertés du Continent. Ah quand cette indépendance sera établie vous verrez que nous ne sommes pas un peuple ingrat et qu'un monument public dédié à cet ami immortel de la France et de l'Irlande attestera à l'Europe et à la postérité la reconnoissance éternelle que nous lui devons.

Je dois vous dire que le Citoyen Williams,[1] envoyé extraordinaire des Irlandois et dont je vous ai présenté le mémoire par le Ministre de la Marine,[2]

[1] i.e. William James MacNeven.

[2] Shortly after his arrival in Hamburg towards the middle of July with instructions from the United Irish executive MacNeven drew up a memorandum for a French landing in Ireland which he gave to the French ambassador, Reinhard, for presentation to the Directory. In it he pointed out Oyster Haven, Lough Swilly, Killybegs and Galway as suitable landing places, and asked for five to ten thousand

en s'en retournant dans son pays prit le chemin de Westlar. Je lui avois donné une lettre pour le Général. J'en ai reçu deux de sa part depuis qui confirment d'une manière particulière les assurances générales que j'avois eu de la part de ce grand homme dans une lettre qu'il m'avoit écrite quelques jours auparavant. Mon ami me mande qu'il l'avoit chargé de m'instruire' et le Comité Exécutif des Irlandois à son retour, qu'il feroit l'impossible pour être prêt à partir de Brest le 20 d'octobre avec 10,000, et tout ce qui seroit nécessaire en fusils, canons, amunition &c. et qu'il n'attendroit pas la sortie de la flotte hollandoise. Il étoit même convenu de l'endroit du débarquement avec mon ami. Il sera absolument nécessaire que je sois autorisé de votre part d'instruire le Comité si sa mort doit changer ces dispositions. Je vous prie de m'accorder la permission de m'entretenir un quart d'heure en particulier avec vous à ce sujet et à celui d'un projet du Général Daendels, dont j'ai déjà parlé avec le Ministre de la Marine.

> Salut et respect
> Edwd Jos. Lewines
> nommé par le Comité Exécutif des Irlandois
> Ministre Plénipotentiaire de l'Irlande auprès
> de la République Françoise

4 de Vendémiaire An 6.

Je viens de recevoir dans l'instant une lettre de la part du Général Debelle, du 30 Fructidor, qui me mande que le Général Hoche alloit envoyer son Adjutant Général Smyth à Paris pour les affaires de mon pays et pour communiquer avec moi. Je viendrois ce soir chercher une réponse chez le portier que vous aurez la bonté d'addresser au Citoyen Giauque. C'est le nom que je porte à Paris.

To Matilda Tone, 27 September 1797

Tone (Dickason) papers.

À Bruxelles, ce 6 Vendémiaire, an 6

Dearest Love,

All the gods have conspired to cross my impatience to see you and my babies. I have arrived everywhere just in time to be *too late* for the diligence. At last after fighting my way thus far, I have secured a place for the 8th inst., and I am, in the meantime, to pass these two days as I may.

French troops, 'a numerous staff, engineers and general officers', to be commanded by Hoche. He confirmed the position of Tone as well as that of Lewines. (*Castlereagh corr.*, i, 277–86, 295–306; Paul Weber, *On the road to rebellion: the United Irishmen and Hamburg* (Dublin, 1997), pp 77–8).

Leaving this the 8th I hope to be in Paris the 11th. I dined with Mr Sheé three or four days ago and found *one* letter of yours dated the 11th of June, viz. above three months since, but a letter from you is never out of season. It was *prince of letters*. I wrote, in consequence of your orders, to Madgett, to thank him for his civility to you &c. For the death of your mother,[1] as she is gone, I will only say that she never gave you much cause to regret her.

Tell Mme Sheé that her little boy[2] is delightful and that he and [I] are the best friends in the world. We helped to plant the Tree of Liberty together at Bonn and dined afterwards with the Municipality, the Commission Intermédiaire and its worthy President.[3]

Adieu, my Life and soul, I reserve all my news till we meet; in the meantime '*live unbruised and love my babies*'.[4] If you see Messrs Giauque & Co.[5] remember me affectionately.

Your loving spouse
J. Smith

From Édouard François Simon, 28 September 1797

Tone (Dickason) papers.

Simon, having been told by Sheé that Tone is in a predicament for want of acquaintances and friends, suggests that he see Chérin and Debelle in Paris.

Coblentz, le 7 Vendémiaire, 6ᵉ année rép[ublic]aine

J'ai vu hier, mon cher Shmit, le Citoyen Sheé qui m'a parlé de vous et m'a témoigné de l'inquiétude sur l'embarras où vous pouvez vous trouver faute de connaissances et d'amis qui puisse vous faire approcher des personnes auxquelles vous avez à faire. Je me suis chargé de vous écrire en conséquence. Chérin, qui revenait à l'armée, est retourné à Paris dès qu'il a appris la fatale nouvelle. Le Général Debelle y va sous très peu de jours, par conséquent, voilà deux appuis. Vous trouverez l'adresse de Chérin, soit au Directoire, soit chez le ministre de la guerre, soit rue de Chabannais, la porte cochère à droite en entrant par la rue des Petits Champs, la dernière dans l'angle. Le Général Debelle logera Hôtel Vauban, rue de la Loi. Voiez-les tous les deux. J'écris au dernier et l'engage à s'occuper des affaires d'Irlande.

---

[1] Catherine Witherington (née Fanning) died on 18 Apr. 1797 in Ash St., Dublin. At the trial of John McCann in 1798 at which her son-in-law Thomas Reynolds (married to Harriet Witherington) was the principal crown witness, John Philpot Curran for the defence tried on slender grounds to suggest that Reynolds had poisoned his mother-in-law. (Thomas Reynolds, junr, *The life of Thomas Reynolds* (2 vols, London, 1839), i, 78, 376–81; H. F. Reynolds, 'Fanning of Dublin' in *Notes and Queries*, 12th ser., vii, no. 131 (16 Oct. 1920), p. 307).   [2] Emmanuel Sheé (1791–1811).
[3] i.e. Henri Sheé.   [4] 'Live unbruised and love my cousin' (*Much ado about nothing*, V, iv).
[5] i.e. Lewines and other United Irishmen in Paris.

Adieu, mon cher. Écrivez-moi quelques fois. Si je ne vais pas bientôt à Paris, mille choses à Giauque.[1] Bonjour.

Simon

From General Hermann Wilhelm Daendels, 3 October 1797

Tone (Dickason) papers.

Daendels despairs at the death of Hoche and at the deteriorating political and military situation in Holland; he sends Tone three letters of recommendation and calls for United Irish representation at the Hague.

No. 2.

La Haye, le 3me octobre 1797
L'an 3me de la Liberté Batave

Le Lieutenant Général Daendels
À l'Adjudant-Général Smith

Vous devez penser, mon cher Smith, combien la mort du Général Hoche me désespère. Dans ce moment tout semble concourrir à contrarier nos projets et vient ajouter encore à cette affliction. Les affaires politiques dans notre païs prennent une direction vraïement allarmante pour la tranquilité publique, et je crains que bientôt notre gouvernement, paralysé au milieu des partis, n'aye pas l'énergie nécessaire pour nous mettre en état d'agir. Déjà il a fait retirer les troupes des cantonnements provisoires où je les avois mis sur les côtes. Elles viennent par son ordre de rentrer toutes dans leur garnisons, ainsi il faut renoncer à l'activité pour cette année, mais au moins il faut nous mettre en mesure, pour pouvoir agir le printems prochain au cas que la France suive toujours ses anciens projets, et c'est à quoi je travaille sans relâche. J'espère que quelques heureux événemens, que quelques mesures rigoureuses, parviendront à déjouer les manoeuvres des malveillans qui nous travaillent ici à peu près avec la même perfidie qu'ils travailloient en France avant le 18 fructidor, et pour que nous puissions aussi les contre-manoeuvrer avec fruit. Il faut que vous me teniez bien exactement instruit de tout ce que vous espérez du côté de Paris.

Je vous envoye trois lettres de recommandation.[2] Usez-en dès que vous serez arrivé. Priez, pressez, sollicitez, pour que nous sachions quelque chose de positif, et dès que nous serons certains ici que la France est déterminé à suivre l'exécution de ses projets, croyez que je ne négligerai rien pour que nous soyons en état de la seconder puissamment.

---

[1] i.e. Lewines.   [2] Below.

156

Il seroit bien nécessaire que nous puissions avoir ici un de vos compatriotes, un Écossais, un Anglais même, qui soyent dans notre sens. Vous devez en avoir beaucoup à Paris qui ne peuvent faire autre chose que d'attendre le résultat de vos démarches et de celles de Giauque,[1] un d'eux seroit plus utile ici, tâchez de nous l'envoyer.

Le Lieutenant Général
Daendels

P.S. J'ai encore 92 florins à vous que le Citoyen Souc[2] qui partira dans quelques jours pour Paris vous remetra.

D.

General Hermann Wilhelm Daendels to Georges René Pléville-le-Pelley, 3 October 1797

Tone (Dickason) papers; copy in Tone's handwriting.

Daendels explains how Tone, because of Hoche's regard for him, came to be employed by him on the Texel. Daendels sent him to Hoche at Wetzlar 'to communicate to him a plan which I had put to our government'. Tone arrived 'only to witness General Hoche's death' and so returned to Paris hoping that it 'would alter in no way the intentions of the government with regard to Ireland'. Daendels recommends Tone strongly.

La Haye, le 3me Octobre 1797
l'an 3me de la liberté batave

Le Lieutenant Général Daendels
commandant l'armée batave
au Citoyen Pléville Péli, ministre de la marine
de la République Française

Citoyen Ministre!

Au moment où nous nous embarquâmes, le général Hoche voulut bien me laisser l'adjudant général Smith, Irlandais, qui l'avait déjà accompagné à son départ de Brest. Le citoyen Smith a constamment travaillé avec le général Hoche à l'expédition d'Irlande, et avant la mort de ce général je le lui avois envoyé, pour qu'il lui communiquât un projet que j'avois proposé à notre gouvernement,[3] d'après lequel j'espérois que nous pourrions toujours agir cette année, quoique la longue contrariété des vents eut enlevé à notre flotte

---

[1] i.e. Lewines.   [2] Citizen Souc (or Soue?) has not been identified.
[3] For Daendels's plan for an invasion of Scotland in order to reach Ireland, see above (pp 132, 142–3).

la possibilité de doubler le nord de l'Écosse. Le citoyen Smith malheureusement n'est arrivé à Wetzlar que pour être témoin de la mort du
Général Hoche, et espérant cependant que cette mort, si malheureuse, ne
changera en rien les intentions du gouvernement a l'égard de l'Irlande, le
citoyen Smith est retourné à Paris. Permettez, Citoyen Ministre, que je le
recommande à vos bontés. J'ai pensé que, si le gouvernement est disposé à
suivre l'exécution de ses projets sur l'Irlande, c'étoit lui rendre un service
que de lui faire connoître le citoyen Smith, qui a le fil de toutes les correspondances, et qui jouit de la confiance de ses compatriotes. J'espère qu'il
méritera la votre, citoyen Ministre, quand vous connoîtrez ses talens, et le
zèle qui l'anime pour arracher son païs à l'oppression.

> Salut et respect
> (signé)
> Le Lieutenant Général
> Daendels

(pour copie conforme, J. S.)

General Hermann Wilhelm Daendels
to Casparus Meyer, 3 October 1797

Tone (Dickason) papers; copy in Tone's hand.

Casparus Meyer was Dutch minister to the French republic, Mar. 1795–Mar.
1798 (*Repertorum der diplomatischen Vertreter aller Länder* (Graz and Cologne,
1965)).

Daendels recommends Tone to Meyer and asks him to recommend him to
members of the Directory and to the minister of the marine.

> La Haye, le 3me Octobre 1797
> L'an 3me de la liberté batave

> Le Lieutenant Général Daendels, commandant l'armée batave,
> au Citoyen Meyer, Ministre de la République Batave près
> la République Française

Permettez, Citoyen et Ami, que je recommande à vos bons offices le Citoyen
Smith, Irlandois expatrié, que le général Hoche avoit bien voulu inviter à
m'accompagner au moment où nous nous sommes embarqués. Il vient de
perdre ce général, avec lequel il a constamment travaillé à l'expédition
d'Irlande, et qui étoit son protecteur naturel auprès du gouvernement.
Comme le citoyen Smith espère que cette mort, si malheureuse, ne changera cependant pas l'intention où est le Directoire d'arracher son païs de

l'oppression, il est retourné à Paris, où il sera sûrement de la plus grande utilité au gouvernement, car il possède tous les renseignemens qui peuvent être nécessaires, et jouit de la confiance de ses compatriotes. Mais à présent il est privé d'appui et de recommandation auprès des personnes qui sont en place, et je vous serois obligé, Citoyen et Ami, si vous vouliez avoir la bonté de le recommander aux membres du Directoire avec qui vous êtes lié, et au ministre de la marine. Je lui envoye aussi des lettres de recommandation pour ces différentes personnes, et j'espère que ces lettres et les démarches que vous voudrez bien faire pour lui, lui attireront la faveur et la confiance que ses talens et son zèle lui méritent.

> Salut et amitié
> (signé)
> Le Lieutenant Général
> Daendels

(pour copie conforme, J.S.)

General Hermann Wilhelm Daendels to Louis Marie de la Révellière-Lépeaux, 3 October 1797

Tone (Dickason) paper; copy in Tone's hand.

Daendels recommends Tone to La Révellière-Lépeaux.

> La Haye, le 3me Octobre 1797
> L'an 3me de la liberté batave

Le Lieutenant Général Daendels, commandant l'armée batave, au Citoyen La Réveillère Lépeaux, membre du Directoire Exécutif de la République Française

Citoyen Directeur!

Permettez que j'abuse encore de vos momens pour recommander à vos bontés le citoyen Smith, adjutant général. Il est Irlandais expatrié, il a constamment travaillé avec le général Hoche à l'expédition d'Irlande. Ce général avait bien voulu me le céder au moment ou nous espérions mettre à la voile, car il nous auroit été de la plus grande utilité pour la réussite de notre expédition si nous avions pu la tenter. Si la France suit l'exécution de ses projets, le citoyen Smith lui sera aussi de la plus grande ressource, car c'est lui qui est le premier agent de l'insurrection, qui a le fil de toutes les correspondances, et la confiance de ses compatriotes. Il méritera la vôtre, citoyen directeur, quand vous connoîtrez et ses talens, et le zèle ardent qui l'anime pour arracher son païs à l'oppression britannique, et j'ai cru que ce seroit vous obliger vous-même, que de vous faire connoître un ami de la liberté, qui peut être si utile au triomphe de sa cause, et si bien seconder les vues du Directoire.

Salut et respect (signé)
Le Lieutenant Général
Daendels

(pour copie conforme, J. S.).

To the Executive Directory, 15 October 1797

T.C.D., Tone papers, MS 2050, f. 17^r.

Tone states what he has been doing during the last few months and asks to be authorised to remain in Paris and to receive there the salary commensurate with his rank. Talleyrand adds a note that Tone 'had the confidence of the late General Hoche and vindicated it in very difficult circumstances'.

L'adjudant général Smith, Irlandais, au Directoire Exécutif

Citoyens Directeurs,

L'adjudant général Smith, attaché au feu général Hoche pour la partie de sa correspondance chez l'étranger, a l'honneur de vous exposer que ce général l'ayant envoyé en Hollande sur une mission particulière, il a resté 54 jours, embarqué au Texel avec le général Daendels, commandant en chef l'armée batave destinée à une expédition secrète; que les circonstances ayant rendu l'exécution de ce projet impraticable, le général Daendels l'a envoyé auprès du général Hoche, chargé d'un mémoire et des instructions verbales, en conséquence de quoi il est arrivé à Wetzlar trois jours seulement avant la mort de son général, dont il ne cessera jamais de déplorer la perte; qu'ayant communiqué le mémoire et les instructions, le général Hoche lui marquait que sous peu de jours il l'enverroit à Paris auprès du gouvernement; qu'en conséquence de ces instructions du général, il a cru être de son devoir de se rendre à Paris pour y suivre l'affaire dont il était chargé par les généraux Hoche et Daendels. L'objet de sa mission n'étant pas encore accompli et sa présence ici pouvant être utile, il vous prie, citoyens directeurs, de l'autoriser de rester à Paris et d'y recevoir les traitemens attachés à son grade.

(signé)
L'adj[udan]t général
J. Smith

À Paris, ce 24 Vend[émiai]re an 6

Apostillé par le ministre des relations extérieures: 'L'adjudant general Smith a eu la confiance du g[énér]al Hoche, et l'a justifiée dans des circonstances très délicates. Signé C. M. Talleyrand, 24 Vend[émiai]re an 6.'

To Charles Maurice de Talleyrand-Périgord, 15 October 1797

Archives des Affaires Étrangères, Correspondance Politique Angleterre, Cote 592, ff 61ʳ–61ᵛ.

Tone gives some information on 'all the Irish refugees in Paris whom I know personally'. One of them is 'Citizen Edwᵈ Jos. Lewines who has taken the name "Giauque" '. He mentions also four Irishmen in prison at Liège.

Au Cᵉⁿ Talleyrand

À Paris, ce 24 Vendémiaire, an 6

Citoyen Ministre,

D'après vos ordres j'ai l'honneur de vous soumettre la liste nominative de tous les Irlandois, réfugiés à Paris, que je connois personnellement, savoir,

Le Citoyen *Edw[ar]d Jos[eph] Lewines*, qui a pris le nom de *Giauque*. Il ne m'est pas nécessaire de vous parler de ce citoyen, puisqu'il est déjà connu de vous. Je dirai seulement que son zèle, son intégrité et ses talens, ont décidé ses compatriotes de l'envoyer près du gouvernement français, pour y remplir les fonctions de leur agent, et qui, si la révolution avait lieu dans l'Irlande, il seroit nommé ministre plénipotentiaire, situation qu'il a bien mérité par ses lumières, et son dévouement entier aux interêts de sa patrie.

Le C[itoy]en *James Napper Tandy*, respectable vieillard, connu par son patriotisme depuis 30 ans; chassé de son pays par le gouvernement anglois en 1794.

Le C[itoy]en *John Tennent*, qui a pris le nom de Thomas Howard, natif de Belfast, jeune homme plein de courage, et dont je connois bien le zèle et le patriotisme.

Le C[itoy]en *Alexander Lowry*, qui a pris le nom d'Alexander Black, natif du comté de Down, jeune homme courageux, et qui s'est beaucoup distingué parmi les Irlandais Unis. Ces deux derniers se sont réfugiés ensemble; je les connois personnellement, et je peux répondre de leur intégrité.

Le C[itoy]en *James Coigley*,[1] prêtre catholique.

Le C[itoy]en *Arthur Macmahon*,[2] qui a pris le nom d'Arthur Redmond, ministre calviniste. Tous les deux très distingués par leur zèle et leur

---

[1] James Coigly or Quigley (1761–98), catholic priest; joined United Irishmen; fled from Ireland, Apr. 1797; returned to assist in making plans for a French invasion, 1797–8; arrested at Margate on 28 Feb. 1798 *en route* for France, tried, convicted of high treason and executed (*D.N.B.;* Brendan McEvoy, 'Father James Quigley' in *Seanchas Ardmhacha*, v, no. 2 (1970), pp 247–68).

[2] Arthur McMahon (*c*.1755–1816?), presbyterian minister at Kilrea, Co. Londonderry, 1789–94; minister at Holywood, Co. Down, 1794–7; fled to France in 1797; commissioned in Irish legion, 1804; prisoner of war in England, 1809–14; retired to Boulogne (W. A. Maguire, 'Arthur McMahon, United Irishman and French soldier' in *Irish Sword*, ix, no. 36 (1970), pp 207–15; note by J.L.G., ibid., x, no. 39 (1971), p. 172).

patriotisme, qui les ont rendu si odieux au gouvernement anglais, qu'ils ont été obligés de se sauver, en passant par l'Angleterre. Je crois, citoyen Ministre, que vous les avez vus, et qu'ils vous ont même donné quelques renseignemens sur l'état actuel des choses en Angleterre et dans l'Écosse.

Voilà, citoyen, tous ceux que je connois. Je vous prie seulement de remarquer la coalition de tous les partis en Irlande, si évidemment démontrée par la réunion d'un Catholique et d'un Presbytérien pour le même objet. Pendant que cette union subsistera, et je crois que maintenant elle est inébranlable, il ne faut jamais se désespérer de la liberté de l'Irlande.

> Salut et Respect,
> J. Smith
> Adj[udan]t Gén[éra]l

J'avais oublié de dire qu'il y en a encore quatre Irlandois dans le prison de Liège, savoir deux, nommés *Byrne*,[1] un nommé *Jackson*,[2] et un nommé *Macan*.[3] Je les crois tous de vrais patriotes, d'après le rapport de ceux qui les connoissent plus intimement que moi.

Charles Maurice de Talleyrand-Périgord to Pierre Sotin, 20 October 1797

Archives des Affaires Étrangères, Correspondance Politique Angleterre, Cote 592, f. 65.

Pierre Jean Marie Sotin de la Coindière (1764–1810) was minister of police, 1797–8 (*Dict. parl. franç.*).

The italicised words in the heading are printed in the MS. The crest bears the words 'République Française' and 'Relat[ions] Ext[érieures]'.

Talleyrand passes on the information contained in the letter from Tone of 15 Oct. 1797 (above).

Relations   *LIBERTÉ*   [crest]   *ÉGALITÉ*
Extérieures   *Paris, le 29* vendémiaire *de l'an 5*[4]
Secrétariat-Général   *de la République Française*
1ère Division[5]   *une et indivisible*

Le Ministre des Relations Extérieures

[1] Patrick Byrne (d. 1812) and his younger brother, John Byrne (1776–1834) of Dundalk, Co. Louth; they were in Paris a year later (*Burke's landed gentry of Great Britain and Ireland* (London, 1868); Paul Weber, *On the road to rebellion: the United Irishmen and Hamburg* (Dublin, 1997), pp 102–3).

[2] Perhaps one of the two men of this name, John and James Jackson, listed in the fugitive bill (Madden, *United Irishmen*, 2nd ed., i (1857), p. 581).

[3] Anthony MacCann of Corderry, near Drogheda, Co. Louth (see below, p. 190, n. 1).

[4] *Recte* '6'.

[5] Followed in the MS by 'Nota. L'ordre de la correspondance exige que la réponse relate le no. de la Division ci-dessus indiquée' (printed in italics).

*A*u ministre de la Police Générale

L'adjudant Général Smith, qui avait toute la confiance[1] du feu Général Hoche et qui l'accompagnait lors de l'expédition d'Irlande, m'a remis, mon cher collègue, la liste des Irlandais réfugiés à Paris qu'il connaît et dont il répond. Voici cette liste.[2]

1.° Jacques Napper Tandy
2.° Jacques Tennent qui a pris le nom de Thomas Howard
3.° Alexandre Lowry qui a pris le nom d'Alex Black
4.° Jacques Coigley prêtre catholique
5.° Arthur Mac-mahon qui a pris le nom d'Arthur Redmond.

Ces cinq Irlandais sont dévoués à la liberté et odieux au Gouvernement anglais dont ils ont été obligés de fuir les persécutions. Ils ont déjà rendu et, dans l'occasion, ils rendront encore d'importants services à la France. Je vous invite donc, mon cher collègue, à donner des ordres pourqu'ils puissent résider à Paris sans être inquiétés et qu'ils y trouvent au contraire la protection qui leur est due.

Quatre autres Irlandais doivent être dans les prisons à Liège. Le citoyen Smith croit, sur le rapport de ceux qui les connaissent plus intimement que lui, qu'ils sont tous de vrais patriotes. Deux se nomment Byrne, un troisième Jackson, le quatrième Macan. J'ignore les motifs de leur détention. Je vous engage, mon cher collègue, à vous en faire rendre compte, afin de les mettre en liberté, s'ils en sont dignes.

Salut et fraternité
C. M. T.

To General Hermann Wilhelm Daendels,
21 October 1797

Tone (Dickason) papers.

Tone thanks Daendels for some letters. He states that on arriving in Paris he gave Barras the verbal instructions and memorandum entrusted to him by Daendels and, at the request of Debelle, made a memorandum of the instructions, a copy of which he subjoins below. He expresses optimism despite recent reverses. He submits to Daendels his ideas ('somewhat daring'), which are that, not later than the beginning of February, 5,000 elite troops should be embarked secretly and a northerly passage taken for Ireland. Tone adds a

---

[1] In the MS the words 'homme de confiance' have been altered to 'qui avait toute la confiance'.
[2] In the MS the first item on this list was originally '1⁰ Edmund Joseph Luwines qui a pris le nom de Giauque'. This has been crossed out and the subsequent items renumbered. A marginal note in the same hand reads: 'Vous connaissez déjà, mon cher collègue, Edmund Joseph Luwines qui a pris le nom de Giauque et [*several words not deciphered*] la liste ci-dessus n'est pas d'ailleurs un réfugié, il est venu en France sur l'invitation du feu G[énér]al Hoche'.

footnote to say that his first idea ('even more daring') was to leave straightaway. He admits that he regards an invasion as 'almost impossible'. A number of compatriots have arrived in Paris, two or three of them 'members of the insurrectionist committee'. They agree that with 5,000 armed men landing in Ireland revolution would succeed. Tone praises Daendels for his fortitude and assures him of his eagerness to follow his orders. Referring to Daendels's last letter stating his desire for a person able to advise him on Scotland, Tone informs him that he knows such a person, one who is 'known personally to all the patriotic leaders of the country, where he has spent some years'. Tone undertakes to refer political matters to 'Citizen Giauque'.

No. 1

Paris, ce 30 Vendémiaire, an 6

L'adjudant général Smith au général Daendels

Général,

J'ai l'honneur de vous remercier très sincérement des lettres que vous avez bien voulu m'envoyer,[1] et que j'ai présenté aux citoyens respectifs auxquels elles étoient adressées. J'ai toute raison d'être content de ma réception, surtout de celle que m'ont accordé les citoyens Réveillière et Meyer. Comme je vous ai cru maintenant très occupé, je me suis abstiné de vous écrire, espérant toujours d'avoir quelque chose digne de vous communiquer; jusqu'ici, cependant, rien ne m'est parvenu. Tout ce que je sais, c'est ce dont tout le monde est instruit, savoir, que les vaisseaux français sont rentrés dans le port de Brest, et qu'on a loué pour quatre mois aux particuliers les frégates de la république pour être armées en course. Il paroît, d'après tout cela, qu'on ne pense à rien, au moins avant le printems prochain; en attendant je tâche d'obtenir un ordre de rester à Paris, et j'espère d'y réussir.

Dès mon arrivée je me suis adressé au citoyen Barras, et je lui ai remis le mémoire que vous m'avez confié, aussi bien que toutes les instructions verbales. Il m'a écouté très attentivement, et m'a renvoyé jusqu'à l'arrivée du général Debelle, qui me suivit de très près. Le général Debelle, à son arrivée, m'a ordonné de lui faire un mémoire de tout ce que je lui disois verbalement; en conséquence je lui ai présenté le mémoire, dont j'ai l'honneur de vous transmettre, ci-jointe, une copie.[2] Bientôt après survint la nouvelle du combat entre les flottes anglaise et batave,[3] dont le résultat ne nous étant pas favorable, j'ai crû être de mon devoir, de ne faire aucune démarche, sans avoir reçu vos ordres ultérieures.

Maintenant, général, il n'est plus question, à ce que je pense, de forcer un passage. Cependant je suis bien loin de désespérer à cause de nos derniers

---

[1] Above, pp 144–5, 154–5. [2] No copy has been found.
[3] On 11 Oct. 1797 the Dutch fleet was defeated by a British fleet at Camperdown (Kamperduin), in the Texel roads.

revers, et je crois vous connoître assez, pour être convaincu que vous saurez bien prendre votre parti dans ces circonstances difficiles. Ce sont les grands malheurs qui font déployer les grandes ressources, et maintenant il ne s'agit plus de moyens ordinaires.

Je vais, sans préface, vous soumettre mes idées; elles sont peut-être un peu hardies, mais dans les circonstances actuelles, il ne nous reste d'autre parti à prendre que celui de l'audace.

Maintenant les Anglais sont certainement sans inquiétude, du côté de la Hollande; la saison, et l'état de la flotte batave depuis le dernier combat, les met à leur aise à cet égard, cependant toutes vos frégates, et peut-être quelques-uns de vos vaisseaux sont encore en état de tenir la mer, voilà donc ce que je proposerai:[1] d'arranger tout de manière à être prêt, au plus tard pour les premiers jours de février prochain, de faire embarquer avec le plus grand secret 5,000 hommes d'élite, de toute arme, avec les armes et les munitions destinées pour la dernière expédition, de tenter le passage par le nord, et de vous rendre dans l'Irlande, où vous pouvez être sûr d'être accueilli d'une manière à ne pouvoir pas manquer de porter un coup mortel à la domination anglaise, et de faire bien payer à cette nation orgueilleuse tous les maux qu'elle a causé à votre patrie et à la mienne.

Je sais bien que cette entreprise est des plus hardies, à ne pas dire téméraires; mais c'est sur cette raison, précisément, que je fonde mes espérances d'y réussir; je le pose, pour principe, que nous ne saurons jamais forcer un passage: la saison est moins redoutable que l'ennemi, et si nous ne pouvons pas brusquer l'affaire de la manière que je propose, ou de quelqu'autre pareille, je vous avoue franchement, général, que je regarde toute invasion, soit en Angleterre, soit en Écosse, soit en Irlande, comme une chose à peu près impossible.

Depuis que je suis à Paris, il vient d'arriver un nombre de mes compatriotes, forcés comme moi-même de se soustraire de la persécution anglo-royaliste; parmi eux se trouvent deux ou trois membres du comité insurrecteur. Ils sont tous d'un accord unanime qu'avec des armes et des munitions, et cinq mille hommes, ou même un plus petit nombre, pour en protéger la distribution, la révolution ne peut pas manquer de s'opérer. Les horreurs qu'ont fait les Anglais dans le pays, loin d'abattre l'esprit public, n'ont fait que d'aigrir, au dernier point, tous les citoyens, même les moins exagérés. Le mécontentement est à son comble, et il ne faut absolument au peuple irlandais

---

[1] Footnote by Tone: NOTE. Mes premières idées étoient encore plus hardies. Les voilà! 'De faire embarquer le plutôt possible, et avec le plus grand secret, 5,000 hommes d'élite avec les armes et les munitions destinées pour la dernière expédition, *de sortir le premier instant que le passage seroit libre*, de tenter la route par le nord, et de vous rendre dans l'Irlande, &c.' Si le secret auroit pu être gardé, comme les Anglais, sans contredit, n'auroient jamais compté de nous voir reprendre l'offensive, après un si rude echec que celui que nous venions d'essuyer, je ne suis pas du tout sûr que le coup, tout téméraire qu'il étoit, n'auroit pu réussir; mais, *dis aliter visum!* Je ne puis plus me rapeller, à cette intervalle, pourquoi j'ai changé mon plan, car mes premières idées me paraissent maintenant les plus justes.

30 Germinal an 6

que l'apparition d'un petit corps d'armée, avec des armes pour se soulever, comme un seul homme, et terrasser à jamais leurs oppresseurs.

L'amitié que vous m'avez témoigné, général, me fait infiniment désirer que vous eussiez la gloire d'une expédition aussi brillante que celle dont je vous parle, et dont la réussite affermiroit pour toujours la liberté et la prospérité de la France, de la Hollande et de ma patrie. Je sais que vous avez ce courage, et surtout cet enthousiasme ardent, sans quoi, dans les cas difficiles, on ne fait jamais rien de grand. C'est cette conviction que j'ai de votre caractère, qui m'enhardit de vous soumettre cette légère esquisse, sur laquelle je vous prie de me donner, au plutôt possible, votre avis. Il ne m'est pas nécessaire de vous dire que si vous adoptez ce plan, toutes fois en le corrigeant et l'améliorant de votre manière, je ne désire rien autant que d'y concourir de tous mes moyens, soit en agissant ici, sous vos ordres, soit en vous accompagnant, si l'expédition, après un mûr examen, auroit lieu.

Vous me dîtes, dans votre dernière lettre,[1] que vous souhaitez beaucoup, d'avoir près de vous une personne capable de vous donner des renseignemens sur les affaires de l'Écosse. Je connois ici une telle personne[2] qui en est parfaitement instruite, comme il paroit d'après les mémoires de sa composition que Giauque[3] vous a dernièrement transmis. C'est un homme de talens, d'un patriotisme, et d'une intégrité à toute épreuve, et très connu, personnellement, de tous les chefs patriotes du pays, où il a passé quelques ans. Si les derniers événemens n'ont rien changé à votre plan, et si vous désirez encore le voir, il ne fera aucune difficulté de se rendre auprès du gouvernement batave, mais, pour cela, il faudra lui faire passer les fonds nécessaires pour son voyage, n'étant pas, lui-même, en état d'y subvénir. Vous me ferez le plaisir de me marquer, dans votre réponse, ce qu'il me faudra faire à cet égard. Je vous garantis, encore, les talens et l'intégrité de l'homme en question, et si vous pensez encore à votre plan, il sera pour vous une acquisition très précieuse.

Je me rapporte au citoyen Giauque, qui vous écrit aussi par ce courrier, pour tout ce qui regarde la politique, et la décision du gouvernement français, à l'égard de notre affaire, autant qu'il en est, lui-même, instruit, je crois que les détails qu'il vous donnera vous intéresseront beaucoup.

Salut et respect.

J. S.

Memorandum

The following memorandum ('which contains the advice I was charged by General Daendels to communicate to the late General Hoche') refers to two plans for an expedition to Scotland. The first is in the memorandum received by Barras. Details of the second are given. In the absence of the English fleet,

[1] Daendels to Tone, 3 Oct. 1797 (above, pp 154–5).
[2] Probably John Aherne, identified above as Eugene Ahern; he seems to have spent some time in Scotland and to have associated there with radicals (see above, vol. II, p. 150, n. 2).
[3] In fact Lewines (see above, p. 161).

about 15,000 Dutch troops are to go to Scotland soon followed by 10,000 to 15,000 troops of the French *armée du Nord*. The war has badly affected Scotland's trade. It is asserted that at the instance of the United Irish in Ulster ('in origin a Scottish colony') the Scots are forming themselves into baronial committees. In Scotland disgust at the horrors of the military regime nearby in Ulster and a new law requiring enlistment in the militia have given rise to bloody riots. A French and Dutch army would therefore be welcomed. But even without help from the Scots the presence of England's enemy would have an adverse effect on England's finances. It is essential for the success of the expedition that it take place as soon as possible, as Scotland is almost devoid of regular troops and next spring England will again be blockading our ports. An expedition to Ireland is undoubtedly of first importance, but an expedition to Scotland has the merit of being easily effected in the present circumstances; moreover it would not, if successful. prevent an Irish expedition but would be a diversion and would deplete Ireland of regular troops. Tone adds that Hoche regarded this plan as 'very feasible'.

Attaché au N° 1

Copie du Mémoire que j'ai présenté, le 28 Vendémiaire, an 6, au général Debelle, d'aprés les ordres du Citoyen Barras, président du Directoire Exécutif, et qui contient les renseignemens que j'étais chargé par le général Daendels de communiquer au feu général Hoche.

Il y a deux plans à l'égard de l'expédition contre l'Écosse.

Pour le premier, je me rapporte au mémoire du Général Daendels entre les mains du citoyen Barras; pour le second, le voici:—

Il est proposé de profiter du premier moment de l'absence de la flotte anglaise, pour faire passer dans l'Écosse, à l'endroit marqué, dans le mémoire susdit, l'armée expéditionnaire batave, qui peut consister d'environ 15,000 hommes de toute arme; de les faire suivre le plus près possible par 10 à 15,000 hommes de l'armée du nord, ce qui portera l'armée entière à 25 ou 30,000 hommes, environ; avec cette force on compte bien, pour les raisons et d'après la manière exposées dans le mémoire, ou de se maintenir dans le pays, ou de pénétrer dans le nord de l'Angleterre, en cas que les circonstances dont je vais parler, rendroient une telle mesure praticable.

Il est connu généralement qu'il y avait dans l'Écosse, il y a trois ou quatre ans, un esprit très révolutionnaire, qui n'étoit alors réprimé que par l'exécution de quelques-uns des chefs, et la déportation de plusieurs autres.[1] Cet esprit, quoique réprimé, ne paroît être pas du tout éteint.

---

[1] In Aug. 1793, Thomas Muir was sentenced in Edinburgh to fourteen years' transportation to Botany Bay for sedition; next month another radical, Thomas Fyshe Palmer, a Unitarian minister, was sentenced by a Perth court to seven years' transportation; early in 1794, William Skirving and two other radicals who had been delegates to the British Convention held in Edinburgh received similar sentences.

La guerre a été très funeste au commerce de l'Écosse; c'est surtout dans les grandes villes manufacturières, telles que Glasgow, Paisley, &c., qu'existoit l'esprit révolutionnaire, qui a été, certainement, très augmenté par la détresse et la misère, produites parmi la classe ouvrière, par la suspension, ou au moins la grande diminution, de ces travaux qui leur fournissoit les moyens de vivre.

Il y a eu, depuis un an environ, des communications fréquentes et suivies entre les Irlandais Unis de la province d'Ulster (qui sont originairement une colonie écossaise) et les Écossais de cette partie du pays, qui est vis à vis de l'Irlande. En conséquence de ces communications, les Écossais se sont formés, à l'instar des Irlandais Unis, en comités baroniales, comitiales &c. Au mois du juin dernier ils étoient même avancés au point d'avoir formé un comité provincial. Il paroît d'après les rapports faits par des gens affidés, envoyés par les Irlandais Unis, pour fraterniser avec les Écossais, que l'objet de ces derniers étoit, décidément, de bouleverser le gouvernement actuel, et de fonder une république, sur les grandes bases de la liberté et de l'égalité.

Les Écossais, justement révoltés des horreurs du régime militaire qui se sont passés journellement devant leurs yeux, pour ainsi dire, en Irlande, viennent d'être attaqués, chez eux-mêmes, par la loi dernièrement promulguée, qui ordonne un enrôlement général de la milice dans l'Écosse. En conséquence le peuple s'est soulevé dans plusieurs endroits, et il y a eu des affaires très sanglantes, notamment à Tranent, dans lesquelles la troupe a fait main basse sur les paysans, et en ont massacré un très grand nombre,[1] ce qui ne peut qu'augmenter infiniment leur détestation de la domination anglaise, et ressusciter l'esprit révolutionnaire qui s'est montré dans l'Écosse plusieurs fois depuis l'établissement de la République Française, et specialement en 1793.

Pour toutes ces raisons il paroît très vraisemblable qu'une armée française et batave, venant dans le pays seulement pour aider les Écossais à se souliver, et à briser définitivement le joug anglais, seroit non seulement bien accueillie, mais qu'avec des arrangemens convenables on pourroit augmenter ses forces, par l'assistance des patriotes écossais, au point même de pouvoir attaquer les Anglais chez eux, et peut-être par ce moyen, de faire écrouler le gouvernement, d'autant plus qu'il y a en Angleterre, et à Londres même, un très fort parti de mécontens, sur lequel le Directoire doit avoir reçu, dernièrement, des communications importantes.

Mais supposé même qu'on ne pouvoit compter sur l'assistance des Écossais, ce seroit toujours un coup mortel pour l'Angleterre, que de voir un ennemi dans ce pays. 1,200 forçats, débarqués il y a quelques mois dans le pays de Galles,[2] ont suffi pour fermer la banque d'Angleterre, qui depuis ce tems là ne paie qu'en papier. On peut bien juger de cet échantillon, quel effet produiroit

---

[1] There were anti-militia riots in Scotland in August and September, one of the disturbed areas being the district of Tranent in East Lothian. A number of the rioters were brought to trial in October. (*Scots Magazine*, 1797, pp 704–5, 778–81).

[2] An allusion to Tate's landing at Fishguard in Wales on the night of 22–3 Feb. 1797 with a French force made up partly of convicts taken from prisons in and around Brest. See above, vol. II, p. 397, n. 4.

un débarquement de 15 jusqu'à 30,000 hommes dans un pays très mécontent, et qui à cette heure même paroit être à deux doigts d'une insurrection ouverte et générale. Il seroit dans ce cas absolument impossible pour le ministre anglais de négocier le moindre emprunt, à cause de la dépréciation du papier-monnaie, qui suivroit inévitablement, et à l'instant même, la débarquation; et on sait bien que c'est par ce moyen seul, d'emprunt, que le gouvernement anglais existe.

L'entreprise, sous ce point de vue, est de la plus haute importance; reste à voir si elle soit praticable, ce que je crois, fermement, pour les raisons suivantes.

Puisqu'il est impossible pour la flotte anglaise de tenir la mer pendant l'hiver, il ne faut que de profiter du premier coup de vent, qui les fera rentrer dans leurs ports, et de sortir toute suite pour effectuer le débarquement. Le voyage du Texel en Écosse se fait avec facilité dans deux, ou, tout au plus, trois jours; mais je le regarde comme indispensable pour la réussite de l'expédition, qu'elle ait lieu le premier moment possible, si on attend le printems prochain, ou tout autre époque, c'est un coup manqué; les Anglais nous bloqueront encore, et tout sera fini, maintenant l'Écosse est à peu près dégarnie de troupes régulières; il n'y en a que celles qu'on a fait marcher derniérement pour comprimer l'esprit insurrecteur, qui venoit de se montrer, et qui ne sont nullement en état de résister à une force imposante, telle que celle, dont il s'agit maintenant; mais si on laisse passer l'occasion actuelle, sans tenter un coup de main, je ne m'attends pas du tout que le secret sera si bien gardé, que l'Angleterre ne soit pas averti à tems, et qu'elle ne fasse dans l'Écosse des préparatifs qui rendroient toute entreprise dans ce pays à peu près impossible.

L'expédition d'Irlande est sans doute l'objet de la première importance, mais celle dans l'Écosse, quoique moins brillante que l'autre, a dans sa faveur cette grande recommandation, qu'elle peut s'exécuter facilement, dans les circonstances actuelles, et sous peu de tems, d'ailleurs cette dernière, si elle avait lieu, et si elle réussissoit à notre souhait, loin d'empêcher l'expédition d'Irlande (qui pourroit et qui devroit la suivre de très près) serviroit comme une diversion puissante, et en dégarnissant l'Irlande des troupes anglaises (qui dans ce cas seroient certainement rappellées, presque toutes, pour défendre l'Angleterre elle-même) elle rendroit la réussite de l'expédition irlandaise presqu'inévitable.

Pour le présent je me borne à cette légère esquisse, en vous priant de relire le mémoire du général Daendels, ci-dessus mentioñné, et de le comparer avec la carte du pays; j'ajouterai seulement que le brave général que la mort vient de nous enlever, et dont l'opinion doit être presque décisive, regardoit ce projet comme un plan *très exécutable*.

(signé)
J. Smith
adj[udant] gen[era]l

Au
Gén[éra]l Debelle
&c., &c., &c.

From General Hermann Wilhelm Daendels, 4 November 1797

Tone (Dickason) papers.

Daendels refers to the many difficulties that make a new Dutch expedition impossible while seeing some hope in the desire of the Dutch to repair their fleet and the possibility that the French government, having concluded a peace with the Emperor, will direct all its energies against England. Daendels advises Tone in the event of Bonaparte taking command of the 'army of England' to confer with him or, failing this, with Desaix or Berthier. He asks whether some of Tone's compatriots—'an Englishman, a Scotsman and an Irishman in the confidence of the different secret committees of their countries'—could come to the Hague and engage in a correspondence.

No. 3

La Haye, ce 4 novembre 1797
L'an 3me de la Liberté Batave

Le Lieutenant Général Daendels
À l'Adjudant Général Smith

Il est de toute impossibilité, mon cher Smith, de songer à l'activité pour cette année; vous connoissez à peu près quel est notre gouvernement. La sortie imprévue de notre flotte, les revers qu'elle a éprouvés,[1] l'ont déjà mis trop en but aux reproches pour qu'on puisse jamais le décider à donner l'ordre d'une expédition aussi hazardouse [sic] que celle que vous proposez. D'ailleurs il faut, pour que cette expédition réussisse, le secret le plus absolu, et l'Angleterre entretient chez nous un si grand nombre d'agents, qu'il est impossible qu'elle n'aye pas bientôt connoissance d'un embarquement de 5 mille hommes, qu'elle ne soit même avertie à tems de la sortie des vaisseaux qui les portent comme Mr Duncan l'a été de la sortie de notre flotte, ainsi elle pourroit toujours prendre des mesures pour intercepter ce convoi dans sa marche. Si l'on veut faire un coup de surprise notre païs est le moins propre à le faire réussir. La longueur et la difficulté de la navigation que nous avons à faire pour doubler le Nord de l'Écosse, la multiplicité des relations de nos habitants avec l'Angleterre, la position actuelle de notre gouvernement, tout s'oppose à un succès de cette nature, mais nous pourrons encore puissamment seconder la France, si comme je le pense, elle veut développer tous ses moyens contre l'Angleterre. L'esprit public a pris une nouvelle énergie par les revers que nous avons essuyés. Une foule de citoyens offrent des sacrifices

---

[1] On 11 Oct. 1797, Admiral Duncan had completely defeated the Dutch fleet at the battle of Camperdown.

considérables pour le rétablissement de notre flotte, et si le gouvernement veut, au mois d'avril elle pourra être réparée. Mais pour activer davantage ces préparatifs, il nous faudroit être certains de ceux que fait aussi la France. La paix qui vient d'être conclue avec l'Empéreur[1] va laisser au gouvernement la possibilité de développer toute son énergie contre l'Angleterre. Déjà il a créé une armée destinée à opérer contre elle. Si Buonaparte en vient bientôt prendre le commandement, tâchez, mon cher Smith, de conférer avec lui, ou à son défaut avec le général Dessaix,[2] ou le général Berthier. Assurez l'un et l'autre des efforts que nous ferons ici pour les seconder de tous nos moyens. Dès qu'ils s'occuperont de l'organization de leur armée, j'entrerai en correspondance avec eux, mais en attendant tenez-moi, autant qu'il vous sera possible, instruit des préparatifs, et mandez-moi, si depuis la conclusion de la paix on n'a pas revoqué à Brest l'ordre de désarmement.

Je vous demandois si quelques-uns de vos compatriotes ne pourroient pas venir ici, parceque si l'on suit l'exécution des grands desseins que l'on annonce, je crois qu'il seroit très utile que nous puissions entretenir une correspondance directe avec les trois royaumes. Nous aurions besoin pour cela d'un Anglois, d'un Écossois, d'un Irlandois, qui eussent la confiance des différents comités secrets de leur païs, nous aurions toutes les facilités possibles d'entretenir une correspondance active et suivie dont on pourroit tirer le plus grand fruit, et dès que le Directoire aura fait à notre gouvernement des ouvertures sur l'opération, c'est une des premières mesures que je l'engagerai à prendre, et je ferai accorder des fonds pour cet objet, alors je vous prierai de m'indiquer les hommes.

Mille amitiés pour moi au Citoyen Giauque.[3] Je n'ai point reçu la lettre que vous m'annoncez de sa part et j'en ai grand regret. Priez-le de m'en envoyer un duplicata et daignez tous les deux m'écrire le plus souvent possible. Informez-moi surtout si le Général Dessaix viendra bientôt s'occuper de l'organisation de l'armée d'Angleterre.

> Salut et amitié!
> Le Lieutenant Général
> Daendels

From General Louis Nicolas Hyacinthe Chérin, 22 October 1797 or later

Tone (Dickason) papers.

For the date of this letter, see below, p. 172, n. 1.

Chérin invites Tone to contribute to a life of Hoche which is in progress.

---

[1] See below, p. 176, n. 7.

[2] Louis Charles Antoine des Aix or Desaix (1768–1800), général de brigade, 1793; général de division, 1794; provisionally in command of the *armée d'Angleterre*, Oct. 1797–Mar. 1798; killed at Marengo (Six, *Dict. des généraux & amiraux*).   [3] i.e. Lewines.

ARMÉE   ÉTAT-MAJOR GÉNÉRAL
D'ALLEMAGNE   LIBERTÉ   [crest]   ÉGALITÉ

Au Quartier-général à Offembourg
le 1 [ ] *l'an* [6] *de la République Française,
une et indivisible*[1]

CHÉRIN, *Général de Division, Chef de l'État-major général*
au Citoyen Smith, adjudant-général, Cul de Sac Notre Dame des Champs
No. 1390, près du Luxembourg à Paris

Un écrivain patriote[2] occupé de composer la Vie du général Hoche vient
d'arriver à notre armée. Il vient recueillir dans la mémoire de ceux qui ont
approché ce général vertueux les souvenirs qu'il leur a laissés. Notre dernier
devoir est d'aider cet ouvrage de tous nos moyens, de l'éclairer de toutes
nos lumières.

Si les Républicains qui ont moins vu Hoche que nous s'empressent
de payer à sa cendre le tribut de la reconnoissance, la dette que nous avons
à acquitter est bien plus sacrée. Nous avons à prouver que nous fûmes
dignes de l'amitié de ce grand homme, et qu'il n'est point mort dans notre
coeur.

Personne n'a plus droit que vous, Citoyen, d'apporter votre part à cette
contribution de souvenirs honorables et chers à tous les amis de la liberté.

Je vous invite aussitôt la réception de ma lettre à vous recueillir quelques
momens, et fixer aussitôt sur le papier les faits intéressants pour la Vie du
général Hoche qui peuvent revenir à votre pensée. Vous l'avez connu d'une
manière intime et vous avez été à même de l'observer de très près. Rien
n'est minutieux de ce qui a rapport à un grand homme. Ses paroles, ses
habitudes domestiques, ses gestes mêmes, tout l'indique, tout le montre.
Les détails qui paroîtroient les plus indifférens au premier coup d'oeil sont
souvent ceux qui servent le mieux à prononcer le caractère de l'homme.

J'espère que vous ne laisserez échapper aucun de ces traits précieux pour
l'histoire. Vous prendrez Hoche depuis l'époque où vous avez commencé à
le connoître jusqu'à celle où vous l'avez perdu de vue, depuis sa jeunesse,
sa naissance même jusqu' aux derniers momens de sa vie.

Si quelque chose pouvait ajouter au plaisir que je crois vous offrir, je vous
dirois que vous feriez une chose très agréable au général en chef. Il vous a

---

[1] The writer has inserted the day ('1') but has not added the month and year. From the date of
publication of the book mentioned by Chérin, it is inferred that the year was Year 6 in the republican
calendar. As Hoche died in Wetzlar in Hesse on the so-called third complementary day of Year 5,
i.e. three days before 1 Vendémiaire Year 6, and as Chérin was far away in the south of Germany
when he was writing, the earliest possible date of the letter must be 1 Brumaire Year 6, i.e. 22 Oct.
1797.
[2] Alexandre Charles Omer Rousselin de Corbeau de Saint-Albin (1773–1847), civil servant,
attached as 'réquisitionnaire' to Hoche's staff (*Dict. biog. franç.*). In the first edition of his *Vie de
Lazare Hoche* (2 vols, Paris, an VI (1798)), he does not mention Tone. In the third edition (Paris,
an VIII (1799)), he refers to him with admiration.

jugé l'un des plus dignes coopérateurs de cette oeuvre républicaine, il vous invite à y mettre la plus grande célérité.

Le travail que je vous annonce, sans être trop long, doit avoir l'étendue nécessaire pour comprendre les faits qui sont à votre connoissance: peu de mots, mais beaucoup de choses. Il faut suivre, comme dans tout le reste, la devise de notre ami, *Res non verba.*

Aussitôt que vous aurez terminé la rédaction que je vous demande, vous voudrez bien me l'adresser sur le champ au quartier général, en mettant sur l'enveloppe, *Affaires personnelles.*

Chérin

Vous avez, Citoyen, sur la position de l'Irlande, sur le naturel des habitans du pays, sur leur antipathie avec les Anglois et sur mille autres choses importantes des détails précieux que vous seul pouvez donner et que rien ne peut suppléer. Je vous invite à les remettre au porteur de ma lettre sur le champ.

To General Napoléon Bonaparte, 12 November 1797

T.C.D., Tone papers, MS 2050, f. 18.

Tone offers his services to Bonaparte, who is in command of the 'army of England' established by a decree of the Executive Directory.

L'adjudant général Smith, Irlandais, attaché au feu général Hoche pour la partie de sa correspondance chez l'étranger, au Général Buonaparte, commandant en chef [de] l'armée d'Italie.

Citoyen Général,

Ayant eu l'honneur d'être attaché au général Hoche pendant les derniers dix-huit mois de sa vie, et de l'accompagner dans son expédition d'Irlande, je m'empresse, d'après l'arrêté du Directoire Exécutif, qui crée une armée d'Angleterre, et vous en confie le commandement, de vous offrir mes services. J'ose espérer qu'à votre arrivée à Paris vous aurez lieu de me croire de quelqu'utilité. Au surplus je me rapporte, et pour ma conduite et pour ma moralité, à la bienveillance des citoyens directeurs Barras et La Réveillére.

Salut et respect,
James Smith

À Paris, ce 22 Brumaire, an 6 (pour copie conforme)

To General Louis Alexandre Berthier,
12 November 1797

T.C.D., Tone papers, MS 2050, f. 19.

Louis Alexandre Berthier (1753–1815), army officer before the revolution; général de division, 1795; chief of staff to Bonaparte in Italy and Egypt; marshal of the empire, 1804 (Six, *Dict. des généraux & amiraux*).

Tone asks Berthier to forward a letter to Bonaparte.

Cul de Sac Notre-Dame-des-Champs, No. 1390, près du Luxembourg

ce 22 Brumaire an 6

L'adjudant-général Smith au général Berthier, chef d'état-major de l'armée d'Italie

Général,

Permettez-moi de vous adresser un petit mémoire[1] que je voudrois faire parvenir au général-en-chef. Si dans la multiplicité de vos occupations vous ne vous ressouveniez plus de moi, je vous prierai de vous rappeller que j'ai eu l'honneur de vous être présenté il y a quelques jours par le général Hédouville.[2]

Salut et respect
J. Smith

(pour copie conforme)

Diary, 30 September–29 November 1797

T.C.D., Tone papers, MS 2049, ff 281ᵛ–284ᵛ; *Life*, ii, 449–53.

The diary entries for the period to 21 Nov. 1797 were evidently written up in arrears.

21 Nov. 1797[3]

It is today two months since I made a memorandum, which is downright scandalous, for many important circumstances have happened in that time. The only good in my journals is that they are written at the moment and represent things exactly as they strike me, whereas when I write after an interval of some time——; but I am going into an essay on journal writing

---

[1] Above.   [2] See Diary for 9 Nov. 1797 (below, p. 177).
[3] In the MS the date (in the form 'November 21ˢᵗ') is followed by an exclamation mark.

instead of minding my business. Let me endeavour to take up as well as I can from memory the thread of my story:

30 Sept. 1797

or thereabouts I arrived in Paris,[1] where I had the satisfaction to find my wife and little babies in health and spirits. Went to Lewines, who is in high favor here with everybody. He is all but acknowledged as minister from Ireland, and I am heartily glad of it, for I have an excellent opinion of his integrity and talents; he has the *entrées libres* with Barras, the Minister for the Marine Pléville Lepaley, and Talleyrand Périgord, Minister for Foreign Affairs,[2] whom I saw in Philadelphia when we were both in exile. In a day or two we went together to the Minister for the Marine in order to ask him to give me a note of introduction to Barras, but we were not able to beat it into his head that we did not want him to present me formally to the Directory as an agent from some foreign power, on which I set him down in my own mind for a dunce. In consequence of his refusal we determined to go ourselves to the Luxembourg, which we did accordingly two or three evenings after. We found Barras at home giving favorable audience to Madame Tallien,[3] with whom he retired into an inner room, where they continued, I have no doubt, very seriously employed for about half an hour. On his return we presented ourselves and I delivered him the memorial which General Daendels had entrusted me with for Gen[era]l Hoche,[4] and I at the same [time] detailed to him fully all the verbal instructions I had received from Gen[era]l Daendels. He heard me very attentively and told me in reply that he expected Gen[era]l Debelle (brother-in-law to Gen[era]l Hoche) in town every day, who had the thread of our affairs in his hands and that at his arrival I should address myself to him. We then took our leave after a short conversation between him and Lewines. Lewines tells me that he has Barras's word that if the Directory can make a separate peace with the Emperor,[5] they never will quit England until our independance shall be recognised, which is going a very great length on their part.

5 Oct. 1797

or thereabouts, Gen[era]l Debelle arrived and I immediately waited on him agreeably to Barras's orders. After telling him all I was instructed to do, he desired me to make a note of it, which I did accordingly and delivered it to him a day or two after. Some short time after he told me, *generally*, that the

---

[1] Tone was in Brussels on 27 Sept. when he wrote to his wife that he had secured a place in a Paris-bound diligence for the 29th and expected to arrive on 2 Oct. (see above, p. 155).

[2] *Life*, ii, 449, reads more clearly: 'Barras, Pléville Lepelley, Minister for the Marine, and Talleyrand Périgord, Minister for Foreign Affairs'.

[3] Jeanne Marie Ignace Thérèse Cabarrus (1773–1835) married in succession the marquis de Fontenay (from whom she was divorced), Jean Lambert Tallien, a member of the Convention, and the comte de Caraman, later prince de Chimay (*La grande encyclopédie*).

[4] See diary for 21 Aug. and 3 Sept. 1797 (above, pp 131–2, 142–3).

[5] Peace between France and Austria was in fact signed on 18 Oct. 1797 (see below, p. 176, n. 7).

Directory were determined to take up our business, and that most probably it would be Simon, Adj[utan]t Gen[era]l in the army of Sambre & Meuse, and who was in the same capacity with us in the *Armeé expéditionnaire*,[1] who would be charged with the command. I saw clearly the fact was that Debelle knew nothing of the determination of the Government; however, I received his information thankfully, and told him, as indeed the fact was, that I had a very good opinion of Simon, and that if they were decided to try an expedition on a small scale, I would not desire a better general to command it. Debelle set off for the army in a day or two after, and I have not seen him since. As it was now time to think a little of my own affairs, I applied to Gen[era]l Hédouville, whom I had known at Rennes and Brest, and who has been just nominated to the command of St Domingo, to obtain me an order to stay at Paris, in order to follow up the affair wherewith I was charged by Gen[era]ls Hoche and Daendels, and to receive the arrears of my appointments[2] which are due to me &c., &c. Gen[era]l Hédouville charged himself with my business in a manner so friendly that I shall never forget it. Besides speaking to Barras, he brought me to the Luxembourg and presented me to La Reveillère Lépaux, to whom he spoke of me in terms of great commendation. La Reveillère received me with attention and desired me to draw up a memorial stating my request, and to get it certified by the minister at war, and for foreign affairs, and it should be done. In consequence on the 15th

15 Oct. 1797[3]

Gen[era]l Hédouville introduced me to Talleyrand Périgord, who signed my memorial immediately, and the same day to Schérer,[4] minister at war, to whom he presented my memorial.[5] Schérer took it and promised to expedite it directly, but from that to this (viz. Nov[embe]r 21st) he has given himself no concern about it, which delay on his part I attribute to the circumstance of my being attached to Gen[era]l Hoche, whose very memory Schérer abhors, and to [my] having spoken respectfully of him in my memorial. If that be so, it is shabby to the last degree in Schérer, but we shall see more about it.[6]

The peace[7] is at last concluded with the Emperor, and England only remains. With the conditions of the peace, strictly speaking, I have nothing

---

[1] *Life*, ii, 450, substitutes 'expedition to Bantry Bay' for '*Armée expéditionnaire*'.
[2] i.e. allowances.
[3] MS reads 'on the 15th'. The heading is supplied by the editors in the usual form.
[4] Barthélemy Louis Joseph Schérer (1747–1804), an officer before the revolution; général de division, 1794; commanded the army of Italy, 1795–6; minister of war, 1797–9 (Six, *Dict. des généraux & amiraux*).
[5] Very probably the memorial he wrote for the Executive Directory on 15 Oct. (above, p. 160).
[6] In the MS the next paragraph is in darker ink and was probably written later.
[7] The treaty between the Emperor and France, signed on 18 Oct. 1797 at Campo-Formio, was published in the *Moniteur*, 28 Oct. 1797. Austria ceded Belgium and Milan to France, recognised her annexation of the left bank of the Rhine and received the western part of the former Venetian Republic.

to do, my great object and wish being confined to the prostration of the English tyranny; yet it is a great satisfaction to me to see that they are as favorable as, I think, any reasonable man can desire. The Cisalpine Republic is acknowledged, and I fancy we have got the Rhine for our limit. Venise goes to the Emperor, which is bad, if it could be helped, but we cannot have everything. Gen[era]l Berthier is the bearer of this great news. Firing of cannon, bonfires, illuminations &c., &c. Paris is today in great glory.

28 Oct. 1797[1]

This day, viz.[2] the day after the proclamation of the peace, I see an *arrêté* of the Directory ordaining the formation of an army, to be called *l'armée d'Angleterre*,[3] and appointing Buonaparte to command it. Bravo! This looks as if they were in earnest! Gen[era]l Desaix, from the Army of the Rhine, who distinguished himself so much by his defense of Kehl against Prince Charles[4] in the last campaign, is ordered to superintend the organisation of this army until the arrival of Buonaparte. All this is famous news.

3 Nov. 1797

This day Matt[5] joined me from Hambourg, where he arrived about a month ago. It is a great satisfaction to me, and I hope he arrives just in time to take a part in the expedition.

9 Nov. 1797

This day Gen[era]l Hédouville brought me to Gen[era]l Berthier and presented me to him, recommending me in the warmest manner. We had very little conversation,[6] but he promised to speak of me to Gen[era]l Buonaparte, whom he sets off to join in three or four days. Two days after I called and left for him a memorial of about five lines addressed to Buonaparte,[7] offering my services &c. It is droll enough that I should be writing to Buonaparte.

---

[1] This date is inferred from what follows. The heading is supplied, in the usual form, by the editors. Tone gives no date explicitly and there is no heading in the MS.

[2] The preceding three words, which come at the beginning of a new page in the MS, are omitted from *Life*.

[3] i.e. 'the army of England', the French army intended to invade Britain or Ireland.

[4] Tone seems to mean Archduke Charles (or Karl) of Austria.   [5] Mathew Tone.

[6] Berthier was a few years later described by an Irishwoman who met him in Paris as 'a little slouch'd-looking man, brusque in his manners and abrupt in his address' (*An Irish peer on the Continent, 1801–1803; being a narrative of the tour of . . . Earl Mount Cashell through France, Italy etc. as related by Catherine Wilmot*, ed. T. U. Sadleir (London, 1920), p. 47).

[7] Above, p. 173.

20 Nov. 1797

This day Gen[era]l Hédouville presented me to Gen[era]l Desaix, who is arrived within these few days. I could not possibly desire to meet a more favorable reception. He examined me a good deal as to the locality[1] of Ireland, the face of the country, the facility of finding provisions &c., on which I informed him as well as I could. He told me that he had not directly the power, himself, to name the officers who were to be employed in the army of England, but that I need not be uneasy, for I might rely I should be of the number. His expression, at my parting him, was *'Laissez-moi faire; nous arrangerons tout cela'*,[2] so I may happen to have another offer at John Bull before I die. God knows how I desire it! I like Desaix at least as well, if not better, than of any of his confrères that I have yet seen. There is a soldier-like frankness and sincerity in his manner, from which I auger everything favorable.

25 Nov. 1797

This day we (viz. Lewines, Lowry, Tenent, Orr,[3] Teeling and myself) gave a grand dinner at Meol's[4] to the Gen[era]ls Desaix, Hédouville, Watrin, Mermot,[5] Dufalgua[6] and one or two of their aid-de-camps. Watrin and Mermot we asked as being friends of Gen[era]l Hoche and embarked in the expedition of last year. Our dinner was superb, and everything went off very well. We had the Fort of Kehl represented in the dessert in compliment to Desaix &c., &c.

29 Nov. 1797

This day received my arrears for 4 months, so now I am at my ease as to cash; çy 2,330 livres.

To General Hermann Wilhelm Daendels, 4 December 1797

Tone (Dickason) papers.

---

[1] *Life*, ii, 453, has 'localities'.   [2] 'Leave it to me, we'll arrange all that.'
[3] Joseph Orr (d. 1799), a brazier and leading United Irishman in Londonderry; member of the national directory; fled to avoid arrest, July 1797; his application in Apr. 1798 to remain in Paris was supported by Paine; he was said by Samuel Turner to be 'a clever, sensible strong-minded man' (38 Geo. III, c. 80; Breandán Mac Suibhne, 'Up, not out: why did north-west Ulster not rise in 1798?' in Cathal Póirtéir (ed.), *The great Irish rebellion of 1798* (Cork, 1998), pp 86, 88; Archives Nationales, F⁷ 7293; P.R.O., HO 100/70, f. 341).
[4] Meol's is not mentioned in 'a list of the best restorateurs or chop houses' given in *A practical guide during a journey from London to Paris* (London, 1802), p. 104.
[5] Or Mermet? See above, vol. II, p. 317, n. 2.
[6] Louis Marie Joseph Maximilien de Caffarelli Du Falga (1756–99) served as an officer in the engineers before the revolution; lieut, 1781; capt., 1791; lost his left leg in action, 1795; général de

Tone states that General Hédouville, now in Paris, has taken an interest in him 'as if I were his closest relation' and introduced him to Barras and La Révellière, to the ministers of external relations, war and marine, and to Generals Berthier and Desaix, giving him hope of employment in the 'army of England'. He mentions Moira's recent speech at Westminster and arrests in Scotland, praises Dewinter for his 'heroic courage' and asks Daendels to keep in touch.

No. 2

Paris, ce 14 frimaire, an 6

L'adjudant général Smith au Général Daendels

Général,

J'ai reçu, il y a trois semaines environ, la lettre que vous avez eu la bonté de m'écrire, en date du 4 novembre dernier.[1] Depuis ce tems il n'est rien arrivé d'extraordinaire qui ne soit connu de tout le monde. Quant à moi, personellement, j'ai quelque chose à vous communiquer qui vous fera, j'espère, plaisir.

Le général Hédouville, ancien chef de l'état-major du Général Hoche, que j'ai connu à Brest lors de notre expédition, est maintenant à Paris, étant nommé par le Directoire Exécutif au commandement de St Domingue; il a eu la bonté de s'intéresser pour moi, comme si j'étais son plus proche parent. Il m'a présenté aux citoyens Barras et Réveillière, aux ministres des relations extérieures, de la guerre, et de la marine; il m'a aussi présenté au général Berthier, avant son départ pour joindre le général Buonaparte, comme une personne qui pourroit être de quelque utilité dans les circonstances actuelles, et ce général a eu la complaisance de se charger d'un très court mémoire, que j'ai adressé au général en chef offrant mes services; dernièrement le général Desaix étant arrivé à Paris le général Hédouville m'a encore présenté, et lui a parlé de moi d'une manière que je souhaiterois fort de pouvoir mériter. J'espère, en conséquence de tout cela, que je serai employé dans l'armée d'Angleterre. En attendant le Directoire m'a autorisé de rester à Paris, jusqu'à nouvel ordre.

Depuis l'arrivée du général Desaix, j'ai eu plusieurs entretiens avec lui sur l'état actuel des choses dans son pays, et je lui ai donné tous les renseignemens en mon pouvoir là-dessus. Je suis content de lui, on ne peut pas plus. Il a dans sa manière une sensibilité, une simplicité que je suis sûr vous trouveriez infiniment à votre gré, et comme vous lui écrirez, sans doute, vous me ferez en même tems un grand plaisir et un service d'avoir la bonté de me charger de lui présenter votre lettre; d'après tout ce que j'ai pu remarquer, vous pouvez lui parler à coeur ouvert, et avec la plus grande confiance.

brigade, 1795; commanded engineers attached to the *armée d'Angleterre*, Jan.–Mar. 1798; served in Egyptian expedition (Six, *Dict. des généraux & amiraux*).

[1] Above, pp 170–71.

Quant à la décision du gouvernement français, vous en serez instruit par le citoyen Giauque[1] autant qu'il la sait lui-même. Je suis presque sûr qu'ils ne quitteront jamais le gouvernement anglois avant que de l'avoir bouleversé et qu'ils feront l'impossible pour y réussir. Enfin, général, je suis intimement persuadé que vous pouvez, de votre côté, prendre les arrangemens nécessaires avec la dernière certitude de la sincérité du Directoire et de la chaleur, de l'acharnement même, qu'ils mettront dans tout ce qui pourroit accélerer la chute prochaine de cet ennemi du genre humain et de la liberté et la prospérité du monde. Quant à moi, je n'ai pas la moindre doute là-dessus; je compte sur le Directoire comme je compterois sur vous, et il ne faut pas dire davantage.

Je viens de lire dans les dernières gazettes anglaises un discours du Lord Moira, dans la Chambre des pairs à Londres, sur l'état des choses en Irlande.[2] Vous le trouverez, je crois, dans le journal intitulé the *Courier* en date du 23 novembre, et je vous prierai, général, de le faire remarquer à ces membres de votre gouvernement qui savent l'anglois. Vous verrez là comment les misérables Irlandais sont tourmentés par leurs tyrans implacables; vous verrez en même tems que le nombre des Irlandais Unis est plus que triplé depuis que la conspiration a été dénoncée par le ministre anglois. Vous verrez aussi, dans les mêmes gazettes, qu'un nombre de personnes assez considérable vient d'être arrêté dans l'Écosse pour avoir commencé un système pareil à celui des Irlandais Unis,[3] et vous vous souviendrez sans doute des conversations que nous avions à ce sujet, au Texel, avec mes amis et de tout ce qu'ils vous disoient alors. Vous voyez que quoiqu'ils n'ayent parlé qu'avec beaucoup de retenue ils avaient bien raison en tout ce qu'ils vous ont conté, il me semble, Général, que dans la distribution des grands momens qui vont avoir lieu, ce sera l'Écosse qui doit le plus naturellement attirer toute votre attention, pour des raisons qui sautent aux yeux. La personne dont je vous ai parlé dans ma dernière lettre[4] sera toujours prête à recevoir vos ordres; il pourra vous communiquer des renseignemens précieux sur tout ce qui concerne ce pays.

Quant à l'égard des choses à Brest, je n'en suis pas instruit. Je crois, cependant, qu'on y fait maintenant fort peu de choses, et que rien ne sera prêt avant le printems. Je ne sais, non plus, quand on commencera l'organisation de l'armée d'Angleterre. Aussitôt que j'en connoîtrai quelque chose, je ne manquerai pas de vous en avertir.

J'avais oublié de vous dire, Général, dans ma dernière lettre, que le citoyen Meyer m'a remis 92 florins de votre part; je vous en fais mes remercimens.

---

[1] i.e. Lewines.

[2] In a debate in the British house of lords on 22 Nov. 1797, Moira urged the government to adopt a conciliatory policy in Ireland (*Parliamentary History*, xxxiii, 1050–66).

[3] George Mealmaker, a leader of the United Scotsmen, a body that owed much to the influence of the United Irishmen, was arrested at Dundee in November 1797; more arrests followed at Perth, Dundee and Edinburgh (Elaine W. McFarland, *Ireland and Scotland in the age of revolution* (Edinburgh, 1994), pp 140, 153–62, 167).

[4] Probably John Aherne; see Tone's letter to Daendels of 21 Oct. (above, esp. p. 166, n. 2).

Si vous le jugez convenable, vous aurez, j'espère, la bonté de m'envoyer la lettre que vous écrirez au général Desaix. Il vous instruira, sans doute, de tout ce qui concernera l'organisation prochaine de l'armée. Je lui ai déjà montré votre dernière lettre.[1] Si l'amiral De Winter revient à la Haye comme il est dit dans les journaux anglois, je vous prie, général, de lui présenter mes très sincères amitiés. Tout le monde ici est d'accord sur le courage héroïque qu'il a montré dans le dernier combat,[2] mais je crois ne devoir pas vous cacher qu'on est fort étonné de la sortie de la flotte batave sans aucun objet majeur, ni motif déterminé, comme il parait, et qu'on en dit bien de choses et de très sévères même; mais rien de tout cela ne tombe sur le brave de Winter, qu'on loue ici, à l'envie, et avec bien de raison.

Je vous prie, Général, de m'écrire de tems en tems. Comptez toujours sur le zèle que je mettrai à exécuter vos ordres, si vous m'en donnez, aussi bien que sur le sincère estime que j'ai pour vous, et la reconnoissance que je sens de toutes vos bontés.

Salut et respect.

J. S.

Diary, 10–12 December 1797

T.C.D., Tone papers, MS 2049, ff 284ᵛ–285ʳ; *Life*, ii, 453–4.

10 Dec. 1797

This day was a grand fête to receive the ratification of the treaty of peace by the Emperor,[3] which has been brought up by Buonaparte in person to the Directory.[4] It was superb, and I am particularly pleased with Barras the president's speeches, wherein there reigns a spirit of the most determined hostility to England. As far as I can observe, all parties in France are sincerely united in this sentiment.

12 Dec. 1797

Called this day with Lewines on Gen[era]l Desaix and gave him Taylor's map of Ireland.[5] He tells us to be under no anxiety; that the French government will never quit the grip they have got of England till they humble her to the dust; that it is their wish and their interest, that of all France, as well as of Ireland; that the government had now means, and powerful ones,

---

[1] Above, pp 170–71. [2] At Camperdown on 11 Oct. 1797.
[3] See above, p. 176, n. 7.
[4] The Directory welcomed Bonaparte in the courtyard of the Luxembourg, Bonaparte making a short speech and Barras a long one (*Moniteur*, 12, 13 Dec. 1797).
[5] Probably Alexander Taylor's *A new map of Ireland . . . for the use of travellers* (London, 1793).

particularly money, and they would devote them all to this great object; it might be a little sooner or a little later, but that the success of the measure was inevitable. Barras has lately in one or two different conversations gone as far with Lewines as Desaix has done today.

From General Hermann Wilhelm Daendels, 12 December 1797

Tone (Dickason) papers.

Daendels congratulates Tone on the news conveyed in his letter of 4 Dec. (above, pp 178–81) and thinks Scotland most likely to fall to an attack.

> La Haye le 12ᵉ Décembre 1797
> L'an 3ᵐᵉ de la Liberté Batave

Le Lieutenant Général Daendels
à l'Adjudant Général Smith

Recevez toutes mes félicitations, mon cher Smith, pour ce que vous m'annoncez d'heureux et pour vos intérêts et pour ceux de votre patrie. Vous devez sentir, combien je me rejouis de voir que le gouvernement français s'occupe sérieusement d'abbattre le seul ennemi qui peut encore opposer des obstacles à la prospérité de nos deux républiques, et j'espère que l'énergie qu'il montre dans ses résolutions en inspirera aussi la nôtre. Mais je crains bien que l'absence d'une constitution, que nos misérables divisions de partis, ne viennent encore augmenter notre lenteur nationale dans l'adoption ou l'exécution des mesures que nous avons à prendre pour être à même de seconder les entreprises de la France. Il seroit très instant que le Directoire put faire des ouvertures à notre gouvernement sur les opérations qu'il médite et sur la nécessité de hâter ses préparatifs. Nous n'avons pas même assez de tems, si nous voulons réparer pour le printems prochain les pertes qu'a essuyé notre flotte. C'est ce qu'il faudroit faire sentir au Général Dessaix, et c'est ce que je lui témoigne dans la lettre que vous trouverez ci–joint. Mais vous, qui avez été à même de connôitre l'indécision et la lenteur des formes de notre gouvernement provisoire, vous pourrez facilement lui développer ce qui seroit inutile et ennuyeux à dire dans une lettre, et lui faire sentir la nécessité de stimuler notre pas, non pas notre zèle, qui est assez chaud, mais l'énergie de notre gouvernement pour le mettre en pratique.

J'envoye au Général Dessaix copie de la carte d'Irlande dont le Général Hoche m'a fait présent. Je lui offre d'autres objets de ce genre qui peuvent lui être utile. Je désire bien, qu'à mesure que les préparatifs se font, que les opérations se méditent, nous puissions entretenir une correspondance particulière entre nous deux, qui nous éclairant mutuellement, serviroit peut-être à mettre de l'ensemble dans les idées et les mesures des deux gouvernements, et nous ameneroit à des résultats utiles, soit pour la célérité des préparatifs, soit pour le succès de l'expédition elle-même.

Je pense bien que si l'on médite une attaque générale, ce sera l'Écosse qui nous tombera en partage, et quoique j'aye une collection déjà assez complette de cartes et de mémoires sur cette partie, je vous serois très obligé, si vous pouviez me procurer les plans des trois forts du Nord, St George, Williams et August.[1] J'ai déjà ceux de Sterling et de Édimbourg.

Adieu, mon cher Smith, comptez toujours sur la plus grande estime et la plus sincère amitié.

Le Lieutenant Général
Daendels

Diary, 13–17 December 1797

T.C.D., Tone papers, MS 2049, f. 285^r; *Life*, ii, 454.

13 Dec. 1797

Talleyrand-Périgord sent for Lewines this morning to tell him that the Directory were positively determined on our business, that the arrangements were all concluded upon, and everything would be ready for April next, viz. about four months from this. All this is very good.

17 Dec. 1797

Called with Lewines on Gen[era]l Desaix and gave him a letter from Gen[era]l Daendels. Desaix repeated the assurances which Talleyrand had given on the 13th, and told us further that Buonaparte and the Directory were now occupied in the organisation of the Marine and the funds, and that, when that was arranged, the military part of the business would be easily settled; finally he desired us to set our hearts at ease, for that every thing was going on as well as we could possibly desire it.

From General Hermann Wilhelm Daendels, 20 December 1797

Tone (Dickason) papers.

Daendels tells Tone that he is taking an opportunity to send him duplicates of letters sent few days ago, one of them for Desaix; he asks Tone to tell

---

[1] *Recte* 'George, William et Augusta'.

Desaix that he has found an opportunity to get from England a collection of maps.

La Haye, le 20 X^bre 1797

Le Lieutenant-Général Daendels

À l'Adjudant-G[énér]al Smith

Le Citoyen Vichery,[1] adjudant-g[énér]al du G[énér]al Dumonceau, se rendant à Paris, je profite de cette occasion, mon cher Smith, pour vous envoyer un duplicata des lettres que je vous ai adressées il y a quelques jours. Parmi ces lettres vous en trouverez une pour le g[énér]al Dessaix, et si la première s'étoit égarée celle-ci pourra toujours vous être utile pour la lui présenter de ma part. Vous pourrez lui dire aussi que j'ai trouvé une occasion pour me faire venir d'Angleterre une collection de cartes la plus complette indépendamment des atlas généraux. Je dois avoir les cartes particulières des différens comtés; je dois avoir aussi des cartes maritimes de toutes les côtes. Dès que ces cartes me seront parvenues, si le général le désire, je lui en ferai faire des copies.

Vous rappellerez sûrement d'avoir vu le C[itoye]n Vichery et vous savez qu'il jouit de la confiance entière du g[énér]al Dumonceau et de la mienne. Ainsi je vous serois obligé de le présenter au G[énér]al Dessaix et de lui dire qu'il peut avoir avec lui toutes les ouvertures et obtenir par lui une intimité de renseignemens que la brièveté d'une lettre et l'incertitude de son arrivée empêche ordinairement de donner par écrit.

Adieu, mon cher Smith, recevez l'assurance de mon inviolable amitié.

Daendels

Cul de Sac Notre-Dame-des-Champs No. 1390, près du Luxembourg

Diary, 21–3 December 1797

T.C.D., Tone papers, MS 2049, ff 285^r–287^r; *Life*, 454–6, 451–2, 456.

21 Dec. 1797

Gen[era]l Desaix brought Lewines and me this morning and introduced us to Buonaparte at his house in the Rue Chantereine. He lives in the greatest simplicity; his house is small, but neat, and all the furniture and ornaments

---

[1] Louis Joseph Vichery (1767–1831), *sous-officier* before the Revolution; *sous-lieutenant*, 1792; aide-de-camp to Dumonceau, Oct. 1793 to Feb. 1794; entered Dutch service, June 1796; lieut col., July 1797; commanded under Davout in Grand Army; created baron, 1817 (Six, *Dict. des généraux & amiraux*).

in the most classical taste. He is about five feet six inches high, slender and well made, but stoops considerably; he looks at least ten years older than he is, owing to the great fatigue he underwent in his immortal campaign of Italy. His face is that of a profound thinker, but with no marks of that great enthousiasm and that unceasing activity by which he is so much distinguished; it is rather to my mind the countenance of a mathematician than of a general. He has a fine eye, and great firmness about his mouth; he speaks low and hollow. So much for his figure and manner. We had not much discourse with him, and what little there was, was between him and Lewines, to whom, as our ambassador, I gave the *pas*.[1] We told him that Tenent was about to depart for Ireland and was ready to charge himself with his orders, if any he had to give. He desired us to bring him the same evening and so we took our leave. In the evening we returned with Tenent, and Lewines had a good deal of conversation with him, that is to say, Lewines *insensed* him a good deal on Irish affairs, of which it appears he is a good deal uninformed; for example, he seems convinced that our population is not more than *two* millions, which is nonsense.[2] Buonaparte listened but said very little. When all this was finished he desired that Tenent might put off his departure for a few days, and then turning to me he asked whether I was not an adjudant general, to which I answered that I had the honor to be attached to Gen[era]l Hoche in that capacity. He then asked me where I had learned to speak French, to which I replied that I had learned the little I knew since my arrival in France about 20 months ago. He then desired us to return that next evening but one at the same hour, and so we parted. As to my French, I am ignorant whether it was the purity or the barbarism of my diction that drew his attention, and as I shall never inquire, it must remain as an historical doubt, to be investigated by the learned of future ages.

22 Dec. 1797

Good news today! The merchants of Paris have presented a famous address to the Directory encouraging them to the war with England, and,[3] which is the criterion of their sincerity, offering to advance money for that purpose. The Directory, of course, received them with the greatest respect and made a flourishing reply, which, as well as the address, they transmitted immediately to the two Councils,[4] where the news was received with great applause and

---

[1] i.e. gave priority.

[2] The recollection in 1812 of an Irishman who twice met Bonaparte in 1802 was that 'he seemed to understand nothing of this noble island of Ireland more than to have a general idea of its religious differences with England. He erroneously thought the entire country Catholic. I afterwards knew that he entertained a very poor idea of the Irish nation.' (John Bernard Trotter, *Memoirs of the latter years of the right honourable Charles James Fox* (London, 1811), pp 264, 271, 342; idem, *Walks through Ireland in the years 1812, 1814 and 1817* (London, 1819), p. 199).

[3] Ampersand in MS.   [4] i.e. the Council of Five Hundred and the Council of Ancients.

satisfaction.[1] I regard this as of great consequence, not so much on account of the money (25,000,000#,[2] as I understand), tho' that sum is very convenient just now, as on account of the spirit which dictates the loan, and above all of the confidence which it seems the monied men (no bad judges in such affairs) have in the establishment of the Government. I have no doubt but, in this point of view, it will produce a great effect on the mind of every thinking man in England. It will prove that the republic and the Directory have taken an *assiette*, an *aplomb*, as the French call it, which may embarrass John Bull not a little in his future discussions with the Great Nation, as the French have begun latterly, and not without great reason, to call themselves. This without doubt is the *money* to which Desaix alluded the other day.

23 Dec. 1797

Called this evening on Buonaparte, by appointment, with Tenent and Lewines and saw him for about five minutes. Lewines gave him a copy of the memorial[3] I delivered to the Government in February 1796 (viz. nearly two years since) and which fortunately has been well verified in all the material facts by everything which has taken place in Ireland since. He also gave him Taylor's map, and shewed him half a dozen of Hoche's letters, which Buonaparte read over. He then desired us to return in two or three days with such documents relating to Ireland as we were possessed of, and in the meantime that Tenent should postpone his departure. We then left him. His manner is cold, and he speaks very little; it is not however so dry as that of Hoche, but seems rather to proceed from languor than anything else. He is perfectly civil however to us, but from anything we have yet seen or heard from him, it is impossible to augur anything good or bad. We have now seen the greatest man in Europe three times, and I am astonished to think how little I have to record about him. I am sure I wrote ten times as much about my first interview with Charles De la Croix,[4] but then I was a greenhorn. I am now a little used to see great men, and great statesmen, and great generals, and that has in some degree broke down my admiration. Yet after all it is droll that I should become acquainted with Buonaparte!

It is singular enough that I should have forgot to mention in its place the famous battle[5] fought on the 11th of October between the English fleet under Admiral Duncan and the Dutch commanded by De Winter. It shews the necessity of making memorandums on the moment. There never was a completer victory than that gained by the English. The fleets were equal in

---

[1] A deputation to the Directory from the Paris chamber of commerce expressed its willingness to subscribe to a loan raised to pay for the invasion of England, the proud tyrant of the seas (*Moniteur*, 23 Dec. 1797).   [2] i.e. 'livres', as amended in *Life*.

[3] Above, vol. II, pp 61–70, 88–97.

[4] In fact Tone wrote only two sentences describing Delacroix in his diary for the day of their first meeting, 15 February 1796; the description he wrote after meeting him again two days later was also brief (above, vol. II, pp 54, 56).   [5] At Camperdown.

number, but the enemy had the advantage in number of guns and weight of metal. De Winter fought like a lion, and defended himself to the last, but was at length forced to strike, as were *nine* of his fleet out of sixteen whereof they[1] consisted. With him were taken the Admirals Reyntjies[2] (who is since dead) and Meunez.[3] Bloys[4] lost his right arm, and Story[5] is the only one who came off clear; the last two were not taken. I cannot conceive why the Dutch government sent out their fleet at that season, without motive or object, as far as I can learn. My opinion is that it is direct treason and that the fleet was sold to Pitt; so thinks Barras, Pléville le Pelley and even Meyer, the Dutch ambassador, whom I have seen once or twice. It is well I was not on board the *Vryheid*. If I had, it would have been a pretty piece of business! I fancy I am not to be caught at sea by the English, for this is the second escape I have had, and by land I mock myself of them.

This time twelvemonth I arrived in Brest from my expedition to Bantry Bay. Well, the third time, they say, is the charm; my next chance, I hope, will be with the *armée d'Angleterre*! Allons, vive la république! I write no memorandums now at all, at all, which is grievous, but I have nothing to write &c., &c.

From Colonel Henri Sheé, 25 December 1797

Tone (Dickason) papers.

Bonn of 5th Nivôse 6th year

My dear Friend,

I am indebted to you this month past of an answer to your letter of ye 22d ul[tim]o,[6] but you must forgive the miserable condition I have been in with the gout in both hands & therefore under an impossibility of writing.

Altho' you could get no admittance near the person[7] I had given you a letter for, he answered me but in such terms as convinced me that, whatever may be the reason, he is entirely out of credit near the present members who lead the Republ[ic], which I am heartily sorry for, believing him an upright honnest man; however mistakes in a revolution are unavoidable, wittness what happened my nephew[8] for whose true patriotism & candour I would pledge my head. Notwithstanding his momentary disgrace, I know

---

[1] Corrected in *Life*, ii, 452, to 'it'.

[2] Commander of the *Jupiter* at the Texel in 1797 (see Tone's diary for 14 July 1797, above, p. 101).

[3] Not identified.

[4] Jacob Arnout Bloys van Treslong (1756–1825), commander of the *Brutus* (*Nieuw Nederlandsch biografisch woordenboek*, v, 39).   [5] Commander of the *Staaten Generaal* (see above, p. 101).

[6] Not found. It must have been written on the same day as Tone's letters to Bonaparte and Berthier, 12 Nov. 1797 (above, pp 173–4).   [7] Not identified.

[8] Henri Clarke, whose closeness to Carnot had cost him his employment after the coup d'état of Fructidor.

that he stands on distinguished terms with Buonaparte & that his recommendation will go far with s[ai]d general. So I advise you to try your chance on that side. To be sure it is a thousand pity [*sic*] that one who shew'd your zeal & constancy in the pursuit of a cause so interesting for the French republ[ic] must sollicit & crave to be permitted to contribute powerfully towards the success of it. But let not that discourage you, consider it is the wellfare of your country that is at stake & that after all you have rubbed through these two years you must like a brave Irishman gain your point in spite of all the obstacles laid in your way.

Would to God my miserable limbs could support the wishes of my heart & I would very readily take my chance of another campaign in hopes of seeing my countrymen revenged of the proud tiranical English government, but alas my situation of health is so desperate that I am forced to give up all hopes of being one among ye. May every success attend you wherever you strike the blow. My warmest wishes will follow you wherever the fortune of war will conduct you, remember that you leave at this side of the water a sincere lover of his country & a true friend.

Sheé

Au Citoyen Smith, adjutant général
Cul de Sac Notre Dame des Champs
No. 1390 près du Luxembourg
À Paris

Charles Maurice de Talleyrand-Périgord to Pierre Sotin, 28 December 1797

Archives Nationales, Police Générale, F⁷ 7293, dossier B⁴ 2671; copy ('duplicata') in Tone (Dickason) papers.

An earlier version, dated 7 nivôse an 6, is in Archives des Affaires Étrangères, Corresp. Politique Angleterre, cote 592, f. 139.

Talleyrand instructs the minister of police to seek Tone's advice on each Irishman claiming to be a refugee patriot.

Paris, ce 8 nivôse an 6 de la
République Française

Le Ministre des Relations Extérieures
 au Ministre de la Police Générale

Vous sçavez, mon cher collègue, qu'il se trouve en France un certain nombre d'Irlandais qui tous se disent patriotes réfugiés et prétendent avoir embrassé et servi la cause de la liberté.

Cela demande un examen que vous seul pouvez faire.

Je dois vous prévenir que l'intention du Directoire Exécutif est que vous veuilliez bien appeller le citoyen Smith, adjudant général du feu général Hoche, et prendre de lui des renseignemens sur chaqu'un des dits Irlandois.

Vous jugerez dans votre sagesse, mon cher collègue, du parti qu'il conviendra de prendre à l'égard de ceux dont le citoyen Smith ne garantirait pas le civisme et l'attachement à la République.

Salut et fraternité
Ch. Maur. Talleyrand

Diary, 1–13 January 1798

T.C.D., Tone papers, MS 2049, ff 287ᵛ–288ᵛ; *Life*, ii, 456–8.

1 Jan. 1798

I wish myself the compliments of the season—a merry Christmass and a happy new year! Received a letter from my sister,[1] wherein she informs me that my father has at last received a letter from Will,[2] from whom I have not heard since 1794. He is alive and well, in the service of the Mahrattas[3] with a liberal appointment of £750 p[er] annum, and this is the whole of what she tells me and, I suppose, of what she knows. It is most provoking that they did not send her his letter, or at least a copy of it. I do not even know the date. I cannot express the satisfaction I feel at this news, which is certainly not diminished by the reflection that he is not in the British service. Poor fellow! Well, we may meet yet, for our family, I see, are not to be sunk. We are, to be sure, a strange set, for proof of which see the History of my Life and Opinions, written by myself (which buy).[4] Wrote to my sister, desiring her, of all love, to procure and forward to me a copy of Will's letter.

One or two things have happened lately which give me personally some pleasure. The minister for foreign affairs[5] has written to the minister of police[6] that whereas Pitt may probably endeavour to slide in some of his emissaries, under the character of refugee United Irishmen, none are to be permitted to remain but such as I may vouch for, which shews they have some confidence in me, and the minister of police has given his orders in consequence. The

---

[1] Mary Giauque, who was living in Hamburg.

[2] A letter from William Henry Tone to Peter Tone, 25 Jan. 1797, is printed above (pp 8–11); a rather similar letter, dated 1 Jan. 1797, is printed in R. R. Madden, *The United Irishmen*, 3rd ser. (London, 1846), i, 182. Neither, however, seems to be the letter referred to here.

[3] The Mahrattas were a Hindu confederacy dominant in central India.

[4] Last two words omitted from *Life*. The 'History of my life and opinions' to which Tone refers is the document usually described as his 'Autobiography'; it is printed above (vol. II, pp 260–306, 320–41).   [5] Talleyrand.

[6] Sotin de la Coindière.

first use I made of this was to apply for the liberty of two lads, named Burgess and Macan,[1] who are detained at Liège, and I am in hopes they are enlarged before this. Another thing is, a young man, whom I do not know, named Mc Kenna[2] who was recommended, as he says, by Tallien,[3] applied to Buonaparte to be employed as his secretary and interpreter. Buonaparte after some discourse gave him for answer to address himself to me, and that I should report thereupon to him, Buonaparte. All this is very good. I have not seen the general since but I expect I shall in a few days.

6 Jan. 1798

Called on my old friend Gen[era]l Clark[e], who is at last returned to Paris. His close connexion with Carnot has thrown him out of employment and I am heartily sorry for it, for I have a very good opinion of him; he is however very well with Buonaparte, to whom he tells me he has spoken of me in the stongest manner, for which I feel most sincerely obliged. Buonaparte, among other things, asked him whom he had most confidence in as to Irish affairs, and Clarke answered, in me by all means. I thanked Clarke heartily for all this, and at the same time explained to him the nature of Lewines's mission and my wish to cede him the pas on all occasions, &c. We talked a great deal of Hoche, of our Bantry Bay expedition &c., &c., and parted the best friends in the world. I was very glad to see Clarke, and it is a great pity and loss that he is not employed.

13 Jan. 1798

Saw Buonaparte this evening with Lewines, who delivered him a whole sheaf of papers relative to Ireland, including my two memorials of 1795,[4] great part of which stands good yet. After Lewines had had a good deal of

---

[1] Thomas Burgess (d. 1848) and Anthony MacCann, both of Drogheda, Co. Louth, had fled to Hamburg and then proceeded to Paris to offer their services to the republic. They attached themselves to Tandy and served on his expedition to Rutland Island in Sept. 1798. Later Burgess studied music and painting, while MacCann became the business partner of Thomas Ridegway, owner of the *Providence*, a smuggling vessel operating between Hamburg and the British Isles. In 1800 MacCann met Thomas Campbell, the Scottish poet, at Altona, and inspired his melancholy verses, 'The exile of Erin'. In 1837, in his autobiographical notes, Campbell recalled MacCann as 'an honest, excellent man—who is still, I believe, alive—at least I left him in prosperous circumstances at Altona a few years ago' (*Life and letters of Thomas Campbell*, ed. William Beattie (3 vols, London, 1849), i, 330–31; Miles Byrne, *Memoirs* (3 vols, Paris, 1863), iii, 48–50; Paul Weber, *On the road to rebellion: the United Irishmen and Hamburg* (Dublin, 1997), pp 122–4, 173, 185–6).

[2] Perhaps Thomas McKenna, a native of Maghera, Co. Londonderry, who entered the Irish College, Paris, in 1785 and was the spokesman of students there in 1790. He was adjutant to Tandy on his expedition to Rutland Island in 1798; he became a wealthy merchant and in 1807, when Miles Byrne met him at Boulogne-sur-Mer, was a shipowner and privateer. (Liam Swords, *The green cockade* (Dublin, 1989), pp 33–5, 56, 128, 134, 236–7, 247; *Castlereagh corr.*, i, 406–9; Byrne, *Memoirs*, ii, 50, iii, 165–6). [3] Jean Lambert Tallien (1767–1820), member of the Convention.

[4] Probably Tone means his two memorials of Feb. 1796 (above, vol. II, pp 61–70, 88–97).

discourse with him, I mentioned the affair of McKenna, who desires, it seems, to be employed as secretary and interpreter.[1] Buonaparte observed that he believed the world thought he had fifty secretaries, whereas he had but one. Of course there was an end of that business; however, he bid me see what the young[2] man was fit for and let him know. I took this opportunity to mention the desire all the refugee United Irishmen now in Paris had to bear a part in the expedition and the utility they would be of in case of a landing in Ireland. He answered that undoubtedly they would be all employed and desired me to give him in, for that purpose, a list of their names. Finally I spoke of myself, telling him that Gen[era]l Desaix had informed me I was carried on the *tableau* of the army of England.[3] He said I was. I then observed that I did not pretend to be of the smallest use to him while we remained in France, but that I hoped to be serviceable to him on the other side of the water; that I did not give myself to him at all for a military man, having neither the knowledge nor the experience that would justify me in charging myself with any function. *'Mais vous êtes brave'*, said he, interrupting me. I replied, when the occasion presented itself, it would appear. *'Eh bien'*, said he, *'ça suffit'*. We then took our leave.

To Pierre Sotin, 16 January 1798

T.C.D., Tone papers, MS 2050, ff 20ʳ–20ᵛ.

Tone replies to two letters received the previous day about 'Irishmen who have just arrived in France and who desire to have passports'. Of Captain Macdermott he is uncertain; of a certain Sunderlin he knows nothing. Being in a dilemma when asked an opinion on persons with whom he is not acquainted, Tone suggests they all be sent 'to some frontier town like Guise or Péronne'. Finally, he asks the minister to give suitable protection to John Ashley and James Maguire.

27 Nivôse an 6

Au ministre de la police

Citoyen ministre,

J'ai reçu hier deux lettres que vous avez voulu bien écrire au sujet des Irlandais qui viennent d'arriver en France et [dés]irent avoir des passeports. Quand [*sic*] au Capitaine Macdermott,[4] je n'ai pas l'avantage de le connoître; tout ce que je sais, c'est qu'il y [a] une famille irlandaise très respectable qui porte ce nom et dont les principes sont patriotes, mais j'ignore s'il soit

---

[1] *Life*, ii, 458, reads 'who desires to be employed as Secretary'.   [2] *Life* omits 'young'.

[3] In a decree of the Directory, dated 12 Jan. 1798, the text of which was dictated by Bonaparte and corrected in his own hand, 'Smith' (i.e. Tone) is listed among the senior officers of the *armée d'Angleterre* or 'army of England' (*Correspondance de Napoléon 1ᵉʳ* (32 vols, Paris, 1858–70), iii, 480).

[4] Possibly the Citizen MacDermot, retired infantry captain (possibly 87th regiment), who in Thermidor an 6 (19 July–17 Aug. 1798) was ordered to go to Brest (Archives de la Guerre, dossier).

de cette famille ou non.[1] Cependant, s'il m'est permis de vous offrir mon opinion, je crois qu'il n'y aura pas d'inconvénient de le laisser venir à Paris, d'autant plus que je n'ai jamais connu un officier des ci-devants régiments irlandais au service de la France qui ne détestoit cordialement le gouvernement anglais. À l'égard du nommé Sunderlin,[2] dont il est question, je l'ignore absolument, mais s'il est marin, comme il dit, je crois que le meilleur moyen d'en tirer parti seroit de l'envoyer à Brest; s'il est ami de la liberté il pourra y montrer son zèle et son courage dans la cause de la république.

Je profite de cette occasion, Citoyen Ministre, pour vous soumettre une idée qui se présente. Comme il est presque certain que dans la crise actuelle il y aura beaucoup de véritables patriotes, tant Irlandais qu'Anglais et Écossais, qui tâcheront de passer en France, ne fût-ce que pour concourir dans la grande expédition qui se prépare il est plus que vraisemblable que Pitt tâchera de faire glisser parmi le nombre quelques faux frères pour espionner l'état des choses; or puisque vous me faites l'honneur de me consulter, je serai dans le cas, ou de garantir le patriotisme des gens que je ne connois pas, ou d'être la cause innocente du renvoi d'autres qui pourront bien être d'excellens sujets et des patriotes qu'on pourroit utilement employer. Voilà donc, je crois, un moyen d'éviter cet embarras. Si je connois les individus qui pourroient demander des passeports &c., je vous dirai franchement toute la vérité à leur égard; si je ne les connois pas, le meilleur moyen, il me semble, sera de les envoyer tous à quelque ville frontière, comme Guise ou Péronne,[3] où ils seroient en sûreté et à même d'être surveillés; s'ils sont des bons patriotes, l'inconvénient ne sera pas grand pour eux, et s'ils sont des mauvais sujets il seront mis hors d'état de faire du mal.[4]

Il vient d'arriver dernièrement deux réfugiés qui se sont adressés à moi, l'un anglais nommé John Ashley[5] ci-devant secrétaire de la Société Populaire de Correspondance Générale à Londres, et qui est connu pour être tel par Thomas Paine, ex-député; l'autre nommé James Maguire,[6] Irlandais qui m'est envoyé spécialement de ce pays. Ils viennent directement de la Haÿe avec des passeports du Citoyen Charles de la Croix. D'après la permission que vous avez voulu bien m'accorder, de m'adresser à vous en faveur des réfugiés que je connoisse, je vous

---

[1] An allusion to the MacDermot family of Coolavin, Co. Sligo, whose head was Hugh MacDermot (see above, vol. I, pp 153–4). [2] Not identified. The MS is indistinct.

[3] Guise and Péronne, in northern France, were by 1797 no longer frontier towns but they were fortified and so still of military importance.

[4] In the MS the words 'et hors la capacité de faire du mal' follow but are crossed out.

[5] John Ashley (1762?–1829), shoemaker of Red Lion Sq., London, secretary of the London Corresponding Society in 1795 and 1796; he resigned from the society, June 1797, and went to Paris, where he successfully continued his trade (Mary Thale (ed.), *Selections from the papers of the London Corresponding Society, 1792–1799* (Cambridge, 1983), pp xix–xx, 400, 426; B.L., Add. MSS 27814–15).

[6] James Macguire or Maguire took part in Hardy's expedition, sailing on a frigate, was captured, but returned to France in 1799; he was frequently on active service until he retired as a captain in the 3ème régiment étranger in 1811. When in 1812 he applied to be recalled Major William Lawless supported his application, declaring that his conduct was always brave, loyal and exemplary. He is probably the Captain Macguire referred to by Miles Byrne and who died in 1822. (*Life*, ii, 521; Miles Byrne, *Memoirs* (Paris, 1863), iii, 13, 51–2, 66–7; Archives de la Guerre, dossier).

prie, citoyen Ministre, de vouloir bien leur accorder telle protection que vous jugerez convenable, pendant leur séjour à Paris, et je réponds de leur conduite.

Salut et respect

L'adj[udan]t gén[éra]l

J. Smith

Diary, 22 January 1798

T.C.D., Tone papers, MS 2049, ff 289^r–290^r; *Life*, ii, 458–60.

22 Jan. 1798

There has been a 18 fructidor in Holland,[1] and some of those whom I saw at the Hague at the head of affairs are now in arrestation, particularly Becker and Hahn. It was Hahn that drew up the proclamation which was to have been published on our landing in case the expedition had taken place. It is three months at least since Meyer, the Dutch ambassador here, told Giauque[2] and me that this event would take place; and the fact is that it seems to me to have been full as necessary in Holland as it was in France. If the late government was honest (which I very much doubt) they were evidently incapable; witness their conduct in the maritime affairs of their country, and more especially their sending out Dewinter to be sacrificed on the 11th of October,[3] without rhime, reason or apparent object that I can hear of from any quarter. Some time since Daendels sent up Adj[utan]t Gen[era]l Vischery, who brought me a letter desiring me to present him to Gen[era]l Desaix as a person in whom Daendels had the utmost confidence, which I did accordingly, without prying at all into the nature or object of his mission. From the conversation, however, I could collect that the French government were determined at length to speak intelligibly to the Dutch and give them to know that they must adopt a more decided and energetic line of conduct. Desaix's expression was, *'puisque vous ne voulez pas vous faire une constitution on vous priera d'en accepter une, et j'espère que vous ne la refuserez pas'*.[4] I could likewise see that the support of the French was in a manner set up to auction between the party that is *in*, and the party that wants to *get in*, in Holland, and I was very glad to find the price was to be paid in *maritime support*. The party now uppermost offered 25 sail of the line for the approaching campaign, which I learn from Vischery absolutely exceeds the faculties of the Dutch republic to accomplish; however if they promise 25, it is probable they will have 18, or perhaps 20; at least it is certain they will

---

[1] On 22 Jan. 1798 the Dutch convention was purged of twenty-two members unacceptable to the party with which the French were collaborating over the adoption of a new constitution.

[2] Silently changed in *Life*, ii, 458, to 'Lewines'.   [3] An allusion to the battle of Camperdown.

[4] 'Since you do not wish to make yourselves a constitution you will be asked to accept one and I hope that you will not refuse it.'

move heaven and earth to bring it to bear. If the late government had not sacrificed, whether thro' treachery or incapacity, the fleet of Dewinter, there might have been by April next a fleet of at least 25 sail of the line at the Texel, in which case the English would have been obliged to keep one of at least 30 sail in the North seas, for they would not hazard an equality of force; and then what a powerful diversion would that have been for our projected invasion! There is one of the fruits of the incapacity, or, as I rather think, the treachery of the late Dutch government. Well, I hope now they are in a great degree regenerated, and especially as France has interfered with a high hand, that they may conduct themselves better for the future. I cannot blame the French at all for their interposition on this occasion. Having conquered Holland, they had a right, if they pleased, to have thrown it into the Zuyder Zee; instead of that they left the Dutch at liberty to organise their own government and frame their own constitution. After nearly three years independance, they are not farther advanced than they were the first month, the plan of a constitution which they devised having been rejected by an immense majority of the people. Under these circumstances, and especially in a crisis like the present when great and active energy is so necessary, certainly the French are justified in returning on their steps and obliging the Dutch to adopt a constitution, since after three years experiment they have shewn that they want either talents or integrity to frame one for themselves. Individually, I wish most heartily it were otherwise, for I am sorry to see a people incapable to profit of such a great occasion as the Dutch have had in their hands, but if unfortunately the fact be against them, I, once more, must acquit the French for their interposition; and I think I should do so even in the case of my own country, if she were to shew similar incapacity in like circumstances, which however I am far from apprehending would be the case. I do not know how Daendels may stand now, but I hope well, for I have an esteem for him, and should be sorry he were to lose the confidence that his past services and sacrifices have procured.[1] Meyer is decidedly with the new men, and I know he has no great devotion for Daendels. Well, time will shew.

From Colonel Henri Sheé, 26 January 1798

Tone (Dickason) papers.

Bonn, le 7 pluviôse an 6

My D[ea]r Sir,

Your letter of ye 25 ul[tim]o gave me great satisfaction to hear you are well, ready to bid defiance once more to seas, storms & our inplacable enemies the detested English. May God speed you in your noble enterprise. I harbour

---

[1] In fact Daendels supported the coup.

the most sanguine hopes of success this bout & heartily regret not being able to go with you, for my leggs absolutely refuse to support me and if with the approaching spring I even was to recover the proper use of them I could not leave this country before all accounts are given in to the government & accepted, which with the slow expedition of business in all offices at present can hardly be supposed to be performed in less than 3 or 4 months, so that by such time I reckon you will be safely landed & have driven all before you, for I fancy your expedition will be calculated for the time of the equinox or thereabout. However I do not despair yet of seeing you & all friends in the land of milk & honey in full possession of all the rights of a free nation, for if I have it in the world I shall gladly lay it out to see a country before I die that has been all my lifetime the object of my warmest wishes & for the wellfare of which I am willing to undergo any danger.

I learnt with great pleasure that you have seven of our countrymen with you at Paris whose zeal for the cause forced them to fly hither for refuge against tiranny. They are to be sure bold, enterprising men & will with you be of great help to Buonaparte in the expedition. With such a leader and our brave republicans, I make no doubt but you will bear down every obstacle in your way.

We have nothing new in these parts. We wait with impatience the result of the congress at Rastadt,[1] which however can be easily guessed beforehand, for we are, thank God & our brave army, at the sure side of the question, for we are in possession of all the left side of the Rhine. We have nothing more to do than keep what we have & lett the Empire settle all disputes & indemnities between the German princes. If we have anything worth our notice [I] shall let you know. Do the same, pray, on your side & believe me

My D[ea]r Sir, your affectionate friend & countryman

Sheé

From Pierre Sotin, 26 January 1798

Tone (Dickason) papers.

Sotin notifies Tone that he has authorised the issue of passports to four men 'who, you assure me, have been persecuted in their countries'.

LIBERTÉ [CREST] ÉGALITÉ

2ᵉ Division

5 Bureau B 4

Nº 2671.

On est invité à

rappeler en marge de

Paris, le 7 Pluviôse, *an* 6ᵉ

de la République une et indivisible

---

[1] The Congress of Rastadt met between Dec. 1797 and Apr. 1799 with the aim of arranging the details of a peace between France and the empire.

la réponse, le nom de
la Division, du Bureau
et le numéro ci-dessus.

Le Ministre de la Police Générale de la République
    Au Citoyen Smith, Adjudant Général, Cul de Sac Notre Dame des
    Champs No. 1390

    Je vous préviens, Citoyen, que j'ai autorisé le Bureau Central de Paris à
délivrer des cartes d'hospitalité aux Citoyens Mathieu Smith,[1] James
Williams,[2] B. Burke[3] et Theodore Wilkins,[4] que vous m'assurez avoir été
persécutés dans leurs pays pour la cause de la Liberté.
    Vous pouvez les en prévenir, afin qu'ils se présentent au Bureau Central.

Salut et Fraternité,
Sotin

From General Barthélemi Louis Joseph Schérer, 30 January 1798

Tone (Dickason) papers.

This document pertains to the formalities of Tone's appointment to the
'army of England'.

4ᵉ Division
Bureau
des
Officiers
Généraux

Paris, le 11 Pluviôse, an 6 de
la République Française, une et indivisible

Le MINISTRE de la Guerre,
Au Citoyen Smith, adjudant général, Cul de Sac Notre Dame des
Champs nᵒ 1390 à Paris.

Le DIRECTOIRE EXÉCUTIF ayant jugé à propos, Citoyen, de vous employer
en votre grade . . . .
. . . . prés les troupes qui composent

---

  [1] Mathew Tone.
  [2] Nom de guerre of William James MacNeven (Archives des Affaires Étrangères, AE IV, 1671,
ff 100–105).
  [3] It was reported that with Humbert's expedition 'from Rochefort went Teeling, who went by
the name of Burke' (Secret report, *c*. Oct. 1798, *Castlereagh corr.*, i, 409).
  [4] 'Theodore Wilkins, Écossais' sought permission from the minister of police in Mar. 1798 to go
to Carcassonne to purchase 'des biens nationaux', in which application he was supported by Tone;
he was on 9 June 1802 granted permission to travel, for family reasons, from Paris to London; he
gave his age in Jan. 1798 as '37 ans' (Archives Nationales, AN F⁷ 7293 and F¹ 3504). 'Wilkins' was
a pseudonym of Thomas Wilson (see above, p. 24, n. 2).

l'armée d'Angleterre . . . ., j'adresse en conséquence les lettres de service qui vous ont été expédiées au Général commandant en chef cette armée . . . . qui vous les remettra avec ses instructions sur les fonctions que vous aurez à remplir sous ses ordres. Le bien du service exige que vous vous rendiez le plus promptement possible au poste qui vous est assigné.

Vous voudrez bien m'accuser la réception de cette lettre, et m'informer de l'époque de votre arrivée à votre destination.

Salut et Fraternité,
Schérer

Diary, 1 February 1798

T.C.D., Tone papers, MS 2049, ff 291^r–293^v; *Life*, ii, 460–62.

No. 16
From February 1st to April 30th[1]
Nil desperandum!
Paris and Rouen
1798[2]

1 Feb. 1798, Paris

The number of Irish refugees is considerably increased. Independent of Lewines, Tenent and Lowry, of whom I have spoken,[3] there are Teeling of Lisburne, Orr of Derry, McMahon of the Co. Down, Macan and Burgess of the Co. Louth, Napper Tandy and my brother;[4] where is also one Maguire, who was sent by Reynolds from Philadelphia in consequence of my letter to him by Monroe,[5] and one Ashley, an Englishman, formerly secretary to the Corresponding Society and one of those who was tried with Thomas Hardy[6]

---

[1] The Diary entries for 10–11 Feb., 1–4 Mar., 20–24 Mar., 25–6 Mar., 31 Mar.–4 Apr., 6–8 Apr., 15 Apr., 20 Apr. and 24–7 Apr. are given as separate documents (below). There are no entries for 28–30 Apr.

[2] The preceding headings, which Tone obviously added later than 1 Feb., are omitted from *Life*.

[3] See Diary for 25 Nov. 1797, where he also writes of Teeling and Orr, the five of them and Tone himself having given 'a grand dinner' to some officers (above, p. 178).

[4] Mathew Tone.

[5] See Diary for 24 Feb. 1797 (above, p. 28). There is some elaboration of this in a letter from Macguire to the duc de Feltre, 10 Dec. 1810: 'en l'an 5, d'après le désir et la désignation expresse de Wolf Tone (alors adjudant commandant au service de France), je fus envoyé des États-Unis d'Amérique en Irlande pour faire part aux chefs du peuple irlandais de l'expédition que [*sic*], à cette époque, se préparait au Texel et qui avait pour but l'affranchissement de l'Irlande. Je devais ensuite rapporter à Tone en France un état exact de la situation des choses relativement à l'union Irlandaise.' (Archives de la Guerre, Bataillons et régiments étrangers, X^h 16^c).

[6] Thomas Hardy (1752–1832), radical politician; he was tried in 1794 for high treason and acquitted (*D.N.B.*). Ashley was not tried along with Hardy.

in London for high treason.[1] We all do very well together except Tandy, who is not behaving very correct; he began some months ago by caballing against me with a priest of the name of Quigley,[2] who is since gone off, no one knows whither. The circumstances of this petty intrigue are not worth my recording. It is sufficient to say that Tandy took on him to summon a meeting of the Irish refugees at which Lewines and I were to be arraigned on I know not what charges by himself and Quigley. Lewines refused to attend, but I went and when I appeared, there was no one found to bring forward a charge against me, tho' I called three times to know 'whether any person had anything to offer?'. In consequence of this manœuvre I have had no communication since with Tandy, who has also lost ground by this mean behaviour with all the rest of his countrymen; he is, I fancy, pestering the government here with applications and memorials, and gives himself out for an old officer and a man of great property in Ireland, as I judge from what Gen[era]l Murat[3] said to me in speaking of him the other night at Buonaparte's. He asked me did I know one Tandy, *'un ancien militaire, n'est ce pas?'*. I said I did know him, but I could not say that he was exactly an *ancien militaire*, having never served but in the volunteer corps of Ireland, a body which resembled pretty much the Garde Nationale of France at the beginning of the revolution. He then said, *'mais c'est un très riche propriétaire?'*. I told him I believed he was always in easy circumstances, and there the discourse ended. By this I see how he is shewing himself off here. He has got latterly a co-adjutor in the famous Thomas Muir,[4] who is arrived at Paris, and who has inserted three or four[5] very foolish articles relating to the United Irishmen in the French papers,[6] in consequence of which at a meeting of the United Irishmen now in Paris, with the exception of Tandy, who was not summoned,[7] it was settled that Lowry, Orr, Lewines and myself should wait upon Muir and, after thanking him for his good intentions, entreat him not to introduce our business into any publications which he might hereafter think proper to make. Accordingly we waited on him a few days since, but of all the vain, obstinate blockheads that ever I met, I never saw his equal. I could scarcely conceive such a degree of self-sufficiency to exist. He told us roundly that he knew as much of our country as we did, and that he would venture to say he had as much of the confidence of the United Irishmen as we had; that he had no doubt we were very respectable

---

[1] In the MS there follow three lines scored through and rendered illegible except that one word can be distinguished as 'Philadelphia'.   [2] James Coigly.

[3] Joachim Murat (1767–1815), général de brigade, 1796, and aide-de-camp to Bonaparte in Italy; général de division, 1799; marshal of the empire, 1804; king of Naples, 1808 (Six, *Dict. des généraux & amiraux*).

[4] Thomas Muir (1765–98), Scottish radical; sentenced in 1793 to fourteen years' transportation for sedition; escaped from Botany Bay and after an adventurous journey reached France (*D.N.B.*).

[5] *Life*, ii, 461, reads 'two or three'.

[6] *Life* reads 'Paris papers'. At the end of Dec. 1797 a letter from Thomas Muir to the minister of police was published in a Paris newspaper. In this letter, Muir declaring 'I am a United Irishman, I am a Scotsman, I can speak for both nations', promised that the Irish and the Scots would break their chains on the heads of their tyrants. (*Journal des Hommes Libres de tous les Pays ou Le Républicain*, 10 Nivôse an 6).   [7] *Life* omits 'who was not summoned'.

individuals but that he could only know us, as such, having shewn him no powers or written authority to prove that we had any mission; that he seldom acted without due reflection, and that when he had once taken his party, it was impossible to change him; and that as to what he had written relative to the United Irishmen, he had the sanction of, he would say, *the* most respectable individual of that body, who had, and who deserved to have, their entire confidence and approbation, and whose authority he must and did consider as justifying every syllable he had advanced. This *most respectable individual of the body* we presume to be Tandy, for we did not even ask his name. In short after a discussion of near three hours, we were obliged to come away *re infecta*, except that we gave Mr Muir notice that he had neither licence nor authority to speak in the name of the people of Ireland, and that if we saw any similar productions to those of which we complained, we should be obliged to take measures that would conduce neither to his ease nor respectability, for that we could not suffer the public to be longer abused. On these terms we parted, very drily on both sides. The fact is Tandy and Muir are puffing one another here for their private advancement; they are supporting themselves by indorsing each other's credit, and issuing, if I may so say, accommodation bills of reputation. This conversation has given the *coup de grace* to Tandy with his countrymen here, and he is now in a manner completely *in Coventry*. He deserves it. These details are hardly worth my writing, but as there may be question of the business hereafter, I thought I might as well put them down.

To General Hermann Wilhelm Daendels,
3 February 1798

Tone (Dickason) papers.

After acknowledging receipt of two letters Tone relates how he and Lewines were introduced some days ago to Bonaparte. 'He listened to us attentively, he spoke to us very little, and we finished our last conversation by giving him all the memorials and other papers that we had concerning the political and military situation in our country.' Tone states that Desaix has had a search made for plans of forts and asks Daendels to look for charts of the British and Irish coasts.

No. 3

Paris, ce 15 pluviôse an 6

L'adjudant-général Smith au général Daendels

Général,

J'ai reçu vos deux lettres, celle du 12 décembre, et celle du 20,[1] que m'a remis [*sic*] l'adjudant général Vichéry. J'ai apporté toute suite [*sic*] chez le général

---

[1] Above, pp 182–3, 183–4.

Desaix les lettres à son adresse, et deux ou trois jours aprés, j'ai eu l'honneur de lui présenter le citoyen Vichéry, avec lequel il a eu une assez longue conversation, dont vous êtes sans doute déjà instruit. En conséquence je me rapporte, pour tout ce qui regarde les affaires publiques, au citoyen Vichéry, et je me bornerai, pour le présent, à ce qui me regarde personellement.

Nous avons été présentés, le citoyen Giauque[1] et moi, il y a quelques jours, au général Buonaparte par le général Desaix.[2] Il nous a reçu d'une manière aussi favorable que nous pouvions le désirer; il nous a écoutés très attentivement; il nous a parlé fort peu, et nous avons fini notre dernière conversation par lui remettre tous les mémoires, et autres papiers que nous avions, concernant la situation, politique et militaire, de notre pays. D'après cela, il parait qu'il s'en occupe sérieusement.[3] Depuis ce tems le général Desaix m'a dit que j'étois porté pour l'armée d'Angleterre. Tout cela me fait espérer que les choses vont comme nous les souhaitons. Au reste, étant uniquement attaché à une seule affaire, à laquelle je me suis si longtems dévoué, et ne faisant guère des questions, je suis précisément l'homme de toute la république le moins instruit de tout ce qui se passe ici.

Le général Desaix a fait chercher dans les dépôts, tant de la guerre que de la marine, les plans des forts que vous avez demandé[s], mais ils ne s'y trouvent point. Au reste, à l'exception du Fort Augustus, ils ne doivent pas être très considérables, n'étant construits que pour contenir les montagnards du pays, qui, n'ayant guère du canon, n'étaient pas très forts pour les siéger. Le général Desaix vous remercie bien des cartes que vous avez eu la bonté de lui offrir, mais il les a déjà toutes. Si vous avez l'occasion d'en faire venir de l'Angleterre, je vous conseille, général, de chercher surtout les cartes maritimes des côtes de l'Angleterre, de l'Écosse et de l'Irlande faites, d'après les ordres de l'Amirauté anglaise, par le capitaine Joseph Huddart[4] environ l'année 1778 ou 1779. Je vous écris le titre en anglais à peu près: *Survey of the coasts of England, Scotland and Ireland, made by order of the Lords of the Admiralty, by Captain Joseph Huddart, 1778.*

Je vois dans les feuilles publiques qu'un grand événement vient d'avoir lieu chez vous.[5] Puisse-t-il, en ajoutant plus d'énergie et d'ensemble à votre gouvernement, déployer heureusement les moyens et les ressources qui se trouvent, tant dans le caractère des Bataves que dans la situation de leur païs, et en doublant la force de nos deux républiques, terrasser enfin le tyran des mers, at rendre la paix et la tranquillité à l'Europe.

Salut, amitié et respect
J. S.

---

[1] i.e. Lewines.

[2] Probably the meeting recorded in the diary for 13 Jan. 1798 (see above, pp 190–91).

[3] For Bonaparte's knowledge of Ireland, see above (pp 185–6).

[4] Joseph Huddart (1741–1816), hydrographer (*D.N.B.*).

[5] The coup d'état of 22 Jan. 1798, which was supported by Daendels and countenanced by the French ambassador, Delacroix (see above, pp 193–4).

Je vous prie, général, de vouloir bien m'expédier une copie de votre ordre[1] de me rendre auprès du feu général Hoche, qui m'est nécessaire maintenant dans les bureaux de la guerre; il doit être en date du 3 ou 4 septembre, 1797.

From Pierre Sotin, 3 February 1798

Tone (Dickason) papers.

Sotin states that the French minister in Holland has given passports to Macguire and Ashley; he asks whether they have introduced themselves and whether their presence in France is dangerous.

2^c Division
5^c Bureau   LIBERTÉ   [crest]   ÉGALITÉ
B.G.   *Paris, le* 15 Pluviôse, *an* 6^c
No. 968[2]   *de la République une et indivisible*
    Le Ministre de la Police Générale de la République
      À l'Adjudant Général Smith,
        Cul de Sac, Notre Dame des Champs No. 1390

Je vous préviens, Citoyen, que notre ministre en Hollande[3] a délivré des passeports à James Meguire, Irlandais, natif de Dublin, et à John Ashley, Anglais, natif de Londres, pour se rendre à Paris.

Je désire savoir si ces individus se sont présentés devant vous, et si leur présence en France est dangéreuse.[4]

Je vous invite à vouloir bien traiter séparément chaque affaire et à éviter avec soin de réunir, sous le même n[umér]o, plusieurs objets.

Cette marche vous évitera des recherches pénibles et rendra notre correspondance plus rapide.

                                        Salut & fraternité,
                                        Sotin

---

[1] Not found. It is mentioned in Tone's diary for 3 Sept. 1797 (see above, p. 142).

[2] There follows the request: 'On est invité à rappeler, en marge de la réponse, le nom de la Division, du Bureau et le numéro ci-dessus'.   [3] Delacroix.

[4] Macguire recalled over twelve years later that, the defeat of Admiral Dewinter having made the expedition from the Texel impossible, 'il ne me restait qu'à venir à Paris rejoindre Tone, qui me témoigna une entière satisfaction de la manière dont j'avais répondu à son attente. Quelque temps après je l'accompagnai à Brest pour y être embarqué dans l'expédition aux ordres du Général Hardy. Dans cette occasion je fis nommé capitaine au régiment de Lee sous la date du Ier fructidor an 6. Pris dans cette expédition, et n'ayant échappé à la vengeance du gouvernement anglais qu'en prenant le nom et l'uniforme d'un caporal tué dans l'action, je fus échangé sous le même nom après être resté 14 mois prisonnier au château d'Édimbourg' (James Macguire to duc de Feltre, 10 Dec. 1810, Archives de la Guerre, Bataillons et régiments étrangers, X^h 16^c).

Diary, 10–11 February 1798

T.C.D., Tone papers, MS 2049, ff 293ᵛ–296ʳ; *Life*, ii, 462–4.

10 Feb. 1798

Lewines was the other night with Buonaparte, when a circumstance took place which I think, from his relation of it, worth recording. Since the 18 fructidor the Jacobins are in a certain degree more tolerated by government than formerly, and some of the leaders who had been tried at Vendôme with Babœf venture to shew themselves a little.[1] On the evening I mentioned, a person called on the general from the minister of the police and spoke to him for a considerable time in a low voice so as Lewines did not hear what he said, but it appears by the sequel that it was probably relative to some overtures from the *chefs* of that party, for Buonaparte all at once sprung into the middle of the room, with great heat,[2] and said, 'what would those gentlemen have? France is revolutionized, Holland is revolutionized, Italy is revolutionized, Switzerland is revolutionized; Europe will be soon revolutionized; but that, it seems, is not enough to content them. I know well what they want; they want the domination of thirty or forty individuals, founded on the massacre of three or four millions; they want the constitution of 1793, but we will[3] not have it, and Death to him who should demand it![4] We will have the present constitution and we will have no other, and we have common sense, and our bayonets to maintain it. I know these persons, in order to give themselves some little consequence, affect to spread reports of some pretended disunion between the government and the Legislative body. It is false! From the foundation of the republic to this day, there never was perhaps a moment when there reigned such perfect harmony between the constituted authorities, and I may add, since it seems they are so good as to count me for something in the affair, that I am perfectly in union of sentiment and esteem with the government, and they with me.[5] No! We will not have the assistance of those gentlemen who call themselves chiefs and leaders of the people; we acknowledge no chiefs or leaders but those pointed out by the

---

[1] Between Feb. and May 1797 Babeuf and 48 of his fellow conspirators were brought to trial before a high court sitting at Vendôme.

[2] In the MS this word is indistinct and could be either 'heart' or 'heat'. *Life*, ii. 462, has 'heat'.

[3] *Life*, ii, 462–3, has 'they shall' instead of 'we will'.

[4] In the MS a small sheet attached (f. 295) contains the words 'we did not fail to reduce them to order when we had but 1,500 men, and we will do it much easier now, when we have 30,000!'. They are inserted at this point in *Life*, ii, 463.

[5] MS f. 295 (see above, n. 4) contains the words 'he that fears calumny is below me; what I have done, has not been in a *boudoir*, and it is for Europe and posterity to judge me'. They are inserted at this point in *Life*, ii, 463.

constitution, the Legislative body and the Executive Directory; to them only will we pay respect or attention. For the others, we know very well how to deal with them, if necessary; for my part I declare, for one, that if I had only the option between royalty and the system of those gentlemen, I would not hesitate a moment to declare for a king. But we will have neither one nor the other; we will have the republic and the constitution, with which if those persons pretend to interfere, they shall be soon made sensible of their absolute nullity.' He spoke to this effect, as Lewines reports to me, but in a strain of the greatest animation and with an admirable eloquence. From two or three words he let drop, Lewines concludes that Sotin, the present minister of police, will probably not continue long in office.

11 Feb. 1798

In conversation, today, with Gen[era]l Clarke, I mentioned to him how happy I was when the news of the armistice between Buonaparte and the Austrians arrived, as I began to be extremely uneasy at his situation. Clarke assured me I was quite right in that respect; that the fact was the division of Joubert[1] was completely beaten out of the Tyrol by the peasants with no better arms than chance furnished, even down to clubs and sticks, with which they charged the French like madmen and drove before them the very same troops who had so often defeated the best disciplined forces of Austria,[2] of such an uncertain nature is the courage of armies, and so much are they disconcerted by a mode of fighting different from that to which they have been accustomed; that the Venetians were rising *en masse*, and Trieste retaken, so that the communication with Italy was exceedingly embarrassed; that if the army met with the least check in front, it was ruined, and every step that Buonaparte advanced increased his difficulties and multiplied the probabilities against him. I was glad to hear my own opinion confirmed by Clarke's authority, who is a military man of experience and character, and especially who was on the spot at the very time.

To Pierre Sotin, 15 February 1798 (I)

T.C.D., Tone papers, MS 2050, f. 21.

Tone states that he does not know at all Citizen Marguerite Crawford, an Englishwoman lately arrived at Calais. 'I do not mean to dabble in the affairs of the English; I believe it was the intention of Citizen Talleyrand, and your own, to call on me only in the case of patriots and especially of United Irishmen who might take refuge in France.'

---

[1] Barthélemy Catherine Joubert (1769–99) joined the National Guard, 1789, *général de division*, 1796; commanded *l'armée de Batavie*, Jan.–July 1798 (Six, *Dict. des généraux & amiraux*).
[2] Towards the close of Mar. 1797, Joubert advanced to Brixen, where he was attacked by an Austrian force backed by the peasantry, rising en *masse* in arms. Joubert managed to cut his way through to Spital. (R. W. Phipps, *The armies of the first French republic* (5 vols, London, 1926–39), iv, 174–6).

The sense suggests Tone was addressing himself to Sotin, who however had
been succeeded as minister of police two days before by Nicholas Dondeau.

2ᵉ Division   à Paris, ce 27 pluviôse an 6
5ᵉ Bureau   L'adj[udan]t-gén[éra]l Smith
B 5   au Min[istre] de la Police Gén[éra]le
Nº. 2285

Citoyen Ministre,

J'ai l'honneur de vous informer que je ne connois nullement la citoyenne
Marguerite Crawford,¹ Anglaise dernièrement arrivée à Calais.

Au reste, citoyen Ministre, je ne prétends pas me mêler dans les affaires
des Anglais. Je crois que c'étoit l'intention du C[itoy]en Talleyrand, et la
vôtre, de m'appeller seulement dans le cas des patriotes et surtout des
Irlandais Unis qui pourroient se réfugier en France. Pour les autres je ne
prétends pas répondre d'eux.

Salut et respect,
J. Smith

To Pierre Sotin, 15 February 1798 (II)

Archives Nationales, Police Générale, F⁷ 7383ᴰ.

Tone states that neither he nor compatriots in Paris to whom he has
spoken recognise O'Finn, who says he is an Irish refugee.

2ᵉ Division   à Paris, ce 27 pluviôse an 6
5ᵉ Bureau   L'adj[udan]t-gén[éra]l Smith
D 5   au Min[istre] de la Police Générale
Nº. 2119

Citoyen Ministre,

Ne reconnoissant pas moi-même le nommé O'Finn,² se disant Irlandais
réfugié, j'en ai parlé à mes compatriotes qui sont maintenant à Paris, mais ils
ne le connoissent pas plus que moi. Je ne puis en conséquence vous rien dire
à son sujet.

Salut et respect
J. Smith

¹ Not identified.
² Edward Finn or O'Finn (1767–1810), son of a Cork provision merchant; United Irishman; fled
to Holland, Jan. 1798; probably author of a memorandum on the political and strategic situation in
Munster addressed to the French government; briefly an admirer of Tandy; apparently suspected by
the Irish in Hamburg of being a British spy and regarded with contemptuous dislike by some of
the Irish in France; later served in the French army (Miles Byrne, *Memoirs* (Paris, 1863), i, 386;
Seán Ó Coindealbháin, 'The United Irishmen in Cork County—VII' in *Cork Historical and
Archaeological Society Journal*, lvii (1952), pp 91–6; ——to Rufus King, 5 Mar. 1798, P.R.O., FO
32/17; Archives Nationales, AF IV 1671, ff 115–27).

From General Hermann Wilhelm Daendels
and Admiral Jean Guillaume Dewinter,
16 February 1798

Tone (Dickason) papers.

Daendels informs Tone that the Dutch government will prepare to act; he asks Tone to get 'the Scot of whom you have spoken to me' to go at once to the Hague and give information. He states that he has received some maps of Scotland. Dewinter promises money.

La Haye, 16ᵉ Février 1798
L'an 4ᵐᵉ de la Liberté Batave

Le Lieutenant Général Daendels
à
L'Adjudant-Général Smith.

Enfin, mon cher Smith, notre gouvernement est organisé. Maintenant tout notre sistême administratif va prendre une grande activité, et on va travailler sans relâche à accélérer les préparatifs nécessaires, pour que nous soyons prêts d'agir incessament. Nous désirions pouvoir entretenir une correspondance exacte avec l'Angleterre ou l'Écosse, pour être exactement instruits de toutes les mesures que le Gouvernement Anglais pourra prendre pour la défense de ces pays. En conséquence je vous serois obligé, mon cher Smith, d'engager l'Écossois[1] dont vous m'avez parlé à se rendre auprès de nous à la Haye. D'après le témoignage que vous m'en avez rendu, je pense, que nous pourrons avoir une confiance absolue dans ses principes et dans les renseignements qu'il nous procurera. Il aura sûrement des relations avec les patriotes les plus marquant d'Écosse, mais je vous prie, mon cher Smith, de lui procurer surtout les adresses et tous les moyens enfin qui pourront le mettre à même de correspondre avec les comités réunis à Londres des patriotes des trois royaumes, et nous le mettrons à même de pouvoir les entretenir. Il doit partir aussitôt cette lettre reçue. Pour lui procurer les fonds nécessaires pour faire ce voyage vous pourrez, mon cher Smith, tirer sur le Citoyen Pijman,[2] Ministre de la Guerre, une somme de trois ou quatre cent florins de Hollande. Vous pouvez être assuré que l'on fera honneur à cette lettre.

Je n'ai reçu aucune des lettres du Citoyen Vichéry. Si vous le voyez, priez le de me tenir la promesse qu'il m'a faite de m'écrire exactement. Dites aussi au Citoyen Giaucque,[3] que je n'ai point reçu les lettres intéressantes de lui que vous m'annoncez dans votre précédente lettre.

[1] Perhaps Wilson, more likely Aherne who, though not a Scot, had lived in Scotland.
[2] Abraham Jan zorn van Pijman (1750–1839), Dutch minister of war (*Nieuw Nederlandsch biografisch woordenboek*). [3] Probably meaning here Lewines.

J'ai reçu une collection des plus complettes des cartes les plus exactes et les plus détaillées de l'Écosse. J'en fais demander encore celles que vous m'indiquez.

J'espère, mon cher Smith, qu'enfin nous pourrons tirer parti des ressources qui nous restent encore quelques médiocres qu'elles soyent, pour travailler encore utilement à la cause commune.

Salut et Amitié!

Le Lieutenant Général

Daendels

P.S. Désormais envoyez moi vos lettres et celles du Citoyen Giaucque dans le paquet du Ministre Meyer.

N'ayant point trouvé la minute de l'ordre que je vous avois donné pour vous rendre chez le Général Hoche,[1] je vous envoye ci-joint un certificat dont vous ferez l'usage nécessaire.

Mon cher ami! J'ai reçu votre lettre à l'instant. J'ai donné les ordres en conséquence que l'argent vous soit discompté. J'espère que vous en aurez 600; j'ai vu les effects.

Assurez Madame de mes respects et croyez moi toujours

Votre ami

De Winter

Note on Tone's proposal for an adjunct, 18 February 1798

Archives de la Guerre, Archives Administratives.

Tone proposes MacSheehy as his adjunct.

Liberté [*Crest*] *Egalité*

Proposition d'adjoint[2]

L'adjudant général James Smith employé à l'armée d'Angleterre propose pour remplir sous ses ordres les fonctions d'adjoint:

Le C^{en} Mac-sheehy, cap^e à la 48e 1/2 B^{de3} et employé près de lui depuis le 1er f[rim]aire an 5.

Le Ministre est prié d'app[uy]er cette demande et de vouloir bien signer la commission adjointe.

[*initials illegible*]

---

[1] See diary for 3 Sept. 1797 (above, pp 142–3).
[2] The left-hand margin reads: '*Département* | *de* | *la Guerre* | [double rule] | *4e Division* | *Bureau des Off[ici]ers G[énér]aux* | Du 30 Pluviôse an 6e remis au C^{en} Mac-Sheehy le 2 Vent[ôse] an 6.' [3] i.e. 'capitaine à la 48e demi-brigade'.

To General Hermann Wilhelm Daendels, 25 February 1798

Tone (Dickason) papers.

Tone expresses satisfaction at the coup in Holland, assures Daendels that preparations on the coast are advanced and tells him to expect 'the person of whom you have written to me'.

No. 4   Paris, ce 7 Ventôse, an 6

L'adjudant général Smith au général Daendels

Général,

J'ai reçu votre lettre du 16 courant,[1] et je suis, on ne peut plus, content des nouvelles que vous avez la bonté de m'envoyer. Enfin, j'espère, la nation batave va déployer son ancienne énergie, si longtems entravée, soit par la perfidie du Stadthouder et de l'ancien gouvernement, soit par l'ineptie (à ne pas dire davantage) de ceux qui leur ont succédé, et dont votre dernière révolution vient de faire un exemple salutaire et frappant.[2] Avec du courage et de la bonne volonté on vient à bout de tout. De votre côté, vous serez bien aise d'entendre que tout va aussi bien que nous pouvons le désirer.

Les généraux Buonaparte, Kléber et Desaix ont fait une tournée dernièrement le long des côtes pour voir l'état des préparatifs, et ils en sont entièrement contens. Je viens de voir le général Desaix, qui a été à Brest. Il m'a donné des nouvelles des plus satisfaisantes. Partout il a trouvé le plus grand zèle et dévouement, une activité longtems étrangère à nos chantiers, et surtout le meilleur esprit possible dans la marine, à tel point qu'il y a un très grand nombre d'officiers qui, ne pouvant être placés pour le moment, ont demandé la permission du gouvernement de faire la campagne comme simple volontaires, chose qui m'est d'autant plus agréable que j'ai été moi-même, il y a un an, à même de remarquer un esprit tout à fait différent. Enfin, d'après ce qu'il m'a dit, partout où il a passé, il n'a trouvé que le même sentiment de haine et de vengeance contre les Anglais, et il en conçoit, avec bien de raison, les meilleures espérances. Pour moi, j'en suis d'autant plus charmé, que, d'après ce que j'ai pu remarquer de son caractère il ne me semble être pas, du tout, un homme à se bercer facilement, à se tromper lui-même, ni à se laisser tromper par d'autres.

Suivant vos ordres j'ai donné les instructions nécessaires à la personne dont vous m'avez écrit.[3] Il partira dans cinq ou six jours d'ici. Pour ses moyens et ses talens, vous en jugerez vous-même, mais pour son zèle et son intégrité, j'en

---

[1] Above, pp 205–06.
[2] i.e. the coup d'état which had occurred in Holland on 22 Jan. 1798 (see above, pp 193–4).
[3] John Aherne; see Tone to Daendels, 12 Mar. 1798 (below, p. 214).

reponds comme de moi–même; il a, en outre, des connaissances locales qui pourront le rendre singulièrement utile dans l'affaire à laquelle vous le destinez. Comme vous me mandez de l'envoyer, sans perdre du tems, je lui ai donné, moi–même, les 400 florins d'Hollande que vous m'autorisez de lui faire payer, pour ne pas attendre le retour du billet, que vous m'ordonnez de tirer sur le citoyen Pijman, ministre de la guerre. J'ai l'honneur de vous remettre ce billet, ci-joint, et je vous prie, général, de vouloir bien me le renvoyer, aussitôt qu'il sera accepté, à moins que le ministre de la guerre ne juge plus à propos de m'envoyer directement une lettre de change sur Paris pour cette somme, ce qui me conviendra encore mieux. Vous aurez la bonté de me pardonner de vous donner tant de peine, mais c'est toujours pour la cause commune.

Le Citoyen Giauque[1] me charge de vous dire toutes sortes de choses de sa part; il aura le plaisir de vous écrire par la personne en question. Quand vous verrez l'amiral de Winter, veuillez bien lui dire combien je suis sensible à toutes les bontés qu'il a eu pour moi, acceptez mes très sincères rémercimens du certificat que vous m'avez envoyé. Je voudrai seulement être en état de justifier toutes les choses flatteuses que vous avez la bonté de dire en ma faveur. Soyez assuré, général, qu'il y a peu de choses dont je suis plus jaloux que de mériter votre estime. Il y a, en conséquence, fort peu de choses qui me pourront faire autant de plaisir qu'un si honorable témoignage. *'Laus est laudari, a tu, laudato viro'.*[2]

Salut et respect,
J. S.

Toute reflexion faite, général, je prierai le ministre de la guerre de vouloir bien m'envoyer directement une lettre de change sur Paris, n'ayant pas, moi-même, les facilités de négocier celle que vous m'avez ordonné de tirer sur lui.

Diary, 1–4 March 1798

T.C.D., Tone papers, MS 2049, ff 296ʳ–302ʳ; *Life*, ii, 464–70.

1 March 1798

An event has taken place of a magnitude scarce, if at all, inferior in importance to that of the French revolution. The Pope is dethroned and in exile.[3] The circumstances attending this great event are such as to satisfy my mind that there is a special providence guiding the affairs of Europe at this moment, and turning everything to the great end of the emancipation of mankind from the

---

[1] i.e. Lewines.   [2] 'It is praise indeed to be praised by a praiseworthy man like you'.
[3] In Jan. 1798 the Directory ordered General Berthier to occupy Rome. On 10 Feb. the city surrendered and Pius VI was deposed as temporal sovereign. Immediately afterwards he was compelled to leave for northern Italy and then France. In Aug. 1799 he died at Valence.

yoke of religious and political superstition under which they have so long groaned. Some months ago, in the career of his victories, Buonaparte accorded a peace, and a generous one, to the Pope; it was signed at Tolentino, and Louis Buonaparte,[1] brother to the *général*, proceeded to Rome as the first ambassador from the republic. Many people thought at the time, and I was of the number, that it was unwise to let slip so favorable an opportunity as then presented itself to destroy for ever the papal tyranny, but it should seem the necessity of following up close the impression made on the Austrian armies overbore all inferior concerns, and, as I have said already, peace was made with the cabinet of Rome. One would have thought that so narrow an escape as the Pope then had, holding his very existence, as it were, dependent on the breath of Buonaparte, who could with a single word have annihilated him, might have prevented his rashly embarking in a second contest with the Republic. But Providence for its own wise and great purposes, the happiness of man & the complete establishment of civil and religious liberty, seems to have utterly taken away all sense and understanding from the Pope and his councils. After a fruitless attempt to trepan the French ambassador into a fabricated insurrection, they procured a tumultuous mob to assemble under the windows of his palace and within the circuit of his jurisdiction; the guards are immediately called out and begin to fire; the ambassador rushes out attended by Generals Duphot[2] and Sherlock, and some other officers, all dressed in the costume of their respective situations, in order if possible to restore tranquillity, or at least to assert the neutrality of the *enceinte* of the ambassador's palace, which is in all nations privileged ground. They are received with a running fire, which levels Duphot to the ground; he recovers his feet, tho' dreadfully wounded, and while supporting himself on his sabre, a corporal advances and discharges his piece in his bosom. The ambassador and his suite escape the fire, as it were by miracle, and regain the palace by a backway, leaving the body of Duphot at the mercy of his assassins, who cover it with wounds, and have even the barbarity to pelt it with great stones.[3] The unfortunate Duphot had commanded the grenadiers of the army of Italy, and was the next morning to have been married to the ambassador's sister-in-law! That no doubt might remain as to who authorised this massacre, both the captain who commanded the guard and the corporal who committed the murder are rewarded, and the latter is promoted to the rank of serjeant. But now the measure of the folly and wickedness of the papal government was filled, even to running over. The ambassador instantly quit Rome with his family, announcing these events to the Directory, who gave orders to Gen[era]l Berthier to advance with the invincible army of Italy on this ancient capital of the world. A few days put him in quiet possession of Rome, from whence all those concerned in the late abominable transaction had

---

[1] Joseph Bonaparte (1768–1844), not his brother Louis (1773–1846), was appointed ambassador to Rome.

[2] Léonard Duphot (1769–97), chef de brigade, 1794; *général de division*, 1797 (Six, *Dict. des généraux & amiraux*).   [3] This incident occurred on 27 Dec. 1797.

fled, the Pope alone remaining. On his arrival the Roman people, assembled in the Capitole, formally deposed the Pope and declared themselves free and independent, chusing a provisory government, under the ancient Roman names of consuls, prefects,[1] and aediles &c. Two or three days after, the Pope quit Rome, attended by two French aid-de-camps [*sic*], and where he is gone to, I do not yet know. Thus has terminated the temporal reign of the Popes after an existence of above one thousand years. What changes this great and almost unparallelled event may produce on the moral and political system of Europe, I cannot pretend to conjecture, but they must be numerous and of the last importance. It seems to me, once more, to be an absolute fatality which drove that unfortunate and guilty government into this most frantic of all attempts, at the precise time when all the potentates of Europe were obliged to receive the law from the victorious republic; without friends, allies or support, without pretext or excuse, to wantonly commit a most barbarous outrage, in the person of a gallant officer, on the dignity of France, and the allowed rights of all civilised nations, is such a degree of infatuation as I am utterly at a loss to conceive, especially in a court so long celebrated for the depth of its cunning, and its art and address in steering with whatever wind might blow. So it is, however. The fact is certain and the Pope, who has at his will and pleasure so often disposed of crowns and monarchs, is himself deposed without effort or resistance. '*How art thou fallen from heaven, oh Lucifer, son of the morning!*'[2] The Revelations have many fine things on the subject, touching the beast and Babylon, &c., &c. '*Of the Pope's ten horns, God bless us! I have knocked off four already!*'[3] He is now a prelate *in partibus;* his means are gone; his cardinals, his court, his wealth, all disappeared, and nothing remains but his keys. It is a sad downfal for the *servant of the servants of God!* But I scorn to insult the old gentleman in his misfortunes. '*Requiescat in pace!*'

2 Mar. 1798

Received a letter from Gen[era]l Daendels desiring me to send on Ahern to him, without loss of time, in order to be employed on a secret mission. The letter also contained a very favorable testimony to my good conduct during the time I had the advantage to be attached to him in Holland, which certificate I am very proud of, and will carefully keep. Gave Ahern immediately his instructions. He will set off, I expect, in a very few days.

3 Mar. 1798

I have seen lately, in the paper called the *Bien Informé*, two articles relating to Napper Tandy which are most extravagant rhodomontades. They describe him as an Irish general to whose standard 30,000 United Irishmen

---

[1] *Life*, ii, 466, reads 'praetors'.   [2] Isaiah, 14: 12.
[3] 'Of the beast's ten horns (God bless us!) I have knock'd off three already' (Richard Corbett, 'The distracted Puritan', in Thomas Percy, *Reliques* (1767), ii, 2nd ser., bk III, p. 353).

will fly the moment he displays it, and other trash of the like nature.[1] This must come directly or indirectly from himself, for I remember some time ago, at a dinner given him, Madgett and myself by Ahern, as soon as he got warm with wine, he asserted he would answer, himself, for raising all the yeomanry of Ireland, who were at least 30,000 men, viz. precisely the number above stated. This is sad, pitiful work, puffing a man's self in this manner, especially when it is *not true!*

4 Mar. 1798

On the 19th of Feb[ruar]y last (as I see in the *Courier* of the 26th) Lord Moira made a motion of great expectation in the Irish house of lords,[2] tending to condemn the rigorous[3] measures which have been pursued by the British government in that country, and to substitute a milder system.[4] I was exceedingly disappointed at his speech, which was feeble indeed, containing little else than declamation and scarcely a single fact, at a time when thousands of [crimes of] the most atrocious nature have been perpetrated for months over the whole face of the country. In times like ours, half friends are no friends. A man in his situation, who can tell the truth with safety, or even with danger, and does not do it, is a feeble character, and his support is not worth receiving. He must speak out ALL, boldly, or be silent. Independent of this, which I cannot but consider a timid and unmanly suppression of facts which at this great occasion especially, should be sounded thro' Europe, if possible, by every man having a drop of genuine Irish blood in his veins, there is introduced a strained compliment to the virtues of the King, and a most extravagant and fulsome eulogium on the *magnanimity* of his Royal Highness George Prince of Wales, which completely disgusted me.[5] A pretty time, indeed, to come out with a panegyric on the royal virtues, and the virtues of the princely heir, when his ministers and his army were laying the country waste with fire and sword! I hate such *half-faced fellowship.*[6] His Lordship, at the conclusion of this milk-and-water harangue, comes to his conciliatory plan, which is to check the army

---

[1] On 19 Feb. 1798 the *Bien Informé* referred to an Irish general, Napper Tandy, 'qui réunira à l'instant à son drapeau plus de 30 mille Irlandais-unis', and a week later, having mentioned that Tandy had been toasted at a dinner, it went on to say that his opposition to oppression, republican principles and respect for the rights of all his fellow citizens were well known (1, 8 Ventôse an VI).

[2] For the debate in the Irish house of lords, see *The debate in the Irish house of peers on a motion made by the earl of Moira, February 19th, 1798* (Dublin, 1798) and *Report of the debate on Lord Moira's motion for an address to the lord lieutenant recommending conciliatory measures on behalf of the people of Ireland* (Dublin, 1798). In the debate Moira spoke of 'the magnanimity' of the prince of Wales, while Clare referred to the letter written to his friends at Belfast in 1791 by Tone 'who is now a fugitive for high treason and was lately an adjutant general in Hoche's army and bore a command in the Dutch service'.   [3] *Life*, ii, 467, reads 'vigorous'.

[4] Moira was informed by William Sampson, who had been informed by Whitley Stokes (see below, p. 256).   [5] In the MS there follows one line scored through.

[6] In *Life*, ii, 467, this sentence is set in italics between quotation marks, which suggests that it was taken from a literary work.

in their barbarities and to grant catholic emancipation and parliamentary reform. It is really amusing to see the various shifts and struggles, and turns and twists, and wry faces the noble lord makes before he can bring himself to swallow this last bitter pill. This kind of conduct will never do well at any time, but it is downright folly[1] in times like the present. His Lordship has mortally offended one party, and not at all satisfied the other, as will always be the case in similar circumstances. I am sorry for all this, because I esteem him personally; politically I must give him up, the more as *he ought to have known better*. But if Lord Moira speaks in this half and half style, the Chancellor[2] on the other side appears not to have been so reserved; he openly calls the United Irishmen *rebels*, and says they should be treated as such; he mentions me, by name, as having been *adjudant général* in Hoche's expedition, and again in the armament at the Texel, and says I am at that very moment an accredited envoy at Paris from that accursed society, who had also, as he is pleased to say, their envoys at Lisle, by whose insidious and infernal machinations it was that Lord Malmesbury's negotiation was knocked on the head. He also makes divers commentaries on a well-known letter, written by me to my friend Russell in 1791,[3] and which, one way or other, he has brought regularly before the House at least once a session ever since, and which figures in the secret report made by Secretary Pelham in the last one. From all these facts, and divers others which he enumerates, he infers that the design of the United Irishmen is to separate Ireland from Great Britain and that consequently all measures to destroy that infamous conspiracy are fair and lawful, of which opinion it seems the House of Lords was also, Lord Moira's motion being rejected by a large majority.[4] I can hardly, I think, be suspected of partiality to the Chancellor, but I declare I have a greater respect for his conduct on this occasion than for that of Lord Moira; he is at least an open and avowed enemy; he takes his party, such as it is, like a man who expects no quarter, and therefore is determined to give none. Had Lord Moira brought as much sincerity to the attack on that most atrocious of all governments as the Chancellor did to its defence, tho' I am far from thinking he would have been able to influence the decision of the House of Lords, he would at least have been able to scandalise it to all Europe. Instead of that he has trimmed, and by trimming has lost himself, for, to repeat it once more, in terrible times, as ours now are, a man must speak out the whole truth, or be silent. There is no mean, especially when, as in the case of Lord Moira, he may do it with perfect safety to his person. But, to return to my friend Fitzgibbon, tho' his speech be sincere, I cannot think it very wise under all the circumstances of the case. If the people of Ireland had any doubts as to the determination of the French government to support them, he has taken care to remove them all by dwelling on the reception their envoys have met

---

[1] In the MS there follows one line scored through.   [2] John Fitzgibbon, since 1795 earl of Clare.
[3] Tone to Thomas Russell, 9 July 1791 (above, vol. I, pp 104–6).   [4] By 45 votes to 10.

with here. If the United Irishmen, groaning so long under a horrible persecution, might be supposed to relax a little in their resolution, he has been so kind as to raise their drooping spirits by shewing them that a simple emissary from their society has had such influence with the Executive Directory as to outweigh all the offers of his Majesty's ministers to obtain peace, and even to cause the sending away of his ambassador in a manner certainly not the most grateful to his feelings; in short he has let out the grand secret that there is a regular communication between the Patriots, or as he is pleased to call them, the Rebels of Ireland, and the French executive; that the independance of our country is the common object of both which they are determined in concert to pursue until it is attained; and that all the efforts of government to stop the progress of this most fearful event have been and continue to be vain. Whether this candid avowal of such important facts, coming from such authority, be likely to raise the spirits of the adherents to the English govern[men]t and to extinguish all hope in the breasts of the patriots is, I confess, more than I can bring myself to believe. On the whole, I do not think the Chancellor's speech, the speech of a profound and temperate statesman.[1] Such as it is, however, I will take care to submit, or cause it to be submitted, to the eyes of Buonaparte and one or two other republicans here, who, I think, will be edified by the contents thereof. With regard to what he says of Lewines and myself, who, I presume, are the envoys of this pernicious society that he alludes to, his information, wherever he got, or however he came by it,[2] is correct enough; what relates to me is quite right, and as to Lewines, tho' he certainly was not at Lisle, artfully undermining Lord Malmesbury, I do admit he was doing his best to defeat him at the Luxembourg and elsewhere, and I hope and believe with success. What weight his representations might have had, we cannot exactly know, not being in the secret of the Directory; but, without vanity, he may reasonably conclude that some weight they certainly had, and if it was they which turned off my Lord Malmesbury, according to the Chancellor's assertion, Lewines may boldly say that he has in that instance deserved well of his country. The fact is, he and I have both done our best here to serve the cause of liberty in Ireland, but we have neither done as much good nor as much evil as Fitzgibbon is pleased to lay to our charge, and, for example, in the present instance, I do not think in my conscience that it was we that hunted Lord Malmesbury out of the Republic. *Allons!*

---

[1] On Lord Moira's motion, Fitzgibbon made a powerful speech in which he referred to Tone, 'a fugitive for high treason', the founder of 'that pestilent society', the United Irishmen, and stated that 'during the late negotiations at Lille, the plenipotentiary of the Union was there'.

[2] Some at least of the lord chancellor's information seems to have been supplied by Leonard MacNally ('J.W.'), whose source was James Tandy, who from time to time received letters from his father James Napper Tandy (J.W. to——, 3 July 1797, 3 Jan. 1798, Nat. Arch. (Ire.), Rebellion papers, 620/10/121/69, 620/10/121/88).

To General Hermann Wilhelm Daendels, 12 March 1798

Tone (Dickason) papers.

Tone recommends Citizen Aherne who will present this letter.

No. 5 Paris, ce 22 Ventôse, an 6

L'adjudant général Smith au général Daendels

Général,

Vous ayant déjà écrit si souvent au sujet du citoyen Ahern, qui aura l'honneur de vous présenter cette lettre, il ne me reste que de vous assurer, encore une fois, que j'ai mis confiance entière dans sa discretion, sa fermeté, et ses moyens, aussi bien que dans la connoissance locale et personnelle qu'il a du pays,[1] qui, je présume, va devenir l'objet de votre attention. Il vous expliquera l'état de nos affaires ici, du moins en autant que nous le savons nous-même, ce qui me dispense d'entrer dans d'autres détails que de vous assurer de toute l'étendue de mon estime, et de mon attachement.

Salut et respect.

J. S.

From General Hermann Wilhelm Daendels, 12 March 1798

Tone (Dickason) papers.

Daendels asks Tone to see Desaix to obtain from Bonaparte a reply to letters from Joubert and 'our government' asking whether it was for 30,000 men they were to prepare and the exact time they were to be ready, as the 'silence of the French government is paralysing everything'. He and his wife ask Tone to make certain purchases for Mme Daendels and to send them on.

La Haye, ce 12ᵉ Mars 1798
l'an 4ᵐᵉ de la Liberté Batave

Le lieutenant général Daendels à l'adjudant général Smith

Mon cher Smith,

Je réponds à votre lettre du 7 Ventôse,[2] et j'écris en même tems au Général Desaix. Allez le voir, et priez-le de ne rien négliger pour tâcher de nous obtenir du Général Buonaparte une réponse prompte et pressante à deux

---

[1] Scotland.   [2] Above, pp 207–08.

lettres qui lui ont été écrites par notre gouvernement et par le Général Joubert pour savoir de lui si c'étoit pour 30 mille hommes de débarquement que nous devions faire des préparatifs, et l'époque précise ou nous devions être prêts à agir. Vous sentez que nos gouvernans craignent d'engager leur responsabilité en ordonnant les dépenses des préparatifs sans avoir la certitude qu'ils ne seront pas inutiles, et le silence du gouvernement français à cet égard paralyse tout; qu'on nous tire donc de cette incertitude, qu'on nous dise quelque chose de précis et nous aurons une activité d'enfer.

Je vous remercie de la promptitude que vous avez mise à nous envoyer l'homme que je vous avois demandé. Le Citoyen Meyer, notre ambassadeur, recevra peut-être en même tems que vous cette lettre, ou bien peu de tems après l'ordre de vous rembourser vos 400 fls, ainsi vous pourrez vous présenter chez lui pour ce recouvrement.

Mon cher Smith, écrivez-moi toujours le plus que vous pourrez, et tenez-moi au courant, afin que je puisse de mon côté presser autant que possible pour ne pas rester en arrière quand il sera tems d'agir.

Ma femme[1] et moi nous vous prions aussi très instamment de vouloir bien nou faire quelques petites commissions. Je vous fais d'avance toutes mes excuses sur l'embarras qu'elles peuvent vous donner, mais je compte assez sur votre amitié pour vous prier de me rendre ce service.

Voici la note de ces commissions:

Aller chez Madame Bonnecarrère[2] qui demeure rue neuve des Capucins, Chaussée d'Antin n° 479, et lui demander si, comme elle a promis en partant de la Haye à Madame Daendels, elle a eu la bonté de lui faire l'amplette de huit tasses de porcelaine pareilles au modèle qu'elle a emporté; de lui demander aussi si elle a acheté un chapeau pour Mad[ame] Daendels.

Puis, ma femme vous prie de vous informer, soit auprès de Mad[ame] Bonnecarrère ou auprès d'autres d'un bon cordonnier, et vous lui commanderiez quatre paires de souliers en maroquin, de la même grandeur un peu plus étroits à pendant que celui jaune qui est ci-joint.

Vous lui en commanderez en outre six autres paires[3] sur la mesure en papier qui est jointe au paquet.

Vous recommanderez que ces souliers soyent des couleurs les plus à la mode excepté le noir et l'orange.

Puis, je vous prie aussi d'acheter six paires de bas de soie pour femmes, quatres blancs avec des coins de couleur les plus à la mode, deux paires de couleur grise, mais que ces deux paires ne soyent pas cependant du même gris.

Plus, deux paires de bas de soie noir[4] pour homme de la meilleure fabrique de Paris.

---

[1] Aleida Elizabeth Reiniera van Vlierden (1768–1848) (*Nieuw Nederlandsch biografisch woordenboek*).

[2] Possibly the wife of Guillaume Bonnecarrière (1754–1825), a French diplomat who in 1792 was active in organising a revolution in the Low Countries in the wake of Dumouriez's army.

[3] Daendels has a marginal note: 'moitié en soye, moitié en maroquin'.

[4] Daendels has interlined 'noir' but forgotten about agreement, i.e. 'soie noire'.

Vous voudrez bien faire un paquet de toutes ces bagatelles et me l'expédier ici, en m'annonçant la somme que cela vous a coûtée et que je vous ferai rembourser sur le champ par le Cit[oye]n Meyer.

Adieu, mon cher Smith, encore mille pardons de tant d'embarras, mais vous savez que les amis sont quelques fois importuns.

Adieu, je vous embrasse et vous aime.

Le Lieutenant Général
Daendels

P.S. Vous voudrez bien addresser le paquet à Rouget[1] dans le Heerenstraat, maison du citoyen Leib.

Rouget se rappelle à votre souvenir et à votre amitié en vous assurant de la constance de la sienne.

To General Barthélemy Louis Joseph Schérer, 19 March 1798

Archives de la Guerre, 17 yd 14, Tone dossier.

This letter has the appearance of being hurriedly written. It requests authorisation to remain in Paris until the following month for family reasons.

Paris, le 29 Ventôse l'an 6e rép.

L'adjudant général Smith
au Ministre de la Guerre

Citoyen Ministre,

Des affaires de famille d'une importance majeure rendant ma présence absolument nécessaire à Paris pour quelques jours encore, je vous prie de m'autoriser à y séjourner jusqu'au 15 du mois prochain.

Salut & respect,
L'adjudant général
J. Smith

Accord. Congé expédié le
2 Germinal an 6

Diary, 20–24 March 1798

T.C.D., Tone papers, MS 2049, ff 302ʳ–303ᵛ; *Life*, ii, 470–71.

---

[1] Pierre Rouget (1771–1833), who was on the staff of General Daendels (*Nieuw Nederlandsch biografisch woordenboek*).

20 Mar. 1798

It is with the most sincere concern and anxiety that I see in the late English papers that Arthur O'Connor has been arrested at Margate endeavouring to procure a passage to France.[1] The circumstances mentioned indicate a degree of rashness and indiscretion on his part, which is astonishing. It seems he set off from London in company with four others, viz. Quigley, the priest who was some time in Paris and of whom I have no great reason to be an admirer, Binns,[2] of the Corresponding Society, Alley,[3] also of the Corresponding Society, and his servant, of the name of Leary.[4] Quigley called himself at first Cap[tai]n Jones and afterwards Colonel Morris;[5] the others past [*sic*] for his servants. Their first attempt was at a place called Whitstable, where the vigilance of the custom house officers embar[r]assed them; they then hired a cart, which they loaded with their trunks (of which it seems they were sufficiently provided), and crossed the country on foot for 25 miles to Margate. It does not appear they made much mystery of their intended destination, but, be that as it may, at Margate they were arrested by the Bow Street runners Fugim and Rivet, who had followed them, *à la piste*, from London. From Margate they were brought back with their luggage to London, where they were examined two or three successive days before the Privy Council and finally committed to the Tower. Since their committal several other persons have been arrested, particularly a Colonel Despard,[6] a Mr Bonham,[7] a Mr Evans,[8] &c. It is inconceivable that *five* men should attempt such an enterprise, and with such a quantity of luggage; it is equally incredible that they should bring papers with them, of which the newspapers say several have been found, and especially one in the great coat pocket of Quigley purporting to be an address from the Executive Directory of England to that of France, and desiring the latter to give credit to Quigley

---

[1] For the arrests of O'Connor and his companions, see *London Chronicle*, 3, 8 Mar. 1798, and *The trial of James O'Coigly otherwise called James Quigley, otherwise called James John Fivey, Arthur O'Connor, Esq., John Binns, John Allen and Jeremiah Leary, for high treason* (London, 1798). The officers who arrested O'Connor and his companions were John Revett and Edward Fugion.

[2] John Binns (1772–1860), Irish radical; he emigrated in 1801 to America, where he became a well-known journalist (*D.N.B.*).

[3] John Allen (d. 1855), who went by the name of Alley, served his time to a woollen draper in Francis St., Dublin; later joined Irish legion as *sous-lieutenant*, rising, after being held captive by Spanish guerrillas, 1811–12, and seeing action in the Grand Army, 1812–13, to the rank of *chef-de-bataillon* (*Nation*, 24 Feb. 1855; R. R. Madden, *The United Irishmen*, 2nd ed. (London, 1857–60), i, 493; Miles Byrne, *Memoirs* (Paris, 1863), ii, 224, 239).   [4] Jeremiah Leary.

[5] It was in fact O'Connor who called himself 'Colonel Morris'.

[6] Edward Marcus Despard (1751–1803), an officer of Irish origin with a grievance against Grenville arising out of service in the West Indies; he was released from custody after a few weeks but was rearrested later in the year and remained in prison until 1800; he was charged in 1802 with conspiring to overthrow the British government and was executed in Feb. 1803 (*D.N.B.*).

[7] John Bonham (1769–1844), a member of the United Irish club in London and a friend of Valentine Lawless, later Lord Cloncurry (Lord Cloncurry, *Personal recollections* (Dublin, 1849), pp 61, 144–5; *Burke's landed gentry of Ireland* (London, 1912), p. 62).

[8] Thomas Evans (b. 1763?), Plough Court, Fetter Lane, secretary of the London Corresponding Society. In Jan. 1798 he signed an address of the society to the Irish nation. (*Report of the committee of secrecy of the house of commons* (London, 1799), appendix, pp 32–5; *Biographical dictionary of modern British radicals, vol. i: 1770–1830*, ed. J. O. Baylen and N. J. Gossman (Hassocks, Sussex, 1979)).

as being *'the worthy citizen whom they had lately seen'*. These last expressions stagger me, as otherwise I should not believe it possible any man living would leave a paper of such consequence in such a careless, extraordinary place. Other newspapers however say that *no* papers have been found, but still the expressions above quoted shake me a good deal; it is also said that O'Connor has said that his friends may be easy about him, as he has nothing to fear. God send it may be so, but I am very much afraid he will find it otherwise. It is dreadful to think of a man of his situation, character and talents being caught in so extraordinary and unaccountable a manner. I cannot conceive it! Time and time only will explain whether there is any treachery in this business. It is certain Government had notice of their intentions before they set off, for the Bow Street officers left London as soon as they did. The report is that they will be tried at Maidstone by a special commission consisting of Justices Buller, Heath and Lawrence,[1] which is expected to sit before the 10th of April. I expect that event with the most anxious sollicitude. I fear the very worst, for a thousand reasons.

24 Mar. 1798

This day I received my orders to set off for Headquarters at Rouen, where I am to remain *à la suite* of the État-Major until further orders. There is at least one step made.

To General Hermann Wilhelm Daendels, 25 March 1798

Tone (Dickason) papers.

Tone replies to Daendels's letter of 12 March and adds that he has read of many arrests, some of friends, and has just received an order to leave for the headquarters of the 'army of England' at Rouen.

No. 6   Paris, ce 5 Germinal, an 6

L'adjudant général Smith au général Daendels

Général,

J'ai reçu la lettre que vous avez voulu bien m'écrire, en datte du 12 Mars,[2] et je l'ai apportée aussitôt chez le général Desaix; mais ce général étant parti l'avant-veille pour faire une course, j'ai fait un extrait de cette partie de votre lettre qui regardoit le général Buonaparte, que je lui ai présenté avant-hier. Après l'avoir lu[e], il m'a dit qu'il alloit écrire en Hollande incessamment; ainsi j'espère que vous ne tarderez pas de recevoir de ses nouvelles.

---

[1] Francis Buller (1746–1800), John Heath (1736–1816) and Sir Soulden Lawrence (1751–1814) (*D.N.B.*).   [2] Above, pp 214–16.

Quant à nous, tout ce que je sais c'est que je viens de recevoir l'ordre de partir pour le quartier général de l'armée d'Angleterre, à Rouen, pour être à la suite de l'état-major général en attendant des nouveaux ordres. Je compte de partir dans une huitaine de jours, et je vous prie en conséquence de m'envoyer vos lettres toujours sous l'enveloppe du citoyen Meyer.

Je vois dans les gazettes anglaises qu'il y a eu des nombreuses arrestations dans ce pays.[1] Parmi les détenus il se trouve par malheur qu'il y a de mes amis et de ces personnes aussi que je vous ai designé par le citoyen que je vous ai envoyé,[2] il y a quelque tems, et qui doit être maintenant à la Haÿe. C'est à votre sagesse, général, de décider s'il ne faut pas laisser passer un peu l'orage avant que de tenter quelque chose dans ce genre là. Les esprits seront encore trop abattus par ce dernier coup, il me semble qu'il faudra absolument quelque tems pour les rassurer.

Je n'ai pas perdu un instant à exécuter les commissions, dont Mme Daendels m'a fait le plaisir de me charger. J'ai passé chez Mme Bonnecarrière, qui a entrepris d'acheter les souliers, les tasses et le chapeau; pour les bas, je les ai commandés moi-même chez une marchande qui m'a promis de m'en donner de la véritable fabrique de Paris et des plus à la mode. Tout sera prêt pour environ huit jours d'ici, et j'ai été assez heureux de trouver une personne de votre connoissance qui va directement à la Haye et qui a bien voulu se charger au moins de la porcelaine, des bas et des souliers. Pour le chapeau, étant une affaire d'une importance majeure, comme il ne voyage pas dans sa voiture, il craint un peu de l'entreprendre. J'ai tâché de le rassurer de mon mieux à cet égard, appuyant ma demande sur la bonté de Mme Daendels, qui, j'ai osé le promettre de sa part, le pardonnera, en faveur de sa bonne intention, dans le cas de quelque événement fâcheux. J'espère de prévaloir enfin, et qu'en conséquence tout arrivera en bon ordre, et que vous le trouverez à votre gré; j'en donnerai le mémoire à la personne qui aura le plaisir d'apporter à Madame ses commissions, et c'est à lui que vous aurez la bonté de remettre le montant.

Mille amitiés de ma part au Citoyen Rouget, de qui, d'abord, j'ai une petite grâce à demander, c'est de me faire une notte de toutes les uniformes de l'armée batave, infanterie, cavalerie et artillerie, avec la composition de leurs demi-brigades et régimens, la manière de nommer les officiers, &c. J'ai vu aussi à la Haye un livre de gravures contenant le costume de tous les régimens autrichiens; c'était chez un libraire qui demeurait dans une rue à côté, à peu près, de la parade; mais je ne me souviens plus, ni de son nom ni de celui de la rue. Je me suis accusé cent fois depuis, de ne l'avoir pas acheté dans le tems, mais comme je connais Rouget pour être homme de talent, s'il pourrait, d'après ces données imparfaites, déterrer le libraire et le livre, il me fera un grand plaisir de me l'acheter, et de l'envoyer par la première occasion, à l'adresse du citoyen Meyer, chez qui je laisserai toujours la mienne, il doit coûter six florins, environ,

---

[1] For details of arrests in England, see Tone's diary for 20 Mar. 1798 (above, pp 217–18). He seems however to have in mind the arrests that took place in Ireland, of which he gives details in his diary for 26 Mar. (below, pp 220–21).   [2] i.e. Citizen Aherne.

et je tiendrai toujours cette somme à sa disposition pour être employée ici d'après telle manière qu'il jugera la plus avantageuse.

Je vous prie, général, de présenter mes respects à Madame Daendels et ma sincère amitié à l'amiral De Winter, quand vous le verrez. Acceptez les assurances de ma reconnoissance et de mon respect.

L'adj[udant]t gén[éra]l
J. S.

Diary, 25–6 March 1798

T.C.D., Tone papers, MS 2049, ff 303ᵛ–304ᵛ; *Life*, ii, 471–2.
These two entries show signs of having been written up in arrears.

25 Mar. 1798

Received my letters of service from the War Office, as *adjudant général* in the *Armée d'Angleterre*. That has a lofty sound, to be sure, but God knows the heart! Applied to the Minister at War for leave to remain a few days at Paris to settle my family,[1] which he granted me.

26 Mar. 1798

I see in the English papers of this day[2] news of the most disastrous and afflicting kind, as well for me, individually, as for the country at large. The English government has arrested the whole committee of United Irishmen for the province of Leinster,[3] including almost every man I know and esteem in the city of Dublin. Among the names are Emmet, McNevin, Jnᵒ Sweetman, Bond, Jackson[4] and his son.[5] Warrants are likewise issued for the arrestation of Edward Fitzgerald, McCormick and Sampson, who have not, however, yet been found. It is by far the most terrible blow the cause of liberty in Ireland has yet sustained. I know not whether in the whole party it would be possible to replace the energy, talents and integrity of which we are deprived by this most unfortunate of all events. I have not received such a shock from all that has passed since I left Ireland. It is terrible to think of, in every point of consideration.

---

[1] Probably the letter from Tone to Schérer dated 29 Ventôse, i.e. 19 Mar. (above, p. 216).

[2] Note by Tone: 'March 17th from Irish papers of the 13th'.

[3] On 12 Mar. 1798 the Leinster provincial committee was arrested when meeting at Oliver Bond's house in Church St., Dublin.

[4] Henry Jackson (d. 1817), iron-founder of Old Church St.; he had by 1798 a foundry 'wrought by a steam engine, the first erected in Dublin'; he was banished by 38 Geo. III, c. 78, and went to America (Madden, *United Irishmen*, 2nd ed. (1857–60), iii, 183, iv, 153, 165–9; R. B. McDowell, 'The personnel of the Dublin Society of United Irishmen, 1791–4' in *Irish Historical Studies*, ii, no. 5 (Mar. 1940), p. 36).

[5] Perhaps Hugh Jackson who ran the Jackson family business in Dublin after 1800 (Suspects book, Nat. Arch. (Ire.), Rebellion papers, 620/12/217).

Government will move heaven and hell to destroy them. What a triumph, at this moment, for Fitzgibbon! These arrestations, following so close on that of O'Connor, give rise to very strong suspicions of treachery in my mind. I cannot bear to write or think longer on this dreadful event! Well, if our unfortunate country is doomed to sustain the unspeakable loss of so many brave and virtuous citizens, woe be to their tyrants, if ever we reach our destination! I feel my mind growing every hour more and more savage. Measures appear to me now justified by necessity which six months ago I would have regarded with horror. There is now no medium. Government has drawn the sword and will not recede but to a superior force—*if ever that force arrives.* But it does not signify threatening. Judge of my feeling as an individual when Emmet and Russell are in prison and in imminent peril of a violent and ignominious death! What revenge can satisfy me for the loss of the two men I most esteem on earth? Well, once more, it does not signify threatening. If they are sacrificed, and I ever arrive, as I hope to do, in Ireland, it will not go well with their enemies. This blow has completely deranged me—I can scarce write connectedly.

To General Hermann Wilhelm Daendels, 29 March 1798

Tone (Dickason) papers.

Tone states having read in the latest English papers of arrests of several of his friends in Dublin, he asks Daendels to expedite payment of 400 florins owing him, and promises to send within a few days the purchases commissioned by Mme Daendels.

No. 7

Paris, ce 9 Germinal an 6

L'adjudant général Smith au général Daendels

Général,

J'ai eu l'honneur de vous écrire en datte du 5 courant.[1] Depuis ce tems, il n'est arrivé rien ici de nouveau.

Je viens de lire dans les dernières feuilles anglaises, avec une douleur inexprimable, les nouvelles de l'arrestation de plusieurs de mes meilleurs amis à Dublin. Il n'y a presque pas un échappé et cela m'afflige d'autant plus qu'indépendamment de mon estime et de mon amitié pour eux. Ce sera un grand embarras pour tout ce qu'il y a de patriote dans le pays. Il ne faut pas croire, cependant, que ce malheur, tout grand qu'il est, peut arrêter le progrès de la grande cause. Les principes de la révolution sont

---

[1] Above, pp 218–20.

trop répandus maintenant pour dépendre de l'existence de qui que ce soit, mais cela ne m'empêche pas d'être vivement affligé de cette nouvelle, qui est bien la plus fâcheuse qui me soit jamais arrivée. J'ignore encore la cause de leur arrestation, mais comme je connois bien l'acharnement du gouvernement anglais contre eux, je suis sûr qu'on remuera le ciel et l'enfer pour les perdre. J'attends avec la dernière impatience les éclaircissemens qu'amèneront, probablement, les premiers journaux anglais.

Le citoyen Meyer, qui a la bonté de se charger de celle-ci, n'avait pas, avant son départ, reçu l'ordre de me faire payer les 400 florins. Je vous prie, général, de me les faire expédier le plutôt possible, étant à la veille de mon départ pour l'armée, où j'espère d'arriver sous quatre ou cinq jours. Je laisse la quittance entre les mains de Mme Smith. Au reste je n'en parlerois pas, si je n'étois véritablement à cette heure un peu gêné sur le chapitre de l'argent, ce qui vous fera, j'espère, mon excuse.

Je compte d'expédier sous très peu de jours les commissions dont Mme Daendels m'a honoré. Veuillez, général, l'assurer de mon respect, et agréez en même tems les assurances de mon estime, et de ma sincère amitié.

Salut et respect,
J. S.

Diary, 29 March 1798

T.C.D., Tone papers, MS 2049, f. 304ᵛ; *Life*, ii, 472.

29 Mar. 1798

The last arrestations seem to be followed up by others.[1] I believe my brother-in-law, Reynolds,[2] is among the number, and James Dixon of Kilmainham. Government will now stop at nothing.

To Charles Maurice de Talleyrand-Périgord, 31 March 1798

T.C.D., Tone papers, MS 2050, ff 22ʳ–23ᵛ.

This is a copy or draft in Tone's hand. It is possible that he wrote this letter in anticipation of handing it to Talleyrand when meeting him later

---

[1] In *Life* the following sentence is omitted.

[2] Thomas Reynolds (1771–1836), West Park St., Dublin, poplin manufacturer; represented St Nicholas' parish at the Catholic Convention; married Harriet Witherington on 25 Mar. 1794; joined the United Irishmen, 1797; gave information to the government leading to the arrest of the Leinster provincial directory at Oliver Bond's house on 12 Mar. 1798; he was arrested himself on 5 May and was the principal crown witness at the trials of Bond and others in July (*D.N.B.*).

the same day or of finding him unavailable. In it he rejects accusations by
'persons here' of intrigue and asks Talleyrand to believe 'my conduct here
has been that of an honourable man'.

Paris, ce 11 Germinal an 6

L'adjudant-général Smith au Citoyen Talleyrand, ministre des relations
extérieures de la République Française

Citoyen Ministre,

Après m'être dévoué pendant six ans à la grande cause de l'indépendance
de ma patrie, pour laquelle j'ai sacrifié ma femme et mes enfans. J'ai subi
l'exil, la ruine de ma petite fortune, et tout ce que pourroit susciter contre
moi l'esprit persécuteur du gouvernement anglais, ce n'est qu'avec quelque
douleur, mêlée en même tems d'un peu d'étonnement, que je viens
d'apprendre qu'il y a des personnes ici qui m'accusent d'être un intrigant,
et d'avoir sacrifié la cause de ma patrie à mes intérêts personnels. Comme
une telle accusation, toute fausse qu'elle est, peut avoir pour moi des suites
infiniment fâcheuses, j'espère que vous me permettrez une très courte
exposition des faits, comme ils existent. La-voici—

Je ne parle pas de ma conduite antérieurement à l'époque où j'ai eu l'avantage
d'être connu de vous. Il suffira, j'espère, de dire que j'ai eu la confiance du
général Hoche pour tout ce qui regardoit les affaires de mon pays, confiance
qu'il a conservée à l'heure même de sa mort. Le suffrage de ce grand homme,
qui pour sûr n'aimait pas les intrigans, sera, j'espère, une justification de ma
conduite, pendant le tems que j'ai eu l'honneur de lui être attaché. Après sa
mort, il y a environ six mois, quand je suis venu à Paris, chargé des dépêches
du gén[éra]l Daendels, le général Hédouville, encore un homme à ne pas
protéger les intrigans, a eu la bonté de me présenter d'abord au citoyen Barras,
auquel j'ai remis mes dépêches, et puis au citoyen Réveillère. Depuis cette
heure jusqu'à celle que j'écris, je n'ai jamais mis le pied chez ni l'un ni l'autre
de ces directeurs. Ce n'étoit pas à beaucoup près que j'étois insensible à
l'honneur et à l'avantage qu'il seroit pour moi d'être connu des hommes dont
le courage et les talens avaient si puissament contribué à élever la grande nation
à l'hauteur [sic] de ses destinées; j'en étois pénétré; je savois même que je
manquois, en quelque sorte, à mon juste devoir envers eux, mais tant j'ai
toujours craint d'encourir même le plus léger soupçon d'intrigue, que je me
suis privé volontairement d'un avantage, que bien de personnes auroient
souhaité avec ardeur, et j'ai noté dans mon obscurité, désirant qu'on me
demandât, non pourquoi j'y allois, mais pourquoi je n'y allois pas?

Dans le même tems, citoyen ministre, j'avois l'honneur de vous être
présenté, aussi par le général Hédouville, de la protection duquel, d'après
sa réputation bien connue, je ne puis m'empêcher d'être un peu fier. Comme
c'est à vous même que j'écris, je ne vous dirai pas les motifs puissans de
toute espèce, que j'aurois eu de vous faire ma cour; vous savez bien, cependant,

si je vous ai obsédé de mes visites, ou si dans aucune d'elles, j'ai jamais parlé de moi, de mes services, ou de mes intérêts.

Depuis ce tems j'ai vu, une seule fois, le ministre de la guerre, une seule fois le ministre de la marine, tous les deux pour affaire de service et dans la présence du gén[éra]l Hédouville, qui m'a présenté. Le ministre de la police, Sotin, j'ai aussi vu une seule fois; c'étoit pour lui présenter la lettre dont vous m'avez chargé, lettre très intéressante pour mes malheureux compatriotes, et qui a empêché bien de désagrémens à plusieurs d'eux, mais qui malheureusement ne m'a pas attiré, à moi, cette bienveillance de la part de quelques-uns que j'aurois espéré d'avoir méritée.

Voilà, citoyen ministre, un abrégé de mes intrigues auprès du gouvernement français, de l'exacte vérité duquel vous pouvez vous satisfaire, et dont je réponds de ma tête. Vous voyez que je ne parle ni de mérite, ni de services, ni de sacrifices. Il n'y a personne plus sensible que moi combien peu j'ai à me vanter de ce côté là, mais pour l'intégrité et le désintéressement, je n'ai assurément rien à m'accuser d'y avoir jamais manqué. C'est à votre bienveillance, citoyen ministre, que je m'adresse maintenant. Si vous croyez que ma conduite ici a été celle d'un honnête homme, qui a tâché, selon ses faibles talens, de servir la cause de la liberté et de sa patrie, sans s'abaisser jamais à des vils moyens d'y parvenir, j'oserai vous prier, avec instance, de vouloir bien répondre à cette lettre de la manière que vous jugerez convenable, et qu'une telle conduite vous sembleroit mériter. Dans les circonstances actuelles je ne vois que vous à qui je pourrai m'adresser, mais aussi votre témoignage en ma faveur sera la réponse la plus victorieuse à toute calomnie, et dont je me ferai toujours le plus de gloire.

Salut et respect,
James Smith

Diary, 31 March–4 April 1798

T.C.D., Tone papers, MS 2049, ff 304ᵛ–307ᵛ; *Life*, ii, 472–5.

31 Mar. 1798

Called with Lewines on Talleyrand, the minister for foreign affairs, to take leave previous to my setting off for the army, and met with a gracious reception. I took that opportunity to tell him that I had reason to think that Lewines and I (*as is the fact*) were exposed to some little dirty intrigues here, and that all we desired was that he would judge us, not after any calumnious report, but after our conduct, such as he himself had observed it. He replied [that] we might make ourselves easy on that head; that he had heard nothing disadvantageous with regard to us, but even if he had he should pay it no attention, the opinion of Government being made up in our favor. This is pleasant, the more so as poor Lewines and I have been tormented latterly with dirty cabals and faction, which I scorn to commit to paper. We have, God knows, done our best to content everybody, but we find it impossible while one of us is *adjudant général*, and the other is well received, and with attention, by the French government. I solemnly declare I believe these are our sole offences, but also they are offences not to be forgiven. I hate such pitiful work, and I am heartily glad I am getting off to the army, where I shall be out of the reach of it. If I would dirty my paper with them, I could record some anecdotes which are curious enough, were it only for their singular meanness; but I will not. Let them die and rot! My conduct will stand the test, and to that I trust. When a man knows he has nothing to accuse himself, it is not very difficult to bear the malevolence of others, with which profound observation I dismiss this chapter.

2 Apr. 1798

Lewines waited yesterday on Merlin,[1] who is President of the Directory for this *trimestre*, and presented him a letter of introduction from Talleyrand. Merlin received him with great civility and attention. Lewines pressed him as far as he could with propriety on the necessity of sending succour into Ireland the earliest possible moment, especially on account of the late arrestations, and he took that occasion to impress him with a sense of the merit and services of the men for whom he interested himself so much on every account public and personal. Merlin replied that as to the time or place of succour, he could tell him nothing, *it being the secret of the state*; that as to the danger of his friends, he was sincerely sorry for the situation of so many brave and virtuous patriots; that however, tho' he could not enter into the details of the intended expedition, he would tell him this much to comfort him—*that France never would grant a peace to England on any terms short of the independance of Ireland.* This is great news! It is far more direct and explicit than any assurance we have yet got. Lewines made the proper acknowledgements, and then ran off to me to communicate the news. The fact is, whatever the rest of our countrymen here may think, Lewines is doing his business here, fair and well, and like a man of honor. I wish others of them that I could name had half as good principles.

3 Apr. 1798

Lewines is determined to take a journey to Holland, or perhaps to Hamburgh, on his private affairs; he will probably set off about the same time I do. He waited in consequence, today, to take leave of Barras, who, by the bye, it seems has been looking for him these some days. From Barras, in the course of the conversation, he received a confirmation of the assurance that Merlin had given him a few days since—*that the French government would never*

[1] Philippe Antoine Merlin, known as Merlin of Douai.

make peace with England until our independance was acknowledged, which indeed
Barras had promised, himself, conditionally, before the peace with the Emperor
(vide   ).[1] My name happening to be mentioned, Lewines spoke of me, as
he thought. Barras replied that the French government was sensible of the
merit of Adj[utan]t Gen[era]l Smith. All this is *damned fine*, as poor Will[2] used
to say. Well, we shall see. Apropos! of Lewines's private affairs. He has been
now on the continent for the public business above 15 months at his own
expence to the amount of at least £500, during which time his colle[a]gues at
home have not thought proper to remit him one farthing, and it is now, in
order to raise money, that he is going to Holland. It is to me most unaccountable how men under whose good faith and authority he came here can
so neglect their engagements, the more so as McNeven, when he was here,
undertook to remind them of their duty and that proper remittances should
be made. It is the less excusable as several of the individuals concerned are not
only in easy but in affluent circumstances. So, however, it is; and what is better, Lewines is accused here by some of his own countrymen and fellow-sufferers
of neglecting, if not sacrificing, the public cause to his own private interests.[3]
To be sure, if anything could shake the determination of a man who has made
up his mind on our question it would be the pitiful and mean persecution that
he and I find ourselves exposed to here for some time back. There is no sort
of *désagrément* that we have not suffered. Well; it is no matter. That will all
pass away, and in the long run it will be seen whether we have not, each of
us in his vocation, done our best for the country. Certain it is, however, that
the pleasure I formerly felt in pursuing this great object is considerably diminished by recent experience. But no matter, once more! It is my duty to go on,
and go on I will, arrive what may! I hope yet to do some good and prevent
some mischief, and I foresee sufficient grounds to exercise me, both at one and
the other. At all events I will do my duty and discharge my conscience, and
then, come what come may, I can abide the consequence.

4 Apr. 1798

This day at three o'clock, having previously received my letters of service,
order to join, *frais de route*, &c., I set off for the headquarters of the Army of
England at Rouen, and, after travelling all night, arrived at 12 next day and
took up my lodging at the Maison Wattel. Met Gen[era]l Kilmaine by accident who invited me to dinner where I found Gen[era]l Lemoine,[4] Beyssières,[5]
comm[andan]t of the *guides* of Buonaparte &c., &c. Comedy in the even[in]g.

---

[1] See above, p. 176, n. 7. *Life* omits '(vide)'.   [2] Probably William Henry Tone.
[3] Footnote by Tone in parentheses: 'in which accusation, by the bye, I have the honor to find
myself included, but as to that, *je m'en fiche! Allons!*'
[4] Louis Lemoine (1754–1842), a *sous-officier* before the revolution; *général de division*, 1796; with
armée d'Angleterre, 1797–8; count, 1818 (Six, *Dict. des généraux & amiraux*).
[5] Jean Baptiste Bessières (1768–1813), capt. in National Guard, 1789; chosen by Bonaparte to
command the company of guides attached to his person, 1796; marshal of the empire, 1804 (ibid.).

To Matilda Tone, 6 April 1798

Tone (Dickason) papers.

Rouen, 17 Germinal, an 6

Dearest Love,

I arrived here yesterday, as tired as a horse, after my journey all night, in which I met with no adventures. I found Gen[era]ˡ Kilmaine here, who asked me to dinner and treated me very civilly, and there is the history of the twenty-four hours I have spent in Rouen.

I come now to business. The moment you receive this, let Matt set off to Giauque,[1] in case my letter is time enough to catch him, and desire him by all means to call on Gen[era]l K——, who is gone this morning to Paris, and hold with him a discourse to the same effect as mine in our last interview with our friend in the rue de Bacq.[2] He will see the expediency of this himself and beg of him not to neglect it. Another thing—I find myself here without pistols, which are notwithstanding, in time of danger, a pretty convenience. He has a pair belonging to a valuable and unfortunate friend of ours, for which he (Giauque) has no present occasion. If he will entrust them to my keeping, I will esteem it as an act of kindness, and, as I expect, or at least I hope, to see the right owner before he will, I engage to deliver them safe and sound into his hands. In case Giauque obliges me in this, let Matt take charge of the weapons until further orders.

Also—let Matt go to the ci-devant fencing school, and take away a pair of sandals and a blue jacket which belong to me. I paid for a foil also, which he may take if he chuses, and a glove. I hope you have got the 400 florins, or at least news of them, by this. The gross sum of what you ought to receive is as follows: Giauque[3] 266#; Burke[4] 240#; MacSheehy 84#; Black,[5] for his share of Meot's dinner[6] 88#; the Dutch ambassador[7] 800#; total 1,478#. Let Matt remind Black of his part, as he may have forgot it, but in a manner not at all to press him.

I am, and shall be until I hear from you, in the utmost uneasiness about your lodging. I hope you may get soon fixed to your mind. It is curious to think of the enterprise I have embarked in, who could not in a month's search find out a lodging for you in Paris and finished at last by being the dupe of that idiot, your landlady. Well, what will you have of it? *'One man has one way of thinking, and another has another, and that is all the difference.'*[8]

---

[1] i.e. Lewines. [2] Where the ministry of foreign affairs was situated.
[3] Probably Lewines. [4] Bartholomew Teeling (see above, p. 196, n. 3).
[5] Alexander Lowry (see above, p. 161). [6] See Diary for 25 Nov. 1798 (above, p. 178).
[7] Meyer. [8] Source of this quotation not traced.

Do, dear Love, try if you cannot succeed better than I was able to do, and relieve me from the anxiety which I shall feel until you are fixed.

Tell Matt to be making all arrangements, as to his kit, by means of Maguire, Ashley, &c. I have not yet reconnoitred the ground so as to guess when his departure may be necessary, but I shall on Gen[era]l K——'s return, which will be, he tells me, within this week. Let him keep himself ready to cut and run at the first signal. The moment your Hamburgh friends[1] arrive, let me know and I will send G—— all necessary instructions how to proceed. And this is all the business I recollect.

I have got well lodged here. *'My landlord is civil, but dear as the devil'*,[2] which is more than poetically true. I intend to see nobody that I can avoid, and to read, write and paint like a horse. You see, dearest Love, I do not say one word about your spirits; I am sure they are good, and I desire you to keep them so. All will go, I am sure, as you would wish it. Depend upon it, *ça ira!*

Adieu, Life and soul. Take care of the Babies, and let Maria stick like a leech to her music; a month's loss now would not be recovered in six at three years hence, but indeed I must say she wants no incentive on that head. Make the boys mind their books, *'for when both house, &c., &c.'*.[3] If ever I come to be anything, it will be all along of my learning. Adieu, dearest Life. Your ever affec[t]

J. S.

Direct to me, *au Citoyen Smith, maison Watel, à Rouen.* My sincere love to Giauque, if this is in time to catch him, and especially to Matt—for the others! I do not however include Howard[4] & Wilkins.[5]

A la Citoyenne Smith
Cul de Sac, Notre Dame des Champs
No. 1390 près du Luxembourg
À Paris

Diary, 6–8 April 1798

T.C.D., Tone papers, MS 2049, ff 307ᵛ–308ᵛ; *Life*, ii, 475–6.

6 Apr. 1798

Strolling about the town,[6] which is large, ugly and dirty. It wears however a great appearance of manufactures and commerce, which I have no doubt in time of peace is considerably augmented. The Cathedral is a beautiful relic of ancient architecture. I have seen the inside of Westminster Abbey

---

[1] His sister, Mary, and her husband, Jean Frédéric Giauque.
[2] Swift, 'Epigram on a window at an inn at Chester' (1726?).
[3] Samuel Foote, *Taste* (1752), i, 1.   [4] i.e. John Tennent.   [5] i.e. Thomas Wilson.
[6] Rouen.

and Notre-Dame, as well as several in Germany and elsewhere, but I prefer the inside of the cathedral at Rouen to them all. It is a magnificent *coup d'oeil*. But what is provoking, between the body of the church and the choir, some pious archbishop who had more money than taste has thrown a very spruce colonnade of pure Corinthian architecture which totally destroys the harmony of the building and ruins what would otherwise produce a most magnificent effect. This little specimen of Grecian architecture is more truly Gothic than all the rest of the edifice.[1]

8 Apr. 1798[2]

On a second inspection of the Cathedral this day, I find that the Corinthian colonnade which is described in terms of such just indignation in yesterday's journal turns out to be Ionic, but all's one for that. The archbishop, I still hold, is a blockhead, in all the dialects of Greece, and all the orders of architecture, and moreover he is a fellow of no taste. N.B.[3] Heard part of a sermon, this being Easter Sunday, V.S.[4] Sad trash! A long parallell, which I thought would never end, between Jesus Christ and Joseph, followed by a second equally edifying between the same personage and the prophet Jonas, shewing how the one lay three nights in the tomb, and the other three nights in the belly of a great fish, &c., &c., at all which I profited exceedingly. The church was full of women, but I did not remark twenty men. I wonder how people can listen to such abominable nonsense.

Apropos! I should have mentioned in its place that Lewines called, a day or two before I left town, on Buonaparte to endeavour to interest him in behalf of our unfortunate friends now in arrestation and to try whether it would be feasible to obtain a declaration from the Directory similar to that which they issued in the case of the patriots of the Pays de Vaud, for whose safety they made the aristocracy of Berne personally responsible.[5] Buonaparte replied that the case was totally different. With regard to the Swiss, France was in a situation to follow up the menace by striking instantly; with England it was not so; she was a power of the first rank, and the republic must never threaten in vain. Under those circumstances he thought any interposition on the part of the French government in favour of the Irish patriots might injure them materially by enflaming still more the English government against them, and

---

[1] A choir screen or jube with six Ionic columns was erected in Rouen cathedral, 1775–7. By the early nineteenth century it was being strongly criticised and it was taken down in 1884. (A. P. M. Gilbert, *Description historique de la cathédrale de Rouen* (2nd ed., Rouen, 1837); 'La cathédrale de Rouen: sauvetage, restauration, 1939–55' in *Les monuments historiques de la France*, ii (1956), 115–19).

[2] *Life*, ii, 475, has 7 Apr.

[3] *Life* omits 'N.B.' and inserts 'April 8', the date on which Easter Sunday fell.

[4] i.e. *vieux style* ('old style').

[5] On 28 Dec. 1797 the Directory decreed that the French minister to the Swiss Confederation should inform the cantonal authorities of Berne and Fribourg that they would be held personally responsible for the safety of those inhabitants of the Pays de Vaud who had placed themselves under the protection of the French republic (*Moniteur*, 30 Dec. 1797).

could at the same time do them no possible service. In this reasoning Lewines was obliged to acquiesce, and in fact the argument is weighty. Lewines has however the consolation to think he has left nothing on his part untried to rescue our unfortunate friends from the peril which menaces their lives. It is a melancholy comfort, but still it is some comfort.

To Matilda Tone, 12 April 1798

Tone (Dickason) papers.

Rouen, ce 23 Germinal, an 6

Dear Love,

I have just received yours, which is so artfully worded that I cannot divine whether you received a letter I wrote you on the 17th;[1] however I presume you did, as you say nothing to the contrary. I am delighted with all your operations. *'I looked wistfully on the little arrangement you had made, and then gave a sigh!'*[2] Your situation appears as pleasant as you can reasonably desire, and the convenience of the river, if it be feasible, is a great object. I am glad you have taken Marianne, for I have a better opinion of the poor unchaste than many people entertain; let her not, however, buy for you, whatever you can discreetly buy for yourself, for certain reasons. Her wages, I believe, are reasonable enough. For your music master, I think your best way will be to give him 24#[3] a month, at the same time letting him know, in a mild and determined manner, that you expect he will attend very regularly, that he will give *a full hour* at each lesson and also that he will keep the pianoforte in tune, for it is a vile business to strum on an instrument out of tune. At the same time if he will take 21# (viz. half a crown more than his present engagement) I do not insist on your giving more, but I mean you should not break off even at the 24#. Touching your finances, all goes well, and it will be better when you have the money in your hands. I do not want any, nor do I suppose I shall; on the contrary I hope to remit you regularly your share of my appointments, but I have as yet seen nobody on that head, nor shall I before the return of Gen[era]l Kilmaine which I expect in the course of a few days.

As to my operations, I spend almost the whole day in my room, reading, writing or painting my *états militaires*. I find sufficient amusement in that, and besides I have been twice at the play. I have made no acquaintance as yet but with the waiter, however tomorrow I mean to sally out and pay a visit to the colonel of Buonaparte's *guides* whom I met at dinner the day of my arrival at Gen[era]l Kilmaine's,[4] in order to reconnoitre a little the position of things.

---

[1] Above, pp 227–8. [2] Sterne, *A sentimental journey* (1768), 1. [3] i.e. 24 livres.
[4] See Tone's diary for 4 Apr. (above, p. 226).

Adieu, Dearest Love. Take care of yourself and the babies, of whom, by the bye, you tell me nothing, and love me always,

Yours ever and most affectionately,
J. Smith

To Mathew Tone, 12 April 1798

Tone (Dickason) papers; added to the preceding letter.

D[ea]r Matt,

I thank you for your note. It was not quite as it ought to be in Giauque[1] to fight shy about the pistols, and as for those that he *would* give me, if he had them, when he *would not* give me those he had, I shall try to do without them. I believe MacSheehy has a scurvy pair which belong to me, see about them. I think he said he had sent them to Burke's lodgings.[2] If you can find a bed at Matty's new lodgings,[3] remain there by all means until further orders; the difference of expence to her will be but trifling, and everything here is dearer than at Paris. Tell Maria to look out for a little square lump of Indian inks, about as big as a hazel nut, which I forgot in her drawing box, and let her send it to me very carefully by MacSheehy when he comes, if indeed he means to come. When Gen[era]l Kilmaine returns I shall endeavour to learn something with regard to your distinctions and that of the other Irish emigrants. Have they presented their memorial declaring off unless they were to be employed in Ireland?

I am exceedingly pleased with the account you give me of Matty's new landlord and family, and I hope she will be at her ease. As for Desaix, he is gone in consequence of a wager of six livres which he laid in the Café de Foy to measure the height of the Grand Pyramid. I know it is surmised by some that he is taken, as you say, with a passion for mummies but I rather fancy the former solution to be the true one.

As for my spirits, they are always level, and I assure you I regard it as no small comfort to be removed from the dirty *tracasseries* I am exposed to for some days before I left Paris. Definitively, have you got my letter of the 17th[4] and is Giauque[5] set off on his *'long gurney to the north'*?[6] I send this, happy go lucky, to your new lodgings.

Adieu, dear Matt,
Yours sincerely
J. Smith

---

[1] i.e. Lewines.   [2] 'Burke' may be Bartholomew Teeling (see above, p. 196, n. 3).
[3] At Chaillot, on the right bank of the Seine, 4 km W.N.W. of Notre-Dame de Paris.
[4] Above, pp 227–8. Evidently Tone intended this sentence for Matilda Tone.
[5] Lewines, who was to set off for Holland about the same time as Tone was to leave for Normandy (see above, pp 225–6).
[6] 'Mistress says, we are going on a long gurney to the north' (Smollett, *Humphry Clinker* (1771), i, 157).

À la Citoyenne Smith
Rue des Batailles, No. 29
À Chaillot
près Paris

To General Hermann Wilhelm Daendels, 12 April 1798

Tone (Dickason) papers.
Tone tells of being assailed by cabals and schemers and encloses a letter to
Delacroix, which he asks Daendels to read and, if he approves the contents,
to forward.

No. 8

Au Quartier général de l'armée d'Angleterre
à Rouen, ce 23 Germinal, an 6

L'adjudant général Smith au général Daendels

Général,

Vous n'êtes pas sans doute arrivé à la situation éminente que vous tenez
avec tant d'honneur à vous même, et d'avantage à votre pays, sans avoir être
exposé parfois aux entraves de la malveillance et de l'envie. Dans le cas d'un
homme tel que vous rien de plus naturel, mais qu'un être aussi obscur, aussi
inconnu que moi, se trouve en butte à des attaques pareilles, voilà, par exemple, quelque chose d'extraordinaire. Cependant la chose se trouve ainsi. Depuis
quelque tems je suis travaillé par des cabales, des intrigailles, dont ni la matière
ni les agens (qui, par malheur, sont de mes propres compatriotes) valent la
peine de vous en occuper. Peu de gens ont le bonheur de pouvoir faire du
bien, mais malheureusement il n'y a presque pas d'être si vil, qui ne pourroit quelquefois faire du mal. Tout en méprisant les tracasseries dont on tâche
de m'embarasser ici, je le regarde comme une mesure de prudence de me
mettre à même de les repousser victorieusement en tems et lieu, et surtout
dans le cas de mon retour dans mon pays. Comme je me trouve accusé, prin-
cipalement, d'avoir agi à Paris comme un intrigant, et d'avoir sacrifié les
intérêts de mon pays à mes intérêts personnels, j'ai écrit la lettre ci-jointe au
citoyen Charles Delacroix,[1] auquel comme ministre des relations extérieures,
je me suis adressé dès mon arrivée en France.[2] Je vous prie, général, comme
mon ami, de la lire, et si vous approuvez le contenu, vous aurez la bonté de

---

[1] Below. [2] See Tone's diary for 15 Feb. 1796 (above, vol. II, pp 53–4).

la cacheter et de la faire passer au ministre français. Je ne sais, d'abord, s'il se souviendra de moi, mais si vous le voyez, vous pourrez lui rappeler que c'étoit au mois de ventôse, il y a deux ans, que j'ai eu l'honneur de lui présenter une lettre en chiffre de la part du citoyen Adet,[1] alors ministre de la République Française auprès des États Unis à Philadelphie. Si le ministre a la bonté de m'accorder le témoignage que je demande, et que je crois même avoir mérité de sa part, je vous prierai, général, de vouloir bien vous en charger, et de me le faire passer dans votre première lettre.

Je dois vous demander mille excuses de vous troubler d'une telle manière, mais vous m'avez toujours montré tant de bonté, que je me trouve enhardi de m'adresser à vous, dans la circonstance actuelle, d'autant plus que je me sens vivement touché de la méchante fausseté de la calomnie, que je désire de me mettre à même de repousser. Loin d'avoir sacrifié mon pays à mes intérêts personnels, je lui ai sacrifié tout ce que j'avais de plus cher, ma femme, mes enfans, mon bien, modique à la vérité, mais enfin tout ce que j'avois, j'ai subi l'exil, étant chassé de chez moi par le gouvernement anglais; j'ai deux fois traversée l'Atlantique pour soumettre la triste situation de ma patrie aux yeux du Directoire même, et implorer son secours; depuis que je suis en France, il n'y a pas eu un seul coup medité pour sa libération, où je ne me suis trouvé de ma personne, j'ai plus d'une fois hasardé ma vie, et je suis aujourd'hui, et je serai toujours, prêt à faire de même encore. Après une telle conduite, j'aurois peut-être du espérer que l'envie eût attendu jusqu'à ce que j'eusse reçu, ou au moins demandé, quelque récompense; mais non! Il parait qu'on veut m'accabler par anticipation et me barrer le chemin avant même que j'y suis entré.

Il est vrai que le Directoire, de sa propre volonté, m'a fait, d'abord, chef de brigade; que le général Hoche m'a nommé depuis adjudant général, et que dernièrement le Directoire a encore bien voulu me continuer dans cet grade; mais je vous assure, général, que tout cela s'est passé sans la moindre application de ma part. Il s'en faut tant qu'après que l'expédition de Brest avait manqué, j'écrivis au général Hoche pour lui résigner le grade qu'il m'avait accordé, et c'étoit seulement d'après ses ordres positifs que j'ai consenti de rester à mon poste, car j'étois loin de m'attribuer les qualités et surtout l'expérience qui me fallaient, pour remplir dignement la situation où je me suis trouvé, mais enfin c'étoit à mon général de décider, et sa decision une fois prise, je n'avois que de m'y soumettre. Vous ne verrez pas dans tout cela, j'espère, l'allure d'un intrigant.

Pardon, encore, général, mille fois de cette lettre, mais c'est un véritable soulagement pour moi de m'épancher dans le sein d'un homme; comme vous, de ce petit nombre que je me ferai toujours un devoir de regarder avec estime, amitié et respect.

L'adj[t] gen[l]

J. S.

---

[1] Pierre Auguste Adet to Committee of Public Safety, 14 Dec. 1795 (above, vol. II, pp 34–5).

To Charles Delacroix, 12 April 1798

Tone (Dickason) papers.

In anticipation of returning to Ireland, Tone asks for a testimonial to his dedication to Ireland's interests while in France.

Au Quartier général de l'armée d'Angleterre, à Rouen,
ce 23 germinal, an 6

L'adjudant général Smith, Irlandais,
  au citoyen Charles De la Croix, ministre plénipotentiaire de la
  République Française auprès la République Batave

Citoyen Ministre,

  Le Directoire Exécutif m'ayant fait l'honneur de m'employer dans l'armée d'Angleterre, je commence enfin à jouir de l'espérance de revoir encore ma patrie après un triste exil de trois années. Comme c'étoit à vous que je me suis adressé lors de mon arrivée en France, et que j'avais l'honneur de vous présenter les seuls mémoires que j'ai adressés au gouvernement français sur l'état de l'Irlande, ce seroit pour moi en même tems le plus grand service, et la plus douce satisfaction, de pouvoir emporter chez moi un témoignage de votre approbation de ma conduite durant le tems que j'ai eû l'honneur de vous entretenir sur la situation de mon pays. C'est à vous, citoyen ministre, de décider si j'ai tâché de soutenir, avec zèle, ses intérêts, d'exposer avec chaleur ses besoins, de supplier avec instance le gouvernement français, de lui accorder la protection de la grande nation. Vous savez bien, surtout, si j'ai jamais avili la cause de ma patrie en y mêlant de mes intérêts personnels. Si, donc, vous croyez, citoyen ministre, que ma conduite a été celle d'un homme véritable-ment dévoué à la cause de l'indépendance de sa patrie, cet objet si intéressant en même tems pour la république française, pourrai-je vous prier de vouloir bien m'accorder le témoignage de votre approbation dont je sens bien toute la valeur, et que, pour cette raison, je suis si jaloux d'obtenir?

  Agréez, citoyen ministre, les assurances de mon sincère respect et de ma vive reconnoissance de l'accueil favorable dont vous m'avez toujours honoré.

Salut et respect,
J. S.

Diary, 15 April 1798

T.C.D., Tone papers, MS 2049, ff 308ᵛ–309ʳ; *Life*, ii, 476–7.

15 Apr. 1798

This day I have got lodgings, by order of Adjutant Gen[era]l Boulant,[1] *provisoirement chef de l'état-major*, in the house of Citizen Bigot.[2] It is a large hotel, and I am well lodged. Mine host invited me to dinner, which passed *tête à tête*. He has been *président à mortier* in the ci-devant *parlement* of Normandie. His father has been, I believe, *maire* of Rouen under the ancien régime, and they have lost a considerable property, besides lying eleven months in prison during *la terreur*. It is easy to judge from all these anecdotes that my host is no great admirer of the revolution, which he always qualifies with the title of *malheureuse*. I forgive with all my soul aristocrats of his description, who really were something before the Revolution and who find themselves now nothing or worse; besides he seems a man of a gentle, not to say a timid, temper, and I rather fancy his sufferings and his fears have weakened his mind. If it be not so, justice must have been strangely administered in France in times when men of his capacity could arrive at the first stations in the law; he is downright *weak!* However, I sat him out with great civility, tho' it was a terrible *corvée* to me, and we parted very good friends. He has asked me again for the day after tomorrow, when there is to be company. I was glad of that circumstance, for in truth I have no great stomach for another dinner *tête à tête*. My landlord is a *fit!*

To Matilda Tone, 18 April 1798

Tone (Dickason) papers.

Rouen, ce 29 Germinal, an 6

Dear Love,

I have received two letters from Matt and you of the 24 & 25 inst. In the first place I congratulate you both on the safe arrival of our friends,[3] to whom you will of course present my sincere and affectionate regards. It is an unspeakable satisfaction to me that you are settled to your mind. For your slave,[4] you know *'young ravens must have food'*.[5] Subject to the caution I gave you of not employing her to buy more than is necessary, I dare say she will answer you as well as another, and I do not love strangers; it appears her *Giautism* is

---

[1] *Recte* Boulart, i.e. Jean François Boulart (1776–1842), artillery officer attached to the right wing of *l'armée d'Angleterre*, 1798; created a baron of the empire, 1810 (Six, *Dict. des généraux & amiraux*).

[2] Alexandre Robert Emery Bigot de Sommesnil (1749–1820), member of a great legal family in Normandy which supplied five presidents to the *parlement* of Rouen. His father was mayor of Rouen in 1779. He himself was a president of the Rouen *parlement*, was arrested in 1791, emigrated in 1792 but was removed from the list of *émigrés* in March 1797. (H. de Frondeville, *Les présidents du parlement de Normandie, 1499–1790* (Paris, 1953)).

[3] Perhaps an allusion to his sister and brother-in-law, Mary and Jean Frédéric Giauque (see Tone to Mathew Tone, 18 and 23 Apr. 1798, below, pp 236–7, 242–3).

[4] Apparently her servant, Marianne (cf. Tone to Matilda Tone, 12 Apr. 1798, above, p. 230).

[5] *Merry wives of Windsor*, I, iii.

admitted.[1] Touching my visit to Paris, I think upon it. You may be sure I shall embrace the first proper opportunity, for which you are not more anxious than I am. If Gen[era]l Kilmaine returns here speedily, I shall, I hope, settle it at once; if not, *'I shall find, said he, some other way to get it off'*.[2] *'By the Lord, lads, I'm glad you've got the money'*,[3] the Ambassador's, I mean. Keep your own secret thereupon &c., &c.

I wrote a few days since to Gen[era]l Clarke and I transcribe a part of his answer, of the 22d inst. 'Quant à mes sentimens pour vous, mon cher Smith, je vous dois de les consigner dans la présente, et je vous assure que je me ferai un plaisir d'annoncer en toute occurrence, que non seulement vous avez plaidé avec éloquence la cause des républicains d'Irlande, mais que vous avez cherché à leur être utile par un devouement dont j'ai été longtems témoin et un zèle assidu. Je dirai plus, vous avez, dans une position qui pouvoit si facilement vous donner l'apparence de l'intrigue, su éviter cet écueil, et vous vous êtes placé à mes yeux dans l'état de dignité et de désintéressement, qui seul convenait au caractère dont vous étiez revêtu, à la cause des hommes libres, que vous défendiez, et à l'estime que cette conduite vous a mérité des personnes qui vous ont connu particulièrement et que le gouvernement français a mis en rapport avec vous, &c.'[4]

All this is pleasant, *n'est-ce pas?* Clarke is a good fellow. He expects Mr Sheé immediately, which makes me more and more desirous to visit Paris, for you know my esteem for that truly respectable man. One of these times which are justly denominated *'odd come shortlys'* I will make a race to visit you. *'I will, by the god of war!'*[5]

Do you write a letter to Howard[6] & Wilson[7]? They will be much more pleased thereat than at one from me, and you know all the news.

Love to all the Babies. Yours ever affectionately,

J. Smith

To Mathew Tone, 18 April 1798

Tone (Dickason) papers; added to the preceding letter.

Citizen J. Smith to Citizen M. Smith

Citizen,

That I take to be a true republican commencement. I have received your letter, announcing your various misadventures in pursuit of glory and Gen[era]l Kilmaine, in which you tell *'of moving accidents by flood and field,*

---

[1] Perhaps an allusion to Giauque, who seems to have been careless with money.
[2] Sterne, *A sentimental journey* (1768), ii.   [3] *1 Henry IV*, II, iv.
[4] This letter from Clarke testifies to Tone's probity. There is an English translation in Marianne Elliott, *Wolfe Tone, prophet of Irish independence* (New Haven, 1989), p. 371.
[5] Cf. John O'Keeffe, *Love in a camp* (1785), I, iii.
[6] *Nom de guerre* of John Tennent.   [7] Probably Thomas Wilson.

of being taken by the insolent foe, &c.,[1] in all which I truly sympathise with you; however, as you have already had the honor to lie ten months upon straw in a prison in the same great cause,[2] you can the better bear these petty mortifications, which I can well imagine are not so easily digested by your fellow-sufferers. The fact is they look on themselves as of more consequence than I am afraid the Directory does, and that being the case, I am sure their situation is very far from a pleasant one. However, pleasant or unpleasant, it is a great satisfaction to me to be out of the way just now, for one way or another, a part of their ill humour would have fallen upon me, and I am already more than sufficiently weary of *finding and proving*.

Give my sincere regards to Giauque and Mary.[3] As to my return to Paris, I shall see about that in a few days. If General Kilmaine were here, I would apply for leave at once, but I do not wish to ask a permission of strangers. In the meantime if Giauque wishes I should write to Chaumont & Cie with regard to the bill for the 17,000#,[4] let him send me a copy of the letter, which I will dispatch by the next post.

Do not budge from where you are until further orders. You do not tell me where, or how, Giauque has disposed of himself. Tell him or Mary to write to me thereupon.

Touching the other Giauque,[5] whom you are to call in future James Brown, you never tell me a word of him. Is he gone or not? You and Matty are vile correspondents in matter of business.

Call on Black,[6] to whom I promised to write, and tell him I would do so if I had one syllable to say, but in truth I have not. I see as yet no trace here of the formation of our *état-major* but if it be true, as I see in the papers, that Gen[era]l Berthier is arrived, I suppose we shall soon hear something upon that head.

Adieu, dear Matt; your slave and dog
J. S.

À la Citoyenne Smith
Rue des Batailles No. 29
À Chaillot
près Paris

To Citizen La Janiette, 18 April 1798

Archives Nationales, F⁷ 7422; copy in T.C.D., Tone papers, MS 2050, f. 24.

La Janiette was in charge of the 5th bureau (passeports) in the Département de la Police Générale. Tone asks him whether a report of Lord Edward

[1] *Othello*, I, iii.
[2] Mathew Tone had left Ireland for France in Aug. 1794 (when Britain and France were at war) with the intention of entering the French army but was put in prison at Dunkirk under suspicion of being a British spy and held until May 1795. [3] Their brother-in-law and sister.
[4] i.e. 17,000 livres. [5] Lewines. [6] *Nom de guerre* of Alexander Lowry.

Fitzgerald taking refuge in France is true, in which case 'I will ask the minister of police to facilitate his going to the Executive Directory'.

Au Quartier Général à Rouen, ce 29 Germinal an 6

L'adjudant-général Smith, Irlandais
au Citoyen La Janiette à l'Hôtel du Ministre de la Police Générale,
Quai Voltaire

Citoyen,

Je viens de lire dans les journaux un article annonçant que le lord Edward Fitzgerald s'est sauvé de la poursuite du gouvernement anglais, et s'est réfugié en France.[1] Veuillez bien me dire si cette annonce soit vraie, et dans le cas de son arrivée, je prierai le ministre de la police de vouloir bien lui faciliter les moyens de se rendre auprès du Directoire Exécutif, qui l'accueillera, je ne doute nullement, de la manière que ses talens, son dévouement et son courage ont si bien méritée.

Salut et fraternité
J. Smith

[*Endorsed*]: Répondre après avoir vérifié avec document qu'on n'a pas connaissance que cet individu soit arrivé en France. 21 Flor[éal].

Diary, 20 April 1798

T.C.D., Tone papers, MS 2049, ff 309ᵛ–310ʳ; *Life*, ii, 477–8.

20 Apr. 1798

I pass my time here *'worse than the mutines in the bilboes'*,[2] but there is no remedy, so *'what cannot be cured, must be endured'*, as the poet sweetly sings.[3] Seeing yesterday in the papers an article that Lord Edward Fitzgerald had made his escape from Ireland and got safe into France,[4] I wrote[5] immediately to the chef de bureau in the police charged with the foreign departm[en]t to know if the report were true, and in that event praying the minister to shew Lord Edward every attention, &c, but I am afraid it is too good news to be true. Walked out this evening, along the river, to see the *bateaux*[6] which are building here for the descent. There are 10 of them, 4 of which are launched. I judge the whole might be ready in three weeks, or a month at farthest. They

---

[1] It was reported in *Bien Informé* that Lord Edward Fitzgerald had escaped arrest and was in London (*Bien Informé*, 3 Apr., 15 June 1798).   [2] *Hamlet*, V, ii.
[3] Possibly Tone was recalling these words from George Colman, *Phormio* (1765), II, ii.
[4] See above, n. 1.   [5] Tone to La Janiette, dated 29 Germinal (above).
[6] *Life*, ii, 477, reads *'batteaux plats'* (*sic*), signifying flat-bottomed boats.

cost 13,000# a piece,[1] viz. £541 13[*s*]. 4[*d*]. Apropos! of the expedition. I am utterly at a loss what to think since my departure from Paris. Desaix, whom I hoped to find here, seems certainly to be at Toulon, and the report in the papers of this day, as well as in my brother's[2] letter, is that Buonaparte is to set off in three days to join him, and take the command of this inconceivable armament which is preparing in the ports of the Mediterranean, the destination of which nobody knows. It is certain that Buonaparte's *guides* set off from this on the road to Paris three days ago. In the meantime it seems General Kilmaine commands, par interim, the Army of England. All this, I confess, utterly derouts me. I am *'lost in sensations of troubled emotion'*.[3] The prevailing opinion in the Paris papers is that Egypt is the object of this armament, and that the Turk is to concur with us in the expedition. If it were not for our own business, I should like extremely in that case to be with General Desaix— but that is *castle-building*. What if, when all is embarked, Buonaparte were suddenly to turn to the right towards Gibraltar and surprise Lord St Vincent's with a visit one of these fine mornings? But I am afraid he won't. The thing is however possible. His Lordship would in that case find himself between two fires, and may be, at last, those miserable Spaniards might make an exertion. But no! Well, time will shew more, which observation I take to be a very safe one, on my side. It is not a fortnight since the Directory passed a decree conferring the command of both fleet and army on Buonaparte, with orders to render himself at Brest in ten days. How is that to be reconciled with the present reports? At any rate, all this is well calculated to puzzle John Bull. I am sure I am puzzled with a vengeance. In short I will torment myself no more with conjectures, in which I only lose myself. Once more, time will explain all.

To Matilda Tone, 22 April 1798

Tone (Dickason) papers.

Rouen, 3 floréal, an 6

Dear Love,

I have received yours of the 30th Germinal, and am surprised you have not heard from me more regularly. I have written to you, or to Matt, on the 17th, the 23d, the 29th of last month,[4] and the 1st of this, so at least you see, it has not been my fault. I saw the news you mention in the *Bien Informé* a few days since, but I mentioned in my last, that I did not give much credit to it. I am very glad poor Hamilton[5] has got safe thus far; say everything friendly to him

---

[1] *Life*, ii, 477, reads '13,000 livres apiece'.
[2] William Tone expands this to 'my brother Mathew's' (ibid.).
[3] Source of this quotation not traced.   [4] Above, pp 227–8, 230–31, 235–7.
[5] William Henry Hamilton (see above, vol. I, p. 502, n. 8). A member of the London Corresponding Society, he fled, in consequence of O'Connor's arrest, to Hamburg, proceeded to the Hague and had

on my behalf. I think *your people*[1] would do very well to go home, for any good I see they are doing, or likely to do here; however I shall be very far from taking upon me to advise them, and of course you and Matt will observe the same discretion. If there be any truth in this news, which once again I do not believe, we shall soon be certified of it, and in that case I will see what is fit to be done. I will therefore in all events wait here for a few days, and in case it should after all turn out to be true, I will immediately set off for Paris and see with the Government what they mean to do, and regulate my conduct accordingly.

I expect letters from Giauque[2] (whose name is Brown at present) with great impatience. In your conversation with Hamilton, you will soon see what line to take. He certainly *was*, as you say, a man of honor, and I hope is so still; besides we have heretofore obliged him. I think therefore you may speak freely to him, but after all it must be your own discretion which will determine you.

I confess the change in Buonaparte's destination totally surpasses my comprehension.[3] It is certain that here, at least, there is a suspension of the preparations for the grand expedition, nor do I see that another general taking the command necessarily implies that the scheme is given up.[4] At the same time this unaccountable change totally derouts me. I have left off guessing, in despair, and I let myself float blindly at the mercy of events over which I have no control.

I am sorry to see you are more discomposed by our present separation than you ought to be. Surely, dear Love, it is nothing in comparison of our former ones. I assure you I have far more reason, on every account, to regret it than you, for I spend my time here as bad as if I were in a gaol, whereas you have your people, and especially your babies, with you. Don't say *poor Matt* any more or wish there was *no Matt*, but take care of your body, and especially keep up your spirits, the more so as, one way or other, I will contrive to see you all, and that speedily.

What can be the reason that I have not had one line from Giauque (properly so called) nor Mary, since their arrival? They must have been extremely occupied these ten days. I am more distressed than I can express about poor Russell, poor fellow![5] But what good does my compassion do him, and if we

conversations there with Delacroix and Daendels, eventually reaching Paris on 17 Apr. He took part in Hardy's expedition to Lough Swilly, Sept.–Oct. 1798, and was captured but, mistaken for a Frenchman, released. He took part in Emmet's insurrection in 1803, was imprisoned, 1803–06, went to South America to join Bolívar's forces, 1820, and died there of fever on 26 Dec. 1825. (*Enniskillen Chronicle and Erne Packet*, 20 Apr. 1826; Madden, *United Irishmen*, 3rd ser. (1846), ii, 210–11, 217, 227; Paul Weber, *On the road to rebellion: the United Irishmen and Hamburg* (Dublin, 1997), pp 103–4; Nat. Arch. (Ire.), Rebellion papers, 620/14/194, 620/20/23; see also below, p. 245).

[1] Perhaps his sister Mary and brother-in-law Jean Frédéric Giauque.

[2] Lewines, whose *nom de guerre* had been 'Giauque' but recently been changed to 'James Brown'; he is not to be confused with Tone's brother-in-law Jean Frédéric Giauque; see Tone to Mathew Tone, 18 Apr. 1798 (above, p. 237).   [3] Napoléon Bonaparte was bound for Egypt.

[4] By 'grand expedition' he means the expedition to Scotland or Ireland to be undertaken by the *armée d'Angleterre* ('army of England').

[5] Russell had been in prison since Sept. 1796. In a letter to a friend dated 14 Feb. 1798, Russell states: 'my illness was only of three days duration, but for part of the time so severe that I thought it would have been my last' (Madden, *United Irishmen*, 3rd ser. (1846), ii, 196).

were to lose him, what degree of vengeance would recompense his loss? You know I am no threatener beforehand; it leads to nothing. Let us therefore say no more on this subject.

I am very well satisfied that you have taken Will into your own hands. I believe it is time. This is a most uncomfortable letter, and I will finish it here. I am completely puzzled this day, so that I scarcely know what I write. The next post must I suppose bring some definite news, and then we shall all see what we have to do.

> Adieu, dearest Love,
> Yours ever affectionately
> J. S.

[*Addressed on reverse*]:

À la Citoyenne Smith
Rue des Batailles, N° 29
À Chaillot
près Paris

To General Charles Joseph Kilmaine, 22 April 1798

Tone (Dickason) papers.

Rouen, 3 floréal an 6

Gen[era]l Kilmaine

Gen[era]l,

I have just received letters from Paris which mention the arrival of a friend and countryman of mine,[1] who brings, it seems, a report that the revolution is commenced in Ireland. Tho' I do not entirely give credit to this intelligence, yet after all it is possible it may be true. I therefore beg, General, you will have the goodness to inform me whether it be authentic, or not, and if it should prove to be so, I presume you will think it advisable to send me an order to return to you at Paris where my presence may perhaps be in some degree serviceable.

> Health & respect
> J. S.

[1] William Henry Hamilton (see below, p. 245).

To Mathew Tone, 23 April 1798

Tone (Dickason) papers.

Rouen, 4 floréal an 6

D[ea]r Matt,

I have just received your letter and do not lose a moment to answer it. With regard to the person you mention,[1] he is both a ruffian and a bully, and deserves to be punished; nevertheless, under the present circumstances, it is impossible, for a thousand reasons. The length of time which has elapsed, the disgrace of any quarrel among the few Irish now in France, and especially, what weighs with me more than all the rest, the bringing Mary's name at all in question in such an affair, decide me positively, and will, I am sure, you also, when you reflect a little, on the necessity of letting the matter die in silence. There are two further reasons, if they were necessary; first, that her honor is by no means compromised, and secondly, if it were, it is her husband who is charged with her defense.[2] On the whole, keep the peace & avoid, quietly, all intercourse with your adversary.

For your Irish news, it is of no great importance. I am not surprised at the event of the combat, for you know my opinion on that subject. As my poor friend Russell used to say, *'We are certainly the bravest nation in Europe'*. I think still however that the assistance of a few thousand French would do us no harm, were it only to look on, and see how we would beat the English, and not all the Cisalpine treaties in the world will beat us out of that prejudice, if it be one. I wish we were as well off as even the Cisalpines this day.

Tell Giauque I am very glad to hear from him, at last. I began to wonder at his silence! You know my ignorance of all manner of affairs, so that I can pretend to advise him in nothing farther than that I understand a man having the command of ready money can make more of it at Paris than anywhere else. Let him read the *petites affiches*, but I need not, I suppose, caution him to be well on his guard, for there are adventurers without end, and very dexterous ones to be met in all quarters here. Messrs Chaumont and Co. are confoundedly negligent, to my knowledge, for I have had sundry walks after them, and if Giauque's bill depends on their diligence, I think his chance is but a dull one. If he can conveniently he ought by all means to take it out of their hands, and either follow his claim himself or else find some more active substitute.

---

[1] Not identified.

[2] Differences among the Irish in Hamburg and Paris were having repercussions on Jean Frédéric Giauque, who from his arrival in Hamburg acted as an intermediary. Giauque was accused of lack of caution by the French minister at Hamburg, Reinhard, who was under the influence of Samuel Turner, a United Irishman resident in Hamburg and supplying information to the British government. How the honour of Mary Giauque, Tone's sister, might have been compromised is unclear. (Marianne Elliott, *Wolfe Tone, prophet of Irish independence* (New Haven, 1989), pp 369–70, 467–8).

There is one thing I would observe—that loss of time on the present occasion is loss of everything. Independent of the expense of living on his capital, he may be sure the moment of a general peace the price of land will rise infinitely, as it has indeed already risen. There was my folly not to have brought my family and the fragments of my property when I came myself into France, and to have realised it immediately. Let him profit by my mistake.

I wrote last post to Gen[era]l Kilmaine,[1] requesting an order to join him at Paris in case the news of the revolution being commenced in Ireland was true, which I observed at the same time I did not believe. I suppose I shall have an answer in a post or two; but I am not sure, if the order comes, that I will make use of it, at least for some short time, until I see what turn things take here, where by the bye, I lead the life of a dog, for I do not know one living soul, which is truly agreeable. I wrote also to Matty last post,[2] and my letter was deplorable, but I could not help it, for I was in the horrors. She complains of not hearing from me, which surprises me, for this is my sixth letter to you or her since I am here,[3] and my third within this present month, surely that is punctuality.

You have one fault in your correspondance; you never date your letters from any place, so that I never know where you are; however, I direct my letters, happy go lucky, to Chaillot. Where are G— and Mary lodged? Are they incognito or do they see *the rest*? If they have not yet seen them, I am sure they have no great reason to covet their company. If Giauque 2d[4] be arrived from the Hague, let him write to me instantly and bring me *au courant*. I know the exertion will be terrible to him, but I insist upon it. I do not write to Matty, as she owes me a letter. My love to G—, Mary and their son & heir. Adieu, dear Matt

Yours sincerely
J. S.

Have you heard anything of your *cadres* yet?

[*On back*]:

Another fault in your correspondance, you *never* acknowledge the receipt of my letters which is very disagreeable. I beg you may remember this and quote them by the date: '*yours of the 4th I received and note its contents*'.

My love to Matty and the Babies ten thousand times.

Au Citoyen M. Smith
Rue des Batailles, N°. 29
À Chaillot
près Paris

---

[1] Above, p. 241.   [2] Above, pp 239–41.
[3] Four of the five other letters which Tone states he wrote to Mathew or Matilda Tone after arriving at Rouen on 5 April have been found and are printed above; they are dated 6, 12, 18 and 22 April.   [4] i.e. Lewines.

Diary, 24–7 April 1798

T.C.D., Tone papers, MS 2049, ff 310^v–315^r; *Life*, ii, 478–84.

24 Apr. 1798

The last Paris papers mention that Buonaparte is decidedly set off to take the command of the expedition which is preparing in the Mediterranean. It is to consist, I learn, of three divisions; one to embark at Toulon commanded by Buonaparte in person; another at Genoa, by Kléber; and the third at Civita Vecchia, by Desaix. The object declared is Egypt and Syria. With regard to this last country, in which Palestine is included, I see today an article in the *Telegraphe* which has struck me very much. It is a proposal to invite the Jews from all quarters of the world to return to the parent country and restore the ancient temple.[1] It has not struck me so much in a political point of view as in one far different. I remember Stokes more than once mentioned to me an opinion of his, founded on an attentive study and meditation of the old and new Testament,[2] that he did not despair, even in his life time and mine, of seeing this great event take place, and I remember I laughed at him heartily for his opinion, which, however seems this day far less visionary than it was at that time, in 1793. It is now not only possible, but highly probable, that the Jews may be once more collected and the Temple restored. The French will naturally take care to stipulate for advantages in return, and there is a giant's stride made at once into Asia, the extent and consequences of which I am at this moment utterly unable to calculate, or perhaps to comprehend. I see every day more and more that after ten years' war, and the defeat of all the despots of Europe united, the French revolution is but yet begun, that Hercules is yet in swaddling bands. What a people! Combining this intended measure with the downfal[l] of the Pope actually[3] accomplished, I have no doubt but a person who had made the prophecies and revalations his study (Stokes, for example) might build very extraordinary systems. For my part I know happily nothing of Daniel and his seventy weeks, nor of St John in his Island of Patmos.[4] I leave divinity to those who have a turn that way and confine my humble speculations to the state of this world. I do not see the prodigious good sense of the Grand Turk in abetting and encouraging, as he seems to do, this grand operation. I do not think the neighbourhood of the

---

[1] In the *Courier* (London), 19 June 1798, there is reprinted an article from a French journal on the possibility of the Jews returning to Palestine and establishing there a national government.

[2] Whitley Stokes had interests in biblical studies and was the author of a pamphlet, *Observations on the necessity of publishing the Scriptures in the Irish language* (Dublin, 1806).

[3] *Life*, ii, 479, reads 'already'.

[4] Daniel, 9: 24; Revelation, 1: 9.

French will be wholesome for the crescent, but that is his affair. Moreover, if the Jews are restored, as their wealth is immense in Europe, and in Asia incalculable, the republic will of course exact certain *'shekels of gold'*[1] before they consent to the elevation of the Tabernacle, which will be convenient. I would I had a good map of Asia to see how far it is from Jerusalem to Madrass, for I have a great eye upon the Carnatic. Once again I lose myself utterly in the contemplation of the present position of the republic. What miserable pigmies we unfortunate Irish are! But that is no fault of ours. We may be better yet! It is a great consolation to me the assurance of Barras and Merlin with regard to our independance. I count upon it firmly.

25 Apr. 1798

W[illia]m Hamilton, who is married to John Russell's daughter,[2] is arrived a few days back in Paris. He was obliged to fly from London in consequence of the arrestation of O'Connor and his party. On his way he met Lewines at Brussells, and also saw in an English paper of the 3d that the revolution in Ireland was commenced, having broke out in the South, and that Gen[era]l Abercrombie[3] and the army were in full march to suppress it. Both he and Lewines believe it. For my part I do not. It is at most some partial insurrection and so much the worse. I wrote however to Gen[era]l Kilmaine to request an order to join him at Paris, in case the news were true, which however I am sure it is not. My brother[4] writes me word that there is a person who waits for Lewines at the Hague who has made his escape with plans, cartes[5] and other military information, and that Lewines is expected with him in Paris every day. Who can this be? I wish Lewines was returned with all my heart.[6]

26 Apr. 1798

I see in the Paris papers today extracts from the English ones of a late date by which it appears, as I suspected, that the news of an insurrection in Ireland was at least premature. Nevertheless things in that country seem to be drawing fast to a close; there is a proclamation of Lord Camden's, which is tantamount to a declaration of war, and the system of police (if police it can be called) is far more atrocious than ever it was in France, in the height of the Terror. There is however no authentic account of any hostilities, except at a place called Holy Cross,[7] where the people were easily dispersed by the Cashel

---

[1] These words appear in Numbers and in four other books of the Old Testament.
[2] Mary Ann Hamilton née Russell (*c.*1776–*c.*1840), the only surviving daughter of Thomas Russell's brother John; she married Hamilton in Co. Fermanagh on 29 Jan. 1794 and then moved with him to London (*Journals and memoirs of Thomas Russell, 1791–5*, ed. C. J. Woods (Dublin, 1991), pp 66, 144).
[3] Sir Ralph Abercromby (1734–1801), commander-in-chief in Ireland, Nov. 1797–Apr. 1798; he later defeated the French at Aboukir (*D.N.B.*).   [4] Mathew Tone.
[5] i.e. maps or charts?   [6] *Life* omits 'with all my heart'.
[7] The clash at Holycross occurred on 28 Mar. (*Saunders' News Letter*, 5 Apr. 1798).

fencible cavalry and a party of the Louth militia with the loss of three killed and above twenty wounded and prisoners, but that is nothing. I see it is the policy of the government to employ such Irish troops as they can depend upon, to avoid, or at least lessen, the odium which would otherwise fall on the English and Scotch. It should seem however that they cannot reckon on all the troops, for in the same papers there is a report (but it is *only* a report) that several regiments of militia have refused to march against the people. What they ought to do, if they were in earnest, would be to march as far as the people and then join them. On the whole, notwithstanding the menacing appearance of things in Ireland, it is my belief that there will be no serious hostilities there unless the French arrive. Then indeed it would not be Lord Camden's proclamation which would stop our revolution. I see also in the papers that Arthur O'Connor is transferred to Maidstone, where his trial and that of the others will come on immediately. I attend the result with the most anxious expectation. Whatever may be O'Connor's fate he will at least sustain the dignity of his situation and, in the worst event, he will bear it like a man.

27 Apr. 1798

I am sadly off for intelligence here, having nothing but the imperfect extracts in the Paris papers. I see today, and I am very glad to see it, that my friend Sir Laurence Parsons has resigned the command of the King's County militia in consequence of the sanguinary measures about to be adopted by the English government, in which he will take no share.[1] His example should be imitated by every country gentleman in Ireland, but they have neither the sense nor the virtue to see that. Alarming as the state of Ireland really and truly is to the English government, I have no doubt on my mind but that it is their present policy to exaggerate the danger as much as possible in order to terrify the Irish gentry out of their wits, and, under the cover of this universal panic, to crush the spirit of the people and to reduce the country to a state of slavery more deplorable than that of any former period of our unfortunate history. They take a chance against nothing; they see that Ireland will escape them without a struggle if they adopt lenient measures. They therefore prefer force. If it succeeds, well and good; if it fails, still it is Ireland [who] is the material sufferer; it is she that bears all the actual calamities of war, and if England must renounce at last her sovereignty, at least she will desolate what she cannot subdue. It is a most infernal policy, but no new one for her to adopt. In this point of view, the conduct of the English government,

[1] Sir Lawrence Parsons resigned command of King's County militia at the end of Mar. 1798 (*Saunders' News Letter*, 2 Apr. 1798). It was stated in a French newspaper that it was to be assumed that the reason for Sir Lawrence's resignation was that a general officer gave him orders of a kind which he could not bring himself to execute (*Gazette de France*, 7 floréal an VI). In fact Parsons resigned because of the commander-in-chief's comments on the 'relaxed discipline' of the King's County militia (Lawrence Parsons to lord lieutenant, 27 Mar. 1798 (Birr Castle, Co. Offaly, Rosse papers, F32/14)).

tho' atrociously wicked, is by no means deficient in point of system and arrangement. They have begun by seizing almost the whole of the chiefs of the people, and now they are about to draw the sword in order to anticipate the possibility of assistance and reduce the people to that state that, if assistance should at length arrive, they may be unable to profit of it. In this last part,[1] however, I am sure they will find themselves mistaken. The spirit is, I think, too universally spread to be checked now, and the vengeance of the people, whenever the occasion presents itself, will be only the more terrible and sanguinary. What miserable slaves are the gentry of Ireland! The only accusation brought against the United Irishmen by their enemies is that they wish to break the connexion with England, or in other words to establish the independance of their country, an object in which surely the men of property are the most interested. Yet the very sound of independance seems to have terrified them out of all sense, spirit, or honesty. If they had one drop of Irish blood in their veins, one grain of true courage or genuine patriotism in their hearts, they should have been first to support this great object; the people would have supported them. The English government would never have dared to attempt the measures they have since triumphantly pursued and continue to pursue; our revolution would have been accomplished without a shock, or perhaps one drop of blood spilled, which now will succeed, if it does succeed, only by all the calumities [sic][2] of a most furious and sanguinary contest, for the war in Ireland, whenever it takes place, will not be an ordinary one, the armies will regard each other not as soldiers but as deadly enemies. Who then are to blame for this—the United Irishmen, who set the question afloat, or the English government and their partisans, the Irish gentry, who resist it? If independance be good for a country, as liberty for an individual, the question will be soon decided. Why does England so pertinaciously resist our independance? Is it for love of us? Is it because she thinks we are better as we are? That single argument, if it stood alone, should determine any honest Irishman. But it will be said the United Irishmen extend their views farther; they go now to a distribution of property and an agrarian law. I know not whether they do or not. I am sure in June 1795, when I was forced to leave the country, they entertained no such idea. If it has since taken root among them, the Irish gentry may accuse themselves. Even then they made themselves parties in the business; not content with disdaining to hold communication with the United Irishmen, they were among the foremost of their persecutors; even those who were pleased to denominate themselves Patriots were more eager to vilify and, if they could, to degrade them than the most devoted and submissive slaves of the English government. What wonder if the leaders of the United Irishmen, finding themselves not only deserted but attacked by those who for every reason should have been their supporters and fellow labourers, felt themselves

---

[1] In *Life*, ii, 481, 'design' is substituted for 'part'.　　[2] *Recte* 'calamities' or 'calumnies'?

no longer called upon to observe any measures with men only distinguished by the superior virulence of their persecution? If such men lose, in the issue, their property, they are themselves alone to blame. By deserting the first and most sacred of all duties, the duty to their country, they have incurred a wilful forfeiture; by disdaining to occupy the station they might have held among the people and which the people would have been glad to see them fill, they left a vacancy to be seized by those who had more courage, more sense and more honesty; and not only so, but by this base and interested desertion they furnished their enemies with every argument of justice, policy and interest to enforce the system of confiscation. Besides, if the United Irishmen succeed, there is no rational man can doubt but that a very short period will suffice to do away the evils inseparable from a contest, and that in seven years, or less, after the independance of Ireland is established, when she can apply all her energy to cultivate her natural resources, her trade, commerce, agriculture and manufactures will be augmented to a degree amply sufficient to recompense her for the sacrifices she will be undoubtedly obliged to make in order to purchase her liberty. The example of America is an evidence of this truth, and England knows it well; it is one reason why she is so eager in the contest. On the other hand, if the English party succeed, and the United Irishmen are put down, what will be the consequence to Ireland? It will be the eternal prostration at the feet of her tyrant, without a prospect of ever being able to rise. What then is to be said of a faction to whom defeat is extermination and whose victory would be but the perpetuation of their slavery? At least, the United Irishmen have a great and glorious object to terminate their prospect and which sanctifies almost any means they may take to attain it. The best that can be said in palliation of the conduct of the English party is that they are content to sacrifice the liberty and independance of their country to the pleasure of revenge and their own personal security. They see Ireland only in their rent rolls, their places, their patronage and their pensions. There is not a man of them that in the bottom of his soul does not feel that he is a degraded being in comparison of the men whom he brands with the name of incendiary and traitor. It is this stinging reflection that, among other powerful motives, is one of the most active in spurring them on to revenge. Their dearest interests, their warmest passions are equally engaged. Who can forgive the man that forces him to confess that he is a voluntary slave, and that he has sold for money everything that should be most precious to an honorable heart; that he has trafficked in the liberties of his children, and his own, and that he is hired and paid to commit a daily parricide on his country? Yet these are charges which not a man of that infamous cast can deny to himself before the sacred tribunal of his own conscience. At least the United Irishmen, as I have already said, have a grand, a sublime object in view; their enemies have not as yet ventured, in the long catalogue of accusation, to insert the charge of interested motives; while that is the case, they may be feared and abhorred, but they never can be despised, and I believe there are few men that do not look upon contempt as the most insufferable of all evils.[1] Can the English faction say as much? In vain do they crowd together and think by their numbers to disguise or to lessen their infamy. The public sentiment, the secret voice of their own corrupt hearts has already condemned them. They see their destruction rapidly approaching and they have the consciousness that when they fall no honest man will pity them. *'They shall perish like their own dung; they that have seen them shall say, where are they?'*[2]

From General Hermann Wilhelm Daendels, 1 May 1798

Dickason (Tone) papers.

Daendels states that he has forwarded Tone's letter to Delacroix, who has promised to send Tone the requested testimonial, and that Mrs Tone has received the 400 florins that Tone wished to pass on to a compatriot.

La Haye, ce 1ᵉʳ May 1798
L'an 4ᵉ de la Liberté Batave

Le Lieutenant Général Daendels
à
L'Adjudant Général Smith

Je me suis empressé, mon cher Smith, de remettre votre lettre au Citoyen Delacroix,[3] qui m'a promis de vous envoyer le certificat que vous demandez, et j'espère que le témoignage, qu'il rendra à vos sentimens et à votre conduite, sera assez puissant pour vous faire triompher de vos ennemis.

Madame Smith a reçu les 400 fl. que vous avez bien voulu avancer à votre compatriote,[4] car sa quittance nous est parvenu. Je m'empresserai aussi d'acquitter les dépenses que vous avez bien voulu faire pour moi.

Vous vous êtes déja rendu à Rouen, mais j'espère que vous ne vous êtes nullement ressenti du malheureux accident qui vient d'y arriver.[5] Daignez m'écrire pour me rassurer à ce sujet, et continuez je vous prie à me donner toujours des nouvelles et de vos intérêts particuliers et de ceux de la cause commune, qui vous le savez me sont bien chers.[6]

Diary, 1–17 May 1798

T.C.D., Tone papers, MS 2049, ff 316ʳ–319ʳ; *Life*, ii, 484–6.

---

[1] *Life*, ii, 484, reads 'all human evils'.   [2] Job, 20: 7.
[3] See Tone to Daendels and to Delacroix, 12 Apr. 1798 (above, pp 232–4).
[4] See Tone to Matilda Tone, 6 Apr. 1798 (above, pp 227–8).
[5] Perhaps the repulse of the French naval force attempting to take back the Isles Saint-Marcouf (see below, pp 255–6).   [6] No more found.

No. 17
From May the 1st to June 30th, 1798[1]
Nil desperandum!
Paris, Rouen et Havre
1798[2]

1–17 May 1798[3]

Having obtained leave of absence for two decades,[4] I have spent the last twenty days deliciously with my family at Paris. During the time, we received a letter from my brother William, dated at Poonah, the 7th of January 1797,[5] viz. sixteen months since, at which time he was in health and spirits, being second in command of the infantry of the Peshwa, or chief of the Mahratta state, with appointments of 500 rupees a month, which is about £750 a year.[6] I cannot express the pleasure which this account of his success gave us all. Great as has been his good fortune, it is not superior to his merit. Six years since he went to India, a private soldier, unknown, unfriended and unprotected; he had not so much as a letter of introduction to a mortal that could serve him;[7] but talents and courage like his were not made to rust in obscurity. He has forced his way in spite of every obstacle[8] to a station of rank and eminence, and I have no doubt but his talents and his views are extended with his elevation. The first war in India, we shall hear more from him. He complains of never having received a letter from me (his being addressed to James Bell[9] in Dublin), by which I see that one I wrote to him in June 1795, when I was on the point of sailing for America, never came to his hands. I wrote to him on the 8th instant, in as clear a manner as I durst venture, mentioning simply that my adventures had been nearly as romantic as his own; that in consequence of my political conduct I had been obliged to go into exile in America after narrowly escaping with my life from Ireland; that, since, I had come to France, where after some time I had risen to the rank of adjutant general, which I then held, and that I thought about a year would settle my fate definitively, for good or evil. I desired him to write to me under cover to Mr Geo[rge] Meyer,[10] at Mr Edw[ar]d Simeon's,[11] Bishop's Gate St., London, and also, in case of meeting an American ship at Bombay, to

---

[1] The Diary entries for 18–21 May, 23 May, 25 May, 26 May, 28 May, 29 May, 30 May, 31 May–1 June, 2 June, 3 June, 4–5 June, 6 June, 8 June, 12–13 June, 16 June, 18 June and 19–30 June are given as separate documents below.

[2] The preceding headings, which Tone obviously added later than 1 May, are omitted from *Life*.

[3] In the MS the year is repeated and the date is given as 'May 1st–17th'. The diary was evidently written up on 17 or 18 May. [4] i.e. twenty days in the republican calendar.

[5] Cf. William Henry Tone to Peter Tone, Bombay, 25 Jan. 1797 (above, pp 8–11).

[6] See also Tone's diary for 1 Jan. 1798 (above, p. 189).

[7] *Life* omits 'to a mortal that could serve him'.   [8] *Life* omits 'in spite of every obstacle'.

[9] Possibly James Bell, an attorney living in North Cumberland St., Dublin (*Wilson's Dublin Directory*).   [10] Probably a Hamburg merchant (see below).

[11] Edward Simeon, merchant, Salvatore House, Bishopsgate (*New Annual Directory* (London, 1800)).

Mr Benj[ami]n Franklin Bache,[1] at Philadelphia. This letter, to which everybody added a postcript, I sent to Meyer[2] at Hamburg to be forwarded to his brother at London, and so, by way of the India House, to Leonard Jaques Esqr at Bombay,[3] who is, it seems, Will's agent and to whom he desires Bell to address his answer. It is very uncertain whether my letter will ever reach him, having so many difficulties to encounter on the way, and our name being a suspicious one in the English post office. At any rate my father, mother and Bell can write to him with greater certainty, so one way or other I am in hopes he will hear of us. His letter was inclosed in one from my mother to Mary, by which I see she and my father are in health & spirits.

Two or three days after the receipt of Will's letter, we were agreeably surprised by one from poor Arthur, of whom we had had no news of a long time, viz. since Matt parted from him at Philadelphia some time in July last, at which period he spoke of making a voyage to the West Indies, where he had been already once. His letter is dated from Hamburg, where Meyer, Giauque's correspondent,[4] had shewn him all possible friendship and kindness. We answered it immediately, desiring him to come on directly to Paris, where I judge he may arrive in about a month. Poor fellow! He is but sixteen years of age, and what a variety of adventures has he gone through! It is now two years and a half since he and I parted at Philadelphia, when I sent him home in the *Susannah*, Capt[ai]n Baird, to notify to my friends my immediate departure for France. It was a delicate commission for a boy of his age, and he seems to have acquitted himself well of it; at least I have heard no complaints of his indiscretion. When the first arrestations took place in Ireland, in September 1796, when my dear friend Tom Russell, Neilson and so many others were arrested in Belfast, those of my friends in Dublin who were in the secret, dreading the possibility of the Government's seizing on Arthur and, either by art or menaces, wringing it from him, fitted him out and sent him again to America with the consent of my father and mother, who were, with reason, afraid for his personal safety. In America, where he arrived after my wife and family had sailed for Europe, he met with Matt, and, after some little time, embarked on board a sloop bound for the West Indies; on his return from this voyage, he again met with Matt, at Philadelphia, who was on the point of sailing for Hamburg,[5] in consequence of my instructions. At Philadelphia they parted, and what poor Arthur's adventures since have been I know not. He is however, at least, safe and sound, having supported himself these two years without assistance from anybody. When I saw him last, he was a fine manly boy, with a beautiful countenance. I hope and trust he will do well. If we ever come to have a navy in Ireland, he is the very

---

[1] Benjamin Franklin Bache (1769–98), journalist at Philadelphia; editor of *Aurora;* very pro-French (*D.A.B.*).

[2] Perhaps Daniel C. Meyer, who in Sept. 1799 was Hamburg's consul-general in Paris (W. J. Fitzpatrick, *Secret service under Pitt* (London, 1892), p. 70, n. 2).

[3] Messrs Jacques and Wooler were Bombay merchants (*The Bombay Kalendar . . . for the year 1807* (Bombay, [1807])).   [4] In *Life* 'Giauque's correspondent' is omitted.

[5] MS reads 'from Hamburg', which is obviously an error and so is corrected here.

stuff of which to make a Jean Bart.[1] I do not yet know what we shall, or can, do for him, but when he arrives we shall see. Perhaps I may be able to accomplish something thro' Citizen Bruix, who is now minister of the marine, and with whom I became acquainted at Brest at the time of our last expedition, the nautical part of which he in effect conducted. I see in the papers that Citizen Bedout, who commanded the *Indomptable*, on board of which I was embarked, is returned from a cruise in the West Indies and promoted to the rank of rear admiral, which his services have well merited. Perhaps by one or both of these channels I may be able to fix him, especially if Bedout takes a part, as I sincerely hope he may, in the present expedition. I am not superstitious, yet I cannot but remark the singularity of the circumstance that Mary, Matt, Arthur and myself, with my family, should, under such a diversity of strange events, be reassembled in France on the eve of this great expedition, and that precisely at the same period we should have the happiness of hearing from my father and mother, and especially from Will, after a silence of above four years. It is one of the singular *traits* in the history of our family, and increases the confidence I feel that we shall all meet together yet, well and happy, *'which that we may do &c. &c.'*, as the Parson ends his sermon. Well, we shall see.

To Matilda Tone, 18 May 1798

Tone (Dickason) papers.

No. 1

Rouen, 29 floréal, an 6

Dear Love,

I arrived here yesterday at twelve o'clock as tired as a horse, and in all my travels I do not think I ever spent a day so ill. I bear every separation worse than the last. After wandering about the town, without well knowing where I was going, at last the hour of dinner arrived, when, as the sublimest grief you know will at last condescend to eat, and I will add from my own experience, to *drink* also, I made to my inn, and, remembering Voltaire's advice, *'Ou bien buvez, c'est un parti fort sage!'*, I sat down to a mutton chop and a choice bottle of *vin de Beaune*, which I never quit while there was a drop of the contents remaining. I do not wonder that grief drives people to drink, for I found yesterday, experimentally, that wine is a sovereign remedy against despair. I need not, I suppose, assure you that I drank your health with great devotion. In short with the assistance of one bottle (for, after all, it was but one) I got thro' the evening, I do not well know how, and was in bed by eight o'clock. I slept all night like a dormouse, and today I find myself in excellent health and in as good spirits as I expect to be until we meet again.

---

[1] Jean Bart (1650–1702), celebrated French naval officer (*Dict. biog. franç.*).

'My landlord is civil, but dear as the devil.'[1] However, I subdued him yesterday. I have come on a new footing with him. I am, as it were, *en pension* for my dinner at half a crown a day, which is too much, but, in consideration of my rank, I am obliged to sacrifice something to appearances. I have also been thinking of other arrangements and, *I guess*, I shall be able to send you per month about from 250 to 300#.[2] If I can possibly make it more I will, but I am afraid I shall hardly be able, and do you, on your part, endeavour to make your arrangements accordingly. Rouen seems to me about one third dearer than Paris, instead of being as much cheaper, as a provincial town ought to be.

Are all these *détails de ménage* a fit? If they are I ask pardon for it. I have you may well judge no news for you, so I will finish here. I am going to unpack my trunks and get things in their places a little. Give my love to Mary and Giauque; kiss the Babs for me a *milliard* of times; tell Matt to write to me news at his leisure, and let me know when Arthur[3] arrives. Remind Mary in her first letter to give orders to Meyer about the Irish music.[4]

'From my house if I had it, this 6th of December,
Your loving friend
Benedick'[5]

I found a short & friendly letter from Gen[era]l Daendels, dated the 10th floréal,[6] in which he does not say one word of L——.[7] Is not that odd? I will write to Ahern tomorrow.

Number your letters, at the top, as I have done this.

À la citoyenne Smith
Rue des Batailles No. 29
À Chaillot
près Paris

Diary, 18–21 May 1798

T.C.D., Tone papers, MS 2049, ff 319ʳ–322ʳ; *Life*, ii, 486–90.

18 May 1798

Dined today with Adj[utan]t Gen[era]l Rivaud,[8] chef de l'état-major, p[er] interim of the army of England. There were also General

---

[1] Swift, 'Epigram on a window at an inn at Chester' (1726?).   [2] i.e. 250 to 300 livres.
[3] Arthur Tone.
[4] Probably a reference to Edward Bunting, *A general collection of the ancient Irish music* (Dublin, [1797]).
[5] 'From my house if I had it, the sixth of July, your loving friend Benedick' (*Much ado*, I, i).
[6] Probably the letter printed above (p. 249), which however is dated 'Iᵉʳ May 1798', i.e. 12 floréal.
[7] Probably Lewines.
[8] Olivier Macoux Rivaud de la Raffinière (1766–1839) joined the army after the outbreak of the revolution; chief of staff to Kilmaine, 1798; général de brigade, 1798; baron, 1808 (Six, *Dict. des généraux & amiraux*).

Marescot,[1] of the Engineers, and Adj[utan]t Generals Boulan and Dugommier.[2] This last is son to Dugommier[3] who retook Toulon and was afterwards killed in Spain[4] commanding the army of the Pyrennees. The dinner was very pleasant. All the war was talked over, the characters of the generals canvassed, &c. At the battle of Jemappes the French were 50,000, the Austrians 18,000; the French lost 3,500 in killed and wounded, every man of whom might have been spared, as the enemy's position could have been turned, in which case they had no choice but to evacuate their redoubts or be taken prisoners. It is to be observed however in defense of Dumourier that it was absolutely necessary at that time to gain a victory in order to raise the credit of the French arms and the spirit of the soldiers, both of which were sunk very low by a succession of unfortunate events. It is certain that Houchard[5] might have taken the Duke of York and his whole army prisoners at the time of his famous retreat, or rather flight, from before Dunkirk. There was but one passage open by which he could possibly escape,[6] and Jourdan with his division was within half a league of the *débouché*, which he would have stopped hermetically when Houchard's orders overtook him, commanding him to halt instantly on pain of immediate destitution. In consequence he was obliged to stop short in his career,[7] and had the mortification to see the English army defile quietly before him, every man of whom he could have made prisoners. By this account it appears that Houchard, at least, was justly punished.[8] On the whole I got over this day pretty well.

19 May 1798

I do not know what to think of our expedition. It is certain that the whole left wing of the army of England is at this moment in full march back to the Rhine; Buonaparte is God knows where,[9] and the clouds seem to be thickening more and more in Germany, where I have no doubt Pitt is moving heaven

---

[1] Armand Samuel Marescot (1758–1832), an officer before the revolution; *général de brigade*, 1794; *général de division*, 1794; commander engineers in *l'armée d'Angleterre*, 1798; count of the empire, 1808 (Six, *Dict. des généraux & amiraux*).

[2] Jacques Germain François Chevigny Dugommier (1773–1813), adjutant general and chef de brigade, 1795; he reached the rank of adjutant commandant and died a prisoner of war at St Petersburg (Dossier, Archives de la Guerre).

[3] Jacques Coquille Dugommier (1738–94), member of the Convention; captured Toulon, 1793; took Bellegarde, 1794; killed fighting on the Montagne Noire in the Cévennes. The Convention decreed that his name should be inscribed on a column of the Pantheon. (Six, *Dict. des généraux & amiraux*). [4] *Life* omits 'in Spain'.

[5] Jean Nicolas Houchard (1738–93), an officer since before the revolution; he won the battle of Hondschoote in Sept. 1793 but, having retreated shortly afterwards, was arrested and executed (Six, *Dict. des généraux & amiraux*).

[6] In *Life*, ii, 487, what follows reads: 'and Jourdan with his division was within half a league of it when Houchard's orders overtook him'. [7] *Life* omits 'in his career'.

[8] In *Life*, ii, 487, 'condemned' is substituted for 'punished'.

[9] In fact Bonaparte was on board the *Orient* 'en grande rade à Toulon' having sailed out of port early on the morning of 19 May 'avec un beau temps' (*La correspondance de Napoléon 1er* (32 vols, Paris, 1858–70), iii (1859), p. 114).

and earth to embroil matters and divert the storm which was almost ready to fall upon his head. In the meantime Treilhard, principal negociator at Rastadt, is elected into the vacant place in the Directory in the room of François de Neufchâteau, and Syeyes[1] goes to Berlin as ambassador extraordinary, taking Rastadt in his way. Perhaps he may be able to arrange matters; I look for great things from his talents and activity. The Toulon expedition, of which so much was lately said, is no more spoken of, and the others, from Genoa and Civita Vecchia, are said to be given up. The fact is that the gazettes speak in such various and contradictory terms with regard to all that concerns these expeditions that it is impossible to make anything out of them. The only conclusion I draw is that they know nothing whatsoever about the matter. Nearer home, however, there is an expedition the failure of which has vexed me, not on account of the importance of the affair, for it is but a trifle, but for sake of the example.[2] A *flotille* of about 30 sail of gun-boats &c., under the command of Muskein,[3] an officer who had made himself a reputation in that kind of *petite guerre*, sailed from La Hogue to attack the Isles Marcou; he had on board a detachment of the 4th demi-brigade. It appears however that on their arrival before the islands, *five* sail only attacked, and the remainder kept out of the range of the fire; in consequence, after a cannonade of three or four hours, the five sail were obliged to fall back, having lost 6 men killed and 15 wounded. The outcry is now against Muskein, whose conduct the wits of La Hogue say *'smells not of Musk'*.[4] They have *'made ballads upon him, and sung them to filthy tunes'*,[5] and the report is that he is dismissed, and that Rear-admiral Lacrosse[6] takes the command. I know Lacrosse, having seen him in our last expedition, where he commanded the *Droits de l'Homme*, and distinguished himself in the action with two frigates under Sir Edw[ar]d Pellew, which ended in his driving ashore one of the frigates, and being himself driven ashore also; he is one of the boldest officers in the French navy, and is at this moment confined, it appears, to his room, by a wound he received in a rencontre with Gen[era]l Vendan.[7] But to

[1] Emmanuel Sieyès (1748–1836) was nominated ambassador to Berlin, May 1798, and became a member of the Directory, May 1799 (*Dict. parl. franç.*).

[2] During 1797 the French had been building flat-bottomed boats and in Apr. and May 1798 attacks were launched on the two islands of Saint-Marcouf. Lying 6 km off the Normandy coast, they had been seized by Sir Sidney Smith in 1795 and were a useful base for the British navy, threatening French communications between Le Havre and Cherbourg. These attacks were repulsed by the British garrison on the first occasion assisted by the *Adamant* (50 guns) and a couple of frigates. (William James, *Naval history of Great Britain* (new ed., London, 1826), ii, 164–9).

[3] Muskeyn, a Fleming who had served with the Antwerp company in India and in the Swedish navy against Russia (Édouard Desbrière, *Projets et tentatives de débarquement aux îles Britanniques* (4 vols, Paris, 1900–02), i, 171).

[4] Cf. 'They don't smell of musk' (Thomas D'Urfey, *The rise and fall of Massaniello*, pt I (1700), I, i).   [5] *1 Henry IV*, II, ii.

[6] Jean Raymond Lacrosse (1760–1829), a naval officer before the revolution; admiral, Sept. 1796; commanded *Les Droits de l'Homme* in Hoche's expedition to Ireland (Six, *Dict. des généraux & amiraux*).

[7] Dominique Joseph René Vandamme, comte d'Unsebourg (1770–1830), a *sous-officier* before the revolution; *général de brigade*, 1793; in trouble in 1795 'pour sa liberté de langage et ses exactions en pays conquis'; commander of Cherbourg, 1798; count of the empire, 1808; distinguished himself at Waterloo (ibid.).

return to this check. I am sorry for it principally on two accounts; first, that it may have a bad effect on the spirit of the troops, and perhaps disgust them with maritime expeditions; and secondly, on the score of reputation. 'What!', may the English well say, 'you are going to conquer England, and you cannot conquer the Isles Marcou!' It is a bad business, take it any way. I wonder will the Directory examine into it? If they do not seriously establish a rigid responsability in the Marine, it is in vain to think of opposing England by sea. There is a bad spirit existing in that corps, and I see nor hear of no means taken to correct it. *'They do not order this matter better in France.'*[1]

20 May 1798[2]

During my stay in Paris, I read in the English papers a long account, evidently taken from the *Dublin Journal*, of a visitation held by the Chancellor in Trinity College,[3] the result of which was the expulsion of nineteen students[4] and the suspension, for three years, of my friend Whitley Stokes. His crime was having communicated to Sampson, who communicated it to Lord Moira, a paper which he had previously transmitted to the Lord Lieutenant, and which contained the account of some atrocious enormities committed by the British troops in the South of Ireland.[5] Far less than that would suffice to destroy him in the Chancellor's opinion, who, by the bye, has had an eye on him this long time, for I remember he summoned Stokes before the Secret Comm[itt]ee long before I left Ireland. I do not know whether to be vexed, or pleased, at this event as with regard to Whitley. I only wish he had taken his part more decidedly, for, as it is, he is destroyed with one party, and I am by no means clear that he is saved with the other. He, like Parsons and Moira, have either their conscience too scrupulous, or their minds too little enlarged, to embrace the only line of conduct in times like ours. They must be with the people, or against them, and that for the whole truth, or they must be content to go down without the satisfaction of serving or satisfying any party. With regard to Stokes, I know he is acting rigidly upon principle, for I know he is incapable of acting otherwise, but I fear very much that that very metaphysical, unbending purity that can accom[m]odate itself neither to men, times nor circumstances will always

---

[1] Cf. 'They order, said I, this matter better in France' (Sterne, *A sentimental journey* (1768), i, ch. 1).

[2] The text that follows begins at the top of MS f. 321 recto, which is headed 29th. This, however, could be an error for 19th and so the text the beginning of a new entry, as it runs mid-sentence into f. 321 verso, which is headed 19th. Tone may have inserted in arrears the dates appearing in the heads. In *Life*, ii, 488, William Tone dates the entry 20 May, which is also done here.

[3] The chancellor was Lord Clare, acting however as vice-chancellor of Dublin University. For accounts of the visitation, see *Faulkner's Dublin Journal*, 24 Apr. 1798, and *Saunders' News Letter*, 25 Apr. 1798.

[4] Their names are listed in T.C.D., MS 1203. There is a facsimile copy in Jane Maxwell, 'Sources in Trinity College, Dublin, for researching the 1798 rebellion' in *Journal of the Irish Society for Archives*, n.s., v, no. 1 (summer 1998), pp 10–11.

[5] See above, pp 211–12. A conflation of notes of Stokes's interrogation by Clare and Patrick Duigenan (T.C.D., MSS 1203, 3363 and 3373) is given in loc cit., pp 12–13.

prevent his being of service to his country, which is a thousand pities, for I know no man whose virtues and whose talents I more sincerely reverence. I see only one place fit for him, and after all, if Ireland were independant, I believe few enlightened Irishmen would oppose his being placed there; I mean at the head of a system of national education. I hope this last specimen of Fitzgibbon's moderation may give him a little of that political energy which he wants, for I have often heard himself observe that nothing sharpened men's patriotism more than a reasonable quantity of insult and ill usage. He may now be a living instance and justify his doctrine by his practice.

21 May 1798

Rivaud, chef de l'état-major, tells me this morning that the English have landed about 10,000 men near Ostend,[1] undoubtedly with a view to bombard it and to burn the shipping & small craft, which is preparing there for the expedition. I believe the number must be exceedingly exaggerated. Be that as it may, he says 6,000 French are already collected, and that is more than enough to render a good account of 10,000 English. Championnot[2] commands in that division and Gen[era]l Beyssières in the town, where there is a garrison of about 700 men, which is not, by any means enough. If they suffice to prevent the enemy succeeding by a coup de main, that will be sufficient, for a very few days will bring together a force which will make the English remember the attack with a vengeance. In the mean time Rivaud has dispatched expresses to the Directory and to Gen[era]l Kilmaine, commander-in-chief. Tomorrow will let us know more of the matter.

To Matilda Tone, 22 May 1798

Tone (Dickason) papers.

No. 2

Rouen, ce 3 prairial, an 6

Dear Love,

I have this day received yours, No. 1, and am sincerely happy to see that you write in tolerable spirits. For the storm which you mention, that we met with on our passage, I slept the whole time, tho' the heat of the carriage

---

[1] In May 1798 a force of about 1,300 men under Major General Eyre Coote (1762–?1824) (*D.N.B.*) was landed at Ostend. Its objective was the destruction of the gates of the Bruges–Ostend canal. The gates were blown up but the weather conditions prevented the re-embarkation of the force, which was compelled to surrender. (J. W. Fortescue, *A history of the British army* (13 vols, London, 1899–1930), iv, 587–9).

[2] Jean Étienne Vachier Championnet (1762–1800) joined the National Guard at the revolution; *général de division*, 1794; commanded right wing of 'army of England', 1798 (Six, *Dict. des généraux & amiraux*).

obliged me to take my place in the cabriolet before,[1] where I had no defence against the fury of the pitiless elements save a thick leather curtain. However, it proved sufficient to ward the thunder from my head, for I awoke towards morning without having suffered the least accident.

I am glad Burke[2] and Hamilton are behaving as they ought to do. You well know how I detest all bickering, feuding and proving. If the Irishmen in Paris have not agreed, at least I can safely say it has been no fault of mine. I need not request you to be particularly attentive to them and to everybody who may call out to see you.

Giauque is doing very well to lose no time in making whatever purchase he may find to suit him, as every day is diminishing his capital, and you know how our '*poor remains*' were exhausted by a similar conduct. If I had had the luck to bring you all to France when I came myself—but no matter! I hope it is all, still, for the best.

With regard to my spirits, I am quite restored. It is all over now, but in my whole life I never spent a day so ill as that of my arrival in Rouen.[3] I have however since made divers arrangements; that with '*mine host of the Garter*'[4] of which I have already spoken; another at the coffee house; a third at the circulating library, which last, at least, is not dear, being but twenty sols a months, whereby you see I have my learning at a reasonable rate; a fourth at the spectacle, where I am *abonné* with the rest of the état-major, at the rate of 20# a month,[5] which is not dear, neither. It is true the actors are not the Peron,[6] but at all events it serves to pass away the evening, and all I desire, or expect, is to kill the time; on the whole you see I am not very much to be pitied.

Your letter, which I should have had yesterday, I did not receive till [to]day, at twelve o'clock, owing to the carelessness of the *wagon master* of the état-major, '*for which his own gods bless him*'.[7] The courier sets off at one, so I have time to say no more than that I am with my kind love and service to everybody, your dutiful spouse

J. Smith

I have not got Matt's budget of English news; pray him to mind the *dates*. Kiss the Babies for me a thousand times.

À la Citoyenne Smith
Rue des Batailles No. 29
À Chaillot
près Paris

---

[1] i.e. at the front. [2] Pseudonym for Bartholomew Teeling.
[3] Cf. Tone to Matilda Tone, 18 May 1798 (above, p. 252).
[4] *Merry wives of Windsor*, I, iii. The Garter is an inn.
[5] i.e. for which he pays a subscription of 20 livres a month.
[6] Perhaps a reference to Alexius Piron (1689–1773), well-known French playwright.
[7] The source of this quotation has not been traced.

Diary, 23 May 1798

T.C.D., Tone papers, MS 2049, ff 322ʳ–322ᵛ; *Life*, ii, 490.

23 May 1798

Yesterday passed without any news. Today the journals announce that the English have attempted to bombard Ostend,[1] that to this effect they had debarked 4,000 men who were almost immediately attacked and defeated, the general wounded and taken, with 2,000 men, besides between 3 and 400 killed and wounded, 5 or 6 pieces of cannon and about 40 boats.[2] This is all that the journals mention, the news having come by the Telegraphe.[3] Of course we must now wait until the next courier for the particulars. Rivaud, in speaking of the affair today, made a remark which I think worth recording. He said the French generals of today undoubtedly had not the extent and variety of knowledge of those under the old system,[4] but they made up for that deficiency by superior intrepidity, and when the chiefs are intrepid, the French soldier, who is intrepidity itself, will always follow them and undoubtedly beat any troops they meet with. I have no doubt but Rivaud is right. There is a very circumstantial account in the journals today of the arrival of Buonaparte at Toulon,[5] which yet I cannot bring myself entirely to credit; they go so far as to give his speech to the army, which however seems to me somewhat apocryphal; at least, if it be genuine, it is not in his best manner.[6] On the whole I doubt the authenticity of the intelligence, as well as of another article which comes from Dunkirk and mentions the English being off that coast with 8 sail of the line and *four hundred* transports. That seems to me rather much—*four hundred* transports would carry easily 60,000 men, with their horses, stores and artillery, for so short a passage. That the English are off the coasts I well believe, but by no means in the force which is spoken of.

To Matilda Tone, 24 May 1798

Tone (Dickason) papers.

---

[1] See above, p. 257, n. 1.
[2] The *Moniteur*, 23 May 1798, reported that of the 4,000 enemy troops who had landed 2,000 had been taken prisoner.   [3] Probably a kind of semaphore.
[4] *Life*, ii, 490, reads 'regime' instead of 'system'.
[5] By 9 May, Bonaparte had arrived in Toulon (*Correspondance de Napoléon 1ᵉʳ*, iv, 127). On 22 May the *Moniteur* announced his arrival in Toulon.   [6] See below, p. 262, n. 3.

No. 3

Rouen, ce 5 prairial, an 6

Dear Love,

I wrote to you ere yesterday a short letter[1] to which this is a postscript. My appointments are increased 120# per month,[2] so that I can without inconvenience ensure you 300# for yourself. Tell Maria to *'superadd a pair of horns to her capuchin'*,[3] or in other words, to get a dancing master in addition to her music, for she has great need of instruction on that head. When she has made her bargain with the master, let her write me word what is *'the gross amount of what I owe her'*, and I will remit it regularly every month. In return I have a request to make of you, which at a little distance has very much the air of a command, viz. *that you assist regularly, and without fail, in your proper person, at every lesson her dancing master gives her*, a condition on which I positively insist. It would not be much amiss if you did the same at her music, but in all events I am sure you will see the propriety with regard to the other.

I shall send you your money in the course of two or three days by the diligence, giving you due notice by the post.

I thank you for your advice touching the vin de Beaune; it shall not be thrown away. Touching that subject, I made yesterday, *after dinner*, a very profound remark, viz. that the question with regard to the use of wine has never yet been properly investigated; those who write essays do not get drunk, and those who get drunk do not write essays. The sober man is no fair judge, and the man who is drunk is an interested party, so that there is no appeal, and of course no fair decision. The question will therefore never be properly settled.

I have nothing more to add, saving that I read every post, with singular pleasure, that dullest of all journals, the *Journal de Paris*, for no other reason, you may suppose, than that I know you read it every day. It is to me the *'greater bear, favorite of all the constellations, since it recalls you to my view'*.[4]

Adieu, Dear Love, and don't be poor Matt
Your Slave & Dog
J. S.

My kind love and service to everybody. I think I am fairly becoming *'this good prince'*,[5] writing to you every post. *'Well, who would have thought that Miss Molly Jollup, &c., &c.'*[6] Tell Matt to write to me; he is a lazy hound.

---

[1] Above, pp 257–8. [2] i.e. 120 livres per month.

[3] A capuchin was a cloak with a hood. The source of this quotation has not been traced.

[4] The words 'I have also seen the greater bear, favourite of all the constellations' appear in Goethe's *The sorrows of Werter* (2 vols, Dublin, 1781–2), ii, 117, but not the seven words that follow. Cf. Tone's *Belmont Castle* (1790), letter XXXIV.

[5] Perhaps 'this good prince' in Swift's *Gulliver's travels* (1726), ch. 9, who 'was so gracious as to forgive the page his whipping'.

[6] Character in Samuel Foote's *The mayor of Garret: a comedy* (1764).

It seems by the two or three lines per the Telegraph that the English made no prodigious exhibition at Ostend.[1] I wish to God I had been there. But no matter. *'I hope to see a battle yet, before I die.'*[2]

À la Citoyenne Smith
Rue des Batailles, N°. 29
À Chaillot
près Paris

To Aristide Dupetit-Thouars, 24 May 1798

T.C.D., Tone papers, MS 2050, f. 25ʳ.

Having just read in the press that Dupetit-Thouars has command of the *Tonnant* in the expedition being prepared at Toulon, Tone wishes him every success.

Rouen, ce 5 Prairial, an 6

Au Citoyen Du Petit Thouars, commandant le vaisseau de la république, le *Tonnant*, à Toulon

Citoyen,

Je viens dans l'instant même d'apprendre par la voie des feuilles publiques que vous commandez le *Tonnant* dans l'expédition qui se prépare à Toulon.[3] Veuillez en accepter mes très sincères félicitations. Je le regarde comme un grand bonheur pour la république, que de voir des hommes, comme vous, appelés à son service. Plût au ciel que tous vos camarades soient de votre trempe! Vous voilà maintenant dans le cas d'employer vos talens et votre courage contre cet ennemi acharné du genre humain, car je ne saurois douter que l'Angleterre ne soit, en dernière analyse, l'objet de vos préparatifs. Que je voudrois vous accompagner, et que le plaisir, surtout, seroit grand pour moi, de me trouver sur votre bord! Deux fois j'ai été embarqué pour cette entreprise, deux fois j'ai manqué, mais sous les auspices du grand général[4] qui dirige maintenant vos opérations, je ne saurois en douter le succès.

En attendant de vos nouvelles, je m'amuse à bâtir mille beaux châteaux en Espagne. Je vous envoie, d'abord, à Cadix, en passant par Carthagène. Après vous être un peu raffraichi là, je vous vois à Brest. Vous pouvez peut-être, en passant, faire votre petit compliment à sa majesté très fidelle.[5] Cette bonne vieille, toute folle qu'elle est, doit vous devoir quelque chose. Les

---

[1] See above, p. 257, n. 1.   [2] Source of this quotation not traced.
[3] i.e. the expedition preparing to leave for Egypt (not for Ireland as Tone imagined). In fact, it had left a few days before Tone was writing.   [4] Napoleon Bonaparte.
[5] An allusion to Marie-Louise de Parma (1754–1819), wife of Charles IV, king of Spain. She and her favourite, Manuel Godoy Álvarez de Faria, exercised great influence over the king.

mânes plaintives de la pauvre Chercheuse[1] crient encore vengeance. Ayant arrangée cette affaire, de Brest vous irez où vous voudrez, mais dans ce dernier voyage j'espère bien, pour mon individu, d'avoir l'honneur de vous accompagner, le Directoire Exécutif ayant bien voulu me continuer dans mon grade et m'employer à l'état-major de l'armée d'Angleterre.

Les détails de votre situation actuelle doivent vous occuper pleinement; aussi je ne vous occuperai plus. Si cette lettre soit à tems pour vous attraper encore en rade, veuillez bien m'écrire. Je serois véritablement fâché de croire que vous m'eussiez oublié. J'ai la témerité, vous voyez, de vous adresser en françois. Vous aurez de la peine, peut-être, à me déchiffrer, mais vous vous rappellez le tems quand je ne pouvois pas dire trois mots de suite,[2] et quand on a trente ans passés, c'est un peu tard de commencer à apprendre une nouvelle langue, fût-elle même la langue française. Adieu, mon cher du Petit Thouars. Partout où vous irez, comptez toujours sur mon estime et ma sincère amitié.

> Je vous embrasse bien fraternellement,
> J. Smith
> A[djudant] G[énéral]

Diary, 25 May 1798

T.C.D., Tone papers, MS 2049, ff 322ᵛ–323ʳ; *Life*, ii, 490–91.

25 May 1798

It is certain that Buonaparte is at Toulon and embarked since the 14th. His speech, as I suspected, is not as it was given [in] the last journals. The genuine one I read today, and there are two sentences in it which puzzle me completely. In the first, at the beginning of the address, he tells the troops 'that they form a wing of the Army of England'; in the second, towards the end, he reminds them that they have the glory of the French name to sustain 'in countries and seas, the most distant!'.[3] What does that mean? Is he going, after all, to India? Will he make a short cut to London by way of Calcutta? I begin foully to suspect it. He has all his *savans* embarked with

---

[1] Perhaps an allusion to the leading character in *La Chercheuse d'esprit* (1741), a one-act light comedy by Charles Simon Favart. The expression 'chercheuse d'esprit' acquired the wider meaning of 'une jeune fille qui a encore l'ignorance de l'innocence, mais qui commence à éprouver le désir de perdre sa simplicité' (*Larousse du XXᵉ siècle* (6 vols, Paris, 1929), i, 197).

[2] i.e. at the beginning of 1796 on board the *Jersey* bound for Le Havre and on their arrival in France.

[3] Bonaparte's proclamation to the soldiers and sailors of 'l'armée de la Méditerranée', dated 10 May 1798, pointed out that they formed a wing of the army of England, that the Roman legions had fought Carthage on the plains of Zama and that they themselves might serve in the most distant regions (*Correspondance de Napoléon 1ᵉʳ*, iv, 128–9).

him with their apparatus; that can hardly be for England. As for Egypt, of which so much has been said, I never paid much attention to the report. If it be for India, I wish to God I were with him; I might be able to co-operate with Will, and perhaps to be of material service; but what would become of my family in my absence? I am in more perplexity at this moment than I have been in since my arrival in France. I have a good mind to write to the Minister at War, or of the Marine, whom I know. Why not to Barras? *Allons!* I will write to Bruix. Happy go lucky.

To General Charles Joseph Kilmaine, 26 May 1798

Tone (Dickason) papers.

Rouen, 7 Prairial, an 6

To General Kilmaine, &c., &c.

General,

I see in the papers this day the address of General Buonaparte to the army embarked at Toulon, and from one or two expressions contained in it, it seems possible his destination may be for India. I think it in consequence my duty to inform you that I have a brother[1] in that country, from whom I lately received a letter, dated at Poonah, the capital of the Mahratta states, January the 7th, 1797, informing me, among other circumstances, that he was then second in command of the infantry of the Peshwa, or chief of the Mahrattas.[2] As I can assure you he is a man of courage, talents and great enterprise, perhaps the situation he holds may be turned to some account for the glory of the republic. I need not observe to you the importance of securing, if it could be done, an ally in India, capable of bringing into the field from eighty to an hundred thousand cavalry; if there were not a probability of something being done in Europe, I am ready to embark for that country tomorrow, if it should be thought that I could be useful, as perhaps I might, in opening the communication above mentioned.

In short, general, if there be no likelihood of an immediate attack on England, I take the liberty, thro' you, to make an offer to the Government of my services in India, provided you think, under the circumstances, they can be in the least useful. My first object, undoubtedly, is to assist in the emancipation of my own country; if that cannot be attained my next is to assist in the humiliation of her tyrant, and in whatever quarter of the globe the English government exists, there is our enemy.

---

[1] William Henry Tone.   [2] See Tone's diary for 1–17 May 1798 (above, pp 250–51).

I request the favor of an answer as speedily as your leisure will permit, and am, with great respect, your most obedient servant,

J. Smith

I take the liberty to request that, whatever may be your decision, the subject of this letter may remain a secret.

Diary, 26 May 1798

T.C.D., Tone papers, MS 2049, ff 323ʳ–323ᵛ; *Life*, ii, 491–2.

26 May 1798

I have changed my mind and written this day a letter[1] to General Kilmaine acquainting him with Will's present situation in India and offering to go thither if the government thinks that my services can be useful, requesting secrecy and a speedy answer. I know not how this may turn out. It is a bold measure. My only difficulty is my family, but if the Directory accepts my offer, I hardly think they will refuse to pay my wife one half of my appointments during my absense. If they do that, I will go chearfully, notwithstanding that the age for enterprise is almost over with me. My blood is cooling fast. *'My may of life is falling to the sere, the yellow leaf!'*[2] It would be singular if, after all, I were to go out to India. Twice or thrice already, I have narrowly escaped the voyage and I confess my rage for such an expedition is considerably abated; nevertheless, under all the circumstances, I have thought it, on due reflexion, my duty to make the offer, and it rests now with the government to decide. A few days, and I shall probably know the result. In the meantime there is no more question or appearance here of an attempt on England than there is of one on the Moon, and I am, in consequence, devoured with *ennui*. The last papers bring no further news of Buonaparte and his expedition, which seems to be still at Toulon, but I see that Admiral Nelson[3] has joined Earl St Vincents before Cadiz, which will not facilitate much the *sortie* of the Toulon fleet, in case that their destination should be to pass the Straight of Gibraltar.[4] I see also that it was a body of only 300 French of the 46th and 94th demi-brigades which defeated the English before Ostend and made 1,500 prisoners. It was a most brilliant exploit.

To Matilda Tone, 28 May 1798

Tone (Dickason) papers.

---

[1] Above. [2] *Macbeth*, v, iii.
[3] Horatio Nelson (1758–1805), British admiral; created baron, Nov. 1798, and viscount, 1801 (*D.N.B.*).
[4] Nelson joined St Vincent off Cadiz on 30 April and a few days later sailed to watch Toulon.

No. 4

Rouen, ce 9 prairial, an 6

Dear Love,

I send you per the Messagerie of this day £20, or 480#,[1] 300 of which is for your month's pay, and 180 to make ducks and drakes of. I shall be able to send you regularly 300# per month.

They tell me at the Bureau that your *sac* of *écus* will be sent to you, to Chaillot, but for fear of accidents I enclose the card of their address. The money is in a bag sealed up, with a ticket attached with your name and place of abode, &c., so *that in case* of accidents you can send Giauque to see after it. But I dare say it will go safe. I have paid all expence, except the porter who may bring it to you.

This is my third letter since I heard from you, for which I deserve an ovation. Have you got Maria her dancing master? I think *that* may be one of the *ducks* above mentioned.

Having written so often and so lately I have nothing to add but that I am, with my sincere love to everybody

John Elwes[2]

Matt is, as I said in my last, a lazy hound. No news, I suppose, of the *cadres*.[3] That is not right of somebody.

À la Citoyenne Smith
Rue des Batailles, N° 29
À Chaillot
près Paris

Diary, 28 May 1798

T.C.D., Tone papers, MS 2049, f. 324ʳ; *Life*, ii, 492.

28 May 1798[4]

The English having appeared in force before Havre and having attempted to throw some bombs into the town, Adj[utan]t-Gen[era]l Rivaud, who is provisionally Chef de l'état-major, determined to send me off at a moment's warning to join General Béthencourt,[5] who commands the division.

---

[1] i.e. 480 livres.

[2] Obviously a humorous nom-de-plume. John Elwes (1714–89) was a well-known miser (Edward Topham, *Life of the late John Elwes Esq.* (London and Dublin, 1790); *D.N.B.*).

[3] For the *cadres*, see above, p. 100, and below, pp 298–9.

[4] The pen and sense suggest that this entry was written on 29 or even 30 May.

[5] Antoine de Béthencourt (1759–1801), commissioned before the revolution; général de brigade, 1793; in command at Rouen, 1796–8 (Six, *Dict. des généraux & amiraux*).

In consequence, having received my order and made up my kit, I set off post and ran all night.

To Adjutant-General Olivier Macoux Rivaud, 29 May 1798

T.C.D., Tone papers, MS 2050, f. 26ʳ.

Tone informs Rivaud that nothing important has happened and that the English are not now expected today.

À l'Adj[udan]t Gén[éra]l Rivaud, chef de l'État-major de l'armée d'Angleterre

> au Havre, ce 10 Prairial, an 6
> deux heures

No. 1

Général,

Conformément à vos ordres j'ai l'honneur de vous informer qu'il n'y a rien d'important arrivé ici. Nous avons eu seulement une belle fête que les Anglois ne se sont pas avisés de venir troubler et comme l'heure de la marée est long tems passée je ne crois pas que nous les verrons aujourd'hui. Le Gén[éra]l Béthencourt m'a montré beaucoup d'honnêteté. J'écris si mal en français que je vous ferai grâce d'une longue lettre, en vous priant d'agréer les assurances de mon sincère respect.

> Salut et Fraternité
> J. S.

Diary, 29 May 1798

T.C.D., Tone papers, MS 2049, f. 324ʳ; *Life*, ii, 492.

29 May 1798

Arrived this morning at Havre about 4 o'clock. At twelve waited on General Béthencourt, who received me very politely. This being the Fête de la Victoire, all the officers in garrison accompanied the General to the Municipality in order to assist at the ceremony. The president made an excellent discourse full of animosity against the English, which I perceived was most cordially received by the military. In the evening the spectacle. Very bad. On my return home saw two corvettes working out of the bason in order to put to sea. God send them well over it. I am lodged in the same hotel where I put up at my first landing in France.[1] How many scenes have I witnessed since!

To Matilda Tone, 30 May 1798

Tone (Dickason) papers.

No. 5

11 prairial, an 6

Dear Love,

Two days since I received an order to set off for Havre at a moment's warning to join General Béthencourt, who commands there in consequence of the English having appeared in the road. I set off an hour after, but before my departure I had the satisfaction to receive your letter, No. 2. I arrived here yesterday morning and waited immediately on the General, who received me with the greatest civility. I do not know how long I may stay, as I am, of course, under his orders. When you see the lads, you will tell them where I am, at the same time that my change of place makes nothing whatsoever for or against the speedy arrival of the expedition, as I am sent here merely to be near the general, in case of an attack by the English, of which however I have not the least apprehension, as I rather think the lesson they got at Ostend will prevent their exposing themselves to a second rebuke before Havre.[2] As to the expedition itself, I know not a syllable about it more than I did at Paris. Do you hear anything of it?

I am glad you received a pleasant letter from Wilkins,[3] for I have all the disposition in the world to like him. I only suspect, from the gaiety of his style, that he made a mistake in his numeration, and that it was his *second* bottle that was empty before, when he called for pen, ink and paper, and commenced on the *third*. When I write my essay, I shall confer with [him] thereupon, as you prudently suggest.

When you write to Mary, say all manner of things for me. God knows I sincerely wish her happy. If she fixes herself, I think we must quarter Arthur upon her and Giauque, I mean if they are in the country. The inconvenience to them will be but trifling and cannot last long.

Touching *'peace and harmony, peace and harmony'* between you and the lads I am very glad of it; you know if it was ever my fault that it should be otherwise, but I believe I said that in my last.

---

[1] The Hôtel de Paix (see Tone's diary for 2 Feb. 1796, above, vol. II, p. 40).

[2] For the failure of a British attempt in May 1798 to destroy the gates of the Ostend–Bruges canal, see above (p. 257, n. 1.)   [3] Pseudonym for Thomas Wilson.

I am beyond measure delighted with your little *ménage*, and I long more than I can express to take my part in the system, but that happiness is suspended for some little time; that time cannot now possibly be long. *'I would to God my name were not so terrible to the enemy as it is.'*[1] I was just thinking of applying for a fortnight's leave of absence for Paris, when, *voilà*, the cruel *chef de l'état-major*, with his plaguy order to set off for Havre![2] Well, *'if I be not a drudge, let all the world judge'.*[3] I intend to write the history of my campaigns, and have today written the first page, which begins with a misadventure, for I have a foul suspicion that two of our corvettes which sailed last night have been early this morning driven on shore by the enemy;[4] but tomorrow will let us know more. In the meantime we have the town in the best state of defence, all the batteries mounted, the furnaces ready heated, and the garrison in the highest spirits; but, once more I am sure the English will give us no opportunity to try our valour. Remember the story of our corvettes is a secret.

(Sings) *'Oh money, money, money is your friend!'*[5] The money you wot of is the indemnity for my forage, at 4#, per day,[6] which is £5 a month. *'A handsome addition for wine and good cheer!'*[7] I think this letter is made up of nothing but quotations. Don't say *'poor Matt'* and *'don't call me Sir, call me Citoyen!'*

Adieu, dear Love. If Maria does not dance like Gardel,[8] it will be worse for her when we meet; take care of yourself and the Boys; my love to Matt. I see in the French papers today a report of some cannon being seized at Clarke's in King Street.[9] I should be sincerely sorry if anything disagreeable were to happen to him. Adieu, once more, dear love. This is a vile unconnected letter, but it is written *after dinner*, as the style and penmanship will witness. Write to me at the Quartier général, au Havre.

'Yours while this machine is to him.'[10]

J. Smith

My namesake, Sir Sidney, I see is safe arrived in London.[11]

À la Citoyenne Smith
Rue des Batailles, N°. 29
À Chaillot
près Paris

---

[1] *2 Henry IV*, I, ii.   [2] See above, pp 265, 266.   [3] Swift, *My lady's lamentation* (1728).
[4] On 29 May *La Confiante*, 24 guns, commanded by Pevrieux, and *Le Vésuve*, 16, commanded by Lécolier, were engaged by an English squadron. *La Confiante* was lost but *Le Vésuve*, having run aground, was refloated and escaped to Le Havre. An investigatory court absolved Pevrieux of blame. (*Moniteur*, 24 June 1798; O. Troudé, *Batailles navales de la France* (4 vols, Paris, 1867), iii, 132–3).
[5] Swift, *The grand question debated* (1729).   [6] i.e. 4 livres per day.   [7] As n. 5.
[8] Anne Boubert (1770–1833), a well-known dancer, married in 1795 Pierre Gabriel Gardel (1758–1840) (*Dict. biog. franç.*).
[9] William Clarke (d. 1810), brewer, North King St., Dublin. On 11 May 1798 five pieces of cannon were seized in his brewery yard. It was subsequently explained that the cannon had been sent there two years before to Clarke's father to be sold (*Saunders' News Letter*, 14, 16 May 1798; *Cox's Irish Magazine*, Feb. 1810).   [10] David Garrick's adaptation of *Hamlet*, III, ii.
[11] Captain Sir Sidney Smith having escaped from the Temple had arrived in London at the beginning of May.

Diary, 30 May 1798

T.C.D., Tone papers, MS 2049, ff 324ʳ–324ᵛ; *Life*, ii, 492–3.

30 May 1798

This morning at 4 o'clock there was a heavy cannonade to the southward, which continued at intervals until 10. The weather is hazy, so that we can see nothing distinctly. I walked out on the batteries three or four times, but could make nothing of it. I fear however the worst.[1] Dined with General Béthencourt and made after dinner the tour of the ramparts with him and Capt[ai]n Gourège,[2] who commands *L'Indienne*, a 44 now in the bason. He thinks the corvettes are driven ashore. I am as melancholy as a cat upon this news. I see too, in the papers, that all the system of persecution goes on without intermission in Ireland; the government has seized 5 pieces of cannon at Clarke's in King St. and I know not how many pike staves in Bridgefoot St. I hope sincerely poor Clarke may come to no trouble, for I can never forget his kindness to my father. Altogether I am devoured this evening by the blue devils, and I must be on the batteries again tonight at 10 (being the hour of high water) with Gen[era]l Béthencourt. '*Heigh ho! When as I sat in Pabilon! And a thousand vragrant posies,*[3] *mercy upon me, I have a greater mind to cry.*'

Ten at night. Took a walk alone on the batteries to meet the *commandant de la place* and delivered him a message from the general. Home and to bed, where I slept like a top.

To General Barthélemi Louis Joseph Schérer, 31 May 1798

T.C.D., Tone papers, MS 2050, f. 28ʳ.

Explaining that his adjoint, MacSheehy, went away a considerable time ago, Tone requests Fayolle as a successor.

Au Quartier général au Havre, 12 Prairial, an 6

Au Ministre de la Guerre

Citoyen Ministre,

Le citoyen Macsheehy, mon adjoint, étant parti en vertu, probablement, des ordres supérieures, pour une destination qui m'est inconnue, et un tems

---

[1] *Life*, ii, 492, adds 'for our corvettes'.
[2] Commanded the *Aigle* at Ferrol and Trafalgar in 1805 (Troudé, *Batailles navales*, iii, 228, 352, 374).   [3] *Merry wives of Windsor*, III, i.

considérable s'étant écoulé sans que j'ai[e] eu de ses nouvelles, j'ai lieu de présumer qu'il se trouve placé avantageusement qu'il n'étoit près de moi. Je vous prie en conséquence, citoyen ministre, de vouloir bien accorder la demande que je vous fais, de le remplacer dans cette fonction par le citoyen Fayolles,[1] capitaine adjoint, maintenant employé dans cette qualité à l'état-major de l'armée d'Angleterre à Rouen, et de faire expédier à ce citoyen sa lettre de service comme adjoint.

> Salut et respect
> L'adj[udan]t gén[éra]l
> J. Smith

(pour copie conforme)

To Adjutant-General Olivier Macoux Rivaud, 31 May 1798

T.C.D., Tone papers, MS 2050, ff 26ʳ–26ᵛ.

The identity of the addressee of this and subsequent letters in the sequence to which they belong (nos 2 to 11) can be established from Tone to Rivaud, 29 May 1798 (no. 1, above, p. 266) and from the content.

Tone reports an engagement between two corvettes, *La Confiante* and *Le Vésuve*, and five British frigates.

No. 2

12 Prairial, an 6

General,

Le général Bethencourt vous ayant écrit hier, je me sais cru être dispensé de vous troubler d'une lettre d'autant plus qu'il n'y avait rien d'important à vous communiquer. Ce matin de très bonne heure nous avons reçu la nouvelle désagréable que deux corvettes de la république, *La Confiante* et *Le Vésuve*, qui étaient sorties du port avant hier au soir, ayant eu le malheur de rencontrer une division de 5 frégates angloises à quelques lieues d'ici au sud, ont été obligée[s] de faire côte, pour ne pas tomber entre les mains de l'ennemi. L'honneur du pavillon, cependant, n'a rien souffert, au moins à ce qui regarde la *Confiante*, dont le brave capitaine, nommé Pevrieux,[2] s'est battu avec la dernière opiniâtreté et n'a fait échouer sa frégate qu'après un combat de 5 heures, dont la plus grande partie a portée du pistolet. Il n'a

---

[1] Jacques Emmanuel Fayolle (b. 1770), lieut., 1792; adjutant, Year IV; served in the campaigns of the north and the interior, 1792–3; wounded when serving with *l'armée d'Italie*; accompanied Tone to Ireland, Sept. 1798, and was captured (Archives de la Guerre, dossier).

[2] Pevrieux, in command of *La Chiffonne*, captured the *Minerva*, 48 guns, in 1803 (Troudé, *Batailles navales*, iii, 228).

perdu heureusement que 4 hommes de tués et 10 blessés. Le *Vésuve* a infiniment moins souffert et on espère même de la retirer. On a déjà envoyé des charpentiers, des calfats, &c, à cet effet; cependant je doute que les Anglois ne tentassent d'y mettre le feu, et je ne sais si la corvette soit dans une position à être protegée par les batteries de ce côté. Demain probablement nous saurons davantage. Au reste tout est tranquille ici, et quant à moi je ne crois pas que l'ennemi viendra troubler notre repos. Le général cependant de son côté ne néglige rien pour leur assurer une réception des plus chaudes en cas qu'ils se soient avisés de tenter le débarquement, ce qu'encore une fois je suis sûr ils ne feront pas [*sic*].

Me trouvant ici sans adjoint, ce qui m'est très inconvénient, j'écris par cet courier [*sic*] au M[inist]re de la Guerre pour demander le citoyen Fayolles. Je vous prierai, général, de me l'envoyer ici provisoirement, à moins que ses services auprès de vous ne soient absolument indispensables. C'est d'après son désir que j'ai fait la demande au ministre. Si cet arrangement ne vous convient pas vous aurez la bonté de m'écrire là dessus.

Salut & Fraternité,
J. Smith

Diary, 31 May–1 June 1798

T.C.D., Tone papers, MS 2049, ff 325ʳ–326ᵛ; *Life*, ii, 493–5.

31 May 1798

My fears were too true about the corvettes. They fell in with a division[1] of five English frigates, and immediately the captain of the *Vésuve* of 32 guns took fright and ran his ship ashore. His name is L'ecolier.[2] He fired but two broadsides. His comrade, however, who commanded the *Confiante* and whose name is Pevrieux fought his ship in another guess manner. He engaged the *Diamond* within pistol shot for three hours, and it was not until the rest of the division were closing upon him fast that he ran the frigate ashore, where he defended himself still for two hours after, so that the English could not succeed in their attempts to burn her. She is dismasted and torn to pieces with the shot. This affair is the more honorable for him in that the *Diamond* carries 24 pounders and his[3] were but twelves. In the meantime, there are two corvettes gone, tho' there are some hopes that the *Vésuve* may be got off. All this does not promise violently in favor of the invasion, and indeed the English seem by the papers to have no longer any uneasiness on that score. What will be the result, after all? God only knows.[4]

---

[1] William Tone substitutes 'squadron' for 'division' (*Life*, ii, 493).   [2] See above, p. 268, n. 4.
[3] In *Life*, ii, 493, the following three words are replaced by 'ship twelve pounders'.
[4] In the MS the pen changes at this point. What follows was probably written up the next day.

12 at night. Rode out with General Béthencourt and made the tour of the different posts and batteries. *'All's well!'* Returned in perfect safety, having met with nothing worse than ourselves. *'Dan caught nothing in his net!'*[1] Laughed immoderately at that foolish quotation, as we rode along.

1 June 1798

Read this morning an article in a Paris journal of ere-yesterday,[2] which astonishes me more than I can express. It is, in one word, that General Daendels has fled from the Hague, where he is proclaimed *a deserter* by the Dutch government. It seems orders were given to arrest him, which he avoided by flying into France, and it is supposed he is now at Paris.[3] The true reason is also said to be his having given his opinion too unguardedly on the measures of the government.[4] This is the whole of the article, and I confess it does astonish me most completely. Judging from my own experience, I would say that Daendels is an honest men and a good citizen, if there be one existing, and I learn by a letter that I received this morning from Lewines, dated May the 4th and which is in some parts obscure, from a prudent caution on his part, that parties run extremely high in Holland, so that I must conclude he [Daendels] is a victim to his principles. Go now, and make revolutions! Daendels was obliged to fly into France ten years since from the fury of the Orange party. In his absence he was beheaded in effigy. In 1794 he returned triumphant with Pichegru,[5] and was appointed to the chief command of the Dutch army. In[6] 1798, he is again obliged to fly into France, with the disgraceful epithet of *deserter* applied to his name, to avoid the fury of the Democratic party (as I conclude from circumstances). It is with me a great proof of a man's integrity when in times of revolution he is sacrificed alternately by both parties, but certainly what he gains on the score of principle, he loses on that of common sense. In order to do any good with any party, a man must make great sacrifices, not only of his judgement but, which is much worse, I fear of his conscience also. If he cannot bring his mind to this, there is but one line of conduct for him to pursue, which is to quit the field. He is the best politician and the honestest man who does the most good to his country and the least evil, for evil there will be in his despite, and he must at times himself be the instrument thereof,

---

[1] Jonathan Smedley, *Gulliveriana* (1728).   [2] *Life* omits 'of ere-yesterday'.
[3] In May 1798, denouncing the new regime as incompetent, Daendels fled to Paris. Having secured the backing of the Directory, he returned to the Hague early in June and played a leading part in the overthrow of the Dutch Directory, a further purge of the convention (or national assembly) and the installation of a new directory. (Simon Schama, *Patriots and liberators: revolution in the Netherlands, 1780–1813* (London, 1977), pp 308–09, 342–53).
[4] *Life*, ii, 494, reads 'his government'.
[5] Tone has a footnote in parentheses: *'another memorable instance of the change of fortune!'* In *Life*, ii, 494, this is embodied in the text and 'caprices' substituted for 'change'.
[6] *Life*, ii, 494, begins the sentence 'Now in 1798 . . .'.

whatever it may cost him. He must keep, as it were, a sort of running account with his conscience, where he is to set off the good against the bad, and if the balance be in his favor, it is all he can expect. This is but a melancholy speculation for a man at the beginning of his political career, but I am afraid it will be found to be, in effect, the only practicable one. If ever I am thrown by chance into a political situation, God knows how I may act. Thus far at least I have preserved my principles, and therefore I register my opinion beforehand that I may see how my practice will square with it in case, as I have already said, that the occasion should ever present itself of which this day there is very slight appearance indeed. Poor Daendels! I am sincerely sorry for him and I never will give him up on any charge that is not accompanied by an absolute demonstration of his guilt, which I do not apprehend will ever be the case.

I see also in the papers that they have begun to arrest the women in Ireland, for wearing *United Irish rings*.[1] Will the men submit to this, or is it humanly possible for them to resist? I hate to turn my thoughts that way, and avoid it as much as possible. I have already done all that, humanly speaking, I could do to serve my country in France. I can only now wait the event.

To Adjutant-General Olivier Macoux Rivaud, 2 June 1798

T.C.D., Tone papers, MS 2050, f. 26ᵛ.

Tone reports 'nothing new has happened here; the enemy force has merely increased and today numbers eight vessels'.

No. 3

14 Prairial, an 6

Général,

Depuis ma dernière lettre, en datte du 12,[2] il n'est rien arrivé de nouveau ici. La force de l'ennemi est seulement augmentée, étant aujourd'hui au nombre de huit bâtimens, dont un vaisseau rasé et trois ou quatre frégates.

Comme la voiture publique part à six heures du matin, c'est ne presque pas la peine [*sic*] d'écrire que par le courier, à moins d'un événement extra-ordinaire, dans quel cas le gén[éra]l Béthencourt vous enverra un courier exprès. Vous trouverez donc bon que j'aie l'honneur de vous écrire tous les jours pairs seulement. Si le gén[éra]l Kilmaine soit arrivé à Rouen, je vous prierai de lui présenter mes respects. Je lui ai écrit à Paris avant mon départ

---

[1] Some women in Ireland who were arrested as suspects were found to be wearing rings inscribed 'To the United Irishmen' (*Moniteur*, 29 May 1798).   [2] Above, pp 270–71.

pour le Havre, mais, comme je n'ai pas encore eu de réponse, je crains que ma lettre ne soit égarée. Veuillez bien, général, lui en parler.

Salut et fraternité,
J. S.

P.S. Je vous prie avec instance de bien vouloir m'envoyer le citoyen Fayolles incessament. Il faut aussi qu'il fasse venir ses chevaux.

To Matilda Tone, 2 June 1798

Tone (Dickason) papers.

No. 6

Havre, 14 prairial an 6

Dear Love,

I write to you in a hurry to catch the post. You have before this received my letter, No. 5,[1] acquainting you with my arrival here. I had yesterday the pleasure to receive two from you, Nos 3 and 4, with the inclosures. At the same time I saw in the papers an article relating to General Daendels which has astonished me more than I can express;[2] it is inconceivable. I have answered Giauque's[3] letter, and I send it to you open; I know not how to forward it in consequence of this unfortunate event, if it be indeed true, regarding General Daendels. Do you and Matt seal and forward it as you shall see best, but I presume your best chance will be through the Dutch ambassador; or perhaps still better under cover to De Winter, *à la Haye*.

I have heard nothing as yet of Gen[era]l Kilmaine. I suppose he is at Rouen by this. In the meantime all is quiet here, but we keep still a sharp look-out. My fears with regard to our *corvettes* were but too well founded; they were both driven ashore, but we hope to get one of them off; the other was burnt to prevent her falling into the hands of the enemy.

Touching trade affairs,[4] *'I ask not kingdoms, I can conquer those; I ask not money, money I've enough!'*.[5] At the same time, as you have a sum beforehand, I will, if I see it absolutely necessary, profit of the licence you give me and borrow some of your next month's pay; but I do not apprehend I shall have any occasion.

Adieu, dear love, I must finish here. I would not write today, but merely to acknowledge the receipt of yours. My love to Matt, to Mlle Gardel[6] and

---

[1] Above, pp 267–8. [2] See Diary for 1 June (above, pp 272–3).
[3] Jean-Frédéric Giauque's or Edward Lewines's? [4] i.e. money.
[5] Henry Fielding, *Tom Thumb* (1731), I, iii.
[6] Maria Tone. For an explanation of this private joke, see Tone to Matilda Tone, 30 May 1798 (above, p. 268).

the boys. I wish I could see them in their invisible, blue, grey jackets and pantaloons; thank you for *staying* them; it may save you nine stitches;

Adieu, dearest Life, Love me always

Yours ever and truly

J. Smith

Was it not well they did not send me to Dieppe? I might have been tempted to go and take possession of the dame and the château. Unfortunately there are no *châteaux* near Havre.

À la Citoyenne Smith
Rue des Batailles, N° 29
à Chaillot
près Paris

Diary, 2 June 1798

T.C.D., Tone papers, MS 2049, f. 326ᵛ; *Life*, ii, 495.

2 June 1798

Last night walked all around the ramparts and inspected the state of the works with Gen[era]l Béthencourt. Went the rounds with him as far as the battery of La Hêve, which is above a league from the town, *'among the rocks'*,[1] and returned at one in the morning. *'How merrily we live that soldiers be!'*[2] All this afternoon there has been a heavy cannonade to the southward, opposite the point of Dives.[3] We conjecture it is the *flotille* of Muskein which is endeavouring to return and having, as we suppose, fallen in with the English has taken shelter under a little fort of 4 pieces of cannon at the point. Be that as it may, the fire has continued until an hour after dark. Walked out with the general to the battery of La Neige in order to try an experiment, which did not succeed, for setting fire to the enemy's vessels by a kind of combustible machine attached to an 18-pound shot. It will never answer. We are not sure but we may be attacked, ourselves, tonight. I do not, however, apprehend it.

From Adjutant-General Olivier Macoux Rivaud, 2 June 1798

Tone (Dickason) papers.

[1] Source of this quotation not traced.
[2] Opening line of Henry Bate Dudley, *The flitch of bacon* (1779), act I.
[3] The Pointe de Dives is 28 km south-west of Le Havre as the crow flies.

Rivaud acknowledges Tone's two letters, tells him that he may go to Rouen when he wishes and thanks him for keeping him informed.

ARMÉE　　　　　　　　　ÉTAT-MAJOR GÉNÉRAL
D'ANGLETERRE　　　*Au Quartier général à* Rouen, *le* 14 Prairial,
　　　　　　　　　　　　an 6 *de la République Française*
　　　　　　　　　　　　　　　　une et indivisible

L'Adjudant Général, Chef de l'État-Major de l'Armée,
　　　　　　　　　à l'Adjudant Général Smith au Havre

J'au reçu, mon cher camarade, avec vos deux lettres,[1] les détails que vous me donnez sur les entreprises des Anglais contre le Havre et nos deux corvettes parties le 10 pour Cherbourg. Je désire savoir au juste ce qu'elles sont devenues. Aura-t-on pu sauver le *Vésuve?* Apprenez-moi la suitte de cet événement dans lequel il paroît que la *Confiante* a montré autant de courage que le *Vésuve* en a montré peu.

Maintenant que le Havre n'est plus menacé par l'ennemi, vous pouvez, mon camarade, vous rendre à Rouen quand vous voudrez. Je ne puis que rendre hom[m]age à votre activité et aux soins que vous avez pris de m'instruire de ce qui s'est passé au Havre pendant votre séjour.

Salut et amitié,
Rivaud

Port Payé
Arm[ée] d'Angleterre
Citoien Schmith, Adjudant Général
Au Havre

Diary, 3 June 1798

T.C.D., Tone papers, 2049, f. 327^r; *Life*, ii, 495.

3 June 1798

Last night passed over quietly, but this morning at six the cannonade recommenced at the point of Dives, which is about seven leagues to the southward from this.[2] We can see the fire distinctly from the Tower. There are 5 frigates which relieve each other alternately and there are generally three at a time on the poor little fort of 4 guns, for we see no trace of Muskein's *flotille*. At one o'clock, when I write this, the fire still continues with great violence and the fort still holds out. I am astonished it is not torn to pieces long since.[3]

[1] Tone to Rivaud, 29 and 31 May 1798 (above, pp 266, 270–71).
[2] Dives is 28 km south-west of Le Havre.　　　[3] At this point in the MS the pen changes.

At night. The fire slackened soon after one and, the tide of ebb beginning to make, the frigates retired, but a bomb ketch continued to throw shells from time to time until half after two, when she quit also.[1] All quiet for the rest of the day.

To General Barthélemi Louis Joseph Schérer, 4 June 1798

T.C.D., Tone papers, MS 2050, f. 29^r.

Tone asks Schérer to agree to Favory being made his adjoint.

Au quartier général, au Havre, ce 16 prairial, an 6

Au Ministre de la Guerre

Citoyen Ministre,

Ayant à nommer un adjoint, je vous prie de vouloir bien agréer le choix que j'ai fait du citoyen Favory, capitaine adjoint, qui en a déjà rempli les fonctions près de moi, à l'armée de Sambre-et-Meuse, et de lui faire expédier en conséquence sa lettre de service au quartier général de l'armée à Rouen.

Salut et respect
l'adj[udan]t gén[éra]l
J. Smith

To Adjutant-General Olivier Macoux Rivaud, 4 June 1798

T.C.D., Tone papers, MS 2050, ff 26^v–27^r.

Tone reports that the English have set the *Confiante* on fire while another corvette, the *Vésuve*, has anchored near the Pointe de Dives under the cover of coastal batteries; he asks that Fayolles come straightaway and for a copy of the regulations on fortified places.

No. 4

16 Prairial an 6

Général,

J'ai reçu hier votre lettre du 14 courant,[2] et je suis très sensible à la bonté que vous me témoignez. À l'égard du sort des corvettes, il paroît que les Anglois ont mis le feu à la *Confiante* le surlendemain du combat, tout l'équipage est

---

[1] William Tone amends this to 'she fell off also' (*Life*, ii, 495).   [2] Above, pp 275–6.

sauvé avec leurs effets. Le *Vésuve* a eu le bonheur de mouiller à l'embouchure d'une petite rivière près de la pointe de Dives à environ 7 lieues d'ici au sud, où elle est, je crois dans une situation à être protégée par les batteries de la côte, car hier et avant-hier les Anglois ont fait un feu des mieux soutenus pendant plusieurs heures chaque journée sur un petit fort qui se trouve dans cet endroit et ne l'ont quitté que quand la marée en baissant les y a obligés. Sans doute ils reviendront aujourd'hui même; ainsi vous voyez, général, il n'y a pas lieu à présent d'être tout à fait rassuré sur le sort du *Vésuve*.

Comme l'ennemi se trouve toujours en présence, je n'ai pas cru devoir profiter de la permission que vous m'avez accordé[e] de me rendre auprès de vous à Rouen; d'autant moins que le Général Béthencourt a eu la bonté de me dire que je pourrois encore lui être utile ici; je resterai en conséquence jusqu'à nouvel ordre, et je vous prie, général, de m'envoyer incessamment (s'il n'est déjà parti) le Citoyen Fayolles dont j'ai le plus grand besoin. Si vous pouviez en même tems m'envoyer le *Règlement pour le service des places fortes*, vous me feriez un plaisir sensible.

Salut et fraternité
J. S.

Le Gén[éra]l Béthencourt a envoyé hier un officier dans un canot vers la pointe de Dives. Je ne sais s'il est encore de retour. S'il rapporte des détails intéressans, le général sans doute vous en instruira.

Diary, 4–5 June 1798

T.C.D., Tone papers, MS 2049, ff 327ʳ–327ᵛ; *Life*, ii, 495–6.

4 June 1798

Yesterday I received a letter[1] from Adj[utan]t Gen[era]l Rivaud informing me that I might return to Rouen when I pleased. Answered it today, letting him know that, as the enemy continued still before the place, I considered it my duty to remain until further order. Nominated the citizens Fayolles, captain of infantry, and Favery of the Engineers to be my adjoints, and dispatched the letters of nomination to the Minister at War, so now I am fairly afloat. *'If I had bought me a horse in Smithfield, I were manned, horsed, and wived!'*[2] I had like to have forgot!—this is his Majesty's birthday! (Sings) *'God save great George, our king!'*. I feel myself extremely loyal, in the sudden, methinks. Well, God knows the heart! Many a body says *well*, that thinks *ill*, &c., &c.

---

[1] Above, pp 275–6.
[2] 'I bought him in Paul's and he'll buy me a horse in Smithfield; an' I could get me but a wife in the stews, I were manned, horsed and wived' (*2 Henry IV*, I, ii).

5 June 1798

Last night went my round, as *adjudant général*, in all the forms. *'I brought in the boar's head and 'quitted me like a man!'*[1] I do not see, myself, that that quotation is extremely apposite; but no matter. I like the idle activity of a military life well enough, and if I were employed in an Irish army, I should make a tolerable good officer; but the difference of the language here is terribly against me. However, I made myself understood at all the outposts, which is sufficient for my purpose. *'Vive la république!'* I do not know what that sally is for, I am sure. The report in Havre this morning [is] that the Toulon fleet has beaten an English squadron in the Mediterranean and taken 4 sail of the line. *'Would I could see it, quoth blind Hugh.'*[2]

From James Dalton, 5 June 1798

Tone (Dickason) papers.

Dalton tells Tone that in the event of Favory being unable to accept the post of adjoint to him he would replace him.

Paris, le 17 Prairéal an 3 [*sic*][3]

Votre lettre du 13 c[ouran]t m'est parvenue hier, mon cher Smith. Aussitôt Fleury a écrit à Favry, qui sort en ce moment d'ici, pour lui faire connoître que vous étiez dans une position à ne pas vous passer d'adjoint plus longtems, et qu'en conséquence votre intention était qu'il fût prêt à partir incessamment. Il a répondu à cela qu'il ne le pouvait faire qu'hier. D'ailleurs il s'était engagé à être employé dans le corps du Géné[ra]l et adjoint à l'état-major général et qu'il ne partirait pas avant d'avoir son brevet de capitaine. Je lui ai fait part de ma situation, que s'il n'était pas disposé à accepter la place d'adjoint auprès de vous je le remplacerais; que cependant j'allais rejoindre mon corps s'il était dans l'intention d'aller occupper la place que vous lui reserviez. Non, m'a-t-il dit, je vais écrire au G[énér]al Smith pour le remercier en lui notifiant mon refus et je vous engageai de votre côté à lui mander que vous acceptez et que c'est une affaire consommée entre vous et moi. Vous ne doutez pas sans doute, mon cher Smith, de tout mon empressement à vous joindre; en conséquence j'attends votre ordre et votre demande au Ministre en ma faveur. Aussitôt réception, je me mettrai en route pour le Havre. Je n'ai pas besoin de vous dire de me répondre par le retour du courrier. Je suis entièrement libre de partir aussitôt votre ordre reçu. Clarke et Fleury vous diront bien [*three words not deciphered*].

Agréer l'assurance de mon estime et attachement inviolable.

J. Dalton

---

[1] Corinthians, 16: 13.   [2] Swift, *Polite conversation* (1738), dialogue 1.   [3] *Recte* 6.

P.S. Ce n'est que d'après le refus (?)soudain de Favry, comme vous pouvez croire, que j'accepte la place que vous lui destiniez, car malgré tout le plaisir que j'aurai[s] d'être accepté de vous je serais au désespoir de supplanter un camarade.

Je rouvre ma lettre pour vous donner l'état de mon grada. *James Dalton*, lieutenant au Régiment de chasseurs dit Lamoureux. Né le 28 octobre en 1773. Ces renseignemens peuvent être nécessaires pour ma [*word(s) not deciphered*] d'adjoint.

To Adjutant-General Olivier Macoux Rivaud, 6 June 1798

T.C.D., Tone papers, MS 2050, f. 27^r.

Tone reports the situation as unchanged and adds that he has just learnt that the commander at Le Havre has been replaced.

No. 5

18 Prairial, an 6

Général,

Depuis ma dernière lettre, en datte du 16,[1] il n'y a rien arrivé de nouveau ici. Le *Vésuve* reste toujours dans la même station. Aujourd'hui j'apprends que le citoyen Labretêche,[2] commandant des armes au Havre, est destitué, et que le citoyen Favre, capitaine de vaisseau, le remplace. On ne voit ce matin que deux frégates au large. Voilà, général, toutes nos nouvelles.

Salut et fraternité,
J. S.

Diary, 6 June 1798

T.C.D., Tone papers, MS 2049, f. 327^v; *Life*, ii, 496.

6 June 1798

Citizen Fayolle, my adjoint, is arrived from Rouen, so now I am something more at my ease.[3]

---

[1] Above, pp 277–8.

[2] La Bretèche was the 'chef des mouvemens maritimes au Havre' or 'chef de l'état-major de la marine au Havre'; he was replaced in early June by Fabre, probably Jean-Antoine Fabre (1748–1834), engineer (*Moniteur*, 8, 9 June 1798; *Dict. biog. franç.*).

[3] In *Life*, ii, 496, this sentence begins an entry headed 'June 6, 7, 8' and is run on by the first sentence of the entry for 8 June (see below, p. 283).

To Matilda Tone, 8 June 1798

Tone (Dickason) papers.

No. 7

Havre, 20 prairial, an 6

Dear Love,

I received yours and Matt's (No. 5) in course. Matt is like the serjeant: *'Here is a guinea and a crown, beside the Lord knows what renown!'*[1] I do not however apprehend the English to be such fools as to give us the opportunity of gathering a forest of laurels at their expense. Yesterday, it is true, they presented themselves before Havre, about two o'clock, and continued executing divers movements until six in the evening, when they moved off. During all this time they kept a respectful distance, out of cannon shot; however, we were all on the batteries, the furnaces heated, &c., and one time, about four o'clock, I thought they were bearing down on us in right earnest, but they did not, so, as the French say, 'nous fûmes quitte[s] pour la peur'.[2] The battery at La Hêve, about a league from the town, fired five shot at them, which they answered by throwing as many shells, but neither the one nor the other did any harm, the distance being too great. Today all is quiet, and the enemy out of sight.

You may both be sure I shall take no leave of absence while things remain as they are. The day before I received yours I received an order to return to Rouen, but I wrote immediately to request permission to stay here, so long as the port was menaced by the English, so you see I think exactly as you do on that subject.

I have got an adjoint already, and written for another to Paris. I go the round at night, in my turn, like a *skin* officer,[3] and am beginning to fall a little into the track of the profession. I like it well enough, but I should like it far better at home.

I guess, on looking over your letter, that a flourishing postscript in Matt's writing was added *after dinner*. It cost me considerable pains to decypher it, and after all there is one word which I give up. To answer it methodically, I have not yet seen Gen[era]l Kilmaine, but we expect him here, every day, and when he arrives I shall try to learn something touching the *cadres*.[4] I congratulate Will on his taste for music and poetry, as well as the laudable constancy which he manifests in sticking to his old song. Tell Frank I will stay to my soldiers, as he desires, the more so as he, being a general

---

[1] Charles Dibdin, *Poor Vulcan* (1778), I, ii.   [2] 'We escaped with a fright.'
[3] Possibly Tone had in mind the slang expression 'a skin merchant', denoting a recruiting officer.
[4] For the *cadres*, see above, p. 100, and below, pp 298–9.

and my superior in rank, it is for me to obey his orders. I am however curious to know *what* it was he saw in his visit to the palace, for it is not possible, I think, to decypher the word, as it stands in Matt's writing. The nearest guess I can make is 'cochon', which in the language of men signifies *a pig*, but as pigs do not usually frequent palaces, I must wait for your answer to let me know what it was he did see.

I have not a word of news of any kind, nor you neither I believe. I shall be in mortal transes until I hear what is become of Buonaparte. I have bad dreams about him and Lord St Vincents. Write to me the instant anything transpires.

Adieu, Dear Love; service to everybody; has Maria got her dancing master yet?

Yours ever & truly
J. Smith

I copy a passage from a little French play, which I met yesterday and which I think pretty

Colette

Du mariage, moi, je chéris la contrainte,
 Sa chaîne, ses devoirs sont, pour moi, pleins d'attraits;
Qu'il est doux d'obéir à l'objet que l'on aime.
Vivre avec son époux, ne le quitter jamais,
Prévenir avec soin ses plus légers souhaits,
Répondre à son amour, par un amour extrême,
  Ne trouver de félicité
Qu'autant qu'il est heureux lui-même
Un tel bonheur, je crois, vaut bien la liberté.

It put me in mind of you.

À la Citoyenne Smith
Rue des Batailles, No. 29
À Chaillot
près Paris

To Adjutant-General Olivier Macoux Rivaud,
8 June 1798

T.C.D., Tone papers, MS 2050, ff 27^r–27^v.

Tone describes how the previous day eight British ships were off Le Havre precipitating a minor engagement with a shore battery. Generals D'Espinasse, Compère and Béthencourt are now here; Fayolle arrived two days ago.

No. 6

20 Prairial, an 6

Général,

J'ai l'honneur de vous apprendre que, hier à deux heures et demie dans l'après-midi, les Anglois se sont présentés devant le Havre, au nombre de 8 bâtimens, dont 2 bombardes, 1 vaisseau rasé, 4 frégates et 1 brick. Après avoir fait plusieurs manœuvres, toujours hors de portée du canon, ils se sont enfin dirigés vers la pointe de la Hêve, où il y a une batterie qui a tiré cinq ou six coups sur eux, mais la distance étant trop grande, le feu n'a produit aucun effet; l'ennemi, en revanche, a lancé quelques bombes vers la batterie, mais également sans effet. Enfin après une promenade d'environ quatre heures ils ont pris le large vers le[s] six heures du soir, et ce matin on ne les voit plus. Tout le monde étoit aux batteries, et, sans la moindre doute [*sic*], si l'ennemi se fût approché à portée de nos canons, il auroit été chauffé d'une rude manière.

Nous avons ici maintenant les généraux D'Espinasse[1] et Compère,[2] nouvellement arrivés, et le général Béthencourt, mais, s'il soit vrai, comme on le dit, que le gén[éra]l Compère vient pour prendre le commandement du Havre, je présume que le général Béthencourt ne tardera pas de revenir à Rouen.

Je vous remercie, général, de m'avoir envoyé le citoyen Fayolle, qui est arrivé avant-hier au soir. J'ai toute raison d'espérer que nous serons très contents de l'autre. Veuillez bien présenter mes devoirs au général Kilmaine.

Salut et fraternité
J. S.

Diary, 8 June 1798

T.C.D., Tone papers, MS 2049, ff 327ᵛ–328ᵛ; *Life*, ii, 496–7.

8 June 1798

Yesterday the enemy appeared before Havre and from their manœuvres we expected an attack. In consequence all the batteries were manned and the furnaces heated. I was stationed on the Batterie Nationale. About 3 o'clock in the afternoon they bore down on us, within about[3] two cannon shot, but after some little time they hauled their wind and stood off again, so we were quit for the fright.[4] As they passed the battery at the Pointe la

---

[1] Antoine Joseph Marie d'Espinasse (1757–1829), *sous-lieutenant*, 1779; captain, 1788; member of the legislative assembly, the Convention and the Committee of Five Hundred; general, 1797 (Six, *Dict. des généraux & amiraux*).

[2] Louis Fursey Henri Compère (1768–1833), private in artillery, 1784; joined National Guard, 1789; *général de brigade*, 1794; served with *armée d'Angleterre*, 1798 (ibid.).

[3] *Life* omits 'about'.   [4] Cf. 'nous en fûmes quittes pour la peur'.

Hêve, they threw about half a dozen shells to answer as many shot which the battery had fired at them *à toute volée*, but neither the one nor the other did any damage. I saw three of the shells fall in the water, and all the shot. Two of the latter passed very near a bombketch, but the distance was entirely too great, and I wonder the general does not give order never to fire but at a distance to do mischief. If the enemy waste their powder foolishly, that is no reason we should waste ours. *Au reste*, it was a fine sight, and I should have enjoyed it more if it had not been for certain *'speculations on futurity and the transmigration of souls'* which presented themselves to my fancy at times. I defy any man to know whether he is brave, or not, until he is tried, and I am very far from boasting of myself on that score; but the fact is (*and I was right glad of it*) that when I found myself at my battery and saw the enemy bearing right down on us, as I thought to begin the cannonade, tho' I cannot say with truth that I was perfectly easy, yet neither did I feel at all disconcerted, and I am satisfied, as far as a man in that situation can judge of himself, that I should have done my duty well and without any great effort of resolution. The crowd, and the bustle, and the noise, and especially the conviction that the eyes of the cannoniers were fixed on the *chapeau galonné*,[1] settled me at once. It is the etiquette in these cases that the general stands conspicuous on the parapet, while the cannoniers &c. are covered by the *épaulement*, which is truly amusing for him that commands. Nevertheless I have no doubt but it is easier to behave well on the parapet, exposed to all the fire, than in the battery, where the danger is far less.

I had time to make all these and divers other wise remarks during my stay, for it was six in the evening before the English stood off, and, on the faith of an honest man, I cannot truly say I was sorry when I saw them decidedly turn their backs. There were 8 sail, viz. 4 frigates, 2 bombketches, 1 brig and 1 cutter. *Huzza! Vive la république!*

'Thus far our arms have with success been crowned, For tho' we have not fought, yet have we found, No enemy to fight withal.'[2] Huzza! Huzza!

From Marie Jean François Philibert Le Carlier, 9 June 1798

Tone (Dickason) papers.

Marie Jean François Philibert Le Carlier (d. 1799) was minister of police, May–Oct. 1798.

Le Carlier tells Tone that he is certain that Lord Edward Fitzgerald has not arrived in the territory of the republic.

---

[1] Laced hat.   [2] Henry Fielding, *Tom Thumb* (1731), III, vii.

LIBERTÉ   [crest]   ÉGALITÉ

Paris, le 21 Prairial, *an* 6ᵉ.
de la République une et indivisible

Le Ministre de la Police générale de la République
Au Citoyen Smith, Irlandais, adjudant général;
au Quartier Général à Rouen (Seine Inférieure)

Vous avez, Citoyen, écrit à mon prédécesseur pour savoir si la nouvelle que vous avez vue, insérée dans les journaux, de l'arrivée en France du lord Fitzgerald étoit vraie.

Je viens de faire faire des recherches qui m'ont donné la certitude que cet étranger n'est pas arrivé sur le territoire de la République.

Salut et fraternité,
Le Carlier

Au Citoyen
Smith, Irlandais, Adjudant
G[énéra]l
au Quartier Général à Rouen[1]
Seine Inférieure

To Adjutant-General Olivier Macoux Rivaud, 10 June 1798

T.C.D., Tone papers, MS 2050, f. 27ᵛ.

Tone reports the situation as unchanged and, after reminding Rivaud that when sending him here he put him under the orders of Béthencourt, asks whether the arrival of Compère should make any difference.

No. 7

[Au Havre, le] 22 Prairial, an 6

Général,

Depuis ma dernière, en datte du 20,[2] il n'y a rien arrivé de nouveau ici. Les Anglois se sont montrés hier avec 5 frégates, 2 bombardes, 1 brick et 1 cutter. Ils ont fait, comme à l'ordinaire, une promenade sur la grande rade, mais toujours hors de portée du canon. Dans le cours de la journée ils ont fait prier d'un bâtiment neutre.

---

[1] In the MS the words 'à Rouen' are crossed out and 'Havre' interlined. Tone moved from Rouen to Le Havre on 28 May and, though given permission by Rivaud on 2 June to return to Rouen, remained there (see above, pp 265–6, 273–4, 278).   [2] Above, pp 282–3.

Comme l'ordre que vous m'avez donné de me rendre ici porte que je serai aux ordres du gén[éra]l Béthencourt, veuillez bien m'instruire, général, si l'arrivée du gén[éra]l Compère auroit fait quelque changement à cet égard. Je vous prie de présenter mes devoirs au général en chef.[1]

Salut et fraternité,
J. S.

From Adjutant-General Olivier Macoux Rivaud, 10 June 1798

Tone (Dickason) papers; copy in Archives de la Guerre, B^{5*} 115, f. 269.

Tone's report on the enemy's manœuvres is acknowledged on Rivaud's behalf.

ARMÉE   ÉTAT-MAJOR GÉNÉRAL
D'ANGLETERRE   *Au Quartier général à* Rouen *le* 22 Prairéal
                            an 6 de la République française,
                                  une et indivisible

L'Adjudant Général
Chef de l'État-Major de l'Armée
à l'Adjudant Général Smith au Havre

Je vous suis infiniment obligé des détails sur les manœuvres de l'ennemi du 19 de ce mois,[2] et quoique leurs bravades sont toujours sans effet, je vous prie de vouloir bien m'en continuer les rapports.

J'ai communiqué votre lettre au Général-en-chef.[3] Je crois, comme vous, que le Citoyen Fayolle, votre adjoint, aura lieu d'être content de se trouver avec vous.

Salut & fraternité
Pour l'adjudant-général en chef
de l'État-major de l'Armée
le chef de bat[aill]on adjoint
Andrieu[4]

To Charles Maurice de Talleyrand-Périgord, 12 June 1798

T.C.D., Tone papers, MS 2050, ff 30^r–30^v.

Tone asks that his brother, who has just arrived in Hamburg from America, be given a passport to enter France; he adds that he has just learnt from

---

[1] Kilmaine.   [2] Possibly Tone to Rivaud, 20 Prairial (above, pp 282–3).   [3] Kilmaine.
[4] Andrieu, who signs on Rivaud's behalf, may have been Martin Antoine Andrieux (1768–1802), who began military service as a captain of Volunteers in Nov. 1791; he was an adjutant-general in 1799, served in the *armée d'Italie* in 1800, and died on the French expedition to Santo Domingo (*Nouv. biog. gén.; Dict. biog. franç.*).

the newspapers that Arthur O'Connor has been acquitted at Maidstone and Lord Edward Fitzgerald arrested in Dublin; he implores Talleyrand to consider the sorry state of Ireland.

Au Havre, ce 24 Prairial, an 6

Au Ministre des relations extérieures

Citoyen Ministre,

Mon frère,[1] nouvellement arrivé à Hambourg des États-Unis d'Amérique, s'étant adressé au citoyen Roberjot,[2] ministre de la république, pour obtenir un passeport, je viens d'apprendre par une lettre du citoyen Lemaistre,[3] que pour cela il faut une autorisation spéciale du gouvernement. Comme je désire ardemment d'embrasser un frère que je n'ai pas vu depuis près de trois ans, je vous supplie, citoyen ministre, de vouloir bien faire passer vos ordres au citoyen Roberjot, l'autorisant à accorder à ce jeune homme un passeport pour entrer en France. Il se nomme Arthur O'Neil Smith. La bonté avec laquelle vous m'avez toujours accueilli me fait espérer que vous ne me refuserez pas la grâce que j'ose vous demander.

Je viens d'apprendre par les feuilles publiques d'aujourd'hui qu'Arthur O'Connor a été acquitté à Maidstone,[4] et que son digne ami le Lord Edward Fitzgerald vient d'être arrêté à Dublin.[5] La joie que j'aurois sentie de la première nouvelle se trouve presqu'entièrement anéantie par la dernière. Que l'Irlande est destinée à être toujours malheureuse, et comme il est terrible pour moi de voir presque tous mes amis, et les meilleurs amis de leur pays, en fuite, en exil, ou dans les cachots anglais! Souffrez, citoyen ministre, que je vous implore de jeter vos regards sur l'état de ma patrie infortunée. Elle a, j'espère, donné bien d'épreuves de son attachement à la cause de la république. Seroit il possible que la France laisseroit tomber sous le joug impitoyable des Anglais, sans l'espoir de le pouvoir jamais briser, une nation qui lui a servi comme la plus fidelle de ses alliés, qui occupe sans cesse 40,000 hommes des troupes ennemies et qui a déjà coûté au moins vingt millions de livres sterlings à l'Angleterre? Je dois peut-être vous demander pardon, citoyen ministre, de vous troubler de cette manière, mais si je vous semble importun, songez, je vous en supplie, qu'à l'heure même que j'ai l'honneur de vous écrire, la ville capitale de mon pays, où j'ai des parens, des amis, est livrée en proie à toutes les horreurs du régime militaire et à

---

[1] Arthur Tone.

[2] Claude Roberjot (1752–99), *curé* of Mâcon before the revolution; member of Convention and of Council of Five Hundred; minister at Hamburg, Mar.–June 1798; murdered at Rastadt after the collapse of the peace negotiations with the Emperor, Apr. 1799 (*Dict. parl. franç.*).

[3] Jean-Bénédict Lemaître, born in Switzerland, worked in 5th bureau of the Ministry of Foreign Affairs, then became parliamentary secretary to Reinhard, French minister at Hamburg (Frédéric Masson, *Le Département des Affaires Étrangères pendant la Révolution* (Paris, 1877), pp 235, 328, 354).

[4] Charged with high treason, O'Connor had been tried at Maidstone, in the south of England, on 21 and 22 May. Found not guilty, he was immediately rearrested on an Irish warrant.

[5] Fitzgerald was arrested on 19 May. Tone gives more detail in his diary for 12 June (below, pp 292–3).

la licence effrénée d'une soldatesque étrangère, dont j'ai été moi-même, bien dans le cas de connoître toute l'insolence et la férocité.

Pardonnez encore une fois, citoyen ministre, à des émotions que je ne suis pas le maître de contenir, et daignez rappeller aux souvenirs du gouvernement la situation déplorable, où gémit une nation qui, une fois libre et indépendante, seroit plus utile à la république, j'ose le dire avec confiance, que tout le reste de ses alliés, et qui a déjà scellé son attachement à la cause de la liberté, par le sang de tant des plus braves de ses enfans, victimes de leur constance et de la tyrannie anglaise. C'est vers la grande nation que nous regardons, tous, sans cette espérance, il y a longtems succombé. Si elle venoit de nous manquer, nous serions perdus à jamais.

Salut et respect
(signé)
J. Smith

(*pour copie*)

To Matilda Tone, 12 June 1798

Tone (Dickason) papers.

No. 8

Havre, 24 Prairial, an 6

Dear Love,

I received yours, No. 6, yesterday, and at the same time one from Matt,[1] written on the back of Lemaistre's letter to Giauque,[2] relative to Arthur's passport. I write by this courier to the minister for foreign affairs, requesting him to give orders to the minister at Hambourg, but God knows whether he will or not. I begin to suspect from circumstances that the Irish are not in as good odour here as formerly, and I am most heartily sorry for it. It seems, by Lemaistre's letter, that orders are given to let no more of them pass by way of Hambourg. If that were known to those in Paris, it would be instantly said that Lewines was the cause of it, for all misadventures are laid to his charge; do you therefore say nothing of it. All things considered I am not surprised at the French government giving no encouragement to further emigrations. Who knows what juggling and dirty work they may have had occasion to see, and of which we, happily, know nothing? Joe Orr has written to me to get him a passport from the minister of police, which he has been hunting after some time ineffectually. I presume he sees now that it is something more than *ask and have* in the bureaux of the police, and that should

---

[1] Mathew Tone.   [2] Probably Jean-Frédéric Giauque.

teach him to judge more charitably of Lewines with regard to the Liège business.[1] I had a good mind to write him a lecture thereupon, but on reflection I gave it up, for these kind of expostulations only serve to exasperate, and never to correct. I therefore have written him a short letter (enclosing one extremely official for the minister of the police) in which I tell him (Orr) that I hope the letter may be of use to him, at the same time that it is more than I expect, having had no intercourse with the minister for some months, and especially considerable pains having been taken to diminish my credit, if any I might be supposed to have. Let him chew upon that. Do you however, as I shall also do, continue to keep fair with everybody.

I cannot express to you the effect the news of Fitzgerald's arrestation[2] had upon me. My acquaintance with him personally was extremely slight, yet I hardly think had he been my dearest friend I could have been more sincerely affected. I certainly was less so at the arrestation of Russell. Let Matt go to his *cabinet* and copy, word for word, the account of what passed. It should seem, by the *Bien Informé*, that he made a desperate resistance, and was severaly wounded, before he was overpowered. I cannot describe the rage and indignation I felt at reading the paragraph. From all the circumstances, I am satisfied he meditated an attack on Dublin. When I compare his conduct, his situation, his rank, his courage, with that of others, how pitiful they appear in my eyes! Judge what I feel at this moment, when I reflect on the helpless situation I am in here, with my blood boiling within me, and absolutely unable to make the smallest effort. Well, it does not signify blustering, so I will stop here. I was ill all day yesterday with sheer rage and vexation, and I slept none scarcely last night. Think what poor Pamela[3] suffers just now! But if she be the woman I take her to be she will bear it well.

It is some consolation that O'Connor is acquitted.[4] If it were not for the other unfortunate intelligence, my satisfaction would be complete, but I am sure O'Connor himself can scarcely feel pleasure at his own safety, if he is apprised of the danger of his friend. Quigly[5] has redeemed himself completely by his conduct; I see he has the faults and the virtues of his country.

Let us quit this most unfortunate event, on which I hate to think, and which recurs to me a thousand times in the day. I am delighted that you have begun to bathe your boys. I hope you have chosen a place of perfect safety, and, at all events, Matt will do me a great pleasure if he assists every morning at the ceremony for fear of accidents. Have you finished their *greyness*

---

[1] This is probably a reference to the imprisonment of four Irishmen at Liège. There is an earlier reference to this affair in Tone to Talleyrand, 15 Oct. 1797 (above, pp 161–2). Talleyrand for his part wrote to the minister of police, Pierre Sotin, urging him to examine the men's cases with a view to releasing them (Talleyrand to Sotin, 20 Oct. 1797, above, pp 162–3).

[2] On 19 May 1798; see below (p. 292).

[3] Lady Pamela Fitzgerald (1776–1831), wife of Lord Edward Fitzgerald; she was reputed to be the natural daughter of the duke of Orleans ('Philippe Égalité') and Madame de Genlis but in fact her parents were English (*Gent. Mag.*, ci (1831), pt II, suppl. pp 645–6; *D.N.B.*).

[4] Charged with high treason, O'Connor had been tried at Maidstone on 21 and 22 May. Found not guilty, he was immediately rearrested on an Irish warrant.   [5] Coigly.

yet, and how do they look in their *'vests and tunics'?*[1] Touching Maria, you know, *'Had pretty miss been at the dancing school bred, &c.'*.[2] I see no manner of impropriety in your going to the lady's appartment you speak of if she has no objection, especially as you will always be with the Bab. For the price nothing can be more reasonable. How do you get on with your music?

For my part, I have not one syllable of news. The English are always in sight of the port, but I have not the slightest notion that they will venture an attack, as we are perfectly prepared, and they know that as well as we do. It is therefore a mere bravado on their part. If however they should hazard the measure, they will sorely repent it, but, once more they are too well apprised of the state of our preparations to venture.

I pass my time here more stupidly than you can imagine. I have got an adjoint,[3] a very brave lad, and a fool, but good-natured. I have *'excarded Ofrizzle for kicking of Chowder'*,[4] or, in other words I have got rid of Captain MacSheehy, of which I am truly glad, for if ever there was a rascal in the world, devoid of all principle, he is one. I have likewise chosen my second adjoint, Favery, who, you may remember, called on us *with his wife*.[5] He is however an acquisition and I expect him in a few days, having sent him his order to join me without delay, so you see I am getting afloat. I foresee I shall have to borrow money of you, when your next month comes due. Tell Matt I thank him for his cautions, which I shall observe. I have not yet seen Gen[era]l Kilmaine, but we expect him every day. Adieu, dearest Love.

Yours ever
J. Smith

When you hear from Mary let me know. Kiss the Babs for me a *milliard* of times.

À la Citoyenne Smith
Rue des Batailles, N°. 29
À Chaillot
près Paris

To Adjutant-General Olivier Macoux Rivaud, 12 June 1798

T.C.D., Tone papers, MS 2050, f. 27ᵛ.

Tone acknowledges Rivaud's letter of 10 June and reports the situation as unchanged.

---

[1] Laurence Sterne, *Tristram Shandy* (1760), vi, ch. 18.
[2] 'The cobler of Cripplegate' in George Alexander Stevens, *Songs comic and satyrical* (1788).
[3] Fayolle.   [4] Chowder (a dog) and Ofrizzle appear in Smollett's *Humphry Clinker* (1771).
[5] Mme Favery has not been identified.

No. 8

24 Prairial, an 6

Général,

Votre lettre du 22¹ m'est parvenue hier.

Depuis ma dernière, en datte du 22,² tout reste ici dans la même position. L'ennemi se tient fort au large, et en général on ne voit que 2 frégates. Demain, étant la grande marée, amenera peut-être quelqu'événement. S'il arrive quelque chose d'extraordinaire j'aurai soin de vous en instruire sur le champ.

Veuillez bien présenter mes devoirs au Gén[éra]l en chef.³

Salut et fraternité

J. S.

To Marie Jean François Philibert Le Carlier, 12 June 1798

T.C.D., Tone papers, MS 2050, f. 31ʳ.

Tone requests a passport to the interior for Joseph Orr, who is travelling with the intention of purchasing a 'national property' and settling in France.

au Havre, ce 24 Prairial, an 6

Au Ministre de la Police

Citoyen Ministre,

Le ministre des relations extérieures ayant invité votre prédécesseur, le citoyen Sotin, à s'adresser à moi, dans le cas de toute réclamation faite auprès du ministre de la police par des patriotes irlandais réfugiés, je prends la liberté de vous prier de bien vouloir accorder un passeport pour l'intérieur au citoyen James Williams, domicilié depuis quelques mois à Paris.

Comme ce citoyen voyage avec le dessein d'acheter un bien national et de se fixer en France, veuillez bien faire expédier le passeport sous son véritable nom, Joseph Orr, celui de James Williams n'étant qu'un nom supposé, qu'il a été obligé de prendre pour se mieux soustraire à la poursuite du gouvernement anglais; et, comme l'affaire pour laquelle il veut partir est très pressée, je vous supplie, citoyen ministre, de donner vos ordres, pour que son passeport lui soit expédié le plutôt possible.

Salut et respect

(signé)

J. Smith

(copie)

¹ The letter of 10 June written on Rivaud's behalf (above, p. 286).
² Above, pp 285–6.   ³ Kilmaine.

Diary, 12–13 June 1798

T.C.D., Tone papers, MS 2049, ff 328ᵛ–331ʳ; *Life*, ii, 497–500.

12 June 1798

Yesterday I read in the French papers an account of the acquittal of Arthur O'Connor at Maidstone and of his being taken instantly into custody again. Undoubtedly Pitt means to send him to Ireland in hopes of finding there a more complaisant jury. Quigley, the priest, is found guilty. It seems he has behaved admirably well, which I confess was more than I expected. His death redeems him. Alley, Binnes and Leary, the servant, were also acquitted and discharged. O'Connor seems to have behaved with great intrepidity. On being taken into custody, he ad[d]ressed the judges, desiring to be sent to the same dungeon with his brother,[1] who, like him, was acquitted of high treason, and, like him, arrested in the very court. The judge, Buller, answered him, coldly, that their commission expired when the sentence was pronounced and that the court could do nothing further in the business. He was instantly committed. My satisfaction at this triumph of O'Connor is almost totally destroyed by a second article in the same paper, which mentions that Lord Edward Fitzgerald has been arrested in Thomas St., Dublin, after a most desperate resistance, in which himself, the magistrate (one Swan)[2] and Capt[ai]n Ryan,[3] who commanded the guard, were severely wounded. I cannot describe the effect this intelligence had on me; it brought on almost instantly a spasm in my stomach which confined me the whole day. I knew Fitzgerald but very little, but I honor and venerate his character, which he has uniformly sustained and, in this last instance, illustrated. What miserable wretches are the gentry of Ireland beside him! I would rather be Fitzgerald as he is at this moment, wounded, in his dungeon, than[4] Pitt at the head of the British empire. What a noble fellow! Of the first family in Ireland, with an easy fortune, a beautiful wife, a family of lovely children, the certainty of a splendid appointment under the government, if he would condescend to support their measures, he has

---

[1] Roger O'Connor.

[2] William Bellingham Swan (d. 1837), deputy town major, who on 12 March had arrested John McCann, William Michael Byrne and other members of the Leinster provincial committee at Oliver Bond's house; he was inspector-general of excise and a J.P. in several counties (*Freeman's Journal*, 16 Oct. 1798, 28 Dec. 1828; Thomas Reynolds junr, *The life of Thomas Reynolds* (London, 1839), i, 444, ii, 229–33).

[3] Daniel Frederick Ryan (1762?–98), surgeon in 103rd regiment and in Dublin; as a conservative journalist he 'defended the cause of loyalty and honour'; capt., St Selpuchre's yeomanry corps; mortally wounded when taking part in the arrest of Lord Edward Fitzgerald (*Faulkner's Dublin Journal*, 31 May 1798; *D.N.B.*).

[4] MS has 'that' in error.

devoted himself wholly to the emancipation of his country; to that he has sacrificed everything, even to his blood. My only consolation is in the hope that his enemies have no capital charge against him, and that they will be obliged to limit their rage to his imprisonment. The city and country[1] of Dublin are proclaimed and under martial law.[2] When I combine this with the late seizure of the cannon at Clarke's[3] I am strongly inclined to think that Fitzgerald was organising an attack on the capital. Poor fellow! He is not the first Fitzgerald who has sacrificed himself to the cause of his country. There is a wonderful similarity of principle and fortune between him and his ancestor Lord Thomas,[4] in the reign of Henry 8th, who lost his head on Tower Hill for a gallant but a fruitless attempt to recover the independance of Ireland. God send the catastrophe of his noble descendant may not be the same! I dread everything for him, and my only consolation is in speculations of revenge. If the blood of this brave young man be shed by the hands of his enemies, it will be no ordinary vengeance that will content the people whenever the day of retribution arrives. I cannot express the rage I feel at my own helplessness at this moment, but what can I do! Let me if possible think no more; it sets me half mad.

13 June 1798

Yesterday evening, about six o'clock, the enemy approached almost within random shot of the batteries to the number of 4 frigates and 2 bomb ketches. The batteries were immediately manned and the furnaces heated, but the enemy keeping a cautious distance, nothing ensued. We fired two or three shot from the *batterie du nord*, but observing they fell short, we ceased firing. The enemy did not return our gun; at eight they stood off. This morning, about eight o'clock, I was roused by two or three guns; I dressed myself in a hurry and ran off to the batteries, where I arrived before the cannoniers or any of my comrades; the enemy were, as the evening before, something more than a random shot from the line. The gun boats had opened their fire, but to no effect; of at least 100 shot, not one reached aboard, tho' the guns were admirably pointed. By what I can observe, we always begin to fire a great deal too soon. They complain here that the English powder is better than the French in the proportion of near two to one, yet we fire on them at full one third more than the distance. We fired two or three shot from the batteries merely to shew the

---

[1] *Sic*. The sense, however, requires 'county', as in *Life*, ii, 498.

[2] On 15 May 1798 the lord lieutenant, acting under the Insurrection Act (36 Geo. III, c. 20), declared County Dublin a disturbed area; on 24 May the commander of the forces issued a proclamation declaring that he was determined to use all the powers entrusted to him to suppress rebellion and imposing a curfew in the city of Dublin (*Faulkner's Dublin Journal*, 26 May 1798).

[3] See above, p. 268, n. 9.

[4] Thomas Fitzgerald, 10th earl of Kildare (1513–37), known as 'Silken Thomas', in 1534 (during the reign of Henry VIII) renounced his allegiance, was captured and executed at Tyburn (*D.N.B.*).

gun-boats that we were there to support them, but without any expectation of reaching the enemy, who all this time never condescended to return us one gun. After about half an hour, the fire ceased and the enemy stood off. I do not well conceive the object of these two visits last night and this morning. It is now eleven o'clock in the forenoon, and we expect them again with the evening's tide. Maybe we shall then see something. I have been running over in my mind the list of my friends and of the men whom, without being so intimately connected with them, I most esteem. Scarcely do I find one who is not, or has not been, in exile or in prison and in jeopardy of his life. To begin with, Russell and Emmett, the two dearest of my friends, at this moment in prison on a capital charge; MacNeven and John Sweetman, my old fellow labourers in the Catholic cause;[1] Edward Fitzgerald, Arthur O'Connor, Roger O'Connor, whom, tho' I know them less, I do not less esteem; Sampson, Bond, Jackson, his son,[2] still in prison; Robert Simms, William Simms, the men in the world to whose friendship I am most obliged, but just discharged; Neilson, Haslett, McCracken,[3] the same; McCormick, absconded; Rowan, Reynolds, in exile in America; Lewines, Tenent, Lowry, Hamilton, Teeling,[4] in France; others, with whom I have little or no acquaintance but whom I must presume to be the victims of their patriotism, viz. Tandy, Orr, O'Finn,[5] Burgess, Macan, Maguire,[6] McMahon, in France; Byrne,[7] in Germany; Baily,[8] in Holland; Turner,[9] I know not where; not to speak of my own family!; Stokes, disgraced

---

[1] In *Life*, ii, 500, William Tone makes numerous minor changes to Tone's catalogue of United Irishmen.

[2] Probably Hugh Jackson.

[3] Henry Joy McCracken.

[4] Bartholomew Teeling.

[5] Edward Finn or O'Finn (see above, p. 204, n. 2).

[6] James Macguire (see above, p. 192, n. 6).

[7] Patrick or John Byrne (see above, p. 162, n.1).

[8] Probably William Bailey of County Down, late an officer in the East India Company's service; member of the London Corresponding Society; he visited Dublin in Jan. 1798 to present a fraternal address to the United Irish; he went with W. H. Hamilton to the Continent early in Apr. with information on United Irish plans to rise; exempted from the act of pardon (38 Geo. III, c. 55) (*Castlereagh corr.*, i, 409; Marianne Elliott, *Partners in revolution: the United Irishmen and France* (New Haven, 1982), pp 175, 178; Paul Weber, *On the road to rebellion: the United Irishmen and Hamburg* (Dublin, 1997), pp 103–4). A Thomas Bailie signed the address of the United Irishmen in Paris to Mrs Tone, 19 Oct. 1799 (Tone (Dickason) papers).

[9] Samuel Turner (1765?–1810?) of Newry, Co. Down; joined the United Irishmen, 1797, and was admitted to their national directory; he provided the British government with a considerable amount of information. He arrived in Hamburg in June 1797 and was in Paris c.26 July to 19 Sept., returning then to Hamburg where the French minister unwittingly gave him a passport that enabled him to confer in London with both Lord Downshire and Lord Edward Fitzgerald and to return to Hamburg in mid Nov. as a double agent; he was in London again, late Feb. to late Mar. 1798, during which time he met Downshire and Portland; he returned to the Continent, travelling via Hamburg and Holland to Paris, which he reached on 17 Apr.; he stayed until 9 May, leaving via Cuxhaven for London, having failed to gain an audience with the Directory; he arrived in Paris on a third visit apparently at the end of May. In a report he sent from Hamburg on 16 Aug. 1798 he gave information on Tone. (*D.N.B.;* Weber, *On the road to rebellion*, pp 66–73, 79, 81–8, 96–9, 114–15; Samuel Turner to—— ——, 16 June 1803, Nat. Arch. (Ire.), Rebellion papers, 620/11/160/4).

on a suspicion of virtue.[1] It is a gloomy catalogue for a man to cast his eyes over! Of all my political connexions I see but John Keogh who has escaped, and how he has had that inconceivable good fortune is to me a miracle.[2]

Ten at night. I have been these two hours on the batteries but the enemy keeps at a considerable distance. It is downright wearying to be in continual expectation of an attack, and I begin to lose my patience. Tonight I was almost sure we should have had a brush, but it ended in nothing, confound them! They *fit*[3] me. *'My soul's in arms, and eager for the fray'*,[4] and the enemy won't indulge me, which is unkind. It is not that I thirst unreasonably for their destruction, for I am like Parson Adams: *'I would not have the blood even of the wicked upon me'*.[5] Apropos! I should remark that the cannoniers of the town shew the greatest zeal; they were this morning the first on the batteries, and I remarked among them several *collets noirs*,[6] who seemed to desire nothing better than to begin the cannonade. The fact is the French are a most intrepid people, and I forgave the *jeunes gens*[7] a great deal of their frivolity and nonsense in favor of their courage. For my part I was there on my parapet, and I could not help laughing at my own wit, or rather Sheridan's,[8] in a bright quotation I made from Acres, in the *Rivals: 'Oh that I were at Clod Hall now, or that I could be shot before I was aware!'.*[9] *Allons! Courage! Vive la République!*

To Adjutant-General Olivier Macoux Rivaud, 14 June 1798

T.C.D., Tone papers, MS 2050, f. 32ʳ.

Tone reports that the batteries have again been in action against British vessels and that the general in command arrived 'towards midnight yesterday', adding that he hopes to see the general today.

No. 9

26 Prairial, an 6

Général,

Avant hier, le 24, sur les 7 heures du soir, les Anglais se sont présentés devant le port avec 4 frégates et 2 bombardes. Aussitôt tout le monde s'est rendu aux

---

[1] Whitley Stokes was suspended from his tutorship at Trinity College in Apr. 1798 on account of his political opinions.

[2] John Keogh was one of over two thousand catholics who signed an address, dated 30 May 1798, declaring their loyalty to the king and constitution (*Walker's Hibernian Magazine*, Aug. 1798, p. 560).

[3] In *Life*, ii, 500, 'teaze' is substituted for 'fit'.

[4] Colley Cibber's adaptation of Shakespeare's *Richard III* (1700), v, iii.

[5] Henry Fielding, *Joseph Andrews* (1742), bk II, ch. 9.

[6] In *Life*, ii, 500, William Tone adds in parentheses 'royalists'.

[7] Literally 'young people'. For Tone's deeper meaning, see above, vol. II, p. 55, n. 2, and p. 188, n. 3.

[8] Richard Brinsley Sheridan (1751–1816), playwright and politician (*D.N.B.*).

[9] Bob Acres in *The rivals* (1775), v, iii.

batteries et l'on tirait deux ou trois coups sur eux de la batterie du nord, mais voyant que la distance étoit trop grande, on a cessé de faire feu. Ils ont resté dans cette position pendant deux heures environ et puis ils ont pris le large. Hier le 25 ils sont encore revenus sur les huit heures du matin, mais ils ont eu soin de se tenir toujours hors de la portée du canon. Les chaloupes cannonières ont tiré au moins une soixantaine de coups sur eux, mais je n'en ai remarqué aucun qui a porté à leur bord. Après une heure environ ils se sont retirés, sans nous avoir riposté d'un seul coup de canon. Nous nous attendîmes à une autre visite, le soir, mais ils ne sont pas revenus. Aujourd'hui ils sont encore au large mais ils ne font aucun mouvement inquiétant.

Le général en chef[1] est arrivé hier vers minuit. J'espère d'avoir l'honneur de le voir aujourd'hui.

Salut et fraternité
J. S.

To Adjutant-General Olivier Macoux Rivaud, 16 June 1798

T.C.D., Tone papers, MS 2050, f. 32ʳ.

Tone reports that the English have not appeared today and that Kilmaine, Espinasse, Compère and Béthencourt have gone off in the direction of Fécamp.

No. 10

28 Prairial, an 6

Général,

Depuis ma dernière lettre en datte du 26[2] il n'est arrivé rien de nouveau. Les Anglais ne paroissent pas aujourd'hui. Le général en chef vient de partir avec les généraux Espinasse, Compère et Béthencourt pour faire une tournée du côté de Fécamp &c. Je ne crois pas qu'il revienne ici. Veuillez bien, général, faire passer la lettre ci-jointe au Général Grouchy.

Salut et fraternité
J. S.

To General Emmanuel Grouchy, 16 June 1798

T.C.D., Tone papers, MS 2050, f. 33ʳ.

---

[1] Kilmaine.   [2] Above.

Tone expresses pleasure at the news that Grouchy is to command the cavalry of the 'army of England'.

Au quartier général au Havre, [ce] 28 Prairial, an 6

Au Général Grouchy

C'est avec le plus grand plaisir, général, que je viens d'apprendre que vous devez commander la cavalerie de l'armée d'Angleterre. Je regarde cette nouvelle marque de la confiance du gouvernement en vous comme une circonstance du meilleur augure pour la libération de mon pays, ayant eu bien l'occasion de remarquer, lors de notre dernière expédition, le zèle et le dévouement que vous avez montré dans une position des plus critiques. Le sort ne favorisait pas alors votre courage. Vous vous voyiez privé par la fureur des élémens de la gloire d'avoir, avec une poignée de braves, culbuté la puissance anglaise, rétabli la liberté et l'indépendance d'Irlande, et, en créant une nouvelle puissance en Europe, assuré à la république un allié fidèle, utile et reconnoissant. J'espère que l'occasion va bientôt se présenter encore, et que j'aurai le plaisir de me retrouver auprès de vous, dans des circonstances plus heureuses, où vous allez vous combler de la gloire, dont je vous ai vu si indignement frustré dans la baïe de Bantry, tant par la malignité des cieux, que par le méchanceté des hommes.

Quant à moi, général, quoique je ne vous ai pas troublé de ma correspondance, soyez assuré que je n'ai oublié ni le zèle que vous avez montré pour la liberté de mons pays, ni la bienveillance dont vous m'avez honoré personnellement. Soyez également sûr que je n'ai jamais manqué, quand l'occasion se présentait, de faire sentir aux autres toute l'estime et le respect pour votre caractère que je sens moi-même, et que surtout je me suis fait, toujours, un devoir de rendre justice au courage, au zèle et au dévouement que vous avez montré dans des circonstances infiniment difficiles et que personne mieux que moi n'étoit dans le cas de remarquer.

Veuillez bien, général, à vos heures perdues, m'écrire un mot. Je vous prie d'agréer les assurances de mon très sincère respect.

J. Smith

Copy

Diary, 16 June 1798

T.C.D., Tone papers, MS 2049, ff 331ʳ–334ʳ; *Life*, ii, 500–03.

16 June 1798

Last night, at the comedy, I had a conversation with Gen[era]l Kilmaine, who has been here these two days, which did not much encourage me on the present posture of our affairs. We began on the subject of my letter of the 26th May,[1] offering to go to India &c. He said he had not answered it because, the Directory not having communicated to him the object of the Toulon expedition, if he had made the offer on my behalf, it would have looked as if he were fishing for information, but at the same time he would keep it in his mind and would mention it, if he saw a fit occasion. I told him it was not a thing that I pressed, or wished to give for more than it was worth; my object was merely to inform the government that in case nothing were likely to be done in Europe, and an attempt were to be made in India, if they thought under the circumstances that my services there could be of any use, I was ready to go in four-and-twenty hours. Gen[era]l Kilmaine answered that a little time would let us see the object of Buonaparte's plan; that in the meantime there was a supplementary armament preparing at Toulon of 2 ships-of-the-line with some frigates and transports, and if it were destined for India, we would then see what was to be done.

The conversation naturally introduced the subject of the grand expedition against England, or Ireland, of which from Kilmaine's report I do not see the smallest probability. The Marine is in a state of absolute nullity; the late minister, Pléville Lepeley, towards the end of his function, had disarmed all the ships-of-the-line, so that when he was pressed by the Directory, it appeared that nothing was ready, and in consequence, after about a month's shuffling, he was obliged to resign. I mentioned that I had better hopes of the present minister, Bruix, who, besides his being a man of acknowledged talents and activity, was in a certain degree bound in honor to try the expedition, having taken so active a part in conducting the last, and having been even indirectly implicated by his enemies in the failure, which ought naturally to pique him to make the greater exertions. Kilmaine said that was all true, but what could Bruix do? In the first place, he had no money; in the next place, the arsenals of Brest were empty and what stores they had in the other ports they could not convey thither, from the superiority of the naval force of the enemy, which kept everything blocked up; finally, that of 14 sail of the line now in the road of Brest, there were but 3 in a state to put to sea; that the government towards the end of Pléville Lepeley's ministry (being apparently uninformed of the real state of the marine) had ordered him (Kilmaine) to have the army prepared, in consequence of which he had marched about 17,000 men towards the coasts, where they still remained, viz. 6 demi-brigades of infantry, 1 reg[imen]t of dragoons, 1 reg[imen]t of hussars and 1 of chasseurs, besides the artillery, but that there was no manner of appearance of anything being done on the part of the marine. All this is as bad as bad can be. I asked the general then whether he could tell me the determination of the government with regard to the *cadres*[2] formed by Gen[era]l Hoche for the late expedition and whether the young men[3] now in

---

[1] Above, pp 263–4. [2] Expanded in *Life*, ii, 502, to 'cadres of regiments'.
[3] Changed in *Life* to 'Irishmen'.

Paris were to be employed in them or how. He said he had spoke of it twenty times at the Directory; that the fact was the existence of those *cadres* was authorised by no law, and if there was any question about them, the consequence would be their immediate suppression; that if the expedition took place, once there was question of embarking, the matter could be managed, but in the meantime nothing could be done, the constitution being express against employing foreigners, and the jealousy being even carried so far that the Directory were obliged to refuse the offer of a regiment of hussars made to them by the Cisalpines, which in fact I remember myself, and the truth is I cannot blame the French for adopting a principle which is very reasonable in itself. I then mentioned that the situation of those young men now in Paris was very painful and that I was afraid if something were not done in their behalf, that they would be reduced to considerable difficulties. He said he felt all that; at the same time the conduct of[1] the Irish now at Paris had been such as to reflect credit neither on themselves nor their country; that there was nothing to be heard amongst them but denunciations, and if it were true for every one of them separately, all the rest were rascals; at the same time that there was one thing in their favour, that hitherto they had asked nothing for themselves, which in some degree saved their credit; that there was only one person, named O'Finn, who appeared in the light of a mere adventurer and a fellow of no character;[2] that Tandy had also applied for assistance and that he (Kilmaine), believing the poor old man to be in distress, had signed a paper to the minister at war, requesting that Tandy might be employed. I answered that I was heartily sorry for the account he gave me of the conduct of our countrymen, which I had some reason to believe to be not exaggerated, having been myself denounced more than once already, for no other offence, as I believed in my conscience, than the rank I held in the French army, which caused heartburnings among them; that the misfortune was that they came into France with their ideas mounted too high, from having had a certain degree of influence among the people at home, and finding themselves absolutely without any in France, their tempers were naturally soured, and their ill humour vented itself in accusations of each other. I then took occasion to ask the general whether, in the worst event of a general peace leaving Ireland still under the British yoke, he thought the French government would do anything for the Irish patriots who had suffered so much in their cause and who by the number of men they employed, and the quantity of money they had cost England, had served as a powerful diversion in favor of the Republic, without putting her to the expense of one shilling; and I mentioned the example of England after the revocation of the Edict of Nantz,[3] who had received with open arms and given all possible encouragement to the French Protestants, with far less reason than in the present instance. The General answered that in the event I mentioned

---

[1] In *Life*, ii, 502, William Tone inserts 'many of'.
[2] *Life* omits 'and a fellow of no character'. [3] In 1685.

he had no manner of doubt but the French government would give every possible encouragement to the Irish refugees. I then observed to him that I had been thinking whether the islands in the Gulf of Venice, Corfou &c. did not offer a convenient occasion for affording a settlement, especially as their destiny was yet unsettled—at the same time that I merely threw it out as a hint for him to think of, having myself no definite ideas on the subject. He said he would turn it in his mind, and so our conversation ended.

All this is as discouraging as it well can be. I am sworn not to despair. It is my motto, but if it were not for that, I know not what I should do today. It is now twenty-eight days since Buonaparte sailed from Toulon, and the only certain news we have from the Mediterranean is that Lord St Vincent's fleet has been reinforced by 6 sail of the line from England and 4 from Portugal (these last Portuguese); that he has left 18 sail to block[1] Cadiz, and has passed the Straights of Gibraltar with 16 sail, of course his prime vessels. If that be so and he falls in with the French fleet of 13 sail, encumbered with a large convoy, there is an end of the Toulon expedition, even supposing, what I hardly think possible, that the French with that inferiority should not be utterly defeated. It is dreadful!

I should have observed in its place that Gen[era]l Kilmaine told me that the calumnies[2] of the Irish had even reached the government, and had of course lowered the nation in their esteem; he added that Lewines however was not implicated, of which I am heartily glad. I did not ask him how it was with regard to myself.

To Matilda Tone, 18 June 1798

Tone (Dickason) papers.

No. 9

Havre, ce 30 prairial, an 6

Dear Love,

I have received yours, No. 7, as well as Matt's of the same date. I have also read some further details relating to our business in the *Bien Informé*. I will make no remarks here, nor endeavour to describe the situation I have been in ever since. Unluckily Gen[era]l Kilmaine, and Gen[era]l Béthencourt, under whose orders I am at present, had set off from this place the evening before. Had it not been for that, I should have applied for a fortnight's leave of absence for Paris; as it is, I must wait for the return of Gen[era]l Béthencourt, which may be today. I will get from him an order to return to

---

[1] *Life*, ii, 503, reads 'blockade'.   [2] Ibid. reads 'denunciations'.

Rouen, where I expect to find Gen[era]l Kilmaine, and I shall then settle with him whether I shall go to Paris or not, at the same time that, if I were there, I scarcely know what I should have to offer or propose.

The pain which I feel, myself, at these unfortunate tidings is extremely augmented by the impression it seems to have made upon your spirits. You know great occasions demand great efforts, and certainly there are few more trying ones than those in which we find ourselves this day. Tell Matt to keep himself absolutely quiet, and to say or do nothing until we meet, which I expect may be in a very few days; do not, at the same time, say that you expect me. Adieu, dear Love, I cannot bear to write. I suppose my next will be from Rouen. God bless you all

J. Smith

Your old friend, Eyriès,[1] breakfasted with me this morning; he desires his respects to you.

À la Citoyenne Smith
Rue des Batailles, No. 29
À Chaillot
près Paris

To Adjutant-General Olivier Macoux Rivaud, 18 June 1798

T.C.D., Tone papers, MS 2050, f. 32[r]; Archives de la Guerre, B[5*].
Tone reports the situation as unchanged.

No. 11

30 Prairial an 6

Général,

Depuis ma dernière lettre, en datte du 28,[2] tout est ici toujours dans la même position. Je n'ai, en conséquence, rien de nouveau à vous annoncer.

Salut et fraternité,
J. Smith

Diary, 18 June 1798

T.C.D., Tone papers, MS 2049, ff 334[v]–336[r]; *Life*, ii, 503–05.

---

[1] Probably Jacques-Joseph Eyriès (1733 or 1734–98), captain of the port of Le Havre, 1796 (*Dict. biog. franç.*)   [2] Above, p. 296.

18 June 1798

The news I have received this morning, partly by the public prints, and partly by a letter[1] from my wife and brother, is of the last importance. As I suspected, the brave and unfortunate Fitzgerald[2] was meditating an attack on the capital, which was to have taken place a few days after that on which he was arrested. He is since dead in prison, of poison,[3] as it should seem, but whether taken voluntarily by himself, or administered by his enemies, does not appear. Be it as it may, his career is finished gloriously for himself, and whatever be the event, his memory will live for ever in the heart of every honest Irishman. He was a gallant fellow! For us who remain as yet, and who may perhaps soon follow him, the only way to lament his death is to endeavour to revenge it. Among his papers, it seems, were found the plan of the insurrection, the proclamation intended to be published and several others, by which those of the leaders of the people who have thus far escaped have been implicated and several of them seized; among other names I see Tom Braughall, Lawless,[4] son of Lord Cloncurry,[5] Curran,[6] son of the barrister, Chambers and P[atrick] Byrne, printers, with several others whom I cannot recollect. All this, including the death of the brave Fitzgerald, has, it appears, but accelerated matters. The insurrection has commenced formally in several counties in Leinster, more especially in Kildare and Wexford. The details in the French papers are exceedingly imperfect, but I see there have been several actions. At Monastereven, Naas, Clain and Prosperous, the three last immediately in my ancient neighbourhood, there have been skirmishes, generally, as is at first to be expected, to the advantage of the army; at Prosperous the Cork militia were surprised and defeated. The villains! to bear arms against their country! Kilcullen is burnt. At Carlow, 400 Irish, it is said, were killed; at Castledermot 50. In return in the Co. Wexford, where appears to be their principal force, they have defeated a party of 600 English, killed 300 men and the commandant, Colonel Walpole,[7] and taken 5

---

[1] *Life* reads 'letters' instead of 'a letter'. See Tone to Matilda Tone, 18 June 1798 (above, pp 300–01).

[2] Lord Edward Fitzgerald,

[3] *Life* omits 'of poison' and the words that follow as far as and including 'as it may'. Fitzgerald died, on 4 June, as a consequence of wounds sustained at his arrest on 19 May. The finding of the coroner's inquest was that 'two wounds inflicted on the right arm by two pistol balls found lodged near the scapula' caused an effusion on the chest and a fever which proved fatal. (R. R. Madden, *The United Irishmen*, 2nd ed. (1857–60), ii, 415–19, 435–7, 451–2, 458–9).

[4] Valentine Browne Lawless (1773–1853) joined United Irishmen; student at Middle Temple, 1795–8; arrested, 1798 and 1799; succeeded as 2nd Baron Cloncurry, 1799 (*Personal recollections . . . of Valentine, Lord Cloncurry* (Dublin, 1849); *D.N.B.*).

[5] Nicholas Lawless (1733–99), 1st Baron Cloncurry, landowner in Co. Kildare (G. E. C[okayne], *The complete peerage*, 2nd ed. by Vicary Gibbs et al. (13 vols, London, 1910–40), iii, 328–9).

[6] Richard Creagh Curran (1776?–1847), eldest son of John Philpot Curran; scholar of T.C.D., 1796; student at Middle Temple, 1797; called to the Irish bar, 1799 (W. H. Welply, 'Curran and his kinsfolk' in *Notes and Queries*, clxciv (1949), p. 384).

[7] Lambert Theodore Walpole (1757–98), aide-de-camp to Lord Camden, commanded about 400 men marching south to engage insurgents in Co. Wexford; his party was ambushed south of Gorey on 4 June and Walpole and many of the men were killed (*Burke's peerage* (1912), p. 1466; Thomas Pakenham *The year of liberty* (London, 1969), pp 181–2).

pieces of cannon; this victory, small as it is, will give the people courage and shew them that a red coat is no more invincible than a grey one. At Rathmines there has been an affair of cavalry, in which the Irish had the worst, and two of their leaders, named Ledwich and Keogh, were taken and, I presume, immediately executed.[1] I very much fear this last is Cornelius, eldest son to my friend John Keogh and a gallant lad;[2] if it be so, I shall regret him most sincerely, but how many other valuable lives will be sacrificed before the fortune of Ireland be decided? Doctor Esmond[3] and eight other gentlemen of my county have been hanged. At Nenagh the English whip the most respectable inhabitants in the open streets till their blood flows into the kennels. The atrocious barbarity of their conduct is only to be excelled by the folly of it; never yet was a rebellion (as they call it) quelled by such means. The 18,000 victims sacrificed by Alva[4] in the Low Countries in five years and on the scaffold did not prevent the establishment of the liberty of Holland. From the blood of every one of the martyrs of the liberty of Ireland will spring, I hope, thousands to revenge their fall. In all this confusion of events, there is one circumstance which looks well. The English government publish latterly no detailed accounts, but say, in general, that all goes well and that a few days will suffice to extinguish the *rebellion;* at the same time they are fortifying the Pigeon House,[5] in the harbour of Dublin, in order to secure a retreat for the government in case of the worst, which does not savor extremely of the immediate extinction of the rebellion. These are all the details I recollect, and they are of the last importance. What will the French government do in the present crisis? After all, their aid appears to me indispensable, for the Irish have no means but numbers and courage— powerful and indispensable instruments, it is true, but which after all require arms and ammunition, and I fear they are but poorly provided of either. They have an army of at least 60,000 disciplined troops to contend with, for, to their immortal disgrace and infamy, the militia and yeomanry of Ireland concur with the English tyrant[6] to rivet their country's chains and their own; and, to my great mortification, I see some of my old friends in the number, Griffith and his yeomen, for example, in the county Kildare,[7]

---

[1] It was reported that on 24 May a party of insurgents had been dispersed near Rathfarnham and their leaders Ledwich and Keogh captured, tried and hanged (*Faulkner's Dublin Journal*, 26, 29 May 1798). It is evident from other sources however that, while Ledwich, a yeoman, was captured by a posse of the 5th dragoons, tried by court martial as a deserter from the yeomanry and hanged, Keogh was sabred and his body removed on a wagon to Dublin, to Lower Castle Yard, where it revived; Keogh recovered, made a confession and was pardoned (Pakenham, *Year of liberty*, pp 113–14, 123–4; Nat. Arch. (Ire.), Rebellion papers, 620/52/156).

[2] In fact the Keogh who was captured was not a son of John Keogh but was Thomas Keogh, son of a Rathfarnham farmer.   [3] John Esmonde (see above, vol. I, p. 255, n. 2).

[4] Fernando Alvarez de Toledo, duke of Alva (1508–82).

[5] A block-house on South Bull (a sea-wall, jutting into Dublin Bay).   [6] *Life* omits 'tyrant'.

[7] Richard Griffith of Millicent, Co. Kildare, commanded the Clane yeomanry cavalry corps.

and Plunkett in the House of Commons.[1] They may be sorry yet for this base prostitution of their character and talents. If ever the day of retribution arrives, as arrive I think it must, they will fall unpitied victims, and thousands of other parricides like them, to the just fury of the people, which it will be impossible to restrain.[2]

What must I do now? General Béthencourt returns this evening. The English seem to have given up all idea of an attack on this port, so I may go with honor. I will apply for an order to join Gen[era]l Kilmain[e] at Rouen, and when I am there, we will see further.

Authorisation from General Antoine de Béthencourt, 18 June 1798

Tone (Dickason) papers.

Béthencourt authorises Tone to go to Rouen.

15ᵉ Div[ision] Militaire	République Française	[crest]	Obéissance aux Lois

Au Quartier-Général au Havre, *le* 30 Prairial,
an 6 *de la République Française, une & indivisible*

Le Général de Brigade Béthencourt, commandant dans les départements de la Seine Inf[érieu]re & de l'Eure, autorise l'Adjudant Général Smith & son adjoint à se rendre à Rouen près du général en chef de l'armée d'Angleterre.

le G[énér]al de B[riga]de
Béthencourt

From Adjutant-General Olivier Macoux Rivaud, 19 June 1798

Tone (Dickason) papers.

Rivaud tells Tone that if he prefers to remain at Le Havre rather than Rouen he may do so.

ARMÉE
D'ANGLETERRE

ÉTAT-MAJOR GÉNÉRAL
Au Quartier général à Rouen, *le*
1ᵉʳ Messidor, *an* 6 *de le République
Française, une et indivisible*

---

[1] In the Irish house of commons on 22 May 1798, William Conyngham Plunket, when supporting an address to the lord lieutenant thanking him for the measures he had taken to suppress rebellion, declared he was ready to meet treason in the field and would ever resist it in parliament (*Faulkner's Dublin Journal*, 24 May 1798).   [2] In the MS the ink changes at this point.

L'Adjudant Général
Chef de l'État-Major de l'Armée

à l'adjud[ant] Général Smith au Havre

Le Général de Brigade Compère, mon cher Schmith, commandant au Havre les troupes qui dépendent de l'armée d'Angleterre, et, étant vous-même attaché à cette armée, vous devez être sous les ordres du général Compère ou de tout autre officier général de l'armée qui commandera dans cette partie.

S'il vous convient mieux de rester employé au Havre qu'à Rouen je vous y attacherai définitivement. Je pense même qu'il vous plaira mieux de servir sur un port de mer que dans l'intérieur; ce service doit être plus relatif à vos goûts et à vos connoissances.

Je vous remercie, mon cher camarade, de l'exactitude avec laquelle vous m'avez instruit de ce qui s'est passé au Havre depuis que vous y êtes. Je vous prie de recevoir l'assurance de mon estime et de mon attachement.

Salut et amitié
Rivaud

Port-Payé
Arm[ée] d'Angleterre.
Au citoyen
Schmit, adjud[ant] g[énéra]l
au quartier général à Rouen
de l'armée d'Angleterre[1]

Diary, 19–30 June 1798

T.C.D., Tone papers, MS 2049, ff 336ʳ–340ʳ; *Life*, ii, 505–10.

19 June 1798

This morning, at 5, set off for Rouen, having taken leave of Gen[era]l Béthencourt last night, who loaded me with civilities. Arrived at 5 in the evening and met General Rivaud. Gen[era]l Kilmaine is also arrived, so I shall see him tomorrow. Gen[era]l Grouchy, who commanded the *armée expéditionnaire* in Bantry Bay, as is already consigned in my journals of that period,[2] and to whom I was much attached, is also here. I had written him a letter[3] two days ago from Havre to felicitate him on his appointment to the command of the cavalry of the Army of England. Rivaud tells me he was delighted to hear I was employed, and intended to apply for me to be his

---

[1] In the MS this line and the previous one are added after 'au Havre', which is struck through. Tone moved from Le Havre to Rouen on the day the letter was written.
[2] Above, vol. II, pp 401 et seq.   [3] Above, pp 296–7.

adjudant general, of which I am very glad, for a variety of reasons. I will call on him, and on the general-in-chief, tomorrow morning. No news yet of the Toulon expedition! It is inconceivable!

20 June 1798

Today is my birthday. I am thirty-five years of age. More than half the career of my life is finished, and how little have I yet been able to do! Well, it has not been at least for want of inclination and, I may add, of effort. I had hopes two years ago that at the period I write this my debt to my country would have been discharged, and the fate of Ireland settled for good or evil. Today it is more uncertain than ever. I think, however, I may safely say thus far, I have neglected no step to which my duty called me. In that conduct I will persist to the last.

Called this morning on Gen[era]l Grouchy. I find him full of ardour for our business. He has read all the details, and talks of going to Paris in two or three days to press the Directory on that topic. His idea is to try an embarkation aboard the corvettes and privateers of Nantes, on which he thinks at least 3,000 men with 20,000 fusils[1] can be stowed, and he speaks as if he meant to apply for the command of this little armament. What would I not give that he should succeed in the application! I endeavoured once to be of service to Gen[era]l Grouchy when I saw him unjustly misrepresented after our return from Bantry Bay, and he does not seem to have forgotten it, for nothing could be more friendly & affectionate than his reception of me today. We talked over the last expedition. He said he has shed tears of rage and vexation fifty times since at the recollection of the opportunity of which he had been deprived, and there was one thing which he never would pardon in himself, that he did not seize Bouvet by the collar and throw him overboard the moment he attempted to raise a difficulty as to the landing.[2] He also mentioned his intention to apply for me to be his adjutant general, of which I am very glad, and he added that, as he believed he would have the command of the 4th division of the Army of England (besides his command of the cavalry) in which Nantes was included, in case the government relished his offer, we would be at hand to execute our plan, making at the same time a great parade at Brest and elsewhere to divert the attention of the enemy. In short, he shews the same zeal and ardour in our cause that I had occasion to remark in him during the late expedition, and I look upon it as a very fortunate circumstance for me to have the advantage to be attached to him. From Gen[era]l Grouchy, I went to visit the General in chief, Kilmaine, and mentioned to him that under the

---

[1] In *Life* ii, 506, 'muskets' is substituted for 'fusils'.

[2] Admiral Bouvet had commanded the squadron that entered Bantry Bay on 21 Dec. 1796, Grouchy having the military command. Heavy weather made landing difficult but Grouchy was for making an attempt. On the evening of the 25th, Bouvet unexpectedly put out to sea on board his frigate, the *Immortalité*, taking Grouchy with him and leaving behind fourteen other vessels including Tone's, the *Indomptable*. See Tone's diaries for 21–26 Dec. 1796 (above, vol. II, pp 419–20, 422–5, 427–32).

circumstances, especially as there was no appearance of any event at Havre, I had thought it my duty to return near him to receive his orders. He said I did very well, but he was sorry at the same time to tell me that he was much afraid the government would do nothing, and he read me an extract from a letter written by the minister of the marine himself,[1] and which he had received but that very morning, mentioning that in consequence of the great superiority of the naval force of the enemy, and the difficulty of escaping from any of the ports during the fine season the Directory were determined to *adjourn* the measure until a more favorable occasion. I lost my temper at this and told him that if the affair was adjourned, it was lost, the present crisis must be seized, or it would be too late; that I could hardly hope the Irish, totally unprovided as they were of all that was indispensable for carrying on a war, could long hold out against the resources of England, especially if they saw France make no effort whatsoever to assist them; that thus far they had been devoted to the cause of France, for which, if they had not been able to do much, at least they had sufficiently suffered, but who could say, or expect that this attachment would continue, if in the present great crisis they saw themselves abandoned to their own resources; that *now* was the moment to assist them—in three months it might be too late, and the forces which might be then sent, if the Irish were overpowered in the meantime, would find themselves unsupported and would in their turn be overpowered by the English. Gen[era]l Kilmaine answered that he saw all that as well as I did, but what could he do? He had pressed the Directory again and again on the subject, but they were afraid to incur the charge of sacrificing a handful of the troops of the republic, and would not try the enterprise except on a grand scale. He then shewed me two different plans he had prepared, the first for an embarkment of 17,500 men, the second for about 9,500, both of which he had sent by his aid-de-camp to Paris, and that he expected his return. I answer'd I should be heartily glad that either one or the other were adopted, but that I saw infinite difficulties in the way, and that I had always been of opinion that 5,000 men that could be sent were better than 50,000 that could not. I added that one demi-brigade of light infantry, with two or three companies of light artillery, at this moment, might be better than 20,000 men in six months. He shook his head and replied he was morally certain the Directory would attempt nothing on so small a scale. He then gave me the French papers, and after settling to dine with him, I took my leave.

I see in the papers, first of all the safe arrival of my friend General Hédouville at St Domingo, of which I am sincerely glad, for I shall never forget his kindness to me on my return to Paris after the death of Gen[era]l Hoche. Poor Hoche! It is now that we feel the loss of his friendship and influence! If he were alive, he would be in Ireland in a month, if he went with only his *état-major* in a fishing boat. I fear we shall not, after all, easily

[1] Bruix.

meet with his fellow. I see likewise that my friend Daendels is returned in triumph to the Hague, where he has smashed the Dutch Directory like a pipe stalk, dissolved the government and framed a new one, at the head of which he is himself, all this certainly with the approbation of the French government, and, as it appears, with that of the Dutch people also.[1] Charles de la Croix, who was the support of the late Dutch Directory, is recalled and Gen[era]l Joubert, who was of the opposite party, continues in the command of the French troops in Holland. I do not see my way in all this; however, I have the best opinion of Daendels, and, to say the truth, my anxiety for Ireland at this moment leaves me very little leisure or inclination to think of the politics of other countries. Quigley has been executed, and died like a hero. If ever I reach Ireland and that we establish our liberty, I will be the first to propose a monument to his memory; his conduct at the hour of his death clears everything.

> —— Nothing in his life
> Became him like the leaving of it.[2]

Poor Pamela.[3] She is in London, which she has been ordered to quit in three days. The night of her husband's arrestation,[4] she was taken in labour and—— will it be believed hereafter?——not one physician could be found in Dublin who would be hardy enough to deliver her![5] The villains! The pusillan[im]ous and barbarous scoundrels! It was a lady, who was not even her acquaintance, who assisted her in her peril. I do not think in the annals of mankind there is a parallel instance of inhumanity. She is said to be inconsolable for the death of Fitzgerald. I well believe it. Beautiful and unfortunate creature! Well, if Ireland triumphs, you shall have your full share of the victory and the vengeance.[6]

There is also, under the article Waterford, the 2nd of June, an article which gives me the highest satisfaction inasmuch as it proves to me that notwithstanding the death, exil[e] and arrestation of so many of the leaders of the Irish, enough are still at large to conduct their affairs and to give them a consistance, which I was afraid they would have wanted. It is an extract from a proclamation of the Supreme Committee, as it is called in the French papers, consisting of three articles. The first invites all Irishmen absent from their native country to return instantly, or, if that be impossible, to transmit all succour in their power, whether in money or otherwise, in order to assist

---

[1] See above, p. 272, n. 3.   [2] *Macbeth*, I, iv.   [3] Wife of Lord Edward Fitzgerald.
[4] He was arrested on 19 May 1798.
[5] According to the *Bien Informé*, the terror in Dublin was so great that no midwife was prepared to attend to Lady Edward 'et qu'une lady fut obligée de lui en servir' (*Bien Informé*, 27 prairial an 6). Thomas Moore in his *Life and death of Lord Edward Fitzgerald* (London, 1828) does not mention this story. Lady Sarah Napier, writing to Lady Sophie Fitzgerald on 24 Apr. 1798, a few days after the birth of Pamela Fitzgerald's child, stated that, after the arrest of Lord Edward Fitzgerald, Lady Moira, 'who has acted like a mother', sat with Pamela and that the doctor was 'our old Dr Melly, a famous good surgeon and midwife in a second line of life' who 'showed the greatest skill and attention' (Gerald Campbell, *Edward and Pamela Fitzgerald* (London, 1904), p. 148).
[6] Ink changes.

their countrymen to throw off the yoke of English tyranny. The second enjoins all Irishmen now in the British service to quit it instantly under pain of forfeiting their rights as Irish citizens; all Irish now in the British service and employed in Ireland who shall be taken with arms in their hands to be shot instantly. The third is a solemn promise to recompense all, whether soldiers or seamen, who abandon the enemy and join the standard of their country; all ships brought in to be the property of the captors, and preference to be given in the distribution of the national property to those who shall act in conformity to the present proclamation.[1] These three articles are of the highest importance, the more so as they prove to me the existence of something like a regular authority among the Irish. It is curious enough that they are contained almost *verbatim* in the memorial[2] I delivered to the Executive Directory above two years since. I am anxious to see the effect this will produce. It is later in date than any Irish news I have yet seen. The Militia have thus far, as well as the Yeomanry, to their eternal degradation, supported the enemy. If the Irish can hold out until the winter, I have every reason to hope the French will assist them, and effectually. All I dread is that they may be overpowered before that time. What a state my mind is in at this moment! In all this business I do not see one syllable regarding the North, which astonishes me more than I can express. Are they afraid? Have they changed their opinions? What can be the cause of their passive submission at this moment, so little suited to their former zeal and activity? I remember what Digges said to Russell and me five or six years ago: 'If ever the South is roused, I would rather have one Southern than twenty Northerns'.[3] Digges was a rascal, but he was a man of great sense and observation;[4] he was an American and had no local or provincial prejudices. Was he right in his opinion? A very little time will let us see that. If it should prove so, what a mortification for me, who have so long looked up with admiration to the North, and especially to Belfast! It cannot be that they have changed their principles; it must be that circumstances render all exertion on their part as yet *impossible*.

30 June 1798

Having determined to set off for Paris in consequence of the late news from Ireland, I got leave of absence for a fortnight from Gen[era]l Kilmaine and arrived on the [   ].[5] My adjoint, Citizen Favery, called on me the next morning to let me know[6] that the Minister at War had dispatched an order for me to

---

[1] According to the *Moniteur*, 20 June 1798, 'the supreme committee of the United Irishmen' had issued a proclamation inviting Irishmen abroad to return to Ireland at least to send help to the Irish patriots. All Irishmen in the British services were told to leave them at once. If they joined the Irish cause they would be well rewarded.

[2] Tone cues here a footnote reading 'Vide Second Mem[oria]l articles 2nd, 3d and 4th, page 22 and 23'. The 'Second memorial' is given above (vol. II, pp 88–97).

[3] See Diary for 19 Oct. 1791 (above, vol. I, p. 141).   [4] *Life* omits 'was a rascal but he'.

[5] In the MS the ink changes after 'Kilmaine' and the date is blank.

[6] In *Life* ii, 510, the preceding reads: 'the next morning after my arrival to inform me'.

come to Paris in all haste. I waited in consquence on the minister, who told me it was the Minister of the Marine who had demanded me; he gave me at the same time a letter of introduction to the Minister of the Marine.[1]

Adjutant-General Olivier Macoux Rivaud to Barthélemy Louis Joseph Schérer, 28 June 1798

Archives de la Guerre, Tone dossier personnel.

Rivaud informs Schérer that Tone has been in Paris for five days.

ÉTAT-MAJOR GÉNÉRAL
Au Quartier général à Rouen, le 10 messidor
an 6 de la République française, une et indivisible

L'Adjudant Général Chef de l'État-Major de l'Armée
au ministre de la guerre à Paris
Citoyen ministre,

L'adjudant général James Smith à qui vous me dites, par votre lettre du 8 de ce mois, de donner ordre de se rendre à Paris en poste pour y recevoir [*word indecipherable*] de nouveaux ordres, est à Paris depuis cinq jours avec le général de division Grouchy.

J'espère qu'à la réception de cette lettre cet adjud[an]t général se sera présenté chez vous.

Salut et respect
Rivaud

From Admiral Eustache Bruix, 1 July 1798

Tone (Dickason) papers.

For the date of this letter, see below, p. 312.

Bruix states that animosity and brawling between Irish and English prisoners-of-war have made it essential to separate them. He asks Tone to go to camps at Laon, Orleans, Fontainebleau and Versailles in order to identify those wishing to be released 'to serve the cause of freedom', who should then be escorted to Brest.

LIBERTÉ [*crest*] *ÉGALITÉ*

---

[1] The Diary ends here. William Tone adds 'Caetera desunt' (*Life*, ii, 510). In the MS the remaining two-thirds of folio 340ʳ and the whole of folio 340ᵛ are blank.

3ᵉ Division
Bureau des   *Paris, le* [13] Messidor *an* 6ᵉ
Prisonniers de   *de la République une et indivisible*
Guerre

Le Ministre de la Marine et des Colonies
  Au C[itoy]en Smith, Adjudant Général

L'animosité et la haine qui existent entre les Irlandais attachés au parti patriote et les Anglais s'étant développées particulièrement dans les dépôts où les prisonniers de guerre des deux nations sont renfermés, et les rixes qui en ont été la suite, notamment dans le dépôt d'Orléans, pouvant prendre de jour en jour un caractère plus grave, il a paru essentiel de séparer des prisonniers anglais tous ceux qui par leurs opinions politiques seraient exposés à la fureur des autres.

J'ai, en conséquence, cru ne pouvoir mieux placer ma confiance, Citoyen, qu'en vous pour seconder à cet égard les vues du Gouvernement. Je vous invite donc à vous rendre de suite dans le Dépôt de Laon où vous trouverez le C[itoy]en Macdonagh,[1] commandant de ce dépôt, préparé à s'entendre avec vous, cette opération ayant déjà été entamée par lui. Si vous pensez que sa présence puisse vous être nécessaire dans les trois autres dépôts d'Orléans, de Fontainebleau et de Versailles, où vous vous rendrez ensuite, vous êtes autorisé à vous faire accompagner par lui. Vous serez porteur d'ordres particuliers pour les commissaires du Directoire Exécutif, et pour ceux des guerres avec lesquels vous vous entendrez sur les moyens les plus prompts et les plus sûrs de reconnaître les individus irlandais ou autres qui désireront être mis à portée de servir la cause de la liberté. Vous vous assurerez de leur voeu par les questions que vous leur ferez, et déclarerez à ceux que vous aurez jugés susceptibles de cette faveur que l'intention du Gouvernement est de briser leurs chaînes, et de les appeler à partager les travaux de leurs compatriotes. Vous leur annoncerez qu'ils jouiront jusqu'à leur retour dans leur pays, et ce sans restriction, de tous les avantages accordés aux marins français. En conséquence vous vous concerterez avec les commissaires de guerre pour faire expédier sur le champ ces prisonniers sur le port de Brest, avec escorte de Gendarmerie de brigade en brigade. Si cette mesure paraissait leur répugner, vous leur feriez sentir que les moyens de surveillance employés à leur égard pendant la route ont bien moins pour objet la crainte de leur évasion que leur propre sûreté. Au surplus ceux d'entre ces hommes en qui vous reconnaîtrez le plus d'ascendant sur leurs camarades, et dont le patriotisme sera le plus prononcé, seront désignés par vous pour diriger la conduite des autres et en répondre dans le cas où vous penseriez que l'appareil de la force fût superflu et dangéreux.

                                       E. Bruix

---

[1] Charles MacDonagh, sometime an officer in Berwick's regiment, was stationed at St Omer in Nov. 1796 (Archives de la Guerre, dossier personnel).

[Marginal note opposite first paragraph]:

Pour se rendre de suite dans les dépôts des prisonniers de guerre à l'effet d'en distinguer ceux des Irlandais qui désireront d'être mis à portée de servir la cause de la liberté.

From Admiral Eustache Bruix,
3 July 1798

> Tone (Dickason) papers.
>
> Bruix orders Tone to go without delay to Laon and other places as instructed in his letter of 1 July (above).

3ᵉ Division
Bureau des
Prisonniers de
Guerre

LIBERTÉ [crest] ÉGALITÉ

Paris, le 15 Messidor *an* 6ᵉ
de la République une et indivisible

Le Ministre de la Marine et des Colonies
Au Citoyen Smith, Adjudant Général

Vous voudrez bien, Citoyen, vous rendre, sans délai, dans les communes de Laon, Versailles, Fontainebleau et Orléans pour les objets de service détaillés dans ma lettre du 13 de ce mois.[1]

E. Bruix

From General Barthélemi Louis Joseph Schérer,
15 July 1798

> Tone (Dickason) papers.
>
> Schérer orders Tone to go straightaway to Brest.

LIBERTÉ [crest] *ÉGALITÉ*

Paris, le 27 Messidor *an* 6ᵉ
de la République française,
une et indivisible

---

[1] Above. Whether Tone did tour the places mentioned has not been ascertained. About this time and certainly before the end of August, another Irishman, Nicholas Madgett, left Paris on a similar mission; according to an informant of the British government who was on one of the expeditions to Ireland, 'he set out for Orleans to tamper with the Irish prisoners there in order to get them to engage in the expedition on account of their knowledge both of the coast and of the country' (*Castlereagh corr.*, i, 398).

Bureau
des Off[ici]ers
G[énér]aux

Le Ministre de la Guerre,
    Au Citoyen James Smith, Adjudant Général employé à l'armée
d'Angleterre

Vous voudrez bien, Citoyen, à la réception de cette lettre, vous rendre sur
le champ à Brest pour être employé en votre grade. Vous y attendrez des
ordres ultérieurs.

Salut et fraternité
Schérer

To General Barthélemi Louis Joseph Schérer, 17 July 1798

McPeake papers; photocopy in P.R.O.N.I., T/3048/K/5.
This document is said to have been taken from a French archive.
Tone asks that the notification of command issued to him as James Smith
on 15 Jan. 1798 be sent to him as Theobald Wolfe Tone, 'my real name that
the difficult circumstances bringing me to France had forced me to disguise'.

Paris, le 29 Messidor, an 6ᵉ de la Rép[ubli]que

Au Ministre de la Guerre
Citoyen Ministre,
    À la veille d'aller seconder les efforts de mes concitoyens contre leurs
oppresseurs et jaloux de paraître au milieu d'eux avec un titre légal, je vous
prie de vouloir bien ordonner que les lettres de service d'*adjudant général* qui
m'ont été délivrées sous le nom de *James Smith* le 26 nivôse de cette année
me soient expédiées sous celui de *Theobald Wolfe Tone*, mon véritable nom
que les circonstances difficiles qui m'avaient amené en France m'avaient forcé
de déguiser.

Salut et Respect
J. Smith

[*Endorsed:*]

Bureau des Officiers Généraux

James Smith, Irlandais, adjudant général, demande que ses lettres de service
lui soient expédiées sous son véritable nom, *Theobald Wolfe Tone*.

General Barthélemi Louis Joseph Schérer to Admiral Eustache Bruix, 21 July 1798

Archives de la Guerre, Marine BB⁴ 123, f. 151.

Berthier, who writes on behalf of the minister of war, Schérer, states that as 'General James Smith' has asked to resume his real name, his letter of engagement has been addressed to him as 'Theobald Wolfe Tone alias James Smith' and requests that he be enrolled in this name on the list of officers of the staff to which he is attached.

> Paris, 3 Thermidor an 6 de la
> République Française, une et indivisible
> (reçu 3 therm[idor])

Le Ministre de la Guerre au Ministre de la Marine et des Colonies

L'Adjudant Général James Smith, Irlandais, destiné à l'expédition de Brest, ayant demandé, mon cher collègue, à reprendre son véritable nom, je vous préviens que je lui ai fait expédier sa lettre d'emploi sous celui de Théobald Wolffe Tone dit James Smith. Veuillez bien, je vous prie, l'inscrire sous ce nom sur la liste des officiers qui composent l'état-major auquel il est attaché.

> Salut et respect
> Berthier[1]

To Matilda Tone, 2 August 1798

Tone (Dickason) papers.

> Brest, ce 15 Thermidor, an 6

Dear Love,

I write you just one line to let you know that I arrived here last night, safe and sound. As yet I have seen nobody, of course I have no news to communicate, but I will write to you fully by the next courier. I am obliged to set off in a hurry to pay my respects to General Hardy,[2] so that I have time to say no more than that I am, Dear Love,

> Yours most truly
> J. S.

---

[1] Louis César Gabriel Berthier (1765–1819), director of the topographical department in the war office, 1798–1800 (*Dict. biog. franç.*).

[2] Jean Hardy (1762–1802) enlisted as a private, 1783; capt., 1792; chef de brigade, 1793; served with *armée d'Angleterre* from Jan. 1798; had military command of expedition to Lough Swilly, Aug–Nov. 1798; général de division, 1799 (Six, *Dict. des généraux & amiraux*).

I wrote to you from Rennes. Direct to me here *Poste restante*. Kiss the Babs for me *plusieurs fois*. There is a Postscript for you in Howard's best manner.[1] Service to Giauque.[2]

À la Citoyenne Smith
chez le Citoyen Chevalier,[3]
Rue des Batailles, No. 29
À Chaillot
près Paris

To Matilda Tone, 7 August 1798

Tone (Dickason) papers.

No. 3   Brest, ce 20 Thermidor, an 6

Dear Love,

Two days ago Hamilton, Maguire and Corbett[4] arrived here and delivered me your letter. I need not tell you the pleasure it gave me to see that you appeared in tolerable spirits. A day or two before I had received another of your letters which we thought had miscarried; it followed me from Havre, so now our correspondance is, as the French say, *au jour*. I wrote to you & Giauque[5] from Rennes on the 11th and to you from this place the 15th;[6] but I have not as yet had an answer, nor indeed did the time permit it.

I have not as yet one syllable of news for you. I see General Hardy every day, and I like him a great deal better on acquaintance than I expected. If we were at our destination, I have no doubt but we shall do very well together; in the meantime we are at work on divers proclamations and other *'inflammatory branches of learning'*.[7] We have likewise overhauled some ancient mischief, intended to be made use of eighteen months ago,[8] which we find still serviceable; so that it seems treason, like Anderson's pill, will *'keep good*

---

[1] Not found. 'Howard' was the *nom de guerre* of John Tennent.

[2] Probably Lewines.   [3] Not identified.

[4] Very probably Thomas Corbet (1773?–1804), who, with his brother William Corbet (1779–1842), arrived in France in 1798; he went on Hardy's expedition to Lough Swilly, his brother on Tandy's expedition to Rutland Island. Hamilton, Maguire and Corbet were, according to an informant of the British government who sailed with William Corbet, picked out by Tone to accompany him on the expedition to Lough Swilly. (R. R. Madden, *The United Irishmen*, 3rd ser. (Dublin, 1846), i, 15–62; *Castlereagh corr.*, i, 399).   [5] Jean Frédéric Giauque or Edward Lewines?

[6] Above.

[7] One of them, an address of General Hardy to the United Irishmen, is given below, pp 316–18. The words quoted are Mrs Malaprop's in Sheridan's *The rivals* (1775), I, ii.

[8] Tone's pamphlet, *An address to the people of Ireland on the present important crisis* (Brest, 1796). It is given above, vol. II, pp 375–92. A copy was later found on board the *Hoche*, the ship on which Tone sailed to Lough Swilly.

for years in any climate'.[1] I will take an opportunity to send you copies of all that, when God sends time.

I see in the papers that the business still goes on in Ireland, but the accounts are very mutilated and meagre. If Giauque[2] can come at any more detailed and authentic let him write to me the contents or at least let him communicate them to you.

I thank you a thousand times for your attention in sending the books and music. If I had a grain of gallantry in my composition I would tell you I should study both with a double interest on your account, but I believe you know me sufficiently to render all declarations of that kind unnecessary.

I shall be very uneasy until I hear from Mary, Matt and Arthur. Of course you will write to me the instant you learn anything concerning them.

I do not write to Giauque as you will shew him this of course. Tell him, from me, that Montecuculli,[3] in his maxims, lays down one principle which we here find, experimentally, to be true. He says in order to carry on war, three things are necessary; 1st *money;* 2d *money;* and 3d *money.* If Giauque will send us about 300,000#,[4] he will marvelously serve and oblige us.

I spend my time here stupidly enough and with so little incident of any kind that I have not even written, as yet, one line in my journal. A little time (I know not how little or how much) will probably give me some employment. In the mean while I am, dearest Love

> Yours ever and most truly
> J. Smith

I will send you in time and place the necessary details as to our force, destination, &c., &c., &c. Kiss the babies, always for me. Love to Maria; she is a good bab.

À la Citoyenne Smith
chez le citoyen Chevalier
Rue des Batailles, No. 29
À Chaillot
près Paris

Address of General Jean Hardy to the United Irishmen, 7 August 1798

The Dickason papers include A, a dated MS in French, B, a MS translation in English and C, a contemporary print of B (one folio sheet). There is

---

[1] Anderson's pill, 'left to posterity' by Patrick Anderson (d. 1635), physician to Charles I (*D.N.B.*), was advertised in the *Hibernian Journal*, 22 Mar. 1793, where it was described as 'highly useful in all disorders of the stomach and bowels'. [2] Probably Lewines.
[3] Raimondo Montecucculi (1609–80). He makes the observation Tone quotes in his *Memoirs* (first published 1703), bk I, ch. 2. [4] i.e. 300,000 livres.

also a copy of C in T.C.D., MS 2050, f. 36 (folio size) and f. 39 (octavo size). Version B has the following note at the head:

no. 460 $\begin{cases} \text{2000 in folicare} \\ \\ \text{2000 in 8°} \end{cases}$

Versions A and C are printed below. There is another copy, in English and in a hand resembling Tone's, formerly at Convoy House, Convoy, Co. Donegal, and now in the possession of Miss Anne Crookshank. It was probably seized after the capture of the *Hoche* off Lough Swilly in October 1798.

[Version A]

(Copie)   20 Thermidor, an 6, à Brest

Le Général commandant l'armée française en Irlande
aux Irlandais Unis

Irlandais!

Les persécutions que vous éprouvez de la part d'un gouvernement atrocement perfide ont excité des sentimens d'indignation et d'horreur dans l'âme des amis de l'humanité. Tous les hommes libres déplorent votre pénible situation en admirant votre constance. Vos cris plaintifs ont retenti dans toutes les parties du globe, mais votre cause est devenue particulièrement celle du peuple français. C'est pour vous donner de nouvelles preuves de son affectation, c'est pour seconder vos généreux efforts, que le Directoire Exécutif de la République Française m'envoie vers vous. Je n'aborde point votre île précédé de l'effroi, dans le dessein d'y porter le ravage et de vous dicter des lois. Compagnon et ami du brave et malheureux Hoche, je viens, marchant sur ses traces, remplir ses engagemens, et vous tendre une main, amie et secourable; je vous apporte des armes, des munitions, et les moyens de vous affranchir du joug barbare qui vous opprime.

Je vous présente mes braves compagnons. Ils ne connoissent que le chemin de l'honneur, et celui de la victoire. Vieillis dans l'art de vaincre les tyrans, sous quelque forme qu'ils se présentent, ils joindront leur courage au vôtre, ils mêleront leurs bayonettes à vos piques, et *l'Irlande sera libre pour toujours*!

Victimes infortunées du plus exécrable despotisme, vous qui gémissez dans les affreux cachots, creusés à chaque pas par la férocité du gouvernement anglais, ouvrez vos coeurs à l'espérance. Vos fers vont être brisés. Habitans malheureux, qui avez vu vos propriétés dévorées par les flammes, vos pertes vont être réparées.

Appaisez vous, mânes innocens de Fitzgerald, de Crosbie,[1] de Coigley, d'Orr,[2] d'Harvey![3] Votre sang, versé pour la cause sainte de la liberté,

---

[1] Edward William Crosbie (*c.* 1755–98), baronet; charged with treason; tried by court martial and executed in June 1798. His family vehemently denied that he was in any way implicated in the rebellion. (*An accurate and impartial narrative of the apprehension, trial and execution of Sir Edward William Crosbie, bart, . . .* (Bath, 1802); G.E.C [okayne], *Complete baronetage* (6 vols, Exeter, 1900–09), ii, 378).

[2] William Orr (1766–97), United Irishman; executed at Carrickfergus in Oct. 1797 for administering a treasonable oath to two soldiers (*D.N.B.*).   [3] Beauchamp Bagenal Harvey.

cimentera l'indépendance de votre patrie; il circule dans les veines de tous vos compatriotes et les *républicains unis* vont punir vos bourreaux.

(signé)
Hardy

[Version C]

LIBERTY, EQUALITY, FRATERNITY, UNION

*The General Commanding the French Army in
Ireland to the United Irishmen*

UNITED IRISHMEN!

The persecution which you experience on the part of a government atrociously perfidious has excited sentiments of indignation and horror in the breast of every friend of humanity. The lovers of liberty, while they admire your fortitude, deplore the situation to which you are reduced. The complaints of your suffering country are heard in all parts of the world, but your cause is become more particularly that of the French people. It is to give you new proofs of their affection, it is to second your generous efforts, that the Executive Directory of the French republic has sent me among you. I do not enter your country with hostile views, to spread terror and desolation around me; I come not to dictate the law. Companion and friend of the gallant and unfortunate Hoche, I follow scrupulously the line of conduct which he had chalked out; I come to fulfil his engagements, to offer you friendship and assistance, to bring you arms, ammunition and all the means necessary to break the barbarous yoke under which you groan.

I present to you my brave companions. They know no other road but that of honor and of victory. Long trained in the art of humbling tyrants, under whatever form they may present themselves, they will join their courage to yours, they will mix their bayonets with your pikes, and IRELAND SHALL BE FREE FOR EVER!

Unhappy victims of the most execrable despotism, you who groan in the hideous dungeons, where at every moment you are plunged by the ferocious cruelty of your English tyrants, let hope once more revisit your hearts. Your chains shall be broken.

Unfortunate inhabitants who have seen your houses, your properties, wrapped in flames by your pitiless enemies, your losses shall be repaired.

Rest in peace, gallant and unspotted spirits of Fitzgerald, of Crosbie, of Coigley, of Orr, of Harvey! Your blood, shed for the sacred cause of Liberty, shall cement the independance of Ireland; it circulates in the veins of all your countrymen, and the UNITED REPUBLICANS swear to punish your assassins.

Hardy

To Matilda Tone, 9 August 1798

Tone (Dickason) papers.

No. 4   Brest, ce 22 Thermidor, an 6

Dear Love,

I wrote to you ere yesterday, No. 3.[1] Today I have been made happy by your letter, No. 1, of the 16th. I am delighted with your calculations and accounts. There is *talk* here of three months' pay, but God knows the heart. If it arrives I shall be able to make you a remittance of, I know not yet how much. *'Here take five guineas to those warlike men, &c.'*[2]

That cruel Giauque,[3] not to write to me! His indolence is insufferable. I am anxious to learn about my arms, &c., of which I hear nothing. If they be not sent immediately, in all human probability they will come too late, and that will be a thousand pities.

I am glad to learn the arrival of Lawless,[4] as Corbet[5] gives me the best account of him. If you see him, present him my best regards. Tho' I have not the advantage to know him, I understand his exertions in our common cause demand every respect.

I shall most sincerely rejoice if my old and valuable friend Dick[6] reaches Paris in safety; him I am sure you will see and you will of course assure him of my sincere and unvarying esteem for him. His arrival will explain to you many facts which, I have no doubt, have been egregiously misrepresented.

Touching my *fits*, they are completely so; I am endeavouring to get them on board.[7] You would hardly believe that Corbet reproaches Maguire (to whom I have scarcely spoken) with being my creature. I am in consequence done with Mr Corbet. However, I take no notion to him, or any one. The others had probably the same opinion of him and with just as much reason. But this trash is not worth troubling you about.

For Mr Turner,[8] he is a lucky man. He has the secret of fern *seed:* he walks invisible.

---

[1] Above, pp 315–16.   [2] George Villiers, *The rehearsal* (1672), V, i.
[3] Jean Frédéric Giauque or Lewines?
[4] William Lawless (1772–1824), United Irishman; professor of anatomy and physiology at the Royal College of Surgeons in Ireland, 1794–9; in order to escape arrest he fled to France, 1798; entered French army; appointed captain in the Irish legion, 1803; lost a leg at Löwenberg, 1813; retired as *général de brigade* (*D.N.B.*; C. A. Cameron, *History of the Royal College of Surgeons in Ireland* (Dublin, 1886), p. 480).   [5] Thomas or William Corbet?
[6] Probably Richard McCormick, who left Ireland in Feb. 1798 to avoid arrest.
[7] Tone's meaning has not been determined. He earlier uses the word 'fit' of his landlord (see above, p. 235).   [8] Presumably Samuel Turner (see above, p. 294, n. 9).

Do not wait for my answers, but write when anything occurs. For Giauque,[1] I put no trust in him, but at least let him communicate what is necessary to you and do you let me know what is going forward.

If he, Lawless or Dick wish to write home, let them send me their letters directly. If I arrive safe I will forward or deliver them and, in all events, they shall not fall into the hands of the enemy.

There is at present a sort of stagnation in our affairs here, proceeding, I rather more than suspect, from want of money. However I understand we are moving heaven and earth and of course a short time will suffice to remove our difficulty. When I have anything worth while to communicate I will let you know. All I can tell you at present is that things are hoping 'an appearance'.

The reason why you did not find the map, at least one of the reasons, was that it was not in the box. Fayolle had the precaution to bring it with him, which showed more common sense than I gave him credit for. My other adjoint, Favory, is arrived today but he brings no news, having left Paris the 12th inst. I was in hopes he would have brought me the pistols but he had heard nothing about them.

Tell Giauque[2] that when everything is definitively settled here, I will write him a letter extremely official, in which I will communicate to him fully our designs, our force, our destination, *'Mr Nisby's opinion thereupon'*, &c., &c.[3] I will likewise enclose him copies of all papers, proclamations, &c., but as yet I cannot venture to do it for fear of accidents.

Adieu, my dearest Love. Kiss the babies for me a thousand times; take care of yourself and keep up your spirits. When this expedition is over I will stay with you always. *'I will, by the god of war!'*[4]

Once more, remember me affectionately to Giauque and Dick if he be arrived. Let Bab pick at her music. As for yourself (sings), *'Madam, you know my trade is war'* &c., &c.[5] Adieu, Life and soul.

Your own
J. Smith

One of these times, which are justly denominated *odd come shortly's*, I mean to change my name. You need not therefore be surprised if you receive a letter from me with a new signature.[6]

---

[1] Contrary to the distinction between the two Giauques Tone draws in letters to Mathew Tone on 18 and 23 Apr. and Matilda Tone on 22 Apr. (above, pp 237, 240, 243), this is probably not Jean Frédéric Giauque but Edward Lewines, as suggested in the next sentence and in the sentence below in which Tone states 'I will communicate to him fully our designs, our force, our destination'.

[2] Lewines.

[3] *Spectator*, no. 317 (4 Mar. 1712).   [4] Cf. John O'Keeffe, *Love in a camp* (1785), I, iii.

[5] Charles Dibdin, *Poor Vulcan* (1778), II, iii.

[6] Tone had informed the French authorities of his wish to revert to his original name; see Tone to Schérer, 17 July 1798 (above, p. 313).

À la Citoyenne Smith
chez le Citoyen Chevalier
Rue des Batailles, No. 29
À Chaillot
près Paris

To Matilda Tone, 14 August 1798

N.L.I., MS 36094/1; formerly in McPeake papers; facsimile in Richard Hayes,
Irish swordsmen of France (Dublin, 1941), p. 297.

ARMÉE   *ERIN GO BRAH!*
FRANÇAISE   *LIBERTÉ* [crest] *ÉGALITÉ*

> *Au Quartier général à* Brest
> *ce* 27 Thermidor an 6

L'ADJUDANT-GÉNÉRAL T. WOLFE TONE[1]
À sa bien aimée

Dearest Love,

This day, at twelve o'clock, we embark, but I do not yet know when we shall put to sea; probably it will not be long.

I send you by the diligence which leaves this the 29th a packet containing copies of all papers &c., some of which remain since our last expedition. You will likewise find one or two coins enclosed for the Bab. You will give a copy of each to Giauque,[2] *who has never written me one line*. I write to him however by this post: he will of course shew you my letter. Your packet ought to arrive the 5 or 6 Fructidor.

Touching money matters, I have not yet received a *sous*, and last night I was obliged to give my *last* five guineas to our countrymen here. I can shift better than they can. I hope to receive a month's pay today, but it will not be possible to remit you any part of it. You must therefore carry on the war as you can for three or four months, and before that is out we will see further. I write (in French) to Giauque on that head. I am mortified at not being able to send you a remittance but you know it is not my fault.

We embark about 3,000 men, with 12 pieces of artillery, and I judge about 20,000 stand of arms. We are enough, I trust, to do the business if we arrive safe.

With regard to myself personally I have every reason to be satisfied. I stand fair with the General[3] and my *camarades;* I am in excellent health and spirits; I have great confidence in the success of our enterprise, and, come what come may, at least I will do what is right.

---

[1] For the first time that is known, Tone is using his own headed notepaper, his rank and name being printed in capitals.   [2] i.e. Lewines.
[3] Hardy.

The time is so short that I must finish this. I will if possible write to you again, but if we should unexpectedly sail, my next will be, I hope, from Ireland. Adieu my dearest Life and soul. Kiss our babies for me always. I doat upon you all.

Yours ever and most truly
T. Wolfe Tone

To Matilda Tone, 19 August 1798

Tone (Dickason) papers.

No. 7

ERIN GO BRAH!
LIBERTÉ   [crest]   *ÉGALITÉ*

ARMÉE
FRANÇAISE

*Au Quartier général a*bord le vaisseau
le *Hoche*[1] à Brest *ce* 2 Fructidor *an* 6

L'ADJUDANT-GÉNÉRAL T. WOLFE TONE

À sa bonne amie

Dearest Love,

I wrote to [you] yesterday No. 6, and an hour after my letter was dispatched I received yours, No. 3. I had already got No. 1, but No. 2, which you tell me you confided to Lewines, has not yet reached me. More than one half of my last was taken up in scolding him, as well on my own account as on behalf of Simon, who complains, with some reason, that he has used him worse than a dog. But if I had been aware of the injury he had done me, in keeping back your letter, I should have added an extra half sheet of *vituperation*. He is downright insufferable on the score of indolence and inattention.[2]

Since my last, nothing new. We have been regaled this morning with a procession of above twenty sail of English men-of-war, which have been parading slowly before us. I suppose they thought our French blood would get up and that we would turn out in a rage and fight them, but we know a trick worth two of that. They may parade and be hanged. When the time comes they shall hear of us. *En attendant* we make it out as well as we can, at anchor in the Road.

I forget to tell you our commodore aboard whose vessel the *état-major* is embarked is named Bompard.[3] He distinguished himself very much at the

---

[1] The *Hoche*, 74 guns, took part in the Bantry Bay expedition in 1796, when it was called *Le Pégase*; it was on the stocks at Toulon in 1793 when the port was controlled by the British fleet (*Saunders' News Letter*, 2, 19 Nov. 1798; see also above vol. II, p. 418).

[2] Miles Byrne states that visiting Lewines two days before he died he 'found him reading Wolfe Tone's memoirs in his sick bed' and repeatedly saying 'what a true Irishman Tone was!' (Miles Byrne, *Memoirs* (Paris, 1863), iii, 20–21).

[3] Jean Baptiste François Bompard (1757–*fl.*1834), commissioned in the navy before the revolution; captain, 1793; chef de division, 1796; commanded *Hoche* in expedition to Lough Swilly, 1798 (*Dict. biog. franç.*).

breaking out of the war in an action which he fought off Sandy Hook with the Boston frigate. The English captain, Courtenay,[1] sent him a challenge, which was filed in the Coffee House at New York, and cost him his sweet life, as he was killed in the action. I like Bompard very well; he is a smart little man and puts me a good deal in mind of Griffith of Millicent.

My adjoint, Citizen Favory, took a thought the very day we got the order to go on board, and respectfully declined embarking. In consequence, after telling him a piece of my mind, we parted on very indifferent terms, and I have taken James Dalton in his place. If Lewines sees General Clarke he may tell him this piece of news. Dalton is a very good lad and in the main I believe I have gained by the exchange.

To recompense me for the loss of my adjoint, I have taken unto myself a servant named Louis with whom I am well pleased. He is very civil and quiet and ties my hair, &c., so that I am not badly off. He has already been at sea, which will be convenient on our voyage.

I wish you had mentioned the date of Matt's letter from Rochefort.[2] Cap[tai]n Bompard assures me the squadron sailed the 17th, which can hardly be, according to the calculations I have made, as you tell me you received it the 25th, and allowing six days for the post it must have been written the 19th.[3] But I have often had occasion to remark that ladies never trouble their heads about dates, which are notwithstanding sometimes, at least, convenient; but I scorn invidious remarks.

Matt's name brings to my mind the luminous project mentioned by Lewines to reimburse you the sum, to wit £15, as I remember, advanced to him on his departure. I am not quite certain as to the etiquette, but I leave it to Lewines himself. In all events, let him add the five guineas advanced [by?] him to the United Irishmen to the ten I disbursed at Paris on the same account; that is to say, if Matt's money is to be included, he will have to pay you £30, but if not, the sum will be reduced to £15. I wish you had that same.

It gives me sincere pleasure to hear of Mary's recovery. Write to her to that effect in your next letter.

I hope Arthur[4] may arrive speedily. I give full power to Lewines to use all his influence, as well with De Winter as with Daendels and the Dutch government, in his behalf. Do you write a friendly letter to Jack Ahern,[5] and

---

[1] William Augustus Courtney (d. 1793), commanding *Boston*, 32 guns, was killed in engagement with *Embuscade*, 36, commanded by Bompard (William James, *Naval history of Great Britain* (6 vols, London, 1826), i, 142–7).

[2] Mathew Tone was a member of the thousand-strong force commanded by Humbert which left Rochefort on the west coast of France on 6 Aug. 1798 and landed in Killala Bay on the west coast of Ireland on 22 Aug.

[3] These dates are in the month of Thermidor in the French republican calendar. According to the Gregorian calendar they are 4, 12 and 6 Aug. respectively. It appears from this that Mathew Tone's letter was written on the day he sailed.   [4] Arthur Tone.

[5] Probably the John Ahearn who died at Metz in 1806 (see above, vol. II, p. 150, n. 2).

tell him the catastrophe of his pin. He will be better pleased with a letter from you than from me. Recommend Arthur to his friendship and remember me to him affectionately.

Take care of my letter from the Minister at War, and lay it with the other papers.

I am sorry the North appears to have done a *cochonnerie* in the business, which I am pretty clear they have.[1] It is however some comfort that our friend Simms is out of the scrape.[2] Under the circumstances I am glad the country are coming in, as you mention; if we win I do not think it will materially impede our progress, and if we do not, it may save the poor fellows' lives. I see citizen M[   ][3] gave us a spice of comfort in his last harangue. *'La belliqueuse Irlande!'*—that has a lofty sound! I hope in time and place we may justify his good opinion.

I feel precisely as you do with regard to our separation. I have a sort of a blind confidence, which sustains me, I know not how, nor why, but, I am sure, one way or other we shall succeed. I do not for this reason write sentiments to you, nor affect an unhappiness that I do not feel. The greatest satisfaction I can enjoy, in your absence, is to be assured that you do not make yourself miserable on that account. The true and the best way, and [con]sequently the way you have adopted, to shew your love for me is by taking care of our babies in my absence. Adieu, Dear Love, I doat on you and them. My love to Maria, and Will, with his hair *à la Titus*, and Sir Fant. Adieu, my life and soul.

T. W. Tone

[*On the back*]:

I advise Bab to play her harpischord *d'une belle manière*, and to dance *d'une furieuse force*. If she does not it will be worse for her when we meet.

À la Citoyenne Smith
chez le Citoyen Chevalier
Rue des Batailles, No. 29
À Chaillot
près Paris

---

[1] The insurrection in Antrim and Down lasted for only one week, from 7 to 13 June.

[2] Robert Simms resigned on 1 June as adjutant-general of the United Irishmen in Antrim (*Commons' jn. Ire.*, xvii (1798), p. dccclxvii; Charles Dickson, *Revolt in the north* (Dublin, 1960), pp 204–5).

[3] This name, which begins with the letter M, has not been deciphered. The person referred to could be Michel Mathieu Lecointe-Puyraveau (1764–1827) who on 12 Aug. 1798, in a speech delivered in the Conseil des Anciens, assured the Irish that they would not be abandoned, that the blood of Fitzgerald and O'Connor would be revenged and Ireland freed (*Procès-verbal des séances du Conseil des Anciens*, Thermidor an 6, p. 182).

To Matilda Tone, 22 August 1798

Tone (Dickason) papers.

No. 9

ARMÉE
FRANÇAISE

ERIN GO BRAH
LIBERTÉ   [crest]   *ÉGALITÉ*

*Au quartier général a*bord le vaisseau le Hoche à Brest
ce 5 fructidor *an* 6

L'ADJUDANT GÉNÉRAL T. WOLFE TONE

À son épouse

Dear Love,

I am prime of correspondents, this is No. 9. No. 8 I dispatched yesterday with an account of our cruise, which lasted exactly fourteen hours. At night I received yours, No. 4, with Arthur's enclosed. I need not say what pleasure it gave me. Nevertheless I was better pleased with your last because it was evidently written in better spirits. Why should you think it incumbent on you to be miserable in my absence? It is the last proof of affection which I wish to receive at your hands. I am not miserable in yours, and yet I do not love you the less because of that; and I should be sorry most sincerely that you should suffer more than me. I have already wisely observed that in our separation the true way to testify our affection for each other is for me, on my part, to endeavour to distinguish myself, for your sake, and for you, on yours, to take great care of our dearest babies. I believe that is nearly as sincere and as respectable a method as many others which appear more sentimental, a style for which neither you nor I have inclination nor talents. Love me always but never be unhappy, for unhappiness is a great *fit*.

I am exceedingly pleased with poor Arthur's letter, and I beg of Giauque[1] to try his and my interest with De Winter to place him, if possible, in the Dutch navy. With regard to Ahern, I have already charged you with that correspondance. I am sure he will take all possible care of Arthur if he arrives at the Hague. On reflection I will send, by the next courier, for it is too late for today, two letters on the subject for Daendels and De Winter, which you and Lewines will read together, and either suppress or forward, as you see good.

---

[1] He seems to mean Lewines, who spent some time at the Hague as United Irish envoy. Lewines is mentioned in the following sentence in the same context.

Tell Lewines I honor our friend Braughall for his unbending integrity. I know very well that when his conscience is satisfied no human force will make him swerve from the line of conduct which he has once adopted. It is with the sincerest pleasure that I hear of this additional proof of his honesty and his courage. I think my old masters of the Committee[1] will turn out well, if ever the occasion presents itself. I have a secret leaning to that side, which is not diminished by Mr Lawless's report of the state of things.

What are the terms which the prisoners have agreed to?[2] Your letter, No. 2, which I presume contained the news, and which you understand to having *miscarried*, as might be expected. As for him,[3] *I have not yet received one line of his writing*; but I am weary of complaining, so I shall say no more on that score. I do not know whether the letter I sent him is to his mind, but if not, as I have a copy, let him suggest any alteration he would wish made and I will send him another accordingly, at the same time that I think he much overrated the value of my testimony; however, such as it is, he deserves it and has a right to it notwithstanding the neglect he has shewn me since we parted. Of the pistols, I have not yet heard anything, but I do not accuse him of that. I wish I had them, however——

I perceive your eldest son is assuming that ascendancy over you which is his birthright, for all your anecdotes are about him. I am delighted with them. I am in hopes he will turn out well. Take care however, at the same time, of his *vilain cadet*. Honestly speaking, does Frank know his four and twenty letters? I do not think he promises to shine as much, in the literary world, as Will, but in return, as you have well remarked, he will tye his cravat a great deal better, and one cannot have all the good things of this life together. How is the Bab? Does she pick at her music? Let her mind the time, '*One, two, three, four,—one, two, three, four.*' She is a darling Bab, and I doat on her.

I will not burn your letter, because it is not a *fit*, whatever you may think. '*Never came a fit on board the Hoche in the likeness of a letter from your grace.*'[4] I am not yet in Christian charity with Lewines for that which he has made me lose.

Adieu, dear Love; remember me kindly to Howard.[5] What have you done with Wilkins?[6] If he is with you, assure him of my sincere esteem. Remember me always to Mary, when you write. Take great care of yourself and the Babies, and love me always.

'*Thine and my poor country's ever*[7]

T. W. Tone

---

[1] i.e. the Catholic Committee.

[2] Towards the close of July 1798 an agreement was entered into between the state prisoners in Dublin and the government. It provided that if William Byrne and Oliver Bond, who had been sentenced to death for high treason, were pardoned and Samuel Neilson was not brought to trial, the prisoners would give the fullest information, without implicating individuals and accept perpetual banishment (*Correspondence of Charles, first marquis Cornwallis*, ed. Charles Ross (3 vols, London, 1859), ii, 372–8). [3] i.e. Lewines.

[4] Literary quotation?   [5] i.e. Tennent.   [6] i.e. Wilson.   [7] *Macbeth*, IV, iii.

There is no date to Arthur's letter; the dog! he writes like *a lady*. Make a little book and whenever you write, enter the date and the no. I do so and find it very convenient.

À la citoyenne Smith
chez le citoyen Chevalier
Rue des Batailles N°. 29
À Chaillot
près Paris

Mathew Tone to Matilda Tone and others, 22, 23 August 1798

T.C.D., Sirr papers, MS 872, ff 147ᵛ–148ᵛ; P.R.O., London, PC 1/44/A/155; *Report on the manuscripts of J. B. Fortescue* (H.M.C., London, 1905), iv, 329–30.

All three versions contain additional wording and so none can be an exact transcription of the original. The T.C.D. version, which is printed by Bulmer Hobson (*The letters of Wolfe Tone* (Dublin, [1920]), pp 127–30), has been followed and significant variants in the P.R.O. version noted.

> Donegal Bay
> 5 Fructidor
> 6 o'clock, morning

Dear Friend[s] Giauque and Matty,[1]

The day I embarked at Rochelle, I wrote to you.[2] In that letter I gave you an account of our force, but, as it might have miscarried, I shall repeat its contents. We are nine hundred infantry and about one hundred chasseurs and can[n]oniers, with twenty or thirty officers *à la suite*.[3] We have, besides, three field pieces, 6,000 stand of arms, and a very adequate quantity of ammunition. I should also mention a large quantity of helmets and odd clothing of various colours which the General[4] found in the magazines at Rochelle.[5] Pat will look droll[6] in a helmet without any corresponding articles of dress.

To come to our actual situation. Yesterday morning we arrived at the mouth of the bay after a passage of thirteen days without seeing anything. We stood up toward Killibegs Harbour with a light breeze and got within two[7] hours' sail of our landing place when the wind died away. This is damned unlucky, as it has entirely deprived [us][8] of the advantage of surprise. The wind springing up contrary in the evening, we stood right across the

---

[1] P.R.O. MS reads 'Dear Mattey & Friend Giauque'. Whether this Giauque is Jean Frédéric Giauque or Edward Lewines is unclear.
[2] Probably the letter referred to by Tone in writing to his wife on 19 Aug. (see above, p. 323).
[3] P.R.O. MS adds 'making in all one thousand & thirty men'.   [4] Humbert.
[5] P.R.O. MS reads 'La Rochelle'.   [6] P.R.O. MS reads 'very drole'.
[7] P.R.O. MS reads 'six'.   [8] P.R.O. MS reads 'robbed us'.

bay to the County Mayo,[1] where Killala, I believe, affords a place proper to debark.

Night and the want of a pilot obliges us to anchor in the middle of the bay. This morning, we are under way again and endeavouring to get into Killala, the wind not very good. I refer you to the map, where you will see that we are both in sight of Killibegs and Killala Bays without the power of entering either——.[2] Pause here, my friends, and pay a compliment to my patience which suffers me to write in such a situation. You cannot expect any coherency.

We are surrounded on all sides by very high mountains. If there is any aristocrat within ten leagues of us [he is][3] with his glass on the top of some hill watching our motions and sending expresses in every direction—these are pleasant speculations. I hope the rogues won't have the wit to destroy all the fishing boats round the bay, for we are in great need of some to help us to debark. We have not as yet seen a single boat round the bay.[4] *On dit* that we shall be in Killala in a couple of hours. Our grenadiers will debark in their[5] own boats, and if there be any fishermen the rascals shall be made useful. I have no more to add. You shall have a line from me written on the back of my hat—I have seen a print of Buonaparte in that attitude.

One o'clock in the afternoon

My D[ea]r Friends,

I ask pardon of the gods for having repined. We are close in with Killala and have taken a little brig, a thing absolutely necessary, as our frigates are too large to run close in. We have also some fishing boats. The pilot, who is *up*,[6] gives us the best intelligence in the world. [There are] scarcely any troops to oppose us and Jemmy Plunket[7] is at the head of the insurgents who are up in the County of Roscommon. We have also taken a lieutenant in the Prince of Wales' Reg[imen]t of Fencibles,[8] going from Sligo to Killala[9] to take the

---

[1] P.R.O. MS reads 'County Mayo side'.   [2] P.R.O. MS reads 'being able to enter either'.

[3] P.R.O. MS reads 'he's'.

[4] P.R.O. MS has 'and be damned to them' in place of 'round the bay'.

[5] P.R.O. MS reads 'our'.

[6] '*Up* was a popular expression well understood and synonymous with the word *united*' (C. H. Teeling, *Personal narrative of the Irish rebellion of 1798* (London, 1828), p. 60).

[7] James Plunkett (see above, vol. I, p. 308). P.R.O. MS reads 'Johnny Plunket'. An Irish correspondent of a London newspaper, the *Courier*, reported some days later: 'Colonel Plunket is a man of much coolness and bravery well known in Dublin, and is a complete military scholar of the French school, having spent many years in the service of the late king'. Later however the report was amended, Plunkett having 'surrendered himself about a fortnight since to the bishop of Elphin'. (*Courier*, 8, 17 Sept. 1798).

[8] Lieutenant Sills (probably George Sills) of the Leicester or Prince of Wales Fencibles (Sir Herbert Taylor, *pseud.* An Officer who Served . . . under . . . Marquis Cornwallis, *Impartial relation . . . of the military operations . . . in Ireland* (Dublin, 1799), pp 4–5).

[9] In P.R.O. MS the sentence continues 'to take the command of (or rather join) a company or two of infantry. There was his servant and a gentleman of Sligo (a yeoman) with him.' These were Henry Waldron and a Mr Bourke, both of the Tyrawley Cavalry (Nuala Costello (ed.), 'Little's diary of the French landing in 1798' in *Analecta Hibernica*, no. 11 (1941), p. 77). The latter may have been, as stated by Bishop Stock, 'Mr John Bourke of Summer-hill about two miles from Killala,

command, or rather to join a company of infantry there, ditto a gentleman of Sligo with him, a yeoman. The[y], I believe, are aristocrats. I offered to lay a guinea that if we please, we will be masters of Sligo tomorrow without [the enemy] firing a shot at us.[1] God bless you. [My] postscript shall be dated from Killala. *En attendant* I apprize you that we hear nothing of any other squadron having arrived.[2] Burke[3] considers this letter as from himself.

Killala, 6 Fructidor

Yesterday evening we landed and drove 60 yeomen and regulars like sheep before us. A few of our grenadiers only were landed and engaged. We killed 20[4] and made a dozen prisoners. The people will join us in myriads, they throw themselves on their knees as we pass along and extend their arms[5] for our success. We will be masters of Connaught in a few days. Erin go braugh.

M. Tone

[*Endorsed*]

Mr Tone to la Citoyenne Smyth[6]

To Matilda Tone, 23 August 1798

Tone (Dickason) papers.

Though Tone states 'I do not reckon this as a letter', it is treated here as such, as it appears on a separate folio and is separately addressed. It seems to have been written mainly to cover another letter, which has not been found. The place, date and salutations are in the middle of the letter, as given here.

No. 0, for I do not reckon this as a letter. My last was No. 9.[7] This makes *five* times I have written to you in *six* days; that is, I hope, handsomely done.

☞ Take great care of the printed papers &c. that I sent you by the diligence and do not give a copy to mortal but to Giauque,[8] for reasons.

---

a Protestant of good property'. He was, Stock believed however, 'the only gentleman in the barony capable of bearing arms who had not joined some yeoman corps . . . He was in Sligo when he heard of the invasion, from which town he hastened away to his own house and immediately set about the defence of it.' (Joseph Stock, *Narrative of what passed at Killala* (Dublin, 1800), p. 82).

[1] In P.R.O. MS the preceding two sentences read: 'the yeoman, tho' I believe an aristocrat, offered to lay a guinea that if we please we will be masters of Sligo tomorrow morning without their firing a cartridge at us'.   [2] Expeditions were also to set out from Brest and Dunkirk.
[3] *Nom de guerre* of Bartholomew Teeling (see above, p. 196, n. 3).
[4] P.R.O. MS reads '2' (a more likely figure), possibly Henry Rogers and H. Smith, yeomen, mentioned by James Little ('Little's diary', pp 77–8). The latter may have been Henry Smyth, gentleman, Lackancahill, whose will was probated on 16 Nov. 1799 (Patrick Smythe-Wood (ed.), 'Index to Killala and Achonry wills' in *Irish Genealogist*, iii, no. 12 (1967), p. 516).
[5] P.R.O. MS adds 'praying'.   [6] This endorsement is in P.R.O. MS only.
[7] Above, pp 325–7.   [8] Probably Lewines.

Brest, 6 fructidor, an 6

Dear Love,

Read the inclosed and give it to Giauque. I wrote to you yesterday and *have nothing to add*. Kiss the babies for me and love me alway.

Thine, while this machine is to him![1]
T. W. Tone

Is poor Russell at last out of the scrape? I hope he may not bully Pelham again.[2] Would he were in Holstein, with all my soul.[3] I am afraid he would break parole and come to Paris, if it were only to see you and Maria. If that should happen take care of him and let him imbibe. '*The dog has given me medicines, &c. Yes I have drank medicines*',[4] or rather indeed champaigne with him. *Poor Tom, bless his five wits, &c.* Is not that extremely sprightly on my part?

À la Citoyenne Smith
chez le Citoyen Chevalier
Rue des Batailles No. 29
À Chaillot
près Paris

To Matilda Tone, 29 August 1798

Tone (Dickason) papers.

No. 10

ARMÉE

FRANÇAISE

ERIN GO BRAH!

LIBERTÉ   *ÉGALITÉ*

*Au Quartier général a*bord le vaisseau le Hoche à Brest
ce 12 Fructidor *an* 6

L'ADJUDANT-GÉNÉRAL T. WOLFE TONE

À son épouse

Dear Love,

I have this moment received yours dated the 6th instant with a postscript from the Bab. Your letter is not numbered nor does it cite the number of

---

[1] *Hamlet*, III, ii.

[2] Apparently there had been, in Jan. or Feb. 1798, a proposal, involving Thomas Pelham, to release Russell from prison, which however came to nothing (*Drennan–McTier letters*, ii, 363).

[3] It was likely that in the event of Russell being released from prison a condition imposed by the Irish government would be that he should not go to France; he might however be free to go to the duchy of Holstein, part of the neutral kingdom of Denmark. The important town of Altona, which was situated in Holstein and beside Hamburg on the Elbe, attracted republicans from all over Europe (Paul Weber, *On the road to rebellion: the United Irish and Hamburg* (Dublin, 1997), pp 24–5).

[4] *1 Henry IV*, II, 2.

mine to which it is a reply, which puts me in some confusion but I see clearly that several of yours and all Lewines's (if he wrote) have miscarried. I have received of yours, No. 1; No. 2 never reached me; Nos 3 and 4 I have, which with your last of the 6th makes four in all, tho' you tell me you have written six if not seven times. No. 2, which miscarried is, I presume that of the 23d Thermidor, which you mention to be of some importance. I fancy, after all, you had better write me no news, for I see there is no trusting the Post Office. Do you get my letters regularly? Of my pistols I have heard nothing; if they have been sent, which I very much doubt, who-ever sent them should have written me a letter of advice. However I will go ashore today and search all the bureaux of all the Messageries; perhaps they are lying somewhere waiting for me.

I am sorry to see by the style of your letter that it was written in great agitation. I am not a man to despise danger more than another, but I do assure you I see very little in our expedition. Our only difficulty is the passage and our commodore has this morning received a courier extraordi-nary, which has put that on a footing that according to all reasonable probability must, I think, succeed. I therefore expect to have the pleasure of sharing with you the task of educating and providing for the Babs, at the same time that, if anything were to happen to me, I assure you I rely with the most implicit confidence both on your courage and conduct; but all this, between us, is quite unnecessary.

Is not your lover Reynolds a fine fellow?[1] I can hardly conceive such villainy and from a fellow not driven to it by absolute hunger. I am well off with my two brothers-in-law,[2] the hounds! Matty, don't love them tho' they are of your kindred. I am morally sure that Harriet[3] is at the bottom of all this foul business, for, from the little I saw of Reynolds, I am sure he is inca-pable of originating anything, good or evil—the unfortunate dog!

The storms which you mention have not reached us; on the contrary the weather is most provokingly fine, which embar[r]asses us not a little. For my part I am here, like gargantine Panurge,[4] praying for a gale of wind. *'Ah, si quelqu'un venait de faire naufrage! Le beau souhait!* (Sings) *'Dans nos climats, il ne tonne jamais!'*, &c.

I come now to trade affairs. Inclosed you have a letter of Gen[era]l Hardy to the Minister of War, a copy of said letter certified by me, and an extrait of my *livret*, containing the last payment which has been made to me. Let Lewines get a line of introduction from Talleyrand or the Minister of the Marine, or anybody, and let him bring you in his hand and present you to

---

[1] Thomas Reynolds, who was married to Matilda Tone's sister Harriet, had been the principal crown witness at the trials of Oliver Bond and other United Irishmen.

[2] Thomas Reynolds and Edward Witherington.

[3] Harriet Reynolds née Witherington; she married Reynolds on 25 Mar. 1794 and died on 29 July 1851 (H. B. Swanzy, *The families of French of Belturbet and Nixon of Fermanagh* (Dublin, 1908), p. 19). [4] A character in Rabelais's *Pantagruel* (1546–64).

the Minister at War, Rue Varennes, to whom you will shew Gen[era]l Hardy's letter, and he will give the necessary orders that you may receive one half of my appointments during my absence. *Remember, in the Minister's bureaux, to give only the certified copy of the letter and to keep the original.* This arrangement sets my mind at ease on your account. If they allow you barely my pay, at the rate of 583#,[1] you will have about 290# a month, but if they allow the indemnity for forage at 120#, you will have 60# more (viz. one half) which makes 350# a month, in which case I shall look on you as rich. Let Lewines endeavour to wheedle the Chef de bureau to pay you on the latter footing. At all events you will have 290# a month— *'a handsome addition for wine and good chear!'.*[2] As this argument will set you more at your ease, if there is any little accomplishment you wish to give the Bab, I do not see how 50# a month can be better laid out than on her education, *'for when both house and land is spent &c.'.*[3] By the bye she is losing her English, for there were *three* words wrong spelled in her postscript; you must put her in a class with the Boys. It is very right she should learn French but she must not forget her mother tongue. *'Save, if she understands anything it is the substraction of her vernacular idiom and a nice derangement of epitaphs.'*[4]

You do not tell me whether Lewines received mine of the 27th Thermidor enclosing two others, one of which was the letter he desired to have from me; neither do you tell me whether you got mine of the same date with a letter of attorney enclosed, all which is very puzzling to me. Do number your letters, and refer to mine by the numbers also. Tell Lewines, neither Simon nor I have received, as yet, one line from him, but whether it be his fault or that of the Post Office, I leave to God and his own conscience. I have written to him the 11th Thermidor, from Rennes, the 27th from Brest, as above mentioned, and the 6th ins[tan]t, from on board,[5] which last, for greater security, I enclosed to you. The others I addressed to him at his lodgings, Rue Pépinière. I hope he has received them.

I have nothing in the world to add. We are here for some time yet, so write to me. You ought to have a heap of letters from me; this is my *eleventh*, tho' it is numbered 10. I put a *nought* to my last, as it was so short. Adieu, dear love, God bless you, take care of yourself and the Babs, keep up your spirits and love me always.

Your slave and Dog
T. W. Tone

---

[1] i.e. 583 livres.   [2] Swift, *The grand question debated* (1729).
[3] Samuel Foote, *Taste* (1752), i, 1.
[4] 'Sure if I reprehend anything in this world, it is the use of my oracular tongue and a nice derangement of epitaphs!' (R. B. Sheridan, *The rivals* (1775), III, iii).
[5] i.e. 29 July, 14 Aug. and 23 Aug.

Did you receive the packet I sent you by the diligence of the 29th Thermidor? If not, let Lewines call for it at the Bureau, Rue Notre Dame des Victoires, near the Rue Vivienne.

[*Not addressed*]

To Maria Tone, 29 August 1798

Tone (Dickason) papers; added to the preceding letter.

Dear Bab,

I received your postscript with great satisfaction. You may be sure I will take care of your *little* and your *big* when we arrive *là-bas*. Consult with your mama about getting a better music master, as for example the father of your present one. '*I tell you he is no more a music master than I am a music master.*'[1] I hope your mama will be rich enough to get you well taught.[2] I think you might learn to draw a little if you found you had any turn for it, and it was not too dear. But I leave all this to you and your mama. Adieu, dear Bab, god bless.

T.W.T.

To Matilda Tone, 2 September 1798

Tone (Dickason) papers.

No. 11

ARMÉE   *ERIN GO BRAH!*
FRANÇAISE   *LIBERTÉ*   [crest]   *ÉGALITÉ*

*Au Quartier général a*bord du vaisseau le Hoche à Brest
ce 16 fructidor, *an* 6

L'ADJUDANT-GÉNÉRAL T. WOLFE TONE

A Madame, sa très honorée épouse

Dear Love,

I received this morning your two letters, Nos 7 and 8, acknowledging mine down to No. 9.[3] Before this you have doubtless my No. 0 and 10,[4] so at last

---

[1] Isaac Bickerstaff, *Love in a village* (1763), II, ii.
[2] Catherine Wilmot, who twice visited Matilda and Maria Tone in Paris in 1802, was favourably impressed by Maria's 'harp, guitar and pianoforte', which, she wrote, 'spoke her occupations in the line of taste' ('Kitty Wilmot's journal, 1801–1803', Royal Irish Academy, MS 12/L/32, p. 87).
[3] Above, pp 325–7.   [4] Above, pp 329–33.

our correspondance is pretty regular. Yours No. 2 is gone to the dogs; I have no doubt but it is in bad hands but it cannot be helped, so let us think no more about it. I have written to Lewines four letters; let me know in your first whether he has received them and especially whether he is satisfied with his certificate, and if not, what alterations he would desire to be made therein. As for a direct correspondance with him, I give it up as I believe the post office will take care to cut off the communication, if there were no other obstacle. I decyphered your last without difficulty. Of my pistols I have heard nothing, and I earnestly desire Giauque[1] to stick to that business like a leech; let him offer to send them himself provided Chérin will only get them; or if he can have a line from Barras to the Minister at War he will get them at once and without difficulty. I will settle things here so that, in case we should be gone before they arrive, they shall be sent back to you. Touching my appointments, I presume my last enclosing Gen[era]l Hardy's certificates &c. has removed all difficulty on that head as I shall receive but one half of my appointments here (more indeed than I shall want), it is no longer matter of favour but of right. I presume it is settled by this. I am glad General Kilmaine thinks well of me. The friendship of almost any man is worth having in these times, and much more of a man who fills an eminent station. I never supposed General Chérin would come to Brest so his change of destination does not surprise me. If circumstances allow Giauque[2] to reimburse you £20, keep it for Arthur, in case of his arrival at the Hague; if he can give you but a part, make it up to £20 from your own stock, provided you are to receive, as I doubt not but you will, my appointments. If however it will at all embar[r]ass Giauque, let him keep the money by all means, as we can do without it for the present, in which case you must make an exertion to spare £20 yourself which you will send to Arthur, and Ahern will take care to see how he lays it out. *All this is on the supposition* that there is any chance of his entering the Dutch navy, which I throw entirely on yours, Giauque's and Ahern's shoulders; if that misses, as he will come on to France, you need send him no money unless he should happen to want it for his *frais de route*. Apropos! Does Mary never tell you what they are doing *là-bas*?[3] They will remain there idling and living on their capital till it is so far diminished as to disable them from doing anything. You remember how we managed our affairs in America. I hope they may profit by our error. Write to Mary seriously on this head and let her know my uneasiness on her account.

I am glad and I may say in some degree flattered by your visit from Paine. You will of course remember me to him respectfully the first time you see him. I think you would do well to give him, Lewines and Lawless a dinner

---

[1] Probably John Frédéric Giauque.
[2] Jean Frédéric Giauque or Lewines?
[3] This, and what follows, suggests that his sister Mary and her husband, Jean Frédéric Giauque, had left Paris. Giauque, however, was present there in 1799.

one of these days and drink copiously to the success of our enterprise. I am not surprised at Bache's adventure.[1] You will see one of these days Reynolds, Rowan & Co. sent out of the country under the Alien act.[2] That bladdering Bonneville[3] has been printing some trash about the American envoy of whom you speak. I presume, if he be a man of sense, he can hardly wish to figure already in the *Bien Informé* beside Napper Tandy. Apropos! of Bonneville, I see your *pin* figures again in Boulay Pati's report on the state of the Marine, where he speaks of the Harp of Elin &c.[4] Your pin may say with John Gilpin, *'He little dreamt, when he set out, of running such a rig.'*[5]

It is with the most sincere pleasure that I hear of my father and mother's welfare. I have no doubt but they have both suffered a great deal and especially my mother. What astonishing luck she has had thus far, that not one of us happened to be in Ireland in these turbulent times! It is true one of us is probably there by this,[6] and another may soon follow, but if we arrive it will be on a footing totally different from the brave and unfortunate victims who have been sacrificed by their British tyrants. I have already written to you or Lewines, I do not remember which, a long letter touching our friends who have, I hope, by this recovered their liberty. I am only sorry they are obliged to go to that abominable climate, country and people.[7] I mentioned Holstein in my letter[8] as a desirable place. What a delightful society, for I must not say colony, we could form out of the number. If ever we meet again I will form a club of Big-endian exiles,[9] for notwithstanding all their misfortunes I do not think they will ever condescend, more than myself, to break their eggs at the convenient end. For Reynolds, it is too vile to speak of, but I cannot express the satisfaction I feel at poor Harry's[10]

---

[1] On 26 June 1798 Benjamin Franklin Bache was arrested on a charge of libelling the president and executive of the United States (*D.A.B.*).

[2] An American act concerning aliens, approved on 25 June 1798, empowered the president to expel aliens suspected of being dangerous to the United States.

[3] Nicholas Bonneville (1760–1828), journalist (*Dict. biog. franç.*).

[4] *Sic* in MS. On 3 Aug. 1798 Pierre Sébastien Boulay-Paty (1763–1830) presented to the Council of Five Hundred a report on the expenses of the navy for the coming year. He emphasised France's naval strength and pointed out that as a result of French intervention Holland, Italy and Switzerland had regained their liberty and that England, jealous and Machiavellian, was striving vainly to keep the war alive. (*Moniteur*, 25 Aug. 1798).   [5] William Cowper, *John Gilpin* (1785), a ballad.

[6] Mathew Tone. He landed on 22 Aug. and on 2 Sept. was in Co. Mayo travelling from Killala to Castlebar (see above, p. 329, and below, p. 345).   [7] i.e. the United States of America.

[8] In his letter to Matilda Tone dated 23 Aug. (above, pp 329–30).

[9] The Big-endians are in *Gulliver's travels* (1726), pt I, ch. 4.

[10] Henry Witherington (d. 1809), younger brother of Matilda Tone; cornet, 9th dragoons, 1797; ensign, 2nd foot, 1799; then lieut., Monmouthshire militia. Commissioned a lieut. in the 63rd foot, Dec. 1808, he served in the Walcheren expedition and on returning to England died of fever. 'In him', it was written, 'his majesty has lost a most spirited and active officer, an ornament to his profession.' At Bond's trial in July 1798 he gave evidence for the defence, suggesting that his mother had been poisoned by her son-in-law, Reynolds, the principal crown witness. (*Faulkner's Dublin Journal*, 26 July 1798; William Ridgeway, *A report of the proceedings in cases of high treason at a special commission* (Dublin, 1798); *Gent. Mag.*, lxxix (1809), p. 1084; Thomas Reynolds, junr, *The life of Thomas Reynolds, Esq.* (2 vols, London, 1839), ii, 238–46, 252).

behaviour; he is a noble little fellow, and the more so from the contrast he presents with every member of his family, yourself excepted. How did you and he contrive to escape the contagion? If ever we succeed in Ireland, it will be one of my great pleasures to cultivate the friendship of that young man. '*I can't say so much of him at the next stand*',[1] for I do not think Ned[2] and I will ever draw kindly together. Your brother the Captain, *ne vous en déplaise*, is a pimp, but poor Harry is, once more, a noble little fellow.

I see by the papers you have had terrible storms, with lightning &c., while all here has been for above six weeks in a stark calm. I am not at all angry, why should I, at your last letters, but I was sorry to see you so agitated. I beg once for all you will keep up your spirits, for my sake. I have quoted it already fifty times but I must add once more, '*Dost think Hauser Trunnion that has stood the fire of so many floating batteries, runs any risque from the (something that sounds like drowsy) pops of a landsman?*'[3] You may be sure we will not expose ourselves to be *x x oiled x x x x basted x x* &c. *Pas si bête.* We will take our own time. *Do not hurry us and we will spin you a good even thread.* Tell Lewines I am very well contented with Gen[era]l Hardy. Adieu, dearest Love. Kiss the babies for me.

Yours ever
T. W. Tone

To Maria Tone, 2 September 1798

Tone (Dickason) papers; added to the preceding letter.

Dear Bab,

I have written your Mama such a long letter that I have no room left to say anything to you. In my last I recommended to you concerning your music to perform the part of '*Ca—Ca—Cacalyban*'.[4] Let me see will you find out that quotation. Continue in your dancing to perform the part of *the King*. Take care of your Mama and your Boys and love your Fadoff always.

Yours truly,
T. W. Tone

What is become of Mr Wilson?[5] I asked Mama already about him. If he is at Paris remember me to him kindly.

---

[1] The source of this quotation has not been traced.   [2] Edward Witherington.
[3] Tobias Smollett, *Peregrine Pickle* (1751), ch. XXXVI. The forgotten word is 'lousy'.
[4] Possibly an allusion to Caliban in Shakespeare's *The Tempest*.   [5] Thomas Wilson.

To Matilda Tone, 5 September 1798

Tone (Dickason) papers.

There are no headings. Dated in another hand 'Sep. 5th '98?'.

No. 12

À Madame, son épouse

Dear Love,

I wrote to you the 16th ins[tan]t a long letter.[1] Since that time nothing has occurred; everything remains here in statu quo, and I cannot pretend to guess how long it may continue so; all depends on the wind and weather. I write to you this time by order of Gen[era]l Hardy, to desire that you may address yourself to the Minister of the Marine with regard to your moiety of my appointments, as the Minister at War, I believe, rather sets his face against the measure, notwithstanding the obvious justice and humanity of it. He has even, I understand, given very short answers to the wives of one or two officers who, like myself, have given up a share of their pay to their families. However, as General Hardy has already written to the Minister of the Marine on the subject, I presume Giauque[2] will be able to get it settled for you without further difficulty.

I have not one word more to say to you. Take care of yourself, dear Love, and of your Babies. Kiss them for me a thousand times, and love me always

Your affectionate spouse
T. W. Tone

Your last were Nos 7 and 8, which I received by the same courier four days since.

À la Citoyenne Smith
chez le Citoyen Chevalier
Rue des Batailles N°. 29
À Chaillot
près Paris

To Matilda Tone, 9 September 1798

Dickason (Tone) papers.

---

[1] His letter to Matilda Tone of 2 Sept. 1798 (above).   [2] i.e. Lewines.

No. 13

ARMÉE
FRANÇAISE
ERIN GO BRAH
LIBERTÉ   [crest]   *ÉGALITÉ*

*Au quartier général a*bord du vaisseau le *Hoche* à Brest
ce 23 fructidor *an* 6

L'ADJUDANT-GÉNÉRAL T. WOLFE TONE

À Madame son épouse

Dear Love,

I received yours, No. 9, yesterday, and I presume by this you have mine, Nos 10, 11 and 12,[1] particularly that enclosing Gen[era]l Hardy's certificate with regard to your appointments. Your addressing yourself to the Minister of the Marine need not prevent Gen[era]l Kilmaine's interesting himself, in case he will take that trouble, and that the Minister at War should make any difficulty, as I trust he will not. Whenever you are obliged to go into any of the bureaux, whether of the minister, commissary at war, or others, always bring Lewines with you, seeing that there is nothing I more dislike than to see women alone in such places.

I am very well pleased with the posture of our affairs at Paris. As for us here, we are still in *statu quo*, waiting on the wind, so that we may stay a month longer, or we may be off at an hour's warning, in which case you will excuse me the needless formality of a letter, taking leave and assuring you that I will always love you and entreating you to do as much by me. '*You are my true and honorable wife.*'[2] That is saying enough. Besides, neither you nor I have the talent nor the inclination for writing sentimental letters &c., so let us come to business.

I am very glad Gen[era]l Daendels has not forgot me. I hope Lewines will have the grace to write, at least to him, in which case I request him to present always my very sincere and unfeigned respects. I wish as you say, that he would recommend Arthur particularly to him. I feel infinitely obliged to Admiral De Winter for his kindness and I beg of Lewines to wait on him and thank him heartily in my name. I approve entirely of all you have done for Arthur, and especially of what you have written to Ahern, to whom you will always remember me.

There is no harm in your shewing the papers[3] to the persons you mention. There is none of them any great things, especially being written near two years ago, before the British had committed such horrors in the country, but such as they are they are better than nothing; at least they will do no harm. Let me know what you have determined with regard to writing to our exiles. I am always of the same opinion with regard to America.

---

[1] Above (pp 330–37).   [2] *Julius Caesar*, II, i.   [3] Not identified.

I am extremely edified by the anecdote of your son Frank; I think he bids fair to attain the reputation of his uncle William, of being, according to Kitty Finegan, '*an amorous young man*'.¹ It is very odd, the marked difference of character between him and Will, and so early developed. I *guess* we shall have divers *escapades* to overlook on his account, and I hope we may have the good sense to do so.

It gives me great pleasure that you find yourself at least tolerably tranquil, but do not imagine that you ever *fitted* me with complaints. I told you already, '*Never came a fit on board the Hoche, in the likeness of a letter from your grace*,' and I repeat it to you again. So far from being fitted, I am delighted with the courage which you have all along shewed and which I am sure you will continue to shew to the end.

I will keep my mouth shut, as Lewines desires, on the subjects you mention. In return tell him from me that I read yesterday a most frantic article in the *Bien Informé* concerning some unknown *armée des Vengeurs* and Napper Tandy.² It is undoubtedly a thing to be desired that all authentic intelligence, and especially all favorable intelligence, relating to Ireland should be published, but I never will believe that any cause can be served by forgery and falsehood, especially when it is wrapped up in such impenetrable nonsense. Is there no way of reducing that idiot Bonneville to reason? Would it not be well if Giauque³ got it signified to him *by authority* to be more on his guard, and not by his egregious trash and lies to throw at once a burlesque and a discredit on our business? I beg of Lewines to think on this. I have written to you so regularly that I have nothing to add, especially leading as I do such a monotonous life on ship-board. I will therefore leave off here, assuring you of my sincere and unalterable affection.

Yours most truly
T. W. Tone

Love to the Babies. What is become of Wilson? Pray remember me to him affectionately when you see him. My best regards to Howard⁴ and W[illia]m Lawless. I am seriously vexed with Lewines for his laziness, and what is worse Gen[era]l Hardy and Simon are still more so, but as he is incorrigible on that head, I will say no more.

---

¹ The sources of this and the following quotation have not been traced.

² The *Bien Informé* explained that it had received several proclamations prepared by French and Irish generals. One of these, issued at the headquarters of 'l'armée des vengeurs', began with the words 'Liberty or death' and went on to say that the soldiers of the great nation had disembarked on the Irish coast with Napper Tandy at their head (*Bien Informé*, 16 Fructidor year 6).

³ Probably Tone means here not his brother-in-law Jean-Frédéric Giauque but Edward Lewines, as the next sentence suggests. There seems to be confirmation of this in the following letter (see below, p. 341). What he means by 'his egregious trash and lies' has not been determined.

⁴ i.e. John Tennent.

À la Citoyenne Smith
chez le Citoyen Chevalier
Rue des Batailles No. 29
A Chaillot
près Paris

To Matilda Tone, 16 September 1798

Dickason (Tone) papers.

No. 16 or 17

ARMÉE   *ERIN GO BRAH!*
FRANÇAISE   *LIBERTÉ*   [crest]   *ÉGALITÉ*

*Au Quartier général a*bord du *Hoche*, Baie de Camaret
ce 30 fructidor *an* 6

L'ADJUDANT-GÉNÉRAL T. WOLFE TONE

À son épouse

Dear Love,

You see by the date of this that we are still here. It is not however the enemy who keeps us at present, for he has not appeared for some days, but we are becalmed, now for the third day without a breath of wind. Judge of my impatience. This morning I received yours No. 12 with the news of Humbert's success.[1] I hope it may be confirmed, as it will most materially facilitate our operations in case we arrive. According to all appearance the news is highly probable, and my satisfaction would be complete if we were on our way to second him.[2]

In my last[3] I mentioned to you my opinion of the *new converts*. Whatever reason I have individually not to admire them, you may be very sure it will in no degree influence my conduct with regard to them. I am only sorry that many more of the same description did not adopt the same conduct long since. It would have saved us much trouble, the country much blood and confusion, and perhaps in the long run they would have saved their own lives and fortunes. They had fair warning long since, to my knowledge, for I took some pains to *insense* one of those you mention a year before I

---

[1] Humbert, whom Tone had known in Bantry Bay (above, vol. II, p. 432), had the command of a small expeditionary force that, sailing from La Rochelle, landed at Killala on the west coast of Ireland on 22 Aug. 1798. Having moved inland and defeated a larger British force at Castlebar five days later, he was forced to surrender to Lord Cornwallis at Ballinamuck on 8 Sept.
[2] In fact Tone sailed later that day.   [3] Not found.

left Ireland. However, better late than never; if they are honest I for one shall be glad of their co-operation.

I am heartily glad your business is settled at the War Office. Touching my pistols, if you have not sent them off, keep them for me; if they should be gone let Lewines write to Adj[udan]t-gen[era]l Mayer[1] at Brest to be so good as to send them back to your address, for I should be sorry to remain here long enough to receive them.

Touching the Mon,[2] I have already given you and Lewines *carte blanche* and I have only to repeat my caution of committing [?]him. Remember, *not a scrape of a pen* above all things. I see infinite difficulties, but if it be necessary the risque must be run; for Matt I feel no alarm.

I have so often and so fruitlessly laboured to content the four persons of whom you speak,[3] and who I judge from your letter are now at Paris, that I give up all further effort. There is not a man of them that would not rejoice to see me hanged, and I am sure not one of them could assign a reason for it, at least a just one. If they call on you, you will, as you have always been, be civil to them, but avoid all communication with them as far as you can without absolutely breaking with them.

I have of course received Lewines's postscript, and you will of course shew him this. Neither Simon nor I have had a line from him, which is, I see now, the fault of the post. I wrote him four times since I left Paris. I am not at all surprised at the treachery he speaks of. It was before the 18 Fructidor that the communication took place, and you may be very sure that Pitt was apprised by his friends in the Directory of every syllable that passed. Let him recall what General Hoche said to him on that subject: '*Mon ami, nous sommes trahis!*'.[4] It appears now he had great reason to say so.

Tell Lewines that my anger is entirely abated in consequence of his writing '*those few lines that he has penned*'.[5] I wish I had the duplicates he mentions as well as the information brought by his friend, but I do not see how it is possible. I scolded him like a dog in my last, but he discovered it, poor fellow, and so I forgive myself, and I desire he may do the same. Recommend to him, from me, to have no more feuding or [?] proving about the business of Liège,[6] but to let it lie on a line ball, and those who wish him ill, let them make their most of it; if his enemies have never more hold on him than for that affair, his soul may be in perfect tranquillity. I do not know exactly whether this is No. 16 or No. 17, but I believe it is the latter. I write to you famously. The last before this announced to you my picture, which I hope you have received. It is not very like, but it seems to me a sort of a

---

[1] Joseph Sebastien Mayer (1763–1834), lieut, 1778; adjutant-general, 1795; *général de brigade*, 1813 (Six, *Dict. des généraux & amiraux*).

[2] The context here and in the postscript suggests that by 'Mon' he means Arthur Tone.

[3] Not identified.   [4] 'My friend, we are betrayed!'

[5] Samuel Richardson, *Pamela* (1741–2), i, letter XXX.

[6] In Oct. 1797 four United Irishmen were being held as prisoners at Liège (see above, p. 162).

likeness; however you will judge for yourself. It cost me but two louis. Apropos of money, if the Minister at War *comes down the ready* for the business you wot of, there is no occasion for you to disburse; however you will see into that yourself, remembering always that a *store is no sore*.

Give my love to Mary always when you write. Kiss the Babies for me and love me always.

Your affectionate spouse
T. W. Tone

I made a mistake above. I believe it was in my last that I enclosed you the letter which you had required of me touching Will, the Mon &c., &c.

À la citoyenne Smith
chez le citoyen Chevalier
Rue des Batailles No. 29
à Chaillot
près Paris

George Holdcroft to ——, 18 September 1798

Nat. Arch. (Ire.), Rebellion papers, 620/40/70.

George Holdcroft (1751?–1810) was postmaster of Kells, Co. Meath (ibid., 620/49/21; Rosemary Ffolliott, 'Some monumental inscriptions from Kells, Co. Meath' in *Irish Genealogist*, iii, no. 11 (1966), p. 444).

Kells, September 18th, 1798

Dear Sir,

This country continues very much in the same situation as when I last wrote to you. The neighbourhood of Summerhill has been much disturbed and partys of rebels frequently assemble . . . . [1]

Yesterday evening Lord Maxwell[2] was drove into this town in a chaise-and-four from Virginia having with him on his way to Dublin Mr Tone,[3] second brother to the celebrated traitor to his country Counsellor Theo. W. Tone. He was made a prisoner by a party of Killeshandra Cavalry within three miles of Ballinamuck, where the French and Rebels were defeated,[4] the particulars of which appeared in the papers. Mr Tone is a low, thin, smart man about twenty-six years old, of an animated intelligent countenance, and seems to possess very good abilities. He appeared to have very little reserve,

---

[1] The remainder of the paragraph relates to local disturbances.
[2] John James Maxwell (1755–1823), styled Viscount Maxwell; capt., 2nd Ballyjamesduff yeomanry corps, 1799–1800; succeeded as 2nd earl of Farnham, 1800 (*A list of the counties of Ireland and the respective yeomanry corps* (Dublin, 1798); *Burke's peerage* (London, 1912)).
[3] The MS seems to read 'Mʳ Tone' or even 'Mt Tone' ('M[a]t[hew] Tone'). The former reading is more plausible in the circumstances.
[4] The French defeat occurred at Ballinamuck, Co. Longford, on 8 Sept. 1798.

answered every question asked him readily, yet whenever such questions were asked as at all involved his party in Ireland his answers were distorted by uncommon shrewedness, screening his party and aiming at an appearance of plausible sincerity. From observations I made here I am certain uncommon pains will be taken to prevent his making discoverys that probably he may be well enough inclined to do if he is kept clear of designing people—altho' but a year since he last went to France he has very much the appearance of a Frenchman, and has acquired a good deal of their gasconade. He spoke much of the great superiority of the French rapidity of charging with bayonets and instanced several victories they obtained by it in which that of Castlebar in this kingdom the other day was not forgot, and in a half-reluctant, half-consenting manner most certainly spoke with great contempt of the King's troops, officers and soldiers engaged in that business. It was a subject he choose to introduce and liked to speak on, to take the opportunity of impressing on every person who heard him that if 1,030 French c[oul]d do so much, advance so far, and engage so much the attention of a great number of the army and generals of the kingdom, what might a large French army effect here? Another subject he liked to introduce was that pikes were the best weapons or arms the people of this country c[oul]d make use of, and that when taught the proper use of them and to form and stand together in proper position they w[oul]d be irresistable. He slept at Captain Molloy's[1] last night and this morning at 4 o'clock set off with Lord Maxwell and I suppose arrived early this day in Dublin.[2] They were escorted to Navan by a detachment of our yeomen [*sic*] cavalry. The [same?] day Captain Faris[3] of the Killishandra Cavalry and a Mr Armstrong[4] and another of that troop that made Mr Tone a prisoner passed thro' this town on their way to Dublin to give evidence respecting Mr Tone.[5] We are informed two companys of the Carlow militia are to be quartered here. I hope not. They are not fit for this country in its present situation, when a party are ready to rise here to destroy and murder us the first opportunity. The Carlow militia arriving here at this time might encourage and hasten outrage in this neighbourhood.

With very best wishes, I am dear Sir,

most truly your obed[ien]t, humble servant
George Holdcroft

[P.S.] My son[6] went to town this day.

---

[1] Henry Molloy (1746–1814) of Castlepole and Lennoxbrook, sovereign of Kells and captain of the Kells yeomanry (J. C. Shaw, 'The Molloy family of Kells' in *Irish Genealogist*, iii, no. 5 (1960), p. 188).

[2] He was lodged in the Provost at Dublin barrack (*Saunders' News Letter*, 21 Sept. 1798).

[3] William Faris, captain, Killeshandra cavalry; J.P. for Co. Cavan (*A list of the officers of the several regiments . . . of militia, and of . . . fencible cavalry and infantry, upon the establishment of Ireland* (Dublin, 1797?); *Gentleman's and Citizen's Almanack* (Dublin, 1795), p. 96).

[4] Thomas Armstrong, yeoman cavalry (see below, p. 346).

[5] On 14 Mar. 1803, Faris was paid £20 6s. 3d. in reimbursement of the 'expense of bringing up Mathias Tone' in Sept. 1798 (J. T. Gilbert (ed.), *Documents relating to Ireland, 1795–1804* (Dublin, 1893), p. 40).   [6] Not identified.

Statement of Michael Burke relating to the French expedition under Humbert, September 1798

Nat. Arch. (Ire.), Rebellion papers, 620/52/123 (two copies); printed in Richard Hayes, *The last invasion of Ireland* (Dublin, 1937), pp 63–4.

Michael Burke of Loughrea, Co. Galway, was a government informant who gave evidence at Mathew Tone's court martial (see below, pp 345–6).

[No heading]

Michael Burke joined the French at Castlebar on Friday, 31st August. [He] addressed himself first to Roach[1] and afterwards to Teeling,[2] and sat during the night in the same apartments with Teeling. The officers who spoke English were the most active, and the others amused themselves. He thinks that 5 or 6,000 of the country people joined them at Castlebar . . .

Tone[3] was also with the French and had arrived with them. Had much conversation with him about the trials and who were the Directory;[4] said he was brother to Tone who had fled; that himself had gone to France about 4 years ago, was taken up as an English spy and confined nine months in prison, made his escape to America, where hearing from H[amilton] Rowan that his brother was safe in France he proceeded there in the first vessel that sailed and went to Paris; was much surprized to find that it was Reynolds[5] who had married T. Tone's wife's sister that had betrayed Lord E[dward] F[itzgerald]. Tone and Teeling particularly spoke of McNevin, O'Connor, Emmet and some others and reprobated them for betraying the cause and turning informers for the sake of saving their lives.[6] They applauded much Lord E. F. and said the others ought to have died like him. It did not appear that these men had any communication with the prisoners in Dublin or that they knew anything about them except from the public prints. Tone said that Doctor Troy was a great scoundrel and that Grattan had acted shamefully on the trial of O'Connor[7] in not having given more evidence, that any man could have done as much good as he did there and that he seemed on this occasion to have been merely an aristocrat and not a true republican. Tone said that six embarkations were to take place in the ports of France at the same time for the purpose of invading Ireland in the parts least protected, that his brother was to come with one and seemed rather to think

---

[1] *Nom de guerre* of John Sullivan.   [2] Bartholomew Teeling.   [3] Mathew Tone.
[4] Perhaps an allusion to events in France since the *coup d'état* of 22 Floréal Year VI (11 May 1798).   [5] i.e. Thomas Reynolds.
[6] This sentence is omitted by Hayes.
[7] The trial at Maidstone in May 1798 of Arthur O'Connor (see above, p. 292).

that he must have been arrived by this time and N[apper] Tandy with another.[1] Other Irishmen, he said, would also be on board.

Remained with the French at Castlebar ... [and] on Tuesday at daybreak marched with them on the road to Swineford ...[2]

Proceedings at the court martial for the trial of Mathew Tone, 21, 24, 26 September 1798

T.C.D., Court-martial proceedings, 1798, MS 872, ff 133ᵛ–141ᵛ.

Friday, 21st September 1798. The Gen[era]l Court Martial, of which Col. Maginnis[3] was president, met pursuant to adjournment and proceeded to the trial of Mathew Tone brought prisoner before the Court for having acted traiterously, rebelliously and hostiley against his Majesty's Government.

The prisoner being duly arraigned pleaded not guilty. The prisoner prayed the Court to allow him until Monday next to prepare for his trial and procure coun[se]l, which was granted.

Monday 24th Septʳ the Court met pursuant to adjournment.

Col. Maginnis, president

Lord Gosford[4]   Lord Enniskillen
Col. Jones[5]   Lieut Col. Daly[7]
Major Armstrong[6]   Captain Pack[8]

The prisoner acknowledges to be a natural born subject of this realm. Mich[ae]l Burke sworn.

T.A.: Do you know the prisoner?

Answer: I do, I saw him at Castle Bar. I arrived at Castlebar the 31st of August last. The prisoner was not there [that] day or the day following. On Sunday he came there from Killala, as he informed me; he told me that

---

[1] Tandy left Paris for Dunkirk on 17 July but did not sail until 4 Sept.; he briefly landed on 16 Sept. on Rutland Island off the Irish coast before heading out to sea again.

[2] What follows relates to Burke's experiences after leaving Castlebar. Mathew Tone is not mentioned again.

[3] Hugh Magennis, capt. of corps invalids in Ireland; held rank of colonel in the army (*Army list*, 1798).   [4] Viscount Gosford (see above, vol. II, p. 370, n. 3).

[5] Possibly Col. Love Parry Jones, 2nd (Queen's Royal) foot.

[6] Major John Armstrong, 5th dragoon guards.

[7] Peter Daly, corps of invalids in Ireland (*Army list*, 1798). This may have been Peter James Daly (1769?–1846) of Castle Daly, Co. Galway, listed in 1793 as a major in the Military Department; he was M.P. for Galway borough, 1792–7 (Edith Mary Johnston-Liik, *History of the Irish parliament, 1692–1800* (Belfast, 2002), iv, 12–13).

[8] Denis Pack (1775–1823), 5th dragoon guards; commanded a force against insurgents, May–June 1798; promoted major, 4th Royal Irish dragoon guards, 25 Aug. 1798; major-gen., 1813; knight, 1815 (*D.N.B.*; *Burke's landed gentry of Ireland* (London, 1958), p. 76).

he had quit this country about 4 or 5 years ago and had arrived in France, that after his arrival there he had been taken up as an English spy and was committed to prison where he remained for 6 or nine months, and that he then effected his escape out of prison and sailed for America, where he arrived and remained for some time, that he had met in America a Mr Hamilton Rowan who had informed him that his brother Mr Theobald Woulfe Tone had arrived in Paris, that upon receiving that information from Mr Rowan, he took the first opportunity of leaving America for France, and arrived there accordingly, where he remained for some time until the intended invasion of this country, when he and other Irish gentlemen did shake hands with each other at Paris, intending to take diff[eren]t routs for six diff[eren]t destinations from where armaments were to be settled out for the invasion of this kingdom, and told me he came here as a French officer embarked from Rochelle, that they were three weeks at sea before their landing in Ireland. I saw him, the prisoner, on Monday the day after his coming to Castle Bar, inspecting the martialing of the rebels who had joined the French force, in Lord Lucan's Lawn, on which day he told me that it had been very unfortunate for them, the French, to be joined by so savage disposed set of people as the rebels, whose dispositions only led them to plunder and murder the Protestants, and that necessity alone had compelled the French to give commissions to persons totally unworthy of them. I saw the prisoner march from Castle Bar as a French officer, and at Killoony I saw him inspecting the distribution of spirits amongst the rebel chiefs. I left the French at Killoony and saw no more of them. I saw the prisoner distributing those spirits before the action took place at Killoony.

Thomas Armstrong, yeoman cavalry, sworn.

T.A.: Do you know the prisoner?

Answer: I do. On Saturday the 8th of Sept[embe]r, the day of the battle of Ballinamuck, I was returning home with two other yeomen, and accidentally on the road met the prisoner. One of the party asked him where [he] came from; he said from Killala, upon which we took him into custody; he then acknowledged that he had been amongst the rebels, and that he had a captain's commission under the French government, upon which we deliv[ere]d him up to the commanding officer of the district at Belturbet. He was disguised in the cloaths of a peasant, and acknowledged that he had thrown away his French uniform, his sword and pistols.

The prosecution being closed, and the pris[one]r called to his defence prayed the court to grant him till Wednesday next to prepare his defence, which the Court complied with.

Wednesday, 26th Sept[embe]r, the Court met pursuant to adjournment. Prisoner's defence.

1st witness, Peter Tone, sworn.

Q. Pres[ident]: Do you know the pris[one]r and have you had any and what conversation or intercourse with him?

Answer: I am the prisoner's father.

Q. do.: What age is the pris[one]r?

Answer: About twenty-six or twenty-seven years of age.

Q. do.: Do you know the pris[one]r to have left this country, to go to any other country and what country and about what time?

Answer: He left this country about six years ago as I best recollect to go to America.

Q. Pres^r: What was the occasion of this pris[one]r's leaving this country?

Answer: Having failed in his circumstances.

Q. do.: Had you any knowledge of the prisoner's habits previous to his leaving the country?

Answer: I always considered the pris[one]r a quiet, attentive young man, diligent and careful in his business untill things went wrong with him.

Q. Presr: Was he a man who insisted himself in politics?

Answer: Not to my knowledge.

Q. do.: Did you ever know him to belong to any political society?

Answer: I never did, and I do think from the connexion and intercourse that subsisted between him and me I must have known it if he did.

The Presr: addressed the Court on the words of which the annexed paper marked X X A is a copy.[1]

Mr President and my Lords and Gent[leme]n of the Court Martial.

Duly[2] relying on your justice and liberality that I shall have the full benefit of the objection which I have been advised to make to your jurisdiction, and that having made that objection, it will not prejudice any claims which I may have to the justice or even humanity of this Court, or of Governm[en]t, I shall proceed to state, not so much a defence of my conduct, as a plain and candid account of what it has been. Before however I do this permit me to observe that in pleading to your jurisdiction, I did not mean to deny that you are a court known to the constitution & recognized by Common Law. I merely meant to say that though you are so known & so recognized, you can only act under certain circumstances which do not exist in my case and that there is no difference between a court utterly unknown to the law and one acting beyond the powers given it by that law.

I have already admitted that I was born in Ireland, unsuccessfull in my endeavours to acquire an establishment in my native country and left it & went to America some time before the war between England and France was declared. This, my first emigration, was rather the effects of necessity than choice. Politicks had nothing to do in it. After remaining some time in America I quit it with an intention of going to France.[3] On my arrival there I was thrown into prison as stated in the evidence. In that prison I remained

---

[1] See below (pp 349-52).   [2] Erroneously 'Juley' in MS.

[3] T. W. Tone states that Mathew Tone returned to Ireland after spending twelve months in America and that he left Ireland for France on 3 Aug. 1794, which was eighteen months after war was declared between England and France (see above, vol. II, pp 264–5).

several months and at length escaped back to America. It cannot be supposed that if I had gone to France with views hostile to Ireland, or with any previous intention of throwing off my allegiance, or in any way [ ]¹ by persons holding a treasonable correspondence with France, I would have been arrested there as a spy and treated with all the severity usually employed ag[ain]st such characters. It is well known with what readiness France received all those who admitted her principles, with what zeal she adopted them, with what favour she promoted them, she would not make prison in her country reward treachery in yours. After residing some time in America and failing in my views of establishing myself there I went to Hamburg in consequence of an invitation rec[eive]d from my sister who had married a mer[chan]t in that city. In this place however I could not continue long, I had no means of independant support, I felt myself a burthen on those whom it would [have] been much more my wish to assist than oppress. I had failed in my endeavours to obtain subsistance in Ireland, I could not steadily look poverty in the face and accepted a commission in the French army for bread. Having thus accepted of a commission in the French army I became necessary subject to their military law. Orders were given that I should embark for Ireland. I obeyed those orders. I solemnly declare that I never was consulted upon or in any degree promoted the expedition. It cannot be conceived that so obscure an individual and one so long absent from Ireland would be consulted upon such an occasion, although my knowledge of two languages might induce and did induce those who planned the expedition to require my co-operation, [and I] would not refuse it without the forfeiture of my life.

It is also plain that being landed and in the midst of a French camp I dare not be inactive but has there been any fact adduced in evidence to shew that my acting was officious and more tha[n] what might be expected from a man circumst[a]n[ce]d as I was? Does it appear that I committed or countenanced any depredation, does it appear that I headed any attack, that I was cordial to the rebels or that I approved of their conduct, was I not averse to the rebels' measures and expressed my detestation of them?

Is it not also to be inferred fairly from the evidence that as soon as an escape from the army and the rebels was practicable I made it? Untill the French troops were in disorder and the rebels dispersed it was impossible, and then to have remained would have been perilous, for instant death without any investigation of my conduct and situation might have been the consequence. I therefore assumed the character of a peasant in order to escape to some magistrate or person of authority to give myself up. The evidence [is] that when I was met by the yeomen I instantly gave myself up, I told them I came from Killala, which discovery was not consistent with my disguise if my purposes was not to elude the rebels & give myself up when I might escape abuse and avoid falling into the hands of a ferocious rabble whose

---

¹ MS blank.

conduct and machinations I execrated and these my sentiments & conduct cannot be denyed, for nothing is more clear than that my discovery was voluntary and that my escape in the end through the medium of the rebels was certain if I could have persuaded so desperate and execrable a body.

You have now before you a candid and permit me to say an awfully sincere exposition of my conduct. Born to inheritance, an emigrant from necessity and led on by circumstances which no prudence could foresee and which the ordinary firmness of the human character could not resist, I entered into the army of France out of necessity, not out of choice. I was no fomentor of broils, no concealed conspirator against the state. I acted in obedience to an authority which necessity had imposed upon me and strictly confined myself to what that situation required. If I have not said sufficient to secure me against the rigour of publick law I trust there is at least enough to mitigate the harshness of private judgement & to soften where the power exists of a legal sentence.

Mathew Tone

The Court having taken into consideration the evidence adduced in support of the charge preferred ag[ain]st the pris[one]r Mathew Tone & also what was offered by the pris[one]r in his evidence find that the pris[one]r is guilty of the crimes alledg'd ag[ain]st him and therefore adju[d]ge him to suffer death at such time and place and in such manner as Lieut Gen[era]l Craig[1] shall direct.

Hugh Maginnis, Col.
Fran[ci]s Patterson,[2] A[dvocate] Gen[era]l & T. Martial

What follows (MS 872, ff 138ᵛ–141ᵛ) is a larger version of the legal argument contained in Mathew Tone's address to the court martial. It differs considerably in detail and style from the relevant portion of the address given above and is probably 'the annexed paper marked X X A' referred to by the president (see above, p. 347). The attention it gives to legal matters suggests that it was composed by a lawyer. There is further evidence of this in the existence of another version in the Burrowes papers in which textual variants are slight or barely significant. According to Eyre Burton Powell, writing to Francis Dobbs on 24 September, Mathew Tone received advice from Peter Burrowes (see below, p. 353). Significant variants in the version in the Burrowes papers (Royal Irish Academy, MS 23/K/53) are noted.

Mr President and Gentlemen of the Court Martial

I feel that I am acting respectfully to this Court in stating an objection to your competency to try me for the offence with which I am charged

---

[1] Peter Craig (d. 1810), major-general, 1793; lieut-gen., 1798; later col., 67th foot (*Army list; Gent. Mag.*, lxxx (1810), pt II, p. 592).

[2] Francis Patterson, called to the Irish bar, 1779; judge advocate general, 1788–1820 (Rowley Lascelles, *Liber munerum publicorum Hiberniae* (2 vols, London, 1852), ii, pt VII, p. 151; R. B. McDowell, *The Irish administration* (London, 1964), p. 19).

before I answer the allegations and before the question of my guilt or innocence shall be investigated.

If I postponed this objection, it might be said I voluntary waived my right and submitted to the jurisdiction and it's obvious that if my objection be well founded (and I really believe it is) that it is a preliminary objection and that it ought now to be made.

I hope it will not be conceived that a doubt of your perfect impartiality has the slightest influence in urging me to this measure. Were I to select a jury by which I was to be tried I would exult in seeing such men as you impannelled upon my life. The best proof I can offer of the sincerity of these professions is under the circumstances I am placed relying upon an objection which as it derogates from the power of this court would offend weak, prejudiced, proud men, but which I am persuaded receive a patient and unprejudiced hearing from you who derive no importance from this transitory authority with which you are now invested but who have a great and permanent interest in the laws and constitution of this country.

The ground of any objection is merely this. It is not pretended that I am or ever was a soldier in the British or Irish armies or in any way subject to the articles of war. I am as little liable to be tried under these laws for high treason as any man in the community. To extend their provisions to me would be to extend them to every man but unnecessarily to universaly and a code which is only deemed consistent with the free constitution of this country because it is limited, because it is necessarily limited.

Upon this ground there cannot be any difficulty, but it may be said being a native of this country and owing it allegiance I was found among rebels, that I accompanied an invading enemy under whom I held commission, that by the laws of war I might instantaneously [have] been shot and that therefore by the law of nations, recognized by the Common Law of England, I am triable by martial law. Such are the facts alleged against me. The truth or falsehood are totally irrelevant to the present question because if they were all true it would not follow that I ought to be tried by a military court.

It cannot be denied but the Common Law committee have jurisdiction of this offence, that commissions of oyer and terminer are now actually in existence and trial by jury daily had nay that an assizes will be immediately held in the very country in which the offence is alleged to have been committed and that Common Law judges are actually invested with authority to hold such assizes.

I say therefore, admitting as I readily admit than when the civil courts are shut and cannot act upon offences and upon offenders in consequence of rebellion or invasion that during the necessary inaction of such courts, offences like this and perhaps all offences are triable by martial law, admitting also that all persons joined in such rebellion or invasion may be seized and instantly and summarily indentified and executed by martial law, admitting I say that while there is no alternative but impunity and encouragement to crimes or a temporary surrender even of our most valued privileges, the British laws and constitution will tolerate the latter, it does not follow that where a prisoner has been taken and placed in the custody of the law and where he can be tried by a jury of his country acting under the guidance of a judge of the land, that a military tribunal should be resorted to and that he should be deprived of the various advantages which, in the course of such a trial, the benignity of the British laws and institutions give to every man in my situation.

The same necessity which introduces and justifies martial law defines its objects and sets bounds to its duration. If it be resorted to without or continued beyond such[1] necessity, 'tis arbitrary power.[2] If it may be continued a single day or applied to a single case beyond the principle of necessity which gives its birth and denote[3] it as a legitimate offspring of our constitution, it may be extended to any number of cases and continued for any length of time, and it would follow that when unhappily martial law is introduced for a single hour into a country it must depend upon the description[4] of the power which wields the sword whether universal and perpetual dispositions[5] shall not prevail. This is not fanciful theory, 'tis agreeable to the reasonings and opinion of the most esteemed writers upon general law and coincides with sentiments of every distinguished English judge or[6] lawyer who ever wrote or spoke upon the subject. Hence it is that Sir Edward Coke,[7] the highest authority in the English law, has said, 'a rebel may be slain in the rebellion but if he be taken he cannot be put to death by the martial law, and when the courts are open martial law cannot be executed'; and Lord Chief Justice Rolls[8] has expressly said, 'if a subject be taken in rebellion if he be not slain in the time of his rebellion he is to be tried after by the Common Law', and hence it is that the attainder of the Earl of Salisbury[9] founded upon the conviction[10] of a court martial was reversed in the reign of Henry the 5th upon the alleged ground, amongst others, *that he was a day and a half in prison after his apprehension and was put to death without trial at law contrary to the Magna Carta.*

I shall not trouble you with reference to authors upon the subject, to one book only shall I refer you, namely to Rushworth's *Historical Collection*, volume 3, page 76,[11] because there you will find collected the opinion and arguments of several of the most eminent legal men in England, three of whom were afterwards chief justices of the highest character and all of whom support and fortify my reasoning. I could cite various other authorities of the highest repute decisive upon the subject, but that I do not expect or wish that you will found

---

[1] R.I.A. MS reads 'that' instead of 'such'.   [2] R.I.A. MS reads 'lawless and arbitrary power'.
[3] R.I.A. MS reads 'adopts' instead of 'denote'.
[4] R.I.A. MS reads 'discretion' instead of 'description'.
[5] R.I.A. MS reads 'despotism' instead of 'dispositions'.   [6] R.I.A. MS has '&' instead of 'or'.
[7] Sir Edward Coke (1552–1634), chief justice of the king's bench, 1613–16 (*D.N.B.*).
[8] Sir Henry Rolle (1589?–1656), chief justice of the king's bench, 1648; lord chief justice of the upper bench, 1649 (ibid.).   [9] John de Montague (1350?–1400), 3rd earl of Salisbury.
[10] R.I.A. MS reads 'commission' instead of 'conviction'.
[11] The opinions of Coke and Rolle on martial law and the case of the earl of Salisbury are to be found in John Rushworth, *Historical collections, 1618–48* (7 vols, London, 1659–1701), iii, 79, 81.

your decision upon any argument or authority proceeding from me or any person whom I may consult in my defence. All I can hope (and in that hope I am sanguine indeed) is that you will maturely weigh this very important question. Is it presumption for a man whose life may be implicated in the decision to suggest that this question is worthy of being inferred to the twelve judges of Ireland? Does it not relate to them and their jurisdiction even more pointedly than to me? The life of an individual so obscure as I am is of but little consequence; how that life is disposed of in a country governed by law may be of the utmost consequence. This point never has been made by any man circumstanced as I am and consequently never has been decided upon and permit me to say that the oldest man alive has not witnessed the decision of any question of more universal concernment to every subject of the realm. I must not suggest that the question of my guilt or innocence is to you totally indifferent if you have no jurisdiction, and that to punish even a criminal without jurisdiction is in law as criminal an act as if he were innocent. In deciding upon this question I well know[1] that you will not be affected by the freedom [with] which I may have discussed it or any opinion you may entertain of what ought to be the decision of the tribunal before which I contend that I ought to be tried, upon that question it being totally irrelevant at present. I have not uttered one syllable in making this preliminary objection, I have discharged a solemn duty to myself and to the public. In deciding upon it you will[2] discharge a duty equally solemn.

Math. Tone

Eyre Burton Powell to Francis Dobbs, 24 September 1798

Nat. Arch. (Ire.), Rebellion papers, 620/40/114.

Eyre Burton Powell (*c*.1767–*c*.1800) was called to the Irish bar in 1790 (*Wilson's Dublin Directory*, passim).

Francis Dobbs (1750–1811), a political writer with millenarian beliefs, was M.P. for Charlemont, 1797–1800 (*D.N.B.*).

Dublin, Sept[r] 24th, 1798
6, Belvedere Place

My Dear Sir,

I am sure you will pardon the liberty I take in writing to you on a subject in which your philanthropy has been so much exerted, that of obtaining remission of sin for your unfortunate deluded countrymen . . . [3]

---

[1] R.I.A. MS reads 'I trust' instead of 'I well know'.   [2] R.I.A. MS reads 'have to' instead of 'will'.

[3] The omitted matter concerns 'a very young man of some respectability . . . now an object of the fugitive bill'.

This day's packett has brought something *like* an authentic account of a victory[1] by Admiral Neilson over the fleet in which Buonaparte was, but yet I dread giving it too much audit. But it is beyond doubt that this day Teeling[2] was executed, for I saw him hanged at Arbour Hill; he died with the greatest philosophy, declaring that he suffered for his principles. Tone[3] was on his trial today. When called on to plead to the charge exhibited against him, he offered something in the nature of a plea to the jurisdiction by the advice of Peter Burroughs, which was in substance that having been made a prisoner and detained as such from the scene of warfare and the courts of justice being sitting nothing to prevent the jurisdiction of the ordinary tribunals over the crime of high treason alleged against him, he ought not to be prevented the benefits allowed in each case by statute, and should be tried by the court of criminal judication, the Common Law allowing no such courts as courts martial but ex necessities which did not now exist.

I have tresspassed on your time with this intelligence as some excuse for the trouble of the former part of my letter, and requesting your answer

I remain with sincere respect
Yours very truly
Eyre Burton Powell

[*Addressed to*]:

Francis Dobbs Esq[r], M.P.
Carrickfergus

Mathew Tone to ——, 28 September 1798

T.C.D., Madden papers, MS 873/319; printed in Bulmer Hobson (ed.), *The letters of Wolfe Tone* (Dublin, [1920]), p. 131.

Matthew Tone

Letter of Tone after conviction, the 28th of Sep[tembe]r 1798, to the agent[4] who conducted his defence

Dear Sir,

As I know from experience that suspense is the worst of all states, I hasten to relieve my friends from it. The business is determined on and tomorrow

---

[1] Battle of the Nile, fought on 1 Aug. 1798.
[2] Bartholomew Teeling.   [3] Mathew Tone.
[4] Not identified. It is possible that this letter was acquired by Madden from Peter Burrowes.

is the day fixt.[1] I request that no friend may come near me. Sorrow is contagious, and I would not willingly betray any weakness on the occasion.[2]

Accept a thousand thanks for the interest you have taken in my affairs.

Farewell,
Matthew Tone

Londonderry Journal report of Sir John Borlase Warren's victory off Lough Swilly (10–20 October 1798), 23 October 1798

Londonderry Journal, 23 Oct. 1798.

Sir John B. Warren's victory[3]

In our last,[4] we gave the public such intelligence as had then reached us respecting the late glorious and important naval engagement on our coast. We have since taken some pains to procure from the best authorities further particulars of this most interesting event which we hope will be acceptable to our readers.

The information received from various parts of the coast and which excited such interest in the publick mind was fully confirmed by the arrival of the *Canada* and *Foudroyant* men-of-war in Loughswilly on Tuesday last. On that day, Mr Waterhouse,[5] second lieutenant of the *Canada*, passed through this city with dispatches for the Admiralty. To describe the enthusiastic joy that animated all descriptions of people on receiving the glad tidings is utterly impossible: never have we witnessed such general or such hearty expressions of gratitude; the city superbly illuminated; and that and the following evening were devoted to loyalty and exultation. On Wednesday, a Common Council was held at which the freedom of the city was unanimously voted to Sir J. B. Warren in a gild box, and the several captains of his squadron were at the same time complimented with their freedoms.

Sir John Borlase Warren's squadron consisted of the following ships, viz.

---

[1] Mathew Tone was hanged on 29 Sept. at Arbour Hill (*Saunders' News Letter*, 1 Oct. 1798).

[2] According to Buckingham, Mathew Tone, when he was about to be hanged, 'refused a priest and said he gloried in the principles and name of a Frenchman' (Buckingham to Grenville, 29 Sept. 1798, *Report on the manuscripts of J. B. Fortescue, esq.*, iv (H.M.C., London, 1905), p. 329).

[3] Sir John Borlase Warren (1753–1822) commanded the British squadron cruising off Cape Clear, Sept.-Oct. 1798. Created baronet, 1775, Warren entered the navy, 1777, and was commodore, 1794; he gave British naval support to French royalists in the Vendée, June-Oct. 1794; rear admiral, 1799. (*D.N.B.*).   [4] *Londonderry Journal*, 19 Oct. 1798.

[5] Probably John Wilmot Waterhouse, commissioned lieutenant, 1793 (*Steel's original and correct list of the Royal Navy*, July 1798).

Canada, 74 guns	Sir J. B. Warren
Foudroyant, 80	Sir Thomas Byard[1]
Robust, 74	E. Thornborough[2]
Magnanime, 44	Hon. M. de Courcy[3]
Amelia, 44	Hon. C. Herbert[4]
Anson, 44	P. C. Durham[5]
Ethalion, 38	J. Countess[6]
Melampus, 36	G. Moore[7]

The *Amelia* and *Ethalion*, frigates, left the coast of France at the same time that the French fleet got out (Sept[ember] 17th) and were soon after joined by the *Anson*. This little squadron dogged the French fleet throughout its whole course, and was so close upon its rear that it re-took two American brigs soon after they had been captured by the French. The *Boadicea* left the coast of France at the same time with the others, and came to the South of Ireland, as our readers may recollect, with the first intelligence of the sailing of the fleet.

The *Amelia* joined Sir J. B. Warren's squadron on the 9th inst., and gave him most accurate information respecting the enemy's fleet. The *Ethalion* and *Anson* came up just before Sir John came in sight of the French.

On the evening of the 10th Oct[ober] it was that Sir John B. Warren first discovered the enemy off the Rosses, steering for Blacksod Harbour (Co. Mayo) and within six hours sail of land; he immediately gave chase, which continued the whole of the 11th October and till early in the morning of the 12th, when the action commenced. The brig from which Napper Tandy had landed at the Rosses led the van of the French fleet when it first hove in sight; but it was the first to fly, together with a small schooner, neither of which have been since seen.[8]

At the time the action commenced, from the circumstances of the long chase, and of the rough weather that prevailed, both the fleets were a good deal scattered; the action of course was a running one; it was however vigorously supported, and especially by the *Hoche*, which fought for three hours.[9]

---

[1] Byard died shortly afterwards (see below, p. 359).

[2] Edward Thornborough (1754–1834), commissioned lieut, 1773; commander-in-chief of Irish station, 1810–13 (*D.N.B.*).

[3] Not identified.   [4] Not identified.

[5] Philip Charles Durham (1763–1845) entered navy, 1777; commissioned, 1793; cr. knt, 1815; admiral, 1830 (*Steel's original and correct list of the Royal Navy*, July 1798; *D.N.B.*).

[6] *Recte* George Countess, otherwise not identified.

[7] Graham Moore (1764–1843) entered navy, 1777; cr. knt, 1815; admiral, 1837; he was brother of Sir John Moore (*D.N.B.*; see below, pp 422–4).

[8] The *Anacréon*, a brig-rigged corvette, landed Tandy and a small party on Rutland Island on 16 Sept. 1798; she was, according to George Orr, who accompanied Tandy, 'one of the fastest-sailing corvettes in all the French navy', capable of sailing 'eight or nine knots close by the wind' (*Castlereagh corr.*, i, 406–8; Rupert Coughlan, *Napper Tandy* (Dublin, 1976), pp 122, 126).

[9] On board the *Hoche* was Tone. 'During the action', wrote William Tone, 'my father commanded one of the batteries and, according to the report of the officers who returned to France, fought with

The *Robust* and *Magnanime* bore the chief brunt of the action with her, but she struck to the *Canada*, and immediately on that event happening the rest of the French fleet betook themselves to flight. Sir J. B. Warren then sent his first lieutenant and some men on board the *Hoche*, and having made signal for the *Robust* to take her in charge, he proceeded in pursuit of the rest.

The *Anson* frigate had lost her mizen mast in the chase, and was not in sight when the action began; but at this moment she appeared again in the van of the enemy, to whose flight she gave a most important check. This is the frigate of which our correspondent wrote in such terms of admiration (see our last) and well she merited the highest eulogium; disabled as she was, she engaged 5 of the enemy's ships successively and had three of them on her at once for a long space of time. The gallant officer[1] who commands this ship is brother to Colonel Durham[2] of the Fifeshire Fencibles, a gentleman to whose conduct and courage the city of Derry and the whole province of Ulster can bear the most ample testimony.

Soon after the pursuit began, three of the French frigates struck, which Sir J. Warren made signals to our ships to take possession of, and then pursued the rest to the Westward with his own ship and the *Foudroyant* for 36 hours. The whole of them would probably have been taken had they not lightened themselves by throwing overboard their arm–chests, spare masts, stores of every kind &c. Quantities of papers were also thrown overboard and seen floating, supposed to have been trash similar to that circulated by Napper Tandy at his landing. Even their boats were thrown overboard, and some wheels for mounting field pieces were also discovered floating. Sir John Warren at length finding further pursuit vain, returned to Loughswilly, which he had previously appointed as the place of rendez–vous for his squadron and their prizes.

One French frigate (the same which attempted to land men at Mount Charles, see our last) was pursued into Donegal Bay by the *Melampus* frigate and taken. This makes the whole number captured one ship of the line (the *Hoche*) and four frigates.

The inhabitants of this city and neighbourhood had been in hopes of seeing the prizes brought into Loughswilly, but the winds which have prevailed for several days past made it impossible for them to make the Lough, though they have been seen beating about from many parts of the coast. Despairing of being able to effect their design, they have changed their destination, and late accounts have been received from four of them stating that they were off Fair Head, steering up Channel, and intending either to go up the Clyde, to put into Belfast Lough, or to sail for England,

---

the utmost desperation, and as if he was courting death' (*Life*, ii, 524). Details of the action are given by Hardy in reports to the Directory dated 19 Nov. 1798 (below: pp 427–31).

[1] Philip Charles Durham.

[2] According to Mrs Martha McTier, writing to her brother on 31 May 1798, Col. James Durham was 'well thought of' in Belfast (*Drennan–McTier letters*, ii, 409).

as the weather might permit. As to the *Hoche*, she has been seen towards the North of Scotland much shattered and in charge of the *Robust* and *Doris*; we shall probably have the satisfaction of seeing her in Loughswilly.

On the 17th inst. a most gallant action was fought about 40 leagues W. of Tory between *Mermaid* frigate, of 32 12-pounders, and one of the *Raze*'s [*sic*] (a 74-gun ship cut down but carrying 44 guns of weighty metal) which had escaped Sir John Warren. The *Mermaid*, with the *Révolutionnaire* and *Kangaroo* frigates, had chased for 48 hours; having fallen in with two of the enemy, the *Révolutionnaire* parted in pursuit of them; the *Kangaroo* was soon after disabled by a shot from one of the enemy's stern charges, which carried away her fore-topmast; the *Mermaid* of course left her behind and singly pursued and came up with the enemy: a most obstinate action ensued; the French ship at length struck; but the *Mermaid* was so much damaged as not to be able to take possession of her prize, which she left almost a wreck. She herself arrived on the 20th in Loughswilly and is refitting for sea with great expedition.

The *Révolutionnaire* is a fine frigate carrying 40 18-pounders, and we have no doubt that she will give a good account of the ship which she pursued.

The *Foudroyant* yesterday returned from a cruise and is now in Loughswilly with the *Canada* and *Mermaid*.

The French Admiral Savary,[1] who commanded the three frigates which brought the handful of troops under General Humbert to Killalla, had returned to Brest a few days before the enemy sailed, when he was immediately sent for by express and put in command of this squadron that was then destined to invade our country.[2]

On this whole affair, so honourable to the British flag, so singularly important to this quarter of the Empire, we shall not insult our readers by offering a single reflection. To the feelings, to the gratitude, to the admiration of every subject—let these details speak for themselves.

Londonderry Journal report of Tone's landing in Ireland (3 November 1798), 6 November 1798

Londonderry Journal, 6 Nov. 1798.

---

[1] Daniel Savary (1743–1808), naval commander at Rochefort; served with the French East India company before the revolution; *contre-amiral*, 1802 (Six, *Dict. des généraux & amiraux*).

[2] A second expedition under Savary's naval command left Rochefort (not Brest) on 12 Oct. Intended to reinforce Humbert and Hardy, it reached Killala on the 25th but, on receiving news of Humbert's defeat, turned back for France. Despite being intercepted on 28 Oct. by a British squadron, all four vessels reached the French coast by mid Nov. (F. W. van Brock, 'Dilemma at Killala' in *Irish Sword*, viii, no. 45 (1968), pp 261–73).

On Wednesday last [31 October] his Majesty's ship *Robust* and the *Hebé* and *Doris* frigates, with the French Admiral's ship *La Hoche* in tow of the latter, arrived in Loughswilly. They had been beating about in the offing, unable, in consequence of the disabled state of *La Hoche*, to work into the harbour against the adverse winds which have prevailed since the engagement on the 12th ultimo.

On Thursday and Friday the weather being uncommonly boisterous prevented any communication between the ships and the shore, but on Saturday the wind falling, 500 of the prisoners were landed and escorted to this town by a party of the Breadalbane and Somersetshire Fencibles. Some of them are well looking, others wretched in their appearance. They are coarsely and variously cloathed, the uniform most distinguishable is blue, fac'd with white; they seemed delighted by getting on shore, and many of them declared they were happy in being made prisoners, having been forced into the service and expecting to be led to certain slaughter.

Yesterday morning 200 of those who arrived on Saturday were transmitted under a strong escort to Lifford, and in the evening about 150 came in here from the ships; more are to be sent up today, so as to make the whole that have been landed at Loughswilly 800, which will be forwarded in different detachments to Newry, and from thence they will be shipped off to England.

This day the *Hebé* frigate is to sail from Loughswilly for Liverpool, with General Hardy, his suite and all the other officers of the French army on board, and such of the other prisoners as have not been landed.

The only Irishman as yet discovered among the prisoners is the celebrated Theobald Wolfe Tone, who about four years since was, through the leniency of government, permitted to retire to America, and to prove his gratitude for that leniency, he now with the rank of adjutant-general in the French army, and under the name of Smit or Smith, once more revisits his native country, fortunately a prisoner. On landing he was immediately recognized by many of his College and Bar acquaintances.

He is styled in the *role d'équipage* 'Adjutant-Général Theobald Wolfe Tone, dit Smit (called Smith), County Kildare, Ireland'. Yesterday he was transmitted from the place for Dublin, under an escort of dragoons, and in charge of Major Thackery.[1]

Sir George Fitzgerald Hill to Edward Cooke, 3 November 1798

Nat. Arch. (Ire.), Rebellion papers, 620/51/239.

[1] Elias Thackeray (1771–1854), B.A. Cambridge, 1796; served in Cambridge Light Dragoons; took holy orders; vicar of Dundalk, 1803–54 (J. A. Venn, *Alumni Cantabrigienses*, pt II (6 vols, Cambridge, 1940–54), vi, 144; J. B. Leslie, *Armagh clergy and parishes* (Dundalk, 1911), p. 282).

Sir George Fitzgerald Hill (1763–1839), 2nd baronet, graduated B.A. at
T.C.D., 1783; he was M.P. for Londonderry city, 1795–8; chief clerk of the
Irish house of commons from Jan. 1798 (Edith Mary Johnston-Liik, *History
of the Irish parliament* (6 vols, Belfast, 2002), iv, 422–3).

Edward Cooke (1755–1820), under-secretary in the military department at
Dublin Castle, 1789–96, then in the civil department, 1796–1801 (*D.N.B.*).

My Dear Cooke,

Untill this moment such has been the stormy weather that for two days
no boat has been on shore from *Le Hoche*. This morning some hundreds of
the prisoners are just landed. The first man who step[p]ed out of the boat
habited as an officer was T. W. Tone. He recognised me and addressed me
with as much sang froid as you might expect from his character. We have
not yet *ascertained* any other Hibernian to be of his party, but suspect one
of them to be a person named Durham;[1] it is also thought a man named
Duckett[2] is on board, but in such a crowd it is impossible to make all the
scrutiny which on this occasion is requisite. The *Ethalion* frigate is turning
into the Lough with *La Bellone*, French frigate, one of those she chased.

Yours &c.,
G. F. Hill

Tone is sent off to Derry under a strong escort; he called himself Gen[era]l
Smith.

Buncrana, Saturday Nov. 3, twelve o'clock

We yesterday disfranchised Henry Grat[t]an from the privileges of our
ancient & *loyal* Corporation.[3]
Sir Tho[ma]s Bayard[4] died on board the *Foudroyant*. The *Canada* &
Foudroyant are in pursuit of the squadron which was in Killala.

To Major-General the earl of Cavan,
3 November 1798

*Proceedings of a military court held in Dublin Barracks on Saturday the tenth
of November for the trial of Theobald Wolfe Tone* (Dublin, 1798), pp 21–2.

Richard Ford William Lambart (1763–1836), 7th earl of Cavan, was
commissioned ensign in the Coldstream Guards in 1779; he commanded a
brigade at Londonderry, 1798–9 (*D.N.B.*).

[1] Not identified.   [2] Duckett was not with the expedition.
[3] On 2 Nov. 1798 the common council of Londonderry ordered that Henry Grattan, a freeman of
the city, be disfranchised (*Faulkner's Dublin Journal*, 10 Nov. 1798).
[4] Early in Nov. 1798 it was reported that Sir Thomas Byard, captain of the *Foudroyant*, one of the
ships in Warren's squadron, had died (ibid.).

Derry Prison, 12 Brumaire, an 6[1] (3d Nov. 1798) N.S

My Lord,

On my arrival here, Major Chester[2] informed me that his orders from your Lordship, in consequence, as I presume, of the directions of Government, were that I should be put in irons. I take it for granted those orders were issued in ignorance of the rank I have the honour to hold in the armies of the French Republic. I am, in consequence, to apprize your Lordship that I am breveted as Chief de Brigade in the Infantry since the 1st Messidor, an 4; that I have been promoted to the rank of Adjutant General the 2d Nivôse, an 6; and finally, that I have served as such, attached to General Hardy, since the 3d Thermidor, an 6, by virtue of the orders of the Minister at War. Major Chester, to whom I have shewed my commission, can satisfy your Lordship as to the fact, and General Hardy will ascertain the authenticity of the documents.

Under these circumstances, I address myself to your Lordship as a man of honour and a soldier, and I do protest, in the most precise and strongest manner, against the indignity intended against the honour of the French army in my person; and I claim the rights and privileges of a prisoner of war, agreeably to my rank and situation in an army not less to be respected in all points than any other which exists in Europe.

From the situation your Lordship holds under your Government, I must presume you have discretionary power to act according to circumstances, and I cannot for a moment doubt but what I have now explained to your Lordship will induce you to give immediate orders that the honour of the French nation and the French army be respected in my person; and of course I shall suffer no coercion other than in common with the rest of my brave comrades whom the fortune of war has for the moment deprived of their Liberty.

I am, my Lord,
With great respect,
Your Lordship's most obedient servant,
T. W. Tone
dit Smith, Adj. Gen.

From Major-General the earl of Cavan, 3 November 1798

Proceedings of a military court held in Dublin Barracks on Saturday the tenth of November for the trial of Theobald Wolfe Tone (Dublin, 1798), pp. 22–3.

---

[1] i.e. 3 Nov. 1797. Assuming the letter was written on 3 Nov. 1798, this is an error for '13 Brumaire an 7'.

[2] Harry Chester (d. 1821), commissioned as ensign in Coldstream Guards, 1790; lieut and capt., 1793 (*Army list; Gent. Mag.*, xci (1821), pt I, p. 93).

Buncranna, Nov. 3, 1798

Sir,

I have received your letter of this date from Derry Gaol in which you inform me that you consider your being ordered into irons as an insult and degradation to the rank you hold in the army of the French Republic; and that you protest in the most precise and strongest manner against such indignity. Had you been a native of France, or of any other country not belonging to the British Empire, indisputably it would be so; but the motive that directed me to give the order I did this morning for your being put in irons was that I looked upon you (and you have proved yourself) a traitor and rebel to your sovereign and native country, and as such you shall be treated by me.

I shall enforce the order I gave this morning, and I lament as a man the fate that awaits you. Every indulgence shall be granted you by me individually that is not inconsistent with my public duty.

I am, Sir,
Your humble servant,
Cavan, Major-Gen.

Londonderry Journal report of Tone's conduct on board the *Hoche* (October 1798), 13 November 1798

Londonderry Journal, 13 Nov. 1798.

In our last paper[1] we mentioned that Theobald Wolfe Tone having been taken in the *Hoche*, had arrived in Loughswilly, a prisoner on board the *Robust*, and from thence transmitted in charge of Major Thackeray to Dublin. However infamous (and no character more infamous than that of traitor), however criminal may be the untried culprit, to prejudge him, or to influence the public mind against him, is contrary to that benign spirit which so eminently distinguishes the British code, both in law and custom.

Impressed with these ideas, we declined inserting a few particulars relative to Tone which had been communicated to us previous to his being sent to Dublin, but having received accounts that the trial of this arch traitor is over, though the sentence has not transpired, we no longer hesitate in publishing such circumstances respecting him as have come to our knowledge.

---

[1] Above, pp 357–8.

After giving some particulars relating to Tone, his connexion with William Jackson, his departure for America and his exertions in France to promote an invasion, the report continues as follows:

We have learned from some of the French officers themselves that in this last expedition amongst other stimulatives to urge them forward with spirit, Tone painted to them in glowing colours the beauties of the fair sex in this country and boasted the good reception he could procure from them for his brother soldiers. Is there another trait requisite to stamp this villain?

Conscious of being detected, this wretch used no means to conceal himself. Had he done so they must have been fruitless. On landing at Buncrana, he was identified by numbers, and on being brought to the Castle, where Lord Cavan resided, he affected a considerable degree of ease, but was obviously agitated in the extreme.

Lord Cavan told him he was under the necessity of taking measures with regard to him which would be rather disagreeable. Tone said, 'My Lord, you know your duty; I mine'. He then enquired from a gentleman present, whom he had formerly known, respecting all his old Bar acquaintances, talked of them and Irish affairs very freely, as if he had been an Irishman; but afterwards giving an account of the action with Sir J. B. Warren he resumed all the manners and feelings of a Frenchman.

After remaining a short time at Buncrana, he was conducted to the gaol here by Lord Cavan's aid-de-camp, Capt. Chester, who, committing him, directed that he should be put in irons. Against this he remonstrated violently, insisted that being a subject of France, and holding a commission as general in the French Army, he should be treated as a prisoner-of-war and even threatened retaliation in case he was not. Being indulged with materials for writing, he addressed a letter to Lord Cavan on the subject, couched in the genuine terms of republican insolence.

His audacious style of proceeding availed him but little—he however did not share it—for on being informed he must be treated as traitors usually are, he divested himself of an elegant republican uniform, saying that 'it should not be disgraced', and when the irons were fastened on his leg, he declared that to wear such a badge of distinction was preferable to being invested with the Star and Garter.

Elias Thackeray's recollection of Tone's journey from Derry to Dublin (5–8 November 1798)

John Mitchel to Thomas Davis, 7 Sept. 1845, printed in Sir Charles Gavan Duffy, *Young Ireland: a fragment of Irish history, 1840–1850* (London, 1880), pp 682–3.

This letter recounts a conversation between Mitchel and Elias Thackeray in which Thackeray recollected accompanying Tone on his journey from Londonderry to Dublin in November 1798. Though it is not a contemporary document, it is included here for its value as a primary source.

There is a later version of Thackeray's recollection in John Mitchel to John Blake Dillon, 17 Dec. 1845 (T.C.D., Dillon papers, MS 6455/18a). Significant variants are noted below.

Banbridge, 7 September 1845

My dear Davis,

I wish you had *called* on old Mr Thackeray and examined him by what they call in chancery 'personal interrogatories'. He would have remembered far better and been a thousand times more communicative. To me who was a perfect stranger to him, but a good listener, he talked most freely and answered each question by a number of anecdotes. Perhaps you will get a letter of introduction and go to him yet.

I will set down what I distinctly remember. Mr Thackeray was an officer in the Cambridgeshire militia and was quartered in Derry when Tone was taken in Lough Swilly. He was *present* at Lord Cavan's quarters at Letterkenny when the French officers were assembled for breakfast at Lord Cavan's along with the English officers.

Sir George Hill's *brother*[1] (not himself as Tone's life has it[2]) was the person to recognise and discover him.[3] Lord Cavan immediately informed him that he was regarded not as a prisoner-of-war but as a traitor and rebel, and was not to sit in company with the other officers.[4] I forget whether Mr Thackeray confirms the story of his being ironed; but he certainly said that Tone took the matter very quietly,[5] that he was provided his breakfast at a small table apart from the rest, and that 'by the same token' he made a very hearty breakfast.

Mr Thackeray was the person who commanded the party[6] which conducted Tone from Derry to Dublin.[7] He was taken *through the city of Derry* (but not I think any further) with his legs ironed under his horse's belly, and was dressed in his uniform as chef de brigade. The journey from Derry to Dublin occupied four days. Mr Thackeray rode by his side all the way, and says he never spent pleasanter days or met a more delightful companion, which it is not hard to believe.

---

[1] John Beresford Hill (1765–1806), B.A., T.C.D., 1787; rector of Lower Langfield, 1796–1806 (J. B. Leslie, *Derry clergy and parishes* (Enniskillen, 1937), p. 62).

[2] *Life*, ii, 524–5; cf. Sir George Hill's own account (above, pp 358–9).

[3] 'Sir George Hill's brother . . . entered the breakfast room [and] walked up to Tone to address him by his name' (Mitchel to Dillon, 17 Dec. 1845).

[4] 'His whole conduct was perfectly calm and disdainful' (ibid.).

[5] Later version reads 'Lord Cavan and the officers treated him with insolent hauteur and he was not permitted to breakfast at the table with the other prisoners and their entertainers'.

[6] Later version specifies 'escort of dragoons'.

[7] Thackeray was paid £28 8s. 9d. on 12 Nov. 1798 in expenses for escorting Tone from Derry (Madden, *United Irishmen*, 2nd ed., i (1857), p. 373).

On the morning of the last day they breakfasted in the Old Man of War Inn——thirteen miles from Dublin.[1] Tone had hitherto worn plain clothes (since leaving Derry) but on this morning, after breakfast, he went upstairs and came down in the full dress French uniform. Mr Thackeray says *he knew* that this was done in order that he might be known *and rescued* by the people before reaching Dublin, a very improbable thing, and that therefore he was determined not to go with him in that dress. They had however been up to that time on so friendly and familiar terms that he had much reluctance in addressing him in any other tone. But at length he observed that the morning was cold and that Mr Tone had better not travel without any outside coat or cloak. Tone replied that he felt not at all cold and would ride on as he was. Then Mr Thackeray told him he could not permit that, and if he persisted force must be used.[2]

The old gentleman here became more reserved in his communication, and merely said that the remainder of the journey was painful.[3] I did not press for further particulars but concluded that poor Tone was fettered here again.

The only point in which all this differs from the other accounts is the making Tone's detector to be Sir George Hill's brother. I intended writing to you soon on this subject but did not know that you were already engaged upon poor Theobald.[4] It is a sad story, but hardly sadder than the one which has fallen to my lot to tell (Life of Hugh O'Neill).[5] 'What curse is on our land and us?' I am going to put the motto you sent me upon the title page, though I think it looks somewhat pedantic for a man who knows not a word of Irish. Of all shabby pretensions, that of pretending to know what one does not know is about the shabbiest.

Faithfully yours,
John Mitchel

From General Jean Hardy, 4 November 1798

Archives de la Guerre, B¹¹ 2; copy in N.L.I., MS 13258.

Hardy acknowledges Tone's letter of 2 November informing him of his arrest, states his intention of making representations to Cornwallis and assures Tone that he will not be abandoned.

[1] For an earlier breakfast visit by Tone to the Man of War, on 9 July 1792, see above, vol. I, p. 207. It was about 27 km north of Dublin, or about 13 Irish miles.

[2] Later version states that Thackeray's remonstrance was 'in vain and means had to be used to force him to alter his dress'.

[3] Later version reads 'told me nothing more than that all conversation between them ceased and that the pleasure of the journey was over'.

[4] Davis had made a plan for a life of Tone, which however his early death on 16 Sept. 1845 (only nine days after Mitchel wrote) prevented him from carrying out (Sir Charles Gavan Duffy, *Young Ireland* (London, 1880), pp 679–83; idem, *Thomas Davis* (London, 1890), pp 199–201).

[5] John Mitchel, *Life and times of Aodh O'Neill, prince of Ulster* (Dublin, 1845).

Des bords du lac Swilly,
le 14 Brumaire an 7ᵉ de la République

Le général Hardy à l'adjudant général Wolf Thone, dit Smith

C'est avec la plus vive douleur, mon cher Smith, que j'apprends par votre lettre du 12 de ce mois que l'on a employé des moyens aussi rigoureux pour s'assurer de votre personne. Je vais faire à l'instant des démarches auprès du général Cornwallis pour que votre sort soit adouci.

La loyauté, la franchise et les autres qualités que toujours j'apprécierai en vous me persuadent que vous saurez soutenir la dignité de votre caractère. J'aime à croire que les mesures qu'on a prises à votre égard ne sont que de précaution et que bientôt vous triompherez de vos détracteurs.

Vous êtes de droit citoyen et officier français, et à ces deux titres vous devez être convaincu que vous ne serez abandonné ni du gouvernement qui vous a adopté ni de votre général.

Hardy

General Jean Hardy to Marquis Cornwallis, 4 November 1798

Archives de la Guerre, B¹¹ 2; copy in N.L.I, MS 13258; printed in *Mémoires militaires du général Jean Hardy, 1792–1802* (Paris, 1883), pp 10–11.

Hardy requests that Tone be treated with due respect as a French citizen, a member of the French army and a prisoner-of-war.

Des bords du lac Swilly, nord de l'Irlande,
le 14 brumaire an 7ᵉ de la République française

Le général Hardy au Lord Cornwallis, commandant en Irlande

Milord,

L'adjudant-général Wolf Thone [*sic*] dit Smith, attaché à l'état-major de l'armée expéditionnaire dont le gouvernement français m'a confié le commandement, et fait avec moi prisonnier de guerre sur le vaisseau le *Hoche*, réclame mon intervention près de vous contre les mesures de rigueur qui ont été employées pour le traîner dans les cachots et l'y charger de chaînes. Je n'entre pas dans la question de savoir si vous avez des griefs à imputer à cet officier, mais il est citoyen français, il fait partie de l'armée française, il est prisonnier de guerre, et, sous ce triple rapport, il mérite des égards et des respects. J'aime à me persuader, Milord, que vous reviendrez à des idées plus justes sur son compte et que l'esprit de prévention ne l'emportera pas sur la droiture qui doit caractériser les hommes que le mérite ou la fortune ont placés sur un grand théâtre.

L'adjudant-général Wolf Thone est un honnête citoyen. Sa bravoure et des actions d'éclat lui ont mérité la confiance du gouvernment français et l'estime de tous les militaires qui ont l'honneur pour guide, et je ne dois pas vous celer la surprise qu'il me cause en m'apprenant que vous le faites traiter ignominieusement comme un scélérat.

Je réclame au nom du gouvernement français toute votre équité à l'égard de cet infortuné citoyen. Si le sort des armes vous a favorisé au combat du 21 vendémiaire, je ne puis croire que vous veuilliez vous prévaloir de ce succès pour avilir la nation française dans la personne de l'adjudant-général Wolf Thone. C'est néanmoins ce qui résulte de l'acte infamant qui vient d'être commis à son égard.

J'ose espérer, Milord, que vous prendrez ma lettre en prompte considération et que vous me procurerez l'avantage d'informer le Directoire Exécutif que votre conduite envers l'adjudant-général Wolf Thone est fondée en principes de justice.

Hardy

Sir George Fitzgerald Hill to Edward Cooke, 6 November 1798

Nat. Arch. (Ire.), Rebellion papers, 620/41/21.

My Dear Cooke,

There is a damned clever fellow second in command to Hardy taken on board the *Hoche* named Simon; he with the other officers were to sail for England in the *Hébé* this morning. Simon told me that Tone was with Hoche at Bantry. Simon was the confidential friend of Hoche and with him in all his expeditions and constantly about his person; he was at Bantry with him, Quiberon, La Vendée &c., &c. He likewise assured me that Lord Ed[ward] Fitzgerald (with whose fate he was acquainted and upon whose activity they had had great reliance) was not one of the Irish agents with whom Hoche had an interview at Frankfort. Simon was present at the interview which did take place there and observed to me as a droll circumstance that Col. Crawford[1] who was wounded was in the same hotel at the moment. He also mentioned that one of Hoche's aid-de-camps was in Dublin when they were in Bantry, say that he had travel[l]ed from London in the same carriage with a person who had been sent over to watch and arrest him without being

---

[1] Sir Charles Gregan Craufurd (1761–1821), lieut-col.; he went on a special mission to the Austrian army, 1795–6, and was so severely wounded at the battle of Amberg on 24 Aug. 1796 that he was invalided home (*D.N.B.*).

discovered,[1] at that time both Simon and Tone urged strongly to have the expedition sent to the north but they did not chuse to risque their fleet so far from the coast of France, their destination on this last occasion was positively Lough Swilly. Being forty leagues to the north of the lough at the time Warren met them, they were steering southward of east to gain the latitude of Tory Island and then to stand for the lough. Hardy says they have numerous friends in Ireland who hold their tongues, particularly about Belfast and even in Derry, said this Gen[eral], altho' you *pretend* to dislike us, I would not be in any hurry to let this batch of officers be exchanged, they sli[p]ped out in two days, that I dined with them at Cavan's a number of curious observations such as Lough Swilly being a finer harbour than they had ever expected and out of the notice of Gt Britain, without a town upon it, and the surrounding inhabitants oppressed Catholics, &c.

I told Lord Cavan you had a museum stuf[f]ed with badges and relicks of Irish conspiracy and rebellion. He will accordingly send you the flag of Erin.

Simon told me and swore to it roundly that Gen. Coote was attacked by only [?]300 men; he acknowledges the damage done to the canal was considerable but might but for the fault of the engineer [have] been of infinitely more consequence.[2]

Yours in haste,
G. F. Hill

Derry, Nov. 6th.

We have got their pilot,[3] who says he is an American, just now under examination.

[*Addressed to*]: E. Cooke, Esq[r]

Earl of Cavan to Edward Cooke, 7 November 1798

Nat. Arch. (Ire.), Rebellion papers, 620/41/23.

My Dear Cooke,

Understanding from George Hill that you have a museum of French curiosities that were imported by them for the revolution of this country, I will send you by the Derry coach that leaves this Thursday and arrives on

---

[1] A reference to Bernard MacSheehy (see above, vol. II, pp 316, 367–9). MacSheehy in fact had left Dublin for France by the time Hoche sailed. The official with whom he shared a carriage was a king's messenger named Thomas Wagstaff. (*Exshaw's English Registry, 1796* (Dublin, 1796), p. 88; C. J. Woods, 'The secret mission to Ireland of Captain Bernard MacSheehy' in *Cork Historical and Archaeological Society Journal*, lxxviii (1973), p. 101).

[2] See above, p. 257.   [3] See below, p. 368, n. 3.

Saturday a green flag with the harp without the crown taken on board the *Hoche*. I understand each ship had one. The upper part of it was torn by the prisoners. I hope you will be amused with Tone and that he will amuse Dublin by his execution. He wrote me an impudent letter[1] I thought, for a man in his situation, a copy of which I sent Mr Alex[r] Knox[2] with my answer, and I dare say he will shew it you. All the French officers were to sail this day in the *Hebé* for Liverpool except Bompard and the French ones who seem to remain in the *Robert*.

Believe me
Y[ou]rs very much obliged
Cavan

Derry, Nov[r] 7, '98.

[*Addressed to*]:
Edwd Cooke, Esq[r]
Castle
Dublin

Sir George Fitzgerald Hill to Edward Cooke, 8 November 1798

Nat. Arch. (Ire.), Rebellion papers, 620/41/25.

My Dear Cooke,

A man styled Col. Waldryn[3] who says he is an American is amongst the French prisoners. I examined him yesterday. He gave very contradictory accounts of himself; he is a seafaring man and was no doubt one of Buonaparte's pilots for this coast. He was in this country he says ten years ago, not since. I suspect he has some acquaintance with the Belfast gentry. I think it might be as well to have him sent to Dublin, or if you consider that too troublesome I can take his deposition to enable you to judge whether anything can be made of him. He says he has been two years and a half in France,

Yours &c.,
G. F. Hill

Derry, Nov[r] 8th.

You will oblige me by any attention you will shew to Major Thackery who went to Dublin with Tone.

---

[1] Above, pp 359–60.   [2] Alexander Knox (1757–1831), private secretary to Castlereagh (*D.N.B.*).
[3] A note dated 8 Messidor an 6 (26 June 1798) in the Archives de la Marine refers to A. W. Waldrhyn as an Irishman from Armagh who knew the Irish coast better than anyone in France and who was recommended by Monroe and Citizens Paine and Muir (Vincennes, Archives de la Guerre, Marine, BB[4], 122, f. 306).

Tone's trunk is sent off this day directed to you by the Derry coach. There is a bag with 240 French crowns in it, his uniform and cloaths. Keep the cap & uniform for your museum.

[*Addressed to*]: Ed Cooke, Esq

Faulkner's Dublin Journal report of Tone's arrival in Dublin (8 November 1798), 10 November 1798

Faulkner's Dublin Journal, 10 Nov. 1798.

Thursday [8 November] Theobald Wolfe Tone was brought to town prisoner from Derry under a strong escort of cavalry and conveyed to the Castle for examination;[1] from thence he was shortly afterwards transmitted to the Provost Marshalsea, at the barracks,[2] preparatory to his trial by Court Martial, which is expected to take place this day. He was dressed in French uniform, greatcoat with a gold-laced hat.[3]

To Viscount Castlereagh, 9 November 1798

N.L.I., MS 36094/3/A; formerly in McPeake papers; T.C.D., Courts-martial proceedings, 1798, MS 872, ff 143v, 145; printed in Bulmer Hobson (ed.), *The letters of Wolfe Tone* (Dublin, [1920]), pp 136–7.

Provost [Prison], Dublin Barr[ac]k, Nov. 1798

My Lord,

I take the liberty to address your lordship a letter for Citizen Niou,[4] commis[sar]y for the ex[chang]e of French prisoners, inclosing one for the Minister of the Marine and a short memor[ia]l to the Executive Directory. As I send them open your lordship will be apprized of my situation here, and I rely in consequence that no measure will be adopted by the Irish government

---

[1] William Drennan told his sister on 8 November of hearing 'that Tone came into the city this day under a strong military guard, dressed in rich French regimentals, and the carriage passed the Four Courts just as the lawyers were coming out. It is said he looked well and unembarrassed.' (*Drennan–McTier letters*, ii, 424).

[2] For a debate on the exact location of the room where Tone was held, see E. Tobin, 'The barracks and posts of Ireland—11: Arbour Hill' in *An Cosantoir*, xxvi (1966), pp 486–506; P. D. O'Donnell, 'Wolfe Tone's Provost prison: some recent research' in *Irish Sword*, xi, no. 50 (1973), pp 21–31.

[3] Tone 'wore a blue surtout coat and a large hat with a French national cockade' (*Saunders' News Letter*, 9 Nov. 1798).

[4] Joseph Niou (1749–1828), member of legislative assembly, the Convention and the Council of Ancients; deputy on mission; commissioner in London for exchange of prisoners (*Dict. parl. français*).

as to me, untill the decision of the Directory be known. The honor of the French nation is pledged to support me as a citizen and an officer. I trust therefore his excellency the Lord Lieutenant will be pleased to give the necessary orders that I may be treated as a prisoner-of-war with such attention as is due to the rank I have the honor to hold in the armies of the French Republic, in order to avoid the distress and confusion which must otherwise arise at the moment when so many thousand prisoners of both nations are in expectation of a speedy exchange. I mention this with the more confidence from the generous manner in which our government has behaved to such British officers as the fortune of war has thrown into our hands.

I have the honor to be

Your lordship's humble serv[an]t
T. W. Tone
Adjt. Gen[era]l

[*Endorsed*]: No. 7. T. W. Tone to Lord Castlereagh

To Joseph Niou, 9 November 1798

N.L.I., MS 36094/3/B; formerly in McPeake papers.

Tone asks Niou to forward a letter to the minister of the marine and to see that nothing is decided about him by the British government before the decision of the Directory is known.

De la prison de Dublin
ce 19 Brumaire an 7

L'adjutant-général T. W. Tone, dit Smith, au Citoyen Niou, commissaire pour l'[é]change des Français prisonniers de guerre en Angleterre

J'ai l'honneur, citoyen, de vous addresser ci-joints un mémoire et une lettre que je vous prie de vouloir bien faire passer le plutôt possible au Ministre de Marine. Je vous prie en même tems, dans votre qualité de commissaire pour l'échange des Français prisonniers de guerre, de prendre telles mesures que vous jugerez convenables pour que rien ne soit statué à mon regard par le gouvernement anglais, avant que la décision du Directoire Exécutif soit connue. Vous aurez la bonté de vous concerter, pour tout ce qui me regarde, avec le général Hardy, auquel j'ai eu l'honneur d'être attaché en qualité d'adjutant général. Je me recommande à votre zèle et à votre patriotisme.

Salut et fraternité
L'adjutant général
T. W. Tone, dit Smith

[*Endorsed*]: No. 8. T. W. Tone's 1st letter to Citizen Niou

To the Executive Directory,
9 November 1798

N.L.I., MS 36094/3/C; formerly in McPeake papers.

Minor spelling errors have been silently corrected below.

Tone draws the attention of the Directory to his plight and expresses confidence that it will take measures to have him treated as a French officer.

ce 19 Brumaire, an 7 de la République française

L'adjutant-général T. W. Tone, *dit Smith*, présentement prisonnier de guerre à Dublin en Irelande, au Directoire Exécutif de la République française

Citoyens Directeurs,

Ayant été pris sur le *Hoche*, dans l'affaire du 21 Vendémiaire, le gouvernment anglais aussitôt notre arrivée en Irlande a donné des ordres de me séparer de mon général, de me faire débarquer seul, de me mettre aux fers, et de me transporter à Dublin où j'ai toute raison de croire qu'on est dans l'intention de me mettre en jugement. Dans ces circonstances je me suis d'abord réclamé auprès du général anglais comme adjudant général français et j'ai demandé à être traité, comme tel avec les égards dus à mon grade. J'ai eu soin en même tems d'en instruire le général Hardy, qui, de son côté, je suis persuadé, a fait les démarches nécessaires pour appuyer ma réclamation. Mais comme on me garde encore et comme on parait vouloir me regarder plutôt comme prisonnier d'état que comme prisonnier de guerre, je m'adresse à vous, Citoyens Directeurs, dans la ferme assurance qu'aussitôt que vous serez instruits de ma situation vous prendrez les mesures nécessaires auprès du gouvernement britan[n]ique pour que l'honneur de la nation et celui de ses armes soient respectés en ma personne et qu'on [me] traite comme officier et comme citoyen français d'une manière convenable à mon grade et à la dignité de la grand[e] nation à laquelle j'ai l'honneur d'appartenir.

Salut et respect
L'adjudant général
T. W. Tone, dit Smith

[*Endorsed*]: No. 9. T. W. Tone's memorial to the Directory

Peter Burrowes to Thomas Russell, *c.*9 November 1798

T.C.D., Sirr papers, MS 868/2, ff 279ʳ–280; printed in Hobson (ed.), *Letters of Wolfe Tone*, pp 138–9.

Dear Russel,

I shall not hesitate to give our friend every assistance in my power. Much as I condemn his late proceedings, I cannot forget how estimable a man he was & how much he was my friend. I must, however, fairly tell you that I think his case totally hopeless and that postponement untill a tryal by jury can be had is the utmost to be hoped. In a letter to Lord Cornwallis he has announced himself a French officer, & the nature of the expedition in w[hic]h he was engaged cannot be doubted. The nature of his departure from this country will not furnish any legal advantage, and will raise the strongest prejudice ag[ains]t him. I understand he has given directions that no person shall be permitted to see him; yet I expect he will send for me. It is the most tortuous service I ever engaged in but I shall not decline it & if I learn anything consolatory (of w[hic]h I despair) will put you in poss[essi]on of it.

Y[ou]rs truly,
P. Burrowes

[*Addressed to*]: T. Russel, Esqʳ

Thomas Addis Emmet to Thomas Russell, *a.*10 November 1798

Nat. Arch. (Ire.), Rebellion papers, 620/15/2/15.

My Dear Russell

It is impossible for anyone to be more concerned or more anxious than we all are about the fate of Tone. There is not a thing that would appear to us to have any chance of succeeding in saving his life that we would not gladly do. But it is owing to that very feeling that your letter has embarrassed us most exceedingly; because it seems to imply that you and your fellow prisoners imagine some such thing could be done, while we have no doubt that any such application would if possible do injury. When we negotiated for Bond's life we had something to give—our banishment and our information.[1] What have we to give

---

[1] See above, p. 326, n. 2.

now? If we cannot make it a matter of truck, surely you cannot suppose we could obtain it as a favour when we have been in vain soliciting the very small favour of good faith being kept with us. I am sure Gov[ernmen]t hate us & if we asked such a favour they would doubly rejoice in the opportunity of gratifying their own vengeance against him & dislike against us. The day we were at the Castle, the Chancellor[1] mentioned that Tone had before he left the kingdom signed such a confession of his own treason as would & was intended to hang him in case of his ever returning, so that I am sure the points on which you rely would avail nothing. Indeed I am convinced it would not be in the power of any interest to ransom him—even retaliation (the only chance) I think will not avail—but if it should have any weight our interference would injure it. These are our fears & have prevented our doing anything because we see nothing we can do, but if you or your friends with you can point out anything which you think would have any chance of success draw it up & send it to us & I assure [you that] it is not a trifle will prevent our signing it.

> Yours &c.
> T. A. Emmet

[*Addressed to*]: T. Russell, Esq[r]

William Wickham to Viscount Castlereagh, 10 November 1798

Memoirs and correspondence of Viscount Castlereagh, second marquess of Londonderry, ed. Charles Vane, marquess of Londonderry (12 vols, London, 1848–53), i, 434.

Robert Stewart, Viscount Castlereagh, was entrusted with the duties of the chief secretary in July 1797 and succeeded to the office on 3 Nov. 1798.

> Whitehall, November 10, 1798

Secret

My Lord,

I am directed, by the Duke of Portland, to forward to your Lordship the enclosed letter,[2] written by Mr Theobald Wolf Tone [*sic*] and found among General Tate's papers. If the handwriting can be established, it may be a material paper to produce and prove on Tone's trial; and it is in the possibility of its being made use of in that manner that his Grace wishes it to be submitted to the Lord Lieutenant.

> I have the honour to be,
> William Wickham

---

[1] Lord Clare.   [2] Above, pp 7–8.

P.S. Your Lordship will have the goodness to return the letter as soon as it shall have been done with.

TONE'S TRIAL

Tone's capture, trial and death were reported widely and at length in newspapers and magazines. Two reports of his trial appeared in pamphlet form. William Tone, when reporting the trial in *Life of Theobald Wolfe Tone*, ii, 528–32, follows with small variations the account printed in *Conseil des Cinq-cens: Motion d'ordre faite par L[ucien] Bonaparte pour la veuve et les enfans de Téobald Wolf-Tone: séance du 9 Brumaire an 8* (Paris, 1799), which seems to have been based on the report in *Le Moniteur*, which was of course taken from British and possibly Irish newspapers.

In this edition there are reprinted an official record of the court-martial proceedings together with accounts of the trial given in the two pamphlets referred to and in *Faulkner's Dublin Journal* and the London *Morning Chronicle*.

See also esp. *Courier* (London), 14–16 Nov. 1798, and *Walker's Hibernian Magazine*, Nov. 1798, pp 737–44.

Proceedings at the court martial for Tone's trial, 10 November 1798

T.C.D., Courts-martial proceedings, 1798, MS 872, ff 152^r–152^v.

Saturday, 10 November 1798. Proceedings of a Gen[eral] Court Martial held in the Barracks of Dublin by order of Lieutenant-Gen[era]l Craig.

Major-Gen[eral] Loftus,[1] President

Col. Vandeleur[2]	Col. Wolfe[3]
Lt Col. Daly	Lt Col. Tytler[4]
Major Armstrong	Captn Corry[5]

---

[1] William Loftus, col., foot guards; major-general on the staff in Ireland, 1796–1800 (J. Philippart, *Royal Military Calendar* (2 vols, London, 1815), i, 106).

[2] John Ormsby Vandeleur (1767–1822), lieut.-col., 5th dragoon guards; landowner in Co. Kildare and M.P. for Granard, 1790–97 (Edith Mary Johnston-Liik, *History of the Irish parliament, 1692–1800* (6 vols, Belfast, 2002), vi, 463).

[3] John Wolfe (1753–1816) of Forenaughts, Co. Kildare; M.P. for Co. Kildare 1783–90, later for Carlow borough, 1798–1800; app. col., Kildare militia, 1796, on resignation of duke of Leinster (ibid., vi, 550–51).

[4] 'Tytler' is probably an error for 'Taylour', i.e. Robert Taylour (1760–1839), lieut.-col. of the 5th dragoon guards and brigadier-general on the staff of the army in Ireland; he was a son of the earl of Bective, and M.P. for Kells, 1791–1800 (*Army list*, 1798, p. 56; Johnston-Liik, *Hist. of Ir. parlt*, vi, 383–4).

[5] Marcus Corry, 5th dragoon guards. Perhaps he was Marcus Corry (1770–1847), later lieut.-col. in Down militia (A. S. Hartigan, *The family of Pollock of Newry and descendants* (Folkestone, 1901)).

Francis Paterson, Esq., J[udge] Ad[vocate] Gen[eral] &
P[rovost] Martial

The court being met & duly sworn proceeded to the trial of Theobald
Wolfe Tone, brought prisoner before the court for having acted traiterously
& hostilely against his Majesty's Gouvernment.

The pris[oner] being arraigned pleaded Guilty & addressed the court from
a paper which is hereunto annex'd—No. 1.[1]

The pris[one]r also handed into the court three diff[eren]t papers here-
with sent—Nos 2–3–4.[2]

The prisoner Theobald Wolfe Tone having pleaded Guilty, the court do
find the prisoner Theobald Wolfe Tone guilty of the crimes alledged against
him & do therefore adjudge him to be hanged, his head to be struck off,
fixed on a pike & placed in the most conspicuous part of this city

William Loftus
Major General

Fra[nci]s Paterson
Adv[oca]te Gen[eral] & P[rovost] Martial

Faulkner's Dublin Journal report of Tone's trial on 10 November 1798

Faulkner's Dublin Journal, 13 Nov. 1798.

Theobald Wolfe Tone

Saturday, Mr Theobald Wolfe Tone came on his trial before a military
court martial at the Barrack of Dublin.[3]

The Court was composed of the following members:

Major-General Loftus, President

Colonel Vandeleur	Colonel Wolfe
Lieutenant-Colonel Daly	Colonel Tytler
Major Armstrong	Captain Corry.

The charges having been read by the Clerk of the Court against Mr Tone
implicating him as a natural-born subject of our Lord the King, having

---

[1] Probably Tone's address to the court.

[2] Probably his brevet and letter of service (see below, p. 382).

[3] William Tone's account sets the scene: 'at an early hour the neighbourhood of the barracks was
crowded with eager and anxious spectators. As soon as the doors were thrown open, they rushed in
and filled every corner of the hall.' (*Life*, ii, 528). The Dublin Barracks were situated on the north
bank of the Liffey near the main entrance to the Phoenix Park.

traitorously entered into the service of the French Republic at open war with his Majesty, and being taken in open war bearing arms against his king and country and assuming a command in an enemy's army approaching the shore of his native country for the purpose of invasion, and acting in open resistance to his Majesty's forces with several other charges of a treasonable nature. On the conclusion of the charges read against him, he was called to plead whether guilty or not guilty?

Mr Tone, bowing to the Court,[1] said he presumed this was the time in which he might read to the court the statement of a few points which he had committed to paper for the occasion of his trial.

He was asked in the first instance if he would plead to the charge against him, guilty or not guilty? He answered that it was not his wish to avail himself of any subterfuge, or to give the court any unnecessary trouble; he was ready to admit the whole of the charge exhibited against him.

He was then asked what was his object in his reading the paper in his hand, was it anything he wished to offer in his defence, was it anything which his own sense must tell him might be improper for the Court to hear?

Mr Tone answered the paper was certainly drawn up with a view to vindication, though possibly it could not be considered as a defence against the accusation on which he was now called to trial. He could not say whether it was that kind of defence which the Court might chuse to hear. He had endeavoured, in the formation, to be as collected and moderate as his feelings could possibly admit; and if the Court would do him the honor of permitting him to read the paper, its contents would best suggest how far it was admissible as to the reading, and the Court would have the opportunity to check him where any part of the reading seemed to them improper.

The Court was pleased to admit the reading, and Mr Tone proceeded to read the paper.

It stated 'that he had been from his infancy bred up in an honourable poverty, and since the first dawn of his reason he had been an enthusiast to the love of his country. The progress of a classical and academic education confirmed him still stronger in those principles and spurred him on to support by actions those opinions he had so strongly conceived in theory— that British connexion, in his opinion, was the bane of his country's prosperity, and it was his object to destroy this connexion, and in the event of his exertions, he succeeded in rousing three millions of his countrymen to a sense of their national debasement.'

Here he was interrupted by the Court with an admonition that anything so inflammatory could not be heard, as it would only tend to foment the

---

[1] He was dressed in full ceremonial French uniform: 'a large and fiercely-cocked hat, with broad gold lace and the tricoloured cockade, a blue uniform coat, with gold and embroidered collar and two large gold epaulets, blue pantalons with gold laced garters at the knees, and short boots bound at the tops with gold lace' (*Courier*, 15 Nov. 1798).

seditious spirits of persons of a certain description who might have gained admittance to the Court.

Mr Tone said, 'he was convinced no persons of the description alluded to were present there, but stood corrected, and said he should proceed to the remainder, which was exempt from such objections. He wished, however, first to return his thanks to that religious body of Irishmen whose oppressions had first interested his zeal for his country's cause.'

Here he was again stopt, and Mr Patterson, Judge Advocate, admonished him that, as it was useless for him to attempt pressing on the Court irrelevant matter of a nature to which the Court could not attend and which, as it must go before the Lord Lieutenant, a part of the matter on which the Court should found its verdict—would tend rather to injure than serve his cause. He reminded Mr Tone of certain points mentioned by him in a private conversation yesterday, and advised him to confine himself to those points as more material to his purpose.

Mr Tone bowed again and said he should not take up the time of the Court by any subterfuge to which the forms of the law might entitle him. He admitted the charge of coming in arms as the leader of a French force to invade Ireland, but said it was as a man banished, amputated from all natural and political connection with his own country, and a naturalized subject of France bearing a commission of the French Republic under which it was his duty implicitly to obey the commands of his military superiors.

And he produced this commission constituting him an adjutant-general in the French service, and also his written orders to join the Army of England, at three separate periods—first under Buonaparte, secondly under Hoche, and lastly under Kilmaine, who was a native of Ireland and who commanded the last expedition for this country.

He said he knew from what had already occurred to the officers, natives of Ireland, who had been made prisoners on this expedition what would be his fate.[1] On that, however, he had made up his mind. He was satisfied that every liberal man who knew his mind and principles would be convinced in whatever enterprize he engaged for the good of his country, it was impossible he could ever have been combined in approbation or aid to the fanatical and sanguinary atrocities perpetrated by many of the persons engaged in the recent conflict. He hoped the Court would do him the justice to believe that from his soul he abhorred such abominable conduct. He had, in every public proceeding of his life, been actuated by the purest motives of love to his country—and it was the highest ambition of his soul to tread in the glorious paths chalked out by the example of Washington in America and Kosciusko in Poland. In such arduous and political pursuits success was the criterion of merit and

[1] Bartholomew Teeling and Mathew Tone, both of whom received commissions in France, served in Ireland under Humbert and were made prisoners after the French defeat at Ballinamuck, were tried by court martial for treason, convicted and executed by hanging.

fame; it was his lot to fail, and he was resigned to his fate. Personal considerations he had none. The sooner he could meet the fate which awaited him, the more agreeable to his feelings; but he could not repress his anxiety for the honour of the nation whose uniform he wore and the dignity of that commission he had the honour to bear as adjutant-general in the French service. As to the sentence of the Court which he so fully anticipated, he had but one wish, that it might obtain the approbation of the chief governor to be inflicted within one hour; but the only request he had to solicit of the Court was that the mode of his death might not degrade the honour of a soldier. The French army did not feel it contrary to the dignity or the etiquette of arms to grant similar favours to emigrant officers taken on returning under British command to invade their native country. He recollected two instances of this in the cases of Charette and Sombreuil,[1] who had obtained their request of being shot by files of grenadiers. A similar fate was the only favour he had to ask, and he trusted that men susceptible of the nice feelings of a soldier's honour would not refuse his request. As to the rest, he was perfectly reconciled.

Mr Tone, thus concluding, bowed respectfully to the Court, who immediately made up their judgment, which, together with the grounds on which it was formed, has been laid before his Excellency the Lord Lieutenant for his approbation.

The Court Martial which on Saturday tried this unfortunate man was on Sunday generally understood to have found him *guilty* of the crime with which he was charged and which his speech upon his trial fully confessed— 'that of having served in the army of the enemy against his King and Country'.

About eight o'clock yesterday morning[2] it was discovered that T. W. Tone had endeavoured to avoid the sentence of public execution by an attempt to take away his own life; he was found by the keeper of his prison exhausted by loss of blood, his windpipe completely cut across, and the veins of his neck slightly wounded by a pen-knife, which was found in his hand.

The order for his execution had been issued, the front of Newgate was the place appointed and everything was prepared for his reception at the awful spot when Mr Curran[3] moved [at] the Court of King's Bench 'for an *habeas corpus* directed to the keeper of the Prévost Marshalsea to bring up the body of Theobald Wolfe Tone with the cause of his detention'.

Soon after this writ had issued as a matter of course, another application was made to the Court, founded on an affidavit filed by the father of Tone, stating that upon delivering of the writ to the Brigade-Major[4] at the barrack,

---

[1] Charles Virot de Sombreuil (d. 1795), royalist officer; he was in command of an émigré force and was shot after being captured at Quiberon (*Biographie nouvelle des contemporains*, xix (Paris, 1825), pp 244–5).   [2] Monday, 12 Nov.
[3] John Philpot Curran.
[4] William Sandys (d. 1812), captain, Longford militia; major of brigade in Dublin, 1798; later deputy ranger of Phoenix Park. He was, he pointed out, the only permanent major of brigade on the staff and the only major of brigade commissioned by his majesty. It appears that, unlike other brigade

that gentleman had peremptorily refused to comply with the mandate of the writ, alledging 'that he acted under the order of the General of the Garrison and knew no other power'.

Upon this new application, the High Sheriffs of Dublin were directed by the Court to proceed to the barrack and there enforce the order of the Court by taking into their custody the persons of Theobald Wolfe Tone and his detainees.

The Sheriff[1] shortly after returned with the Surgeon[2] who had been called upon to attend Tone, who deposed to the Court that Tone was in so very dangerous a state as to render his removal of imminent danger to his life.

The Court then respited the return of the *habeas corpus* for four days.

In order to prevent any further attempt at suicide, a strait-waistcoat similar to that usually applied to insane persons has been affixed to Tone in consequence of his attempt towards his own destruction.

Morning Chronicle report of Tone's trial on 10 November 1798

Morning Chronicle (London), 15 Nov. 1798.

Ireland
Private letter
Trial of Theobald Wolfe Tone for high treason

Dublin, Nov. 10
About half past eleven o'clock the Court Martial met and was composed of the following persons, viz.

General Loftus, President

Colonel Vandeleur	Colonel Wolfe
Colonel Daly	Colonel Titler
Major Armstrong	Captain Corry

Mr Tone having been brought in, and the charge of high treason read by the Judge Advocate, the usual interrogation was then put to the prisoner, who replied that it was not his intention to give the Court the trouble of adducing proof to the charge preferred against him. He admitted the facts, as he disdained having recourse to any species of subterfuge. He hoped,

majors, he was not chief of staff to a general commanding a brigade but was in charge of the Provost prison. (*Irish Magazine*, July 1812, pp 335–6; Madden, *United Irishmen*, 2nd ed. (1857–60), i, 481–2, ii, 184–5; William Sandys to Alexander Marsden, 23 Dec. 1799 (Nat. Arch. (Ire.), Rebellion papers, 620/56/189; ibid., Official papers, 23/13, 106/20)).

[1] Frederick Darley (see below, p. 413, n. 2).   [2] Benjamin Lentaigne (see below, p. 391, n. 2).

if that was the proper stage, to be indulged in reading to the Court a paper which contained the motives of his action, and he trusted that this indulgence would be the readier granted, as he had endeavoured to preserve the utmost moderation of language which his situation admitted of; nor would the paper advert to anything that was not already to be found in the reports of the legislature of the country.

President: 'Perhaps the paper may contain matter not proper for the Court to hear.'

Mr Tone: 'The Court will, no doubt, reserve to itself the power of stopping me, if that should be the case; but I repeat that I have taken care to be as moderate as possible in my expressions, and if any shall be found too strong, notwithstanding my caution, I will not hesitate to adopt such as shall be more consonant to the feelings of my auditors.'

Judge Advocate: 'Do you mean, Mr Tone, that the paper should go before his Excellency the Lord Lieutenant, along with the decision of the Court?'

Mr Tone: 'I have no objection; let the Court in that respect be directed by its own discretion.'

A member (Col. Daly): 'You don't intend, I suppose, by the paper which you want to read, to deny the charge made against you? You plead Guilty of acting traitorously against your King and Country?'

Prisoner: 'I have admitted the facts, which certainly is an admission of the charge which you have technically described.'

After some short and whispered conversation between the members, permission being given, Mr Tone read the paper, to the contents of which the following report by no means renders adequate justice:—

'Mr President and Gentlemen of the Court: It is not my intention to give you any trouble respecting proof of what has been here advanced against me. My admission of the charges prevents a prolongation of those forms which could not possibly prove more irksome to you than they would to me. What I have done has been from principle, and a conviction of its rectitude. I seek not mercy; I hope I am not an object of pity; I anticipate the consequence of my capture, and am prepared for the event. The great object of my life has been the independence of my country, and to that object I have made every sacrifice. Placed in honourable poverty, the love of liberty was implanted by nature and by education in my heart; no seduction, no terror could banish them from thence (and seduction and terror have not been spared against me); and to impart the inestimable blessing to the land of my birth, I braved difficulties, bondage, and death. After an honourable combat, in which I strove to emulate the bravery of my gallant comrades, I was made captive and dragged in irons through the country, not so much to my disgrace as that of the persons by whom such ungenerous and unmanly orders were given. What I have written and said on the state of Ireland I here reiterate. The connexion with England I have ever considered the bane of Ireland, and have done every thing in my power to break it, and to raise three millions of my countrymen to the rank of citizens.'

President: 'The Court cannot listen to this.'

A member: 'To me it appears as if this paper was read for the purpose of sending abroad impressions of a dangerous nature, through the means of persons who may be attending here for the purpose.'

President: 'I think there cannot be any persons of that description here.'

Prisoner: 'I too think there *cannot*.'

Judge Advocate: 'If what is to follow be of a similar nature with that which you have read, I rather think, Mr Tone, that it must operate to your prejudice.'

Mr Tone: 'What immediately follows may be deemed exceptionable by the Court, but I think should not—it is but the expression of my thanks to the Roman Catholics of Ireland, a body of men whom I had once the honour to serve.'

President: 'We shall take care not to introduce anything that does not apply to the case before us—what you speak of is not at all relative, we cannot hear it.'

Prisoner: 'I have not said anything. I do not wish by this paper to say anything that has not already been mentioned by both houses of Parliament, where my name has been so often quoted, and not always with the temper and decency befitting grave deliberation. I wish to know whether I am permitted to proceed?'

President: 'You must confine yourself to such matter as the Court can hear. You may proceed, Mr Tone.'

Here Mr Tone resumed as follows: 'Having considered the resources of this country, and being convinced that she was too weak to effect her independence without assistance, I sought that assistance in France, and without any intrigue, but acting in the open honesty of my principles, and that love of freedom which has distinguished me, I have been adopted by the French Republic; and in the active discharge of my duty as a soldier, have acquired what is to me invaluable, and what I will never relinquish— the friendship of some of the best men in France, and approbation and esteem of my brave comrades in arms. It is not the sentence of any court that can weaken the force or alter the nature of those principles on which I have acted, and truth will outlive the hostility of those prejudices which rule for the day; to her I leave the vindication of my fame, and I trust posterity will not listen to her advocation without being instructed. It is now more than four years since persecution forced me from this country, and I need hardly say that personally I cannot be involved in anything which has happened in my absence. In my efforts to accomplish the freedom of Ireland I would never have had recourse to any other than open and manly war. There have been atrocities committed on both sides, which I lament; and if the generous spirit which I have assisted to raise in the breasts of Irishmen has degenerated into a system of assassination, I believe that all who have any knowledge of me from my infancy to the present day will be ready to admit that no man in existence would more heartily regret that any tyranny of circumstances or policy should pervert the natural dispositions of my countrymen. I have little more to say. Success is all in this life, and unfavoured by her, virtue becomes vicious in the ephemeral estimation of those who attach every merit to prosperity. In the glorious race of patriotism I have pursued the path which Washington has trod in America and Kosciusko in Poland. Like the latter I have failed to effect the freedom of my country; and unlike both, have forfeited my life. I have done my duty, and I have no doubt the Court will do theirs; and I have only to add that a man who has thought and acted as I have done, should be armed against the fear of death.'

Mr Tone having here ended from the written paper, the Judge Advocate asked him if there was anything else which he wished to say? to which the prisoner replied that if he was not to be brought up again, previous to the determination of the Court, he would take the present opportunity of offering a few words more.

The President desired him to proceed.

Mr Tone: 'I believe that I stand under the same circumstances of our émigrés in France, and I only wish to experience that indulgence which the sympathy of honourable feeling and the magnanimity of the French Republic granted to Charette and Sombreuil, in allowing them the death of a soldier. In requesting to be shot, I yield to no personal feeling, and am only directed by a respect for the uniform which I wear and the brave army in which I have had to honour to serve. From the papers which I yesterday delivered to the Brigade Major, it will be seen that I am as regularly brevetted an officer in the French service as any who now hear me have been in the British service; and it will also be seen that I have not sought or obtained my commission as a protection against the consequences of coming to this country in a hostile character.'

Judge Advocate: The acceptance of a commission in the French service amounts to a positive proof of the charge against you; but I suppose its production is merely intended to shew that you are an officer of France.

Here the papers alluded to were produced, which were a Brevet and Letter of Service, signed by the President of the Directory and the Minister of War, by which it appeared that the prisoner was Chef de Brigade.

The President having asked why those papers applied to the prisoner the sirname of Smith, as well as that of Tone, he replied that he went to France from America, and it having been necessary that he should have a passport, he took the first he could get, which ran in the name of Smith; and on arriving in France, he was necessarily registered by that name; indeed, he said, it was very common with French soldiers to have what they term a *nom de guerre*. 'I know', said Mr Tone, 'that I reap no protection from producing my commission, and as I can have no doubt of the decision of the Court, the sooner the Lord Lieutenant's approbation of the sentence can be obtained the better. I could wish, if possible, that my fate were determined in an hour.'

To this the President replied, 'That the Court would immediately proceed to a consideration and judgment of the case, and would make no delay in transmitting the result to his Excellency.'

Mr Tone having then thanked the Court for the attention with which he had been heard was remanded to the Prevot, and the Court was cleared of all but the members.

Throughout the whole of the proceedings the prisoner preserved the greatest fortitude and collection of mind and manner; indeed at first he appeared a little agitated, but it was a defection of nerve, not courage; but in a very little time, he was perfectly assured. He was dressed in the French uniform suited to his rank, being a long blue coat, buttoning half way down the front; the cape and cuffs scarlet richly embroidered, and on each shoulder a very rich epaulet; his pantaloons were blue, with embroidered bands at the knee, and the tops of his half boots were also laced; he wore a large cocked hat with the tri-coloured cockade.

I shall conclude this letter by quoting the public testimony which a member of our parliament[1] bore in his place in the House to the character and disposition of Theobald W. Tone: 'In boyhood he was the companion of my bosom, in manhood he was my friend; and whatever political errors his enthusiasm may have led him into, a greater genius or a better heart no man ever possessed. Alas! that they should have led him to a scaffold.'

Reynolds the informer[2] and Tone are married to two sisters,[3] and it is said the former is using all his influence to save the life of the latter.

Proceedings of a military court held in Dublin Barracks on Saturday the tenth of November [1798] for the trial of Theobald Wolfe Tone

The title and text are taken from the original pamphlet (t.p. + 24 pp).

The pamphlet was advertised in *Saunders' News Letter*, 15 Nov. 1798, as 'just published . . . 1s. 1d.' with the further information that it contains 'a striking likeness of Mr Tone sketched while on his trial'.

Tone's letters to and from the earl of Cavan of 3 Nov. 1798 are printed on pp 21–3. As they have been given above (pp 359–61), they are omitted here.

---

[1] Charles Kendal Bushe (1767–1843) on 24 March 1797 in the debate on the repeal of the insur- rection act (*Report of the debates in the house of commons of Ireland, session 1796–7* . . . (Dublin, 1797), pp 196–7). [2] Thomas Reynolds.

[3] Harriet and Martha Witherington.

PROCEEDINGS
OF A
MILITARY COURT
HELD IN DUBLIN BARRACKS ON SATURDAY THE
TENTH OF NOVEMBER
FOR THE
TRIAL
OF

THEOBALD WOLFE TONE,

FORMERLY
Barrister at Law and reputed FOUNDER of the
THE LATE IRISH UNION
AND
AN ADJUTANT GENERAL IN THE SERVICE
OF THE
French Republic
ON A
CHARGE

'that he being a Natural Born Subject of our Lord the King, . . . taken Traitorously acting in open Arms, commanding an Hostile Force, for the Invasion of this Kingdom'.

DUBLIN: PRINTED BY
VINCENT DOWLING, NO. 5, COLLEGE GREEN,
THE CORNER OF ANGLESEA STREET,
Of whom may be had every new Book
And Pamphlet

1798

INTRODUCTION

AS every circumstance attending the final catastrophe of a man whose name, as the founder of the late Irish Union, will claim a distinguished mention in the history of Ireland, like that of Erostratus, the ambitious Ephesian who burnt the Temple of Diana to perpetuate his own name, the following tolerably accurate sketch of Mr Tone's trial, 'tis hoped, will not be unacceptable to the public.

The manner of that trial, and the brevity in which it was decided by the very prompt acknowledgment of Mr Tone of the truth of the charges against him, afforded no opportunity for that display of eloquence and legal knowledge which so eminently distinguished the trials of so many of his colleagues in revolutionary views; therefore it cannot have so much to interest curiosity. It will, however, form a necessary link of the chain of that history wherein Mr Tone has taken so conspicuous a part, and will afford more characteristical traits of the enthusiasm which actuated this man, from his first conception of the extraordinary project he avows of separating this country from Great Britain to his final failure in the defeat and capture of that hostile squadron to which he acted as the guide; and in the failure of which Mr Tone has found the termination of his political career, and the issues for which he must have been prepared as the alternative of success, in an enterprize in which nothing short of phrenzy could have taught him to expect completion to his wishes.

Of the court before which Mr Tone was tried he has himself acknowledged the candour and indulgence. Indeed nothing could more strongly feature that indulgence than the patience and attention in which he was allowed to profess the immutability of his principles and his pertinacious confidence in their rectitude.

This trait may serve to account for a conduct on the part of Mr Tone for which even those who were his friends and perhaps the dupes of his opinion cannot excuse him either on the score of honour, good sense or gratitude.

Mr Tone's departure from this country about four years since, immediately after the catastrophe of the traitor Jackson, was, as is confidently alledged on the best authority, to have been in consequence of the lenient forbearance of Government to prosecute him for high treason, though with ample evidence for his conviction in their hands. Through the interference of a right hon. officer of the crown,[1] now a noble lord in high judicial authority, who had been the friend of Mr Tone's youth and the admirer of his talents, Mr Tone was permitted to quit this country unmolested, but upon the express condition of never more returning to any part of those dominions whose separation and ruin he had meditated and contrived. How, to this nice honour of a soldier, of which Mr Tone has professed so much proud jealousy, he can reconcile such a breach of *parole*, as not only to return to this country in violation of the compact on which he had accepted pardon and life but that he should come bearing a commission in an hostile army for the purpose of carrying invasive war into the heart of his native country and overturning that government to whose mercy he owed his life is not easy to conceive.

Mr Tone, however, appears to have been a man impelled by wayward fate to the gratification of an enthusiasm not to be restrained by any consideration

---

[1] Arthur Wolfe, appointed chief justice of the king's bench, 2 July 1798, and created Baron Kilwarden, 3 July.

of prudence or propriety; and his last act in attempting his own life to elude the ignominy of a public execution evinces a mind which, however fitted for arduous adventure, was not eminently gifted with fortitude or philosophy.

To those aged parents who have lived to see their hopes blasted in the fate of two of their children on whose education they spared no expence and in whose talents they were taught to expect a prosperous harvest to the unremitting assiduities of parental attention, the end of this man will be a severe blow. Another son,[1] we understand, still remains to console the grey hairs of his afflicted parents and compensate in some degree the anguish occasioned by his brothers. This gentleman is an officer in the East India service[2] and, even at the distance which he is removed from domestic duty, has evinced by frequent remittances his zeal to assist those parents in the decline of life whose tender attention to his earlier years fitted him to pursue the honourable road to his present success.

THE
TRIAL
OF
THEOBALD WOLFE TONE

Court-Room
DUBLIN BARRACK, Saturday November 10th.
The Court was composed of the following members:
Major-General Loftus, President

Col. Vandeleur	Col. Wolfe
Lieut. Col. Daly	Col. Tytler
Major Armstrong	Captain Corry

Mr Tone was brought into Court under a corporal's guard from the Provost Marshalsea, where he had been confined. He was dressed in the French uniform—a large and fiercely-cocked hat, with broad gold lace and the tricoloured cockade; a blue uniform coat, with gold embroidered collar, and two large gold epaulets; blue pantaloons, with gold-laced garters at the knees, and short boots, bound at the tops with gold lace.

At first he seemed a good deal agitated and called for a glass of water, having drank which he seemed much composed and recollected.

The charges having been read by the Judge Advocate against Mr Tone, implicating him as a natural born subject of our Lord the King having traitorously entered into the service of the French Republic at open war with His Majesty and being taken in the fact bearing arms against his King and Country and assuming a command in an enemy's army approaching

---

[1] William Henry Tone.

[2] In fact by 1798 he was no longer in the service of the East India Company but was in the service of an Indian prince, the peishwa of Poona, head of the Mahratta confederacy (see above, p. 9).

the shore of his native land for the purpose of invasion and acting in open resistance to his Majesty's forces, with several other charges of a treasonable nature. On the conclusion of the charges read against him he was called to plead whether guilty or not guilty?

Mr Tone, bowing to the Court, said he presumed this was the time in which he might read to the Court the statements of a few points which he had committed to paper for the occasion of his trial.

He was asked in the first instance if he would plead to the charge against him guilty or not guilty. He answered that it was not his wish to avail himself of any subterfuge, or to give the Court any unnecessary trouble; he was ready to admit the whole of the charge exhibited against him.

He was then asked what was his object in his reading the paper in his hand; was it anything he wished to offer in his defence; was it anything which his own sense must tell him might be improper for the Court to hear? Mr Tone answered the paper was certainly drawn up with a view to vindication, though possibly it could not be considered as a defence against the accusation on which he was now called to trial. He could not say whether it was a kind of defence which the Court might chuse to hear. He had endeavoured in the formation to be as collected and moderate as his feelings could possibly admit; and if the Court would do him the honour of permitting him to read the paper its contents would best suggest how far it was admissible as to the reading.

Court—Sir, before you read that paper, you will do well to consider whether it contains any matter irrelevant to the question now at issue, or anything which your own good sense may suggest the Court ought not to hear.

Prisoner—In what I am about to read I trust there is nothing irrelevant to my situation, nor anything but what I should hope the Court will not think improper to hear. I have endeavoured to be as collected and moderate as possible, and I should not wish to offer any language offensive to the Court.

Judge Advocate—Is there anything in the paper which you wish should go before his Excellency the Lord Lieutenant?

Prisoner—I have no objection.

A member—You have already pleaded guilty to the charge of having acted traitorously; do you mean by anything contained in that paper to retract that plea?

Prisoner—Certainly I have admitted the charge and consequently the appellation by which I am technically described.

President—It is not the wish of the Court, Sir, to deny you any indulgence which consistently with their duty they can grant, but they must reserve to themselves the power of stopping you if you should utter anything irrelevant to the case before them, or unfitting for them to listen to.

Prisoner—The Court, no doubt, will reserve to itself that discretionary power, but I repeat that I have endeavoured to be as moderate as possible, and if any of my expressions should happen to appear objectionable I shall be willing to substitute others less so.

Here the President having given permission, the prisoner read the paper, which was as follows:

Mr President and Gentlemen of the Court,

It is not my intention to give this court any trouble respecting the purport of what has been alledged against me. My admission of the charge prevents a prolongation of those forms which could not be more irksome to you than they would to me. What I have done has been purely from principle and the fullest conviction of its rectitude. I wish not for mercy. I hope I am not an object of pity. I anticipate the consequence of my caption and am prepared for the event. The favourite object of my life has been the independence of my country, and to that object have I made every sacrifice.

Placed in honourable poverty, the love of liberty was implanted by nature and confirmed by education in my heart. No seduction, no terror could banish it from thence—and seduction and terror have not been spared against me. To impart the inestimable blessings of liberty to the land of my birth I have braved difficulties, bondage and death.

After an honourable combat, in which I strove to emulate the bravery of my gallant comrades, I was forced to submit and was dragged in irons through the country, not so much to my disgrace as that of the person by whom such ungenerous and unmanly orders were issued.

Whatever I have written and said on the fate of Ireland, I here reiterate.

The connexion of England I have ever considered as the bane of Ireland, and have done everything in my power to break it, and to raise three millions of my countrymen to the rank of citizens.

Here he was stopped by the Court; and Mr President said—Mr Tone, it is impossible we can listen to this.

A member—It appears to me that this paper has been produced here with a design of making injurious impressions on the minds of persons who may be in this room.

President—I cannot think there are any persons of that description here.

Prisoner—I do not think either that there are any such persons here, nor have I read the paper with the intention imputed to me. What follows will be found less exceptionable.

Judge Advocate—If what follows be of such a nature as you described to me yesterday, I really am of opinion, Mr Tone, it must operate to your prejudice; you will therefore do well to consider before you read it.

On the further advice which the Court and the Judge Advocate humanely urged, the prisoner consented to cancel part of the most exceptionable of what he read and also some subsequent matter which he said was only the expression of his thanks to the Roman Catholics, a body whom he had once, he said, the honour of serving. He then desired to know if he might proceed.

President—It is a principle by which we shall be scrupulously ruled to avoid most carefully everything not immediately relative to your case and the ends of justice; and it is but fitting that we expect you to confine yourself simply to the charge made against you—a reverse conduct can tend to no good purpose.

Prisoner—I have said nothing, nor do I mean to say anything, that has not been already uttered with respect to me in both houses of Parliament, where my name has been so often quoted.

He was then suffered to proceed.

Having considered the resources of the country and being convinced they were too weak to effect her independence without assistance, I sought that assistance in France. And without any intrigue but asking in the open honesty of my principles and that love of freedom which has ever distinguished me, I have been adopted by the French Republic, and in the active discharge of my duty as a soldier acquired what is to me invaluable and what I will never relinquish but with my existence—the friendship of some of the best characters in France and the attachment and esteem of my brave companions in arms.

It is not the sentence of any court that can weaken the force or alter the nature of those principles in which I have acted, and the *truth* of which will outlive those ephemeral prejudices that may rule for the day. To her I leave the vindication of my fame,[1] and I trust posterity will not listen to her advocation without being instructed.

It is now more than four years since persecution drove me from this country and I need hardly say that personally I cannot be involved in anything that has happened during my absence. In my efforts to accomplish the freedom of my country, I never have had recourse to any other than open and manly war. There have been atrocities committed on both sides, which I lament, and if the generous spirit which I had assisted to raise in the breasts of Irishmen has degenerated into a system of assassination, I believe all who have had any knowledge of me from my infancy to the present hour will be ready to admit that no man in existence could more heartily regret that any tyranny of circumstances or policy should so pervert the natural dispositions of my countrymen.

I have little more to say. Success is all in this life—and, unfavoured of her, Virtue becomes vicious in the ephemeral estimation of those who attach every merit to prosperity.

In the glorious race of Patriotism I have pursued the path chalked out by Washington in America and Kosciusko in Poland; like the latter I have failed to emancipate my country and unlike both I have forfeited my life. I have done my duty, and I have no doubt the Court will do theirs; and I have only to add that a man who has thought and acted as I have done should be armed against the fear of death.

A Member—This paper then which you have read contains nothing in denial of the charge made against you.

Prisoner—What I have once done I would be ashamed to deny.

---

[1] *Recte* 'name'?

Here the prisoner having been been asked by the Judge Advocate if there was anything else which he wished to offer to the Court, he replied that if he was not to be brought up again before the decision of the Court, he would wish to say a few words more, which being permitted the prisoner proceeded.

I conceive that I stand here in the same light with our émigrés, and if the indulgence lay within the power of the Court, I would only request what French magnanimity allowed to Charette and to the Count de Sombreuil, the death of a soldier and to be shot by files of grenadiers. This is the only favour I have to ask and I trust that men susceptible of the nice feelings of a soldier's honour will not refuse the request. It is not from any personal feeling that I make this request but from a respect to the uniform which I wear and to the brave army in which I have fought. From papers which I yesterday delivered into the hands of the Brigade Major, it will be seen that I am as regularly breveted an officer in the French service as any here is in the British army, and it will be seen that I have not my commission as a protection.

Judge Advocate—I wish you to be aware that your acceptance of a commission in the French service amounts to positive proof of the charge advanced against you, but from your admissions already I suppose that by the production of those papers you merely want to shew that you were an officer in the French army.

Prisoner—Nothing more.

The papers were then produced and were a brevet for the rank of *chef de brigade* and a letter of service, both bearing the signatures of the President of the French Directory and the Minister of War. By one of those it appeared that his last appointment was to proceed to Brest to join the Army of England; and to some questions asked of him, he answered that he had been appointed to three several armies, destined on three several expeditions [*sic*], under Buonaparte, Hoche and Kilmaine, an Irishman. Having been asked why he was designated in the brevet and letter of service by the name of Smith together with that of Tone, he explained by saying that in proceeding from America to France it was necessary that he should have a passport and accordingly took the first that *fell in his way*, which *happened* to be made out in the name of Smith; on entering France he was accordingly registered by that and his real name, which he had added thereto. 'Indeed', said he, 'almost every soldier in France has what they call a *nom de guerre*'. He repeated his desire to be indulged with death in the most honourable manner, and as he had no doubt of the decision of the Court, he expressed a wish that the confirmation of it by the Lord Lieutenant might be had as soon as possible, and execution of the sentence immediately follow, within an hour if it were practicable.

The President replied that the Court would forthwith proceed to a consideration and judgment of his case, after which no delay would take place in transmitting the proceedings to his Excellency and that it was probable whoever went with them would bear back the Lord Lieutenant's determination on the subject.

The prisoner then thanked the Court for the indulgence which had been extended to him; he was brought back to the Provost Marshalsea.

Further particulars relative to this unfortunate gentleman:

Mr Tone retired from his trial surrounded by the guard which escorted him there, leaning on the arm of Brigade Major Sands. There was a considerable number of yeomanry officers and other loyal citizens assembled to witness this termination of career in the political race of a man viewed as uniting in his own person the Alpha and Omega of the Irish Union. He walked with an air of unconcern and seemed to feel his situation as one who had fully made up his mind to the worst.

The whole of Saturday and Sunday, however, he expressed much anxiety to learn the decision of his Excellency the Lord Lieutenant concerning the request he had made as to the mode of his execution, having no doubt at all as to the sentence of the Court and its confirmation by his Excellency.

On Sunday evening he was informed that his conviction and sentence of death were confirmed by his Excellency but that his request as to the mode of execution could not be complied with; that he must suffer the same fate with the other traitors who were taken in war against their king and country; and that the peculiar circumstances of his case rendered it necessary his execution should be in the most public manner for the sake of a striking example. He must be executed in front of the New Prison, where his former accomplices had forfeited their lives to the justice of their country.

This, however, was an arrangement for which all his fortitude and philosophy could not string the nerves of Mr Tone. Such a torrent of public ignominy was too much for reflection, and he took the resolution of anticipating the execution by his own hand and relieving his mind from the intolerable load of horror which the manner of his approaching fate impressed, for when the sentinels who watched in his room went to rouse him on Monday morning, he [*sic*] found him exhausted, weltering in blood with his throat cut across and apparently expiring. The centinel immediately alarmed the Provost Martial.[1] A military surgeon[2] of the 5th Regiment of Dragoons immediately attended and, on examining the wound, pronounced it not mortal, though extremely dangerous, to which Mr Tone faintly answered, 'I find then I am but a bad anatomist'.

The wound, which was inflicted with a penknife, intersected the windpipe between two of the cartilaginous rings which form that organ and amounts to what surgeons style the operation of bronchotomy;[3] it was dressed but only

---

[1] Thomas Reed, Esq., provost martial general.

[2] Benjamin Lentaigne (1773–1813), assistant surgeon to the 5th dragoon guards. Born at Caen, Normandy, he left France owing to the revolution, arrived in Ireland in 1797 and was in private practice in Dublin from 1799. (R. R. Madden, *The United Irishmen* (2nd ed., Dublin and London, 1857–60), ii, 140–41; *Burke's Irish family records* (London, 1976)).

[3] It was reported in a newspaper that a razor (not a penknife) was used, Lentaigne deposing that Tone 'was incapable of being removed in consequence of his making an attempt on his life, having

with a view to prolong life till the fatal hour of one o'clock appointed for execution, to which end the cart was prepared and an escort of cavalry and infantry under orders to attend it. But in the meantime a motion was made in his Majesty's Court of King's Bench, then sitting, to arrest execution, grounded on an affidavit sworn by the father of the prisoner, that he had been tried, convicted and sentenced to death on a charge of high treason before a military court of seven members sitting in the Barrack of Dublin, though he did not belong to his Majesty's army, while his Majesty's Court of King's Bench was sitting, before which the prisoner might have been tried in the ordinary way. Mr Curran, who ably argued the point, moved that an *habeas corpus* do issue forthwith to bring up the prisoner *instanter*.

The Court immediately complied, and the officer who served the order on the Provost Martial returned with answer that Brigade Major Sands said he would comply with no orders but those of the commander-in-chief of the Garrison; the Court immediately directed the Sheriff to repair to the Barrack, take Mr Sands into custody and bring him before the court. The Sheriff on his return reported that he had seen General Craig, at whose instance he accompanied the surgeon to Mr Tone, and that the surgeon reported the prisoner could not be removed to court without danger of instant death.

The surgeon attended and made affidavit to the same effect, and the return of the writ of *habeas corpus* was postponed for four days.[1]

Minutes of the court martial held last Saturday, 10th November [1798], at the barracks of Dublin, with the speech made upon that occasion by Theobald Wolfe Tone, Esq.

The title and text are taken from the original pamphlet (t.p. + 8 pp.).

MINUTES
OF THE
COURT MARTIAL
HELD
LAST SATURDAY, 10th NOVEMBER

with a razor cut his throat across, nearly from ear to ear, and also separated the windpipe' (*Dublin Evening Post*, 15 Nov. 1798).

[1] A copy of this pamphlet in the R.I.A. is annotated at this point 'Mem: Mr Theobald Wolfe Tone lingered until Monday, November the 19th, when he died, after which his body was on the application of his mother delivered to her and buried'. The title-page is inscribed in the same hand 'Chamb. Walker, Nov' 22d 1798'. The inscription and note are probably by Chamberlain Walker (1738?–1812), rector of Rathconnell (J. B. Leslie, *Ossory clergy and parishes* (Enniskillen, 1933), p. 344).

10 November 1798

AT THE

BARRACKS OF DUBLIN

WITH THE

SPEECH

MADE UPON THAT OCCASION

BY

THEOBALD WOLFE TONE, Esq

TAKEN IN SHORT HAND

BY A

BARRISTER

DUBLIN:

PRINTED FOR JOHN RICE,

NO. 111, GRAFTON STREET

1798

ADVERTISEMENT

The curiosity of the public is too powerfully excited on the present occasion to make it necessary on the part of the editor to offer any apology for the hasty sketch which, in compliance with their anxiety, he ventures to offer them.

Court Martial

General Loftus, President

Col. Daly	Col. Vandeleur
Maj. Carter	Capt. Wolfe
Maj. Price	Capt. Corry[1]

THE Court sat about eleven o'clock, when Mr Tone was introduced by Major Sandys splendidly dressed in the French uniform—a blue coat highly ornamented with gold, a blue and white waistcoat, blue pantaloons and short boots bound with gold and gold tassels. At first entrance he appeared a good deal agitated and asked for a glass of water, which was immediately procured for him. He afterwards appeared perfectly collected.

The charge was then read to him in the usual form by the President— of adhering to the King's enemies—attempting to levy war within the kingdom &c., &c. When asked whether he pleaded guilty or not guilty, he seemed to hesitate at the term, but at length pleaded guilty and immediately after, producing a paper, he spoke nearly to the following effect:

If any expression which may eventually wound the feelings of this Court should find its way into this paper, I entreat them to stop me, and I will erase them; but I imagine there are few material facts which have not been

---

[1] The names are given incorrectly. Major Armstrong and Col. Tytler are missing and are replaced by Major Carter and Major Price. The latter have not been identified.

proved before the Houses of Parliament. The Court shall have no trouble in substantiating the facts that are alledged. I admit them all, and in their fullest extent, and am aware of the consequences. When I embarked in the cause I foresaw the danger, and I trust I shall meet it with becoming fortitude. I think it, however, incumbent upon me to offer a few reasons for my conduct, for never will I disavow the principles by which I have been invariably actuated. I have reviewed, and with all the precision of a man who is soon to die, every action of my life, and there is not one which at this moment does not convey to me satisfaction and triumph, for they have all with unvarying solicitude tended to the emancipation of my native country.

The influence and the connection of Great Britain I have ever considered the bane of the prosperity and happiness of Ireland. These it has been the first wish of my heart to destroy, and the moment I found the *proper resources* of the country inadequate to the conflict, I applied to a nation who had the will and the power to assist her; that generous nation honoured me with its esteem and confidence. I acknowledge it with pride, I acknowledge it with gratitude. Born to an humble but honourable poverty, I had not only to struggle with penury but with temptation; but it now gratifies my heart, and consoles me under what otherwise would be a deep affliction, that I have refused offers certainly dangerous to the virtue of a man in my obscure situation. The good of my country was the first object of my life—for this I became an exile—for this I submitted to poverty—for this I left the bosom of my family—my wife!—my children!—all that made life valuable!—to procure the aid I thought essential to the welfare of Ireland. I braved the dangers of the deep—the fire of the enemy—with my brave, my faithful *camarades*. I embarked for my native country in the delightful hope of raising from abject slavery *three millions* of my fellow-men! . . . [1]

Here the Court interfered. He was told that he was criminating himself and desired[2] to reflect how much such expressions would necessarily injure him. He continued—

But in life, success is omnipotent. I have made an attempt in which Washington succeeded and Kosciusko failed—the deliverance of my country.

I thank the Court for the attention with which they have honoured me. I shall not trouble them much longer. No individual deplores more sincerely than I do the enormities that have been perpetrated—my object was fair and honourable war, and I am shocked to find the contest has degenerated into murder, pillage and assassination. I shall make but few comments on my treatment since I was made a prisoner—I was loaded with irons, but this I consider as disgraceful only to him who issued the orders. To my *masters*, the Roman Catholics of the country, I offer my heartfelt thanks. And I trust that you, Mr President, and the other members of this honourable court will accept my grateful acknowledgements for the indulgence I have experienced. You must do your duty, I trust I shall fulfil mine.

---

[1] Dots appear in original.   [2] i.e. 'he was desired'.

Here he produced three commissions—1st, as chief de brigade, 2d as adjutant general of the army of Ireland, and 3d, as commissary of the army of England and the order to join issued by the Minister of the Marine. He added that he was in the army of England when commanded first by Buonaparte and latterly by General Kilmaine.

Question by one of the Court.[1] Why do these commissions all run in the name of Smyth?

Answer. I assumed the name of Smyth in America and continued it in France; it is usual to assume a *nom de guerre*, and I was better known in the army by the name of Smyth than by my own.

I shew these commissions to prove to you beyond a doubt that I stand here as a French soldier and must consider myself, and trust I shall be considered by you, precisely in the situation of a French émigré in France. That nation had the noble mindedness to vouchsafe Sombreuil and Charette the death of a soldier.

I hold my commission by a title as valid as any of the members of this Court. My situation, Gentlemen, is a military one. I request and I expect a military execution. After a pause he added: the Court must be sensible I have given no unnecessary trouble or impeded their proceedings with chicane or subterfuge; in return, it is my wish that the sentence may if possible be executed within an hour.

Here the Court explained the necessity of the Lord Lieutenant's ratification &c. and then broke up.

Mr Tone is about two and thirty[2] and has left a wife (sister-in-law to Mr Reynolds)[3] and three children in Paris.[4]

Tone's address to the court martial, 10 November 1798 (I)

British Library, Add. MS 38355, ff 21ʳ–22ᵛ.

Inscribed: 'Mr Tone's Address to the Court, 10 Novʳ 1798, received from Sir J. Blaquiere'.

Mr Tone's address to the Court Martial, 10 Nov. '98

I shall not trouble the Court to adduce evidence in support of the charges preferred against me. I acknowledge the allegations and shall submit to my doom. It is not my intention to disavow those principles by which I have been invariably actuated but on the contrary declare my inducement for the

---

[1] According to the report of the trial in the *Morning Chronicle*, this question was put by the president, Loftus (see above, p. 382).

[2] *Recte* 'thirty-five'.   [3] Thomas Reynolds.

[4] In the copy of this pamphlet held by the R.I.A. the title-page is inscribed 'Chamb. Walker, Novʳ 23, 1798'.

conduct I have pursued to be a sincere regard for the independance and liberties of my fellow subjects.

Upon all occasions have I endeavoured to subvert and destroy the connection which subsists between Great Britain & Ireland, convinced as I am that such a connection is totally inimical to its prosperity, its liberty and its happiness.

With those sentiments forcibly impressed upon my conviction I became an exile in order to procure that assistance which I thought necessary for the assertion of the liberties of Ireland.

For a series of years did I maintain in honorable poverty the sentiments I now profess.

With pride I acknowledge the confidence & regard I have experienced from the French Nation & its Directors. That regard has been manifested by my promotion to a situation of importance and confidence. Success in this world is everything. I have endeavoured to pursue the conduct in which Washington has succeeded and Kosciusko has failed.

I came here with the consoling reflection of being enabled to rescue from slavery and to plan in the honorable rank of citizens *three millions* of my fellow subjects. I have not been successful.

I beg leave only to add that I lament those acts of outrage & assassination which have dishonored my countrymen. I understand that acts of atrocity have been committed on both sides. I lament it. The treatment I have experienced during my conveyance to Dublin reflects disgrace on the order which induced it.

I beg to take this opportunity to return my sincere thanks to the Roman Catholicks of Ireland.

I return my grateful thanks to the members of the Court for the indulgence I have experienced, I am convinced they will do their duty, I trust I shall do mine.

Mr Tone requested the Court would sentence him to be shot, and that execution might be ordered within an hour.

Tone's address to the court martial, 10 November 1798 (II)

P.R.O., HO 100/79, ff 96ʳ–97ʳ.

Covering this document is a letter from Capt. Herbert Taylor to William Wickham, 12 Nov. 1798. Taylor (1775–1839) was a captain in the 2nd dragoon guards, 1795–1801, and secretary to Cornwallis, 1798–9 (J. Philippart, *Royal Military Calendars* (2 vols, London, 1815), ii, 123; *D.N.B*).

Mr President & Gentlemen of the Court Martial,

It is not my intention to give the Court any trouble. I admit the charge against me in its fullest extent. What I have done I have done, and I am prepared to stand the consequences.

The great object of my life has been the independence of my country. For that I have sacrificed everything that is most dear to man. Placed in an honourable poverty, I have more than once rejected offers considerable to a man in my circumstances, where the condition expected was in opposition to my principles. For them I have braved difficulty and danger; I have submitted to exile and to bondage; I have exposed myself to the rage of the ocean and the fire of the enemy; after an honorable combat that should have interested the feelings of a generous foe, I have been marched through this country in irons to the disgrace alone of whoever gave the order; I have devoted even my wife and my children. After that last effort it is little to say that I am ready to lay down my life.

Whatever I have said, written, or thought on the subject of Ireland I now reiterate: looking upon the connexion with England to have been her bane I have endeavoured by every means in my power to break that connexion. (Here the Court interfered and the prisoner struck out what appears within the lines.)[1] I have laboured in consequence to create a people in Ireland by raising three millions of my countrymen to the rank of citizens. I have laboured to abolish the infernal spirit of religious persecution by uniting the catholics and the dissenters. To the former I owe more than can ever be repaid. The services I was so fortunate as to render them, they rewarded munificently but they did more; when the public cry was raised against me, when the friends of my youth swarmed off and left me alone, the catholics did not desert me; they had the virtue even to sacrifice their own interests to a rigid principle of honor; they refused, though strongly urged, to disgrace a man who whatever his conduct towards the government might have been had faithfully and conscientiously discharged his duty toward them, and in so doing though it was in my own case, I will say they shewed an instance of public virtue and honor of which I know not whether there exists another example. But to return.

Having considered the resources of this country and satisfied that she was too weak to assert her liberty by her own proper means, I sought assistance where I thought assistance was to be found. I have been in consequence in France, where without patron or protector, without art or intrigue I have had the honor to be adopted as a citizen and advanced to a superior rank in the armies of the Republic. I have in consequence faithfully discharged my duty as a soldier; I have had the confidence of the French government, the approbation of my generals and the esteem of my brave comrades; it is not the sentence of any court, however I may personally respect the members who compose it, that can destroy the consolation I feel from these considerations.

---

[1] What follows, from 'I have laboured' to 'another example', is printed in *Correspondence of Charles, first marquis Cornwallis*, ed. Charles Ross (2nd ed., 3 vols, London, 1859), ii, 435.

Such are my principles, such has been my conduct; if in consequence of the measures in which I have been engaged misfortunes have been brought upon this country, I heartily lament it, but let it be remembered that it is now nearly four years since I have quitted Ireland and consequently I have been personally concerned in none of them; if I am rightly informed very great atrocities have been committed on both sides, but that does not at all diminish my regret; for a fair and open war I was prepared; if that has degenerated into a system of assassination, massacre and plunder I do again most sincerely lament it, and those few who know me personally will give me I am sure credit for the assertion.

I will not detain you longer; in this world success is everything; I have attempted to follow the same line in which Washington succeeded and Kosciusko failed; I have attempted to establish the independence of my country; I have failed in the attempt; my life is in consequence forfeited and I submit; the court will do their duty and I shall endeavour to do mine.

[*Endorsed in margin*]: Dublin Castle, Nov. 12th 1798.

Sentence of the court martial on Tone, 10 November 1798

T.C.D., Courts-martial proceedings, 1798, MS 872, f. 151ʳ.

At a General Court Martial held in the Barracks of Dublin by the order of L[ieutenan]t Gen[era]l Craig, Saturday, 10 Nov[embe]r 1798

The Court having consider'd the evidence for & against the prisoner Theobald Wolfe Tone did find him guilty of the crimes laid to his charge, [and] did therefore sentence him [to] suffer death in such manner, time & place as L[ieutenan]t Gen[eral] Craig should direct.

(sign'd) Loftus, Major Gen[eral] &
President

To the Executive Directory, 10 November 1798

Archives de la Guerre, Bⁱⁱ 2; Tone (Dickason) papers; T.C.D., Courts-martial proceedings, MS 872, ff 149ʳ–149ᵛ; copy in P.R.O.N.I., T 3048/J/15.

The copy in the Tone (Dickason) papers is an official extract from the Archives Impériales dated 10 Aug. 1811. It seems to have been acquired by Matilda Tone in response to a letter she wrote to Napoleon on 21 July 1811 (Archives de la Guerre, Bⁱⁱ 2). Probably it was used to make the English translation in *Life*, ii, 536–7, reprinted in *The letters of Wolfe Tone*, ed. Bulmer Hobson (Dublin, [1920]), pp 139–41.

Tone informs the Directory that he has been sentenced to death, expresses gratitude for their confidence in him and states that his and his brother's deaths will justify it. He asks them to consider the fate of his wife and children. 'I have sacrificed for the Republic', he continues, 'all that is dearest—my wife, my children, my liberty, my life'.

De la Prison prévôtale de Dublin
20 Brumaire an 7

L'adjudant-gén[éra]l T. W. Tone dit Smith au Directoire Exécutif Français

Citoyens Directeurs,

Le Gouvernement anglais s'étant décidé à ne pas respecter mes droits comme citoyen et comme officier français et m'ayant traduit devant un conseil militaire, je viens d'être condamné à la mort. Dans ces circonstances je vous prie d'accepter mes remercimens de la confiance dont vous m'avez honoré et qui [*sic*] j'ose dire maintenant j'ai bien mérité. Je servi [*sic*] la République fidèlement et ma mort est [*sic*] celle de mon frère (victime comme moi ayant été pareillement jugé il y a [1½][1] mois environ) le prouveront assez. J'espère que le les [*sic*] circonstances dans lesquelles je me trouve me justifieront en vous suppliant, Citoyens Directeurs, de jetter vos regards sur le sort d'une femme virtueuse [*sic*] et de trois infans réduits par ma mort à la dernière misère. Je dois vous rappeller que c'est pour avoir voulu servir la République que j'ai été chassé de ma patrie, que c'était par l'invitation du Gouvernement que je suis venu en France, que depuis que j'ai eu l'honneur d'être au service j'ai fidèlement rempli mes devoirs et avec l'approbation de tout mes chefs, qu'enfin j'ai sacrafié [*sic*] pour la République tout ce qu'il y a de plus cher à l'homme, ma femme, mes infans, ma liberté, ma vie. Dans ces circonstances je m'adresse à votre justice et à votre humanité en faveur de ma famille bien convaincu que vous ne les abandonnerez pas. C'est le [*sic*] plus grande consolation qui me reste en mourant.

Salut et respect
L'adjudant-général
Signé T. W. Tone dit Smith[2]

To Admiral Eustache Bruix, 10 November 1798

T.C.D., Courts-martial proceedings; MS 872, f. 150[r].

Tone sends Bruix a memorandum explaining his situation and asks him to intervene with the French government on behalf of his wife and children and to forward some enclosed letters.

---

[1] Blank in MS.
[2] The copy in the Tone (Dickason) papers continues: 'Pour copie conforme à la minute deposée aux Archives Impériales à St Cloud le 10 Août 1811. Le Ministre Secrétaire d'État'. The signature has not been deciphered.

Dublin, ce 20 Brumaire an 7

L'adjudant-gén[eral] T. W. Tone dit Smith au Ministre de la Marine de
la République française

Citoyen Ministre,

Le mémoire[1] que j'ai l'honneur de vous adresser ci-joint vous expliquera
assez ma situation actuelle. Le tems ne me permet que de vous supplier de
vous intéresser auprès du Gouvernement en faveur de ma femme et de mes
enfans. Bon époux, bon père vous-même, vous pouvez bien juger de ce que
je sens dans [ce] moment; mon seul espoir est dans votre amitié et dans [la]
bienveillance du Directoire, mais c'est un espoir que je suis sûr ne me trompera
pas. Le Gouvernement français n'abandonnera jamai[s] la famille d'un homme
qui s'est sacrafié pour la République.

Salut et respect
L'adjudant-gén[éral]
T. W. Tone dit Smith

Veuillez bien, Citoyen Ministre, faire passer les lettres ci-jointes[2] à leurs
adresses respectives.

To General Charles Joseph Kilmaine, 10 November 1798

N.L.I., MS 36094/3/E; formerly in McPeake papers; T.C.D., Courts-martial proceedings, MS 872, f. 151ᵛ.

Provost Prison, 20th Brumaire an 7

Dear General,

Before this reaches you I shall be no more. You are doubtless already
acquainted with the fate of our expedition which has brought on mine. I write
now relying on you as a friend and countryman to assist and protect my wife
and children by supporting with your interest a memorial which I have addressed
in their favour to the Executive Directory. I have also written to the Minister
of Marine to request his interference, as my family in losing me lose their only
support. The shortness of the time prevents my saying more, but I think I
know you enough to be satisfied that what I have said is sufficient.

I am, dear General, with great respect
Y[ou]r most obed[ien]t serv[an]t,
T. W. Tone, dit Smith
Adj[udant]-gen[éra]l dans l'armée expédit[ionnaire]

---

[1] Not found.   [2] Probably some of the letters given below.

General Kilmaine &c., &c., &c.

[*Endorsed*]: 15. T. W. Tone to General Kilmaine

To Colonel Henri Sheé, 10 November 1798

N.L.I., MS 36094/3/F; formerly in McPeake papers.

> Provost Prison, Dublin Barracks
> 20th Brumaire an 7

Dear Sir

This letter will only reach you in the event of my death. As my wife and children will be in consequence left totally destitute I rely upon your friendship to advise as to the best manner of applying to the Executive Directory for such assistance as the sacrifice of my life in the service of the Republic may seem to deserve. You will please to communicate this letter to my friend General Clarke, who I am sure will interest himself warmly in the fate of my family, as no man in France better knows my conduct and principles. I presume the application will be best made through the Minister of the Marine,[1] who as an excellent husband and a fond father can appreciate what I feel in writing this letter.

> Adieu dear Sir. God bless you
> Your sincere friend
> T. Wolfe Tone

Mr Sheé

[*Endorsed*]: 16. T. W. Tone's letter to Mr Sheé.

To Joseph Niou, 10 November 1798

T.C.D., Courts-martial proceedings, MS 872, f. 150ᵛ.

Tone asks Niou to forward as soon as possible 'to the Minister' (Bruix, minister of the marine) a memorandum and letter enclosed and, in a postscriptum, letters enclosed addressed to his wife, Kilmaine and Sheé.

> Dublin, ce 20 Brumaire an 7

L'adjudant-gén[éra]l T. W. Tone dit Smith au Citoyen Niou, commissaire pour l'échange des Français prisonniers de guerre en Angleterre

Je vous prie, Citoyen commissaire, de vouloir bien faire passer le plutôt possible au Ministre le mémoire et la lettre que je vous adresse ci–joints.

---

[1] Bruix.

Salut et fraternité,
L'adj[udan]t-gén[éra]l
T. W. Tone dit Smith

Veuillez bien aussi faire passer au Ministre les lettres ci-jointes adressées à ma femme, au Gén[éra]l Kilmaine et au Citoyen Sheé.

To Thomas Addis Emmet, William James MacNeven, Arthur O'Connor and John Sweetman, 10 November 1798

N.L.I., MS 36094/3/G; formerly in McPeake papers.

Provost['s Prison], Dublin Barracks
Novr 10th, 1798

To Thomas Addis Emmett, Wm James McNevin, Arthur O'Connor and John Sweetman

My dear friends,

The fortune of war has thrown me into the hands of Government, and I am utterly ignorant of what fate may attend me, but in the worst event I hope I shall bear it like a man, and that my death will not disgrace my life. I know not what may be your situation nor how the last three years may have affected your circumstances.[1] I learn only that you are to go to America with permission. I address myself therefore to you and request if you are suffered that you may communicate this letter to all your brother exiles.[2] If I die I leave a wife whose merit is known to some among you. I leave three infant children utterly destitute. As Irishmen, as men of honor, I rely you will according to your means do for them what I as your friend wou[l]d do for your families in similar circumstances. I add no more, for I know your hearts. Adopt my boys, give them that education which I had promised myself to bestow on them, but especially protect my wife and daughter, whose sex and whose weakness give them a double claim on your humanity. I have said enough. I am indeed incapable to say more.

May God bless and protect you all
Your sincere friend
T. W. Tone

[*Endorsed*]: 17. T. W. Tone to O'Connor, Emmett, Sweetman &c.

---

[1] Emmet and the others had for six months or more been under arrest.

[2] In fact, though the Irish government had been willing to release them to emigrate to the United States, the American minister in London, Rufus King, a strong federalist, asked Portland in Sept. 1798 not to suppose that they would be considered desirable immigrants. They were therefore sent,

To Matilda Tone, 10 November 1798

Tone (Dickason) papers; N.L.I., MS 36094/3/D; *Life*, ii, 537–8.

Both MS copies appear to be in Tone's hand. The N.L.I. copy was formerly in the McPeake papers.

Prevôt Prison, Dublin Barracks,
le 20 Brumaire an 7 (10 Nov[r], 1798 v.s.)[1]

Dearest Love,

The hour is at last come when we must part. As no words can express what I feel for you and our children, I shall not attempt it. Complaint of any kind would be beneath your courage or mine. Be assured I will die as I have lived, and that you will have no reason to blush for me.

I have written on your behalf to the French government, to the Minister of the Marine,[2] to Gen[era]l Kilmaine,[3] and to Mr Sheé;[4] with the latter I wish you especially to advise. In Ireland I have written to your brother Harry, and to those of my friends who are about to go into exile and who I am sure will not abandon you.[5]

Adieu, dearest Love. I find it impossible to finish this letter. Give my love to Mary, and above all things remember that you are now the only parent of our dearest children and that the best proof you can give of your affection for me will be to preserve yourself for their education.

God almighty bless you all.

Yours ever
T. W. Tone

I think you have a friend in Wilkins[6] who will not desert you.[7] Remember me to Lewins affectionately.[8]

---

in Mar. 1799, to Fort George in Scotland, where they were detained until 1802. (R. B. McDowell, *Ireland in the age of imperialism and revolution, 1760–1801* (Oxford, 1979), p. 657).

[1] i.e. 'vieux style'.   [2] Above, pp 399–400.   [3] Above, pp 400–01.
[4] Above, p. 401.   [5] Above, p. 402.
[6] *Sic* in MS, but Tone evidently had in mind Wilson, and this is what William Tone prints in *Life*, ii, 538. 'Theodore Wilkins' was a pseudonym of Thomas Wilson who married Matilda Tone in her widowhood. Matilda Tone quotes from this letter in her 'Narrative' in *Life*, silently emending the penultimate sentence to 'I am sure you have a friend in Wilson, who will never desert you' (ibid., ii, 576).
[7] Note by William Tone (*Life*, ii, 538): 'Nobly did this pure and virtuous man, and he alone of all those whom my father had depended upon, fulfil the expectation of his friend. He was to my mother a brother, a protector and an adviser during the whole period of our distress; and when, at the close of eighteen years, we were ruined a second time, by the fall of Napoleon, he came over from his own country to offer her his hand and his fortune and share our fate in America.'
[8] This sentence has been carefully but discernibly cut away from the Dickason copy and is omitted from *Life*.

À Madame Smith
chez le citoyen Chevalier
Rue des Batailles N°. 29
à Chaillot[1]

To Peter Tone, 10 November 1798

N.L.I., MS 36094/2; formerly in McPeake papers.

Prévôt prison, Dublin Barracks
Novr 10, 1798

Dear Sir,

I hope you will not be offended that I have positively declined seeing you since my arrival in this place. The fact is I had not the courage to support a meeting, which could lead to nothing, and would put us both to insufferable pain. I shall give orders on the arrival of my effects to have them sent to you; what money I have (about £50) I will share between you and my wife. I beg my sincerest and most respectful duty to my mother.

Your affectionate son
T. W. Tone
Adj[t] Gen[era]l

Nothing can exceed the attention which I have received since my arrival in Dublin from Major Sandys, to whom I have been given in charge. He is so good as to promise me he will send my effects &c.

Mr Peter Tone

To Matilda Tone, 10 or 11 November 1798

Tone (Dickason) papers; *Life*, ii, 538.

No. 2

Dearest Love,

I write just one line, to acquaint you that I have received assurances from your brother Edward of his determination to render you every assistance and protection in his power; for which I have written to thank him most sincerely. Harriet[2] has likewise sent me assurances of the same nature and expressed

---

[1] This address is lacking in the N.L.I. copy, which is endorsed '14. T. W. Tone to his wife'.
[2] Sister of Matilda Tone and wife of Thomas Reynolds. *Life*, ii, 538, reads 'Your sister' instead of 'Harriet'.

a desire to see me, which I have refused, having determined to speak to no one of my friends, not even my father, from motives of humanity to them and myself. It is a very great consolation to me that your family are determined to assist[1] you. As to the manner of that assistance, I leave it to their affection for you, and your own excellent good sense, to settle what manner will be most respectable for all parties.

Adieu, dearest Love. Keep your courage, as I have kept mine; my mind is as tranquil this moment as at any period of my life. Cherish my memory, and, especially, preserve your health and spirits for the sake of our dearest children.

Your ever affectionate
T. W. Tone

10th[2] Nov[r], 1798

Madame Smith
Rue des Batailles No. 29
À Chaillot
près Paris[3]

Marquis of Buckingham to Lord Grenville, 10 November 1798

Report on the manuscripts of J. B. Fortescue, esq., iv (H.M.C., London, 1905), pp 369–70.

The author and addressee of this letter are identified in a heading supplied by the editors of the Fortescue manuscripts, who also give the date.

Buckingham was in Ireland in 1798 as colonel of the Buckinghamshire militia regiment; he was an elder brother of Grenville (*D.N.B.*; see above, vol. I, p. 30, n. 2).

[Dublin]

I say nothing upon your very interesting packet, which I got yesterday, as I have been very hard at work upon it . . .[4]

Tone has just been tried. He desired to give the court martial no trouble, acknowledged that he was an Irishman and in the service of the French Republic, gloried in having been the instrument of uniting three millions of his fellow citizens against the oppression and tyranny of England, and of having

---

[1] *Life*, ii, 538, reads 'support' instead of 'assist'.
[2] In the MS '10th' is an alteration from '11th'. William Tone prints it as '11th' (*Life*, ii, 538).
[3] This address is omitted from *Life*.
[4] The omitted matter is mainly a complaint about Cornwallis for what Buckingham sees as an apathic attitude to public affairs. He alleges that 'his excellency does not now come to Dublin more than twice a week and sees no one in the Park'.

procured from 'the great nation' that assistance for the recovery of their liberty which had so unfortunately failed. He was stopped in parts of his declamation addressed to the Catholics of Ireland, for whom, he said, he was happy to lay down his life; and requested of the court that they would copy the humanity of the French Directory and government who, in judging to death Charrette, Sombreuil and others who had fought in opposition to them, had reconciled their death[s] to the feelings of a soldier; and he therefore begged to be shot 'not so much from his private feelings as from a sense of respect to the uniform he wore'. He finished by requesting that the sentence might be sent to Lord Cornwallis instantly and hoped his excellency would confirm it and order it to be executed within the hour. Notwithstanding all this he was much agitated, and I cannot help thinking that he means to destroy himself before Monday, on which day it is supposed he will be hanged.

Grace Joy to Mary Ann McCracken, 10 November 1798

T.C.D., Madden papers, MS 873/102.

Grace or Grisel Joy (1772–1832), youngest daughter of Henry Joy, owner of the *Belfast News Letter*, writes to her first-cousin Mary Ann McCracken (1770–1866), daughter of John McCracken and sister of Henry Joy McCracken (Mary McNeill, *The life and times of Mary Ann McCracken* (Dublin, 1960), pp 200–01, folder).

My dear Mary,

We yesterday received the piece of plaid muslin and liked it so well that I thought it unnecessary to send your letter to the factor . . .

The trial of the unfortunate Mr Tone came on today. It occupied the court but a very short time, as he pleaded guilty to all the charges. He was dressed as a French officer in a superb and beautiful suit of regimentals and behaved in the most firm and dignified manner.[1] He read his defence which was at once inflammatory and eloquent. He came, he said, to raise three millions of his countrymen to the rank of men! In enterprises of this kind, he continued, success is everything. Washington succeeded! Kosciusko failed! Perfectly aware of the fate that awaited him, he had only one request to

---

[1] A similar impression was created on 'a warm-hearted Irishman' named Harden whom Matilda Tone's friend Eliza Fletcher found living beside her in Westmorland in 1834: 'he saw your noble boy as you once called him—your husband!—demand the death of a soldier. He says he never shall forget his countenance and whole deportment. He loves to speak of those exciting times, and feels for Ireland almost as you do.' (Tone (Dickason) papers, Eliza Fletcher to Matilda Tone, 26 Oct. 1834). For John Harden (1772–1847), who belonged to a landed family of Borrisoleigh, Co. Tipperary, and settled in the English Lakes as a watercolourist, see Michael Quane (ed.), 'Tour in Ireland by John Harden in 1797' in *Cork Historical and Archaeological Society Journal*, lviii (1953), esp. pp 26–7.

make, that as a French officer he might be shot. 'This is the death', said he, '*we* give *our* emigrants. Sombreuil had the honor of falling before a file of French grenadiers & Castris[1] the same. I am in a similar situation in this country and ought to be treated in the same manner.' To obtain this favor he begged leave to lay his commission before the lord lieutenant and requested the sentence might be executed as soon as possible.

Harry[2] meant to have attended the trial but as he was late of going it was ended before he reached the barrack. The particulars I have mentioned he had from a gentleman who was present. If I can procure a copy of Mr Tone's defence I will send it you, as I suppose it will not be published. You will not allow me to say I *pity* such a man.[3] I certainly feel the deepest regret at his unhappy fate and the sincerest commiseration for his wife and family.

Harriet and Harry join me in love to my uncle, aunt[4] and all the family. Don't forget to give Kissy Joy's love to Mary and Ann, and believe me, dear Mary, with warmest affection.

Yours
G. Joy

Temple Street, Saturday night

[P.S.] I have not yet heard what reason the lord lieutenant returned to Mr Tone's request. It is generally supposed his execution will take place on Monday.

Miss Mary Ann McCracken
Belfast

Admiral Jean Guillaume Dewinter to Matilda Tone, 10 November 1798

Tone (Dickason) papers.

Dewinter tells Mrs Tone that the news that 'my friend, your dear husband', was on board the *Hoche* and that the vessel was taken is overwhelming; he is asking the Dutch minister in Paris to get the French government to demand Tone's release.

---

[1] She means Charette, captured by Hoche and shot. Charles Eugène Gabriel de la Croix, marquis de Castries (b. 1727), émigré royalist, was from 1797 chef de cabinet of the émigré Louis XVIII; he died however in 1801 (*Dict. biog. franç.*).

[2] Her brother, the barrister Henry Joy (1766–1838), for whom she and her sister Harriet (b. 1768) kept house in Dublin (McNeill, *Mary Ann McCracken*, p. 200, folder).

[3] Eighteen months previously Mary Ann McCracken had referred to Tone, together with Arthur O'Connor and a Dr Bell, as 'three little men possessing much genius' (Mary Ann McCracken to Henry Joy McCracken, 16 Mar. 1797, quoted in ibid., p. 127).

[4] John McCracken and his wife, Ann (1730–1814) (ibid.).

Amsterdam, le 10 nov^bre 1798

Madame!

On ne peu pas être plus sensible et prendre plus de part dans vos afflictions que je ne fais. La nouvelle que mon ami, votre cher mari, se trouvit à bord du *Hoche* et que ce vaisseau a dû succomber devant la force supérieure de l'ennemi m'a terrassé.

J'écris en conséquence à notre ambassadeur Schimmelpennick[1] à Paris, pour qu'il seconde mes démarches pour obtenir, d'après votre désir, que le gouvernement français le réclame comme un officier français. Je fais des voeux sincères pour que cela réussisse, en me flattant aussi de voir réaliser la nouvelle qui nous instruit que l'équipage de la *Hoche* a seu arracher ce vaisseau 24 heures après le combat au pouvoir de l'ennemi.[2] Espérant que votre mari y est resté à bord. Ne doutez pas que je ferai tout mon possible pour satisfaire à votre demande et que je serai toujours un ami sincère et très respectueux concitoyen

De Winter

Captain Herbert Taylor to Lieutenant-General Peter Craig, 11 November 1798

N.L.I., Kilmainham papers, MS 1134, p. 182; printed in *An t-Óglach*, 5 July 1925.

Dublin Castle, Novr 11th, 1798

Lieut Gen[era]l Craig &c., &c.

Sir,

Having laid before Lord Cornwallis the proceedings of a general court martial held upon Theobald Wolfe Tone for having acted traiterously and hostilely against his Majesty's government, I am directed to acquaint you that his Excell[enc]y is pleased to confirm the sentence of death pass'd upon the said Theobald Wolfe Tone but to remit that part of it which directs that his head shall be struck off, fixed on a pike & placed in the most conspicuous part of this city. His Excellency desires the prisoner may be executed tomorrow the 12th inst[an]t.

I have the honor &c., &c.

H. Taylor
sec[retar]y

---

[1] Rütger Jan Schimmelpennick (1761–1825).

[2] The news was false; the *Hoche* did not escape but was taken in tow by the *Doris*. After her capture, it was reported that she was to be taken to England to be refitted. Later she was renamed the *Donegal* and in 1805 'participated with distinction in the mopping-up operations after Trafalgar' (*Saunders' News Letter*, 19 Nov. 1798; Paul M. Kerrigan, 'The capture of the *Hoche* in 1798' in *Irish Sword*, xiii, no. 56 (1978), p. 123).

Order for Tone's execution on 12 November, 11 November 1798

T.C.D., Courts-martial proceedings, MS 872, f. 151ʳ.

His Excell[ency] the Lord Lieutenant having approv'd of the above sentence, I order it to be carried into execution by hanging the said Theobald Wolfe Tone on Monday the 12 ins[tant].

Given under my hand this 11 Novʳ 1798.
Peter Craig
Lieut[enant] Gen[eral]

Capt. Reed, Prov[os]t M[a]r[tial] Gen[era]l or his de[put]y

Tone's will, 11 November 1798

T.C.D., Courts-martial proceedings, MS 872, f. 145ʳ; printed in *The letters of Wolfe Tone*, ed. Bulmer Hobson (Dublin, [1920]), p. 145.

Tone's will

I request Major Sandys may take the trouble on the arrival of my trunk to send it with the contents to my father except £25 which he will have the goodness to remit to Citizen Niou, Commissary for the Exchange of French Prisoners, in London. He will write to Citizen Niou to send the money by means of the Minister of Marine to my wife, whose address I subjoin:

Madame Smith chez le Citoyen Chevalier
Rue de[s] Batailles N° 29 à Chaillot

Près Paris

The remainder of the money in my trunk amounting about the same sum is for my father.

T. W. Tone
Adj[utant] Gen[era]l

11 Nov. '98

To Major William Sandys, 11 November 1798

N.L.I., MS 36094/3/H; formerly in McPeake papers.

11th Novr 1798

Dear Sir,

I return you a thousand thanks for your kind attention to me since I have been committed to your care; you have acted towards me like a brave man and an officer.[1] I trust my old acquaintance Marsden[2] will not suffer my memory to be unnecessarily insulted. My death clears all, and I hope I shall have died like a man.

Yours most truly
T. W. Tone
Adj[utan]t Gen[era]l

Major Sandys &c.

[*Endorsed*]: 18. Letter from T. W. Tone before he cut his throat. To Major Sandys, Dub[li]n Barr[ac]ks

Inscription on Tone's pocket-book, 11 November 1798

National Museum of Ireland; printed in Madden, *United Irishmen*, 3rd ser. (1846), i, 156; facsimile printed as plate in Thomas Pakenham, *The year of liberty: the great Irish rebellion of 1798* (London, 1969), facing p. 304.

On 11 Nov. 1798, the day after he had been sentenced to death, Tone wrote the following in the lining of a pocket-book intended as a keep-sake for John Sweetman:

T. W. Tone
Novr 11th, 1798
'Te nunc habet ista secundum'

The Latin ('This now has thee [Sweetman] as my successor') is from Virgil, *Bucolics*, eclogue II, line 38, omitting the opening words, which, however, Tone evidently had in mind: 'Et dixit moriens'.

Peter Tone delivered the pocket-book to Sweetman with the following unfinished letter:

---

[1] In contrast William Tone, relying on a speech by Curran in Hevey v. Sirr (1802), refers to him as 'the notorious Major Sandys' and characterises his conduct to prisoners as 'insolence, rapacity and cruelty' (*Life*, ii, 526).

[2] Alexander Marsden (1761–1834), called to the Irish bar, 1787; assistant secretary, law department, chief secretary's office, 1798; under-secretary, 1801–06 (B. A. Marsden, *Genealogical memoirs of the family of Marsden* (Birkenhead, 1914), pp 111–13).

Dear Sir,

The enclosed has been ordered by my son to be delivered to you in remembrance of him.

And am your obedient servant,
Peter Tone

The night that——[1]

Morning Chronicle report of proceedings relating to Tone in the court of king's bench, 12 November 1798

Morning Chronicle (London), 17 Nov. 1798.

The Morning Chronicle
London
Saturday, November 17

The intelligence by the Dublin mail which arrived yesterday will be found very interesting. The fate of Mr Tone, which seemed to be decided, has given rise to discussions that are of general concern and involve the liberties of the country. It will be seen from the following particular and detailed account of the proceedings in the Court of King's Bench in Ireland that civil and martial law are now distinctly opposed and their different claims brought to a specific trial. It remains to be seen whether, after rebellion is put down, the lives of Irishmen are to be submitted to the summary investigation of a court martial, or to the solemn verdict of a jury and the sentence of a civil court. The merits or demerits of Mr Tone are totally out of the question in this case. The enquiry is whether men in his situation are to be adjudged to death by a mode of trial dear to freemen, or by a mode of most dangerous application, and which when employed ought never to be endured beyond the most pressing necessity?

The motion made by Mr Curran will be variously accounted for. Some will impute it to the anxiety of Mr Tone's relations; some will perhaps ascribe

---

[1] John Sweetman is identified as the recipient of the inscribed pocket-book and of Peter Tone's letter by R. R. Madden, who in the early 1840s was shown them by Sweetman's son, John (1785–1855). Madden noticed that 'the green silk lining of the book is stained with blood' (*United Irishmen*, 2nd ed., ii (1858), p. 139). The two items were presented to the National Museum of Ireland on 16 October 1936, through Éamon de Valera, by William Sweetman, a descendant of John Sweetman (*Irish Press*, 25 Nov. 1936). The red leather pocket-book (a wallet for carrying papers, cards, banknotes and even notebooks) measures 16 cm × 11 cm and is closed by a flap fastened by a clasp. There are three compartments, two of which would accommodate a small notebook of the kind Tone used for some of his diaries, and a socket for a small pencil, which is also extant. On the inside of the flap, in capitals, is inscribed the original owner's name—'T. W. TONE'.

it to a wish to ascertain a constitutional point. That it was not done with the concurrence of Mr Tone himself is evident from his having attempted his own life as a means of avoiding the execution of a sentence which he thought ignominious to a gentleman and a soldier.[1]

We state the fact, and leave it to our readers to draw their own conclusions. That there was any intention to parade Mr Tone through the streets, which is mentioned in our correspondent's letter as a rumour, is inconceivable. It is not in the nature of Lord Cornwallis to permit such an useless exercise of power, which would have tended rather to more commiseration than to inspire terror, Mr Tone, finding that he was to be hanged, probably thought it better to die in the old Roman way—*conscivit mortem sibi*.[2]

Private letter from Dublin
dated Monday night[3]
King's Bench

Theobald Wolfe Tone, Esq.

The Court of King's Bench opened this day with one of the most important motions that ever occupied a bench of justice in a civilised country. It was simply this:—

Mr Curran observed that on Saturday last the above unfortunate gentleman (as he was instructed by an affidavit of Mr Tone's father) was brought before a bench of officers calling itself a court martial and sitting at the Barracks of the city of Dublin, and was by them sentenced to death. He did not pretend to say that Mr Tone was not guilty of the charges of which he was accused; he presumed the officers were honourable men. But it was stated in the affidavit that it was a solemn fact that Theobald Wolfe Tone had no commission under his Majesty, and therefore, as he contended, no court martial could have cognisance of any crime whilst the Court of King's Bench sat in the capacity of the great criminal court of the land. In times when war was raging, when man was opposed to man in the field, courts martial might be endured; but every law authority was with him when he stood on this sacred and immutable principle of the constitution that 'martial law and civil law were incompatible' and that 'the former *must* cease with the existence of the latter'. This (said Mr Curran) is not the time for arguing this momentous question; my client must appear in this court; he is cast for death this day; he may be ordered for execution whilst I address you. I call on the Court to support the law; I move for a *habeas corpus* to be directed to the Prevôt Marshal of the Barracks of Dublin and Major Sands[4] to bring up the body of Mr Tone.

---

[1] It was stated that Tone had left a note explaining 'that if they had sentenced him to be shot, he would not have shrunk from his fate' (*Courier*, 19 Nov. 1798).   [2] i.e. kill himself.
[3] i.e. 12 Nov.   [4] *Recte* 'Sandys'.

Chief justice:[1] 'Have a writ instantly prepared'.

Mr Curran: 'My client may die whilst this writ is preparing'.

Chief justice:[2] 'Mr Sheriff, proceed to the Barracks and acquaint the Prevôt Marshal that a writ is preparing to suspend Mr Tone's execution, and see that he be not executed'.

A considerable agitation, suspence and anxiety appeared in the Court during the Sheriff's absence.

Mr Sheriff: 'My Lords, I have been at the Barracks in pursuance of your order. The Prevôt Marshal says he must obey General Sands; General Sands says he must obey Lord Cornwallis.'

Mr Curran: 'Mr Tone's father, my Lords, returns after serving the *habeas corpus*; he says General Craig will not obey it'.

Chief justice: 'Mr Sheriff, take the body of Tone into your custody; take the Prevôt Marshal and Major Sands into custody; and shew the order of this Court to General Craig'.

Mr Sheriff: 'I will'.

At the Barracks, Mr Sheriff, we understand, was refused admittance. General Craig sent back the Sheriff with a French emigrant, surgeon of the 9th dragoons.[3]

Mr Sheriff: 'I have been at the Barracks. Mr Tone having cut his throat last night[4] is not in a condition to be removed. As to the second part of your order, I could not meet the parties.'

Emigrant sworn: 'I was sent to attend Mr Tone this morning at four o'clock by General Craig. His windpipe was divided. I took instant means to secure his life by closing the aperture. There is no knowing for four days whether this wound will be mortal. His head is now kept in one position. A centinel is over him to prevent his speaking; his removal would kill him.'

Mr Curran applied for surgical relief to be admitted to Mr Tone exclusive of the Army surgeon who possibly might be a very proper person. Mr Curran likewise stated that no person had admittance to Mr Tone since his confinement and wished his friends might be admitted. Refused.

Chief justice: 'Let a rule be made for suspending the execution of Theobald Wolfe Tone, and let it be served on the proper persons'.

---

[1] Lord Kilwarden.

[2] Frederick Darley (1762?–1841), one of the two sheriffs of Dublin, 1798–9; lord mayor, 1808–09; he was said in an obituary in the *Freeman's Journal* to have attended school in Dublin with Tone and to have acted in the Tone case as recorded here (*Freeman's Journal*, 17 Apr. 1773, 30 June 1841; Jacqueline R. Hill, *From patriots to unionists: Dublin civic politics* (Oxford, 1997), p. 322).

[3] Benjamin Lentaigne.

[4] He was reported to have 'perpetuated the outrage upon himself with a razor that belonged to his brother who was lately executed and confined in the same apartment which T. W. Tone found, we hear, upon the bed in that place' (*Saunders' News Letter*, 16 Nov. 1798).

Since May, courts martial of three and five officers have been sitting in every part of Ireland.

It was universally understood that Mr Tone was to have been publicly paraded through the streets of Dublin previous to his execution, and some assign this to be the cause of his attempt on his life. He seemed at his trial unmoved and unterrified.

Mr Tone towards the close of his address used these words: 'In the cause in which Kosciusko attempted, and Washington succeeded, I have failed'. The Court thought the expression strong, and recommended him to have it erased before the minutes were laid before his Excellency. Mr Tone replied 'Never! He would not.'

Edward Cooke to William Wickham, 12 November 1798

P.R.O., HO 100/79, ff 98^r–99^v; printed in *Correspondence of Charles first marquis Cornwallis*, ed. Charles Ross (2nd ed., 3 vols, 1859), ii, 434–5.

Most private   Dublin, 12 Novr 1798

Dear Sir,

Mr Tone was to have been executed this morning in consequence of a sentence of a court martial. Having contrived to obtain a rasor he cut his throat this morning at 6 o'clock. The wound is very dangerous but not certainly mortal. His execution was suspended. The King's Bench sat at eleven. Affidavits were produced & a *habeas corpus* moved for, which issued & the sheriffs were ordered to prevent the execution. The court could do no otherwise.

Martial law & civil process are now at issue, and I believe it is impossible that the former can be exercised whilst the civil courts are allowed to proceed & hold their sittings. I fear also we shall have much embarrassment from our prisoners on board tenders. They will all move for writs of *habeas corpus*, and it will be a nice point for the courts to decide on the legality of proceedings under martial law.

L[ord] Castlereagh will be in town tomorrow.

Believe me, dear Sir, with [*word not deciphered*] regards

your most faithful & humble servant
E. Cooke

W[illia]m Wickham, Esq.

Marquis of Buckingham to Lord Grenville, 12 November 1798

Report on the manuscripts of J. B. Fortescue, esq., iv (H.M.C., London, 1905), pp 373–4.
The names of the writer and addressee, and the date, are given editorially.

[Dublin, 12 November 1798]

There having been much appearance of ferment this morning, I have only time to tell you that Tone cut his throat but will live to be hanged. However, Lord Cornwallis took so much time to consider whether he would hang him or not that in the meantime Curran moved the court of King's Bench for a *habeas corpus*, which was granted. The Provost-Marshal was directed to make no return, and a *capias* was moved and issued against him, so that our civil and military powers are distinctly pitted against each other. The present orders are to hang him tomorrow, but his Excellency is so versatile on this subject that it is still doubtful. The sentence was that his head should be fixed upon the most conspicuous part of Dublin, *which his Excellency was pleased to disapprove*! What folly is all this.

[Postscript]. Cooke tells me that he warned Lord Cornwallis of this on Saturday!

Reverend Allen Morgan to the Reverend Edward Berwick, 12 November 1798

N.L.I., MS 8505.
Allen Morgan (1761–1830), chaplain to King's Hospital, 1784–1830; dean of Killaloe, 1828–30 (J. B. Leslie and W. J. R. Wallace, *Clergy of Dublin and Glendalough* (Dublin, 2001)).

[No heading]

My dear Berwick,

The unfortunate Tone, by attempting his own life (you no doubt heard of his cutting his throat), did not display that fortitude and magna[ni]mity which his conduct at his trial promised. When a man dares a crime of such a magnitude as his, he ought to be prepared to abide its consequences—he loses the merit of that martyrdom which he seemed to glory in. His wound is by no means dangerous, but a motion was made this day in Court for a writ of *habeas corpus* to bring up Tone on the grounds of the illegality of a court martial, a court of King's Bench sitting. The order was accordingly issued, and the return made that Tone was not in a state to be brought up, on which the Court directed the Sheriff to take care that no execution was had. A motion was made to take Major Sandys into custody, which was also granted. He however eluded the Sheriffs. Military people say that General Craig acted with pusillanimity and that he ought to have obeyed the Lord Lieutenant's warrant for immediate execution and abide an attachment, as any punishment awarded by the Court would be remitted by the Crown, and it is confidently said that his execution will take place under his present sentence. I received your note, which I sent to the Dean[1] and a few lines from myself. I did not get any answer—he is in town I know.

Allen Morgan

[Appendix]

He[2] would not obtrude on the time of the Court by any tedious recital, he only claimed its indulgence and patience in allowing him read a few lines hastily written and under the correction of the Court if any part of what he had to offer was deemed [   ].[3] Everything that he had said or written on the subject of Ireland as detailed in the reports of the secret committees he now reiterated and avowed as the ruling principles of his life from its earliest thinking period, that he ever looked upon the connexion between Great Britain and Ireland as the latter's greatest bane. Possessed of these sentiments and anxious to restore 3 millions of people of this country to the rank of citizens— here he was interrupted by the Court, the matter being inflammatory & irrelevant. He then wished to pay some tribute to the great Catholic body, which was also refused. He accordingly erased the objectionable part & resumed—that solicitations had been made to him & reward offered to desert his principles, which he gloried in having rejected, that blessed in honest poverty, he had become a voluntary exile and had passed over from America to France where, without patronage, without money, without friends; he had been advanced to high rank in the armies of the glorious Republic and had fought her battles under Buonaparte, Dessaix and Kilmaine, an Irishman; that the independence of his country being the first object of his heart, he had gained the confidence of the Directory & sought the aid of the French arms to obtain the freedom of Ireland. For this he relinquished the dearest ties of wife & children, had suffered exile, prison & want, had braved the dangers of the sea and the fire of the enemy. Success in this life was everything,—he had failed. He attempted that in which Washington succeeded and Kosciusko failed. The fortune of battle gave him to the enemy, the Court knew its duty. He trusted he knows his—he had however to complain of the severity of his

---

[1] Not identified.   [2] Erroneously 'It'.
[3] MS blank; missing word probably 'exceptionable'.

treatment, which was mean and cruel—loaded with irons—hurried from one extremity of the kingdom to the other—but he forbore more on the subject, which reflected greater disgrace on those who gave than those who executed orders. He most deeply regretted the glorious cause having degenerated into a religious feud & a system of assassination & massacre quite unworthy of the object & disgraceful to this country; but he begged it to be remembered that he had no personal concern with such horrid deeds, being an exile more than 4 years. (He now broke off, having in the fullest manner admitted the charges and produced his commission of Chef de Brigade, Adj[utan]t Gen[eral] to the Army of England and a letter of service signed by Carnot President of the Directory). Then he said the proving the charges incontestibly had another object—as a soldier in a brave army of which he gloried being a member he had to request that if the Court had any discretionary powers in awarding the measure of its punishment it would pursue a conduct towards him similar to that of the French towards the emigrés Sombreuil & Charette—they were allowed the honor of dying by the fire of a file of French grenadiers. He begged not to die on a gibbet. To him, after the failure of the great object of his heart, life had nothing to make it valuable, he only entreated in addition to the indulgence he had already experienced, that the Court would, if possible, ascertain without delay from the Lord Lieutenant his sentence and that his execution might immediately follow, suppose in an hour.

12 Nov. 1798

To the Revd Mr Berwick
at Mr Bermingham's
Blackrock

Marquis of Buckingham to Lord Grenville, 13 November 1798

Report on the manuscripts of J. B. Fortescue, esq., iv (H.M.C., London, 1905), pp 374–5.
The names of the writer and addressee, and the date, are given editorially.

[Dublin]

The consummation of Lord Cornwallis's incapacity seems drawing on very fast. He has suspended Tone's execution till further orders; he has directed Major Sandys (the acting Provost-Marshal of Ireland) to put in for answer that his reason for not obeying the *Habeas* of yesterday was 'because Tone could not be moved with safety', and he has directed all courts martial now sitting to be suspended. I could not have believed all this if Lieutenant-General Craig had not shewn me his orders, and if Sandys had not shewn me his answer, prepared by Kemys[1] the Crown Solicitor. The consequence of this is an order, moved by Curran, for bringing up Tone in the custody of the sheriff so soon as he can be moved, which order is only delayed under an assurance that it is not intended to carry the sentence of the court martial into execution *for some days*, and a peremptory order made (upon motion) for committing Sandys. In this manner has Lord Cornwallis completely overthrown the whole system of military tribunals that were sanctioned by proclamation, to which the judges were parties, approved by Parliament; and the result of it will be, unless he again changes his system, a general gaol delivery of every suspected person (by *habeas*) not in the custody of the civil power. Such is the firmness and vigour of his conduct in the case of the man who glories to this moment (and so told the court) that he was the man to rouse three millions of his fellow subjects to a sense of their debasement from that bane to all their prosperity, their connexion with Great Britain; that he had first suggested the doing this by French assistance; and that he died happy in having been the instrument to obtain it. And to this glory Tone is too truly entitled, for you know that his assertions are most true. I enclose to you the account drawn up by order of Government for their newspaper and much softened; and yet you will see how strong the language of this man has been stated in their narrative.

Since I wrote this, I am assured that Lord Cornwallis will hang this man *as soon as he is a little better*, and that he means to stand his ground and to abide by the military courts. If so, his conduct is tenfold more unintelligible.

God protect us from such absolute imbecility, the result of which, I will venture to foretell, will shock and loosen the little government now existing.

Postscript. Thank God the Chancellor is landed, and I hope he will at least give this man a little common sense.[2] Holt[3] surrendered himself yesterday and is this morning arrived at the Castle. . . . .[4]

Sir George Fitzgerald Hill to Edward Cooke, 15 November 1798

Nat. Arch. (Ire.), Rebellion papers, 620/41/36.

[1] Thomas Kemmis (1753–1823), Jervis St., Dublin, and Killeen, Queen's Co., crown solicitor for Ireland since 1784 (*Burke's Irish family records* (London, 1976)).

[2] The lord chancellor, Lord Clare, having returned to Ireland, wrote to Lord Auckland on 15 Nov., 'we had got into a little scrape by bringing up Mr Tone for trial to Dublin by a court martial sitting by the side of the Court of King's Bench. We shall probably get out of it by the death of Mr Tone, who was suffered to cut his throat on the day appointed for his execution, and if the vagabond should not die of his wound, we may get out of it, if his majesty's attorney-general will act as he has been advised to proceed.' (B.L., Auckland papers, Add. MS 34455, ff 34ᵛ–35, printed in *Journals and correspondence of William, Lord Auckland* (London, 1861–2), iv, 67–8).

[3] Joseph Holt (1756–1826), an insurgent leader in Co. Wicklow; he was transported to New South Wales (*D.N.B.*).

[4] Mrs Sarah Tighe wrote to Ann Ponsonby on 20 Nov. 1798, 'Tone being dead the reigning topic is General Holt' (N.L.I., 'A short account of the rebellion', MS 4813).

Confidential

My Dear Cooke,

If I communicate candidly what I hear it must be confidential; what I give you as the conversation and opinions of other men if known to come from me might be attributed to me as my own.

The tone of this country upon the points you enquire from me is very inharmonious. Two days ago I wrote you a few lines relative to one of them, a union.[1] People have not yet spoke much out on the subject but they are evidently inimical to the measure, and with the slightest encouragement would violently express themselves.

His Ex[cellency][2] is held in very little respect. The length of time he took to beat Humbert, his subsequent alledged disregard to the rebels in Con[n]ought, his third day's permission to them to cut the Protestants' throats, his orders to the army to retire to the interior on the approach of an invading enemy, his putting the yeomanry off permanant duty in the county of Wicklow, his alledged neglect to the late outrages in Wexford & Kildare, his system of mercy to the rebels contrasted with his severe sentence of censure of Woollaghan's court martial,[3] are universally brought in charge against him in all companys as indicating a determination on his part to render the Kingdom upon system uncomfortable to the Protestants & thereby to force them to become the solicitors for a union. The devil of this language is that it is chiefly held by the most approved friends of Gov[ernmen]t. I do not mean Orangemen, for we have few if any here, I really mean the constitutional loyalists. I do not conceive Lord Cornwallis's character could as here estimated take from the nausea at the measure of a union. Quere, can it be carried by him?

I have received an accurate note of all which passed in K[ing's] B[ench] on Curran's motion. The business has been botched. The authority of Parl[iamen]t, the actual existence of rebellion & invasion should have induced a refusal to obey the King's Bench and execution ought to have taken place. I would have sewed up his neck and finished the business. It will make a desperate outcry to manifest any hesita[tion] to extend to this arch destructive traitor the measure that has been dealt to others not half so mischievous. I wish we had never sent him to Dublin. To save farther trouble it would be happy if he died of his wound. If Tone is to be tryed for his guilt commited

---

[1] i.e. between the Irish and British parliaments.   [2] Cornwallis.

[3] On 18 Oct. 1798, Cornwallis stated publicly that he 'entirely disapproved' of the decision of a court martial to acquit Hugh Woolaghan, a yeoman, of the 'cruel and deliberate murder' of Thomas Dogherty, 'of which by the clearest evidence he appears to have been guilty'; he dismissed Woolaghan from the yeomanry and ordered the court martial to be dissolved (*The genuine trial of Hugh Woolaghan, yeoman, by a general court martial held in the barracks of Dublin on Saturday, October 13, 1798, for the murder of Thomas Dogherty to which is added his excellency Lord Cornwallis's order for the court martial to be dissolved* (Dublin, 1798), p. 27).

on board *Le Hoche* the K[ing's] B[ench] is not the court; they have not authority no more than the court martial, it must be the Admiralty,

> Yours in haste
> G. F. Hill

Derry, Novr 15th.

Viscount Castlereagh to William Wickham, 16 November 1798

Castlereagh corr., i, 445–8.

The addressee is identified in a heading supplied by the editor of the Castlereagh correspondence.

Dublin Castle, November 16, 1798

Sir,

On my return to town, Mr Cooke put into my hands several communications received from you during my absence of which, by the Lord Lieutenant's directions, he had acknowledged the receipt.

You will observe by the papers that T. W. Tone, having been sentenced by a court martial to suffer death, on the morning of his execution cut his throat so as to render his recovery very precarious. On the same day Mr Curran moved to have him brought up by a writ of Habeas Corpus, which was of course granted. The return made to the Court was that he could not be moved from his place of confinement with safety to his life. In this situation the matter rests. The opinion of the Crown lawyers has been taken, and they have advised, in case he is brought before the King's Bench, and that it is purposed, he being in custody of the Court, that he shall be disposed of under the municipal law, to inquire into his treatment rather than bring the question of martial authority to a solemn decision, which would occasion delay, embarrass the Court, and perhaps expose the State to have its summary interference for its own prosecutions deferred in a manner injurious to the public safety.

When the Proclamation of the 24th of May authorizing martial law was had recourse to on the breaking out of the Rebellion, Lord Pery[1] then suggested the expediency of passing a bill to authorize the military authorities to try by court martial persons engaged in the Rebellion, alleging that without such a law, as the exercising of the power could only be justified by the necessity of the case in the strictest sense, and as much doubt and difference of opinion might arise upon what circumstances constituted the necessity so required, he thought it safer to legalize the proceeding by a temporary statute than to

---

[1] Edmond Sexton Pery (1719–1806), speaker of the Irish house of commons, 1771–85; created Viscount Pery, 1785 (*D.N.B.*).

expose the parties exercising those powers to the necessity of coming to Parliament for indemnity.

Whilst the rebels were in the field in force, the necessity of punishment by military tribunals was so obvious as not to admit of a question. Indeed, the degree of public danger was then such as to preclude the ordinary courts of law from sitting. Latterly the rebellion has degenerated, particularly in the counties of Wicklow, Wexford, Kildare, Westmeath and Dublin, into a petty warfare not less afflicting to the loyal inhabitants though less formidable to the State. In those counties, the number of persons taken in the commission of the most shocking crimes still acting upon treasonable and systematic principles has been such as to render it impossible to trust to the usual administration of justice for the punishment of the offenders; indeed, in Wicklow and Wexford it has been found altogether impracticable to hold the assizes. The situation of the district above alluded to, as also those parts of Connaught which were disturbed at the time of the late invasion, has compelled my Lord Lieutenant to punish summarily by martial law at the same time that the general state of the kingdom admitted of the courts being opened in the metropolis and of the judges going their circuits in other parts of the kingdom as formerly.

The two jurisdictions being in activity at the same time could not well fail to clash sooner or later, as has happened in Tone's case. His conviction will be effected with equal certainty by civil as by military law, his trial being had in the metropolis, where the courts are open, and, under the circumstances of the case, it is not of that description upon which it would be expedient to bring the matter to issue;[1] but it certainly deserves to be well considered, should the country remain unsettled for any length of time, whether both jurisdictions are not requisite, and if so, I do not see how they can proceed together without embarrassment, unless Lord Pery's idea is adopted under such restrictions as may be thought necessary. It was before resisted upon the principle that there was less violence done to the Constitution in giving indemnity to those who have acted illegally for the preservation of the State than in enacting laws so adverse to the usual spirit of our legislature. This consideration prevailed; and were the struggle but of short duration, perhaps the inconvenience would be trifling; but if it is to be procrastinated, which there is but too much reason to apprehend may be the case in this kingdom, where religious resentment as well as principles of resistance are so deeply and extensively implanted, it is a question whether military authority, in some degree, is not requisite to keep society together; and, if so, the responsibility of doing an act which, in the eye of the law, is in strictness murder, is too weighty to be encountered in the prospect of future indemnity.

---

[1] This question was settled by the suppression of insurrection bill which was introduced by the government in February 1799 and received royal assent the following August as 39 Geo. III, c. 11. This measure provided that commanding officers might bring insurgents for trial by court martial even though the ordinary courts of law be sitting. (R. B. McDowell, *Ireland in the age of imperialism* (Oxford, 1979), p. 667).

I trust, however, that the internal situation of the country may improve, now the prospect of foreign assistance is in a great measure at an end, and that we may be saved an alternative so unpleasant as that of yielding to this tormenting evil, rather than risk the adoption of a strong remedy, or of being driven to extend the powers of a military code to civil crimes, if crimes can be called civil which are invariably committed in arms.

I have troubled you with these suggestions as the hasty sentiments of my own mind on this question, which connects itself with Tone's case. When I venture to write without much consideration what may meet the Duke of Portland's eye, I trust his Grace will receive it with indulgence.

I have the honour to remain &c.
Castlereagh

Sir John Moore's diary, 16, 25 November 1798

British Library, Sir John Moore papers, Add. MS 57328, ff 122–6; printed, with discrepancies, in *The diary of Sir John Moore*, ed. Sir J. F. Maurice (2 vols, London, 1904), i, 327–30.

Sir John Moore (1761–1809), major-general, Jan. 1798, lieut-general, June 1799; he served in Ireland, Dec. 1797 to June 1799 (*D.N.B.*).

Athlone, 16th November [1798]

The day before I left Dublin, Mr Theobald Wolfe Tone was brought in prisoner, having been taken on board the *Hoche* in the action of the 12th Oct[ober]. I endeavoured to see him, but he was conveyed to the Provost prison before I reached the Castle. He is said to have been one of the principal and first framers of the 'United Irish'. He is the son of a coachmaker in Dublin, but was educated at the college for a lawyer, and, by some writings which are said to be his, he appears to be a man of considerable talent. He was tried by a court martial at the Barracks the day after his arrival, where I understood he conducted himself with great firmness. He had prepared a speech, part of which he was permitted to deliver, the rest being conceived inflammatory. By that part which he delivered he discovered a superiority of mind which must give to him a degree of sympathy beyond what is given to ordinary criminals.

He began by stating that from his infancy he had been bred up in an honourable poverty, and since the first dawn of his reason he had been an enthusiast in the cause of his country. The progress of an academic and classical education confirmed him still stronger in those principles, and spurred him on to support by actions those principles he had so strongly conceived in theory. The British connection in his opinion was the bane of his country's prosperity and it was his object to destroy this connection, and in the event of his exertions he [had] succeeded in arousing three millions of his countrymen to a sense of their national debasement. Here he was interrupted by the Court, and [on his] afterwards going on with something similar he was again interrupted. He then said he should not take up the time of the Court by any subterfuge to which the forms of the law might entitle him. He admitted the charge of coming in arms and as the leader of a French force to invade Ireland, but said it was as a man banished, amputated from his natural and political connection with his own country, and a naturalised subject of France, bearing a commission of the French Republick, under which it was his duty implicitly to obey the commands of his military superiors, & he produced his commission, constituting [him] adj[utan]t-gen[era]l in the French service, his orders, &c., &c. He said he knew, from what had already occurred to the officers, natives of Ireland, who had been made prisoners on this expedition, what would be his fate. On that, however, he had made up his mind.

He was satisfied that every liberal man who knew his mind and principles would be convinced that in whatever enterprise he had engaged for the good of his country, it was impossible he would ever have been combined in approbation or aid to the fanatical and sanguinary atrocities perpetrated by many of the persons engaged in the recent conflict. He hoped the court would do him the justice to believe that from his soul he abhorred such abominable conduct. He had in every public proceeding of his life been actuated by the purest motives of love to his country, and it was the greatest ambition of his soul to tread the glorious paths chalked out by the example of Washington in America and Kosciusko in Poland. In such arduous and critical pursuits success was the criterion of merit and fame. It was his lot to fail, and he was resigned to his fate. Personal considerations he had none; the sooner he met the fate that awaited him the more agreeable to his feelings; but he could not repress his anxiety for the honour of the nation whose uniform he wore and the dignity of that commission he bore as adj[utant]-gen[era]l in the French service.

As to the sentence of the court martial, which he so fully anticipated, he had but one wish, that it might be inflicted within one hour. But the only request he had to solicit the Court was that the mode of his death might not degrade the honour of a soldier. The French army did not feel it was contrary to the dignity or etiquette of arms to grant similar favours to emigrant officers taken on returning under British command to invade their native country. He recollected two instances of this in the case of Charette and Sombreuil who had obtained their request of being shot by files of grenadiers. A similar fate was the only favour he had to wish, and he trusted that men susceptible of the nice feelings of a soldier's honour would not refuse his request. As to the rest, he was perfectly reconciled.

Next morning it was found that he had endeavoured to avoid public execution by an attempt to kill himself. He was discovered with his windpipe cut across. His execution was necessarily postponed.

A motion has since been made in the court of King's Bench by Mr Curran for a habeas corpus directed to the keeper of the Prevost Marshalsea to bring the body of T. W. Tone with the cause of his detention. This is so far fortunate as it is to stop for the future all trials by Court Martial for civil offences, and things are to revert to their former and usual character.

Athlone, 25th Nov. [1798]

Tone died of the wound he had given himself.

Courts martial are not entirely put a stop to. By private orders circulated to general officers we are directed to report the circumstances and have the informations taken by a civil magistrate and forwarded to the Lord Lieut[enant] who will decide whether the trial is to be civil or military.

General Charles Edward Saul Jennings de Kilmaine to the Executive Directory, 17 November 1798

Archives de la Guerre; copies in Dickason (Tone) papers and N.L.I., Tone papers, MS 13258. The copy in Archives de la Guerre is an official extract from Archives Impériales dated 10 Aug. 1811.

Kilmaine believes that Tone should be treated as a prisoner-of-war and that, failing this, the Directory should take reprisals against some English officer held prisoner in France. There are English translations in *Life*, ii, 543–4, and Richard Hayes, 'General Charles Jennings Kilmaine, 1751–1799' in *Studies*, xxiii (1934), pp 486–7.

ARMÉE
D'ANGLETERRE

LIBERTÉ [crest] *ÉGALITÉ*

Au Quartier-général de Rouen, *le* 27 Brumaire, *l'an* 7
de la République française une et indivisible

KILMAINE, GÉNÉRAL EN CHEF,
au Président du Directoire Exécutif

Citoyen Président,

D'après l'assurance qu'a donné le Directoire Exécutif de réclamer d'une manière péremptoire l'Adj[udan]t-général Smith, fait prisonnier abord du *Hoche*, il seroit sans doute superflu de vous en réitérer la prière, mais comme Général en Chef de l'armée dans laquelle il servait avec distinction je me crois en devoir obligé de le faire connaître plus particulièrement au Directoire. Son nom est Tone; il a pris celui de Smith pour que le Gouvernement Anglois ignorât qu'il fût en France, et en conséquence pour épargner à sa famille en

Irlande les persécutions qu'on n'auroit pas manqué de lui faire éprouver, ayant été un des plus zelés et des plus respectables apôtres de la liberté de son pays, il a été obligé pour se soustraire de ses bourreaux de se sauver à l'Amérique septentrionale d'où il a passé en France à la demande même du gouvernement pour coopérer avec le Général Hoche à la première expédition d'Irlande, il fut alors promu au grade d'adjudant-général, et a servi la République dans cette qualité à l'armée d'Angleterre où je l'ai connu de la manière la plus avantageuse, il s'est acquis l'estime et l'amitié de tous les généraux avec lesquels il a servi, par ses talens et ses qualités sociales, il n'a été appellé à l'expédition du Général Hardy que comme officier français, c'est en cette qualité seule qu'il doit être reconnu, il avait adopté la France pour sa patrie, et il a le droit indubitable d'être regardé comme prisonnier de guerre français, et on n'a le droit de le regarder que comme tel. J'ignore le traitement que le gouvernement anglois lui réserve, mais au cas qu'il ne fût pas tel qu'en doit attendre un officier français prisonnier de guerre, je crois qu'il est hors de doutte que le Directoire a le droit de désigner un officier supérieur anglois prisonnier en France pour lui servir d'ôtage et pour subir par représailles le même traittement que le gouvernement anglois feroit subir à l'adj[udan]t général Smith. Par cette démarche l'on conservera à la République un officier des plus distingués, à la liberté un de ses plus éclairés et plus zelés défenseurs, et son père à une famille des plus intéressantes que j'aie connu.

Salut et respect
Kilmaine

P.S. Le citoyen Thompson[1] qui aura l'honneur de vous remettre ma lettre est à même de vous donner des détails plus étendus sur l'Adjutant Général Smith et son intéressante famille.

K.

To Major William Sandys, 18 November 1798

N.L.I., MS 36094/3/I; formerly in McPeake papers.
The McPeake copy is obviously not the original. The writers of the first part and the endorsement have not been identified.

Copy

Tone wrote the following letter to Major Sandys a few hours before his death. The letter is not dated, & was so badly wrote that it was with much difficulty so much of it cou'd be made out.

[1] Lewines.

Sunday morning

I write this letter as labouring under one of the severest sacrifices with which humanity can be afflicted. I have been utterly delirious since Sunday, and I am afraid some one is proposing to [?take advantage] of my blind and miserable state by making [?me do] that which in my senses they could [?not] bring [?me to do], but I see this is all frantic raving. I beg you will come & take charge.

Signed

T. W. Tone

Adj[utan]t Gen[era]l

[*Endorsed*]: No. 19. Letter from T. W. Tone addressed to Major Sandys a few hours before Tone's death.

Saunders' News Letter reports of Tone's death and burial (19, 21 November 1798), 21, 22 November 1798

Saunders' News Letter (Dublin), 21 Nov. 1798.

The miserable career of Theobald Wolfe Tone was on Monday morning [the 19th] terminated by his death. He had been since Friday morning more or less attacked by spasmodic affections in the neck. He experienced great pain during the whole of Sunday and very early in the morning of Monday expired.

Saunders' News Letter (Dublin), 22 Nov. 1798.

Yesterday morning at seven o'clock the remains of Theobald Wolfe Tone were brought from his parents' apartments in High-street and privately interred.[1] At the earnest request of his mother the body was given up a short time after he expired, who had the melancholy consolation of performing the last sad office to his remains.

Viscount Castlereagh to General Peter Craig, 19 November 1798

T.C.D., Courts-martial proceedings, MS 872, f. 153[r]; printed in *The letters of Wolfe Tone*, ed. Bulmer Hobson (Dublin, [1920]), pp 144–5.

---

[1] It was to the house of Peter Tone's brother-in-law, William Dunbavin, 65 High St. (where Peter Tone and his wife may have been living) that the body was removed from the Dublin barracks. It was fetched by Dunbavin and his son Nicholas. William Dunbavin was present at the burial at Bodenstown, some 28 km west-south-west of Dublin in Co. Kildare. Many years later Nicholas Dunbavin informed R. R. Madden of these events and in 1842 accompanied him to Bodenstown. On this evidence, and the testimony of two daughters of William Dunbavin, Madden identifies Bodenstown as the location of Tone's grave. (Madden, *United Irishmen*, 2nd ed., ii (1860), pp 142–3, 160–61).

Phoenix Park, 19 [November]

My d[ea]r Sir,

The Lord Lieu[tenan]t has refer'd your letter in respect to the disposal of W. Tone's body to me.

I see no objection to his body being given to his friends but on the express condition that no assemblage of people shall be permitted, and that it be interred in the most private manner.

I have the hon[ou]r to be, D[ea]r Sir,

Y[ou]rs faithfully
Castlereagh

L[ieu]t Gen. Craig
&c., &c.

General Jean Hardy to the Executive Directory, 19 November 1798 (I)

Archives de la Guerre, B^{II} 2.

Hardy makes a formal report on the progress of the French expeditionary force and gives some details of the battle fought on 12 Oct. off Lough Swilly.

Lichtfield,[1] le 29 Brumaire
an 7ème de la République française

No. 1

19 9bre 1798

Le Général Hardy au Directoire Exécutif

Citoyens Directeurs,

Il y a cinq jours que je débarquai à Liverpool avec l'état-major de l'armée expéditionnaire. Le surlendemain nous fûmes envoyés sur parole à Lichtfield, et ce n'est qu'aujourd'hui que je puis profiter de l'intermédiaire du Citoyen Niou, votre commissaire à Londres, pour vous faire part des évènements malheureux auxquels nous avons été en butte, depuis notre départ de Brest.

Après vingt-neuf jours d'une navigation extrêmement pénible, toujours contrariante et souvent périlleuse, la division commandée par le Citoyen Bompard qui devait porter en Irlande les troupes dont vous m'avez confié le commandement était arrivée le vingt vendémiaire à hauteur et à proximité de l'Isle Tori.[2] Il ne nous restait plus que sept à huit lieues à faire pour entrer

---

[1] Lichfield in Staffordshire, England.   [2] Tory.

dans le Lac Swilly, lieu que, de concert avec le Citoyen Bompard, j'avais choisi pour notre débarquement. Le temps était beau, le vent favorable, depuis deux jours nous avions perdu de vue le vaisseau radé et les deux frégates ennemies qui, depuis l'Isle d'Ouessant,[1] nous avaient constamment observée. Tout semblait nous présager un succès complet, et j'ai été à même de me convaincre par la suite que nous aurions parfaitement réussi.

A midi nous apperçûmes une escadre anglaise composée de huit vaisseaux qui forcèrent bientôt de voiles, les uns pour nous reconnaître de plus près, les autres pour gagner le vent. Dans ce moment même, nous éprouvâmes une avarie irréparable par la fracture et la chute de notre grand mât de hune. Il ne m'appartient pas de vous donner le détail des manoeuvres qui furent faites pour arriver à notre but et remplir vos intentions; je laisse ce soin aux officiers de marine qui vous instruiront beaucoup mieux que je ne pourrais le faire.

Le lendemain vingt un Vendémiaire à six heures et demi du matin, nous nous trouvions par les dix degrés cinquante-trois minutes de longitude occidentale, à vue de terre, et presqu'en face du Lac Swilly.[2] L'ennemi qui nous avait serrés de près pendant toute la nuit, et que nous avions en vain essaié de tromper par une fausse route, ne tarda pas à nous attaquer. Le vaisseau *Le Hoche* fut d'abord assailli par un vaisseau radé et un de 74, nous nous battîmes pendant une heure, sans éprouver beaucoup de perte; mais bientôt l'ennemi fut renforcé par un vaisseau de 80, un de 74 et une frégate de 18; la frégate *La Romaine* qui s'était jointe à nous fut obligée de virer de bord à l'approche du renfort ennemi, et nous nous trouvâmes seuls contre cinq. Le combat devint alors terrible et opiniâtre de part et d'autre; le vaisseau *Le Hoche* vomissait le fer et la flamme de stribord, de bas bord et de l'arrière. Il est impossible de trouver plus de courage et d'activité dans nos soldats de terre et de mer, plus de fermeté et de sang froid dans tous les officiers placés aux différentes batteries, ni plus d'ordre dans une action aussi chaude que meurtrière; l'espérance de la victoire allait toujours croissant dans l'équipage et chacun travaillait avec une ardeur égale à ses désirs.

Cependant le vaisseau avait déjà près de cinq pieds d'eau dans la cale, le poste des chirurgiens était encombré de blessés, toutes les manoeuvres étaient coupées, les voiles en lambeaux, les batteries en partie démontées, trois fois les gaillards avaient été complettement balaiés, les sabords de la 2ème batterie n'en formaient presque plus qu'un; les mâts et les vergues fortement endommagés menaçaient d'écraser l'équipage par leur chute. Enfin réduit à l'impossibilité de gouverner, prévenu pour la seconde fois qu'il n'y avait plus de place au poste pour les blessés, ne pouvant plus compter sur le secours de

---

[1] Ushant.

[2] In the MS 'occidentale' (meaning 'west') is interlined. The orientation given by Hardy (10° 53′ West) is an error for 9° 53′ East, i.e. east of the Isle de Fer (Hierro) meridian, the line of longitude reckoned as zero by French geographers (*Nouvel atlas portatif* (Paris, 1790)). Lough Swilly, which extends directly inland from the north coast of Donegal, lies 7° 34′ west of the Greenwich meridian, or 9° 53′ east of the Hierro meridian.

nos frégates dont quelques unes étaient déja aux prises, forcé de céder au nombre qui l'accablait, le Chef de Division Bompard se détermina à amener le pavillon national, après en avoir défendu l'honneur avec son intrépidité ordinaire pendant trois heures quarante-cinq minutes.

Aucune de nos frégates excepté *La Romaine* n'a eu part à cette action; mais à peine *Le Hoche* fut-il rendu qu'à leur tour elles furent enveloppées par les forces ennemies. J'ai appris depuis que plusieurs d'entre elles avaient également succombé.

Tout ce qui était à bord du *Hoche* s'est vaillamment battu; on ne saurait donner trop d'éloges aux officiers et aux soldats.

Notre perte s'élève à environ cent trente hommes dont trois officiers. Parmi ces derniers se trouve le Citoyen Vildey,[1] lieutenant au 6ème Régiment d'artillerie, jeune homme d'un mérite rare et qui donnait les plus hautes espérances. La République perd en lui un brâve défenseur et un zélé parti-san. Avant d'expirer il a recommandé sa famille à la sollicitude du gouvernement, puis il est mort avec le calme de la philosophie et la tranquillité d'un homme qui a toujours rempli ses devoirs avec honneur et sans reproche; il emporte l'estime de ses chefs et l'amitié de tous ses camarades.

Je m'occupe en ce moment de recueillir, autant que possible, les noms de ceux qui se sont particulièrement distingués. J'aurai l'honneur de vous en remettre la liste, lors que je pourrai jouir de l'avantage de revoir ma patrie.

Recevez, Citoyens Directeurs, l'expression des regrets bien sincères que j'éprouve de n'avoir pas été mieux secondé par la fortune dans la tâche que j'avais à remplir, et de m'être trouvé dans l'impossibilité de justifier la confiance dont vous m'avez honoré en fournissant la carrière que vous m'aviez ouverte.

Salut et Respect
Hardy

General Jean Hardy to the Executive Directory, 19 November 1798 (II)

Archives de la Guerre, B¹¹ 2; partial copy in N.L.I., Tone papers, MS 13258.

Hardy continues his report, relating that the officers were transferred to the British vessel, *Robust*, which twice escaped shipwreck near the Scottish coast, while the *Hoche*, severely disabled and on tow by another vessel, almost sank, such was the weather for 18 days; on their returning to Lough Swilly, Simon and Tone were summoned ashore by the British commander; Tone was sent to Londonderry and put in prison in irons. Hardy concludes stating he sent letters to Cornwallis and Tone, adding as a *post scriptum* the text of the reply just received from Cornwallis.

[1] Not further identified.

No. 2

Lichtfield, le 29 Brumaire
an 7ème de la République française

Le Général Hardy au Directoire Exécutif

Citoyens Directeurs,

Nos malheurs devaient trouver leur terme dans le combat du 21 Vendémiaire, si la fortune capricieuse se fût contenté[e] d'une victoire, et nous eût permis d'arriver au port; mais elle avait résolu de nous persécuter et de nous poursuivre à outrance jusqu'à la fin; il manquait à son triomphe de nous éprouver par d'autres revers.

Aussitôt que nous fûmes, les officiers, sous-officiers et moi, transférés à bord du vaisseau anglais *Le Robuste*, le capitaine voulut faire voile pour Portsmouth, en passant par la Mer d'Irlande; mais les vents se déclarèrent incontinents contre nous et nous rejettèrent dans le nord. Ce n'est que par miracle que nous y échappâmes deux fois au naufrage, tant sur les Isles Bischop (ou de l'Evêque) que sur celles voisines de l'Écosse. *Le Hoche* était avec nous, dans un état si déplorable qu'à chaque instant nous appréhendions qu'il ne fut englouti. Cette crainte était d'autant plus fondée qu'il ne lui restait pour toute mâture qu'un tronçon de son artimon environ de dix pieds de hauteur, qu'il n'avait pas six aunes de voilure, et que le volume d'eau s'augmentait de plus en plus dans la cale. La mer était toujours violemment agitée, et les vents soufflaient avec une impétuosité extraordinaire, une frégate que nous avions rencontrée par hasard, et qui avait pris *Le Hoche* à la remorque, était à tout moment forcée de l'abandonner à la fureur des flots pour ne pas s'exposer à périr avec lui. Telle est la tourmente que nous avons éprouvée pendant dix-huit jours. Ajoutez à cette cruelle position, que les vivres étant sur le point de manquer, on avait été obligé de réduire la ration au quart. Enfin après cette lutte pénible, les vents se calmèrent un peu, et nous pûmes, le 10 Brumaire,[1] regagner le Lac Swilly, où nous trouvâmes un excellent mouillage. À la vue de cette baie, j'éprouvai un regret d'autant plus sensible qu'il y existe une place sur la quelle dix mille hommes peuvent débarquer facilement, et que nous y aurions trouvé infiniment plus de ressources que je ne m'y étais attendu lorsque je n'avais consulté que ma carte.

Le lendemain de notre arrivée au Lac Swilly, les Adjudans Généraux Simon et Wolf Thone dit Smitt furent appelés à terre par le général[2] commandant l'arrondissement de Londonderri, qui se trouvait alors au village de Buncranagh.[3] Simon resta 24 heures chez le général; il y fut traité avec beaucoup d'égards, et on envoya Smitt à Londonderry, où il fut jetté dans

---

[1] i.e. 31 Oct. 1798.   [2] The earl of Cavan.   [3] i.e. Buncrana.

un cachot et chargé de fers. Dès qu'il m'eut fait part de ce traitement affreux, je descendis moi-même à terre et écrivis au Lord Cornwallis la lettre dont je joins une copie.[1] J'en adressai une autre[2] à ce malheureux officier pour le rassurer et l'engager à supporter avec courage la rigueur du sort qui l'accablait instanément.

Je sais pertinemment que malgré mes réclamations, l'Adjudant Général Smitt a été traîné de prison en prison jusqu'à Dublin. Il est doué d'une âme forte, et je suis persuadé qu'il déploiera un grand caractère dans cette occurrence; mais ses ennemis sont tellement acharnés contre lui qu'on ne saurait prendre des mesures trop promptes pour lui sauver la vie. Je laisse à votre prudence et à votre sagesse, Citoyens Directeurs, à faire en faveur de cet officier les démarches que vous croirez convenables.

Salut et Respects
Hardy

P.S. Au moment où le courrier alloit partir, je reçois du Lord Cornwallis la réponse à ma lettre du 14. Voici littéralement ce qu'il me dit par l'organe de son secrétaire:[3]

'Quant à Theobald Wolf Tone, Son Excellence ne le connoît que sous le rapport d'un traître qui vouloit revenir en Irlande pour tenter par la force des armes ce à quoi il n'a pu réussir par les intrigues, qui n'a cessé de chercher à y semer la rebellion et la discorde, et qui vient enfin d'y être conduit pour y recevoir la punition due aux crimes dont il sera rendu coupable envers son roi et sa patrie.'

H.

Receipt signed by Edward Witherington for some possessions of Tone, 19 November 1798

T.C.D., Courts-martial proceedings, 1798, MS 872, f. 145ᵛ.

Rec[eive]d from Major Sandys one hundred and sixteen crowns and a gold watch being the dividend of the property of the late T. W. Tone intended for his wife by his order.

Edw[ar]d Witherington

November 19, 1798

---

[1] Hardy to Marquis Cornwallis, 14 Brumaire 7 (above, pp 365–6).
[2] Hardy to Tone, 14 Brumaire 7 (above, pp 364–5).
[3] i.e. Herbert Taylor.

Peter Tone to Marquis Cornwallis, *p*.19 November 1798

T.C.D., Courts-martial proceedings, 1798, MS 872, ff 156ʳ–156ᵛ; printed in Hobson, *Letters of Wolfe Tone*, pp 146–7.

Punctuation is absent in the original and has not been supplied except for apostrophes.

To His Excellency Cha[rle]s Marquis Cornwallis Lord Lieutenant Gen[eral] & Gen[eral] Governor of Ireland

The Petition of Peter Tone of the City of Dublin [Gent]leman Humbly Sheweth

That your petitioner's unfortunate son Theobald Wolfe Tone having entrusted to the care of W[illia]m Sandys Esqr Prevote Major a letter for Petitioner & his wearing apparal & some cash the s[ai]d Sandys deliver'd to your Petitioner the s[ai]d letter, cash & some few trifling articles of wearing apparal not exceeding in value what your Petitioner was obliged to pay for the carriage of the trunk containing them but the principal articles & which are of considerable value he has detain'd & declines giving them to your Pet[itione]r on the ground of their being forfeited property though if it c[oul]d be supposed that in so small a matter a claim on behalf of the Crown would be put in such claim w[oul]d not as your Pet[itione]r is advised be establish'd no forfeiture having attach'd because y[ou]r Pet[itioner's] s[ai]d son was not convicted of any offence previous to his death.

May it therefore please your Ex[cellen]cy to direct the s[ai]d Sandys to give y[ou]r Pet[itione]r an authentick inventory of all his s[ai]d son's effects & to deliver to y[ou]r Pet[itione]r the part he retain'd thereof

                                    & y[ou]r Pet[itione]r will pray
                                          Peter Tone

Receipt signed by Peter Tone for some possessions of Tone, *p*.19 November 1798

T.C.D., Courts-martial proceedings, 1798, MS 872, f. 145ᵛ; printed in *The letters of Wolfe Tone*, ed. Bulmer Hobson (Dublin, [1920]), p. 147.

There are two copies. In the other the sum received is given as 'one hundred and seventeen'.

Rec[eive]d from Major Sandys one hundred and sixteen crowns and a trunk of clothes, the property of T. W. Tone.

Peter Tone

Courier report of inquest on 20 November 1798 into Tone's death on 19 November

Courier (London), 26 Nov. 1798.

Extract from letter from Dublin 20 instant.

At eight o'clock last night the unfortunate and much-pitied Tone died in the Provost Marshal; and this morning at eleven o'clock, the Coroner called an inquest on the body. Major Sands[1] and the sentinel who guarded Tone on the night when he attempted the suicide were sworn and deposed in substance that as soon as he was secured from offering further violence, he acknowledged 'that he had given himself the wound in his throat with an intention to kill himself, and that he regretted extremely that he had not been able to effect his purpose'. Three surgeons[2] were also sworn to the cause of his death and it was their unanimous opinion that he died of the wound in his throat.[3] They probed the orifice made in the wind-pipe, and examined it very minutely; it appeared that nearly three-fourths of the circumference of the wind-pipe had been cut. Surgeon Lake,[4] who was one of the surgeons before the jury, said that had the orifice been made a quarter of an inch wider, the patient's death must have been instant.[5]

Courier summary of Tone's will

Courier (London), 27 Nov. 1798.

The late Mr Tone had made, previously to the event that caused his death, a disposition of his little property. He left about thirty pounds in French

---

[1] *Recte* Sandys.

[2] One of the three was probably Benjamin Lentaigne (see above, p. 391, n. 2). Another was probably William Leake (see below, n. 4).

[3] When Tone's wound was discovered, by the sentinel, a surgeon was called at 4 o'clock in the morning 'who stopped the blood and closed it. He reported that, as the prisoner had missed the carotid artery, he might yet survive but was in the extremest danger. It is said that he murmured only in reply, "I am sorry I have been so bad an anatomist" ' (*Life*, ii, 539).

[4] Probably William Leake (d. 1824?), Pitt St., Dublin, city surgeon for many years; he was a member of the Royal College of Surgeons in Ireland; his wife was the eldest sister of Grattan (*Watson's Gentleman's and Citizen's Almanac*, passim; *Walker's Hibernian Magazine*, Dec. 1811).

[5] It was reported that 'the body of Mr Tone was on Tuesday delivered to his friends to be buried' (*Dublin Evening Post*, 22 Nov. 1798). Tuesday was the 20th.

crowns and dollars to be divided between his aged parents and his unhappy wife. He left his sword, uniform &c. to his father, and his ring, ornamented with General Hoche's hair, he gave to Counsellor Emmet. I understand, however, that Brigade Major Sandys claimed them as his property by a sort of *droit d'aubaine*;[1] but he has been disappointed; nor has he been gratified by seeing a stake driven through the body of the deceased in consequence of the verdict of the Coroner's inquest that he had committed suicide. The humane Cornwallis does not delight in trampling on the ashes of the dead.[2]

Viscount Castlereagh to William Wickham, 22 November 1798

Castlereagh corr., ii, 11–15.

The addressee is identified in a heading supplied by the editor of the Castlereagh correspondence.

Phoenix Park, November 22, 1798

My dear Sir,

As the Duke of Portland will naturally be anxious to learn the manner in which the officers of the English Militia are impressed on the question of their return . . . .[3]

His Lordship [Lord Buckingham][4] adverted to Mr Tone's case, and observed that, the proclamation of martial law being superseded by the King's Bench, the English Militia were exposed to the vexations of the civil courts for all those acts of general policy not justifiable by ordinary course of law which they were directed to execute. I assured him the Lord Lieutenant[5] by no means considered the proclamation as in any degree superseded; that, whatever might have been the decision upon Tone's individual case, had he lived, his Excellency was desired not on any account to abdicate that summary discretion, although the courts were sitting, the necessity for which Parliament had recognised, and which the public safety still required; that he had, since the case in question, approved of sentences by court martial, and directed them to be executed in

---

[1] A *droit d'aubaine* was a right to the belongings of a deceased foreigner.

[2] Another report on Tone's death and its aftermath begins 'the inflammation arising from the wound extended itself to the lungs, and is said to have been the immediate cause of his death. He was buried in the same vault with his brother.' (*European Magazine*, Dec. 1798, p. 427). The brother referred to was Mathew Tone, executed in Dublin on 29 Sept. 1798 (see above, p. 354, n.1) The vault was presumably at Bodenstown churchyard, where their grandfather, William Tone, was buried (William Sherlock, 'Bodenstown graveyard: a place of Irish pilgrimage' in *County Kildare Archaeological Society Journal*, vi (1909–11), pp 223–9, illus; see also above, p. 426, n.1).

[3] This letter deals mainly with the English militia serving in Ireland. Only the passage relating to Tone's case, the final part of a long postscript, is printed after these words.

[4] For Lord Buckingham, see above, p. 405.   [5] Cornwallis.

other parts of the kingdom; and that his Lordship might depend on the Militia being justified and protected to the utmost, in the execution of those orders which the Lord Lieutenant felt it his duty to impose, whether strictly legal or not, for the security of the metropolis. His Lordship was perfectly satisfied.

I trust the Lord Lieutenant will shortly receive directions how to act on this most important question.

Earl of Clare to Lord Auckland, 26 November 1798

British Library, Auckland papers, MS 34455, ff 38–39ᵛ; printed in D. A. Fleming and A. P. W. Malcomson (eds), '*A volley of execrations': the letters and papers of John FitzGibbon, earl of Clare, 1772–1802* (Dublin, 2005), pp 359–60.

This letter is printed also in *Journals and correspondence of William, Lord Auckland* (London, 1861–2), iv, 81, where however what follows 'where he landed' is omitted.

William Eden (1744–1814), 1st Baron Auckland, was chief secretary for Ireland, 1780–82 (*D.N.B.*).

I very much fear that Lord Cornwallis's reserve will not tend much to what I am very confident is his object. He seems to be impressed with an opinion that the minds of gentlemen with whom he must act in his government are so heated and warped by passion and prejudice that their opinions are not the safest by which we can act, and therefore his determination is made to act solely from himself. I fear also that he much mistakes the nature of the people in supposing that they are to be brought back to submission by a system nearly of indiscriminate impunity for the most enormous offences. . . [1]

Nothing could be so preposterous as the whole proceeding with respect to Tone. He should certainly have been hanged on the shore where he landed. But after he was brought up to be tried by a military tribunal in Dublin upon what principle was his execution delayed from Saturday to Monday?[2] Nay more, there then was full time to execute him on Monday after it was known that an application would be made to the King's Bench and before it was made. And what do you suppose prevented it? The opinion of a surgeon's mate that a man whose throat was cut could not die of hanging. . . . .

Dublin, Novʳ 26th, 1798

[P.S.] You have heard I suppose that Tone is dead.

---

[1] The omitted matter relates largely to the rebellion in County Wicklow.

[2] i.e. from 10 Nov., when sentence of death was passed by the court martial, to 12 Nov., when Tone's case came before the court of king's bench.

Catherine Heaviside to Matilda Tone, 30 November 1798

Tone (Dickason) papers.

November 30th 1798
Holles Street
[Dublin]

My Dear dear Sister,

I have tried in vain to write to you but 'tis impossible. What my heart feels for you and your darling children I need not attempt to express. Enclosed is the most valuable gift I could send you—a lock of your dear Tone's hair. Be careful for yourself—'tis his last request. Would to God you were with us now. If you could know what we all suffer and feel for you. Be careful of your health. God forever bless and comfort you.

Most affectionately yours
Catherine Heaviside

Thomas Addis Emmet to Alexander Marsden, 3 December 1798

Nat. Arch. (Ire.), Rebellion papers, 620/15/2/16.

Dear Marsden,

On seeing a letter from me, you will probably suppose I am going once more to tease you about Government's performing its conditions with me and my fellow prisoners. Such however are not my intentions. I have so often and so vainly applied on that subject that I am but little disposed to spend more time in unprofitable solicitations, and if I am compelled to make another application respecting it, I will not do so thro' those channels that have hitherto failed. My present motive for troubling you is of a very different kind, and gives me reason to hope I may succeed, because it can be no object to Government that I should not. I accidentally read this morning in the *Courier*[1] that a friend whose memory I shall never cease to esteem & love— Tone, directed before his death, that a ring which he wore should be given to me. If this be true it is the first intelligence I received of his affectionate

---

[1] See above, p. 434.

remembrance, and I request that his wish may be complied with. Were it ever so dangerous, I should not hesitate to avow my attachment for Tone— he was dear to me in his misfortunes, his magnanimity has encreased & his death has perpetuated my affection. But there can be no such danger to me. His Majesty's ministers know my political principles, and my inability to act according to them. The ring that was worn by my unfortunate friend (even tho' it should contain a lock of Hoche's hair) cannot advance those principles or diminish that inability. It is not from political motives I wish to possess it, but merely as the last token of remembrance from a beloved friend, and as such I trust there will be no objection to its being forwarded to me. Perhaps however I am misinformed, & that the fact is not so. If that be the case, you will much oblige me by letting me know it.

Believe me yours very sincerely
Thoˢ Addis Emmet

Kilmainham
Monday, Decʳ 3ʳᵈ 1798

[*Addressed to*]:

Alexʳ Marsden Esqʳ.
Dublin Castle

ADDITIONAL DOCUMENTS

Announcement of premiums at Sisson Darling's Mercantile Academy, April 1773

Freeman's Journal, 17 Apr. 1773.

For Tone's career at Darling's academy, see Autobiography (above, vol. II, p. 267). No attempt has been made to identify the 'young gentlemen' named.

MERCANTILE ACADEMY, MABBOTT STREET

Public Examinations ended the 2th inst. [*sic*] when premiums and certificates were adjudged to the young gentlemen in the following branches, viz. BOOKKEEPING, premium Wybrants 1, Wilson, Watson 2, cert. Stewart 1, Ashworth, Brown 1. ARITHMETIC. *Exchange*, prem. Quin, cert. Wybrants 2. *Practics* and *Fractions*, prem. Richardson, cert. Wybrants 2. *Proportion*, prem. Cole, cert. Stewart 1. *Reduction*, prem. Tone, cert. Watson. *Four Rules*, prem. Antrobus, cert. Burton. WRITING, prem. Quin, Wybrants 3, Stewart 1, Edwards 2, McDaniel, Darley 1, McMahon 2, Green 2, cert. Close, Antrobus, Stuart 2, Richardson, McMahon 1, Clancey 2, Crooks, Henry. MATHEMATICKS, *Euclid*, prem. Quin, Edwards 2, Watson 2, cert. Edwards 1, Burroughs. *Geometry*, prem. Quin, Spencer, cert. Tyler. *Trigonometry*, prem. Tyler, cert. Quin. *Navigation*, prem. Tyler, cert. Spencer. *Use of the Globes*, prem. Spencer, Watson 2, cert. Quin, M'Gomery. *Fortification*, prem. Edwards 2, Wybrants 1, cert. Edwards 1. SPEAKING, head prem. Quin, prem. Watson 1, Antrobus, Allen, Tone, Irvine, cert. Owen, Watson 2, Clancey 2. READING, *Gray's Elegy*, prem. Quin. *Milton*, prem. Edwards 2, cert. Owen. *Spectator*, prem. Tone, cert. Brown. *Bible*, prem. Whelan, cert. Stewart 1. *Psalms*, prem. Green 2, cert. Bowen. *Grammar*, prem. Quin, Tone, Irvine, McMahon 1 and 2, cert. Allen, Wilkinson, Gibbons, Green 1. *Spelling*, prem. Cuff, Henry, cert. Tone, Green 2. CATECHISM, *Explanation*, prem. Tone, cert. Brown 1. *Plain*, prem. McMahon 2, cert. Henry. HIST., *English*, prem. Tone. POLITE ACCOMPLISHMENTS, *French*, prem. Thornton, Blackwood 1, cert. Blackwood 2. *Dancing*, prem. Whelan, cert. Bornford. *Drawing*, prem. Quin, cert. Bornford. *Fencing*, prem. Powel 1, cert. Owen.

Resolutions for the catholics of Dublin, 29 October 1792

Hibernian Journal, 5 Nov. 1792.

For Tone's authorship and the date, see Diary for 29 Oct. 1792 (above, vol. I, p. 319).

At a meeting of the Catholic inhabitants of the City of Dublin, duly convened by public summons, Wednesday, October 31, 1792

Thomas Broughall in the Chair

A copy of the letter of the Corporation of the City of Dublin dated September 11, 1792, and addressed to the Protestants of Ireland having been read from a public print, a committee consisting of

Randal McDonnel	Thomas Ryan
John Keogh	Thomas Warren
Hugh Hamill	Charles Ryan[1]
Edward Byrne	John Ball

was ordered to prepare an answer to said publication and to report the same forthwith and the committee having reported accordingly RESOLVED
That the declaration which follows be published as the unanimous act of this meeting;
That we embrace this opportunity to repeat our thanks to the illustrious characters in both houses of Parliament who have nobly stood forward in support of Catholic emancipation and the right of the subject to petition for redress of grievances;
That our warmest gratitude is due and hereby respectfully offered to our countrymen the citizens of Belfast for the uniform and manly exertions which they have on all occasions made in support of our cause and for the example of liberality and genuine public spirit which they have thereby shewn to the kingdom at large;
That our sincere thanks are likewise due to the different Volunteer corps lately reviewed in Ulster, to the societies of United Irishmen of Dublin and Belfast, to the Protestant freeholders of Cork, [to] the different gentlemen who at Grand Juries and County Meetings have supported our cause and to all others among our Protestant brethren who have manifested a wish for our emancipation, and we trust we shall evince by our conduct that we are not insensible nor unworthy of the kindness which they have shewn us;
That our chairman be ordered to transmit copies of this day's proceedings to the chairman of the Town Meeting of Belfast, the chairmen of the different societies of United Irishmen, the different reviewing officers in Ulster and the other distinguished characters who have interested themselves in the cause of Catholic emancipation.

by order of the meeting
Simon Maguire, secretary

---

[1] Charles Ryan (d. 1810), apothecary, Old Church St., Dublin; member of Dublin Society of United Irishmen (C. J. Woods, 'The personnel of the Catholic Convention, 1792-3' in *Archivium Hibernicum*, lvii (2003), p. 69).

Address to the people of Ireland, late 1794

Life, ii, 295–316.

The references in this document to Edmund Burke's pension and to a report 'that it is now the intention of the British minister to allow the Roman Catholics the utmost extent of their original demands', together with the absence of any mention of the appointment of Earl Fitzwilliam to the Irish viceroyalty, suggest that it was composed towards the end of 1794.

Address to the people of Ireland

People of Ireland,

With a most fertile soil, rich in population and in every natural blessing which can give happiness and ought to diffuse wealth, your country has for ages been plunged into all the wretchedness of poverty, at the contemplation of which humanity shudders.

To what malignant influence can this be ascribed if not to the tyrannical dominion of a country which avails itself of a pretended relationship in order to monopolize your trade and whose Government with respect to you has always proved the most flagrant despotism?

From the first invasion of your island by the English[1] till the epoch of their Revolution,[2] when they changed one despot for another, let its circumstances alter as they would, you were ever marked out as the devoted victims of its ambitious system. When you remained attached to the family of the Stuarts, how were you treated by the English Republican faction?[3] And when it pleased the English to restore that family to the crown,[4] how was the fidelity of the Irish recompensed? Did not the son establish the very persons who had pursued his father to death in the possession of the property of those who had died in his service? When England dismissed the second James,[5] a more just conception of their own interest than has ever yet guided Irish politics seems to have been adopted, for they[6] gave him an asylum, and notwithstanding the care of the English to destroy every record of the Parliament held by him in Dublin,[7] enough still exists to prove that their

---

[1] In 1171, when Henry II of England arrived in Ireland.

[2] The overthrow and execution of Charles I and accession to power of Oliver Cromwell (1649).

[3] An allusion to the loyalty of the Confederate catholics to Charles II in his exile and treatment of catholics in Ireland by the Cromwellians (1649–60).

[4] In 1660, when Charles II returned from exile.   [5] In 1688, at the Glorious Revolution.

[6] i.e. the Irish catholics.

[7] In 1695 the Irish parliament enacted that all the acts and proceedings of the 'pretended' parliament held by James II in Dublin should be destroyed (7 William III, c. 3).

object was *the independence of Ireland*.[1] This Parliament was composed of Catholics and dearly has their overthrow cost the nation. A timid king leading a disunited people, still sore with mutual injustice, fell an easy sacrifice to Britain; and every year has added to the weight of those penal laws which enslaved the people almost to brutality. The Catholics, however, were not the only sufferers. The Presbyterians were also included in several disqualifying statutes, because their sentiments were free and their race Republican. They were therefore held up as scarecrows against republicanism to the loyal Catholics, whilst the monarchial Catholic was exhibited to the Dissenter as the advocate of despotism. Thus mutual hatred and distrust were excited to keep them both more easily under subjection, and the reign of superstition and fanaticism prolonged to foment divisions.

Engrossed then by intestine broils, the Irish did not think of opposing their common enemy till at length the radiance of the French Revolution dispelled the cloud and, each party viewing the other through a new medium, the Catholic became the friend of the Presbyterian, and the Presbyterian, more accustomed to political discussion, the steady advocate for the rights of the Catholic on the broad basis of natural justice. The people began to be enlightened by these forcible appeals to common sense, and tyranny trembled on its throne until corruption came to its assistance. Great praise has been given, particularly at this period, where very little was merited, on account of the relaxation of the penal code; as if it were a benefit done to the people to repeal laws so disgraceful to humanity, that there were very few of them which the softened spirit of the times would permit to be mentioned, much less executed, according to the letter; but in what respect has this relaxation, produced by the natural melioration of manners which directs the progress of public opinion, benefitted the peasant? Does he find the Catholic landlord more easy to deal with and less exorbitant in his demands than he found the Protestant? Or does the Catholic magistrate distribute justice more impartially for being of the same persuasion? Have tythes been abolished or regulated? Has the hearth money collector passed by the poor man's cottage, where there was not the luxury of a chimney to demand his entrance?[2] Have the manufactures of the country been encouraged and protected? Where then are the vaunted favors yielded by the English to damp the enthusiasm for liberty that is spreading itself throughout Europe? Is not their present conduct on the contrary only a continuation of the system adopted by the British faction that presides in Ireland, the annihilation of which is necessary to save a people whose talents and spirit have ever

---

[1] Tone seems to have derived his knowledge and understanding of the Jacobite period from Curry and Leland.

[2] In 1793 many occupiers of one-hearth houses were exempted from the payment of hearth money (33 Geo. III, c. 14). In 1795 all occupiers of one-hearth houses were exempted from the tax (35 Geo. III, c. 1).

been bowed down by the short-sighted policy of an invidious neighbour? Always thrown into the background as subordinate, your very individual value as men has only been known when you fought the battles of England and conquered for your taskmasters, or when your unfortunate outcast sons fell covered with wounds in the ranks foreign armies.

Liberty, equality and independence are within your reach. Lose not the golden moment. Seize upon independence and every good will follow. Let every man, rich and poor, possess his rights by equal laws and be obliged to perform the duties of a citizen; then will commence the reign of true equality, and talents and industry having fair scope, the aristocracy fostered by English tyranny will insensibly be undermined. Roused by the voice of reason that is making itself heard on the world, will the mass of the Irish nation still bear the yoke which is dragging their friends and neighbours to America in search of a spot of uncultivated land and freedom when, by a little exertion, they may become free and prosperous at home? No, it cannot be! Irishmen are brave, generous and determined. Courage and prudence will establish independence, liberty and equality in their native soil under the shade of their own mountains.

The French Republic has risen above still greater difficulties. Despots have attempted its overthrow but, disappointed in their views, now tremble at its strength. France, in declaring war to tyrants, offers you alliance and assistance, for where could it find a more oppressed people? And will you still remain the slave of a power that for seven centuries has availed itself of all your vigour to man its fleets and to recruit its armies, to protect a commerce in which you are not permitted to share? Will you not rather raise your drooping head and enable your country to rank again as a nation amongst the nations of Europe? Rescue it from oblivion or contempt. Assert the rights of man and secure the possession of those rights by establishing *a representative legislature*, the only legitimate government, and form an alliance with the Republic of France to promote your commercial interest whilst confirming your independence.

To lead you to form this resolution it is only necessary to turn your attention towards yours wrongs and to arouse you from the stupor that perpetuates them and unmans yourselves; it is sufficient to appeal to reason, bringing forward truths that are felt, to enforce its arguments. From the time of the descent of the English during the reign of Henry the Second until the present moment it has ever been the policy of Britain to excite animosities and encourage jealousies amongst the inhabitants of Ireland in order more effectually to secure to itself the enjoyment of all your natural advantages. Not allowed to live under the protection of the laws of the country which assumed a dominion over you, your very existence has been undervalued. The accidental killing of an Englishman was punished by death on the Irish culprit, whilst the penalty incurred by the murder of an Irishman by an Englishman was only the fine of a few shillings. The crime of the one was high treason against the state, and the other merely a petty misdemeanour.[1]

In a later period, when humanity began by degrees to draw man to man and it was observed that several of the English had mixed with the Irish, preferring the justice and simplicity of the old Brehon law to the despotic government of their co-settlers, severe penalties were enacted against all those who should, by marriage or otherwise, connect themselves with the Irish families and as recreant Britons they became liable to numerous disqualifications; nay even those Irishmen who lived within what it pleased the English to denominate their Pale were obliged to drop their native distinctive names and to adopt some common English appellation as Carpenter, Smith, Black, Brown, Bush.[2]

At length Ireland was permitted to partake of the benefit of the British constitution, and the English monarch changed the name of Lord for that of King of Ireland.[3]

The family of the Stuarts, and particularly Charles the Second,[4] exercised the prerogative of the crown and erected several corporations to which was granted the privilege of sending members to Parliament. But these grants were generally made to some English minion under the pretext of encouraging new settlers and of civilizing the country, though they were in reality enacted in order to secure to Great Britain a legislative dominion over that nation; it became consequently the interest of the proprietor of each district to which the privilege was annexed to prevent the increase of population to secure more completely to himself the nomination of the members sent to Parliament as the representation of the people. This abuse, being favourable to the mistaken sinister policy of England, has always been countenanced by it. Man was never the object of improvement in Ireland; on the contrary every talent which gives dignity to the human species has been not only disregarded but discouraged as destructive to the interest of Britain; and even nature herself has been made to take retrograde steps to prevent the advance of civilization which must necessarily have led them[5] to struggle for independence. That the country might be entirely devoted to the raising of flocks and herds every effort in favour of the agriculture or commerce of Ireland has been opposed by England; nay, even that branch of trade which consists of the manufactory of the raw materials produced on her own soil is denied to Ireland and absorbed by England. Her raw hides and her wool in the state of yarn, which part of the labour demands many hands and is not paid one hundredth part of the profit, can only be sent to the English gulph.[6] Death is the penalty attending the exportation of wool elsewhere.[7]

---

[1] See Sir John Davies, *Historical tracts* (Dublin, 1787), p. 82, and, for a modern view of the question, G. J. Hand, *English law in Ireland* (Cambridge, 1967), ch. 10.   [2] 5 Edw. IV, c. 3.

[3] In 1541 by an act of parliament (33 Hen. VIII, c. 1) the king of England was declared to be king of Ireland.   [4] *Recte* James 1.

[5] Presumably Tone means 'the Irish'.   [6] The meaning of this expression is unclear.

[7] The illegal exportation of wool from Ireland was punished by the forfeiture of the ship carrying the wool and £500 fine (10 Will. III, c. 10 [Eng.]).

England is, of course, their only market and therefore it fixes its own price. In pursuance of the system above animadverted upon a vote of Parliament was procured by British influence which declared that any person who demanded tythe for agistment or grazing cattle was an enemy to his country,[1] though when the poor farmer applied to the Parliament to be exempted from tythe during the short period of three years for such barren ground as he should reclaim into tillage the bill was thrown out without a division.[2]

The British Revolution of 1688, which is said to have given a constitution and restored liberty to England, had indisputably a contrary effect in Ireland and plunged that people into a state of misery and suffering scarcely to be imagined.

At the epoch of the Reformation, the Irish Catholics had indeed been cruelly treated; but it was the tyranny of a haughty conqueror, chasing a whole people from their home and property in order to recompense his followers with their spoil. The expulsion of the inhabitants of the five northern counties and the driving them over the Shannon in the reign of Elizabeth was not so intolerably arbitrary as that infernal system of the penal code which was introduced into Ireland after the Revolution.

A few instances will give some faint idea of the sufferings of the Catholics under that accumulation of legal injury. Deprived of all the blessings of freedom, they were denied the possession of arms; they had no right, civil, political or religious, to defend; arms were therefore unnecessary and might become dangerous to their masters should they aim at regaining them. They were also debarred of education and thus, as it were, systematically brutalized.

Did a Catholic ride a horse of more than five pounds value, if a Church of England man who had perhaps taken a fancy to it offered him that sum he was obliged to dismount and yield it to this authorized robber.[3] In like manner if a man of the same description, a favoured son of the religion wedded to the crown, wished to dispossess him of his farm the iniquity of the law was such that he could be ejected and his lease become void to prevent the growth of Popery.[4] With still greater refinement of cruelty, the ingratitude of children was stimulated and rewarded. If the son recanted the errors of Popery and embraced those of the established church, the property of the father devolved immediately to him; and this not once but as often as, by succession or industry, it should have accumulated, so often the father was obliged to be accountable for it to his child.[5]

---

[1] In 1735 the house of commons resolved that title of agistment was a grievance.

[2] Barren land bills, bills exempting reclaimed land from tithe for a certain number of years, were rejected in the sessions of 1788, 1789 and 1791, but in the session of 1793 it was enacted that waste land converted into arable or meadow would be exempted from tithe for seven years.

[3] 7 Will. III, c. 5.

[4] A catholic could not hold a lease for more than 31 years or on terms which allowed that the profits exceeded one third of the rent (2 Anne, c. 6).

[5] The eldest son of a catholic could, if he became a protestant, turn his father into a life tenant (2 Anne, c. 6).

444

If it did not savour[1] of ridicule, though it will serve to show the wanton sportings of tyranny, the proposal might be cited, made by the famous Harrington in Cromwell's time, of selling Ireland and its inhabitants to the Jews,[2] and the bill which was proposed in Parliament as a means to prevent the growth of Popery to castrate all the Catholic clergy.[3] Besides, an act was really passed to regulate the conduct of judges and magistrates which directed that whenever any doubts should arise respecting the expressions used in any of the laws against the Catholics, the most rigorous construction should be adopted, an injunction directly opposed to the principles and even the practice of Great Britain in the enforcing of any penal statute.[4]

Let us now follow the Irish peasant to his hut and calculate his resources. Let the average of his wages through the year be fixed at sixpence per day, which is a high rate; deduct Sundays, holidays, wet days[5] and the time he is occupied in his own garden and his annual gain will not amount to more, if as much, as six pounds per annum. Let us afterwards examine his disbursements. If he be happy enough to get a cottage and half an acre of bad ground[6] for which he is charged two pounds per annum, he generally, to make up the rent, works through the year for the person from whom he holds it; and, as he holds it at will, he is, in a manner, an indentured servant. If his industry has procured him a cow, his obligation to his landlord is increased by his permitting it to graze on the outskirts of the farm at the rate of two pounds per annum more.[7] A rood of potatoe ground, for which we suppose him to have the necessary manure, will cost him sixteen shillings; and half an acre of what are called corn acres, that is some spot which the farmer has nearly run out by tillage and is now to be laid down with grass seed, will cost him for seed, ploughing &c. at least thirty shillings more. Rate his taxes and tythe at ten shillings and it will be found that his

---

[1] Erroneously 'favor' in *Life*, ii, 300.

[2] James Harrington (1611–77), political theorist, remarks in the introduction to his *The commonwealth of Oceana* (1656) that Panopean (i.e. Ireland), 'the soft mother of a slothful and pusillanimous people', should be planted with Jews (*D.N.B.*).

[3] It was proposed by the Irish privy council in Aug. 1719 but soon dropped (W. P. Burke, *Irish priests in the penal times* (Waterford, 1914), pp 198–201).

[4] Tone may have had in mind the dictum of Baron Mountney that the acts to prevent the growth of popery 2 Anne 6 and 8 Anne 3 'were not to be considered penal laws, but for the advancement of religion and to be extended to promote that end' (G. E. Howard, *Several special cases on the laws against the further growth of popery in Ireland* (Dublin, 1775), p. 102).

[5] Footnote by Tone: 'It is the custom in Ireland, when the day's work is broken by the inclemency of the weather, to discharge the labourers and to allow them for only half a day's work.'

[6] Footnote by Tone: 'In general those angles of great farms which are made by intersecting roads or marshy, unprofitable and unhealthy spots are marked out by the proprietor for the purpose of erecting cabins on. The building, roofing &c of some of these huts may cost about twelve pounds.'

[7] Footnote by Tone: 'I have known a person of the first, and formerly most opulent, family of Ireland turned from the squire's office and pursued with the lashes of a horsewhip across her bare legs, already swollen by the cold, in so inhuman a manner as to carry the scars with her to the grave, merely because there was a deficiency of a few shillings of the rent she ought to have paid for the grazing of a cow, the sole property and support of herself and two orphans'.

disbursements exceed his annual receipt fifteen shillings per annum, not reckoning the clothing of his family, his firing and other incidental expenses. How is this overplus to be furnished? The cow produces a calf which is fattened to make veal; whilst the calf is feeding the family are starving, for they are deprived entirely of their milk and butter; potatoes and water become then their only support. By this parsimonious economy, however, and the sale of his calf, his butter, his eggs, his poultry and a hog, which has been not only his inmate but his messmate, he is enabled to make good his engagements and to drag on an existence from year to year. I have here pictured the peasant in his most favorable situation, where he can find a ready sale for everything his industry and frugality enables him to take to market and when his daily wages are paid to him in cash.

Now let the haughty and self-sufficient Englishman, or the more despicable character, the renegade Irishman, look at this picture; and if they cannot prove that it is overcharged, surely they must blush at recollecting that they have represented the Irish peasant as idle, dissolute and dishonest; nay, if a spark of humanity remain alive in their hearts, they must feel some remorse for having dared to make what is the effect of oppression a plea to perpetuate it.

Such being the situation of the Irish peasant in his prosperity, let us cast our eyes on him whose habitation is reared against some high bank, whose dwelling is the ditch, whose roof is covered with sods taken from the margin of the road, whose bed is potatoe stalks and nightly covering only an old cast-off horse rug from the squire's stable; while the mantle that barely covers the mother of the family, and the tattered remnant of a frieze great-coat which hangs reluctantly on the shoulders of the father sufficiently apologize for the nakedness of the children: the only thing of value which the eye can trace is an iron pot, from which the family are fed; and how often has the hearth-money collector seized this single necessary and sold it at the door under its value to pay the tax of two shillings for a hearth that did not exist! It may appear like exaggeration to say that for want of the trifling sum of two shillings he is reduced to this necessity; but the fact is notorious; and the well-known cause is that instead of paying him for his labour, his master furnishes him with potatoes, turf, grain &c. and contrives to keep the wretched object forever in his debt.

It will rather seem astonishing that the Irish peasant, thus superlatively miserable and oppressed, can value his existence or preserve any attachment to his native soil. The slaves in the West Indies are clothed and fed by those who benefit by their labours; and the expense attending the replacing of them makes their lives valuable to their masters. Some of the planters who reside on their own estates, we are told, render their old age comfortable. Whether this be the fact or not, in Ireland it is certainly the contrary; a labourer is seldom employed unless he be in his prime; and if illness and premature old age overtake him, he depends upon the charity of his fellow labourers for relief, whose own wants are so pressing, and he sinks into the grave from extreme misery, perhaps on the very estate where his ancestors have lived in feudal pomp and on which he had himself been reduced to daily labour at five pence per day.

Under such circumstances is it to be wondered at that the Irish peasantry exhibit the most wretched appearance of any people where civilization has made the smallest advances, or that the ferocity called forth by cruelty and rendered characteristic by ignorance should produce acts of barbarity which furnish their tyrants with a fresh pretext to depress them below the level of improvement?

The situation of the Irish Catholic farmer is not much more enviable than that of the peasant; exorbitant rents, short tenures and high taxes are not his only grievances. A Catholic does not go to market upon equal footing with his Anglican neighbour; nothing is more common than for a person who has land to let to say to the Catholic, 'I can have as much from a Protestant and a vote into the bargain',[1] or to see advertised 'a tract of ground to be let to a Protestant tenant only' and a *nota bene* 'that no preference will be given', meaning that the person whose improvements and the benefit of whose labour has now fallen into the lord shall certainly be turned out if another will offer a trifle more. Add to this the usually adopted mode of letting grounds, which is to receive written proposals and on a certain day to name the tenant.

The number of absentee landlords is also most severely felt by all descriptions of Irish farmers; and it is not merely the absence of the lord but the extravagance occasioned by his residing at a foreign court which makes it generally necessary for him to employ that agent who can remit him the most money. The man who does not reside on his own estate, having no social duties to exercise, easily forgets, in the search of pleasure to vary his idle existence, that reciprocal duties ought to bind him to his tenantry, or he becomes the leech of industry. But instead of making this obvious reflection, he chooses some needy country gentleman or shrewd attorney to be his agent, who generally emulates the state of the proprietor, without having the same resource to support the expence; partly by power, partly by selling as favour indulgencies which the proprietor would not, and indeed could not, refuse to grant, and partly by holding a farm, in the cultivation of which he calls for the assistance of the tenantry, and perhaps employs them in saving his harvest or drawing his turf whilst their own lies rotting in the field, he contrives to maintain his hounds, to drink, game and partake of all the vices and extravagance of his titled neighbours. At last, if either his dissipation or his dishonesty occasion his removal, it frequently happens that a whole tenantry are ruined by being called upon by his successor, or the proprietor of the estate, to settle accounts and pay off arrears which have

---

[1] However, after the passing of Hobart's relief act (33 Geo. III, c. 21, 9 Apr. 1793) catholics were enfranchised subject to the same qualifications as protestants.

been already at least partly discharged but for which they have not received any regular receipts and did not dare to demand them lest they should incur the resentment of their petty tyrant against whose injustice they had no appeal.

The system, indeed, of a well-known character[1] in Ireland was as landlord still more infamous, for whenever a farm fell into his hands he cultivated it to the highest degree of perfection; a farmer dazzled with the prospect of immediate profit consented to give an exorbitant rent for it; he brought his flock upon the farm, which in the course of a few years was seized and sold for an arrear of rent and the farmer and his family, who had in vain implored to be released from the inconsiderate bargain, thrown upon the world without a penny, whilst the baronet put the farm again into a condition to allure and ruin some new adventurer. What name can we give to such a man?

The mercantile then appears to be the only line in which the Catholic is so nearly on a par with the merchant of the established church as to hope that his exertions may produce some degree of independence; but does this proceed from British justice or benevolence? Surely not—on the contrary, the Protestant and Dissenter have to lament in common with the Catholic that selfish British system which has prevented Ireland from enjoying any share of the prosperous English commerce and has ever cramped her internal industry so much as to render the situation of a trader always precarious and too frequently ruinous.

But had this order of men the full liberty of cultivating every advantage which nature has lavished on our country in the spontaneous fertility of her soil, her numerous and well-situated harbours, how inconsiderable would the number of persons thus benefited be when compared with the mass of the Irish nation beaten down by the British selfishness, whether acting through English absentee proprietors or the more despicable willing slaves to England of the established church who inhabit Ireland and call themselves Irishmen but whose short-sighted policy makes them assist in the depression of their country lest others should participate in those emoluments and dignities which England now bestows exclusively on the Anglo-Irish[2] aristocrats.

It is true that within these fourteen years[3] not only no statutes have been enacted against the Catholics alone, but they have in appearance obtained from Government some alleviation of their former restrictions. Apparent favours have been granted to them with that dexterous or rather sinister policy which has served to raise the jealousy of their fellow-sufferers, the Presbyterians, and excite the hatred of their lordly masters of the established church. The free exercise of their religion and a permission to purchase estates for any term not exceeding nine hundred and ninety-nine years were

---

[1] Not identified.   [2] This is the only instance of Tone using the term 'Anglo-Irish'.
[3] The allusion in the same paragraph to the catholic relief act of 1778 suggests that by 'these fourteen years' Tone means the period 1778–92.

granted to the Catholics as favours of the greatest magnitude.[1] But to estimate these at their proper value, it will be but reasonable to examine the grants themselves as well as their natural tendency; and it will then be found that instead of conferring favours on them, the English Government has increased their duties and added to their grievances.

The penalty formerly incurred by those who assisted, or those who celebrated, the rites and ceremonies of the Romish church were abrogated and the permission of possessing places allotted for the worship of the Deity according to their own manner necessarily implied the permitting a clergy to perform the rites and ceremonies which had been thus legalized and consequently the Romish clergy were then authorized to demand subsistence from the state.[2] But by whom was this provision to be supplied? By the Catholics undoubtedly, as the persons who benefited by their appointment, and on them alone the burthen ought to fall. But by a parity of reason that sect ought to have been relieved from the payment of any other clergy than their own, so that during the existence of that most burthensome and arbitrary tax of tythe the Catholic priest ought at least to have shared the pillage of the farmer with the church of England clergyman, instead of which the Catholic finds himself obliged to pay both and is thus reduced exactly to the same situation as the French farmer was in before their glorious Revolution, when the pressure of *corvées*, *gabelles*, mortmains and all the extortions attending an avowed despotic government with feudal tenure left him for himself just one twentieth share of the crop to stimulate and reward his industry.

It may be urged that the English Catholic is in a similar or worse situation as he pays a double land tax. The individual hardship is certainly the same in both cases; but the number of the sufferers in proportion to those of Ireland is so inconsiderable as to render the grievance almost imperceptible; besides, the established is indisputably the national church; the increase of the land tax being a stated sum is little felt; and the tythes in England materially differ from those in Ireland, both in the sums assessed and in the mode of assessing. In England the tythe is commonly settled by a modus or ancient custom; still even there it is most severely felt, though paid by Englishmen to Englishmen of the same persuasion.

But the mode of levying tythes in Ireland is still more oppressive than the tythes themselves; the crop is no sooner ripe than the proctor enters the field, surveys the crop and sets an imaginary value upon it, and then demands a certain sum as an equivalent to the tythe. It may be said that if the sum demanded be extravagant the farmer at the worst may give the tythe in kind, which has nevertheless been calculated to amount to one third of the profit of the whole crop; but this cannot be done in Ireland. Independent of the

[1] 17 & 18 Geo. III, c. 49, known as Gardiner's act (14 Aug. 1778).
[2] 21 & 22 Geo. III, c. 24 (4 May 1782).

trouble, vexation and expense which it is in the power of the tythe proctor to give the farmer, the latter has calculated the quantity of the hay, grain and straw which is necessary for his consumption, and if any part of this be taken from him he has no market to recur to; each of his neighbours is in the same predicament; his wants, therefore, if urgent, must be supplied from the haggart of the rich at an exorbitant rate, and not having the command of money, this rate becomes double from being paid in service.

It has been before observed that the impost of tythe paid to the clergymen of the established church is not so severely felt in England as in Ireland, not only from the different mode of collecting it but likewise on account of the majority of the people belonging to that church whose ministers receive the imposition; and it may be very fairly inferred that the grievance is greatly aggravated in Ireland by another circumstance: the whole Episcopalian clergy of that country may be said to be Englishmen, or at least they are persons appointed by their interest,[1] who have no natural relation with the community on whom the imposition falls.

In general, the Irish bishoprics are filled up by the private tutor, the domestic chaplain, or perhaps the profligate pander to some *viceroy*, sent to revel on the spoil of the people he corrupts. Following the example of his patron, therefore, the only object of the bishop is to drain as much money as he can from the see to which he is appointed. He fills up the vacant benefices either with his needy relations or perhaps sells them at a half public sale through the medium of his lady's maid or his own valet. Even a virtuous man, when he knows that he is presenting a clergyman to a living where all the inhabitants are of a different religious opinion, may be led to look upon it as naming to a sinecure and [think] that it is not so necessary to scrutinize the morals or the manners of the person whom he instals as if he was to become the confidential adviser, as well as spiritual father, of the parishioners from whom he draws his support and who are thus constructively committed to his care.

The second concession made by Great Britain to the Irish Catholics, that of being enabled to possess property for any term not exeeding nine hundred and ninety-nine years, is not perhaps liable to equal objections with the former; but evidently, it can only prove favorable to the rich and must increase the market price of land by inducing many who have realized money in trade to become purchasers; and owing to the depression of the manufactures, the proportion of farmers is already greater than it ought to be in a well-regulated state.

At the approach of the present war with France, when everything was to be dreaded by the English from the desperate situation of the Irish peasantry should that island be attacked by those who professed to be the harbingers of independence and equality, of liberty and peace, and whose conquering

---

[1] i.e. England's interest.

arms were to be directed only against the tyrant's palace, whilst they respected the cottage of the oppressed people—at such a time, it was necessary again to lull the Catholics to sleep on their chains; and as none of the old intrigues could prevent the meeting of the Catholic convention,[1] the next consideration was to render their design abortive. That body was therefore insidiously prevailed upon to send a deputation to throw themselves at the foot of the throne and pray for a redress of grievances. In this deputation, as it is affirmed, the English Minister had contrived to procure a secret influence where it was least to be expected. It was well known that many of the Catholic bishops and priests had been gained over to the side of Government; some had accepted pensions and others sums of money. From the natural adherence of the priesthood to the aristocracy, by which they were chiefly supported, many had attached themselves to Lord Kenmare and the party that had declared against all the popular proceedings of the Catholics.[2] Five laymen were therefore appointed, three of whom[3] were independent country gentlemen, the fourth[4] one of the first merchants in Dublin, and the fifth[5] a person who had retired from trade with an ample fortune of whose zeal and integrity no one then doubted. The rumour which has since gained ground of his having been corrupted by the English Minister appears, however, not to be entirely void of foundation, for notwithstanding the prudent secrecy with which the debates of the convention were conducted, it transpired that this man was denounced by one of his co-deputies for having had some private interviews with the secretary of the Minister, the result of which he had not made known to the rest of the deputation.[6] Besides, another circumstance which gave a decided influence to the Minister in the debates of the Catholic body was their application to Edmund Burke to become their mediator, who, it is since known, was at that very time pensioned by the British Government under a fictitious name to betray the cause of the people who, grateful for his former exertions in their favour which had obtained the repeal of some of the most absurd penal laws, had a most perfect confidence in his honour.[7]

The political farce then commenced with the usual mock solemnity. In pursuance of a recommendation from the throne in the King's speech at the opening of the ensuing sessions of Parliament, a bill was brought in which was found to contain a few indemnities; yet even these only extended to the upper class, such as allowing them to become magistrates, grand jurors, free-holders and members of corporations; trifling and limited, however, as these concessions must appear to the eye of justice, they were obstinately and in

---

[1] In Dec. 1792.   [2] See above, vol. I, p. 325, n. 1.

[3] Christopher Dillon Bellew, James Edward Devereux and Sir Thomas French.

[4] Edward Byrne.

[5] John Keogh, who retired in Dec. 1787 aged 47 (*Dublin Evening Post.*, 11 Dec. 1787).

[6] See Diary for 21 to 31 Jan. and 4 to 6 Feb. 1793 (above, vol. I, pp 398–403, 405–6), where Tone comments severely on Keogh's conduct.   [7] Burke did not receive a pension till 1794.

some instances most illiberally opposed by the servants of the Government. Is it then carrying suspicion too far to conclude that the whole scene was a finesse of the British cabinet devised to allay the heat rising amongst the Catholics at as low a rate as possible and to make them believe that the King alone was the friend of the people of Ireland whose good intention the Parliament had thwarted? So prevalent was this opinion that before the adjournment of the convention they voted a sum of two thousand pounds sterling to be laid out in erecting a statue to the honour of his Majesty, never reflecting that the Chancellor alone, their decided but honourable because their avowed enemy, could nominate magistrates; that grand jurors are appointed by the sheriffs, who are named by the aristocracy of the country; and, further, that forty-shillings freehold could only be acquired through the favour of those Anglican proprietors of land whose interest it was, and whose determination it became, to prevent all interlopers and particularly Catholics from participating of their power. And as for the admissions into corporations, it was doubly nugatory, because the city of Dublin, without whose brevet merely an admission into a corporation secured no privilege, had loudly and frequently declared against their admission and had even instructed their representatives to oppose the bill. Besides, the bill itself was illusory, not having repealed all those acts which made certain oaths necessary that a conscientious Catholic could not take yet which it was incumbent on him to take in order to fill even the office of a beadle in the corporation of which he was now allowed to become a part.

Such was the reality of the former grants. The report is that it is now[1] the intention of the British Minister to allow the Roman Catholics the utmost extent of their original demands, which were for an unlimited participation of the privileges of their Anglican neighbours. This design, if the report has any foundation, must be considered as a fresh manœuvre to ensure the subjection of Ireland at this critical juncture when rumour has spread abroad that an invasion of Ireland is meditated by the French Republic. Should, therefore, the obsequious Parliament, now they have got their cue, no longer shackle the good will of his gracious Majesty towards his people of Ireland, it is but just to apprehend that this favorable disposition will only last till they no longer dread the effect a sense of repeated injuries might produce whilst the conquering arms of France are flying on the wings of victory.

Is it indeed reasonable to take for granted that Pitt or any other British minister would seriously think of re-establishing the Roman Catholics in all their rights of citizenship when it would be in fact to overturn that whole system of government and patronage, the extension of which has made the English cabinet so tenaciously contend for the dominion of Ireland? Is it to

---

[1] The date of Tone writing this sentence has not been ascertained. It seems to have been some time towards the end of 1794, when after the formation in July of a coalition between Pitt and the Portland whigs, it was proposed that Fitzwilliam should be lord lieutenant of Ireland.

be even supposed that when a system at the expense of millions has been brought to bear it will be calmly abandoned, especially when the patronage exercised in Ireland gives so helping a hand to undermine liberty at home? Is it probable that the English court would thus exasperate the aristocracy of Ireland, that is the members of the established church, who are the chief proprietors and have the power and profit of the state at their disposal? Exasperate men who have ever been the willing slaves of the crown of England in favour of a new set of men amongst whom, if some were found as corrupt as those of the establishment, it would still be necessary to advance the purchase money anew; whilst others, who had perhaps been taught by oppression to aspire to freedom, might assist in leading their country on to *independence*, the only change which would essentially benefit the Irish nation.

It is then for unequivocal independence that every patriotic Irishman ought to struggle; and, prostituted as has been the name of patriot to vanity and self-interest, Ireland still contains many generous hearts and firm spirits that can feel with true enthusiasm the value of the blessing they would risque their lives to purchase for their country. Glowing with resentment for injuries, and indignantly marking the strides of injustice, one spark of hope would light the glorious flame that leads on to certain victory.

Why then hesitate to rouse the sleeping fire? For was the real state of Ireland made known to France, there is every reason from her conduct and declarations to conclude that she would assist to emancipate a people oppressed by her mortal enemy and Ireland might become again a free and independent nation governed by her own laws after having established the constitution which should appear to the convened people best adapted to their circumstances and situation. There is little doubt but that this constitution would be upon a popular basis. Notwithstanding the Catholic clergy are so fully and so beneficially to themselves occupied in preaching up submission to those who are put over us and uttering violent philippics against the principles and the conduct of the French Revolution, their aim is obvious; yet it is to be lamented that these invectives have received great force and all the colouring to which their success is owing arises from a momentary deviation from one of the principles of the French Republic, a solemn renunciation of conquest. But the reign of liberty, justice and truth is restored to France and tyrants tremble on their thrones.

In such a case, it is certain that France and Ireland would find their mutual interest in a treaty of amity and commerce upon the basis of equality; and an alliance, offensive and defensive, between two nations that had escaped from a bondage equally ignoble must be founded on just principles. The idea of Ireland becoming a department of France (the enemies of that wretched country have laboured to insinuate this fear) would be as unjust as impolitic, nor is it to be dreaded, for the most superficial observer must clearly perceive that the motives of the Republic of France can only be effected with respect to Ireland by restoring to her her natural and her ancient energy, which would be equally cramped whether she were a colony of England or a department of France. But when, on the contrary, once free and independent, she began to govern herself, religious toleration in the most extensive sense would take place; and the people would only have to pay their own clergy and that in whatever manner they should judge most expedient. All church and college lands would probably be divided into small farms[1] and thus an existence secured to every individual; all would be eligible to the honours and offices of the state; and talents and industry, called forth by encouragement, might naturally be expected to produce their usual effects. The abolition of tythes must follow of course; and all being equally under the care of the law, the disfranchising statute of Henry VI rendering a freehold of forty shillings necessary to become a voter at the election of the representatives of the people could no longer be in force. Taxes also being equally levied, which is the corner-stone of freedom, and the poor not obliged to pay out of the scanty pittance of misery for the luxuries of the rich,[2] emigration would become less frequent till emulation taking place of discouragement, and plenty of penury, Ireland would soon exhibit a scene of happiness to refresh the benevolent heart saddened by the present view.

Did the people once act in concert, all the Irish seamen and soldiers who are in any foreign service would, of course, be recalled and all those who have property would naturally return. Indeed, the known love of Irishmen for their native country and their enthusiastic attachment to liberty, awakened by hope, would soon induce all the sons of Ireland to return to a place which misery and oppression alone had forced them to abandon. The military force of England must consequently be considerably diminished and her marine lose nearly two thirds, whilst the army and navy of Ireland would be augmented in the same proportion.

The suppression of pensions and all the stipends held under the present government necessarily follow so that Ireland would in a short time be enabled to fit out a naval force to protect her trade, which, joined to that of France, must wrest from England that tyrannical dominion she has hitherto exercised over the ocean.

---

[1] Footnote by Tone: 'The church and college lands are supposed to be about one third of Ireland and the distressed families to amount to six hundred thousand'.

[2] Footnote by Tone: 'The taxes which the farmers of Ireland labour under are very unequally levied in the different baronies; nor are all to contribute to the public weal, as, for example, if a new road is desired by some proprietor, the expense attending the purchase of the ground is paid to the proprietor and levied upon the farmer; and the expense likewise of making the road and all its future repairs are levied upon him at the same time he pays rent for it, for it is always measured into his farm. An estate belonging to a parish has been mortgaged to erect a steeple to ornament a Protestant church, when the mass-house, where the people attended worship, was without a roof. This steeple was beat down by a storm and the Catholic people were taxed to rebuild it. The expense occasioned by the taking or engraving a map of the country is, by act of Parliament, laid on the farmers and paid in general by persons the whole area of whose houses would be covered by the map after it was printed!!!'

Can there be an Irishman whose heart does not glow at the prospect of his country's recovering her primitive rights? Let his persuasion be what it will, he must be convinced from a recollection of the oppressive and perfidious manner in which the Irish have ever been treated by England that their prosperity depends upon a total emancipation from her dominion.

During the American war, when Ireland was drained of all her troops and left to her own energy, though she still paid for her defence, the Ministry was little aware of the consequence which might attend the levying of fifty thousand volunteers who then turned out in arms. The discussion of the subject of American independence naturally made them think of their own oppressions and led them to call for independence and a free trade.[1] The artful Minister[2] apparently granted their demand and offered a set of propositions to serve as the basis of a treaty of commerce between the two countries.[3] These being, however, founded on a system of equality, which it was far from the intention of the Minister to establish, he contrived, in his usual way, to get them opposed in the most decided manner when brought before the English House of Commons for their sanction. The number of the articles were therefore increased to destroy the tendency and spirit by weakening and confusing plain demands; and one was added which he well knew would render the whole nugatory; for it was proposed to be enacted that all the laws relative to the trade of both nations should emanate solely from the Parliament of Great Britain and that the Parliament of Ireland should confirm them in every point. But the Irish tool of the Minister had taken advantage, immediately upon the passing of the first proposition, of the good humour of the nation and procured a grant of four hundred thousand pounds to assist Britain to protect their mutual commerce, which the Admiralty of England was to receive and in no case whatever to be accountable for the use of it to the Irish Parliament. Thus, according to his constant evasive plan, he shuffled off at that critical moment the further pursuit of the commercial treaty and got into his hands the four hundred thousand pounds to recompense his minions and silence recreant patriots.

Several of the foregoing particulars have been dwelt minutely upon in order that the Irish of all persuasions may be put on their guard against the offers now said to be held out to them by the English Government and, by showing the fallacy of every grant which has hitherto been made to the Irish nation, to set before them the absurdity of confining their views to partial benefits when the grand remedy for all their ills is probably so near their reach.

---

[1] For the free-trade question, see R. B. McDowell, *Irish public opinion, 1750–1800* (London, 1944), pp 55–62.
[2] Thomas Orde (1746–1807), chief secretary for Ireland, 1784–7; created Baron Bolton, 1797 (*D.N.B.*).
[3] Orde laid the commercial propositions before the Irish house of commons on 7 Feb. 1785.

After having thus considered the various abuses of an illegitimate second-hand government, it would be absurd to turn our attention towards partial remedies. Alleviations have been too long artfully held out to repress murmur; and laws they could not venture to defend have been allowed to become obsolete. The rigour of others has been disguised to silence the menacing growl of the populace and pretended concessions made to lull suspicion asleep. But what does all this avail? Or, what would it avail were the concessions real and the professions of permitting Ireland to participate of the prosperity of her sister kingdom sincere? But these are evidently empty professions, for it is easy to prove that this artificial, miscalled relationship, instead of producing affection, stirs up all the little degrading passions which generate family hatred, and even that it is impossible, with the purest views and most enlightened understanding, to render a delegated government tolerable.

The permission to legislate for themselves only increases the evils of colonial government by giving the semblance of free will to the resolves of a majority corrupted to render the representation nugatory; and the corruption does not rest here, for it is not unfair to infer that a venal senator will become a tyrannical landlord.

The root, then, of the evil, the moral, nay, physical cause of the wretchedness which stops agricultural improvements in Ireland and retards the general melioration of manners that leads to a more perfect civilization is her dependence on another country. Dependence, we say, the import of which the English would fain persuade us is merely an amicable alliance, the natural dependence of a lesser on a greater power, when in fact it is the subordination of slavery, and the more severe for not being avowed. Dependence, or the paying a certain price for protection, can only be useful when it is an alliance to prevent the encroachments of an ambitious neighbour and when a reciprocation of benefits permits sincerity. But when one party is at the discretion of the other, friendship quickly slides into despotism and the interest of the feeble dependant is sacrificed to the caprice of the pretended supporter.

Not, however, to weaken the clear perception of truth by argument, it is sufficient to assert that we do equal violence to natural justice and common sense when we take from a people the right of forming and directing their own social institutions. Is there in short any other way to call the moral and physical powers of a people into that action which strengthens their faculties than that of leaving them free to secure their own interest by the formation and execution of the laws which their situation suggests? Is there any other mode of promoting the felicity and improvement of a country? In order that life and heat should be equally distributed to all the members of the body politic, the government, the heart of society, ought to be in its own centre; the contrary savours of absurdity: it seems like endeavouring to prove the truth of an axiom that is self-evident. Yet accustomed to see their country speciously enslaved, Irishmen rail at partial arbitrary acts, passing over the source from whence they sprung.

Let us state some simple facts to open the eyes of those who do not clearly perceive that a delegated government must ever be tryannical. Dependence obliges you to receive a viceroy; that is, a kind of political monster; a something between a king and a minister. Instead of a magistrate of your own, you are forced to acknowledge the authority of a set of men, creatures of the reigning English Minister, who are often sent to recruit a shattered fortune as a reward for having betrayed their country. It is not therefore extraordinary that such men should wish to provide for their parasites with the same disregard of justice; consequently, the taxes wrung out of poverty are lavished on foreign sycophants who do not even scatter it abroad, amongst mechanics and artists, in search of luxuries which alleviate the oppression in England, as it did in France; but on the contrary, the fruit of industry is carried clear out of your social circle, to pamper your tyrants and render others more keen in their pursuit of plunder. Your national representation is made to consist partly of foreigners in order to pillage your coffers with more impunity. Your very bishops are mostly Englishmen far from being of the most respectable class; and placemen are pensioned on you who have only injured your country. Your trade has been shackled with every possible embarrassment; and your national respectability kept down. And to all this you submit because lures are held out to the aristocracy, who, allowed to oppress their countrymen, crouch to the power that abuses by sustaining them. What indeed does this system produce but a race of landholders, the most despotic, a set of petty tyrants, who are not bound to their country by sentiment or principle, by ambition or vanity? Several examples already adduced will illustrate this observation to every thinking or benevolent man, coming home more forcibly to his bosom and interest.

But were Ireland once free, what a different face would everything wear. The centre of emulation being within her own limits, national talents would be a national advantage; and the virtues brought forth by independence give dignity to the agreeable qualities which distinguish the national character. Until this takes place, the nourishment of Ireland, her vital heat, will constantly be drawn off and her energy, only extended to half-way measures, will but tend to increase the present misery by riveting the chain which no sophistical reasoning can ever make appear a band of fraternity; besides, alliances drawn too close are ever the traps set for well-meaning ignorance by cunning self-interest. That friendship is destructive which renders an individual inactive; but when it concerns a nation it is as absurd for one nation to pretend to govern another as for one man to eat to nourish another. I am again bringing forward, unawares, a truth that does not admit of illustration, which will always be the case when the principles of politics are sought for, and natural justice resorted to, as the base of government.

The question respecting the happiness and emancipation of Ireland may in short be reduced to one point: if the government of one king, however he may identify himself with the people, will infallibly become a tyranny, what must be the situation of a people who have a whole nation of kings to lord it over them? And what ought to be the conduct of a people when they feel their misery and despise their slavery? It would be an insult to the good sense of the nation to add that it is their duty to take advantage of the moment when their haughty conquerors are humble and by boldly daring deserve to be free.

Brief notes on prospects in America, probably August 1795

Tone (Dickason) papers.

Tone seems to have written these notes (which are in a rough hand) during his first month in America, when, expecting to settle there, he 'made many inquiries' (Tone to Thomas Russell, 1 Sept. 1795, above, vol. II, p. 11).

The best station about 100 miles westwards of the sea in Virginia between James River and the Potomack in or about the Water of the Shanandoa.[1] All necessaries better bought on the spot. Not more than 10 p[er] cent dearer.

No doubt but a man had better settle in the Wild than a colonised[?] country if he looks [*word not deciphered*] to the establishment of a family. Are there men of [*word not deciphered*] if he can find 3 or 4 men of similar sentiments as [*word not deciphered*] himself.

Winchester in Virginia ex[empli] gr[atia] a good station for a lawyer.

Leonard MacNally to Thomas Pelham, 17 September 1795

Nat. Arch. (Ire.), Rebellion papers, 620/10/121/29.

This is one of a series of reports by Leonard MacNally on disaffection. For his authorship, see below, p. 460, n. 2.

Dublin, Sept[r] 17th, 1795

The proceedings at the last assizes in the midland counties shew, in the strongest light, the disaffection of the common people there, and the acquittal of several persons charged with defenderism at London-Derry by a jury of wealthy men, against evidence and a strong charge from the judge, evinces the disposition of even the upper classes in that part of the country. This verdict is likely to produce a serious business. The judge ordered the sheriff

---

[1] In fact the district he has in mind lies about 250 km north-west of the sea.

to post up the jurors' names in the court-house as persons unfit to serve in future, the sheriff obliged and the jurors have determined to bring actions against him for libelling them.[1]

I apprehend that the ensuing winter will be marked with very frequent and with very cruel acts of depredation. As to the executions which have taken place, they have in[tim]idated but have not deterred. The flame is not quenched but confined and I fear from innumerable symptoms that come daily under my observation that it will break out very suddenly. Jackson's memory is held in veneration.[2] O'Connor's sufferings are considered as martyrdom.[3] His declarations from the dock after conviction which I saw republished in the *Star* (of London) are genuine and his conduct in death was equally spirited. He was offered provision for his wife and family if he would make discoveries, and answered, 'he who feeds the young ravens in the valley will provide for them'.[4]

A kind of seditious convention is now forming in America composed of Hamilton Rowan, Napper Tandy, Doctor Reynolds, Wolfe Tone and other fugitives from Ireland.[5] These men have it in their power, and no doubt it is their wish, to give every possible information and assistance to France. Tone is a keen, sensible man, argues with plausibility and cunning, and writes with perspicuity and elegance. At the time he was secretary to the Catholic Committee he drew up a state of Ireland for France,[6] which was produced against Jackson on his trial. He is acquainted intimately with all the private proceedings of the catholics, no man in Ireland knows so well their resources, or the real situation of the country, of course no man [is] so capable to further the scheme of an invasion, and I shall not be surprized to hear of his being shortly at Paris.[7]

I this day communicated to our friends a matter of a very serious and interesting nature which will be transmitted this night to England and of course will be communicated to you; it is a plan for the enumeration of the inhabitants of the kingdom, and when executed will not only shew their

---

[1] There were reports almost daily in the newspapers of depredations by Defenders and measures against them taken by the authorities. The *Freeman's Journal*, 20 Aug. 1795, reported grimly: 'the Defenders, alias the Offenders, of the neighbouring counties of Louth, Meath and Kildare have been woefully disconcerted by the result of the assizes and the hempen exit of so many of their companions in arms'. It went on to predict that 'about 150 of those deluded wretches will make their exit by the rope in the course of the present month'.

[2] For the Jackson affair, see above, vol. I, pp xxxvii–xxxix.

[3] For Laurence O'Connor, see above, vol. II, p. 18, n. 4.

[4] Perhaps a conflation of Job, 38: 41, and *As you like it*, II, iii, 44.

[5] Cf. Tone to Thomas Russell, 1 Sept. 1795, and Autobiography (above, vol. II, pp 14, 336).

[6] Above, vol. I, pp 504–8.

[7] MacNally was able to report to Dublin Castle on 3 July 1797 that 'Theo[bal]d Wolfe Tone has been a considerable time in Paris'. MacNally's source of intelligence (letters received by James Tandy from his father James Napper Tandy in Hamburg) revealed that Tone 'had been some time at Brest previous to the French expedition to Bantry and that he "was actually on board one of the ships" on that expedition' (Nat. Arch. (Ire.), Rebellion papers, 620/10/121/69).

gross number, but the comparative numbers of the catholics with the protestants and dissenters.[1] This plan has been approved of by Mr Edmund Burke and Earl Fitzwilliam, considerable progress has been made in it and the whole will very shortly be compleated.

J. W.[2]

[*Addressed to*]:

Rt Hon. T. Pelham, Esq.
London

To James Reynolds, *c.*23 February 1797

John Burk, *History of the late war in Ireland* (Philadelphia, 1799), pp 52–61.

Burk identifies the author of this letter as Theobald Wolfe Tone ('one of those rare spirits which nature sends on earth to instruct a million') and the addressee as 'his friend in America'. It is unmistakably the eight-page letter to Reynolds mentioned by Tone in his diaries for 22 February and 5 March 1797 and in some detail in his diary for 24 February (see above, vol. III, pp 28, 31). Tone entrusted it to James Monroe, who probably left Paris for Philadelphia during the second week of March.

In this letter, of which the opening lines, as well as any conventional salutations, are omitted by Burk, an account is given of the Bantry Bay expedition. There is a similar account in Tone's diaries for 16 Dec. 1796 to 1 Jan. 1797 (above, vol. II, pp 416–20, 422–5, 427–35).

John Daly Burk (1772?–1807), radical journalist; expelled from T.C.D. for blasphemy, 1794, fled to the United States, 1796 (*D.A.B.*).

In consequence of this intercourse, I was by consent of the Directory named *chef de brigade* on the 1st of Messidor last and received orders to join General Hoche at Rennes in a short time after; from Rennes I proceeded to Brest where I arrived the 10th Brumaire (November 1st). At Brest, General Hoche, with whom I have the good fortune to stand very well, promoted me to the rank of adjutant general, and took me immediately into his family.

At length, everything being prepared for the expedition, we embarked about the middle of Frumaire [*sic*] and on the 26th (December 16th) we sailed from Brest, with 17 sail of the line, 13 frigates and 14 corvettes or transports, having on board 15,000 men picked and chosen, 45,000 stand of arms, 30 pieces of cannon and mortars, with a proportionable quantity of

[1] The plan was drawn up by Edward Hay of Wexford (*The correspondence of Edmund Burke*, viii, ed. R. B. McDowell (Cambridge, 1969), pp 264, 270, 272).

[2] For Leonard MacNally's authorship of this and other letters signed 'J. W.', see Thomas Bartlett (ed.), *Revolutionary Dublin, 1795–1801: the letters of Francis Higgins to Dublin Castle* (Dublin, 2003), pp 38–46.

ammunition &c. The first night we had the misfortune, I know not how, to lose the admiral's frigate, on board of which were the commanders-in-chief by sea and land, the commandant of the artillery, the military chest, the correspondence and in short everything that was most material to insure the success of the expedition. We likewise lost, on a reef of rocks, the *Séduisant* of 74 guns and parted company with half the fleet. The third day in the morning (the 29th) we rejoined the greater part of the missing ships, but had not the good fortune to see the *Fraternité* (on board of which was General Hoche) in the number. However, we proceeded for Bantry-bay, out destination, and on the 1st Nivôs[e] (December 21st) at day break we were under Cape Clear with beautiful weather and a fair wind to the number of 36 sail of all sorts. We could have run up Bantry Bay and anchored the same day, but Admiral Bouvet, who in consequence of the separation of the *Fraternité* commanded in the absence of Admiral Morard de Galles, through what motive I will not pretend to say, instead thereof stood on and passed the mouth of the bay, whereby we fell considerably to leeward and could not recover our station that whole day. The next morning we were pretty well up with the bay, notwithstanding our false maneuvre by which we had lost the advantage of the wind which had thus far been favourable, and at six in the evening we cast anchor to the number of 16 sail, of which 11 were of the line, off Bear Island, and the remaining 20 sail, we expected to work up in the night; but a heavy gale of wind coming on which blew right down the bay, drove the 20 sail out to sea and not one of them ever joined us after. In this manner we remained at anchor, with a head wind until the 4th Nivôs[e] (December 24th] when the weather coming [*sic*] something more moderate, General Chérin, Colonel Vaudré of the artillery and myself passed aboard Admiral Bouvet's frigate, the *Immortalité*, where we found General Grouchy, who being second in command was now our general in the absence of General Hoche. We brought him the returns, by which it appeared that, in consequence of the separation of the fleet, the forces we had were reduced from 15,000 to 6,400 men; our artillery to two 4-pounders and two how-etzers, our spare firelocks to about 12,000 and our ammunition diminished in the same proportion; notwithstanding this alarming difference in our means it was determined unanimously to make the attempt with the remnant of our original force, and I am confident if we had been able to effectuate a landing, even with 6,000 men, we should have succeeded. You can imagine nothing more striking than the spirit and enthusiasm of the French troops at the prospect of commencing an expedition which cautious men might be tempted and almost justified to call desperate. In fact we had nothing but the arms in our hands, but that was full enough, and I have not myself the smallest doubt but we should have beaten thrice the number of such troops as could have been opposed to us; our plan was to have made a forced march for Cork, which, as we were not encumbered with baggage, we could easily reach in three days at most, and having once possession of that city, independent of the *eclat*, it would give our arms, the spirit to our friends, and the discouragement to our enemies, we should have found the abundance of everything which we most wanted; we could from thence either push on for Dublin or by forced marches cross the Shannon, if circumstances obliged us, and so effectuate a junction with our friends in Connaught and Ulster. Everything being arranged accordingly, and a requisition given to Bouvet in writing to put the troops &c. ashore the next morning, we returned to our ship with the joyful news. Unluckily that night the wind, which during the day had been rather more moderate, freshened up again and by morning blew a gale, so that all possibility of landing was out of the question, and at six in the evening Bouvet either parted, or cut his cable, and ran out to sea, ordering by word of mouth the whole squadron to follow him, an order which not a single vessel obeyed. This measure of his was so extraordinary that everyone aboard the fleet thought it was an English frigate that had been lurking in the bottom of the bay, and had taken advantage of the dark night and blowing weather to slip through the squadron, and endeavouring at the same time by hailing us with this extravagant order, to throw us into confusion. Be that as it may, we remained, and when the weather cleared up a little the next day (December 26th) we found it was actually Bouvet who had set off, carrying with him by force General Grouchy, who remonstrated in vain against this flight. In the night of this day (the 26th) three of our 74s broke their cables and were driven out to sea, and the next day the weather coming still more boisterous, and by a shift of the wind, making a lee shore, our general being gone, our artillery being aboard the ships last parted, our numbers reduced to 4,000 men, with scarcely any spare arms or ammunition remaining, we were at length reluctantly forced to quit Bantry Bay, after remaining there without opposition, save from the elements, for five clear days, viz. from the 2d Nivôs[e] (December 22d) to the 7th (December 27th); we were by the various accidents already recounted reduced to 10 sail, of which seven were of the line, one frigate and two luggars, and after struggling with the winds, during three or four days, we at length anchored in Brest water on the 12th Nivôs[e] (January 1st, 1797), being after *all*, the first that returned except Bouvet, who[m] we found arrived safe before us. The rest of the fleet has since returned by twos and threes, and what is very extraordinary, and to me unaccountable, the English during and since the expedition took but one frigate (the *Tortu[e]* of 44 guns, which fought her antagonist, the *Polyphemus* of 64 for an hour and an half) and two or three transports or corvettes. Certainly they took their measures very ill not to have made more captures, considering the distressed and scattered state of our fleet — Bouvet is now in arrest for his conduct and will be speedily brought to trial.

You have now, my dear friend, a brief history of our expedition, which even in its failure would, if I were the British minister, alarm me ten thousand times more than any, or all, of the events which have taken place since the war; we have shewed him of what the Republic is capable; we have shewed him that his wooden walls are not impregnable; notwithstanding his enormous superiority at sea, and the ruined state of our Marine, we sailed from our harbours, we remained near six days at anchor in one of his ports, and nothing but the winds prevented our expelling him and his abettors from that unfortunate country which we went to relieve; we returned in safety, and, with God's blessing, we have not done with him yet. After all it was ultimately the weather, *and the weather only*, which prevented our success. Three hours of a good wind any one day while we were at anchor in Bantry Bay would have carried us up to the landing place, but most unfortunately we had it not even for three minutes. I never saw such dreadful weather, and what is still more extraordinary at this season of the year, the wind was from the eastward, the point of the whole thirty-two the most unfavourable for us, as you will see, if you have a good map of Ireland.

I have now done with what I may call the historical part of my letter. As to my own situation during this expedition, I will not attempt to describe it to you. Figure to yourself what I must have felt, during the whole time we lay at anchor, within five hundred yards of the shore, and utterly unable to reach it! Judge of my sensations the hour we quit Bantry-bay! But this is idle complaining. Let me come to something that will interest you more. In all my communications here, whether with the Directory the minister, or the general, I have had every possible reason to be content; I do not mean merely as to myself, for my present situation speaks that, but with regard to my country. I have the very best opinion of their integrity and principles, and I am satisfied that, if our expedition had succeeded, they would have behaved to us with the greatest good faith and liberality. You know I would not devote myself, as I have done, to endeavour to throw off the English yoke, merely to put on a French one; I am even perhaps unreasonably jealous upon that topic; but I am happy at the same time to assure you that I have not hitherto, and I am confident it will continue so, met with a single circumstance to alarm me on that head. I was a witness to most of their proceedings, I saw all the papers, proclamations, &c., and there was scarcely a measure or a sentence that I would wish to have altered.

Tone and Edward Joseph Lewines to ———, 16 December 1797

Archives Nationales, Police Générale, F⁷, 7293 dossier B⁴ 2671.

Addressing themselves (presumably) to the minister of police, Tone and Lewines seek permission for Burgess, MacCann and the two Byrne brothers to come to Paris. The letter is in Tone's hand except for the signature 'J. Fr. Giauque', the pseudonym used by Lewines.

Rue du Bacq, No. 610, ce 26 Frimaire, an 6

Citoyen Ministre,

Ayant fait une application au Ministre des relations extérieures pour faire accorder une permission de venir à Paris à deux de nos compatriotes qui sont actuellement detenus à Liège, et à deux autres qui doivent y venir incessament, il nous a dit de nous adresser à vous avec l'assurance que vous auriez la bonté de nous accorder sans delai la permission que nous demandions.

Nous répondons, Citoyen ministre, du patriotisme et de la moralité des quatre personnes dont nous parlons. Ils sont les victimes du despotisme du gouvernement anglois, qui les a forcés de fuir leur patrie à cause de leur attachement aux principes de la révolution et de l'indépendance de l'Irlande. Ils s'appellent Burgess, Macan et les frères Byrne, les deux premiers sont actuellement à Liège.

Salut et respect
J. Fr. Giauque
L'adj[udant] géné[ra]l
J. Smith

Mathew Tone to Pierre Sotin, 10 January 1798

Archives Nationales, Police Générale, F⁷, 7293 dossier B⁴ 2671.

This letter is in T. W. Tone's handwriting except for the signature. Mathew Tone requests protection while in Paris. T. W. Tone vouches for Mathew being his brother and for 'his patriotism and integrity'.

Paris, ce 21 Nivôse, an 6

Au Ministre de la Police Générale de la République Française

Citoyen Ministre,

Le soussigné, Irlandais refugié, arrivé dernièrement de Hambourg en vertu d'un passeport du Citoyen Rheinhardt, Ministre de la République Française près les villes anséatiques, vous prie de vouloir bien lui accorder telle prestation [*sic*] que vous jugerez convenable pendant son séjour à Paris.

Salut et respect
Math^w Smith

Je certifie que le citoyen Mathieu Smith est mon frère et je réponds de son patriotisme et de son intégrité.

L'adj[udant] géné[ra]l
J. Smith

To Pierre Sotin, 5 February 1798

Archives Nationales, Paris, Police Générale, F⁷, 7293 dossier B⁴ 2671.

Tone requests that MacCann and Burgess, who were held at Liège but lately released and just arrived at Tone's, be afforded protection in Paris.

À Paris, ce 17 Pluviôse, an 6

L'adj[udan]t gén[éra]l Smith au Ministre de la Police Générale

Citoyen Ministre,

J'ai l'honneur de vous apprendre que les nommés Macan et Burgess, qui ont été detenus à Liège et dernièrement mis en liberté d'après vos orders, viennent d'arriver chez moi. Comme je réponds de leur conduite et de leur moralité, je vous prie, Citoyen Ministre, de vouloir bien leur accorder telle protection que vous jugerez convenable pendant leur séjour à Paris.

Salut et respect
J. Smith

Testimonial for Captain Julius Favory, 1 May 1798

McPeake papers; photocopy in P.R.O.N.I., T/3048/K/2.

This testimonial, which commends Favory for his civism, talents and zeal, is in an unidentified hand except for Tone's rank and signature, which are in Tone's. The endorsement is in Chérin's hand.

Paris, le 12 floréal an 6ᵉ
de la République

Je certifie que le citoyen Favery, capitaine, a été employé près de moi en qualité d'adjoint aux armées de Sambre et Meuse, d'Allemagne et du Rhin et que pendant tout ce tems il a donné des preuves de civisme, de talens et de zèle dans toutes les fonctions dont il a été chargé.

L'adjudant général
J. Smith

Vu par moi, Général de division et chef d'état major, G[énéral] à l'armée de Sambre et Meuse, d'Allemagne et du Rhin. Chérin.

The song of Theobald Wolfe Tone, November 1798

A collection of loyal songs as sung at all the Orange lodges in Ireland (Dublin: W. McKenzie, 1798), pp 117–18.

Printed also in T. C. Croker (ed.), *Popular songs illustrative of the French invasions of Ireland*, pt I (London, 1845), pp 114–16, where a headnote states that it is taken 'from a manuscript copy' and that it is printed in the second volume of *A collection of constitutional songs* (Cork: A. Edwards, 1800), p. 28. Internal evidence indicates that this song was composed after Tone's capture and probably before his trial and death.

The song of Theobald Wolfe Tone[1]

From France to Loughswilly I came,
   And that, by my soul, was a blunder,
But I thought that my high-sounding name[2]
   Would in Ireland perform some wonder;
     I starred, and my friends all look'd *blue*,
When Sir John[3] and his fleet did perceive us,
     For I knew once he got us in view,
The Devil himself could not save us.
     Tol lol de rol, lol de rol lo.

British thunder now roared in my ears,
   Seem'd to shake the world to its foundation,
So I down on my knees to my prayers,
   And begg'd Heav'n to preserve the great nation;
     But all I could say 'twas in vain,
Heav'n deign'd not to hear my petition,
     For I'd follow'd too much of Tom Paine,
That curse to a civilized nation.
     Tol lol, &c.

But who dare attempt to oppose
   Britain's heroes upon their *own* ocean?
As to striving to land on their shore,
   In both they've beat out of the notion;
     And when their envoy comes begging for peace,
Unless in a balloon they can swing him,
     In England he'll ne'er shew his face,
Till they borrow a vessel to bring him.
     Tol lol, &c.

[1] Title supplied by Croker.
[2] Note in Orange version: 'Supposed to be Theobald Wolfe Tone'. The content leaves no doubt.
[3] Sir John Borlase Warren.

Addenda and corrigenda

Vol. I, p. xxiii. Reynolds, though very popular among the Irish at Philadelphia, had seven different addresses between 1796 and 1808 and 'company, losses and disappointments drove him to drink' (*The autobiography of Benjamin Rush*, ed. G. W. Corner (Princeton, 1948), p. 322).

Vol. I, p. xxiv, n. 3. Redding was assistant editor of the *New Monthly Magazine* in the mid 1820s (J. J. Auchmuty, *Sir Thomas Wyse* (London, 1939), p. 78, n. 3).

Vol. I, p. xxvi, n. 3. This source however has been discredited. More reliable on possible ancestors of William Tone (though inconclusive) are references in church registers to a Thomas Tone who was probably living in Dublin about the time of William Tone's birth. This Thomas Tone, son of Hugh and Sarah Tone, was baptised in Dublin on 12 February 1682 and was presumably the Thomas Tone who was buried there on 7 March 1716/17. It is at least possible that he was the father of William Tone, who was born when Thomas Tone was aged about 23. (*The register of S. Catherine, Dublin, 1636–1715*, ed. Herbert Wood (Dublin, 1908), p. 42; *The register of the parish of S. Peter and S. Kevin, Dublin, 1669–1761*, ed. James Mills (Dublin, 1911), p. 214; C. J. Woods, 'Theobald Wolfe Tone and County Kildare' in William Nolan and Thomas McGrath (eds), *Kildare history and society* (Dublin, 2006), p. 396, nn 3, 4.

Vol. I, p. 8, l. 9. 'If you have tears . . .' (*Julius Caesar*, III, ii).

Vol. I, p. 39, l. 5 from foot. The absentee alluded to was William Gerard Hamilton (1729–91), a British M.P. and sometime chief secretary who was chancellor of the Irish exchequer, 1763–84. In 1784 he exchanged this office for a pension of £2,000 a year and was replaced by John Foster. (Lewis Namier and John Brooke, *The history of parliament: the House of Commons, 1754–1790* (London, 1964), ii, 572).

Vol. I, p. 49, n. 2. Molesworth Green died on 22 Nov. 1834 (*Gent. Mag.*, Jan. 1835).

Vol. I, p. 51, n. 2. *For* Nooka *read* Nootka.

Vol. I, p. 56, n. 1. Adam Anderson (1692?–1765) was a clerk in South Sea House; his book was first published in 1764 (*Oxford D.N.B.*).

Vol. I, p. 68, l. 8 from foot. *For* i, 319–42, *read* i, 519–42.

Vol. I, pp 75–6. The original of Tone's letter to W. W. Grenville, dated not 30 Sept. but 1 Oct. 1790, was in the early 1970s in the possession of Dr J.G.C. Spencer Bernard of Nether Winchendon House, Aylesbury, Buckinghamshire. The only other variants are in the penultimate sentence, which reads: 'the duke of Richmond's condescension to me emboldens me to hope that my present application to you will not pass without your notice'. It is addressed to 'William Wyndham Grenville, Esqr, &c., &c., Secretary of State's Office, London'; it is endorsed 'Dublin, 1st Octo[be]r Mr Tone' followed by a seal and the words 'answer'd S.B. if any steps taken respect[in]g his Plan he will hear further on the subject'. S.B. is Scrope Bernard.

Vol. I, p. 103. *Recte* Charity Yorke Bramston (d. 1789 or 1791) (*Oxford D.N.B.* on Richard Griffith; *Burke's peerage and baronetage* (London, 1912), p. 887). It is also possible that 'Mrs R. Griffith' was Elizabeth Griffith (1727–93), mother of Richard Griffith and a well-known actress and playwright; she died on 5 Jan. 1793 at Millicent (Dorothy Hughes Eshleman, *Elizabeth Griffith* (Philadelphia, 1949)). A sketch by Tone of 'Mrs R. Griffith' (d. 1793?) is in T.C.D., MS 3805, f. 24v.

Vol. I, p. 104. This letter covered the set of resolutions for the meeting to be held in Belfast on 14 July 1791. Either the original or a copy came into government hands. There are discrepancies between the original and the version from which extracts were given by Fitzgibbon in July 1793 and January 1797. An inaccurate and incomplete version appeared in a report submitted to the Irish house of commons on 10 May 1797 and was printed in *Commons' jn. Ire.*, xvii (1797); see ibid., pp 137, 151, cclxxviii. How the original came to be in the Burrowes papers has not been ascertained.

Vol. I, p. 106. Some information on the circumstances of Tone's first connexion with Belfast radicals was obtained many years later by a nephew of Russell after he 'became *personally* acquainted with many of Thomas Russell's friends'. He told John Gray (who was preparing a book on Tone) that 'it was through Thomas Russell that he was introduced to the Belfast politicians, as Thomas Russell knew his talents and it was considered that his legal acquirements would be of use in the drawing up the various political documents' (John A. Russell to John Gray, 22 Apr. 1843, T.C.D., Madden papers, MS 873/669, ff 1–2). Gray's interest in Tone is stated in Gray to Russell (ibid., ff 1–2).

Vol. I, p. 108, ll 11–17. From internal evidence the entry headed '14 July 1791' must have been written before that date. From the evidence of Tone's letter to Russell, 9 July, it was written on or shortly after 9 July.

Vol. I, p. 108, n. 2. The correct archival reference for the MS is P.R.O.N.I., Drennan papers, D/591/305.

Vol. I, p. 119, n. 1. 'Burke' is Edmund Burke, to whom there are several references elsewhere.

Vol. I, p. 121, ll 8–9. Cf. 'If it were so, it was a grievous fault and grievously hath Caesar answer'd it' (*Julius Caesar*, III, ii).

Vol. I, p. 126. The words quoted are, with appropriate changes, from Shylock's defence of his fellow Jews in Shakespeare's *Merchant of Venice*, III, i, and from Genesis, 4: 13–15, and Exodus, 20: 5–6.

Vol. I, p. 131, n. 4. It is almost certain that the 'Sinclaire' whom Tone met on his first morning in Belfast was William Sinclair, not his brother. Tone refers in other places to 'W. Sinclair' (pp 139, 142, 145, 146) and elsewhere to 'the Draper' (pp 214, 215–17, 221, 225, 319). William Tone states that 'the Draper' was Tone's 'mock name' for William Sinclair (*Life*, i, 137). It can be inferred from the contexts of some of Tone's references to 'Sinclair' (pp 139, 142, 247) that he is referring to William. The only Thomas Sinclair he unambiguously alludes to is 'Mr Sinclair Senr' (p. 146).

Vol. I, pp 133 and 137. Jonas Paisley or Pasley, wine merchant, Jervis St., was high sheriff of Dublin, 1797–8; it was presumably he who seized Chambers' papers after his arrest in March 1798.

Addenda and corrigenda

Vol. I, p. 134, l. 3. *For* Macabe *read* Met Macabe.

Vol. I, p. 134, n. 8. Jane Greg, in Drennan's opinion 'a smart, volatile, vain and versatile woman', died in Sept. 1817 (*Drennan-McTier letters*, iii, 705).

Vol. I, p. 134, n. 9. Jane Bristowe was perhaps Jane Bristow the wife of Roger Bristow, a customs official at Newry, and sister of James and Hill Wilson of Purdysburn (*Drennan-McTier letters*, i, 162, n. 24).

Vol. I, p. 138, l. 11 of text. *For* a Gentleman who *read* a gentleman whom.

Vol. I, p. 139, last line of text. *For* Fall *read* Fell.

Vol. I, p. 143, l. 5 from foot. 'Stella' was Esther Johnson (1681–1728), a friend of Swift and the addressee in his *Journal to Stella* (first published as such in 1784) (*D.N.B.*).

Vol. I, p. 144, n. 4. Thomas Cleghorn was a nephew and ward of George Cleghorn (1716–89), an eminent professor of anatomy at Trinity College, and brother of James Cleghorn (1764?–1826) who succeeded him in the chair (*D.N.B.*).

Vol. I, p. 148, l. 7. *For* McTier and me *read* McTier, Getty and me.

Vol. I, p. 148, l. 8. *For* dubitante et cetera *read* dubitante et cæteri.

Vol. I, p. 149, l. 3. *For* Digges *read* Digges's.

Vol. I, p. 149. The date of Tone's memorandum is inferred from his presence in Belfast in October 1791. Pearce was a confidant of Tone's friend Thomas Russell. See Russell's journals for Mar. and Apr. 1791 (*Journals and memoirs of Thomas Russell*, ed. C. J. Woods (Dublin, 1991), pp 38–42, 48).

Vol. I, p. 153, n. 9. Hart's forename was Patrick (*Letters of Charles O'Conor*, p. 478).

Vol. I, p. 154. Messrs Dillon & Aylward were a firm of woollen drapers at 5 Francis St., Dublin; one partner, Robert Dillon, represented Co. Leitrim at the Catholic Convention, the other, James Aylward (d. 1794), represented Co. Sligo; both were members of the Dublin Society of United Irishmen (C. J. Woods, 'The personnel of the Catholic Convention, 1792–3' in *Archivium Hibernicum*, lviii (2003), pp 37–8, 45).

Vol. I, p. 155. Mrs Buck was very probably Catherine Buck, sister of Richard Griffith (see vol. I, p. 502, n. 1) and wife of Rev. John Buck (1755?–1842), a fellow of T.C.D., 1781–7, and in 1791 rector of Desertcreat, Co. Tyrone (J. B. Leslie, *Armagh clergy* (Dundalk, 1911), p. 199; *Burke's peerage and baronetage* (London, 1912), p. 886).

Vol. I, p. 187, n. 3. *For* General Introduction *read* p. xxxv.

Vol. I, pp 189–90, 191, 195. No attempt has been made to identify here the men listed. Some are mentioned elsewhere in the documents and are identified appropriately in footnotes. All are identified in R. B. McDowell, 'The personnel of the Dublin Society of United Irishmen' in *Irish Historical Studies*, ii, no. 5 (Mar. 1940), pp 12–53.

Vol. I, p. 192. Cf. 'I saw a long one [i.e. letter] yesterday from Tone to Sinclaire. He mistakes the situation of this town and country around; they are still full of prejudice, which time only can remove.' (Samuel McTier to Drennan, Belfast, 27 Mar. 1792, *Drennan-McTier letters*, i (Dublin, 1998), p. 401).

Vol. I, p. 198. It was asserted by Fitzgibbon in a letter to Pitt, 14 May 1793, that Tone was 'the original projector of the Catholick Convention' and 'drew up the circular letter issued in the course of the last summer in the name of Mr Edward Byrne' (see vol. I, p. 445).

Vol. I, p. 204. For more on Richard Burke, see vol. II, p. 322, n. 1.

Vol. I, p. 213. In giving McCormick the nickname 'Magog' and Keogh 'Gog', Tone is perhaps recalling the 14-foot-high effigies of the two Greek giants on the Guildhall, London, carved in 1708 by Richard Saunders (E. C. Brewer, *Dictionary of phrase and fable* (new ed., London, 1898), p. 531).

Vol. I, p. 213, n. 5. *Footnote should continue:* In Defoe's novel, Friday explains that in his religion the old men pray by saying 'O!' to their god, Benamuckee.

Vol. I, p. 213, l. 4 from foot. 'Worthy to be a rebel' (*Macbeth*, I, ii).

Vol. I, p. 221, n. 1. Another possibility is that 'Mr Lubé' was John Lubé's brother George, who lived at Corcoranstown, Co. Kildare (Liam Chambers, 'George Lubé' in Seamus Cullen and Hermann Geissel (eds), *Fugitive warfare: 1798 in north Kildare* (Kilcock, Co. Kildare, 1998), pp 101–4).

Vol. I, p. 222, n. 2, and elsewhere. The correct title is *The buck's bottle companion*.

Vol. I, p. 228, line 23. Richard Burke's father was the orator and political writer Edmund Burke (1729–97).

Vol. I, p. 229, ll 3–4, p. 249, ll 20–21, and p. 250, l. 2. The '*address to the Defenders*' may be the address 'To the Peep o'Day Boys and Defenders', dated 18 July 1792, and published in the *Northern Star*, 25 July 1792. The circumstantial evidence of Tone writing so much of this genre in 1792 and his sending this particular piece to Byrne for printing suggests that he was the author; but the evidence is inconclusive.

Vol. I, p. 229, n. 4. The date of Warren's death and other information on him is in Thomas Reynolds, junr (ed.), *The life of Thomas Reynolds* (London, 1839), i, 52–3, 80–94.

Vol. I, p. 234, n. 5. He seems to have been a relation (probably a brother) of Charity Bramston (d. 1791?), first wife of Richard Griffith (*Burke's peerage and baronetage* (London, 1912), p. 887; see vol. II, p. 80).

Vol. I, p. 240, l. 15. Lieut-col. John Knox was on his way back from India (see vol. I, p. 209, n. 1).

Vol. I, p. 242. The second and third lines of the verse are taken from Shakespeare's *Coriolanus*, IV, iv.

Vol. I, p. 242, n. 3. Cf. 'Whenas as I sat in Pabilon . . . ' (Shakespeare, *Merry wives of Windsor*, III, i).

Vol. I, p. 242, n. 4. Cabra, or Cabragh, lies 6 km south-west of Rathfriland. Another possibility is that Tone may be thinking of O'Neill Segrave (1767?–93) of Cabra, a northern suburb of Dublin (*Dublin Evening Post*, 31 Aug. 1793).

Vol. I, p. 243, l. 1. 'Mr Linsey' is probably David Lindsay of Tullyhenon, near Banbridge, who died in 1805 (*Walker's Hib. Mag.*, Apr. 1805).

Vol. I, p. 243, ll 3–5 from foot. Tone's quotation seems to be a compound of lines from two authors: 'because she had been saucy and called me skandelous names' (Smollett, *Humphry Clinker* (1771), i, 104), and 'a rare bird upon the earth and very like a black swan' (Fielding, *Tom Jones* (1749), ii, ch. 10).

Vol. I, p. 248, n. 3. A man named Clokey was hanged in 1797 or 1798 (John Burk, *History of the late war in Ireland* (Philadelphia, 1799), p. 76).

Vol. I, p. 251, n. 5. *For* Steele *read* Steel.

Vol. I, p. 252. Philip Francis (1708–73), born in Dublin, was a translator of Horace (*Oxf. D.N.B.*).

Vol. I, p. 264, n. 3. James Dixon was host to many democrats and died *c.*1824 (W. J. Fitzpatrick, *Secret service under Pitt* (London, 1892), pp 124–5, 140–41, 143; C. J. Woods, 'The personnel of the Catholic Convention, 1792–3' in *Archivium Hibernicum*, lvii (2003), p. 46).

Vol. I, p. 270, ll 5–6. The words 'Volumes which I prize above my dukedom' are to be found in the version of Shakespeare's *Tempest* by William D'Avenant and John Dryden (1670), act I, and in the version by Thomas Shadwell (1674), act I, scene ii.

Vol. I, p. 270. The letter headed 'To Margaret Russell' begins as a continuation by Tone of 'Matilda Tone to Margaret Russell' (pp 269–70), but from the sentence beginning 'As for you, Mr Tom' it is clearly a letter from Tone to Thomas Russell. Tone must have expected Margaret Russell to show the letter to her brother Thomas.

Vol. I, p. 271, ll 14–17. The source of the verse is John O'Keeffe's *The farmer* (1787), I, ii. In l. 15 'flintlocks' is a misreading of 'firelocks'.

Vol. I, pp 274, 280. Jonathan Tone's will was dated 20 Sept. 1792. He directed that he was 'to be buried with my family in churchyard of Bodenstown in co. of Kildare, my estate and interest in lands of Whitechurch in co. of Kildare to my brother Mathew, his heirs &c., my estate and interest in lands at Sallins in Co. Kildare to my sister Mary Dunbavin, otherwise Tone, widow of John Dunbavin, deceased, my nephew Theobald Wolfe Tone, Esq., counsellor-at-law, to be sole executor'. Jonathan Tone is stated in the will to be of Cassumsize and a lieutenant in his majesty's 22nd regiment of foot. The will was proven on 15 Oct. 1793. (H. F. Reynolds, 'Irish family history: Tone of Bodenstown, Co. Kildare' in *Notes and Queries*, 12 June 1920, p. 290).

Vol. I, p. 287, l. 2. *For* all Foremen *read* all the foremen.

Vol. I, p. 291, n. 8. Possibly 'Mr Powel' was George Powell (d. 1820?), called to the Irish bar, 1777; he was a member of the lawyers' corps of Volunteers, a member of the Dublin Society of United Irishmen and a friend of Sir Edward Crosbie (*The Volunteers' companion* (Dublin, 1784), p. iii; *An accurate and impartial narrative of the apprehension, trial & execution . . . of Sir Edward William Crosbie, bart* (Bath, 1802), pp 90–93; McDowell, 'Personnel'; Edward Keane et al., *King's Inns admission papers* (Dublin, 1982)).

Vol. I, p. 304. The document is also in *Hibernian Journal*, 19 Oct. 1792. The date given in the document is taken to be an error for 'Monday, October 15, 1792'.

Vol. I, p. 306, l. 22. The paragraph beginning 'For the marvellous events in that journey' was, evidently from its sense and position in MS 2044, written on 11 Oct., after Tone's return to Dublin.

Vol. I, p. 308, n. 1. Peter Lynch died on 5 Mar. 1810 aged 81 (*Walk. Hib. Mag.*, Mar. 1810).

Vol. I, p. 311, n. 2. For *Historal* read *Historical*.

Vol. I, p. 314, line 13. This seems to have been the speech made four weeks previously at a meeting of Wexford freeholders (see above, vol. I, p. 291) and published as *The speech of Edward Sweetman, captain of a late independent company, at a meeting of freeholders of the county of Wexford . . . on September 22, 1792* (Dublin, 1792).

Vol. I, p. 314, n. 8. Possibly Mrs McCarty was a relation of Michael McCarty, merchant, George's Quay, Dublin, who represented Wexford town at the Catholic Convention (Woods, 'Personnel of the Catholic Convention', p. 60).

Vol. I, p. 317. For 'Hurry durry! Nicky Nacky!', see Thomas Otway, *Venice preserv'd* (1682), act IV.

Vol. I, p. 323, ll 9–10. 'This is the day, I speak it with sorrow, That we were all to've been blown up tomorrow' (Henry Brooke, *The contending brothers* (1778), IV, viii).

Vol. I, p. 326, n. 3. Another possibility is Robert Dillon, Francis St., a woollen draper in partnership with James Aylward; he was a member of the Dublin Society of United Irishmen and represented Co. Leitrim at the Catholic Convention (McDowell, 'Personnel', p. 30).

Vol. I, p. 327, n. 3. *Recte* Miles Byrne, *Memoirs* (Paris, 1863), iii, 14–15.

Vol. I, p. 346, headnote. There is internal evidence that these notes, and those of the later proceedings, were made by Tone, e.g. 'see my journals' (vol. I, p. 435).

Vol. I, p. 350, n. 1. The correct source is T. J. Walsh, 'The memorandum book of David Rochfort' in *Cork Historical and Archaeological Society Journal*, lxvi (1961), p. 55.

Vol. I, p. 351. The missing footnote cued on l. 8 from foot should read: ' "Trees of liberty" featured in demonstrations in several Scottish towns in November 1792' (E. W. McFarland, *Ireland and Scotland in the age of revolution: planting the green bough* (Edinburgh, 1994), p. 81).

Vol. I, p. 357, n. 5. Two Bryan Sheehys were delegates and signed the Catholic petition; one represented Cork city and county, the other County Limerick; they were probably Bryan Sheehy (1749?–1806) of Corbally House, Co. Cork, and Bryan Sheehy (d. 1816) of Garden Field, Rathkeal, Co. Limerick (C. J. Woods, 'The personnel of the Catholic Convention, 1792–3' in *Archivium Hibernicum*, lvii (2003), p. 71).

Vol. I, p. 371. Tone states in his diary for 9 Apr. 1796, 'we drew up the Petition and Vindication of the Catholics' at Mount Jerome (vol. II, pp 148–9).

Vol. I, p. 407, n. 6. The Bellew whom Tone mentions is more likely to have been Christopher Bellew's cousin Christopher Dillon Bellew (1762–1826), one of the five delegates who took the petition to London (Woods, 'Personnel of the Catholic Convention', pp 38–9).

Vol. I, p. 416. For 'Dear Dear Friend' read 'My Dear Friend'

Vol. I, p. 416, l. 3. *For* met in *read* met with in.

Vol. I, p. 429, n. 3. John Comerford died in 1795 (*Hib. Mag.*, Oct. 1795, p. 384).

Vol. I, p. 440, l. 14. Sir Thomas Esmonde (1758–1803) of Ballynastragh, near Gorey, Co. Wexford, was the 8th baronet and the elder brother of Dr John Esmonde; he was not a signatory to the petition and so presumably did not attend the previous December (*Burke's peerage and baronetage* (London, 1912); Woods, 'Personnel', p. 48).

Vol. I, p. 440, ll 18–19. Tone's friend Russell states that Tone was voted '1,500£ inclusive of 200£ received and 30 sprugs for a gold medal' (*Journals and memoirs of Thomas Russell*, ed. C. J. Woods (Dublin, 1991), p. 72). By 'sprugs' (from Swift's *Gulliver's travels*) he means 'guineas', 30 guineas being £31 10s. It appears from a published account of the finances of the Catholic Convention that a decision had already been taken to pay Tone £1,500 and that £500 was paid in Jan. 1793 followed by another £206 17s. 6d. two months later (*Proceedings of the General Committee of the Catholics of Ireland which met on Tuesday April 16, and finally dissolved on Thursday April 25, 1793* (Dublin, 1793), pp 6, 12).

Vol. I, p. 444, n. 9. Another possibility is that it means 'up'. For a similar idiomatic usage of 'up', see vol. III, p. 328.

Vol. I, p. 460, ll 3–4: The source of the quotation is *Hamlet*, III, iv.

Vol. I, p. 472. Tone is mistaken in referring to 'O'Gorman of Mayo'. The only O'Gorman elected to the Catholic Convention was James O'Gorman who was both a resident and a representative of County Clare (C. J. Woods, 'The personnel of the Catholic Convention, 1792–3' in *Archivium Hibernicum*, lvii (2003), p. 65.

Vol. I, p. 498. 'Captn de Bo[ ]' is probably John de Birniere, capt., 79th foot, on half pay (*Army list*, 1793).

Vol. I, p. 499. James Reynolds died in fact on 25 May 1808 (*The autobiography of Benjamin Rush*, ed. G. W. Corner (Princeton, 1948), p. 322).

Vol. I, p. 500. For Major John Doyle, who raised the 87th foot in 1793, see vol. II, pp 210–11.

Vol. I, p. 501, n. 2. *For* pp 493–6 *read* pp 491–5.

Vol. I, p. 502, n. 8. Hamilton died in fact on 26 Dec. 1825 (info. supplied by Eric T. D. Lambert in *The correspondence of Daniel O'Connell*, ed. M. R. O'Connell, ii (Dublin, 1972), p. 231, n. 6).

Vol. I, p. 507, l. 18. 'Defenders' is William Tone's error for 'Dissenters'; cf. 'Dissenters' on p. 505, l. 3 from foot.

Vol. I, p. 510, n. 4. Cockayne had been attorney to the duchess of Kingston, to whom Jackson had been secretary; he was still living c.1822 (W. J. Fitzpatrick, *The sham squire* (Dublin, 1866), pp 286–9).

Vol. I, p. 513, l. 21. *For* be might *read* he might.

Vol. I, p. 514, n. 2. According to William Tone, whose source is not stated, Tone and Curran 'were both employed as counsel' at Drogheda assizes in 1794 for Bird and Hamill; Curran 'opened his mind to my father', he states, and 'on the necessity of breaking the connexion with England they *agreed*' (*Life*, ii, 533). In *A full and accurate report of the trial of James Bird, Roger Hamill and Casimir Delahoyde . . . in the criminal court of Drogheda, April the 23d, 1794* (Dublin, 1794), Curran's name heads the list of defence counsel but Tone's is nowhere to be found.

Vol. I, p. 518, l. 2 from foot. Tone was not prosecuted. On 27 June 1794, when on a visit to Dublin, Samuel McTier wrote to his wife Martha in Belfast: 'yesterday was brought into the grand jury bills of indictment for high treason against Jackson, A. H. Rowan, Reynolds and Tone. That against Jackson was found, the other three suspended. I wish with all my heart Tone was with Reynolds.' (*Drennan-McTier letters*, ii, 71). James Reynolds, like Rowan, had fled the country.

Vol. I, p. 522. For William Wentworth-Fitzwilliam (1748–1833), 2nd Earl Fitzwilliam, see vol. II, p. 27, n. 5.

Vol. I, p. 522. Duigenan's speech is also reported in *A report of the debate in the house of commons of Ireland on the bill for the further relief of his majesty's Roman Catholic subjects* (Dublin, 1795), pp 109–23. Another speech animadverting on Tone in some detail, by Robert Johnson (1745?–1833), M.P. for Hillsborough, is reported in ibid., pp 49–59. Robert Johnson, a barrister and later a judge, was a brother of William Johnson (F. E. Ball, *The judges of Ireland* (London, 1926), ii, 333, 340).

Vol. I, p. 533, n. 1. Matthew Donellan (1753?–1827), was a merchant at Clane, Co. Kildare; he was said in 1803 to have engaged recently in United Irish activity; he was held prisoner, Oct. 1803 to Feb. 1804 (Seamus Cullen, *The Emmet rising in Kildare* (Dublin, 2004), pp 28, 97, 122–3, 171–4).

Vol. I, p. 536. The full name of Hamilton's correspondent was Rowland Jackson O'Connor; he was a witness at the first trial of the proprietors of the *Northern Star* (*A faithful report of the trial of the proprietors of the* Northern Star (Belfast, 1794), p. 12).

Vol. II, p. 11, n. 1. Madgett died on 9 Mar. 1813 (Archives Nationales, MC et/1/733, cited in Liam Swords, 'Irish priests and students in revolutionary France' in Liam Swords (ed.), *Protestant, Catholic and Dissenter: the clergy and 1798* (Dublin, 1997), pp 40, 44).

Vol. II, p. 16, n. 4. In fact Charles Teeling settled as a linen-bleacher at Naul, Co. Dublin; he was imprisoned again, Nov.-Dec. 1803 (*Dictionary of Irish biography* (Cambridge, 2008?).

Vol. II, p. 25. From an unpublished memoir written by O'Connor in 1842 it appears that Tone did send this or a similar letter: 'Tone wrote to me to set me right, and in enquiry I found that, to the honour of the Catholic Committee, they, so far from dismissing Tone, upheld him to the last and gave him a handsome sum at his departure for America. I make this amende honourable to a man whose talents, integrity and unflinching principles I set at the head of those who served their country with the sole exception of my beloved Lord Edward.' (O'Connor papers, Château du Bignon, Loiret).

Vol. II, p. 26, l. 10. O'Connor vacated his seat in the Irish parliament soon after making his speech in favour of Grattan's catholic relief bill on 4 May 1795, the bill being defeated the next day (*Northern Star*, 11 and 14 May 1795).

Vol. II, p. 35, n. 1. Tone explained this pseudonym to the court-martial trying him for high treason in 1798 by stating 'that he went to France from America, and it having been necessary that he should have a passport, he took the first he could get, which ran in the name of Smith; and on arriving in France, he was necessarily registered in that name' (vol. III, p. 382). Cf. another version of the trial: ' . . . took the first that *fell in his way*, which *happened* to be made out in the name of Smith' (ibid., p. 390).

Vol. II, pp 36–7. According to police records at Le Havre, Tone travelled under the name 'James Smith, négociant' on a passport issued at Philadelphia on 25 Dec. 1795 (Archives Municipales, Le Havre, Police des Frontières, *PR I² *61).

Vol. II, p. 40, n. 5. Tone's landlord at Le Havre was named Mahon (ibid.).

Vol. II, p. 41, n. 1. Daucourt was Joseph Daucourt (b. 1763?), col., 37ème régiment d'infanterie; he had been commander of the forts at Martinique (Archives Muncipales, Le Havre, Registres des passeports pour l'intérieur, PR I² 35, no. 18/361 du 20 pluviôse).

Vol. II, p. 42, n. 8. Tone's sketch is reproduced in Sylvie Kleinman, 'The accidental tourist: Theobald Wolfe Tone's secret mission to Paris, 1796' in Jane Conroy (ed.), *Cross-cultural travel* (New York and London, 2003), p. 127.

Vol. II, p. 46, ll 1–2. Cf. 'All those things were over now, all past, and just as if they had never been' (Henry Fielding, *Joseph Andrews* (1742), i, ch. 10).

Vol. II, p. 57, ll 11–14. This statement by Tone is not consistent with his statement in his diary for 15 Feb. 1796 that he delivered 'my passport and letters' to Monroe and does not account for the letter from Rowan to Monroe mentioned in his diary for 23 Feb. 1796 (see vol. II, pp 52, 73).

Vol. II, p. 59. Aristide Du Petit Thouars, with whom Tone had became friendly on the voyage from New York and whom he mentions for the first time in his diary for 7 Mar. 1796, records in a letter dated 19 Feb. having dined with Tone and walked with him to the Tuileries; they met again later in the day to go to the Opera but found that it and the other entertainments were full (Bergasse Du Petit Thouars (ed.), *Aristide Aubert Du Petit Thouars, héros d'Aboukir, 1760–1798: lettres et documents inédits* (Paris, 1937), pp 417–18, 454).

Vol. II, p. 110, n. 2. Clarke was remembered by Napoléon Bonaparte on St Helena as 'infatuated with his nobility. He was an admirable clerk. He pretends that he is descended from the ancient kings of Scotland or Ireland and constantly boasts of his nobility.' (Barry E. O'Meara, *Napoleon at St Helena* (2 vols, London, 1888), i, 343).

Vol. II, p. 110, n. 3. An earlier ancestor of Henri Clarke (great-grandfather?) was Gabriel Clarke who d. 1728 and was bur. at Tullaroan, Co. Kilkenny (C. A. Ward, 'The Clarke family and the duc de Feltre' in *Notes and Queries*, 7th ser., iv (July–Dec. 1887), pp 256–8).

Vol. II, p. 122, n. 5. Cf. 'the minister for foreign affairs informs the Convention that Citizen Simonville was, by the intrigues of the ambassadors of Vienna, Berlin and other courts, rejected as ambassador for the French Republic at the Ottoman Porte' (*The chronologist of the present war; containing a faithful series of the events which have occurred in Europe* (London, 1796), p. 84).

Vol. II, p. 143, n. 4. In fact his name was John Sullivan. For his career in France, see vol III, p. 77, n. 1. According to 'a person of veracity' with whom Sir Richard Musgrave was acquainted, he was, in Paris in 1796 (*recte* 1797?), sworn as a United Irishman by James Coigly (Musgrave, *Memoirs of the rebellions* (2nd ed., 1801), p. 601).

Vol. II, p. 150, l. 2. In a document in the Archives de la Guerre, Vincennes (X^n 16a, 15 Nivôse an 12 (6 Jan. 1804)), he corrects the spelling of his surname to 'Aherne'. In the archives his forename is given as 'Eugène' (X^n 14, État nominatif, 19 Vendémiaire an 13 (11 Oct. 1804)); Tone (like Byrne) calls him 'John' or 'Jack' (see vol. III).

Vol. II, p. 194, n. 10. *Recte* Alexander Pope, 'Epistle III to . . . Lord Bathurst' in *Works* (1736): 'The bow'r of wanton Shrewsbury and love'.

Vol. II, p. 230, l. 22. *Recte* 'Divers efforts to sing' (Tobias Smollett, *Peregrine Pickle* (1751), iv, 28).

Vol. II, p. 230, n. 13. The source is in fact William Sampson, *Report of the trial of the King versus Hurdy Gurdy, alias Barrel Organ, alias Grinder* (Dublin, 1794), pp 20, 43.

Vol. II, p. 231, n. 5. Tone is most probably thinking of Ernst Gideon Freiherr von Laudon (1717–90) who, at the head of an Imperial force, captured Schweidnitz, a fortified place in Silesia, from the Prussians on 1 Oct. 1761; Laudon was promoted *Feldmarschall* in 1778 (*Neue deutsche Biographie*, xiii (Berlin, 1982), pp 700–01).

Vol. II, p. 261, l. 18. A younger son of William Tone was Mathew Tone, listed in *Wilson's Dublin Directory*, 1784–5, as a coachmaker, 126, Great Britain St., Dublin. He was a beneficiary in the will of Jonathan Tone dated 20 Sept. 1792, and a member of the Forenaughts yeomanry in 1798 (see 'Addenda', above, p. 471; T. U. Sadleir, 'The family of Tone' in *Kildare Archaeological Society Journal*, xii, no. 7 (1943), p. 326).

Vol. II, p. 265, para. 1. At the public examination that ended on 2 Apr. 1773, as a pupil of the Mercantile Academy, Mabbot St., Tone obtained premiums in Arithmetic (reduction), Reading (*Spectator*), Reading (grammar), Catechism (explanation) and History (English) as well as a certificate in Spelling and a minor award in Speaking (*Freeman's Journal*, 17 Apr. 1773). See vol. III, p. 438.

Vol. II, p. 267, n. 1. *For* until *c.*1785 and *c.*1792 *read* until *c.*1785, and from then until *c.*1792.

Vol. II, p. 272, l. 2 from foot. Tone's wife, called Martha by her parents, Matilda by Tone, was born on 17 June 1769 (*Life*, ii, 591).

Vol. II, p. 272, n. 2. In fact, though William Witherington does not appear in *Wilson's Dublin Directory* after 1793, he survived his wife, who died in Apr. 1797; he was dead by 25 Feb. 1802 (Thomas Reynolds, junr, *The life of Thomas Reynolds* (London, 1839), i, 380–81; H. F. Reynolds, 'Witherington of Dublin' in *Notes and Queries*, 4 June 1920).

Vol. II, pp 276–7. On 25 Mar. 1795, the lord chancellor, Fitzgibbon, warned Westmorland of George Knox, a commissioner of revenue: 'rely upon it, he must be watched. He is as notorious a rebel and democrat in heart as Mr Tone, who is his intimate friend and playfellow.' (D. A. Fleming and A.P.W. Malcomson (eds), *'A volley of execrations': the letters and papers of John FitzGibbon* (Dublin, 2005), p. 225).

Vol. II, p. 277, n. 4. James Wills does not explain how he came to have documents relating to Tone's career. It seems possible that he was doubly a connexion of Tone by marriage,

Tone's aunt Ann Tone having married a Wills and his aunt Mary Tone having had a son, William, who married Ann's daughter Frances (see below, vol. III, p. 489).

Vol. II, p. 281, n. 3. A memorial of the deed of assignment dated 1 July 1789 concerning the premises in Stafford St. is in Registry of Deeds, Dublin, 1789, bk 408, p. 205. The property is described therein as 'all that lot of tenement of ground situate, lying and being in Stafford Street containing in front to Stafford Street 30 ft depth backwards to Stable lane 112 ft together with the coach house and stable then built on said ground and fronting said lane formerly in the possession of Peter Faure, merchant, and lately in the possession of Isaac Ambrose Eccles of Dublin'. A memorial of the deed of assignment dated 14 November 1789 is in Registry of Deeds, 1789, bk 407, p. 406. It refers to Isaac Ambrose Eccles having 'by indenture of lease 19th Sept. 1761 demised to John Templeton of Dublin, merchant', the property in Stafford St., and to John Templeton having 'by deed poll 19th January 1765 assigned to Peter Tone of Dublin, coachmaker, all his right to said premises'.

Vol. II, p. 288, n. 2. *For* MS 3508 *read* MS 3805.

Vol. II, pp 313, 346. Matilda Tone's good opinion of James Reynolds altered when, having approached him in Philadelphia in 1806 for the return of Tone's books and diaries which she had entrusted to him before leaving America for France in 1796, she learnt that he had sold the books and apparently mislaid the diaries (Matilda Tone to John Maclean, New York, n.d., John Maclean junr, *A memoir of John Maclean, M.D.* (Princeton, 1885), pp 40–42).

Vol. II, pp 332, ll 22–5. On 13 March 1794, Drennan, referring to the £1,500 voted to Tone by the Catholic Convention, supposed that it was being paid to him 'in small gales in order to keep him hanging on to their bounty' (*Drennan-McTier letters*, ii, 29). Some time in 1793 or 1794 one member of the convention stated that he and others had 'from our own funds' given Tone 'temporary relief' (Anon. to — , n.d., Nat. Arch. (Ire.), Rebellion papers, 620/51/244).

Vol. II, p. 333, n. 5. Dr James MacDonnell recalled, in a letter to R. R. Madden dated 4 June 1843, being present with Tone and Frank McCracken at Samuel Neilson's house in Belfast the day before Tone left for America. To McCracken's assertion that 'the Irish could free themselves without any assistance from France', Tone replied, 'if you act upon that principle, you may pursue your ropewalks and your sail manufacture long and prosperously enough, for there never will be a effectual struggle in Ireland without invasion'. (Madden, *United Irishmen*, 3rd ser. (1846), i, 130–32). Francis McCracken (1762–1842) was an elder brother of Henry Joy McCracken; he was a Volunteer, played some part in the United Irish movement and was trusted by Russell in 1803 (Mary McNeill, *The life and times of Mary Ann McCracken* (Dublin, 1960), pp 54–5, 134–5, 178, 190, 193–4, 212–14, fldr).

Vol. II, p. 336, n. 3. It was reported in Dublin that Hamilton Rowan arrived in Philadelphia from Le Havre on 17 July 1795; his ship had been boarded by *H.M. Melampos* but Rowan, travelling as 'Mr Thompson of South Carolina', escaped detection (*Freeman's Journal*, 3 Sept. 1795).

Vol. II, p. 345, n. 1. Debelle is also to be found, under 'Belle', in *Dict. biog. franç.*

Vol. II, p. 355, n. 3. Cf. 'in the height of their prosperity the Turks have acknowledged that if God had given them the earth he had left the sea to the infidels' (Edward Gibbon, *The history of the decline and fall of the Roman empire* (6 vols, Dublin, 1788), vi, 191).

Vol. II, p. 360, n. 3. Rowley and William Osborne, Ann St., Belfast, in Nov. 1796 announced their withdrawal from 'the soap boiling and chandling business' (*Northern Star*, 18 Nov. 1796).

Vol. II, p. 360, n. 4. He was very likely the same person as Daniel Shanahan, solicitor, who died at Belfast on 8 Aug. 1835 (*Freeman's Journal*, 18 Aug. 1835).

Vol. II, p. 360, n. 8. According to a family historian, John Pollock died on 18 Dec. 1825 (A. S. Hartigan, *The family of Pollock of Newry and their descendants* (Folkestone, 1901)).

Vol. II, p, 391, n. 1. *Address of the United Irishmen of Dublin to the Friends of the People in London* (London, 1792), p. 12.

Vol. II, p. 397, n. 4. William Tate was born in Ireland; he left for America as a young man (J. D. Ahlstrom, 'Captain and *chef de brigade*: William Tate, South Carolina adventurer' in *South Carolina Historical Magazine*, lxxxviii (Oct. 1987), pp 183–91).

Vol. II, pp 397 and 399. Cf. *Authentic copies of the instructions given by Gen[eral] Hoche to Colonel Tate previous to his landing on the coast of South Wales at the beginning of 1797* (London: Wright, 1797, 4 pp).

Vol. II, p. 400, para. 1. Hoche was from March 1794 a married man, his wife being Anne Adelaïde (née Dechaux) (1778–1859) (M. L. Jacotey, *Le général Hoche* (Paris, 1994), p. 246).

Vol. II, p. 420, n. 2. The words 'Taata Enos' do not appear in James Cook and James King, *A voyage to the Pacific Ocean* (London, 1784); but cf. 'they were *taata enos*, "poor wretches"' (Andrew Kippis, *The life of Captain James Cook* (Dublin, 1788), p. 113).

Vol. II, p. 429, lines 9 to 14. A French force might well have had 'a brush by the way' had it set out from Bantry for Cork. Already there was a British force less than 20 km along the road at Drimoleague, 'the place they mean to make a stand' (Daniel O'Sullivan to Maurice O'Connell, Cooliagh, 24 Dec. 1796, in Mrs M. J. O'Connell, *The last colonel of the Irish brigade* (2 vols, London, 1892), ii, 197).

Vol. III, p. 31. Tone's commission is listed in the *Almanach National*, An VI, p. 129: 'Armée de Sambre et Meuse, Adjudans Généraux, Citoyens . . . Smitt'.

Vol. III, pp 35–6. From about the middle of the diary for 20 March, Tone's handwriting, characteristically neat, becomes increasingly rough, which, together with his complaints of loneliness, suggests inebriation.

Vol. III, p. 65, l. 23. Stairs, more correctly spelt 'stares', are starlings. William Tone (*Life*, ii, 369) misreads the word as 'hares'.

Vol. III, p. 70, l. 23. In the MS the words 'strong government' are heavily underlined. In *Life*, ii, 375, they are not italicised or otherwise emphasised.

Vol. III, p. 153. There is another version of this letter, in another hand and with many textual variations, in Archives Nationales, AF IV cart. 1671, plaq. 2. The addressee is identified from the presence of other letters from Lewines to Barras in this location as well as in the McPeake papers.

Vol. III, p. 172, n. 2. Rousselin's book was presented to the Council of Five Hundred on 1 Apr. 1798 (*Corps législatif: Conseil des Cinq-cens: Motion faite par [Pierre Antoine] Laloy en présentant au Conseil la 'Vie de Lazare Hoche, général des armées de la République', par A[lexandre] Rousselin, Séance de 12 germinal an VI* (Paris, an VI)). In the 4th edition (1800) Chérin himself, who died from wounds in Switzerland on 8 June 1800, is the subject of a memoir.

Vol. III, pp 186–7. The paragraph concerning the battle of Camperdown, evidently an afterthought on Tone's part, is given by William Tone at the end of the diary for 15 October (*Life*, ii, 451–2).

Vol. III, p. 239. Omitted here, and from 'Additional documents', is a letter from Tone to the minister of police, 21 April 1798 (Archives Nationales, F^7 7422 doss. B^5 5921).

Vol. III, p. 264, l. 8 of text of diary. *Life*, ii, 491, reads 'My May of life'; Shakespeare, *Macbeth*, V, iii, 22, reads 'My way of life', which similarly fits the context..

Vol. III, p. 268, n. 8. Her full name was Marie Elisabeth Anne; she was wife of the *maître de ballets* at the Opéra and 'première danseuse de son temps' (*Biographie universelle ancienne et moderne* (85 vols, Paris, 1811–62), supplément).

Vol. III, p. 290, ll 113–14. Tone misquotes Smollett, whose actual words are 'Mistress has excarded Sir Ulic for kicking of Chowder, and I have sent O'Frizzle away with a flea in his ear' (*Humphy Clinker*, vol. i). O'Frizzle was Sir Ulic Mackilligut's 'gentleman' and Chowder was Mrs Tabitha's dog.

Vol. III, p. 292. Swan died on 12 Jan. 1837.

Vol. III, p. 313. Tone's letter to Schérer was offered for sale by Phillips' Fine Art Auctioneers in 1984.

Vol. III, p. 321, headnote. Very probably this letter was given by Matilda Tone to her friend Eliza Fletcher (1770–1858), for it was sold by the latter's great-grandson, the Rev. M. D. Fletcher of Tavistock, Devon, for £58 at Sotheby's on 14 Dec. 1926, to a Mrs McPeake, presumably the wife of Brendan McPeake, a collector of MSS relating to the United Irishmen (P.R.O.N.I., McPeake papers, T/3048/L/2-4). It was offered for sale by Phillips' Fine Art Auctioneers in 1984 and by another London auctioneer in Nov. 1993; it was purchased by N.L.I. in Dec. 1993 from Figgis Rare Books, Dublin.

Vol. III, p. 326. 'What I am truly is thine and my poor country's to command' (*Macbeth*, IV, iii, 147).

Vol. III, p. 328, n. 9. It was reported over three months later that two officers of the Prince of Wales regiment had been liberated from a French frigate, the *Immortalité*, when it was captured by a British frigate, the *Fishguard*; it was explained that 'out of curiosity' they had gone on board the French vessel 'thinking her an English vessel, she having hoisted British colours'. (*Finn's Leinster Journal*, 1 Dec. 1798).

Vol. III, p. 329, n. 4. According to a letter concerning the French landing dated 30 Aug. received by a gentleman in Belfast from a friend at Ballyshannon, 'the yeomanry and a small party of 25 fencibles at and near Killala attempted to prevent their landing, in doing which some of the yeomanry fell, among whom was Andrew Kirkwood, esq., of Kilcummin' (*Courier* (London), 11 Sept. 1798).

Vol. III, p. 344, l. 5 of text. In the omitted matter are mentions of George Blake (of Caracloon), Christopher Crump (of Oury), Michael Gannon (of Louisburgh), James Joseph MacDonnell (of Rossbeg) and James O'Dowd (of Bonyconlon).

Vol. III, p. 363. A local belief, not substantiated by any documentary evidence, is that Tone's journey to Dublin was broken at Laragh, Co. Monaghan (J. H. Murnane and Peadar Murnane, *At the ford of the birches: the history of Ballybay* (Monaghan, 1999), p. 326).

Vol. III, p. 366, ll 6–7 from foot of text. One Irish agent, Lewines, accompanied by Simon, was interviewed by Hoche at Frankfurt; Lewines recounts the episode (which must have occurred in Apr. 1797) in a memorandum he wrote probably in or shortly after Oct. 1797, 'Détails et preuves de ma mission et de pouvoirs dont je suis chargé' (Archives Nationales, Paris, AF IV, 1671, pl. 1).

Vol. III, p. 369, n. 1. An item described as 'French national cockade belonging to Theobald Wolfe Tone, adjutant-general in the French army' was to be found in the McPeake collection. A black-and-white photograph is among the papers collected by the editors and now in T.C.D.

Vol. III, p. 404. The early provenance of Tone's letter to Peter Tone has not been ascertained. It was purchased from Winifred A. Myers (Autographs) Ltd by Brendan McPeake in 1954. After the dispersal of the McPeake collection it was purchased by the National Library of Ireland in Dec. 1993 from Figgis Rare Books, Dublin. A photocopy is in P.R.O.N.I., T/3048/J/8.

Vol. III, pp 411–14. In a brief report of the hearing in *Dublin Evening Post*, 13 Nov. 1798, it was stated stated that the 'application was made by Counsellors Curran and Johnson'. This Johnson was probably William Johnson (1760–1845) who was a member of Tone's political club, 1790–91, and who acted for Defenders on trial at Athy assizes, Aug.–Sept. 1795; he was M.P. for Co. Roscommon, 1799–1800, and a justice of the common pleas, 1817–41 (see vol. I, p. 90, and vol. II, pp 31, 291).

Vol. III, p. 425, n. 1. In a letter from Talleyrand to the new minister of police, 1 Nivôse year 7 (21 Dec. 1798), it is stated that 'le citoyen Thompson' is 'l'agent des Irlandais Unis' and that the Directory's intention is that he be consulted concerning Irishmen wishing to enter or reside in France (Archives Nationales, Paris, F[7]). In a memorandum headed 'Détails et preuves de ma mission' signed 'Édouard Joseph Luines, député des Irlandois Unis près de la République Françoise', prob. late 1797, the writer explains: 'depuis mon service sur le Continent j'ai pris tantôt le nom de Thompson, tantôt celui de Giauque, pour mieux me soustraire au recherches du Gouvernement Anglois' (Archives Nationales, AF IV 1671, pl. 1).

Vol. III, p. 426, n. 1. There is a wood engraving of William Dunbavin's premises at No. 46 High St. in an advertisement in *New City Pictorial Directory, 1850* (Dublin: Henry Shaw,

1850), unpaginated. The front of the building is inscribed 'Dillon, successor to Dunbavin'. The proprietor, John Dillon, states his business to be that of soap boiler and tallow chandler. It appears that the building, previously 65, was renumbered 46. William Dunbavin was listed in the Dublin directories as a tallow chandler until 1841.

Vol. III, p. 433, n. 5. According to Madden, Tone's body 'was kept two nights at Dunbavin's' (*United Irishmen*, 3rd ser. (1846), i, 158). If one of these nights was the 21st, the removal of the remains to Bodenstown and burial there must have occurred during a violent storm. It was reported in the *Dublin Evening Post*, 24 Nov. 1798, that 'a tremendous gale of wind at south-east has blown incessantly for the three preceding days but on the night of Wednesday [21st] it increased to a most dreadful tempest'.

Acknowledgements

The letters from Tone given above in 'Additional documents' (pp 460–65) were contributed by Dr Sylvie Kleinman. The editors are entirely indebted to her for these and for information given as addenda, or elsewhere in this volume, obtained by her from the Service Historique de la Défense at Vincennes and from the Archives Municipales at Le Havre. In particular credit is due to her for notes supplied on John Sullivan from her searches at Vincennes (Certificats de civisme, La Flèche, etc.), for her discovery there of an elusive Tone dossier ('Généraux prétendus', 17 yd 14), for conjuring up a police profile of Tone made when he disembarked at Le Havre, and for drawing attention to Tone material in Bergasse Du Petit Thouars (ed.), *Aristide Aubert Du Petit Thouars, héros d'Aboukir, 1760–1798: lettres et documents inédits* (Paris, 1937). Almost all of the information received is to be found in Dr Kleinman's unpublished Ph.D. thesis, 'Translation, the French language and the United Irishmen (1792–1804)' (Dublin City University, 2006), chs 2, 3 and 4. The editors are indebted also to Sir Richard Aylmer for information obtained by him from the O'Connor papers at the Château du Bignon and given above as an addendum.

Descriptions of Tone and his wife Matilda

1

Archives Municipales, Le Havre, Registre des passeports pour l'intérieur, *PR I² 35, no. 18362 du 20 pluviôse an 4 (9 Feb. 1796).

James Smith [i.e. Theobald Wolfe Tone], . . . 30 ans, 5 pieds 4 pouces, cheveux et sourcils châtains, yeux bruns, nez aquilin, bouche moyenne, menton rond, visage ovale et un peu gravé, front bas.[1]

2

A sister of Sir Philip Crampton, describing Tone in a note intended for R. R. Madden, early May 1843 (T.C.D., Madden papers, MS 873/38). The note is printed in Madden, *United Irishmen*, 3rd ser. (1846), i, 158–9, and 2nd ed., ii (1858), p. 142, except for the words 'like the monkey's'.

He was a *very* slender, angular, rapid-moving man; a thin face sallow and pock-marked; eyes small, lively, bright; forehead very low; the hair cut close & growing up from it like the monkey's; nose rather long, I forget the shape; nothing remarkable; laughed and talked fast with enthusiasm about music and other innocent things, so that one could not possibly suspect him of plots and treasons. Wise he could not be, but he had not a foolish look — he was too lively & animated for that.

3

John Edward Walsh, *Sketches of Ireland sixty years ago* (Dublin, 1847), p. 153.

A slight effeminate-looking man, with a hatchet face, a long aquiline nose, rather handsome and genteel-looking, with lank, straight hair combed down on his sickly red cheek, exhibiting a face the most insignificant and mindless that could be imagined. His mode of speaking was in correspondence with his face and person. It was polite and gentlemanly but totally devoid of anything like energy or vigour. I set him down as a worthy good-natured, flimsy man in whom there was no harm, and as the least likely person in the world to do mischief to the state.

4

Catherine Wilmot's Paris diary, 13 March 1802 (R.I.A., 'Kitty Wilmot's journal, 1801–1803', MS 12/L/32).

[1] 'James Smith . . . 30 years, 5 foot 4 inches, brown hair and eyebrows, aquiline nose, medium-sized mouth, round chin, oval, slightly pock-marked face, low forehead.' In fact Tone was aged 32 when he disembarked at Le Havre.

The widow of the unfortunate Tone . . . is interesting to the greatest degree. She is delightfully affectionate & caressing in her manners, delicately pretty & understanding *so much* of every accomplishment that she has a never ending source of amusement & chearfulness in herself. She is exactly what comes under the name of a *fascinating* creature. Maria her daughter (a girl about 16) is her idol. She is beautiful & gives one exactly the idea of a poet's nymph — long satten auburn tresses, sylph-like figure, inexpressibly speaking eyes & elegance of deportment. They live in almost intire seclusion. I went to see them twice. Maria's harp, guitar & pianoforte spoke her occupations in the line of taste & the rest of their *little & only reception room* was the receptacle of everything that announced happiness & rationality — there were various Italian, French & English authors of the best selection, flowers blowing over the chimney, pet birds in a cage, & everything however great or insignificant that charactiz'd the pol- ish'd inmates of this humble residence — independant of these *agrémens* Mrs Tone is delightful in conversation & professes a rectitude of mind I have sel- dom seen equal'd anywhere.

5

T.C.D., Dillon papers, Charles Hart's diary of his tour of America, 1848–9, MS 6464 unfol.; printed in *Young Irelander abroad: the diary of Charles Hart*, ed. Brendan Ó Cathaoir (Cork, 2003), pp 61–2.

Monday, Mar. 4, 1849. After the inauguration of Gen[eral] Taylor as President I walked out to Georgetown hoping to see Mrs W. Tone . . . Was shown up to the Library, a comfortable room with bookshelves well filled all round . . . Saw Mrs T. . . . She chatted very gaily — spoke with great feeling and affection about Ireland . . . Nothing could be more ladylike than her manner and expressions and she must have had considerable powers of conversation . . . Her face was rather square — a forehead rather broad than high tho' quite sufficiently so — straight and still at 80 years beautifully smooth and fair — nose straight — perhaps a lit- tle thick — under lip slightly projecting, eyes full of light, as was her whole face. Must have been very pretty and most attractive and ladylike in manner. Accent Irish, Dublin, and pleasing. Came away much pleased and rather affected — feeling for the first time some idea of what poor T.W.T. suffered for Ireland and what a heroine his wife was. Lived in fine old house in Georgetown.[1]

---

[1] Matilda Tone died on 18 March 1849.

Iconography of Theobald Wolfe Tone

THE various artistic representations of Tone are listed here in order of execution. The many portraits that are merely derivative, modelled on one or another of those listed here, are omitted.

I

'Mrs Tone and her sons Theobald Wolfe and Matthew from original drawings taken in 1778 in the possession of Mrs Moore', engraved by T. W. Huffam from a portrait executed by an unknown artist probably (to judge from the boys' appearance) somewhat earlier than 1778. The portrait was given or (more likely) lent to R. R. Madden by a Mrs Bull, a daughter of William Dunbavin and sister of Mrs Moore.[1] Madden printed it as a frontispiece in the second series of his *United Irishmen* (1843);[2] he refers to it in his third series (1846),[3] where he identifies Mathew Tone as wearing a sash. The other boy, without a sash and apparently older, must be Theobald. The original was in watercolour (see below); its location is not known. The gown worn by Margaret Tone was deposited in the National Museum of Ireland in 1930 by the Barnardo family of Dublin. The engraving is reprinted in Marianne Elliott, *Wolfe Tone* (New Haven, 1989).

A miniature of Margaret Tone (oval-shaped, 11.5 × 10.5 cm), in water colours, head and shoulders only, and described on the verso in an early or mid twentieth-century hand as 'Mrs Tone the mother of T. W. Tone from a watercolour drawing in the possession of Mrs Bull of Mary St.', is in the National Library of Ireland.[4] It is unmistakably taken from the group portrait. Similarly, in the same collection, there are watercolour miniatures of the two brothers. One, wearing a blue sash, is identified in a late eighteenth-century or early nineteenth-century hand as 'Matthew Tone born 1769 or 1770'; the other, who has no sash, is identified in a twentieth-century hand as 'Theobald W. Tone'. In the same repository is another portrait of the boy without the sash (T. W. Tone), which however is a very poor copy.

2

Theobald Wolfe Tone. Oils. Artist unknown. 78 × 65 cm. Probably *circa* 1792. National Gallery of Ireland. Half length in oval. Left side head-and-shoulder view of Tone, who has reddish brown hair, dark blue eyes, pointed nose, blue coat faced with red, white waistcoat, black cravat tied in a bow.

[1] See below, 'Genealogy'.
[2] R. R. Madden, *United Irishmen*, 2nd ser. (London, 1843), i, frontisp.
[3] Ibid., 3rd ser. (Dublin, 1846), i, 134.
[4] N.L.I., Department of Prints and Drawings, Joly collection.

Reproduced 6 × 5 cm in colour in 'The wearing of the green' in *Ireland of the Welcomes*, xxxv, no. 4 (July–Aug. 1986), p. 37.

A mezzotint and etching by T. W. Huffam, entitled 'Theobald Wolfe Tone from an original portrait representing him in his volunteer uniform in the possession of Mr Burrowes' (unmistakably the portrait now in the National Gallery of Ireland), appears in the second series of Madden's *United Irishmen* (1843).[1] A mounted and framed print (2.27 cm × 13.3 cm) is in the National Portrait Gallery, London. Peter Burrowes (d. 1841), a barrister, was a friend of Tone. But the Volunteer corps has not been identified and the uniform could be that of a Whig club.[2]

3

'The unfortunate Theobald Wolfe Tone, Esq'. Line engraving in *Walker's Hibernian Magazine*, November 1798. Artist unknown. Tone is shown right side view, full-length, arms crossed, in a French military uniform, with large hat, standing before a court-martial on 10 November 1798. A mounted and framed print is in the National Library of Ireland.

A print purchased from a P. Traynor is in the National Gallery of Ireland.

4

Plaster cast (17.5 × 15 × 9.5 cm) made from a death mask taken by James Petrie (d. 1819). Trinity College, Dublin, Manuscripts Department. It was acquired by Trinity in July 1923 under the terms of the will of Katherine Anne Maxwell.[3] She is said to have acquired it from Alfred Webb.

Another plaster cast made from the death mask taken by Petrie is in the National Gallery of Ireland. It was purchased in Dublin in 1899 from a relation of Major Sandys (a Mr P. Traynor?) to whom it had descended.[4]

Another plaster cast, also in the National Gallery of Ireland. Provenance unknown.

Another cast, presumably from the same death mask, is in the American-Irish Historical Society Library, New York.[5] Its provenance is not known.

One of Madden's sources, William Dunnan, a nephew of William Dunbavin[1] and present at Dunbavin's house when Tone's body was to be seen laid out there,

---

[1] Madden, *United Irishmen*, 2nd ser. (1843), i, facing p. 90

[2] The 'Whig club dress' generally worn by Grattan is described by his son as 'blue and buff with a large gilt button on it, the harp surmounted by a crown' (Henry Grattan junr (ed.), *Memoirs of . . . Henry Grattan* (London, 1842), iv, 71). Tone acknowledges that in 1792 he himself possessed a Whig club uniform (see vol. II, p. 306)   [3] See below, 'Genealogy'.

[4] For William Sandys, see above, vol. III, p. 378, n. 4.

[5] Marianne Elliott, *Wolfe Tone* (New Haven, 1989), p. 436, n. 13.

told him that 'a person whose name he does not know was brought to the room where the corpse lay to take a cast of the face. What became of that cast he does not know.' Madden states in his earlier treatment of Tone (1846) that he believed that the cast 'was taken by Petrie and was amongst a large number of casts sold at the auction of Petrie's effects and which eventually came into the hands of Mr T. Ray'.[2] By 'cast' Madden presumably means the 'mask' from which casts could subsequently be made. In his later treatment (1858) he states with greater assurance, 'the cast was taken by Petrie and fortunately came into my hands since the publication of the former edition of this work. From the original work I have had a cast taken [and] daguerreotyped.' Madden prints it in the second edition (or new series) of his *United Irishmen*.[3] It is at least likely that the cast, or mask, held by Thomas Ray (a follower of Daniel O'Connell) and then Madden is the one acquired by Trinity and used as a half-tone illustration in Frank MacDermot, *Theobald Wolfe Tone: a biographical study* (London, 1939).

5

Theobald Wolfe Tone. Miniature. By Catherine Anne Tone (née Sampson). Early or mid 1820s. In the possession of Mrs Katherine Dickason of Short Hills, New Jersey, who died in 1996 and now of her daughter Mrs Katherine Goodale. Left-side head-and-shoulders view of Tone, who has blue jacket, high collar and large gold epaulette. Catherine Anne Tone's granddaughter, Katherine Anne Maxwell, wrote to the art historian W. G. Strickland on 19 October 1906 that this portrait 'is taken from a miniature in colored chalks Tone had made for his wife in 1798 in France'.[4] The original miniature is presumably the picture mentioned ('it cost me but two louis') in the letter Tone wrote to his wife on 16 September 1798.[5]

A copper engraving, by W. Harrison, Georgetown, District of Columbia, is the frontispiece of the first volume of *Life of Theobald Wolfe Tone . . . edited by his son* (2 vols, Washington, 1826). The portrait is there described as 'copied in miniature from a portrait of General Tone by his daughter-in-law Katherine Sampson Tone'. The editor of the volumes was William Tone, whose wife Catherine (b. 1796 or 1798) was the artist. A sister of Sir Philip Crampton, a woman who (in the words of R. R. Madden) 'had a perfect remembrance of Tone', stated in a note written for Madden: 'it does not resemble according to my recollection of him' (*United Irishmen*, 3rd ser. (1846), i, 158–9; T.C.D., Madden papers, MS 873/38). For the details she next gives, see 'Descriptions of Tone' (above, p. 482). It is evident, however, that the artist's intention was

---

[1] See below, 'Genealogy'.   [2] *United Irishmen*, 3rd ser. (Dublin, 1846), i, 158.
[3] *United Irishmen*, 2nd ed., ii (1858), facing p. 143.   [4] National Gallery of Ireland, Archives.
[5] Above, vol. III, pp 341–2.

to depict him in the French uniform he wore when standing trial, of which there are several descriptions in documents given above.[1]

A photograph, in full colour, of this portrait appears on the dust-jacket of Marianne Elliott, *Wolfe Tone* (New Haven, 1989); it appears also, in monochrome, as a frontispiece.

A lithograph ('drawn on stone') by C. Hullandel exists as a print published on 20 March 1827 by Henry Colburn of London, publisher also of a London reprint (1827) of William Tone's *Life*, in which it appears as a frontispiece.[2] Hullandel's lithograph differs from the original in showing Tone's right side.

A watercolour miniature (18 × 15.5 cm incl. case), apparently modelled on the engraving, is in the Ulster Museum. It differs from the original in showing Tone's right side and a scarlet uniform.

6

Bust of Theobald Wolfe Tone. Marble. By Terence Farrell, R.H.A. *Circa* 1852. Trinity College, Dublin.

Miss Katherine Anne Maxwell, in a letter to W. H. Strickland, 19 October 1906,[3] states that it was purchased in 1854 by her mother, Mrs Grace Georgiana Maxwell, daughter of William and Catherine Anne Tone (see 'Genealogy', below). It was exhibited in 1853 at the Dublin Exhibition, where it was described as executed 'for Mr Maxwell of New York'.[4] The person commissioning the bust was Lascelles Edward Maxwell who in 1851 married Grace Georgiana Tone, daughter of William and Catherine Anne Tone.[5] It was acquired by Trinity in July 1923 under the terms of the will of Maxwell's daughter Katherine Anne. An early photograph (mid nineteenth century?) is in N.L.I., Department of Prints and Drawings.

7

Statue of Theobald Wolfe Tone. Bronze. Edward Delaney. *Circa* 1966. Northeast corner of St Stephen's Green, Dublin.

[1] Above, vol. III, pp 376, n. 1, 383, 386 and 393.
[2] *Memoirs of Theobald Wolfe Tone written by himself. . . edited by his son* (2 vols, London, 1827).
[3] As above, p. 486, n. 4.   [4] W. G. Strickland, *Dictionary of Irish artists* (Dublin, 1913), i, 335.
[5] See 'Genealogy', below, p. 491.

Genealogy of Theobald Wolfe Tone

THE main sources used for this genealogy, in addition to Tone's own writings and editorial matter in this edition, are correspondence with and a family tree received from the late Katherine Dickason (mentioned below); Alice L. Milligan, *Life of Theobald Wolfe Tone* (Belfast, 1898), appendix; H. F. Reynolds, 'Irish family history: Tone of Bodenstown, Co. Kildare' in *Notes and Queries*, 12th ser., vi (Jan.-June 1920), pp 288–90; Robert Pierpoint, 'Tone of Bodenstown, Co. Kildare' in ibid., 12th ser., vi (Jan.-June 1920), p. 321; Katherine Anne Tone-Maxwell, 'Tone of Bodenstown, Co. Kildare' in ibid., 12th ser., vii (July-Dec. 1920), pp 432–3; and T. U. Sadleir, 'The family of Tone' in *County Kildare Archaeological Society Journal.*, xii, no. 7 (1943), pp 326–9. One source not used is Frank Jerome Tone, *History of the Tone family* (Niagara Falls, 1944), which relies for pre eighteenth-century ancestry on the work of Gustave Anjou. Anjou (1863–1942) is alleged to have been a forger of genealogies.[1]

On Matilda Tone's family there is more in H. B. Swanzy, *The families of French of Belturbet and Nixon of Fermanagh and their descendants* (Dublin, 1908), p. 19, H. F. Reynolds, 'Fanning of Dublin' in *Notes and Queries*, 12th ser., vii, no. 131 (16 Oct. 1920), pp 306–8, and idem, 'Witherington of Dublin' in *Notes and Queries*, 12th ser., ix, no. 170 (16 July 1921), pp 43–5. Her descent from a speaker of the Irish house of commons is traced in 'Descent of McKisack, Tone & Reynolds from Sir Audley Mervyn, Knt, M.P.' (P.R.O.N.I., McKisack papers, D/1745/7). Matilda Tone (née Witherington) was related by marriage to John Fitzgibbon, Baron Fitzgibbon, later earl of Clare, lord chancellor of Ireland throughout the 1790s. Her mother Catherine's sister Martha or Matilda Fanning married (1762) Blennerhasset Grove, a Dublin linen-draper, whose sister Elinor had married (1743) John Fitzgibbon, a successful barrister, and borne him the future lord chancellor. From Grove's death (1773) until her own death (1786?) Martha Grove lived with her father Edward Fanning, with whom the Witheringtons also lived.

Five members of Tone's family are to be subjects of articles in the *Dictionary of Irish biography* (7 vols, Cambridge, 2008?), viz. Theobald Wolfe Tone himself, his wife Matilda, his brothers William Henry and Mathew, and his son William Theobald Wolfe Tone.

WILLIAM TONE (b. 1705?),[2] a farmer of Bodenstown, Co. Kildare, d. 24 Apr. 1766 aged 60 leaving three sons and two daughters namely

1. Peter Tone (of whom more presently)
2. Mathew Tone, coachmaker in Dublin 1780s; served in Forenaughts yeomanry 1798

---

[1] R. C. Anderson, 'We wuz robbed' in *Journal of the Genealogical Association of Utah*, ix (1991).
[2] Nothing is known reliably of his ancestry. It does at least seem possible that he was a son, or even a younger brother, of a Thomas Tone who was buried in Dublin on 7 March 1716/17 and

3. Jonathan Tone (1754?-92), farmer at Bodenstown, later lieut, 22nd foot; resumed farming 1789; d. Sept. 1792 unm. at Cassumsize, par. Bodenstown, Co. Kildare

4. Mary m. John Dunbavin (d. *a.* Sept. 1792)[1] and was presumably mother of William Dunbavin of Bodenstown who v. prob. m. 1795 Frances Wills[2] and who d. 1830 (*recte* 1840?) at 65 High St., Dublin, leaving three daus[3] and one son, Nicholas (fl. 1847), a builder,[4] who m. and had a son Thomas

5. Ann who m. — Wills and had a dau. Frances who prob. m. 1795 William Dunbavin (see preceding)[5]

6. —— m. 'a Mr Clarendon of the County Meath'[6] and by him had two sons

PETER TONE (d. 1805), coach-builder in Dublin, later a farmer at Bodenstown, Co. Kildare, eventually an inspector of globes in Dublin, m. *c.*1761 Margaret (née Lamport), dau. prob. of James Lamport (d. 1747/8), a sea captain of Drogheda; he d. Aug. 1805 having had by his wife (who d. 1818) four sons and two daughters namely

1. Theobald Wolfe Tone (of whom more presently)

2. William Henry Tone (1764–1802), private in East India Co. army and later an officer in service of various Indian rulers; b. Aug. 1764, killed in battle in India mid 1802 and bur. at Poona

3. Mathew Tone (1769?-98), commissioned in the French army and served on Humbert's expedition, captured at Ballinamuck and hanged in Dublin, 29 Sept. 1798; d. unm. but left an illeg. dau. (fl. 1810)

---

who was possibly Thomas Tone, the son of Hugh and Sarah Tone who was baptised in Dublin on 12 February 1682 (*The register of S. Catherine, Dublin, 1636-1715*, ed. Herbert Wood (Dublin, 1908), p. 42; *The register of the parish of S. Peter and S. Kevin, Dublin, 1669-1761*, ed. James Mills (Dublin, 1911), p. 214). This connexion is made without qualification by Gustave Anjou, who gives more detail of Hugh Tone's family but does not state all his sources and has been accused of forging genealogies (see above, p. 488, n. 1).

[1] Jonathan Tone in his will dated 20 Sept. 1792 refers to 'my sister Mary Dunbavin, otherwise Tone, widow of John Dunbavin deceased' (see above, vol. III, p. 471).

[2] Deed of marriage between William Dunbavin and Frances Wills dated 25 Jan. 1795 (T. U. Sadleir, 'The family of Tone' in *County Kildare Archaeological Society Journal*, xii, no. 7 (1943), pp 326-9).

[3] One of the daus was a Mrs Moore residing in the early 1840s at 147 Abbey St., Dublin, another was a Mrs Bull residing then at Simmon's Court, Donnybrook, both of whom gave Madden family information. Another dau. m. — Dunnan and by him had a son William living 1847 in Francis St. 'in great indigence' and who later, to Madden's belief, 'was an inmate of a poorhouse in Dublin' (*United Irishmen*, 3rd ser. (1846), i, 121; ibid., 2nd ed., ii (1858), pp 160-62).

[4] Nicholas, identified as William's son, was residing at 65 High St. in the late 1840s (Madden, *United Irishmen*, 2nd ed., ii (1858), p. 160). He is listed in *Thom's Irish Almanac*, mid 1840s, as a builder of New Bride St.

[5] Deed of marriage between Dunbavin and Frances Wills (see above, n. 2). It is stated in the deed that Frances's mother Anne is sister to Peter Tone. This would make William Dunbavin and Frances Wills first-cousins, their mothers being sisters, as well as first-cousins to T. W. Tone.

[6] Madden, *United Irishmen*, 2nd ed., ii (1858), i, 160, fn.

4. Arthur Tone (b. Feb. or Mar. 1782), seaman in Dutch and American navies; he was still living in 1811
5. Mary Tone (b. *c.*1775?), who m. 29 Jan. 1797, in Hamburg, Jean Frédéric Giauque, a merchant formerly of Neuchâtel, Switzerland, by whom she had a son; she accompanied her husband in or after 1799 to Saint-Domingue, West Indies, where she d. shortly afterwards
6. Fanny Tone (1784?-92)[1]

THEOBALD WOLFE TONE (1763–98), barrister, publicist, French army officer and diarist, b. prob. 20 June 1763 in Dublin; he m. 21 July 1785, at St Ann's Ch., Dublin, Martha or Matilda (1769–1849), b. 17 June 1769, second dau. in the family of two sons and five daus of William Witherington (d. *a.*1802) of Dublin, merchant, and his wife Catherine (d. 18 Apr. 1797), dau. of Edward Fanning (1709–91), clergyman, by his wife Joanna (née French) (d. May 1776). Counsellor Tone and his family went to the United States of America 1795, Tone went on to France 1796, his family joining him 1797. Mrs Tone m. secondly 19 Aug. 1816, in Paris, Thomas Wilson (b. 1758) of Dullatur, Lanarkshire, Scotland, advocate and merchant, whom she accompanied to America and who d. 27 June 1824.[2] T. W. Tone d. from a self-inflicted wound in Dublin Barracks 19 Nov. 1798 having had by his wife, who d. 18 Mar. 1849 at Georgetown, District of Columbia, three sons and one daughter namely,

1. Richard Tone (b. 1787 or 1789), who d. an infant
2. William Theobald Wolfe Tone (who alone reached adulthood and of whom more presently)
3. Francis Rawdon Tone (1793–1806), known as Frank, b. prob. at Bodenstown, 23 June 1793; he d. in Paris of tuberculosis
4. Maria Tone (1786–1803), b. at Bodenstown; she d. Apr. 1803 in Paris of tuberculosis

WILLIAM THEOBALD WOLFE TONE (1791–1828), French and American army officer, was b. 29 Apr. 1791 in Dublin; served in Napoleon's Grand Army (nom-de-guerre 'Le Petit Loup') and wrote account of campaign in Germany etc.; went to America 1816, commissioned in U.S. army 1819; disappointed at his progress he resigned 31 Dec. 1826; edited, under his mother's supervision, his father's literary remains, published as *Life of Theobald Wolfe Tone*, May 1826; he m. 17 Sept. 1825, at New York, Catherine Anne (b. Sept. 1796?) only dau. of William Sampson (1764–1836), barrister, and his wife Grace (1764?–1855), dau. of John Clarke of Belfast, physician; she d. 16 Dec. 1864 at Brooklyn,

---

[1] Dickason (Tone) papers, Matilda Tone to Catherine Anne Tone, 1 Aug., 22 Dec. 1829, cited in Marianne Elliott, *Wolfe Tone* (New Haven, 1989), pp 194, 424, n. 12, 443, n. 14.
[2] For Thomas Wilson, see Jane Rendall and C. J. Woods, 'The unravelling of a mystery: Thomas Wilson (1758–1824) of Dullatur, the Scottish second husband of Matilda Tone' (to be published).

New York; T.W.T. Tone d. 10 or 11 Oct. 1828 (of an intestinal disorder) at Georgetown having had by his wife one child, a daughter,

GRACE GEORGIANA MAXWELL (née Tone) (1827–1900) of Brooklyn, New York, b. 28 May 1827, m. 19 June 1851 Lascelles Edward Maxwell, a native of Belfast whose Maxwell ancestors came from Portaferry, Co. Down, and by him had seven children; she became, after her mother's death (1864), custodian of the Tone and Sampson family papers, which passed after her own death (29 Mar. 1900) to her eldest child,

KATHERINE ANNE MAXWELL (1853?–1922?), later of Ossining, New York, who contrib. an article on the Tone family to *Notes and Queries* (1920) and d. *c.*1922 having bequeathed a bust of Tone and some of the Tone papers (MSS 2041–50) to T.C.D. (received July 1923). Miss Maxwell's niece, dau. of Mrs Grace Maxwell's eldest son Lascelles Chester Maxwell (1857–1932),

KATHERINE HOGG DICKASON (née Maxwell) (1903–95) of Short Hills, New Jersey, b. 20 Aug. 1903, m. Livingston T. Dickason and by him had three daus; she presented more of the Tone papers (MSS 3805–7) to T.C.D. (July 1964). Mrs Dickason d. 20 Sept. 1995 aged 92. The Tone papers still remaining in America are now held by a granddaughter, Mrs Katherine or Kit Prendergast (née Goodale) of Stillwater, Minnesota, second dau. of Mrs Dickason's second dau., also Katherine.

Chronology of Theobald Wolfe Tone

1763	
June 20	Theobald Wolfe Tone born in Dublin

1769	
June 16	Birth of future wife, Matilda Witherington

1770	
April	Aged 6 attends performance of Bickerstaff's *Lionel and Clarissa*

1773	
April	Gains premiums at Darling's Academy

1781	
February 19	Enters Trinity College, Dublin

1783	
August 8	Acts part in two plays at Galway

1785	
July 25	Marries Matilda Witherington

1786	
February 28	Graduates B.A. at Trinity College
	Daughter Maria born
October 19	Burglary at his father's house at Bodenstown

1787	
January	Arrives in London to read for the bar; admitted to Middle Temple (3 February)

1788	
August	First proposes establishment of military colony in Pacific
December 23	Returns to Ireland from London

1789	
June	Called to Irish bar
July 1	Addresses College Historical Society from chair

1790	
April	Publishes pamphlet, *A review of the conduct of administration*
June	Publishes second pamphlet, *Spanish war*
July	Makes acquaintance of Thomas Russell
August	Stays with family and Russell beside the sea at Irishtown
September	Renews proposal for military colony in Pacific

1790 contd
November   Publishes novel, *Belmont Castle*
December?   Forms 'kind of political club'

1791
April 9   Son William Tone born
July 9   Writes politically compromising letter to Russell
August   Publishes pamphlet, *An argument on behalf ot the catholics*
October 12–27   First visit to Belfast; attends formation of society of
                  United Irishmen (25th)
November 7   Present at preliminary meeting of Dublin Society of
                  United Irishmen

1792
July   Appointed assistant secretary of Catholic Committee
July 10–17   Second visit to Belfast
August 7–20   Visits Drogheda, Newry, Belfast etc. on Catholic
                  Committee business
October 5–10   Visits Connaught on Catholic Committee business
December 3–10   Catholic Convention meets in Dublin

1793
January   Accompanies Catholic delegates in London
February 8   Last extant entry in diary made in Ireland
April 16–25   Catholic Convention meets again
June 23   Son Francis Rawdon born (dies aged 12 or 13 in 1806)
July 10   Denounced by Lord Chancellor Fitzgibbon in Irish house
                  of lords
autumn   Writes memoranda on Irish politics
December   Spends Christmas at Bodenstown with Russell as his guest

1794
April   Compromised in Jackson affair
May 23   Papers of Dublin society of United Irishmen seized by
                  government

1795
January 3   Arrival in Ireland of reforming viceroy, Earl Fitzwilliam
February mid   Recall of Fitzwilliam
March early   Accompanies Catholic delegates to London
April 23   Trial of William Jackson for treason; complicity of Tone
                  exposed
June 14   Sails from Belfast for America
August 1   Disembarks at Wilmington, Delaware
August *c*.8   Visits French ambassador at Philadelphia

1795 contd

October late	Contemplates signing deeds for purchase of farm near Princeton, New Jersey
October or November	Receives letters from Ireland on changing political situation
November late	Decides to go to France
December 16	Arrives in New York and books passage; sails from Sandy Hook (1 January)

1796

February 1	Disembarks at Le Havre
February 12	Arrives in Paris
February 24	Makes acquaintance of Lazare Carnot at Palais du Luxembourg
March–May	Sees sights and attends opera in Paris
June 10	Completes first of several manifestos to Irish people
July 12	Makes acquaintance of Lazare Hoche
July 16	Decree of Directory commissioning Tone *chef de brigade* in French army (from 19 June)
August 7– September *c*.28	Writes autobiography
September 17	Leaves Paris for Brest to embark for Ireland
October 29	Learns of arrest of Thomas Russell; arrives at Brest later same day
November	*An address to the people of Ireland on the present important crisis*
December 16	Sails out of Brest Harbour
December 22–9	In Bantry Bay on board *Indomptable*

1797

January 12	Arrives in Paris after disembarking at Brest
Feb. or March	Appointed by Directory to serve in army of Sambre-et-Meuse as adjoint to Hoche
April–June	Service in Rhineland and Batavian Republic
April 26–9	First visit to the Hague
May 7	Reunited with wife and children at Groninguen in northern Holland
June 1–13	At Friedberg in Hesse
July 8–Sept. 3	On board *Vryheid* at the Texel; revisits the Hague (20–29 Aug.)
September 19	Present at death of Lazare Hoche at Wetzlar
December 21	Makes acquaintance of Napoléon Bonaparte in Paris

1798
March 25   Receives letters of service as adjutant-general in 'army of
                  England'
April 5–June 22   Stationed in Normandy
June 18   Learns of outbreak of insurrection in Ireland
June 30   Final extant entry in diary
July   Apparently in Paris awaiting orders
August 1   Arrives at Brest to embark for Ireland
September 16   Leaves Brest on board *Hoche* for Ireland
October 12   Naval battle off Lough Swilly; *Hoche* disabled and captured
November 3   Arrested after disembarking at Buncrana, Co. Donegal
November 5–8   Final journey to Dublin
November 10   Tried by court martial in Dublin and sentenced to death
November 19   Dies of throat wound in Dublin Barracks; burial at
                  Bodenstown, Co. Kildare (21 or 22 November)

1803
April   Death of daughter Maria in Paris aged 17 or 18

1805
August   Burial of Peter Tone at Bodenstown; large attendance

1807
autumn?   Visit of Matilda Tone to America in search of Tone's
                  papers

1813
January 30   Commission of William Tone as *cornet* in Napoleon's army

1816
August 19   Marriage of Matilda Tone to Thomas Wilson

1826
May   Publication of *Life of Theobald Wolfe Tone . . . edited by his
                  son William* (Washington)

1828
October 10 or 11 Death of William Tone, only surviving child of T. W. Tone

1843
autumn?   Visit of Thomas Davis to Tone's grave at Bodenstown

1849
March 18   Death of Matilda Tone-Wilson at Georgetown, District of
                  Columbia

Bibliography of Theobald Wolfe Tone

THIS bibliography consists of (a) writings by Theobald Wolfe Tone, writings about him and writings by or about other members of the Tone family; (b) other primary sources reproduced, quoted or cited above by T. W. Moody, R. B. McDowell and C. J. Woods in editing Tone's writings or other contemporary documents; (c) a large selection of secondary works cited above and considered to be of wider interest; (d) a few other historical works bearing on Tone's background or career but not cited above; (e) literary works from which Tone quotes or with which, from other evidence, he was familiar.

1. Bibliographies

[O'Reilly, Vincent F.?]. Books from the libraries of Theobald Wolfe Tone and William Sampson added to the society's collection. In *The Recorder: Bulletin of the American Irish Historical Society*, ii, no. 3 (Feb. 1924), pp 5–15.
These books, among which were Sampson's own set of the *Northern Star*, 4 Jan. 1792 to 30 Dec. 1796, were held by the society but are no longer to be found.

Simms, Samuel. A select bibliography of the United Irishmen, 1791–8. In *Irish Historical Studies*, i, no. 2 (Sept. 1938), pp 158–80.
Printed sources only.

MacManus, M. J. Bibliography of Theobald Wolfe Tone. In *Dublin Magazine*, xv, no. 3 (July–Sept. 1940), pp 52–64.
Analytical bibliography of published writings by Tone. Repr. as pamphlet, Dublin, Thom, 1940, 15pp.

Elliott, Marianne. Partners in revolution: the United Irishmen and France. New Haven & London, 1982.

> Bibliography, pp 373–402. Lists MS sources and unpublished theses as well as printed sources.

Whelan, Kevin. A check-list of publications on the 1790s, the United Irishmen and the 1798 rebellion, 1900–2002. In Thomas Bartlett et al. (eds), *1798: a bicentenary perspective* (Dublin, 2003), pp 659–724.

> Limited to Irish politics in the 1790s but includes editions of sources and unpublished theses as well as books and articles.

Woods, C. J. The contemporary editions of Tone's *Argument on behalf of the catholics*. In *Irish Booklore*, ii, no. 2 (1976), pp 217–26.

Madden, R. R. The United Irishmen: their lives and times. 2nd ed., vol. ii (Dublin, 1858).

> 'Literary productions of T. W. Tone', pp 146–8.

O'Kelley, Francis. Wolfe Tone's novel. In *Irish Book Lover*, xxiii, no. 2 (Mar.–Apr. 1935), pp 47–8.

> On *Belmont Castle*.

2. Writings by Tone published during his lifetime

A review of the conduct of administration during the seventh session of parliament addressed to the constitutional electors and free people of Ireland . . . By an Independent Whig. Dublin: Byrne, 1790. Pp iv, 59

> Another ed., Belfast, no name, 1790.

Spanish war!: an enquiry how far Ireland is bound of right to embark in the impending contest on the side of Great Britain . . . By Hibernicus. Dublin: Byrne, 1790. Pp ii, 44.

Belmont Castle; or suffering sensibility containing the genuine and interesting correspondence of several persons of fashion. [By Theobald Wolfe Tone, Richard Jebb and John Radcliffe]. Dublin: Byrne, 1790. Pp 223.

> Ch. 8 and other chapters are identified in Marion Deane (ed.), *Belmont Castle* (Dublin, 1998), as being the work of Tone.

Catholics: an argument on behalf of the catholics of Ireland . . . addressed to the people, and more particularly to the protestants, of Ireland. By a Northern Whig. Dublin: Byrne, 1791. Pp iv, 44.

> Another ed., [Belfast?], no name, 1791. A so-called 5th ed., Dublin, no name, 1792, has Tone's name in full on title-page.

Prospectus of the *National Journal*. [Dublin: Chambers, 1791].

> Copy in P.R.O., HO 100/34, f. 9.

The declaration, resolutions and constitution of the societies of United Irishmen. [Dublin?, 1792?]. Pp 2.
 No title-page. Copy in R.I.A., Charlemont papers, MS 12/R/16.

Nimrod to the gentlemen of the Down hunt—I, a. 4 February 1792. In *Northern Star*, 4 February 1792.

Nimrod to the gentlemen of the Down hunt—II, 14 February 1792. In *Northern Star*, 15 February 1792.

Resolutions of the Society of United Irishmen of Dublin, 24–5 February 1792.
 Copy in Nat. Arch. (Ire.), Rebellion papers, 620/19/62; also in *Hibernian Journal*, 17 February 1792, p. 1.

Notice of a meeting of the Society of United Irishmen of Dublin on 9 March 1792.
 Copy in Nat. Arch. (Ire.), Rebellion papers, 620/53/197.

Notice of a meeting of the Society of United Irishmen of Dublin on 16 March 1792.
 Copy in Nat. Arch. (Ire.), Rebellion papers, 620/19/70.

Notice of a meeting of the Society of United Irishmen of Dublin on 27 March 1792.
 Copy in Nat. Arch. (Ire.), Rebellion papers, 620/19/72.

Notice of a meeting of the Society of United Irishmen of Dublin on 25 April 1792.
 Copy in Nat. Arch. (Ire.), Rebellion papers, 620/19/78.

X.Y. to the editor of the *Northern Star*, 13 July 1792. In *Northern Star*, 14 July 1792, p. 3.

[Tone?] to the Peep o'Day Boys and Defenders, 18 July 1792. In *Northern Star*, 25 July 1792.
 Not positively identified as by Tone but prob. same as *Address to the Defenders*, mentioned in vol. I, p. 229.

X.Y. to the editor of the *Northern Star*, 23 July 1792. In *Northern Star*, 28 July 1792.

To the grand jury of the city and county of Londonderry for the summer assizes 1792. By Vindex. 8 August 1792.
 Copy in library of Queen's University of Belfast; also in *Northern Star*, 11 August 1792.

A Derry farmer to the editor of the *Northern Star*, 15 August 1792. In *Northern Star*, 15 August 1792, p. 3.

X.Y. to the editors of the *Belfast News Letter* and the *Northern Star*, 23 August 1792. In *Belfast News Letter*, 28 August 1792, p. 1; *Northern Star*, 29 August 1792, p. 4.

John Keogh and Tone to the Friends of Peace and Harmony at Newry, 31 August 1792. In *Northern Star*, 5 September 1792, p. 3.

Short guide to the constitution of America, *c*. 6 September 1792. In *Northern Star*, 8 September 1792.

A protestant freeman of Dublin to the corporation of Dublin — I, [15 September 1792]. In *Hibernian Journal*, 21 September 1792, p. 4.

X.Y. to the editor of the *Northern Star*, 20 or 21 September 1792. In *Northern Star*, 22 September 1792, p. 3.

A protestant freeman of Dublin to the corporation of the city of Dublin — II, [23 September 1792]. In *Hibernian Journal*, 24 September 1792, p. 4.

Senex to the printer of the *Hibernian Journal*, [24 September 1792]. In *Hibernian Journal*, 5 October 1992, p. 4.

Declaration of the catholics of the county of Louth, [5 October 1992]. In *Northern Star*, 24 October 1792, p. 3.

Declaration of the catholics of the county of Down, [5 October 1792]. In *Northern Star*, 7 November 1792, p. 3.

Resolutions for the Northern Whig Club, [29 October 1792]. In *Northern Star*, 7 November 1792, p. 3.

To the manufacturers of Dublin. By a Liberty Weaver. March 1793.
    Copy in Nat. Arch. (Ire.), Rebellion papers, 620/20/12.

Society of United Irishmen of Dublin to the people of Ireland, 3 March 1793. In *Society of United Irishmen of Dublin established November IX, MDCCXCI* (Dublin, 1794), pp 74–80.

To the militia of Ireland. By Sarsfield. [1796].
    Copy in Archives Nationales, Paris, Archives du Directoire Exécutif, AF III 186 B, dossier 859.

To the Irishmen now serving aboard the British navy. [1796].
    Copies in Archives Nationales, Paris, Directoire Exécutif, AF III 186 B, dossier 859, and Tone (Dickason) MSS.

Proclamation to the French army intended to effect the Irish revolution. [1796].
    Copy in Tone (Dickason) MSS.

An address to the peasantry of Ireland. By a Traveller. [1796]. Pp 13.
    Copy in Archives Nationales, Paris, Directoire Exécutif, AF III 186 B, dossier 859.

An address to the people of Ireland on the present important crisis. [Brest], 1796. Pp 39.
    Copy in Archives Nationales, Paris, Directoire Exécutif, AF III 186 B, dossier 859.

Address of General Hardy to the United Irishmen, [1798].
Copies in Tone (Dickason) MSS and T.C.D., Tone papers, MS 2050, ff 36, 39.

3. Writings by Tone published since his death

An address to the people of Ireland on the present important crisis. Belfast,
1796 [*recte* 1799]. Pp iv, 28.
No printer or publisher stated. Year of publication probably stated falsely.

Auto-biography of Theobald Wolfe Tone. In *New Monthly Magazine*, xi
(July–Dec. 1824), pp 1–11, 336–47, 417–23, 537–48.
The *New Monthly Magazine* was edited by Thomas Campbell and published by
Henry Colburn in London. Omissions include many names. Some original informa-
tion, partly at least inaccurate, in editorial matter.

Life of Theobald Wolfe Tone, founder of the United Irish society and adjutant
general and chef de brigade in the service of the French and Batavian republics,
written by himself and . . . edited by his son William Theobald Wolfe Tone.
2 vols: i, pp vii, 565, portr.; ii, pp 674. Washington: Gales & Seaton, 1826.
The most complete edition; based on Tone MSS.

Memoirs of Theobald Wolfe Tone written by himself . . . Edited by his son
William Theobald Wolfe Tone. 2 vols: i, pp xvi, 422, portr.; ii, pp 453. London:
Henry Colburn, 1827.
Omits pamphlets.

The life of Theobald Wolfe Tone written by himself . . . Edited by his son William
Theobald Wolfe Tone. London: Hunt & Clarke, 1828. Pp x, 347.
Autobiography, extracts from diaries for 1796–8, William Tone's editorial matter.

The life of Theobald Wolfe Tone written by himself and extracted from his jour-
nals from the American edition of his life and works. Edited by his son William
Theobald Wolfe Tone. London: Whittaker, Treacher & Arnot, 1831. Pp x, 347.
Reprint of Hunt & Clarke's edition with new preface.

The life of Theobald Wolfe Tone, the founder of the 'united Irishmen', written
by himself and extracted from his journals . . . Dublin: James McCormick,
[1846]. Pp 142. (National Library for Ireland—IX)
Autobiography and William Tone's 'Continuation' only.

Extracts from the journals of Theobald Wolfe Tone during his mission to
France . . . Dublin: James McCormick, [1846]. Pp 144. (National Library for
Ireland—X)

Life and adventures of Theobald Wolfe Tone written by himself and extracted
from his journals. Edited by his son William Theobald Wolfe Tone. Glasgow:
Cameron & Ferguson, [1876]. Pp 240.
Contains autobiography, diaries for 1796–8 and William's editorial matter.

Reissued by Washbourne, Glasgow, 19—, and by Burns, Oates & Washbourne, London, [19—].

The autobiography of Theobald Wolfe Tone, 1763–1798. Edited by R. Barry O'Brien. 2 vols: i, pp xxxi, 321; ii, pp 430. London: T. Fisher & Unwin, 1893.
    Autobiography, all the diaries, memoranda of Feb. 1796 and William Tone's continuation of life, index.
    2nd ed., Dublin, Maunsell, vol. i (n.d.): pp xxxi, 321, vol. ii (1910): pp 430. Another ed., London, Unwin, vol. i (1912): pp 354, vol. ii (1912), pp 438.

The Spanish war. Dublin: Cumann na mBan, 1915. Pp 20. (National Series no. 2)

The life of Wolfe Tone written by himself and completed by his son together with extracts from his political writings. Abridged and edited by Bulmer Hobson. Dublin: Martin Lester [1920]. Pp 152.
    Autobiography and extracts from diaries and pamphlets.
    Reissued by Talbot Press, Dublin and Cork, n.d., and by Educational Co. of Ireland, Dublin, n.d.

The letters of Wolfe Tone. Edited by Bulmer Hobson. Dublin: Martin Lester, [1920]. Pp 165.
    Taken from *Life* (1826) and from T.C.D., Sirr, Madden and Courts-martial papers.

Beatha Theobald Wolfe Tone mar do fríth 'na scríbhinní féin agus i scríbhinní a mhic agus ar n-a thionntódh go Gaedhilg do Phádraig Ó Siochfhrada. Baile Átha Cliath: Oifig Díolta Foillseacháin Rialtais, 1932. Pp xvi, 716.
    Irish translation. Reissued, 1937.

Patriot adventurer: extracts from the memoirs and journals of Theobald Wolfe Tone . . . Edited by Denis Ireland. London: Rich & Cowan, 1936. Pp x, 228.

The autobiography of Theobald Wolfe Tone. Abridged and edited by Sean O'Faolain. London: T. Nelson, 1937. Pp 307.
    Based on T.C.D., Tone papers.

Tone got the wrong parcel. By Joseph W. Hammond. In *Irish Press*, 3 October 1955, p. 6.
    Tone to John Chambers, 13 and 17 Oct. 1791.

Tone writes to Russell: Washington as a famous exile saw him. By J. W. Hammond. In *Irish Press*, 4 October 1955, p. 6, 5 October, p. 6.
    Tone to Thomas Russell, 1 Sept. 1795.

The mind of Tone. In *Irish Times*, 20, 21, 22, 23, 24, 25, 27 and 28 June 1966.
    Extracts from autobiography and diaries with illustrations.

An argument on behalf of the catholics of Ireland. Cork: Connolly Books, 1969. Pp 40.

Wolfe Tone letter, 1795. Edited by J. J. St Mark. In *Éire-Ireland*, vi, no. 4 (winter 1971), pp 15–16.
    Tone to Pierre-Auguste Adet, Aug. 1795.

The best of Tone. Edited by Proinsias Mac Aonghusa and Liam Ó Réagáin. Cork: Mercier Press, 1972. Pp 192.
Extracts.

Freedom the Wolfe Tone way. Edited by Seán Cronin and Richard Roche; with an introduction by Jack Bennett. Tralee: Anvil Books, 1973. Pp 242.
Extracts.

Un argomento in difesa dei cattolici d'Irlanda. Edited by Manuela Ceretta. Milan: Guerini, 1998. Pp 108.
Italian translation of *Argument on behalf of the catholics* with much editorial matter.

Belmont Castle; or suffering sensibility. By Theobald Wolfe Tone & divers hands. Edited by Marion Deane. Dublin: Lilliput Press, 1998. Pp iv, 143.

Life of Theobald Wolfe Tone compiled and arranged by William Theobald Wolfe Tone. Edited by Thomas Bartlett. Dublin: Lilliput Press, 1998. Pp lii, 1002.
Reprint of 1826 ed. with reinsertion of some suppressed matter and addition of index.

The writings of Theobald Wolfe Tone, 1763–98. Edited by T. W. Moody, R. B. McDowell and C. J. Woods. 3 vols: i (1998), pp xl, 540; ii (2001), pp xviii, 435; iii (2007), pp xxvi, 599. Oxford: Clarendon Press, 1998–2007.

4. Writings on Tone

THIS section consists of books, pamphlets and articles wholly or largely about Tone. Some of the items listed are of purely historiographical interest. For treatment of Tone as part of larger works, see below (sections 8, 11 and 12), and for writings relating to the Tone family or to other members of it, see below (section 13).

Bartlett, Thomas. The burden of the present?: Theobald Wolfe Tone, republican and separatist. In David Dickson et al., *The United Irishmen: republicanism, radicalism and rebellion* (Dublin, 1993), pp 1–15.

Bartlett, Thomas. Theobald Wolfe Tone. Dundalk: Dundalgan Press, 1997. Pp vii, 89. (Historical Association of Ireland Life and Times series no. 10)

Bartlett, Thomas. Theobald Wolfe Tone: an eighteenth-century republican and separatist. In *Republic*, ii (2001), pp 38–46.

Bartlett, Thomas. Theobald Wolfe Tone. In Mary Cullen (ed.), *1798: 200 years of resonance* (Dublin, 1998), pp 55–62

Birrell, Augustine. Wolfe Tone. In *Contemporary Review*, lxv (Jan.–June 1894), pp 46–57.
A review of R. Barry O'Brien's edition of Tone's writings.

Boyd, Andrew. Wolfe Tone, republican hero or whig opportunist? In *History Today*, xlviii, no. 6 (June 1998), pp 14–21.

Boylan, Henry. Theobald Wolfe Tone. Dublin: Gill & Macmillan, 1981. Pp 145. (Gill's Irish Lives)

Boyle, John. Citizen Tone. In *Threshold*, i, no. 4 (winter 1957), pp 30–38.
    Literary influences on Tone.

Brady, Séamus. Wolfe Tone and Donegal. In *Donegal Annual: Journal of the County Donegal Historical Society*, i, no. 2 (1948), pp 129–32.

Burtchaell, G. D. Theobald Wolfe Tone and the College Historical Society. In *Journal of the Royal Society of Antiquaries of Ireland*, xviii (1887–8), pp 391–9.

Campbell, J. D. S., 9th duke of Argyll. The story of a conspirator. In *Nineteenth Century*, xxvii (Jan.-June 1890), pp 730–55, 1001–25.

Cazotte, Jacques de. Irlande entre indépendance et révolution: Wolfe Tone, 1763–1798, Edward Fitzgerald, 1763–1798. Paris: Maisonneuve & Larose, 2005, Pp 206.

Cooper, Bryan. A rebel's diary. In *Cornhill Magazine*, new ser., xlix (July–Dec. 1920), pp 490–501.

Costello, Con. Wolfe Tone and Naas. In *Journal of the County Kildare Archaeological Society*, xiv, no. 4 (1969), p. 361.
    Followed up by idem, 'Query: Wolfe Tone's house' in ibid., p. 376.

Costello, Con. Wolfe Tone and his local connections. In *Leinster Leader*, 18 June 1983.
    Repr. in Costello, *Looking back: aspects of history, Co. Kildare* (Naas, 1988), pp 87–8.

Cox, Gerard S. Tone: murder or suicide? In Coiste Cuimhneacháin 1798, *1798: essays in commemoration* (Dublin, [1948]), pp 25–7.

Cronin, Seán. Wolfe Tone. Dublin: Dublin Directory Wolfe Tone Bi-Centenary, 1963. Pp 52.

Curtin, Nancy J. The Belfast uniform: Theobald Wolfe Tone. In *Éire-Ireland*, xx, no. 2 (summer 1985), pp 40–69.

De Blacam, Aodh. The life story of Wolfe Tone set in a picture of his times. Dublin: Talbot Press, 1935. Pp 225.
    Serialised in *Wolfe Tone Weekly*, 1937–8.

De Blacam, Aodh. Wolfe Tone, man of Dublin. In Coiste Cuimhneacháin 1798, *1798: essays in commemoration* (Dublin, [1948]), pp 16–22.

De Faoite, Ailfrid, Theobald Wolfe Tone: the man and his work. Dublin: Davis Publishing Co. [1920?]. Pp 16.

Davis, Thomas, *pseud.* The Celt. Tone's grave. In *Nation*, 25 November 1843, p. 104.
Romanticised account, in verse, of visit to Bodenstown. Many repr.

Dunne, Tom. Theobald Wolfe Tone, colonial outsider: an analysis of his political philosophy. Cork: Tower Books, 1982. Pp 77.
Reviewed critically by Marianne Elliott in *Irish Historical Studies*, xxiii, no. 92 (Nov. 1983), pp 376–8. Repr., 1984.

Dunne, Tom. 'In the service of the republic': Wolfe Tone in Bantry Bay. In John A. Murphy (ed.), *The French are in the bay: the expedition to Bantry Bay, 1796* (Cork: Mercier, 1997), pp 73–84.

Elliott, Marianne. The United Irishman as diplomat. In P. J. Corish (ed.), *Radicals, rebels and establishments: Historical Studies XV* (Belfast, Appletree Press, 1985), pp 69–90.
Mainly about Tone as a representative abroad of the United Irishmen.

Elliott, Marianne. Wolfe Tone, prophet of Irish independence. New Haven & London: Yale, 1989. Pp xii, 492, illus.

Elliott, Marianne. A different Tone. In *Fortnight*, no. 279 (Dec. 1989), p. 13.

Elliott, Marianne. Wolfe Tone and the development of a revolutionary culture in Ireland. In L. Bergeron and L. M. Cullen (eds), *Culture et pratiques politiques en France et en Irlande, XVIe-XVIIIe siècle: actes du colloque de Marseille, 28 sept.–2 oct. 1988* (Paris, Centre de Recherches Historiques, 1991), pp 171–86.

Elliott, Marianne. Wolfe Tone and the republican ideal. In Cathal Póirtéir (ed.), *The great Irish rebellion of 1798* (Cork and Dublin, 1998), pp 49–57

Fitzgerald, Sean. Wolfe Tone and Bantry Bay. In *Bantry Historical Society Journal*, i (1991), pp 54–65

Gibbons, Luke. Where Wolfe Tone's statue was not: Joyce, monuments and mourning. In Ian McBride (ed.), *History, memory and Irish culture* (Cambridge, 2001), pp 139–59.

Gogan, L. S. Death of Tone. In Coiste Cuimhneacháin 1798, *1798: essays in commemoration* (Dublin, [1948]), pp 22–4.

Graham, Harry. The first of the Fenians. In *Edinburgh Review*, ccxvi, no. 442 (Oct. 1912), pp 321–39.
Repr. in author's *Splendid failures* (London, 1913), pp 1–30.

Greaves, C. Desmond. Theobald Wolfe Tone and the Irish nation. London: Connolly Publications, 1963, Pp 32.
Repr., 1989.

Hammond, J. W. Tone's throat wound. In *Dublin Evening Mail*, 8 July 1944, p. 2.

Hardy, W. J. A born rebel. In *Blackwood's Magazine*, clxxxix, no. 1148 (June 1911), pp 772–87.

Hayes, Richard. The first republican as catholic champion. In *Irish Press*, 20 June 1932.

Hone, Joseph M. Wolfe Tone. In *Dublin Magazine*, viii, no. 4 (Oct.–Dec. 1933), pp 33–41.

Jacob, Rosamond. Tone and the Catholic Committee. In Coiste Cuimhneacháin 1798, *1798: essays in commemoration* (Dublin, [1948]), pp 27–30.

Joannon, Pierre. Wolfe Tone in Paris, 1796–1797. In Patrick Rafroidi, Guy Fehlmann and Maitiu Mac Conmara (eds), *France-Ireland literary relations* (Lille & Paris, 1974), pp 83–107.

Joannon, Pierre. Theobald Wolfe Tone à Paris: conspirateur exilé ou ambassadeur incognito. In *Revue Cycnos* (Université de Nice), xv, no. 2 (1998), pp 5–18.

Johnson, Robert, *pseud.* Philip Roche Fermoy. A commentary on the Memoirs of Theobald Wolfe Tone, major general in the service of the republic of France, in which the moral and physical force of Ireland to support national independence is . . . examined. Paris: Firmin Didot, 1828. Pt 1. Pp xxxii, 178.
    No more published. 2nd ed., Dublin, McCormick, 1846. Despite its title, this book has little to say about Tone or his memoirs.

Kearney, Richard. Tone's French solution to an Irish problem. In *Irish Times*, 9 August 1989, p. 9.

Kelly, Richard J. An official record of the trial and death of Theobald Wolfe Tone. In *New Ireland Review*, x (1899), pp 305–8.
    Based on Howell's state trials, vol. xxii, 615–26. Part III of six-part series, 'Ideas of a republic', all of which contain significant mention of Tone.

Kelly, Seumas, *pseud.* Quidnunc. Wolfe Tone's wake. In *Irish Times*, 19 June 1944, p. 3.
    Followed by idem, 'Thomas or High Street' in ibid., 22 June 1944, p. 3.

Kiberd, Declan. Republican self-fashioning: the journal of Wolfe Tone. In Oonagh Walsh (ed.), *Ireland abroad: politics and professions in the nineteenth century* (Dublin, 2003), pp 16–35.

Kleinman, Sylvie. The accidental tourist: Theobald Wolfe Tone's secret mission to Paris, 1796. In Jane Conroy (ed.), *Cross-cultural travel: papers from the Royal Irish Academy Symposium on Literature and Travel at National University of Ireland, Galway, November 2002* (New York & London, 2003), pp 121–30.

Kleinman, Sylvie. Pardon my French: the linguistic trials and tribulations of Theobald Wolfe Tone. In Eamon Maher and Grace Neville (eds), *France-Ireland: anatomy of a relationship* (Frankfurt, 2004), pp 295–310.

Kleinman, Sylvie. Sorrow and celebration in the Paris diary of Theobald Wolfe Tone, 1796–1798. In Marie-Claire Considère-Charron, Philippe Laplace and Michel Savaric (eds), *The Irish celebrating: festive and tragic overtones* (Cambridge, 2008?).

Leask, Nigel. Irish republicans and gothic eleutherarchs: Pacific utopias in the writings of Theobald Wolfe Tone and Charles Brockden Brown. In *Huntingdon Library Quarterly*, lxiii (2000), pp 347–67.

Lynch, Bernadette. Wolfe Tone. In *Irish Universities History Students' Congress Bulletin*, iii (1958), pp 5–17.

MacArthur, C. W. The origin of an enduring myth: Wolfe Tone and Lord George Hill. In *Donegal Annual*, no. 54 (2002), pp 17–18.

McCabe, Leo. Wolfe Tone and the United Irishmen: for or against Christ (1791–1798)? London: Heath Cranton, 1937. Pp 258.
Vol. i; no more published.

McCann, Eamonn. What Tone really thought of the men of no property. In *Irish Times*, 18 June 1976.

McCann, Eamonn. What Wolfe Tone and the Ian Paisley of '69 have in common. In *Belfast Telegraph*, 7 December 2006.

MacCauley, J. A. Wolfe Tone: the last phase. In *Irish Sword*, xi (1973–4), pp 185–92.

MacDermot, Frank. Wolfe Tone and the catholics. In *Irish Independent*, 4 Oct. 1937.

MacDermot, Frank. The real Wolfe Tone. In *Ireland Today*, ii, no. 11 (Nov. 1937), pp 35–42.

MacDermot, Frank. Theobald Wolfe Tone: a biographical study. London: Macmillan, 1939. Pp xv, 342; pls 8.
Reviewed by T. W. Moody in *English Historical Review*, lv (1940), pp 316–18, and by R. B. McDowell in *Irish Historical Studies*, ii, no. 5 (Mar. 1940), pp 99–100. An unfavourable review by P. S. O'Hegarty in *Dublin Magazine*, new ser., xiv, no. 4 (Oct. 1939), pp 66–72, brought a reply from MacDermot in ibid., xv, no. 1 (Jan. 1940), pp 60–64.
New edition, paperback, retitled *Theobald Wolfe Tone and his times* (Tralee: Anvil Books, 1968, 306 pp).

MacDermot, Frank. A postscript on Tone. In *Studies*, xxviii (1939), pp 639–50.

MacDermot, Frank. A new life of Wolfe Tone. In *Ireland-American Review*, i (1939), pp 371–7.

MacDermot, Frank. Query: Wolfe Tone's house. In *Journal of the County Kildare Archaeological Society*, xiv, no. 4 (1969), p. 376.

McMahon, Seán. Wolfe Tone. Cork: Mercier Press, 2001. Pp 80.

MacManus, M. J. When Wolfe Tone wrote a novel. In *Irish Press*, Xmas 1934.

[MacManus, M. J.?]. Wolfe Tone's death-bed gift: historic relic presented to National Museum. In *Irish Press*, 25 Nov. 1936.

MacManus, M. J. The man who stole Wolfe Tone's books. In *Irish Press*, 1 July 1942, p. 2.

Marsden, John. The union of religious creeds: Theobald Wolfe Tone and the origins of the Irish republican tradition. In *Search*, xii (1994), pp 25–33.
Repr. in author's *Redemption in Irish history* (Dublin, 2005), pp 25–36.

Milligan, Alice L. Life of Theobald Wolfe Tone. Belfast: J. W. Boyd, 1898. Pp 122.
Includes note (pp 118–21) by Katherine Tone-Maxwell on Tone family.

Molony, J. C. Ireland's tragic comedians. Edinburgh & London: Blackwood, 1934.
Tone, pp 73–149.

Moriarty, Mary, & Sweeney, Catherine. Wolfe Tone. Dublin: O'Brien, 1988. Pp 64.

Ó Baoighealláin, Anraí. Wolfe Tone agus réabhlóid na Fraince. In *Comhar*, xlviii, no. 4 (Apr. 1989), pp 20–22.
Anglice Henry Boylan (see also above).

Ó Briain, Liam. Theobald Wolfe Tone in Galway. In *Irish Sword*, ii (1954–6), pp 228–9.

O'Cathaoir, Brendan. Mitchel letter throws new light on capture of Tone. In *Irish Times*, 30 May 1986, p. 5.
John Mitchel to John Blake Dillon, 17 Dec. 1845 (T.C.D., Dillon papers).

Ó Cuinneagáin, Seosamh. Lecture on the Tones in a decade of Irish history. Enniscorthy: Echo, 1970. Pp 36.
Anglice Joseph Cunningham (d. 1987).

[O'Donnell, F. H.]. More about the Wolfe Tone imposture: Wolfe Tone the informer; the Hoche legend. [Dublin, 1895]. Pp 12.

O'Donnell, Patrick. Wolfe Tone's death: suicide or assassination? In *Irish Medical News*, clxvi, no. 1 (Jan.-Mar. 1997), pp 57–9.

O'Faolain, Sean. Rebel by vocation. In *Bell*, xiii, no. 2 (Nov. 1946), pp 97–114.

Ó Grianna, Séamus. Lá an bhriste mhóir: sgéal Bholfe Tone ghá innsint ag 'Máire'. In *An Phoblacht*, 20 June 1931.

Ollivier, Sophie. Presence and absence of Wolfe Tone during the centenary commemoration of the 1798 rebellion. In L. M. Geary (ed.), *Rebellion and remembrance in modern Ireland* (Dublin, 2001), pp 175–84.

O'Sheehan, J. The story of Theobald Wolfe Tone. Dublin: Emton Press, [1925]. Pp 16.

P.H., *pseud.* Theobald Wolfe Tone. In *Faulkner's Dublin Journal*, 22, 24 and 29 November 1798.

'P.H.', who makes revelations about Tone in the early and mid 1780s, may have been Peter Holmes (1729?-1802), M.P. for Banagher and political associate of Richard Griffith.

Pearse, P. H. The separatist idea. Dublin: Whelan, 1916. Pp 20. (Tracts for the Times, no. 11).

On Tone's political ideas.

Pearse, P. H. Theobald Wolfe Tone: an address delivered at the grave of Wolfe Tone in Bodenstown churchyard, 22nd June 1913. In *How does she stand?: three addresses by P. H. Pearse* (Dublin, 1915), pp 1–7.

Repr. from *Gaelic American*.

Pernot-Deschamps, Maguy. Wolfe Tone, a Francophile at heart. In Eamon Maher and Grace Neville (eds), *France-Ireland: anatomy of a relationship* (Frankfurt, 2004), pp 287–93.

Plehn, Werner. Lexical polarities as linguistic reflexion of social life in Wolfe Tone's writings. In Dorothea Siegmund-Schultze (ed.), *Irland: Gesellschaft und Kultur VI* (Halle, 1989), pp 271–7.

Ponsonby, Arthur. Scottish and Irish diaries from the sixteenth to the nineteenth century. London, 1927.

Tone, pp 153–61.

Putnam, W., *pseud.(?)*. Theobald Wolfe Tone. In Séamus McKearney (ed.), *Ninety-eight: a booklet of short stories, biographies, articles and ballads . . . to commemorate . . . the insurrection of* 1798 (Belfast, [1948]), pp 16–20.

Quinn, James. Theobald Wolfe Tone and the historians. In *Irish Historical Studies*, xxxii, no. 125 (May 2000), pp 113–28.

Rivoallan, Anatole. Un patriote irlandais: Theobald Wolfe Tone (1763–1798). In *Annales de Bretagne*, lxxiv (1967), pp 279–97.

Scott, Marty. Wolfe Tone and the rhetoric of Irish nationalism. Unpublished M.A. thesis, University of North Carolina, 1992.

Sheehy, Edward. Tone and the United Irishmen. In *Ireland Today*, ii, no. 12 (Dec. 1937), pp 37–42.

Sherlock, William. Bodenstown graveyard: a place of Irish pilgrimage. In *Journal of the County Kildare Archaeological Society*, vi, no. 3 (July 1910), pp 223–9, illus.

Stone, George. Theobald Wolfe Tone and Irish nationalism. Unpublished M.A. thesis, Eastern Illinois University, 1964.

Thomas, D., *ed.* State trials: I—Treason and libel. London, 1972.

Ch. 4 deals with Tone's trial.

Tigges, Wim. Public, private and poetic: Wolfe Tone's autobiographical writings. In Joseph Leerssen, A. H. Van Der Weel and Bart Westerweel (eds), *Forging in the smithy: national identity and representation in Anglo-Irish literary history* (Amsterdam, 1993), pp 59–74.

Van Brock, F. W. A proposed Irish regiment and standard, 1796. In *Irish Sword*, xi (1973–4), pp 226–33.
Tone's proposals.

Wakeman, W. F. The grave of Theobald Wolfe Tone. In Wakeman, *Graves and monuments of illustrious Irishmen* (Dublin, [1887]), pp 22–4.
Series repr. from *Evening Telegraph* (Dublin), Oct.-Dec. 1886.

Walsh, Paul. Wolfe Tone and the Irish catholics. In *Irish Theological Quarterly*, xvii (1922), pp 1–11.

Woods, C. J. Tone's grave at Bodenstown: memorials and commemorations, 1798–1913. In Dorothea Siegmund-Schultze (ed.), *Irland: Gesellschaft und Kultur VI* (Halle, 1989), pp 138–48.
Under revision as 'Bodenstown revisited'.

Woods, C. J. Theobald Wolfe Tone and County Kildare. In William Nolan and Thomas McGrath (eds), *Kildare history and society* (Dublin, 2006), pp 387–98.

5. Manuscript sources

(a) Tone and Dickason papers

DUBLIN

National Library of Ireland

Tone papers (MS 3212)
A small, eclectic collection consisting partly of copies of documents held elsewhere.

McPeake papers (MS 36094)
Tone letters formerly owned by Brendan McPeake and purchased by N.L.I. in Dec. 1993.

Trinity College Library

Tone papers (MSS 2041–50, 3805–8), viz

Notebook 'C' (1787–93 and 1790–92, incl. Diaries, Apr. 1789 to July 1791), 10.5 x 19 cm, leather cover (MS 2041)

Diary 'E' (9 July to 4 Aug. 1792, 23 to 26 Aug. 1792), 19 x 12 cm (MS 2042)

Diary 'D' (7 to 20 Aug., 5 to 10 Oct. 1792), 11.5 x 19 cm, leather cover (MS 2043)

Diary 'F' (28 Aug. to 5 Oct. 1792, 11 Oct. to 20 Nov. 1792), 19 x 12 cm, marbled paper (MS 2044)

Diary fragments (Oct.–Nov. 1791, 21 Jan. to 8 Feb. 1793), 19.5 x 13 cm, brown cloth boards (MS 2045)

Autobiography (1796), 18.5 x 12.5 cm, brown cloth boards (MS 2046)

Diary no. 1 (2–15 Feb. 1796), 9.5 x 14 cm, leather cover (MS 2047)

Diary nos 2–3 (16 Feb. to 10 Mar. 1796), 21 x 16.5 cm, brown cloth boards (MS 2048)

Diary nos 4-17 (12 Mar. 1796 to 30 June 1798), 20 x 13.5 cm, brown cloth boards (MS 2049)

Letter-book and miscellanea, 1796–8, 38.5 x 26 cm, brown cloth boards (MS 2050+3807).

Posters, various sizes (MS 2050+3807, folder)

Notebook 'A', Miscellanea and sketches (1789–93), 10.5 x 19 cm, leather cover (MS 3805)

Proposal for Sandwich Islands, Sept.-Dec. 1790, and miscelleanea (MS 3806)

Photographs of bust and grave (MS 3808).
    MSS 2041–50 were received as a bequest from Miss Katherine Anne Maxwell in July 1923; MSS 3805-07 were presented by Mrs Katherine Dickason in July 1964, MS 3808 by her in Apr. 1964.

MINNEAPOLIS, MINNESOTA

In the keeping of Mrs Katherine Prendergast

Tone (Dickason) papers (unnumbered)
    Mainly letters, 1796–8, the remnants of the Tone papers, the bulk of which were made over to Trinity College, Dublin, in 1923 and 1964 (see above). The letters were previously in the keeping of Mrs Prendergast's grandmother, Mrs Katherine Dickason, Sinclair Terrace, Short Hills, New Jersey, who died on 20 Sept. 1995 aged 92. A microfilm is held by Trinity College.

(b) Other collections

BELFAST

Linen Hall Library, Donegall Square North

Joy papers

Manuscript sources

Presbyterian Historical Society of Ireland

Simms papers

Public Record Office of Northern Ireland, Balmoral Avenue

Drennan papers (D/591)

McPeake papers (T/3048/J–L)
    Photocopies of various documents and contemporary copies of documents relating
    to the United Irishmen collected by Brendan McPeake (see below).

DUBLIN

National Archives of Ireland, Bishop Street

Rebellion papers (620 series).
    Previously held in State Paper Office, Dublin Castle, and relocated with all other
    papers papers held there in December 1990.

National Library of Ireland, Kildare Street

Forbes papers (MS 978)

French Invasion papers (MS 705)
    Incl. Tone to Hoche, 19 pluv. 5 (7 Feb. 1797)

'A short account of the rebellion' (MS 4813)

Kilmainham papers (MS 1134)
    British military archives.

Registry of Deeds, Henrietta Street

Memorials of deeds

Representative Church Body Library, Braemor Park

Leslie succession lists (typescripts)

Royal Irish Academy, Dawson Street

R.I.A. Minute Book

Burrowes papers (MS 23 K 53)

Charlemont papers (MS 12 R 16, 23)

'Kitty Wilmot's journal, 1801–1803' (MS 12 L 32)

Trinity College Library

Board Register (MUN/V/5)

Journals of the College Historical Society (MUN/SOC/HIST)

Registry of Degrees, 1743–1834 (MUN/V/10/1)

Sirr papers (MS 868)
Incl. papers of Thomas Russell seized by Sirr.

Courts-martial proceedings (MS 872)

Madden papers (MS 873)

Bishop Stock's Killala diary (MS 1690)

Dillon papers (MSS 6455, 6464)
Incl. Charles Hart's diary, 1848–9 (MS 6464)

T. W. Moody papers (MS 10048)
Correspondence created in connexion with editing, by Moody, R. B. McDowell and C. J. Woods, of *Writings of Theobald Wolfe Tone* and related facsimiles, transcripts and English translations of various documents held elsewhere are in this series. Correspondence of Moody and McDowell with Brendan McPeake is in P.R.O.N.I., McPeake papers, T/3048/K.

CLONALIS, CO. ROSCOMMON

Clonalis House, Castlerea

O'Conor papers

THE HAGUE

Algemeen Rijksarchief

Buitenlandse zaken in de franse tijd

LE HAVRE

Archives Municipales

Registres des passeports pour l'intérieur (PR I² 35)

Police des Frontières (*PR I²*61)

LONDON

British Library, St Pancras

Auckland papers (Add. MS 34455)

Pelham papers (Add. MS 33101)

Place papers (Add. MSS 27814–5)

Sir John Moore's journal (Add. MS 57238)

Oriental and India Office collections (East India Co. embarkation lists)

Frognal House, Hampstead, London N.W.3

McPeake papers.
   An eclectic collection of original documents and contemporary copies relating to the United Irishmen formed by the late Brendan McPeake and apparently dispersed in 1984 at a sale by Phillips Fine Art Auctioneers, London. Photocopies of the entire collection are in the Public Record Office of Northern Ireland, Belfast (T/3048/J–L). A few originals were purchased in Dec. 1993 from Figgis Books by the National Library of Ireland (N.L.I., MS 36094/1–3).

Middle Temple

Admission Register

National Archives (formerly Public Record Office), Kew

Adm. 33/548

FO 27/47

HO 50/365, 100/34, 38, 42–3, 54

PC 1/37

WO 27/73.

Chatham papers (30/8/187, 324)

MAIDSTONE, KENT

Kent Archives Office

Pratt papers (U/840/O/147/4/1)

NEW YORK

New York Public Library

Monroe papers

PARIS

Service Historique de la Défense, Château de Vincennes, Val-de-Marne

   Formerly Service Historique de l'Armée de Terre (S.H.A.T.). Abbrev. 'Archives de la Guerre'.

Expéditions d'Irlande, 1796–7 (B111–2)

Dossiers personnels
   The Tone dossier is in the series 'Généraux prétendus', 17 yd 14. It seems not to have been created until the early 1940s and is rather thin; it contains photocopies of letters of military interest donated in the mid 1960s by Mrs Katherine Dickason.

Marine
  Formerly part of the Archives Nationales.

Archives du Ministère des Affaires Étrangères, Quai d'Orsay

Abbrev. 'Archives des Affaires Étrangères'
Correspondance politique, Angleterre

Mémoires et documents, Angleterre, 1743–1813

Archives Nationales, Rue des Francs-Bourgeois

Directoire Exécutif (AF III 186 B)

Consulat et Empire (AF IV 1671)

Police Général (F⁷)

6. Diaries, letters and other contemporary documents (excluding pamphlets)

THE arrangement of items in this section is chronological by date of publication.

Playbill of Kirwan's Lane Theatre, Galway, 8 August 1783

Belfast politics, 1792–3. [*Ed.* Henry Joy and William Bruce]. Belfast, 1794.

Society of United Irishmen of Dublin established November IX, MDCCXCI. Dublin, 1794.

Paddy's resource; being a select collection of original and modern patriotic songs, toasts and sentiments. [Belfast], 1795.

Authentic copies of the instructions given by Gen[eral] Hoche to Colonel Tate previous to his landing on the coast of South Wales at the beginning of 1797. London, 1797.

Proceedings of a military court held in Dublin Barracks for the trial of T. W. Tone. Dublin, 1798.
  Contains Tone's speech from the dock.

Minutes of the court-martial held last Saturday 10th November at the barracks of Dublin with the speech made upon that occasion by Theobald Wolfe Tone, Esq., taken in short hand by a barrister. Dublin, 1798.
  Contains Tone's speech from the dock.

A collection of loyal songs as sung at all the Orange lodges in Ireland. Dublin, 1798.
  Contains 'The song of Theobald Wolfe Tone' (pp 117–18) with the opening line 'From France to Loughswilly I came'.

Paddy's resource, or the harp of Erin attuned to freedom; being a collection of patriotic songs selected for Paddy's amusement. Dublin, [1803?].

Historical collections relating to the town of Belfast. *Ed*. Henry Joy. Belfast, 1817.

An alphabetical list of the freemen of the city of Dublin. [Dublin, 1824?].

Memoirs and correspondence of Viscount Castlereagh. *Ed*. Charles Vane, marquess of Londonderry. 12 vols, London, 1848–53

The correspondence of the right hon. John Beresford. *Ed*. William Beresford. 2 vols, London, 1854.

La correspondance de Napoléon 1er. 32 vols, Paris, 1858–70.

Correspondence of Charles, first Marquess Cornwallis. *Ed*. Charles Ross. 2nd ed., 3 vols, London, 1859.
　3rd ed., 1899.

Journal and correspondence of William, Lord Auckland. *Ed*. George Eden, 2nd Lord Auckland. 4 vols, London, 1861–2.
　Tone, iv, 67–72.

Un général de Sambre-et-Meuse: mémoires du général Jean Hardy, 1792–1802. Paris, 1883.

Literary remains of the United Irishmen. *Ed*. R. R. Madden. Dublin, 1887.

The O'Conors of Connaught: an historical memoir. *Ed*. C. O. O'Conor Don. Dublin, 1891.
　Tone, pp 301, 302, 313.

The manuscripts of the duke of Beaufort, K.G., the earl of Donoughmore and others. Historical Manuscripts Commission, 12th rep., app. ix, London, 1891.

Hoche: sa vie, sa correspondance. *Ed*. Ernest Cunéo d'Ornano. Paris, 1892.

Documents relating to Ireland, 1795–1804. *Ed*. J. T. Gilbert. Dublin, 1893.

Ulster in '98: episodes and anecdotes. *Ed*. R. M. Young. Belfast, 1893.

The manuscripts and correspondence of James first earl of Charlemont, vol. ii. Historical Manuscripts Commission, rep. 13, app. pt viii, London, 1894.

The writings of Thomas Paine. *Ed*. Moncure D. Conway. 4 vols, London, 1894–6.

Writings of James Monroe. *Ed*. S. M. Hamilton. 7 vols, New York, 1898–1903.

Public Record Office of Ireland. Report of the deputy keeper no. 30, appendix. Dublin, 1899.

Projets et tentatives de débarquement aux îles Britanniques, 1793–1805. *Ed.* Édouard Desbrière. 4 vols in 5, Paris, 1900–02.

Report on the mauscripts of J. B. Fortescue. 4 vols, Historical Manuscripts Commission: London, 1905.

Correspondance intime du général Jean Hardy de 1797 à 1802. *Ed.* General Hardy de Péréni. Paris, 1901.

État militaire de France pour l'année 1793. *Ed.* Léon Hennet. Paris, 1903.

Diary of Sir John Moore. *Ed.* Sir J. F. Moore. 2 vols, London, 1904.

Public Record Office of Ireland. Report of the deputy keeper no. 36. Dublin, 1904.

Recueil des actes du Directoire Exécutif. *Ed.* A. Debidour. 4 vols, Paris, 1910–17.

Marriage entries from the registers of the parishes of St Andrew, St Ann, St Audeon and St Bride, Dublin, 1632–1800. *Ed.* D. A. Chart. Dublin, 1913.

Private papers of George, second Earl Spencer, first lord of the admiralty, 1794–1801. *Ed.* J. S. Corbett. 4 vols, Navy Records Society, London, 1913–24.

Quatre généraux de la Révolution: Hoche et Desaix, Kléber et Marceau. *Ed.* Arthur Chuquet. 4 vols, Paris, 1911–20.

An Irish peer on the Continent, 1801–1803; being a narrative of the tour of Stephen, 2nd earl of Mount Cashell, through France, Italy etc, as related by Catherine Wilmot. *Ed.* T. U. Sadleir. London, 1920.

Public Record Office of Ireland. Report of the deputy keeper no. 55. Dublin, 1928.

The Drennan letters . . . , 1776–1819. *Ed.* D. A. Chart. Belfast, 1931.
Used for vols I and II but superseded by Agnew and Luddy's edition (1998–9); see below.

Aristide Aubert Du Petit Thouars, héros d'Aboukir, 1760–1798: lettres et documents inédits. *Ed.* Bergasse Du Petit Thouars. Paris, 1937.

Two diaries of the French expedition, 1798. *Ed.* Nuala Costello. In *Analecta Hibernica*, no. 11 (1941), pp 11–168.
'Journal de l'expédition d'Irlande', i.e. Capt. Jean Louis Jobit's narrative (pp 11–55) and 'Little's diary of the French landing in 1798' (pp 57–168).

United Irish plans of parliamentary reform, 1793. *Ed.* R. B. McDowell. In *Irish Historical Studies*, iii, no. 9 (Mar. 1942), pp 39–59.

The minute book of the Catholic Committee, 1773–92. *Ed.* R. Dudley Edwards. In *Archivium Hibernicum*, ix (1942), pp 1–172.

Proceedings of the Dublin Society of United Irishmen. *Ed.* R. B. McDowell. In *Analecta Hibernica*, no. 17 (1949), pp 1–143.

Register of admissions to the Honourable Society of the Middle Temple. *Ed.* H. A. C. Sturgess. 3 vols, London, 1949.

The correspondence of Edmund Burke. *Ed.* T. W. Copeland et al. 10 vols, Cambridge, 1958–78.

The papers of James Madison. *Ed.* W. T. Hutchinson and W. M. E. Rachal. 17 vols, Chicago, 1962–91.

Wolfe Tone's diplomacy in America, August-December 1795. *Ed.* J. J. St Mark. In *Éire-Ireland*, vii, no. 4 (winter 1972), pp 3–11.
    James Beckley to James Monroe, 14 Dec. 1795.

A plan for a Dutch invasion of Scotland, 1797. *Ed.* C. J. Woods. In *Scottish Historical Review*, liii (1974), pp 108–14.
    Edition of MS in Tone's hand, though of Daendels' authorship.

Journals and memoirs of Thomas Russell, 1791–5. *Ed.* C. J. Woods. Dublin, 1991.

J. Sarrazin, J. L. Jobit and L. O. Fontaine: La descente des Français en Irlande, 1798. *Ed.* Pierre Joannon. Paris: La Vouivre, 1998 (Du Directoire à l'Empire: Mémoires et Documents, no. 12)
    Narratives of three French officers Jean Sarrazin, Jean Louis Jobit and Louis Octave Fontaine.

The Drennan-McTier letters. *Ed.* Jean Agnew and Maria Luddy. 3 vols, Dublin: Irish Manuscripts Commission, 1998–9.
    Supersedes Chart's edition (1931) used for vols I and II.

Young Irelander abroad: the diary of Charles Hart. *Ed.* Brendan Ó Cathaoir. Cork, 2003.
    Meeting with Matilda Tone (pp 48–9, 55–6, 60–62).

Revolutionary Dublin, 1795–1801: the letters of Francis Higgins to Dublin Castle. *Ed.* Thomas Bartlett. Dublin: Four Courts, 2004.

'A volley of execrations': the letters and papers of John FitzGibbon, earl of Clare, 1772–1802. *Ed.* D. A. Fleming and A.P.W. Malcomson. Dublin: Irish Manuscripts Commission, 2005.

7. Contemporary pamphlets

THE arrangement of items in this section is chronological. Authorship being in so many cases indeterminate or collective, individual authors' names are given after the title.

Letters of Owen Roe O'Nial. [By Joseph Pollock]. [Dublin?], 1779.

A letter to the electors of the borough of Lisburn. [By William Todd Jones]. Dublin, 1774.

The history of the proceedings and debates of the Volunteers delegates of Ireland on the subject of a parliamentary reform. Dublin, 1784.

A letter to the Rt Hon. Thomas Conolly. Dublin, 1789.

Lettre des soldats composant les troupes françaises adressée à l'Assemblée Nationale. Paris, 1789.

Reports of the proceedings and arguments before the lord lieutenant and privy council on the petitions of Alderman James and Howison. Dublin, 1790.

Letter . . . to the Rt Rev. Dr Horsley, bishop of St David's. By R. E. Petre, 9th baron. London, 1790.

Declaration of the society instituted for the purpose of unanimity amongst Irishmen and removing all religious prejudices. [Dublin?], 1791.
   Copy in Public Record Office, London, HO 100/34.

Presbyterio-Catholicon; or a refutation of the modern catholic doctrines propagated by several societies of catholic presbyterians and presbyterian catholics in a letter to the real Roman Catholics of Ireland. Dublin, 1791.
   Partly in reply to Tone's *Argument* (1791).

Reply to an anonymous writer from Belfast signed Portia. By William Todd Jones. Dublin, 1792.

A letter to the societies of United Irishmen of the town of Belfast upon the subject of certain apprehensions which have arisen from a proposed restoration of catholic rights. By William Todd Jones. Dublin, 1792.

Argument on behalf of the Romanists reconsidered; being observations on a pamphlet entitled An argument on behalf of the catholics of Ireland signed A Northern Whig. Dublin, 1792
   A reply to Tone's *Argument* (1791).

Tracts on catholic affairs, viz. Presbyterio-Catholicon, &c. Dublin & London, 1792.

Trial between Richard Martin, Esq., . . . and John Petrie, Esq., . . . for criminal conversation with the plaintiff's wife. Dublin, 1792.

Address of the United Irishmen of Dublin to the Friends of the People in London. London, 1792.

Petition of the Roman Catholics of Ireland intended to have been presented to parliament in February 1792; with a preface. Dublin, 1792.

A brief account of the general meeting of catholic delegates held in Dublin, December 1792. By A Delegate. Dublin, 1793.

A letter from the Right Hon. Edmund Burke, M.P. in the kingdom of Great Britain, to Sir Hercules Langrishe, bart, M.P. Dublin, 1793.

Letters to the inhabitants of the town and lordship of Newry. By Joseph Pollock. Dublin, 1793.

Defence of the sub-committee of the catholics of Ireland. Dublin, 1793.

Proceedings of the general committee of the catholics of Ireland which met on Tuesday April 16, and finally dissolved on Thursday April 25, 1793. Dublin, 1793.

A full and accurate report of the debates in the parliament of Ireland in the session 1793 on the bill for relief of his majesty's catholic subjects. Dublin, [1793].

A refutation of the charges . . . against the secretary to the Sub-committee of the Catholics of Ireland of abetting the Defenders. By John Sweetmen. Dublin, 1793.

Règlement provisoire sur le service en campagne des troupes à cheval du 12 août 1793. Paris, 1793.

Manuel de la cavalerie concernant l'exercise et les manoeuvres des troupes à cheval au service de la République. Paris, 1793.

A faithful report of the trial of the proprietors of the *Northern Star*. Belfast, 1794.

An appeal to the people of Ireland, part 1. By William Paulet Carey. Dublin, 1794.

A full and accurate report of the trial of James Bird, Roger Hamill and Casimir Delahoyde . . . in the criminal court of Drogheda, April 23d, 1794. Dublin, 1794.

Trial of Francis Bellew, Esq., youngest son of Sir Patrick Bellew, Bart, for appearing in arms with a mob of Defenders on the 26th of December 1792. Dublin, 1794.

A candid and impartial account of the disturbances in the county of Meath. By a County Meath freeholder. Dublin, 1794.

Report of the trial of the King versus Hurdy Gurdy, alias Barrel Organ, alias Grinder. By William Sampson. Dublin, 1794
Not a report but a satire.

A reply to Mr Paine's Age of reason addressed to the students of Trinity College, Dublin. By Whitley Stokes. Dublin, 1795.

A full report of all the proceedings on the trial of the Rev. William Jackson. Dublin, 1795.
Tone to William Jackson, 15 Apr. 1794, printed in p. 84.

The trial of the Rev. William Jackson. *Ed*. William Sampson. Dublin, 1795.
Tone to William Jackson, 15 Apr. 1794, on p. 64.

On the defence of Ireland including observations on some other subjects connected therewith. [By Maurice Bagenal St Leger Keating]. Dublin, 1795.

A full and correct report of the debates at the Catholic meeting held in Francis Street Chapel, Dublin, on the ninth of April 1795 with the resolutions at full length. Belfast: Northern Star, 1795.
> In the second of the ten resolutions (p. 36) Tone is thanked for his services.

A vindication of Mr Randolph's resignation. By Edmund Randolph. Philadelphia, 1795.

The trial of William Stone for high treason at the bar of the court of king's bench on Thursday the twenty-eighth and Friday the twenty-ninth of January 1796. *Ed.* Joseph Gurney.

The trial on an action for damages brought . . . by the Right Hon. George Fred., earl of Westmeath, against the Honourable Augustus Cavendish Bradshaw for adultery with the Right Hon. Mary Anne, countess of Westmeath. Dublin, 1796.

The trial at large on an action for damages brought . . . by the Right Hon. George Fred., earl of Westmeath. Dublin, 1796.

A letter to the people of Ireland on the present situation of the country. By Thomas Russell. Belfast, 1796.

Thoughts on the projected union between Great Britain and Ireland. By V. B. Lawless. Dublin, 1797.

A journal of the movements of the French fleet in Bantry Bay from their first appearance to their final departure compiled from notes taken on the spot. By Edward Morgan. Cork, 1797.

The trial of James O'Coigly, otherwise called James Quigley, otherwise called James John Fivey, Arthur O'Connor, Esq., John Binns, John Allen, Jeremiah Leary for high treason. London, 1798.

The trial at large of Arthur O'Connor, Esq., John Binns, John Allen, Jeremiah Leary and James Quigley for high treason. Dublin, 1798.

An accurate and impartial narrative of the apprehension, trial and execution of Sir Edward William Crosbie, Bart. Bath, 1802.

8. Reminiscences, biographies and histories by contemporaries

Barrington, Sir Jonah. Personal sketches of his own times. 3 vols, London, 1827–32.
> Tone, i, 278–82.

Binns, John. Recollections of the life of John Binns. Philadelphia, 1854.

Burk, John Daly. A history of the late war in Ireland. Philadelphia, 1799.
Tone to James Reynolds, Feb. 1797 (pp 53–61).

Burrowes, Peter. Select speeches of the late Peter Burrowes, Esq., K.C., at the bar and in parliament. *Ed.*, with a memoir, Waldron Burrowes. Dublin, 1850.

Byrne, Miles. Memoirs of Miles Byrne. *Ed.* his widow. 3 vols, Paris, 1863.
2nd ed., 2 vols, Dublin, 1906.

Campbell, Thomas. Life and letters of Thomas Campbell. *Ed.* William Beattie. 3 vols, London, 1849.

A Candid Observer. Biographical anecdotes of the founders of the late Irish rebellion. 3rd ed., London, 1799.
Tone, pp 1–10.

Carnot, Lazare. Mémoires sur Carnot par son fils. 2 vols, Paris, 1861–3.
Tone, ii, 80–83; William Tone, ii, 83. New ed., *Mémoires sur Lazare Carnot, 1753–1823*, ed. Hippolyte Carnot (2 vols, Paris, 1907).

Corbeau de Saint-Albin, Alexandre Charles Omer Rousselin de. *See* Rousselin de Corbeau de Saint-Albin, Alexandre Charles Omer.

Curran, John Philpot. The life of the right honourable John Philpot Curran, late master of the rolls of Ireland. By W. H. Curran. New York, 1820.
Preface by William Sampson discusses Tone's death and contains info. on William Tone's career. Footnotes, possibly by Sampson, draw from Tone's memoranda of 1796 and his Diary. The 2nd ed. (Edinburgh, 1822) and later editions omit Sampson's preface.

Grattan, Henry. Memoirs of the life and times of the rt hon. Henry Grattan. *Ed.* Henry Grattan, junr. 5 vols, London, 1839–46.

Grimshaw, William. Incidents recalled; or sketches from memory . . . of the rebellion of 1798 . . . Philadelphia, 1848.

Grouchy, Emmanuel de. Mémoires du maréchal de Grouchy par le marquis de Grouchy. 2 vols, Paris, 1873.

Hardy, Jean. Mémoire militaire du général Jean Hardy, 1792–1802. Paris, 1883.

Hay, Edward. History of the insurrection of the county of Wexford, A.D. 1798. Dublin, 1803.

Kemble, John Philip. Memoirs of the life of John Philip Kemble. 2 vols, London, 1825.

Lapierre de Chateauneuf, A. H. de. Histoire des généraux français depuis 1792 jusqu'à nos jours. 5 vols, Paris, 1809–12.

Lapierre de Chateauneuf, A. H. de. Histoire des généraux qui se sont illustrés dans la guerre de la Révolution: Carteaux, Battin, Pully, Partoureaux, Wolfe Tone, Houdar de la Motte. Paris, 1811.

La Revellière-Lépeaux, Louis Marie. Mémoires de Larevellière- Lépeaux, membre du Directoire Exécutif. 3 vols, Paris, [1895?].

Lawless, V. B., 2nd Lord Cloncurry. Personal recollections of the life and times, with extracts from the correspondence, of Valentine Lord Cloncurry. Dublin, 1849.
> Fitzpatrick asserts that 'it is an open secret that the book known as "Lord Cloncurry's Personal memoirs" was fully prepared by for publication, and its style strengthened throughout, by a practised writer connected with the Tory press of Dublin and who believed that Cloncurry had been wrongly judged in 1798' (W. J. Fitzpatrick, *Secret service under Pitt* (London, 1892), p. 39).

Maclean, John. A memoir of John Maclean, M.D., the first professor of chemistry in the college of New Jersey by his son John Maclean. Princeton, 1885.
> Incl. Matilda Tone to John Maclean, New York, prob. late 1806.

MacNeven, W. J. Pieces of Irish history. New York, 1807.
> Two eds, both with imprint New York, Dornin, 1807, one (1st?) in 10pt type and xxiii, 305 pp, the other in 9pt type and xix, 256 pp.
>
> Incl. T. A. Emmet, 'Part of an essay towards the history of Ireland'.

Moore, Thomas. The life and death of Lord Edward Fitzgerald. 2 vols, London, 1831.

Musgrave, Richard. Memoirs of the different rebellions in Ireland. Dublin, 1801. 3rd ed., 1802.

O'Sullivan, Samuel. Remains of Rev. Samuel O'Sullivan. *Ed.* J. C. Martin and Mortimer O'Sullivan. 3 vols, Dublin, 1853.

Plunket, William Conyngham. The life, letters and speeches of Lord Plunket. *Ed.* David Plunket. 2 vols, London, 1867.

Reynolds, Thomas. The life of Thomas Reynolds . . . by his son Thomas Reynolds. 2 vols, London, 1839.
> Apparently based on family papers.

Rousselin de Corbeau de Saint-Albin, Alexandre Charles Omer. Vie de Lazare Hoche. 2 vols, Paris, An VI (1798); 3rd ed., Paris, An VIII (1798).
> The 3rd and 4th editions are described on the t.p. as 'edition augmentée de quelques considérations nouvelles sur l'état actuel de l'Irlande'.
> Tone, 3rd ed., pp 220–21.

Rowan, Archibald Hamilton. Autobiography of Archibald Hamilton Rowan. *Ed.* W. H. Drummond. Dublin, 1840.

Sampson, William. Memoirs of William Sampson. New York, 1807.
Tone, pp 340–43.

Swinburne, Henry. The courts of Europe at the close of the last century. 2 vols, London, 1864.

Teeling, C. H. Personal narrative of the Irish rebellion. London, 1828.

Teeling, C. H. Sequel to Personal narrative of the Irish rebellion of 1798. Belfast, 1832.

Teeling, C. H. Observations on the History and consequences of the Battle of the Diamond. [Belfast], 1838.

[Walsh, John Edward]. Sketches of Ireland sixty years ago. Dublin, 1847.

9. Official and quasi-official records

(a) Irish

Journal of the house of lords [of Ireland], 1634–1800. 8 vols, Dublin: King, 1779–1800.

Journals of the house of commons of the kingdom of Ireland. 28 vols, Dublin, 1853–91; repr. and contd to 1800, 19vols, Dublin: King, 1796–1800.

The parliamentary register; or history of the proceedings and debates of the house of commons of Ireland, [1781–97]. 17 vols, Dublin, 1782–1801.

The statutes at large passed in the parliaments held in Ireland . . . , [1310–1800]. 20 vols, Dublin, 1786–1801.

A full and accurate report of the debates in the parliament of Ireland in the session 1793 on the bill for relief of his majesty's catholic subjects. Dublin: Jones, 1793.
Appendix contains list of names of members of Catholic Convention.

A report of the debate in the house of commons of Ireland on the bill for further relief of his majesty's Roman Catholic subjects. Dublin: Chambers, 1795.

The debates at large on the catholic bill in the Irish house of commons on Monday, May 4, 1795. Cork: Haly, 1795.

The debate in the Irish house of peers on a motion made by the earl Moira, February 19th, 1798. Dublin: Milliken, 1798.

Report of the debate on Lord Moira's motion for an address to the lord lieutenant recommending conciliatory measures on behalf of the people of Ireland. Dublin: Stockdale, 1798.

(b) British

Journals of the house of lords [of Great Britain].

Journals of the house of commons [of Great Britain].

The statues at large . . . [of Great Britain].

(c) French

Journal gratuit: code militaire, armée de la terre. Paris, 1791.

Bulletin des lois de la République Française.

Lois de la République Française, An IV.

Corps législatif: Conseil des Cinq-cens: Motion faite par [Pierre Antoine] Laloy en présentant au Conseil la 'Vie de Lazare Hoche, général des armées de la République', par A. Rousselin, Séance de 12 germinal an VI. Paris, an VI.

Corps législatif: Conseil des Cinq-cens: Motion d'ordre faite par L[ucien] Bonaparte pour la veuve et les enfans de Téobald Wolf- Ton: séance du 9 Brumaire an 8. Paris, 1799. Paris, an VIII.

Recueil des actes du Directoire Exécutif. *Ed.* Antonin Debidour. 4 vols, Paris, 1910–17.

10. Newspapers, magazines, year-books etc.

(a) Belfast

Belfast News Letter.

Northern Star.

(b) Dublin

Cox's Irish Magazine
    Known also as *Irish Magazine.*

Dublin Chronicle.

Dublin Evening Post.

Dublin Gazette.

Faulkner's Dublin Journal.
    Known also as *Dublin Journal.*

Freeman's Journal.

Hibernian Journal.

Nation.

National Journal.
　　Copies of odd issues in R.I.A. and Maynooth College.

Post Chaise Companion or the Traveller's Directory through Ireland. 3rd ed.,
　　William Wilson: Dublin, 1803.

Saunders' News Letter.

Taylor and Skinner's Maps of the Roads of Ireland surveyed 1777. London &
　　Dublin, 1778.
　　　　2nd ed., 1783.

Universal Magazine and Review.

Walker's Hibernian Magazine.
　　Known also as *Hibernian Magazine*.

Watson's Gentleman's and Citizen's Almanack.

Wilson's Dublin Directory.

(c) Kilkenny

Finn's Leinster Journal.

(d) London

Annual Register.

Army list. London, 1790s (quasi-annual).

Courier.

European Magazine.

Exshaw's English Registry.

Gazetteer.

Gentleman's Magazine.

Lloyd's List.

London Chronicle.

London Gazette.

Morning Chronicle

Morning Herald.

Oracle.

St James Chronicle.

Steel's Original and Correct List of the Royal Navy.

Times, The.

True Briton.

(e) Londonderry

Londonderry Journal

(f) Paris

Almanach National de France An IV.

Bien Informé.

Courier Universel.

Gazette Nationale de France.

Journal des Défenseurs de la Patrie.

Journal des Hommes Libres de Tous les Pays, ou la République.

Moniteur.

(g) Philadelphia

Philadelphia Gazette

Stephens' Philadelphia Directory

11. Special studies

Ahlstrom, John D. Captain and chef de brigade: William Tate, South Carolina adventurer. In *South Carolina Historical Magazine*, lxxxviii (Oct. 1987), pp 183–91.

Anderson, John. History of the Belfast Library and Society for Promoting Knowledge commonly known as the Linen Hall Library. Belfast, 1888.

Aulard, F. V. A. Paris pendant la réaction thermidorienne et sous le Directoire. 5 vols, Paris, 1898–1902.

Benn, George. A history of the town of Belfast. Belfast, 1823.
    2nd ed., 2 vols, London, 1877–80.

Bergounioux, Édouard. Essai sur la vie de Lazare Hoche. Paris, 1852.

Bradley, P. B. Bantry Bay: Ireland in the days of Napoleon and Wolfe Tone. London, 1931.

Cadell, Sir Patrick. Irish soldiers in India. In *Irish Sword*, i (1949–53), pp 75–9.

Calkin, H. L. La propagation en Irlande des idées de la Révolution française. In *Annales Historiques de la Révolution Française*, xxvii (1955), pp 143–60.

Calkin, H. L. Les invasions d'Irlande pendant la Révolution française. Paris, 1956.

Campbell, Gerald. Edward and Pamela Fitzgerald. London, 1904.

Camperdown, Earl of. *See* Duncan, R. A. P. H., 3rd earl of Camperdown.

Carnot, L. H. Lazare Hoche, général républicain. Paris, 1874.

Clark, W. B. In defense of Thomas Digges. In *Pennsylvania Magazine of History and Biography*, lxxvii (1953), pp 381–438.

Colomb, P. H. Naval warfare: its ruling principles and practice historically treated. 2nd ed., London, 1895.
  Tone, pp 157–8.

Compton, Herbert. A particular account of the European military adventurers of Hindustan from 1784 to 1803. London, 1892.
  William Henry Tone, pp 416–19.

Coughlan, R. J. Napper Tandy. Dublin, 1976.

Cullen, Fintan. The Irish face: redefining the Irish portrait. London, 2004.
  Reproduces and discusses two portraits of Tone (pp 155–7).

Curtin, Nancy J. The United Irishmen: popular politics in Ulster and Dublin, 1791–1798. Oxford, 1994.

Dagg, T. S. C. College Historical Society: a history, 1770–1920. [Cork?, 1969?].
  Tone, esp. speech of June 1789, pp 62–3.

Dechamps, Jules. Les îles Britanniques et la Révolution française, 1789–1803. Bruxelles, 1949.

Dickson, Charles. Revolt in the north. Dublin, 1960.

Donnelly, James S. Propagating the cause of the United Irishmen. In *Studies*, lxix (1980), pp 5–23.

Duffy, Sir Charles Gavan. Young Ireland: a fragment of Irish history, 1840–1850. London, 1880.
  Davis's uncompleted life of Tone, pp 679–83.

Duffy, Sir Charles Gavan. Thomas Davis: the memoirs of an Irish patriot, 1840–1846. London, 1890.
Tone, pp 199–201.

Duncan, R. A. P. H., 3rd earl of Camperdown. Admiral Duncan. London, 1898.

Durey, Michael. Transatlantic radicals and the early American republic. Lawrence, Kansas, 1997.

Elliott, Marianne. Partners in revolution: the United Irishmen and France. New Haven & London, 1982. Illus.

Escande, Georges. Hoche en Irlande, 1795–1798, d'après des documents inédits. Paris, 1888.

Falkiner, C. L. Studies in Irish history and biography mainly of the eighteenth century. London, 1902.

Fitzpatrick, W. J. Life and times of Lord Cloncurry. London[?], 1855.

Fitzpatrick, W. J. The sham squire. 3rd ed., Dublin, 1866.

Fitzpatrick, W. J. Secret service under Pitt. London, 1892.

Fortescue, J. W. A history of the British army. 13 vols, London, 1899–1930.

Fox, Charlotte Milligan. Annals of the Irish harpers. London, 1911.

Froude, J. A. The English in Ireland in the eighteenth century. 3 vols, London, 1872–4.

Gill, Conrad. The naval mutinies of 1797. Manchester, 1913.

Godechot, Jacques. Les institutions de la France sous la Révolution et l'Empire. Paris, 1951.

Goncourt, E. and J. de. Histoire de la société française pendant le Directoire. Paris, 1864.

Gribayédoff, Valerian. The French invasion of Ireland in '98. New York, [1890].

Grouchy, A. F. E., marquis de. Le général de Grouchy et l'Irlande en 1796. Paris, 1866.

Guillon, Édouard. La France et l'Irlande pendant la Révolution: Hoche et Humbert d'après les documents inédits des archives de France et d'Irlande. Paris, 1888.
Another ed., *La France et l'Irlande sous le Directoire* (Paris, 1888).

Hammond, J. W. Thomas Braughall, 1729–1803, catholic emancipationist. In *Dublin Historical Record*, xiv (1956), pp 41–9.

Hayes, Richard. Ireland and Irishmen in the French Revolution. Dublin, 1932.

Hayes, Richard. General Charles Jennings Kilmaine, 1751–1799. In *Studies*, xxiii (1934), pp 486–7

Hayes, Richard. The last invasion of Ireland: when Connacht rose. Dublin, 1937.

Hayes, Richard. Irish swordsmen of France. Dublin, 1941.

Hill, Jacqueline. From Patriots to Unionists: Dublin civic politics and Irish protestant patriotism, 1660–1840. Oxford, 1997.

Inglis, Brian. The freedom of the press in Ireland, 1784–1841. London, 1954.

Jacotey, M.-L. Le général Hoche, l'ange botté dans la tourmente révolutionnaire. Paris, 1994.

James, William. Naval history of Great Britain. New ed., 6 vols, London, 1826.

Jones, E. H. Stuart. An invasion that failed: the French expedition to Ireland, 1796. Oxford, 1950.

Jones, E. H. Stuart. The last invasion of Britain. Cardiff, 1950.

Kennedy, W. B. The Irish Jacobins. In *Studia Hibernica*, xvi (1976), pp 109–39.

Kerrigan, P. M. The capture of the *Hoche* in 1798. In *Irish Sword*, xiii, no. 56 (1978), pp 123–7.
  Frontispiece 'The *Hoche* in tow of the *Doris*'.

Lecky, W. E. H. History of Ireland in the eighteenth century. 5 vols, London, 1892–6.

Lynam, Shevawn. Humanity Dick: a biography of Richard Martin. London, 1975.

Macalister, Alexander. James Macartney, M.D. London, 1900.
  Macartney (1770–1843) knew Tone (pp 41–6).

McAnally, Sir Henry. The Irish militia, 1793–1816. Dublin, 1949.

MacDermot, Frank. The church and ninety-eight. In *Ireland Today*, iii (1938), pp 41–4.

MacDermot, Frank. The Jackson episode in 1794. In *Studies*, xxvii (1938), pp 77–92.

MacDermot, Frank. Arthur O'Connor. In *Irish Historical Studies*, xv, no. 57 (Mar. 1966), pp 48–69.

McDowell, R. B. Irish public opinion, 1750–1800. London, 1944.

McDowell, R. B. The personnel of the Dublin Society of United Irishmen. In *Irish Historical Studies*, ii, no. 5 (Mar. 1940), pp 12–53.

McDowell, R. B. Ireland in the age of imperialism and revolution, 1760–1801. Oxford, 1979.

McDowell, R. B. & Webb, D. A. Trinity College, Dublin, 1592–1952: an academic history. Cambridge, 1982.

McFarland, Elaine W. Ireland and Scotland in the age of revolution: planting the green bough. Edinburgh, 1994.

Mac Giolla Easpaig, Séamus. Tomás Ruiséil. Dublin, 1957.

McLoughlin, Thomas. Contesting Ireland: Irish voices against England in the eighteenth century. Dublin, 1999.
> Tone's *Argument on behalf of the catholics*, pp 211–38

McNeill, Mary. The life and times of Mary Ann McCracken, 1770–1866. Belfast, 1960.
> Prints many letters.

McSkimin, Samuel. Annals of Ulster. Belfast, 1849.
> Second ed., as *A history of the Irish rebellion* (1853); new ed., with biographical sketch and notes by E. J. McCrum (Belfast, 1906).

Madden, R. R. The United Irishmen: their lives and times. 1st ed. in 3 series in 7 vols, London and Dublin, 1842–6.
> 1st ser. in 2 vols (1842); 2nd ser. in 2 vols (1843); 3rd ser. in 3 vols (1846).
> Revised ed. in 4 ser. in 4 vols: 1st ser. (Dublin, 1857); 2nd ser. (Dublin, 1858); 3rd ser. (London, 1860); 4th ser. (London, 1860).
> Not all the 'lives' in the 1st ed. reappear in the revd ed.; some in the 2nd ed. are new. For an explanation of the different series, see C. J. Woods, 'R. R. Madden, historian of the United Irishmen' in Thomas Bartlett et al. (eds), 1798: *a bicentenary perspective* (Dublin, 2003), pp 497–512.
> The chapters on Tone are in 3rd ser. (1846), i, 121–84, and revd ed., 2nd ser. (1858), pp 1–173.

Maguire, W. A. Arthur McMahon, United Irishman and French soldier. In *Irish Sword*, ix (1969–70), pp 207–15.
> Further note by J.L.G. in ibid., x (1971–2), p. 172.

Mahan, A. T. The influence of sea power upon the French revolution and empire, 1793–1812. 2 vols, London, 1893.

Maxwell, Jane. Sources in Trinity College, Dublin, for researching the 1798 rebellion. In *Journal of the Irish Society for Archives*, n.s., v, no. 1 (summer 1998), pp 3–22.

Maxwell, W. H. History of the Irish rebellion in 1798. London, 1891.

Millin, S. S. Sidelights on Belfast history. Belfast, 1932.

Moody, T. W. The political ideas of the United Irishmen. In *Ireland Today*, iii (1938), pp 15–25.

[Moody, T. W.]. Crowded years of Wolfe Tone: Moody sums up career. In *Irish Times*, 1 February 1967.
> Report of lecture, 'Theobald Wolfe Tone and his influnce', given by T.W. Moody to Republican Clubs at Trinity College, Dublin, on 31 Jan. 1967.

Mulloy, Sheila. James Joseph MacDonnell, 'the best known of the United Irish chiefs of the west'. In *Cathair na Mart: Journal of the Westport Historical Society*, v (1985), pp 67–78.

O'Brien, R. Barry. Irish memories. London, 1904.
 . Tone, pp 154–80.

Ó Broin, Leon. R. R. Madden, historian of the United Irishmen. In *Irish University Review*, ii (1972), pp 20–33.

Ó Coindealbháin, Seán. The United Irishmen in Cork county. In *Journal of the Cork Archaeological and Historical Society*, 2nd ser., lv (1950), pp 50–61, 73–90; lvi (1951), pp 18–28, 95–103; lvii (1952), pp 87–98; lviii (1953), pp 91–6.

O'Donnell, P. D. Wolfe Tone's provost prison: some recent research. In *Irish Sword*, xi (1973–4), pp 21–31.
 Argues that provost prison where Tone was imprisoned was situated in what became Sergeants' mess at Collins Barracks (formerly Dublin or Royal Barracks).

[O'Sullivan, Samuel]. Rev. Doctor Miller. In *Dublin University Magazine*, xvii, no. 102 (June 1841), pp 683–4.

Pakenham, Thomas. The year of liberty: the great Irish rebellion of 1798. London, 1969.

Parsons, L. H. The mysterious Mr Digges. In *William and Mary Quarterly*, 3rd ser., xxii (1965), pp 486–92.

Pettit, Philip. The tree of liberty: republicanism, American, French and Irish. In *Field Day Review*, i (2005), pp 29–41.

Phair, P. B. A guide to the Registry of Deeds. In *Analecta Hibernica*, no. 23 (1966), pp 486–92.

Phipps, R. W. The armies of the first French republic and the rise of the marshalls of Napoleon I. 5 vols, Oxford, 1926–39.

Pichot, Amédée. L'Irlande et le Pays de Galles. 2 vols, Paris, 1850.
 William Tone, i, 342.

Postgate, Raymond. Story of a year: 1798. London, 1969.

Pursell, C. W., junr. Thomas Digges and William Pearce: an example of the transit of technology. In *William and Mary Quarterly*, 3rd ser., xxi (1964), pp 551–60.

Quinn, James. Soul on fire: a life of Thomas Russell. Dublin, 2002.

Reinhard, M. R. Le grand Carnot. Paris, 1952.

Rogers, Patrick. A protestant pioneer of catholic emancipation. In *Down and Connor Historical Society's Journal*, vi (1934), pp 14–23.
 William Todd Jones (*c.*1755–1818).

Rüdebusch, Eckhardt. Irland im Zeitalter der Revolution: Politik und Publizistik der United Irishmen, 1791–98. Frankfurt-am-Main, 1989.

Ryan, F. W. A projected invasion of Ireland in 1811. In *Irish Sword*, i (1949–53), pp 136–41.
  Suggests awareness of existence of Tone's memoirs in 1811.

St Mark, J. J. The Oswald mission to Ireland from America [*recte* France], 20 February to 8 June 1793. In *Éire-Ireland*, xxiii, no. 2 (summer 1988), pp 25–38.

Senior, Hereward. Orangeism in Ireland and Britain, 1795–1836. London, 1966.

Shaw, Francis. The canon of Irish history: a challenge. In *Studies*, lxi (1972), pp 115–53.

[Smith, George]. Belfast Literary Society, 1801–1901. Belfast, 1902.

Sorel, Albert. Bonaparte et Hoche en 1797. Paris, 1896.
  Tone, pp 256–61.

Stewart, A. T. Q. 'A stable unseen power': Dr William Drennan and the origins of the United Irishmen. In John Bossy and Peter Jupp (eds), *Essays presented to Michael Roberts, sometime professor of modern history in the Queen's University of Belfast* (Belfast, 1976), pp 80–92.

Swords, Liam. The green cockade: the Irish in the French revolution, 1789–1815. Dublin, 1989.

Tobin, E. The barracks and posts of Ireland—11: Arbour Hill. In *An Cosantoir*, xxvi (1966), pp 486–506.
  Argues that the provost prison where Tone died was situated at Arbour Hill, Dublin (pp 489–91).

Van Brock, F. W. Dilemma at Killala. In *Irish Sword*, viii, no. 46 (1968), pp 261–73.

Van Brock, F. W. Captain MacSheehy's mission. In *Irish Sword*, x (1971–2), pp 215–28.

Wall, Maureen. The rise of a catholic middle class in eighteenth-century Ireland. In *Irish Historical Studies*, xi, no. 42 (Sept. 1958), pp 91–115.

Webb, D. A. *See also* McDowell, R. B. and Webb, D. A.

Weber, Paul. On the road to rebellion: the United Irishmen and Hamburg, 1796–1803. Dublin, 1997.

Welply, W. H. Curran and his kinsfolk. In *Notes and Queries*, cxciv (1949), pp 266–8, 290–94, 338–41, 384–7.

Wheatley, H. B. London past and present: its history, associations and traditions. 3 vols, London, 1891.

Witheroe, Thomas. Historical and literary memorials of prebyterianism in Ireland. 2 vols, London, 1879–80.

Wolfe, George. The Wolfe family of County Kildare. In *Journal of the County Kildare Archaeological Society*, iii, no. 6 (1901), pp 361–7.

Wolfe, R. T. The Wolfes of Forenaughts, Blackhall, Baronrath, Co. Kildare. 2nd ed., Guildford, 1893.
  Tone, pp 40–41.

Woods, C. J. The secret mission to Ireland of Captain Bernard MacSheehy, an Irishman French service, 1796. In *Journal of the Cork Archaeological and Historical Society*, 2nd ser., lxxviii (1973), pp 93–108.

Woods, C. J. The place of Thomas Russell in the United Irish movement. In Hugh Gough and David Dickson (eds), *Ireland and the French Revolution* (Dublin, 1990), pp 83–100.

Woods, C. J. The authorship of a letter received by Tone in America in 1795. In *Eighteenth-Century Ireland*, v (1990), pp 192–4.

Woods, C. J. The personnel of the Catholic Convention, 1792–3. In *Archivium Hibernicum*, lvii (2003), pp 26–76.

Woodward, L. D. Les projets de descente en Irlande et les réfugiés irlandais et anglais en France sous la Convention. In *Annales Historiques de la Révolution Française*, viii (1931), pp 1–30.

12. Works of reference

SUCH is Tone's eminence, he has been the subject of entries in numerous reference works, of which a selection is given below.

(a) Encyclopaedias

Dictionnaire Napoléon. New ed., 2 vols, Paris, 1999.
  Esp. Irlande, Campagne naval d', by *Amiral* Dupont.

Enciclopedia italiana. 36 vols, Rome, 1949–52.
  Tone, xxxiii, 1027, by F.M.G.H.

Enciclopedia universal ilustrada europeo-americana. 70 vols, Madrid, 1908–30.
  Tone, lxii, 672.

Encyclopaedia Britannica. 11th ed., 29 vols, Cambridge, 1910–11.
  Tone, xxvii, 2–3, by R. J. McNeill.

Grand Larousse encyclopédique. 10 vols, Paris, 1960–64.
  Tone, x, 377.

Grand Soviet enciclopedia: a translation of the third edition. 32 vols, New York and London, 1973–83.
  Tone, xxvi (1981).

A guide to Irish fiction, 1650–1900. By Rolf Loeber and Magda Loeber with Anne Mullin Burnham. Dublin, 2006.
  Tone, pp 1294–5, esp. *Belmont Castle* (1790).

Historical dictionary of the French Revolution, 1789–1799. *Ed.* S. F. Scott and Barry Rothaus. 2 vols, Westport, Connecticut, 1995.
  Tone, ii, 972–3, by W. D. Griffin.

Meyers Neues Lexikon. 25 vols, Leipzig, 1971–9.
  Tone, xiii (1976?), p. 628.

(b) Biographical dictionaries

Allgemeine Deutsche Biographie. 56 vols, Leipzig, 1875–1912.

Alumni Dublinenses: a register of students, graduates, professors and provosts of Trinity College in the University of Dublin. By G. D. Burtchaell and T. U. Sadleir. 2nd ed., Dublin, 1935.

Bibliothèque musicale du théâtre de l'opéra. By Théodore Lajarte. 2 vols, Paris, 1878.

Biographical dictionary of Irishmen in France. By Richard Hayes. Dublin, 1949.
  William Tone, pp 298–9.

Biographical dictionary of modern British radicals, vol. i: 1770–1830. *Ed.* J. O. Baylen and N. J. Gossman. Hassocks, Sussex, 1979.
  T. W. Tone, pp 488–90, by Stephen O'Neill; Mathew Tone, pp 484–8, by W. B. Kennedy.

A biographical dictionary of modern rationalists. By Joseph McCabe. London, 1920.
  Tone, col. 804.

Biographie nationale publiée par l'Académie Royale des Sciences, des Lettres et des Beaux-Arts de Belgique. 27 vols, Brussels, 1866–1938.

Biographie nouvelle des contemporains. 20 vols, Paris, 1820–25.
  Tone, xx (1825), pp 28–9.

Biographie universelle ancienne et moderne. 85 vols, Paris, 1811–62.
  Tone, xlvi (1826), p. 228, by Louis Gabriel Michaud.

Biographie universelle des musiciens. By F. J. Fétis. 2nd ed., 10 vols, Paris, 1860–84.

Burke's landed gentry of Ireland. 1st ed., London, 1899. 3rd ed., London, 1912. 4th ed., London, 1958.
  The 1st ed. is described on the t.p. as the 9th and is treated as a 2nd vol. of *Burke's landed gentry of Great Britain*.

Burke's peerage and baronetage. London, 1912.

The cabinet of Irish literature. By C. A. Read. 2nd ed., 4 vols, London, 1902–3.
Tone, i, 236–43

A compendium of Irish biography. By Alfred Webb. Dublin, 1878.
Tone, pp 528–34.

Complete baronetage. By G. E. C[okayne]. 6 vols, Exeter, 1900–9.

The complete peerage of England, Scotland, Ireland, Great Britain and the
United Kingdom. By G. E. C[okayne]. 8 vols, Exeter, 1887–98. 2nd ed. by
Vicary Gibbs and others, 13 vols, London, 1910–40.

Dictionary of American biography. *Ed*. Allen Johnson and Dumas Malone.
20 vols, New York, 1928–37.
Not entirely superseded by *American national biography* (24 vols, New York, 1999).

Dictionary of Indian biography. By C. E. Buckland. London, 1906.

Dictionary of Irish biography. 7 vols, Cambridge, 2008?
Project of the Royal Irish Academy. Contains article on T. W. Tone by Thomas
Bartlett, and articles on his brothers William Henry and Mathew, his wife Matilda
and his son William by C. J. Woods, as well as articles on many persons footnoted
above.

Dictionary of Irish literature. *Ed*. Robert Hogan. Dublin, 1980.
Tone, pp 661–3, by Mary Rose Callaghan.

Dictionary of national biography. *Ed*. Sir Leslie Stephen and Sir Sidney Lee.
66 vols, Oxford, 1885–1901; repr. with corrections, 22 vols, Oxford, 1908–9.
Tone by Robert Dunlop. This work superseded by *Oxford dictionary of national biog-*
raphy (60 vols, Oxford, 2004), in which the article on Tone is by Marianne Elliott.

Dictionnaire biographique des généraux et amiraux français de la Révolution et
de l'Empire, 1792–1814. By George Six. 2 vols, Paris, 1934.

Dictionnaire de biographie française. Paris, 1933– .
Published alphabetically in fascicules; by 2007 the letter L was reached.

Dictionnaire de parlementaires français. By Adolphe Robert and Gaston Cougny.
5 vols, Paris, 1889–91.

Dictionnaire des comédiens français. By Henry Lyonnet. 2 vols: i, Paris, 1908;
ii, Geneva, n.d.

Dictionnaire historique ou histoire abrégée des hommes qui se sont fait un nom
par leur génie. By F. X. de Feller. 17 vols, Paris, 1827–9.
Tone, xvi (1828), pp 377–8.

History of the Irish parliament, 1690–1800. By Edith Mary Johnston-Liik. 6 vols,
Belfast, 2002.

The judges of Ireland, 1221–1921. By F. E. Ball. 2 vols, London, 1926.

List of the officers of the Bengal army, 1758–1834. By V. C. P. Hodson. 4 parts, London, 1927–47.

Lives of illustrious and distinguished Irishmen. By James Wills. 6 vols, Dublin, 1840–47.
  Tone, v (1844), pp 395–432.

Neue deutsche Biographie. Berlin, 1952– .

Nieuw Nederlandsch biografisch woordenboek. 10 vols, Leiden, 1911–37.

Nouvelle biographie générale. 46 vols, Paris, 1855–66.
  Tone, xlv (1866), cols 483–4.

Oxford companion to Irish literature. *Ed.* Robert Welch. Oxford, 1996.
  Tone, pp 564–5.

The poets of Ireland. By D. J. O'Donoghue. 2nd ed., Dublin, 1912.
  Tone, p. 457.

Register of admissions to the Honourable Society of the Middle Temple. *Ed.* H. A. C. Sturgess. 3 vols, London, 1949

Soldats ambassadeurs sous le Directoire. By A. Dry, *pseud.* Adrien Fleury, vicomte. 2 vols, Paris, 1906.

Trinity College record volume. Dublin, 1951.

(c) Miscellaneous

Dublin street names dated and explained. By C. T. McCready. Dublin, 1892.

Nouveau dictionnaire historique de Paris. By Gustave Pessard. Paris, 1904.

A new history of Ireland, vol. ix: maps, genealogies, lists. Oxford, 1984.

13. Writings by or on other members of the Tone family

Bullock, Humphrey. Wolfe Tone had a brother. In *Irish Times*, 17 June 1953.
  This article, on William Henry Tone, elicited a letter ('Wolfe Tone's brother') from Patrick Hanley, Tipperary, identifying his grave in a cemetery near Poona for Christian officers in the peishwa's service (*Irish Times*, 24 June 1953).

Butler, P. R. William Henry Tone. In *Studies*, xxxv (1946), pp 259–62.

Concannon, Helena. Women of ninety-eight. Dublin, 1920.
  Matilda Tone. Title-page has Mrs Thomas Concannon.

Curtin, Nancy. Matilda Tone and virtuous republican femininity. In Dáire Keogh and Nicholas Furlong (eds), *The women of 1798* (Dublin, 1998), pp 26–46.

C. E., *pseud*. Some further particulars of the widow and son of Theobald Wolfe Tone. In *New Monthly Magazine*, xii (Jan.-June 1825), pp 267–72.
The author, who knew Matilda Tone and her son in Paris, was probably William Henry Curran, a son of John Philpot Curran.

Fletcher, Eliza. Autobiography of Mrs Fletcher with letters and other family memorials edited by the survivor of her family. Edinburgh, 1875.
Friend and correspondent of Matilda Tone.

Fuller, J. F. The Tones, father and son. In *Journal of the Cork Archaeological and Historical Society*, 2nd ser., xxix (1929), pp 93–101.

Jacob, Rosamond. The rebel's wife. Tralee: Kerryman, 1957. Pp viii, 216.
Semi-fictional biography of Matilda Tone.

Joly, Agnès. Un élève irlandais de l'école de cavalerie de Saint-Germain: William T. Tone. In *Revue de l'Histoire de Versailles et de Seine-et-Oise*, xlv (juillet-décembre 1943), pp 41–68, portr., xlvi (1944), pp 23–71.

Maxwell, Katherine Anne Tone-. Irish family history: Tone of Bodenstown, Co. Kildare. In *Notes and Queries*, 12th ser., vii (July-Dec. 1920), pp 432–3.

Pierpoint, Robert. Tone of Bodenstown, Co. Kildare. In *Notes and Queries*, 12th ser., vi (Jan.-June 1920), p. 321.

Redmond, S[ylvester?]. Theobald Wolfe Tone. In *Notes and Queries*, 3rd ser., xii (July-Dec. 1867), pp 289–90.
Other contributions by E.L.S. in ibid., pp 254, 401–02, and William Pinkerton in ibid., pp 315–16.

Rendall, Jane. 'Friends of liberty and virtue': women and transatlantic correspondence, 1789–1848. In Caroline Bland and Máire Cross (eds), *Gender, the letter and politics* (Aldershot, 2004), pp 77–92.
Letters from Eliza Fletcher to Matilda Tone.

Rendall, Jane, and Woods, C. J. 'The unravelling of a mystery: Thomas Wilson (1758–1824), the Scottish second husband of Matilda Tone' (article pending).

Reynolds, H. F. Irish family history: Tone of Bodenstown, Co. Kildare. In *Notes and Queries*, 12th ser., vi (Jan.-June 1920), pp 288–90.

Reynolds, H. F. Fanning of Dublin. In *Notes and Queries*, 12th ser., vii, no. 131 (16 Oct. 1920), pp 306–8

Reynolds, H. F. Witherington of Dublin. In *Notes and Queries*, 12th ser., ix, no. 170 (16 July 1921), pp 43–5

Sadleir, T. U. The family of Tone. In *Journal of the County Kildare Archaeological Society*, xii, no. 7 (1943), pp 326–9.

St Mark, J. J. The disappearance of Arthur Tone. In *Éire-Ireland*, xx, no. 3 (fall 1985), pp 56–70.

St Mark, J. J. Matilda and William Tone in New York and Washington after 1815. In *Éire-Ireland*, xxii, no. 4 (1987), pp 4–10.

Sampson, William. Matilda Tone. In *Irish Magazine*, June 1810, pp 280–81.

Swanzy, H. B. The families of French of Belturbet and Nixon of Fermanagh. Dublin, 1908.
Matilda Tone's maternal grandmother was a French.

[Swanzy, H. B.?]. Abstracts of wills from the Swanzy collection' in *Irish Genealogist*, ii, no. 3 (1945), p. 85.
The will of Edward Fanning names his granddaus Johanna Witherington, Harriet Witherington, Catherine Witherington and Matilda Tone (p. 85).

Tierney, Moira. From heroic wife to general's widow. In *Irish Times*, 18 November 1997.
Matilda Tone. The author refers to a documentary film she was producing. Entitled 'Matilda Tone', it was made in 16mm, runs for 25 minutes, and was first shown publicly on 29 July 2005 at the Anthology Film Archive, 32 Second Ave., New York.

Tone, Frank Jerome. History of the Tone family. Niagara Falls (N.Y.): the author, [1944]. Pp 192, pls.
There is serious doubt about the accuracy of this work, as the author relies for pre 18th-century ancestry on Gustave Anjou (1863–1942), said to be a forger of genealogies; see R. C. Anderson, 'We wuz robbed' in *Journal of the Genealogical Association of Utah*, xix (1991).

Tone, William Henry. A letter to an officer of the Madras establishment, being an attempt to illustrate some particular institutions of the Mahratta people, principally relative to their system of war and finance; also an account of the political changes of the empire in the year 1796. Bombay: Courier, 1798. Pp 110.
2nd ed., London, 1799. Repr. as 'Illustrations of some institutions of the Mahratta people' in *Asiatic Annual Register . . . for the year* 1799 (London, 1800), pp 124–51. Another ed. as *Illustrations of some institutions of the Mahratta people* (Calcutta, 1818). Transl., abridged, into German as *Bemerkungen über die Mahratten* (Weimar, 1801); transl. into French as *Voyage chez les Mahrattes* (Paris, 1820).

Tone, William Theobald Wolfe. Essai sur la composition de le force armée aux différentes époques de l'histoire. Paris: Imp. de Fain, 1810. Pp 50.
2nd ed., 1813. Another ed., Paris, Magimel, 1814, 68 pp.

Tone, William Theobald Wolfe. État civil et politique de l'Italie sous la domination des Goths. Paris: Imp. de Fain, 1810. Pp 50.

Tone, William Theobald Wolfe. Récit de mes souvenirs et campagnes dans l'armée française. Paris: Paul, 1899. Pp 92.
 French translation of 'Narrative of my services and campaigns in the French army' which he published as an appendix in *Life* (1826), ii, 595–674.

Tone, William Theobald Wolfe Tone. Essay on the necessity of improving our national forces. New York: Kirk & Mercein, 1819. Pp x, 112, illus.

Tone, William Theobald Wolfe. School of cavalry; or system of organisation, instruction and manoeuvres proposed for the cavalry of the United States. Georgetown: Thomas, 1824.
 2nd ed., 1833.

Tone, William Theobald Wolfe, & Tone-Wilson, Matilda. Récit de mes souvenirs et campagnes dans l'Armée française, et Mon entrevue avec Napoléon. Trans. Catherine Paineau–Prévot. [Paris]: La Vouivre, 1997. Pp viii, 108.

Tone-Maxwell, Katherine Anne. *See* Maxwell, Katherine Anne Tone-.

14. Literary works from which Tone quotes

Addison (Joseph)
 Cato (1713)
 The drummer, or the haunted house (1716)

Anon.
 The buck's bottle companion (1775)
 The Kilruddery Hunt (n.d.)
 'A sonnet imitated from the Spanish of Lopez de Vega Menagiana' in *A collection of poems* (1763)

Anstey (Christopher)
 he new Bath guide; or members of the B[lunde]r[hea]d family in a series of poetical epistles (1766)

Beattie (James)
 Epistle to the honourable C.B. (1776)

Bellamy (Daniel)
 The rival nymphs (1739)

Bickerstaff (Isaac)
 Lionel and Clarissa (1748)
 Love in a village (1763)
 The padlock (1768)

Brooke (Henry)
 The contending brothers (1778)
 The fool of quality (1765–70)

Buckingham (George Villiers, 2nd duke of)
 The rehearsal (1671)

Byrom (John)
 Colin and Phoebe (1714). In *Spectator* no. 605.

Carey (Henry)
 The ballad of Sally in our alley (1729)
 Chrononhotonthologos (1734)

Chesterfield (Philip Stanhope, 4th earl of)
 Letters written by the earl of Chesterfield (1774)

Cibber (Colley)
 The lady's last stake (1708)
 Richard III (1700)

Colman (George), the elder
 Tit for tat (1786)
 Phormio (1765)

Colman (George), the younger
 The heir at law (1797?).
 Two to one (1784)

Congreve (William)
 The old bachelor (1693)

Cowper (William)
 John Gilpin (1785)

Cumberland (Richard)
 The brothers (1770)
 The Carmelite (1784)

Defoe (Daniel)
 Moll Flanders (1722)
 Robinson Crusoe (1719)

De Montolieu (Elizabeth J.I.P.)
 Caroline of Lichfield (1786)

Dibdin (Charles), the elder
 The deserter (1774)
 Poor Vulcan (1778)

Dow (Alexander)
 Sethona (1774)

Dryden (John)
 The Spanish fryar (1681)

Dudley (Henry Bate)
 The flitch of bacon (1779)

Farquhar (George)
 The recruiting officer (1706)

Fielding (Henry)
 Amelia (1751)
 Joseph Andrews (1742)
 Tom Jones (1749)
 Tom Thumb (1731)

Foote (Samuel)
 The Englishman in Paris (1753)
 The Englishman return'd from Paris (1756)
 The knights (1754)
 The mayor of Garret (1764)
 Taste (1752)
 A trip to Calais (1778)

Franklin (Benjamin)
 Political, miscellaneous and philosophical pieces (1779)

Gay (John)
 The beggar's opera (1728)
 Fables, 1st ser. (1727)

Goethe (J. W. von)
 The sorrows of Werther (Dublin, 1781–2)

Goldsmith (Oliver)
 Citizen of the world (1762)
 Essays (1765)
 The good-natur'd man (1768)
 She stoops to conquer (1773)
 The vicar of Wakefield (1766)

Gray (Thomas)
 The bard (1757)
 Ode on the spring (1748)

Hawkesworth (John)
 Orounoko (1757)

Home (John)
 Douglas (1757)

Howard (Sir Robert)
 The surprisal (1665)

Jackman (Isaac)
 All the world's a stage (1777)

Johnson (Samuel)
>   A journey to the western islands of Scotland (1775)
>   London: a poem in imitation of the third satire of Juvenal (1738)
>   The vanity of human wishes (1749)

Lee (Nathaniel)
>   The rival queens (1677)

Marana (Giovanni Paolo)
>   L'Espion des grands seigneurs (1684), trans. as Letters writ by a Turkish spy

Milton (John)
>   Paradise lost (1674)

Murphy (Arthur)
>   The apprentice (1756)
>   The citizen (1763)
>   The upholsterer (1758)

O'Keeffe (John)
>   The agreeable surprise (1784)
>   The farmer (1787)
>   Love in a camp (1786)
>   Wild oats (1792)

Otway (Thomas)
>   Venice preserv'd (1682)

Percy (Thomas)
>   Reliques of ancient English poetry (1765)

Pope (Alexander)
>   Autumn, the third pastoral; or Hylas and Aegon (1709)
>   The Dunciad variorum (1729)
>   The Iliad of Homer (1715–20)

Powell (George)
>   Bonduca (1696)

Richardson (Samuel)
>   Clarissa Harlowe (1747–8)
>   Pamela (1741–2)

Rowe (Nicholas)
>   Jane Shore (1714)

Rousseau (Jean-Jacques)
>   Confessions (Dublin, 1783)

Russell (John)
>   Galatea: a pastoral romance . . . translated by an Officer (1791).

Sampson (William)
    Report of the trial of the King versus Hurdy Gurdy, alias Barrel Organ (1794)

Shakespeare (William)
    As you like it (1600?)
    Coriolanus (1608?)
    Hamlet (1602?)
    1 Henry IV (1597?)
    2 Henry IV (1598?)
    Henry V (1599)
    1 Henry VI (1592)
    2 Henry VI (1592?)
    3 Henry VI (1592?)
    Henry VIII (1611?)
    Julius Caesar (1599)
    King Lear (1605?)
    Macbeth (1606?)
    Merchant of Venice (1595?)
    Merry wives of Windsor (1599?)
    Midsummer-night's dream (1594?)
    Much ado about nothing (1599?)
    Othello (1604?)
    Richard II (1594?)
    Richard III (1593?)
    Romeo and Juliet (1593?)
    Timon of Athens (1608?)
    Troilus and Cressida (1602?)
    Twelfth night (1600?)

Shenstone (William)
    A pastoral ballad (1755)

Sheridan (R. B.)
    The critic: tragedy rehears'd (1779)
    The glorious first of June (1794)
    The rivals (1775)
    School for scandal (1777)
    A trip to Scarborough (1777)

Smedley (Jonathan)
    Gulliveriana (1728)

Smollett (Tobias)
    Sir Launcelot Greaves (1762)
    Humphrey Clinker (1771)
    Peregrine Pickle (1751)
    Roderick Random (1748)

Sterne (Laurence)
    A sentimental journey (1768)
    Tristram Shandy (1759)

Stevens (George Alexander)
   The cobler of Cripplegate (1772?)

Swift (Jonathan)
   Epigram on a window at an inn at Chester (1726?)
   The grand question debated (1729)
   Gulliver's travels (1726)
   Horace (1713)
   Journal to Stella (1784)
   My lady's lamentation (1728)
   Polite conversation (1738)
   Tale of a tub (1704)

Vanbrugh (John)
   The provok'd wife (1697)

Voltaire
   Candide (1759)
   La Pucelle (1755)

Wycherley (William)
   The country wife (1675)

Index of persons

ALL persons whose names appear in the documents or in footnotes based on primary sources are listed here. Years of birth and or death, given for positive identification, are taken from various sources. The entry on Theobald Wolfe Tone himself is limited to particulars of his private life. Literary works from which Tone quotes are indicated in the entries on their authors.

A

'Abbé, the', *see* Berwick, Edward

Abercorn, 9th earl of, *see* Hamilton, John James

Abercromby, *Sir* Ralph (1734–1801), iii, 245

Acheson, Arthur (1742?-1807), 2nd Visc. Gosford, ii, 370; iii, 345

Addison, Joseph (1672–1719), ii, 316; quotations from his *Cato*, ii, 244; *Drummer*, ii, 316

Adet, Pierre Auguste (1763–1834), ii, 10, 21, 23, 24, 34, 35–6, 39–40, 53, 77, 81–2, 87, 252, 337, 339–40; iii, 11, 233; letters from, ii, 23–4, 34–5; letter to, ii, 3–7

Adrian IV (d. 1159), pope, ii, 378

Adrien, Martin Joseph (1766–1822), ii, 227, 238

Ahearn, John, *see* Aherne, John

Aherne, Eugene, *see* Aherne, John

Aherne, John (d. 1806?), ii, 150, 158–60, 174, 176, 211, 218, 221; iii, 207–08, 210–11, 214, 253, 323–4, 325, 334, 338, 476; Tone's meetings with, ii, 150, 151, 153–8, 163, 170, 184, 314

Alba, Fernando Alvarez de Toledo, duke of (1508–83), iii, 303

Alexander the Great (356–323 B.C.), ii, 123, 207

Alexander, John (1736–1821), iii, 75

Allen, John (fl. 1790), i, 49

Allen, John (d. 1855), iii, 217, 292

Anderson, — (fl. 1782), ii, 270

Anderson, Adam (1692?-1765), i, 56; iii, 467

Anderson, John William (1736?-1813), ii, 204

Anderson, Patrick (d. 1635), iii, 315–16

Andrews, John, *see* Andrews, Joseph

Andrews, Joseph (d. 180-?), i, 371

Andrieux, Martin Antoine (1768–1802), iii, 286

Anissoy, E. (fl. 1795), ii, 7

Annesley, Arthur (1744–1816), 8th Visc. Valentia & 1st earl of Mountnorris, i, 292

Annesley, Francis Charles (1740–1802), 2nd earl of Annesley, i, 224, 249; letter from, i, 224

Annesley, 2nd earl of, *see* Annesley, Francis Charles

Anson, 1st Baron, *see* Anson, George

Anson, George (1697–1762), 1st Baron Anson, ii, 278

Anstey, Christopher (1724–1805), quotations from his *New Bath guide*, ii, 217, 318

Antonelli, Leonardo (1730–1800), ii, 229

Archbold, James (1752–1804?), i, 354, 367, 438, 439

Archdekin, James (fl. 1792), i, 229, 230, 233

Archer, John (d. 1811), ii, 331

Aristotle (384–322 B.C.), ii, 230

Arkwright, *Sir* Richard (1732–92), i, 134

Armstrong, Edward (fl. 1795), i, 533

Armstrong, John (fl. 1798), iii, 345, 374–5, 379, 386

Armstrong, Thomas (fl. 1798), iii, 345, 346

Armstrong, William Jones (1764?-1827?), ii, 270

Arnold, William (fl. 1792), i, 195

Artois, comte d', *see* Charles X, kg of France

Arthur, Francis (d. 1824), i, 296, 354, 369, 431

Ashley, John (1762?-1829), iii, 192, 197–8, 201, 228

Askew, Ann, *see* Ayscough, Ann (1751–46)

Athy, Edmund Lynch (fl. 1808), i, 369

Atkins, Michael (fl. 1791), i, 138

Atkinson, *Mrs* (fl. 1792), i, 314

Atkinson, Edward (d. 1795), i, 314

Index of subjects

INFORMATION contained both in the documents and, if taken from primary sources, in the editors' footnotes is indexed. Titles of newspapers and pamphlets by Tone are included, but not pamphlets or books by others. Persons are indexed separately (above).

A

Aachen, iii, 36, 44

Acapulco, i, 89

Acts of parliament (Irish), i, 40, 48, 113, 277–9, 305, 390–97, 459, 477; *see also* Catholic relief acts, 1792, 1793; Convention act, 1793; Gunpowder act, 1793

Address to the Defenders (1792), i, 229, 250

Address to the peasantry of Ireland (1796), ii, 347–52, 357

Address to the people of Ireland on the present important crisis (1796), ii, 362, 375–92; iii, 315

'Address to the Roman Catholics of Ireland' (1792), i, 329–42

Africa, ii, 202, 266, 334, 390; *see also* Cape of Good Hope

Agriculture, i, 146, 183, 340, 383, 451; ii, 29–30, 33, 45–7, 233, 235, 261, 338–9, 349–50, 358, 386, 406; iii, 1, 3, 42, 43, 44, 47–8, 56–8, 123, 139, 248, 444–8; *see also* Gardens and orchards; Peasantry; Rents; Tithes

Aix-la-Chapelle, *see* Aachen

Alkmaar, iii, 143

Altona, iii, 6, 330

America, *see* North America; South America; America, United States of

America, United States of, i, 77, 79, 134, 147, 251, 264–6, 283, 451, 510–11, 517; ii, 175, 189, 312–13, 352, 389; iii, 10, 11, 34, 71, 137–8, 140, 197, 335, 338, 346–7, 458; politics, ii, 1–2, 12–13, 30, 33, 53, 195, 204, 225; iii, 29, 335; *see also* American Congress; American people; American revolution; Carolina; Georgia; Maryland; Massachusetts; New Jersey; New York; Philadelphia; Rhode Island; Virginia

American Congress, i, 77, 83, 88, 266–8, 271; ii, 13, 35, 52, 347; iii, 69

American revolution, i, 92, 97–8,–2, 198, 295, 391; iii, 248, 377, 382, 389, 394, 398, 406, 455

American people, ii, 1–2, 11–12, 32, 50, 86, 192, 225; iii, 309, 335; Indians, ii, 14

American war, 1775–82, i, 88, 270, 419, 420, 437; ii, 65, 120, 253, 269, 336, 390, 399; iii, 98, 455

Amsterdam, iii, 58, 60–62, 72–3, 75, 104, 138

Angers, ii, 356

Anglo-American relations, ii, 52

Anglo-French relations, ii, 75, 96, 362; iii, 138, 181, 207; *see also* Peace negotiations

Anglo-Irish relations, i, 60–61, 298, 447, 453, 505, 506; ii, 25–6, 95, 284, 377–92; iii, 440–58

Animals and birds; *see* Bees; Birds; Cats; Fish; Hares; Horses

Antrim, Co., i, 213, 247, 342, 365, 408; ii, 167; iii, 27–8, 126, 324; *see also* Ballycastle; Ballymena; Belfast; Belfast Lough; Broughshane; Carrickfergus; Cave Hill; Lisburn

Arabia, ii, 146, 230; iii, 29

Arbour Hill (Dublin), iii, 353

Architecture, iii, 61, 228–9

Arcola, iii, 30

Ardee, i, 369

Ardennes, iii, 42; *see also* Guise

Ardfinnan, ii, 167, 168

Argentina, i, 87, 88

Argument on behalf of the catholics (1791), i, 132, 137, 145, 150–51, 152, 153, 154, 532; ii, 81, 301–02, 321

Arigna (Co. Roscommon), i, 111

Aristocracy and gentry, i, 107, 140, 235, 241, 243, 249, 309–10, 409; ii, 4, 6, 12–13, 28, 45–6, 65, 70, 101, 107, 110–13, 119–20, 140, 148, 149, 157, 188, 245, 251–2, 295, 298–9, 348, 351, 378, 381–2, 400; iii, 68–9, 100, 235, 246–7, 328, 442, 452–3, 457; *see also* 'Protestant ascendancy'